China Connections

This series between China's Social Science Academic Press and Palgrave Macmillan explores the connections which exist between China and the West, and those which exist between China's heritage and its relevance to the key challenges of our modern world. The books in this series explore China's historical legacy, and how the changes and challenges faced by China, and the lessons learned, are central to solving the global issues we face today in fields as varied as health, education, employment, gender equality, and the environment. This series makes a case for the importance and forms of connections between China and the rest of the world, offering a platform for the active development of research and policy connections which brings together scholars from across the geographical and topical spectrum to showcase the very best of Chinese scholarship to the world.

More information about this series at
http://www.palgrave.com/gp/series/16159

Zhihua Shen
Editor

A Short History of Sino-Soviet Relations, 1917–1991

Translated by Yafeng Xia (Preface, and Parts II and III),
Hongshan Li (Part I), and Xiaohong Liu (Part IV)

社会科学文献出版社
SOCIAL SCIENCES ACADEMIC PRESS (CHINA)

Editor
Zhihua Shen
East China Normal University
Shanghai, China

Based on a translation from the Chinese language edition: 中苏关系史纲：1917~1991 年中苏关系若干问题再探讨 （第三版） by Shen Zhihua. © Social Sciences Academic Press, 2016 All Rights Reserved

The print edition is not for sale in China Mainland. Customers from China Mainland please order the print book from: Social Sciences Academic Press. ISBN of the China Mainland edition: 978-7-5097-8366-5

Published with the financial support of the Chinese Fund for the Humanities and Social Sciences

China Connections
ISBN 978-981-13-8643-5   ISBN 978-981-13-8641-1   (eBook)
https://doi.org/10.1007/978-981-13-8641-1

Cover design: eStudio Calamar

This Palgrave Macmillan imprint is published by the registered company Springer Nature Singapore Pte Ltd.
The registered company address is: 152 Beach Road, #21-01/04 Gateway East, Singapore 189721, Singapore

PREFACE

From the perspective of international relations, no bilateral relationship experienced so many ups and downs as that between the Soviet Union and China during the Cold War period. In the early 1950s, the two countries formed a strategic alliance based on a friendship that was described as "everlasting" and "unbreakable." But with escalating differences and growing conflicts between the leaders of the two countries, within a mere few years the Sino-Soviet alliance collapsed. Thereafter, Sino-Soviet hostilities deepened, ultimately leading to armed border conflicts in 1969. In the 1970s, China adjusted its diplomatic strategy to normalize relations with the United States. Not only did the correlation of power during the Cold War confrontation undergo fundamental changes but the ideological and political conflicts became more pronounced. The all-out showdown between the two nations was a primary factor in Cold War international relations prior to the mid-1980s. When China and the Soviet Union finally normalized relations in the late 1980s, almost simultaneously the global Cold War came to an abrupt end.

The evolution of Sino-Soviet relations is closely related to China's developmental path. Ever since the establishment of the People's Republic of China (PRC) in 1949, the Chinese Communist Party (CCP) pursued the Soviet socialist model to develop its economy, thereby establishing a highly centralized mandatory state planned economic system. Politically, the PRC system followed in the tracks of Soviet proletarian dictatorship and class struggle. But by the late 1950s, when Soviet leader Nikita Khrushchev began to reform and adjust the Soviet political system, there was a rupture in Sino-Soviet relations. China steadfastly insisted on continuing to take the Stalinist road, reaching an apogee during the period of China's "Cultural Revolution." China's "reform and opening" to the outside world in the late 1970s and the normalization of Sino-Soviet relations in the late 1980s are closely related to their respective abandonment of the Stalinist model.

This important yet tortuous historical period, which opens up numerous questions for academic research, has attracted much attention. Nonetheless, due to the paucity of original documents (the archives in the two countries were not open to researchers) and the limitations in research methodology (scholars mainly relied on political science and international relations approaches), little work of academic value was published during the Cold War. Since the end of the Cold War in the early 1990s and with the rise of the "New Cold War History" research approach, during the past decade, several Western scholars, such as Lorenz Lüthi, Sergey Radchenko, Austin Jersild, and Jeremy Friedman, among others, have explored the evolution of Sino-Soviet relations during the Cold War period based on newly released archival sources and have published works of significant academic value.[1]

Within China, due to prolonged ideological restrictions coupled with the lack of access to archival materials, academic research on Sino-Soviet relations remained a "forbidden area," and publications on the subject were considered "revisionist political texts." This situation gradually began to change in the 1980s, and with China's "ideological emancipation" and the declassification of primary archival sources in both China and the Soviet Union, a new generation of Chinese scholars began to open a window to the history of Sino-Soviet relations.

All the authors in this volume, myself, together with Li Danhui, Niu Jun, and Yang Kuisong, were born in the 1950s. We personally experienced and were deeply affected by the legacy of the "revolutionary era." For us, our studies on the history of Sino-Soviet relations are not only an academic activity; they also represent our responses to the intellectual and political issues of the time. It is precisely our concern about such "intellectual issues" that differentiates our work from that of Western scholars.

In the mid-1990s, together with Chen Jian, Niu Dayong, Zhang Baijia, and Zhang Shuguang, we formed close bonds due to our common academic interests. During the last 20 years, we have worked together to mentor a younger generation of Cold War historians in China. The four authors in this volume approach their respective topics with great passion. Li Danhui, Niu Jun, and Yang Kuisong write about the history of Sino-Soviet relations from the perspective of Chinese diplomacy, whereas in Part II, I examine the topic from the perspective of Soviet diplomacy. Together, we frequently attended conferences, participated in trips abroad, shared documents, and debated various issues. This volume represents the fruit of our many years of academic collaboration.

The evolution in the study of Sino-Soviet relations from a "forbidden area" to producing major works attracting the attention of current Chinese leaders and resulting in excellent university textbooks is indicative of the great changes in the understanding of history taking place within mainstream Chinese society. Indeed, this book is a reflection of the academic pursuits by Chinese historians of our generation.

From an academic perspective, our work is characterized by the following:

First, we have made use of declassified and published and unpublished archival sources from Russia, China (including Taiwan), and the United States, as well as eyewitness accounts and oral history materials (including reports by three generations of Russian-language interpreters for Mao Zedong). In addition, we have made great efforts to obtain all available Russian historical materials. During the last 20 years, we have been closely following the progression of declassification and the availability of Russian archival documents, have sought both official and private Chinese historical materials, and have used and promoted the opening of the Chinese archives.

Second, in order to restore the original face of this history, we offer a series of new perspectives and interpretations of many well-known historical events, such as the formation of the Sino-Soviet alliance treaty, the characteristics of Sino-Soviet relations in the 1950s, the Chinese evaluation of the 1956 Twentieth Congress of the Communist Party of the Soviet Union (CPSU), and the Sino-Soviet border negotiations, among others. Although many of our views are still open to debate, they represent a reflection of our current level of understanding. Every generation writes its own history, and this work exemplifies the interpretations of this history by members of our generation. Nevertheless, as scholars, we are making great efforts to offer "value-free" judgments.

Third, this book covers 74 years in the history of Sino-Soviet interactions, that is, from 1917 to 1991. It proceeds chronologically as well as historically. Such a presentation is relatively rare in the currently available Western-language sources on this topic. The main story line is the evolution of the changes in CCP-CPSU relations. Prior to 1949, CCP-CPSU relations and Sino-Soviet state relations proceeded in tandem but at various times they also intersected. After the CCP seized national power in China in 1949, the two relationships merged. Since then, although Sino-Soviet state relations underwent varying periods of alliance, honeymoon, cooperation, divergence, rupture, and conflict, CCP-CPSU party-to-party relations remained dominant. Only when Sino-Soviet state relations were gradually restored in the 1980s did the two sides realize that the party should not take the place of the state and Sino-Soviet state-to-state relations should dominate the bilateral relationship. In effect, this is a more accurate meaning of Sino-Soviet "normalization."

This book is structured on the basis of the above perspective: Part I covers 32 years (1917–1948), whereas Parts II, III, and IV cover only 43 years (1948–1991). This framework better reflects the historical stages, highlighting the dominant role and then the changing status of CCP-CPSU relations.

Fourth, all the authors in this volume are historians, and they have no formal training in international relations theory. Thus, the focus of this book is on the historical process. Nevertheless, the history of international relations and the theory of international relations are closely related. Studies based on the theory of international relations are premised on historical studies, and likewise historical studies cannot be divorced from theory. In this regard, this book attempts to combine both theory and process. For one, we provide a new analytical framework to understand Sino-Soviet normalization based on three factors: the historical structure of state-to-state relations, domestic politics, and China-US-USSR triangular relations. This framework represents a novel and creative innovation in current scholarship. Additionally, in our attempt to analyze the fundamental causes for the rupture of the Sino-Soviet alliance, we seek to break out of the structural dichotomy between "ideology" and "national interest/power" and we propose that there existed a "structural defect" in Sino-Soviet relations—immature and illogical state-to-state relations within the socialist alliance. This often manifested itself in the way that interparty relations controlled state-to-state relations, in how ideology dominated the national interest, and in how sovereignty and equality were subject to "international-ism." This structure led to both the fragility and the turbulence in the socialist alliance during the Cold War.

The Chinese version of the book was first published in 2007 by Xinhua Publishing House. Within less than one year, it was reprinted four times and it won numerous book awards. It attracted much attention from Chinese scholars as well as Chinese political leaders. Since then, due to the more recent release of many archival collections on Sino-Soviet relations, we made major revisions and published a 2011 edition (a later 2016 edition was issued with additional minor revisions) both published by Social Sciences Academic Press. This volume is a condensed translation of the 2016 Chinese edition.

So that the sources will be more accessible to Western readers, we have substituted the Chinese-language footnotes with the relevant English-language literature. Detailed *pinyin* (Chinese romanization) footnotes can be found in Zhihua Shen and Yafeng Xia, *Mao and the Sino-Soviet Partnership, 1945–1959: A New History* (Lanham, MD: Lexington Books, 2015) and Danhui Li and Yafeng Xia, *Mao and the Sino-Soviet Split, 1959–1973: A New History* (Lanham, MD: Lexington Books, 2018). For those in our field who read Chinese, the original Chinese-language sources can be found in the Chinese version of the book. I thank Lexington Books, *The International History Review, Journal of Cold War Studies, Journal of Contemporary China,* and *Modern China Studies* for permission to reprint some of the materials in this new volume.

We wish to thank the three translators of the volume: Xia Yafeng (Preface, and Parts II and III), Li Hongshan (Part I), and Liu Xiaohong (Part IV). We are especially grateful to Nancy Hearst of the Fairbank Center at Harvard for her very careful and professional editing of the manuscript, and we are indebted to the editors at the Social Sciences Academic Press and Palgrave Macmillan for facilitating the entire publication process.

Shanghai, China   Zhihua Shen
August 2018

NOTE

1. Lorenz Lüthi, *The Sino-Soviet Split: Cold War in the Communist World* (Princeton, NJ: Princeton University Press, 2008); Sergey Radchenko, *Two Suns in the Heavens: The Sino-Soviet Struggle for Supremacy, 1962–1967* (Washington DC: Woodrow Wilson Center Press and Stanford: and Stanford University Press, 2009); Austin Jersild, *The Sino-Soviet Alliance: An International History* (Chapel Hill: University of North Carolina Press, 2014); and Jeremy Friedman, *Shadow Cold War: The Sino-Soviet Competition for the Third World* (Chapel Hill: University of North Carolina Press, 2015).

CONTENTS

Preface   v

Notes on Contributors   xiii

Abbreviations   xv

Part I   Uncertain Adversaries, 1917–1948   1

1   Exporting Revolution Against the Backdrop of the
    Establishment of Diplomatic Relations Between China
    and the Soviet Union   3
    Kuisong Yang

2   The Nationalist Revolution Assisted by the Soviet Union   19
    Kuisong Yang

3   Moscow and the Soviet Revolution in China   39
    Kuisong Yang

4   Sino-Soviet Diplomacy Under the Threat of War   55
    Kuisong Yang

5   Sino-Soviet Wartime Cooperation and Conflict   69
    Kuisong Yang

6   China's Civil War and Sino-Soviet and Nationalist-Communist
    Relations   95
    Kuisong Yang

Part II   Comrades and Brothers, 1948–1959   107

7   The Political and Economic Foundations of the Sino-Soviet
    Alliance, 1948–1949   109
    Zhihua Shen

8   Conflicts of Interest and Creation of the Alliance Treaty,
    1949–1950   123
    Zhihua Shen

9   Differences and Cooperation During the Korean War, 1950–
    1953   133
    Zhihua Shen

10 Khrushchev's Policy Toward China and the Honeymoon
    of the Alliance, 1954–1956   147
    Zhihua Shen

11 The Twentieth CPSU Congress and the Eighth CCP
    Congress, 1956   161
    Zhihua Shen

12 The Polish and Hungarian Crises and CCP Political Support
    for Khrushchev, 1956–1957   175
    Zhihua Shen

13 Mao, Khrushchev, and the Moscow Conference, 1957   189
    Zhihua Shen

14 Differences Over Domestic and Foreign Policies, 1957–1959   209
    Zhihua Shen

Part III   From Split to Confrontation, 1959–1978   227

15 Open Struggles and a Temporary Truce, 1959–1961   229
    Danhui Li

16 The Collapse of Party Relations and the Deterioration
    of State Relations, October 1961–July 1964   247
    Danhui Li

17 Mao's Changing Perceptions of Internal Disturbances
   and External Threats, Mid-1963 to the End of 1964   267
   Danhui Li

18 The Schism in the International Communist Movement
   and the Collapse of the Alliance, 1965   285
   Danhui Li

19 The Breakdown of State Relations and the Sino-Soviet
   Military Confrontation, 1966–1973   303
   Danhui Li

Part IV   The Road to "Normalization," 1979–1991   327

20 The Issue of "Normalization"   329
   Jun Niu

21 Embarking on "Normalization"   343
   Jun Niu

22 The Turning Point in "Normalization"   367
   Jun Niu

Further Reading   387

Index   389

Notes on Contributors

Danhui Li is Professor of History at the Institute for Studies of China's Neighboring Countries and Regions, East China Normal University and editor-in-chief of two academic journals: *Lengzhan guojishi yanjiu* (Cold War International History Studies) and *Bianjiang yu zhoubian wenti yanjiu* (Studies of Borderlands and Neighboring Regions). A leading authority on the CCP's external relations during the Cold War, she has written extensively on Sino-Soviet relations and Sino-Vietnamese relations during the Indochina War (in Chinese, Russian, and English). She is the coauthor of *Mao and the Sino-Soviet Split, 1959–1973: A New History* (2018) and *After Leaning to One Side: China and Its Allies in the Cold War* (2011).

Jun Niu is Professor in the School of International Studies, Peking University. He is working on a book project, tentatively entitled, "The Cold War and the Origin of New China's Foreign Policy, 1948–1955." Major publications include *Cong Yan'an zouxiang shijie: Zhongguo gongchandang duiwai zhengce de qiyuan/From Yan'an to the World: The Origin and Development of Chinese Communist Foreign Policy* (Chinese version published in 1992 and English version published in 2005). He is a coeditor of *Towards a History of Chinese Communist Foreign Relations, 1920s–1960s* (1995).

Zhihua Shen is Professor and Director of the Center for Cold War International History Studies and the World History Institute at East China Normal University. He is the leading authority on Cold War history studies in China. The author of a number of major Chinese-language works on Cold War history, he is the author of *Mao, Stalin and the Korean War: Trilateral Communist Relations in the 1950s* (translated by Neil Silver) (2012). He is also the coauthor of *A Misunderstood Friendship: Mao Zedong, Kim Il-sung, and Sino–North Korean Relations, 1949–1976* (2018), *Mao and the Sino-Soviet Partnership, 1945–1959: A New History* (2015), and *After Leaning to One Side: China and its Allies in the Cold War* (2011).

Kuisong Yang is Professor in the Department of History, East China Normal University. A leading authority on CCP's external relations, he is the author of many books, including *Mao Zedong yu Mosike de enen yuanyuan* (Gratitude and Resentment between Mao Zedong and Moscow) (1999) and *Bianyuanren jishi—Jige xiaorenwu de beiju gushi* (Nightmares of Several Ordinary Persons: Social and Political Marginalization in the Early People's China) (2016).

ABBREVIATIONS

AUCP (b)	All-Union Communist Party (Bolsheviks)
CAS	Chinese Academy of Science
CC	Central Committee
CCP	Chinese Communist Party
CGDK	Coalition Government of Democratic Kampuchea
CMC	Central Military Commission
CPSU	Communist Party of the Soviet Union
CPV	Chinese People's Volunteers
CWIHP	*Cold War International History Project*
DPRK	Democratic People's Republic of Korea
DRV	Democratic Republic of Vietnam
FBIS-China	Foreign Broadcast Information Service-China
FRUS	Foreign Relations of the United States
FYP	Five-Year Plan
ILD	International Liaison Department
JCP	Japanese Communist Party
KSČ	Communist Party of Czechoslovakia
LCY	League of Communists of Yugoslavia
MFA	Ministry of Foreign Affairs
NA	National Archives
NSCF	National Security Council Files
PCF	French Communist Party
PHP	Parallel History Project on Cooperative Security
PKI	Communist Party of Indonesia
PLA	People's Liberation Army
PRC	People's Republic of China
SED	Socialist Unity Party of Germany
TFD	Third Front Defense
USSR	Union of Soviet Socialist Republics
WFTU	World Federation of Trade Unions

PART I

Uncertain Adversaries, 1917–1948

On the eve of the establishment of the People's Republic of China (PRC), Mao Zedong, the Chinese Communist Party (CCP) chairman, identified the major factors that made it possible for the CCP to take over the national government. One was the Russian Revolution that "delivered Marxism and Leninism to us." The other was the victory of the Russian Revolution that provided an example. "Take the Russian path, this is the conclusion."

However, the first Chinese who sought assistance from the Russians was Sun Yatsen, a "petty bourgeois revolutionary" who was initially overlooked by the Russian Communists. Moscow began to offer comprehensive guidance and assistance to the Nationalist (Guomindang) Party led by Sun Yatsen in the autumn of 1923. Within four or five years, it managed to turn the small organization that had been operated by Sun for four decades into the most powerful political force in China, with a "party army" that was able to unify the mainland by force.

In sharp contrast, the CCP, established with Soviet help in 1921, had only several dozen members at the beginning and in its early years was forced to operate underground. The party followed Moscow's instructions and allowed many of its members to join the Nationalist Party. It was able to rapidly grow, while at the same time it helped the Nationalist Party to expand. However, its conflicts with the Nationalist Party were inevitable because there was no true loyalty to the latter. As soon as Sun passed away, Jiang Jieshi (Chiang Kai-shek), a military man, became the leader of the Nationalist Party. All Communists were expelled from the Nationalist Party and forced to engage in a Russian-style "Soviet Revolution" in the countryside.

In 1928, the Nationalist Party managed to consolidate its rule over China. The Communists, who could only survive and grow in the rural areas far away from the major cities, found it difficult to effectively challenge the ruling status of the Nationalists. However, as Mao Zedong recognized in his later years, the Japanese invasion significantly changed the political order in China. On the one hand, Moscow immediately readjusted its policy toward China as it too faced grave challenges from the Japanese. On the other hand, as the "Soviet

Revolution" had suffered disastrous defeats, Mao Zedong, a leader who was goot at military strategy, extremely pragmatic, and known for his independent thinking, began to rise within the CCP. Thus, the CCP was gradually resurrected after the War of Resistance Against Japan began in 1937. Within eight years, the number of its members and army soldiers grew from about 20,000 to over 1 million, giving it the power to challenge the Nationalist government, which had lost one-half of China to the Japanese invaders.

The impact of Soviet Russia, later the Soviet Union, on the development of Chinese politics and history between the 1920s and the 1940s is obvious. Both the Nationalist and the Communist parties owed much of their success to Soviet Russia. Their setbacks were also closely tied to the Soviet interventions. However, the political ecology within China and its complex relations with the outside world greatly enriched the history of modern China and left countless stories worth pondering by later generations.

CHAPTER 1

Exporting Revolution Against the Backdrop of the Establishment of Diplomatic Relations Between China and the Soviet Union

Kuisong Yang

Ever since the Opium War in 1840, China had been forced into the status of a semi-colony, constantly bullied and oppressed by the foreign powers. To change this situation, many determined and capable Chinese worked to learn from the West. However, prior to the Russian October Revolution in 1917, China became even more vulnerable because of the ongoing contentious wars among the warlords. When the Chinese again pinned their hopes on the United States and other countries for just treatment after the victorious ending of World War I, the unjust decisions made at the Paris Peace Conference in 1919 forced many radical intellectuals and young students to look to revolutionary Russia, which was moving toward socialism. As Soviet rule expanded from Europe to the Far East, the Russian Bolsheviks, led by V. I. Lenin, based on their belief in world revolution, began to export the Russian revolutionary experience to the Far East. On the one hand, the Soviets had to follow the tradition of the capitalist world when dealing with the Chinese government at diplomatic venues. On the other hand, they firmly held on to their anti-capitalist ideology and worked hard to find allies among the various radical forces in China. Thus, Soviet Russia not only helped organize the Chinese Communist Party (CCP) but it also chose the Nationalist Party, led by Sun Yatsen, to guide China on the track of the world revolution.

K. Yang (✉)
Contemporary China Study Institute, East China Normal University, Shanghai, China
e-mail: yks@vip.sina.com

© The Author(s) 2020
Z. Shen (ed.), *A Short History of Sino-Soviet Relations, 1917–1991*, China Connections, https://doi.org/10.1007/978-981-13-8641-1_1

Chinese Society Shocked by the October Revolution

On 7 November 1917, shelling from the Russian cruiser Aurora woke up the sleeping world. The red flags fluttering in Saint Petersburg startled all bourgeois governments. Fear instantly permeated worldwide media and affected the elite intellectuals in China who had been deeply concerned about the future of Russia since its February Revolution in 1917.

During the first several months of 1917, Chinese newspapers were filled with praise for the overthrow of the Tsar by the February Revolution and the preparations for a constitutional republic. However, beginning in April, newspapers began to pay attention to reports carried by European, American, and Japanese media on the so-called conflict among the "Russian socialist thugs," the "extremists," the "radical leftist party," and the provisional Russian government established after the February Revolution that resulted in "partisan divisions, incoherent government orders, rebellious workers and soldiers," Bolshevik strikes, and major rebellions. Many Chinese intellectuals began to have different attitudes toward the February and October Revolutions, mainly for two reasons. One was that they did not want to see one of the entente powers defeated as China had entered World War I on their side. The other was that they saw the overthrow of the imperial system during the February Revolution as a copy of the Chinese Revolution of 1911 and as a part of a worldwide trend toward democratic republics. They did not want to let this historical process follow the disastrous footsteps of the French Revolution or evolve into a "bloody massacre" simply because the radicals "wanted a foot after getting an inch and wanted a yard after getting a foot."

However, only six months later, the attitude of the Chinese media toward the Russian Revolution gradually began to change again. The anarchists were the first to welcome the victory of the people's revolution in Russia. Because of the collaboration between Peter Kropotkin, a leading figure among the Russian anarchists, and the Bolsheviks, as well as the close attention the new government paid to the interests of workers and peasants, the anarchists were the first to make sympathetic remarks about the October Revolution. By the end of May 1918, the *National Daily*, a newspaper run by the Chinese Revolutionary Party led by Sun Yatsen, also began to change its attitude toward Soviet Russia. Sun even sent a telegram to Lenin, expressing his tremendous admiration for the victory of the socialist revolution in Russia. Thereafter, newspapers and magazines run by Chinese reformers ended their loathing of the "extremist socialists." They predicted that because of the victory of the Russian Revolution, socialism had gained such tremendous momentum that even a falling sky would not be able to stop it.

By the end of 1918, World War I came to an end and democracy overwhelmed authoritarianism as the Austrian-Hungarian empire, the German empire, and the Tsarist government collapsed in succession. At the same time, with the rise of the Russian socialist government, socialist revolutions began to erupt throughout Europe, shocking the capitalist world. All this inevitably made many young Chinese intellectuals aware that "a massive new world trend is now beginning to rise in Eastern Europe" and that "a Russian-style revolution, a socialist revolution, will spread." Li Dazhao, a professor at Peking University who had carefully studied the socialist revolutions in Russia and Europe via Japanese newspapers and magazines, publicly stated that "regarding the current changes in Russia, we should heartily welcome them as the dawn of a new civilization ... and [we] should not be pessimistic simply because of the temporary disorder that is now being observed."

Entering 1919, even the Northern Sea warlords and the Anhui politicians began to organize research associations on socialism. However, the Chinese understanding of a socialist revolution, as Qu Qiubai, a prominent leftist writer said, was not quite clear, just like "observing the morning fog through a screen window. ... The factions and the meaning of socialism are a mess, not quite clear to the Chinese; just like a dam gate closed for a long time, once it opens numerous currents rush out, foaming and thundering, yet without any predetermined direction." However, one thing was clear. Regardless of whether Chinese national feelings would be hurt by the results of the Paris Peace Conference, the rapid rise of a socialist ideology in China and the impact of ideas from the Soviet Russian Revolution on Chinese society had become obvious.

THE ORIGINS OF THE CHINESE COMMUNIST PARTY

The influence of the Russian Revolution and Russian-style socialism on China was a gradual process. Ever since the Opium War, the Chinese had tried various methods, including the overthrow of the Manchu Qing dynasty and the abolition of the imperial system, to introduce advanced Western learning, encompassing the political system to include law and education as well as the military and technology. However, the nation did not become truly independent. Instead, it was further divided because of its separation by the warlords, which greatly aided Japan, a new imperialist country, to implement its aggressive plan aimed at colonizing China. During the 1894 Sino-Japanese War, Japan not only occupied Korea but also took over Taiwan and the Penghu Islands. During the 1904 Russo-Japanese War, Japan seized Lüshun, Dalian, and the South Manchuria Railroad. It forcibly occupied China's Jiaodong Peninsula as it declared war on Germany. Then, in 1915, Japan forced Yuan Shikai's government to sign the "Twenty-One Articles." By signing a secret military treaty with the Duan Qirui government in 1918, Japan obtained the right to engage in military operations in China on the pretext of "mutual defense." Although deeply offended by Japanese behavior, the Chinese could do nothing but pin their hopes on receiving justice from the European and American powers.

During World War I, the Chinese government decided to join the side of the entente. Since most of the entente nations were democratic republics and US President Woodrow Wilson strongly supported "self-determination," intellectual and media circles in China had great expectations for the postwar world order. Thus, when the war ended and the leaders of the entente nations gathered in Paris for the Peace Conference, many elites and reporters, with great hopes for "justice over power," flocked to the city, waiting for the good news that China would be granted justice by the Paris Peace Conference. Therefore, the Chinese were greatly shocked when the Paris Peace Conference ignored the pleas from the Chinese government as well as international law and allowed Japan to continue its occupation of the Jiaodong Peninsula. Once this news spread to China, the entire nation became indignant and many young students poured onto the streets, not only beginning the massive anti-Japanese May Fourth Movement but also radicalizing many young intellectuals and students.

After 4 May, people in China began to pay more attention to socialist ideology. However, since the Soviet Russian Red Army had not yet arrived in the Far East region, information about the Russian Revolution came only indirectly from Japan, Europe, and America. Thus, the minds of radical Chinese intellectuals were filled not with Bolshevism but with anarchism and ideas about "mutual-assistance," "pan-labor," "work-study," "collaboration," and "new villages" were tainted with ideas about anarchism. However, in sharp contrast to the situation at the turn of the century, almost all people participating in discussions about the path for a fundamental reform of Chinese society began to recognize that the laborers were the greatest force in the world and labor was most sacred and honorable. Many Chinese firmly believed that laborers were the creators of everything, whereas capitalists, bureaucrats, warlords, and so forth were nothing but shameful looters. The root cause for social inequality was "private property and private enterprises," and the revolutions in Russia, Austria, Hungary, and Germany were revolutions for the proletariat to completely eliminate such inequalities. Chinese believed, "for sure, this uprising will soon spread here."

Between the summer and autumn of 1919, the Soviet Russian government established a solid footing in the European part of Russia and began pushing toward Asia. In order to help the Chinese public understand that Chinese policy positions were unlike those of the other powers, on 26 August 1919, the Chinese issued a "Statement from the Soviet Russian Federative Socialist Republic Government to the Chinese People and the Governments in North and South China." The statement declared that the Red Army had marched east across the Ural Mountains not to bully or enslave other people but to "let people rid themselves of the shackles of foreign bayonets and foreign money." To demonstrate its willingness to help the Chinese, the Soviet Russian government also declared that it was "willing to return everything looted from the Chinese people by the Tsarist government, either alone or in collaboration with the Japanese and other entente nations." Upon hearing this diplomatic statement by the Soviet Russian government, many Chinese civilians sent telegrams to the Soviet Russian government to express their gratitude, and their positive feelings toward the Russian Revolution grew dramatically.

At the time, Soviet Russia was still focusing on Europe. This was based on the traditional Leninist as well as the Marxist views that a socialist revolution in one country could only be consolidated and win a final victory when socialist revolutions prevailed throughout the world, especially in the advanced capitalist nations of Europe. Therefore, between 1918 and 1919, Soviet Russia used all its economic and political resources to export the revolution to Europe, especially to Germany and Hungary. In March 1919, Soviet Russia even established a World Communist Party, the Communist International (Comintern), devoted to the cause of world revolution. Soviet Russia intended to use the Communist International to centralize leadership and assist the European revolutions. However, in 1920 both the German and Hungarian revolutions ended in failure. When the Soviet Russian Red Army entered Siberia and the Far East, it became aware of the "rice riots" in Japan, the "1 March uprising" in Korea, and the patriotic May Fourth Movement in China. The Soviet Russian Communist Party and the Comintern immediately began issuing revolutionary propaganda and engaging in party organization work in these nations. In the summer of 1919, the Politburo of the Russian Communist Party Central Committee (CC) appointed V. D. Vilensky to be representative plenipotentiary for Far Eastern Affairs and F. I. Gapon to be deputy representative of the Ministry of Foreign Affairs (MFA). They were responsible for (1) making every effort to aggravate the conflicts of national interest among Japan, the United States, and China; (2) attempting to awake the masses in China, Mongolia, and Korea so as to strengthen their liberation movements against oppression by the foreign capitalists; (3) supporting the respective revolutionary movements in these countries, helping them strengthen propaganda and mobilization efforts, and establishing firm ties with their revolutionary organizations; and (4) providing assistance to guerrilla units in China and Korea. As the Red Army began to enter the Far East in the following February, Vilensky arrived at the Far Eastern Bureau of the Russian Communist Party (Bolsheviks) CC in Vladivostok, immediately assuming his new task of exporting revolution.

In April 1920, the Far Eastern Bureau of the Russian Communist Party (Bolsheviks) CC sent Grigori Voitinsky (Wu Tingkang in Chinese) as representative plenipotentiary in China. With help from Russian immigrants, Voitinsky and his entourage got to know Professor Li Dazhao, who then introduced them to Chen Duxiu, the famed chief editor of *New Youth* and former professor at Peking University. Through Chen Duxiu, they were also able to establish contacts with a number of radical intellectuals throughout the country. In the summer, they held the founding conference of the Socialist League in Shanghai, while, at the same time, organizing a Socialist Youth League in China. In order to increase the influence of these organizations and allow more people to understand the Russian Revolution, Voitinsky sponsored the publication of some propaganda materials. He also funded the translation, publication, and dissemination of *The Communist Manifesto* and other theoretical works. Before long, Voitinsky, working with Chen Duxiu and others, organized a preparatory group for the CCP. In November, they issued *The Chinese Communist Party Manifesto*, marking the establishment of the CCP. In the same month, *The Communist Party*, the official publication of the party, began publication as a monthly. But by the following March, the CCP formally parted ways with the anarchists. In July, with the direct involvement of the Comintern representatives, over 50 CCP members in Peking, Shanghai, Guangzhou, Wuhan, and Changsha, who were determined to promote the Chinese Revolution through the use of Russian revolutionary methods, elected 13 representatives. These representatives held the First CCP Congress in Shanghai, raising the opening curtain on the Chinese Communist Revolution.

Troubled Sino-Russian Negotiations

From the very beginning, victorious Communist Russia had to face armed interventions and economic blockades imposed by the European powers, the United States, and Japan. To survive, the Soviet government, under the leadership of the Communist Party, adopted a dual strategy of revolution and diplomacy to handle foreign affairs. Exporting revolution to foreign nations was a logical method for the Communists to ensure the success of their revolutionary ideology. Meanwhile, diplomacy was used to take advantage of the prevailing international practices and to prevent the capitalist powers from forming an anti-Communist united front. Diplomacy also gave Soviet Russia time to regroup before the outbreak of the world revolution. Because it was difficult to send more troops to the Far East, the Soviet Russian Communist Party (Bolsheviks) on 18 February 1920 approved the establishment of the Far East Republic as a buffer state. On 6 April 1920, the Congress of the Laborers in Transbaikalia sent a so-called declaration of independence to all governments in the world. Thereafter, the Far East Republic dispatched a memorandum to the Beiyang government, requesting immediate establishment of mutually beneficial relations, and it sent a mission led by M. I. Yurin, deputy minister of defense and plenipotentiary envoy to China, to engage in "contacts and negotiations."

China did receive some early benefits from the collapse of Tsarist Russia and the armed intervention of the foreign powers in Communist Russia. Similar to other powers, Russia had obtained some special privileges in China. Three of them had posed a grave threat to Chinese sovereignty through the concessions, the Chinese Eastern Railway, and Outer Mongolia.

The Russian concessions were relatively few, located mostly in Hankou, Tianjin, and Harbin. Taking advantage of the confrontations between the new and old Russian immigrant factions in China and the end of the diplomatic authority of the former Russian ambassador and the Russian consuls after the October Revolution, the Chinese government recovered the Russian concessions in Hankou, Tianjin, and Harbin and ended all the extraterritorial rights enjoyed by the Russians.

The Chinese Eastern Railway had been built by Russia when it leased Lüshun (Port Arthur) and Dalian (Dairen) ports in 1898. Passing through Manzhouli (Manchuria) and the Suifen River in China's Heilongjiang province, the railroad connected the Russian Siberian Railroad with the railroads leading to

Dalian and Lüshun in Liaoning province. Because of the Russian defeats in its war against Japan in 1904, the stretch of the Chinese Eastern Railway between Changchun and Dalian was transferred to Japan and renamed the South Manchuria Railway. All that was left for the Russians were the tracks and the land north of Changchun. The authorities in China's Northeast, taking advantage of the confrontations between the old and new Russian factions over the Chinese Eastern Railway after the Russian October Revolution, recovered garrison authority over the railroad and administrative authority over the land concessions along the railway.

Outer Mongolia, according to the 1727 Russo-Chinese Kyakhta Border Agreement, was within the sovereign jurisdiction of China. However, when the 1911 Revolution took place in China, the aristocrats in Outer Mongolia, with support from Tsarist Russia, declared independence on 30 November and established the "Nation of Great Mongolia." On 7 June 1915, the Kyakhta Agreement was signed by China, Russia, and Outer Mongolia. Two days later, Outer Mongolia declared its independence and embarked on self-government. Since no Chinese officials, troops, or immigrants were allowed into the region, China actually lost its power to rule over Outer Mongolia. But as the pro-Russian and pro-Chinese factions began to fight one another after the October Revolution in Russia, the Chinese government in Beijing terminated the Kyakhta Agreement, sent troops to Kulun, and ended the self-government in Outer Mongolia.

Since all these gains were obtained after the Beiyang government joined the entente powers during World War I, China received support from the diplomatic missions of the entente powers in China. Therefore, although most powers did not publicly recognize the Soviet Russian regime or the Far East Republic, the attitude of the Beiyang government to the Yurin Mission was ambiguous. Initially, it rejected the Yurin Mission but then it reversed its position and welcomed the Mission's arrival. Since the Beiyang government wanted to sign a formal agreement with the Far East Republic that would give it legal rights over the Chinese Eastern Railway and other matters, it was obviously willing to conduct negotiations with the Yurin Mission. However, because of the need to stay in tune with the other governments, Beijing had to strictly restrict the scope and level of its negotiations with Yurin. It required that the MFA make the negotiations "appear to focus only on commerce, but in reality, because of the special border relations shared by China and Russia, political issues are to be covered. For example, discussions should be held on all the rights promised to our country by the former Lvov government to serve as a basis for negotiations once the Russian government is formally established." As a result, the two sides could not reach an agreement on the scope of the negotiations after the arrival of the Yurin Mission. It was not until 20 April 1921 that the MFA of the Beiyang government recognized the official status of the Yurin Mission and agreed to negotiate trade issues. However, not long after Foreign Minister Yan Huiqing began discussions with Yurin, the negotiations met another setback because of the sudden eruption of problems in Outer Mongolia.

Due to its resentment over Outer Mongolia's loss of self-government in 1920, the Japanese military, which had been deeply involved in the intervention in Soviet Russia, provided weapons and advisers to Tsarist officer Atman Semenov and in February 1921 persuaded him to allow his troops to enter Outer Mongolia. They took over Kulun (Ulan Bator) and drove out the Chinese troops stationed there. The Mongolian People's Party, established with assistance from Soviet Russia, took advantage of the situation to participate in the battle against the Chinese troops. It declared establishment of the provisional independent Mongolian people's government on 19 March and "invited" the Red Army of Soviet Russia to Mongolia to provide assistance. As early as July 1919, the Soviet Russian government had issued a statement recognizing "Mongolia is a free nation" and opposing foreign intervention in Mongolian domestic affairs. Upon receiving the above-noted "invitation," the Soviet Russian government immediately mobilized Red Army troops in Siberia and sent them, together with the army of the Far East Republic, to Outer Mongolia to assist in the "extermination of the bandits." In July, the Soviet and Mongolian armies jointly occupied Kulun and declared the establishment of an independent Mongolian state. But Yurin was only able to make commitments on behalf of the Far East Republic, and he was not authorized to sign a treaty on behalf of the Soviet Russian government. At the same time, relations between the Hebei and Liaoning warlords deteriorated because of their struggle over control of the Beiyang government. Thus, contacts between the Beiyang government and the Far East Republic were suspended. By the time the war between the warlords had come to an end and the Hebei warlords had taken over the Beiyang government, the Soviet Red Army had already entered the Far East region. With the demise of the Far East Republic, all negotiations with the Chinese government were taken over by the Soviet Russian diplomatic representatives.

NEGOTIATIONS ON UNRESOLVED ISSUES BETWEEN THE TWO NATIONS

Direct negotiations between the Beijing and the Soviet Russian governments began with the release of a second Soviet Russian declaration on China. Entitled the "Memorandum from the Department of the People's Commissioners of Foreign Affairs of the Soviet Russian Federative Socialist Republic," the declaration, which was signed on 27 September 1920, reassured China that all principles articulated in the declaration of the Soviet Russian government of 25 July 1919 would be respected and all territories and concessions obtained from China in the past would be abandoned. This differed from the previous declaration in that the new document required a special treaty on use of the Chinese Eastern Railway.[1] The Beiyang government issued a reply to the Soviet Russian memorandum on 5 February 1921, but it was unwilling to immediately begin negotiations on mutual recognition. It only agreed that Soviet Russia could send delegates to China for talks on commercial issues. After back-and-forth communications, Lenin Aleksandr Paikes, head of the Soviet Russian commercial delegation, and his colleagues finally arrived in Beijing on 12 December 1921. However, by this time the Soviet Red Army had already entered Outer Mongolia and Outer Mongolia had already declared independence. Thus, after its arrival in Beijing, the Paikes Mission faced questioning by Foreign Minister Yan Huiqing of the Beiyang government.

However, as China and Russia were negotiating, the Washington Conference was being held and war between the Hebei and Liaoning warlords was about to begin. Thus, the Beiyang government could not focus on the talks with Paikes or on a solution to the Outer Mongolian problem. It was not until April 1922 that the Beiyang government discovered that Soviet Russia had signed a friendship treaty with Outer Mongolia on 5 November of the previous year. It was only then that it issued a strong protest to the Soviet Russian government. However, just at this time Liaoning warlord Zhang Zuolin was defeated and forced to retreat to Manchuria. As the governor of Mongolia and Manchuria, and garrison commander general of the Three Northeast Provinces, Zhang Zuolin still controlled the Northeast and Rehe, Suiyuan, and Chahar provinces on both sides of the Great Wall. Zhang openly declared that all Manchurian and Mongolian issues had to be handled by the authorities in Fengtian (Shenyang) and he refused to allow the Beiyang government, which was controlled by the Hebei warlords, to make any deals with the Soviet Russian government on Manchuria and Mongolia. At the same time, Paikes insisted that Soviet Russia would not withdraw its troops until a conference between China and Mongolia was convened. As a result, bilateral negotiations came to a standstill.

On 12 August 1922, Adolf Joffe, the famed diplomat who had negotiated the Treaty of Brest-Litovsk with Germany, arrived in Beijing with another delegation sent by the Soviet Russian People's Diplomatic Commission. Gu Weijun (Wellington Koo), the new Minister of Foreign Affairs of the Beiyang government, told Joffe that if Soviet Russia were to withdraw the Red Army from Mongolia and return the Chinese Eastern Railway and all related rights to China, it would thus "create the best opportunity for Sino-Russian friendship and facilitate the resolution of other issues." The instructions received by Joffe also stated that Chinese sovereignty over Mongolia might be recognized. But the legal status of Mongolia and the withdrawal of the Red Army had to be resolved by an agreement signed by Russia, China, and Mongolia. "The exclusion of Mongolia can never be allowed." As for the Chinese Eastern Railway, some rights might be returned to China under certain conditions. Thus, Joffe's reply to Wellington Koo stated that sovereignty over the Chinese Eastern Railway could be returned to China. However, because the railroad was built by Russia, the Russian government would only grant China partial administrative rights. As for the Mongolian issue, Russia objected to China's unilateral termination of the Kyakhta Agreement, which had been signed by China, Russia, and Outer Mongolia. Joffe insisted that Outer Mongolia should regain its self-government status and that the Soviet Russian Red Army would withdraw only if China could ensure that Outer Mongolia would not be used by former Tsarist troops to attack Soviet Russia.

Because China could not accept Joffe's demands, the negotiations came to an end. Soon thereafter, Joffe fell ill. The Soviet Union government (Soviet Russia changed its name to the Union of Soviet Socialist Republics [USSR], or the Soviet Union for short, at the end of 1922) appointed Leo Karakhan, former deputy commissioner of foreign affairs, as the new representative plenipotentiary. He arrived in Beijing on 2 September 1923. However, no progress was made in the negotiations on Outer Mongolia and the Chinese Eastern Railway for quite some time.

Except for the few people who saw the steps taken by the Beiyang government as a necessary action to protect national sovereignty and interests, the overwhelming majority was critical. With formal recognition of the USSR by Great Britain and Italy in early 1924, the international status of the Soviet Union received a huge boost. As a result, public cries to recognize the USSR and to establish diplomatic relations became even louder. Under such pressure, in mid-February the Beiyang government was forced to accept Karakhan's proposal that before they could reopen negotiations to resolve the other issues, each side had to recognize the other. Under these conditions, the negotiation process resumed.

The representative plenipotentiary appointed by the Beiyang government was Wang Zhengting, supervisor of the Sino-Russian negotiations. It was Wang who provided an outline of a draft treaty that aimed to resolve all the existing problems and a draft of a temporary agreement on management of the Chinese Eastern Railway. Karakhan revised and amended Wang's drafts and produced a revised version. By 1 March, both sides were very close to reaching an agreement. They agreed that China would manage the Chinese Eastern Railway after proper payment was made. The Russians asked for 70 million yuan, whereas the Chinese proposed only a little more than 30 million yuan. As for management of the railroad after it was taken over by the Chinese, Chinese sovereignty would be recognized by the Soviet Union, but management would be shared by both sides. There would be 21 section managers and 15 deputy section managers. The Russians wanted to maintain their current positions by reserving the position of director for a Russian who would have real power, and giving the position of supervisor to a Chinese who would have oversight authority. However, the Chinese proposed that all positions had to be shared by both sides. As for Outer Mongolia, the Soviet Union proposed that China and Mongolia would be allowed to negotiate between themselves to resolve the issues. The Soviet Union would respect their decisions and withdraw its army unconditionally if the Chinese government could guarantee that Outer Mongolia would not harbor any people who opposed Soviet Russia. The Chinese demanded an end to the Soviet-Mongolian agreement. While denying that they had ever harbored any Soviet Russian rebel elements, the Chinese promised to do their best to maintain order in Outer Mongolia after its recovery. Both sides agreed that once their agreements were signed, China would immediately recognize the Soviet Union.

On 14 March, Wang Zhengting and Karakhan initialed the Sino-Russian Agreement on an Outline for Resolving All Existing Issues and the Temporary Agreement on the Management of the Chinese Eastern Railway. The former had 15 articles, whereas the latter had 11 articles and seven attachments. But on the next day, the agreements and other documents initialed by Wang Zhengting and Karakhan were strongly opposed by Foreign Minister Gu Weijun and others attending the Beiyang government's State Affairs Meeting. Gu believed that the draft agreements, while abolishing all unequal treaties signed by Tsarist Russia with China as well as all unequal treaties signed by other powers with China, failed to include the repeal of the treaties signed between Soviet Russia and the "independent" Outer Mongolian government, thereby "acquiescing to the treaties between Soviet Russia and Outer Mongolia." The draft agreements provided that once China accepted the terms, Soviet troops would immediately withdraw from Outer Mongolia. However, Gu pointed out that this provision gave an impression "as if it were legal for Soviet Russia to station its army there and it had rights to demand all kinds of conditions before the withdrawal of its troops." According to the draft agreements, all unequal treaties, including the Treaty of 1901, were to be abolished. However, at the same time, as Gu criticized, they also stipulated that the Soviet Union could decide how the Boxer Indemnity should be spent, which meant that the Soviet Union did not cede the Boxer Indemnity. Gu also opposed the stipulations requiring China to turn the assets of the Eastern Orthodox Church over to the government of the Soviet Union and to determine the price set for the Chinese Eastern Railroad. Thus, the State Affairs meeting instructed Wang Zhengting to press Karakhan for further revisions.

The reversal of the Chinese position aroused strong resentment from Karakhan. After several rounds of unsuccessful talks, the negotiations collapsed. With open protests by professors, students, and military personnel in various provinces, criticism of the failed negotiations spread rapidly. Forced by huge public pressure, at the end of March the MFA of the Beiyang government had to send a personal request from Gu Weijun for a meeting with Karakhan so as to restart the Sino-Russian negotiations. During the following ten days, the two sides met 20 times; China finally won partial concessions from Karakhan on the use of the Boxer Indemnity and the repeal of Russian privileges in China.

On 31 May 1924, Chinese and Soviet Russian representatives formally signed the *General Agreement on Solutions to the Unresolved Issues Between China and Russia* (15 articles) and the *Temporary Agreement on the Management of the Chinese Eastern Railway* (11 articles and 7 addenda). According to the agreements, diplomatic relations between the two nations would be restored once these agreements were signed, and bilateral meetings would be held within one month to finalize the detailed measures to settle all unresolved issues. All the treaties and agreements previously signed between China and imperial Russia were to be terminated. The Soviet government was to recognize Outer Mongolia as a part of the Republic of China and to respect Chinese sovereignty over that territory. No institutions, groups, or activities aimed at overthrowing the other government through the use of force would be allowed to exist or to operate in the territory of either party. All sovereignty issues related to the Chinese Eastern Railway would be handled by the Chinese government. China would have authority to buy back, with Chinese capital, the Chinese Eastern Railway and all its other properties. Prior to the buyback, the Chinese Eastern Railway would be operated jointly. Its Board of Trustees and Board of Directors would consist of ten members, with five members appointed by each country. A Chinese would serve as president of the Board of Trustees and chairman of the Board of Directors. A Russian would serve as director of the Railroad Bureau. The Railroad Bureau would also have two deputy directors, one Russian and one Chinese. The positions of department heads would be equally split between Russians and Chinese. The Soviet government would give up all the concessions, privileges, and exemptions the Russian government had obtained in China in the past including the Boxer Indemnity, exterritorial rights, and the consul courts.

The signing of the *General Agreement on Solutions to the Unresolved Issues Between China and Russia* marked official mutual recognition and the establishment of diplomatic relations between China and the Soviet Union. However, the Beiyang government, because of intervention by a consortium of foreign missions, dared not accept the Soviet Union's proposal for an immediate exchange of ambassadors. Instead, until July it continued to try to persuade the Soviet Union to exchange only ministers, just like the other powers. Finally, on 31 July, Karakhan was able to hand a letter of credence to the president of the Republic of China, becoming the first Soviet ambassador to China. The transfer of the Russian embassy building was strongly opposed by the consortium of foreign missions in Beijing that had been taking care of the property. The long and unsuccessful negotiations aroused strong resentment in the Chinese media. The issue was finally settled in September through US mediation.

At the same time, Zhang Zuolin, the warlord in Fengtian, declared autonomy and refused to recognize the agreements signed by the Beijing and Soviet governments. He even claimed that the agreements encroached on Chinese sovereignty and were an insult to the nation. Since operation of the Chinese Eastern Railway had to be approved by Zhang Zuolin, Karakhan sent delegates to Fengtian to begin negotiations with Zhang. The two sides signed the *Agreement Between the Provincial Government of the Three Eastern Provinces of the Republic of China and the Government of the Soviet Socialist Federation* (the Feng-Russian Agreement) on 20 September. It provided that all issues related to the Chinese Eastern Railway would be resolved through negotiations between the Fengtian government and the Soviet Union. It was only then that the Soviet Union was finally allowed to take over the Chinese Eastern Railway.

The Beijing government under the Zhili (Hebei province) warlords opposed this agreement and subsequently, in the same month, a second war erupted between the Zhili and Fengtian warlords. After defeating the Zhili warlords, the Fengtian warlords regained control over the provisional government in Beijing and in March 1925 they announced that the Feng-Russian Agreement would be added as an addendum to the *General Agreement on Solutions to the Unresolved Issues Between China and Russia*.

According to Article 2 of the *General Agreement on Solutions to the Unresolved Issues Between China and Russia*, "a meeting will be held within one month to negotiate detailed solutions to all unresolved issues." However, the meeting did not take place as planned because the second war between the Zhili and Fengtian warlords had broken out in September 1924. One month later, Feng Yuxiang organized a mutiny in Beijing, allowing the Fengtian army to enter North China. With support from the Fengtian warlords, Duan Qirui reemerged as the provisional president of the Beiyang government. Having already established diplomatic relations with China and seeing the Nationalist Army commanded by Feng Yuxiang and the Nationalist Party led by Sun Yatsen in the South as its most reliable ally, the Soviet Union was not in any hurry to start negotiations with the Beiyang government.

SUN YATSEN BECOMES A REVOLUTIONARY

While the Soviet Russian government was seeking diplomatic contacts with the Chinese government in Beijing to negotiate normalization of bilateral relations, the Russian Communist Party and the Comintern, based on principles established by Lenin and the Comintern to "unite with all national liberation movements in the colonies and all oppressed nations," were actively looking for nationalist organizations and forces in China that would be capable of starting an anti-imperialist movement. Moscow put great emphasis on promoting the development of a nationalist movement in China based on the two-stage theory of revolution.[2] It believed that the top priority for China, a backward colonial or semi-colonial nation, was not to build a socialist state but rather to establish an independent democratic republic. The main force behind the revolution could not be the industrial working class which only existed in advanced capitalist countries. Instead, such a role could only be played by Chinese nationalist capitalists who were oppressed by foreign capital. Therefore, it was inevitable that Moscow, with its broad contacts with numerous political forces in China, gradually came to regard Sun Yatsen and his Nationalist Party, both of which had been active in Chinese political life and were known for a long revolutionary tradition, as a potential partner.

Ever since the establishment of the Society for China's Resurrection and the Chinese Revolutionary Alliance, the Nationalist Party had been identified with "revolution." Sun Yatsen's so-called revolution was derived from the goals set by the three most popular ideologies in Europe at the time: democracy, nationalism, and socialism. Sun wanted to win everything in one battle. Integrating these three ideologies with Abraham Lincoln's "of the people, by the people, and for the people," Sun came up with his "Three Principles of the People": nationalism, democracy, and people's livelihood. By limiting people's livelihood to "equal ownership of land," his principles to a large extent reflected the core problems faced by semi-colonial and agrarian China. However, most of Sun's activities and key supporters were located overseas. Thus, after numerous attempts he was able to successfully bring about the Revolution of 1911 and to become the first provisional president of the modern Chinese republic, which then led to the Constitutional Protection Movement,[3] Sun's revolutionary experience was filled with ups and downs. Unable to win strong support either at home or abroad, his activities were always characterized by a life-and-death struggle. In order to increase the possibility that his revolution would be victorious, Sun made every effort to obtain assistance from foreign governments, including the Japanese and American governments. But his efforts failed, even after he promised to grant them special privileges in China in exchange. Under these circumstances, the birth of the Soviet Russian government, which also had used revolution to mobilize the masses, and its victory through revolution not only gave Sun hope for a successful revolution in China but also encouraged him to seek assistance from the Soviet Union.

Collaboration between Moscow and Sun Yatsen began in 1923. The representatives previously sent by the Russian Communist Party (Bolsheviks) to China, such as Voitinsky and others, had all already met with Sun. In the summer of 1920, Liu Jiang was sent to Shanghai by the CCP Organization Bureau that had been established in Russia to meet with Sun and to discuss the possibility of a three-pronged military attack on the Beiyang government from Xinjiang, Mongolia, and South China.[4] Sun promised that he would send two representatives to be stationed in Moscow and they would soon arrive in Blagoveshchensk on the border of China. Li Zhangda, former commander of Sun's Security Regiment and consul of the headquarters of the Grand Marshal was sent to Soviet Russia. Sun instructed Li Zhangda to sign on his behalf a military collaboration agreement with the Soviet Russian government, requesting that the Soviet Russian Red Army in Russian Turkistan enter Xinjiang and then Gansu in the spring of 1921 to assist the revolutionaries in Sichuan province and to promote armed uprisings organized by revolutionaries throughout China. In the summer of 1922, Sun, having just suffered another defeat and forced to retreat to Shanghai, unexpectedly received a letter from Adolph Joffe, the Soviet Russian plenipotentiary diplomatic representative, hoping to establish close contacts. With H. Maring (Henk Sneevliet), a Comintern representative and an assistant to Joffe at the time, serving as liaison, Sun and Joffe, on 26 January 1923 in Shanghai, reached agreement on a joint manifesto. Sun agreed to maintain the status quo regarding the Chinese Eastern Railroad and to allow the Soviet Army to be temporarily stationed in Outer Mongolia. In return, Joffe guaranteed that "Communist organizations, including the Soviet system, are in fact not applicable in China." He also promised that Sun "can count on Russian assistance."

At the time, Sun Yatsen wanted to receive assistance from the Soviet Union to realize his grand project of combining a "long-term plan" and an "emergency plan." The former included establishment of a centralized command mechanism, the strengthening of political and ideological preparation of the Nationalist Party, the organization of its own army, the establishment of a military base in the Northwest, and so forth. The latter aimed at providing immediate funds and delivering weapons to the South to help the Nationalist Party retake Guangdong. Obviously, the CC of the Russian Communist Party (Bolsheviks) saw a bright future for the Nationalist Party under Sun Yatsen's leadership. On 8 March, Moscow formally decided to help Sun Yatsen, whose army had never established a base in the northwest region of China. It agreed to provide Sun with about 2 million gold rubles in aid and to provide military and political assistance to Sun. However, at the time Moscow could only provide 8000 Japanese-made rifles, 15 machine guns, 4 "Arisaka" cannons, 2 armored vehicles, and other related military materials and trainers. In order to organize the new army, in August Sun Yatsen sent Jiang Jieshi, his most trusted military cadre, as the head of a special delegation to Moscow for detailed discussions on cooperation.

Sun Yatsen's plan to establish a military base as well as an army in the Northwest was quickly rejected by the Soviet military after hearing about the Nationalists' concrete designs and practical demands from Jiang Jieshi. The reason for the Soviet rejection was Sun's plan to establish two military bases, one in Kulun (Outer Mongolia) and one in Urumqi (Xinjiang). Since the Soviet Red Army had already entered Outer Mongolia and many Soviet officials were pushing hard for the independence of Outer Mongolia, they certainly would not agree to allow Sun Yatsen to establish a military base in Kulun. The Soviet Union did recognize Urumqi as Chinese territory, but Sun Yatsen's proposal to establish a military base was deemed to be unacceptable by the Soviet military due to the occupation of Urumqi by the Red Army. Ultimately, the Soviet Union agreed to help the Nationalist Party train military cadres both in Moscow and Guangzhou. As the Nationalist Party had just regained control of Guangzhou, Moscow was confident that it could send experts and equipment to the Nationalists via the sea and help the Nationalist Party establish a military school to train officers and organize an army. However, the Soviet Communists who had taken over the government through mass propaganda and general rebellions did not have a truly positive view of Sun Yatsen's revolutionary military thinking. The advice they gave to Jiang Jieshi was that "the most urgent task for Sun Yatsen and the Nationalist Party is to make an all-out effort to carry out political work throughout the nation. Otherwise, under current circumstances any military operations will be doomed to failure."

Jiang Jieshi did not achieve the expected goals from his visit. Moscow's attitude toward Outer Mongolia did not leave him with a good impression of the Soviet Russian government, which was supposedly working toward spreading a world revolution. Not long after his return to China, Jiang told his colleagues that the Soviet Union had a "China policy that sees Manchuria, Mongolia, the areas where Muslims reside, and Tibet as part of the Soviet Union and even has no intention to keep its hands out of China proper. ... Its so-called 'internationalism' and world revolution are nothing but Caesar-style imperialism. Different terms are used simply to confuse the people." Jiang insisted that "it would be impossible for the Chinese Revolution to succeed unless it is carried out independently." However, Jiang's observations of the Soviet Red Army inspired him to become more committed to the idea of establishing an army for the Nationalist Party.

The arrival of Soviet political adviser, Mikhail Borodin, and other military advisers in Guangzhou in early October marked the formal beginning of close collaboration between the Soviet Union and the Nationalist Party. As the Soviet military leaders had proposed to Jiang Jieshi in Moscow, the first action taken by Borodin was to advise Sun to make political work a top priority and to establish a revolutionary party with broad popular support. Sun Yatsen trusted Borodin and accepted his proposal. He not only gave Borodin the title of "Nationalist Party organizer" and authorized him to lead related personnel in drafting the various documents necessary to formalize the mission and organization of the party, but he also began to push for a comprehensive reform of the Nationalist Party by following the Soviet Communist experience as introduced by Borodin. The Soviet military advisers accompanying Borodin, with authorization from Sun Yatsen, began to establish the Nationalists' first military school—the Huangpu (Whampoa) Military Academy—and Jiang Jieshi was nominated by Sun Yatsen to be the first commandant of the academy.

NOTES

1. A 27 September 1920 declaration stated, "The Russian and Chinese governments agree to separately sign a special treaty on use of the Chinese Eastern Railway to meet the needs of Soviet Russia and to allow the Far East Republic, together with China and Russia," to participate in the making of the treaty.
2. The two-stage theory is a Marxist-Leninist political theory which argues that underdeveloped countries, such as Tsarist Russia, must first pass through a stage of capitalism before moving to a socialist stage.
3. The Constitutional Protection Movement was a series of campaigns led by Sun Yatsen to resist the Beiyang Government between 1917 and 1922, resulting in the establishment of another government by Sun in Guangzhou.
4. The Organization Bureau, established in July 1920, was directly under the Russian Communist Party (Bolsheviks).

CHAPTER 2

The Nationalist Revolution Assisted by the Soviet Union

Kuisong Yang

Soviet assistance allowed Sun Yatsen's Nationalist Party to enjoy unprecedented consolidation and growth, to which the young Communists made a significant contribution within a short period of time. But the reorganization of the Nationalist Party by following the Soviet model, the admission of the Communists, and the appointment of the Communists to key positions responsible for the organization and development of the party caused some discontent. Nevertheless, Sun Yatsen clearly understood that the Union of Soviet Socialist Republics (USSR) was indispensable for the success of the Chinese Revolution, and those young Communists could play a role that the Nationalists were incapable of. Thus, he resolutely resisted the opposition within the Nationalist Party. But what Sun did not realize was that his dominant position in the Nationalist Party was, to a large extent, a key factor that prevented Moscow from gaining complete control over the future of the party. After his death, the Nationalist Party broke up because of the lack of leadership and also because it was easy for Moscow's representative to lead the party down an expected yet unacceptable road. This inevitably produced strong resistance within the Nationalist Party and eventually led to a complete split with the USSR and the Chinese Communist Party (CCP). A series of important incidents that took place within the Nationalist Party after Sun Yatsen's death are clearly indicative of this situation. The USSR was certainly the strongest supporter of the Nationalist Revolution. At the same time, it also initiated a process to destroy the Nationalist Revolution and to bring about a complete break between the Nationalist Party and the USSR and the CCP.

K. Yang (✉)
Contemporary China Study Institute, East China Normal University, Shanghai, China
e-mail: yks@vip.sina.com

© The Author(s) 2020
Z. Shen (ed.), *A Short History of Sino-Soviet Relations, 1917–1991*, China Connections, https://doi.org/10.1007/978-981-13-8641-1_2

SUN YATSEN'S POLICY TO ALLY WITH THE SOVIETS
AND TO ACCEPT THE COMMUNISTS

On 20 January 1924, the Nationalist Party held its First National Congress in Guangzhou, formally announcing its reorganization. One of the key components of the reorganization was to allow CCP members to join the Nationalist Party. To a large extent, this policy would determine the fundamental political framework of Chinese society in the following decades. It is only natural that this policy was initiated and advocated by Moscow.

The CCP had made it clear since its founding that Leninism was its ultimate guideline and it would follow the path of the Russian October Revolution and proletarian dictatorship. It advocated the complete elimination of private ownership that had led to unequal distribution. This was accomplished by a revolution launched by the lower proletarian working class against the entire upper exploiting class, just like the Bolshevik Revolution in Russia. The party constitution adopted at the First CCP Congress clearly stated that its goals for the Chinese Revolution were to expropriate the capitalist class and to establish a proletarian dictatorship. The CCP resolutely insisted that it would not compromise or cooperate with the capitalist class.

However, Maring, the Comintern representative, had obvious doubts about the future of this small CCP organization with only 50-plus members. He believed that Soviet Russia could not accomplish anything in China without uniting with Sun Yatsen's Nationalist Party, and the CCP would not have much of a future if it did not integrate organizationally with the Nationalist Party. Maring's proposal was approved by the Comintern. Having formally adopted a resolution in 1922 to recognize the CCP as a branch of the Comintern, the CCP had no choice but to agree to allow its members to join the Nationalist Party, beginning "intraparty cooperation" (*dangnei hezuo*) with the Nationalist Party. In September 1922, with an introduction from Zhang Ji and personal supervision by Sun Yatsen, Chen Duxiu, Li Dazhao, and others joined the Nationalist Party.[1] In the following June, the Third National CCP Congress passed a formal resolution approving of intraparty cooperation. Thereafter, over 400 CCP members and many Socialist Youth League members joined the Nationalist Party.

Even before the convening of the First Congress of the Nationalist Party, the Communists who had joined the Nationalist Party had been given important positions. For example, as soon as Chen Duxiu was admitted to the Nationalist Party, Sun Yatsen appointed him as one of the nine members of the Party Reform Strategy Drafting Committee to participate in the reorganization of the party.[2] Later, Chen Duxiu was appointed consul, Lin Boqu was appointed deputy director of the Service Department, and Zhang Tailei was appointed an official in the Propaganda Department. After the arrival of Borodin, the Communists under his charge became even more active. Although the number of Communist Party and Youth League members only accounted for 2 percent of all registered members of the Nationalist Party, they constituted 10 percent of the delegates to the First Congress. Close to 25 percent of all the members

[handwritten margin note: constituted the minority of Nationalist Party but large political representation]

of the Central Executive Committee elected at the First Congress were either CCP or Socialist Youth League members.[3] A similar situation existed in the Central Headquarters of the Nationalist Party that was established after the congress. Among the six departments and the Secretariat, CCP and Socialist Youth League members held the position of director in two departments (the Department of Organization and the Department of Peasants) and the position of secretary, equivalent to deputy director, in three departments (the Department of Organization, the Department of Workers, and the Department of Peasants). The CCP and Socialist Youth League members also held one-third of the seats on the Standing Committee of the Central Executive Committee.[4] Having the Secretariat and the Department of Organization under Communist leadership clearly demonstrated Sun Yatsen's positive attitude toward such cooperation between the two parties and the important role played by the CCP in the Nationalist Party. This in turn encouraged the CCP and the Socialist Youth League members to attach high priority to the development of the Nationalist Party and to make considerable efforts to accomplish its goals.

Due to great efforts by the CCP and Socialist Youth League members, after its first congress the Nationalist Party quickly established regional, provincial, municipal, and county headquarters throughout the country. Within a year, the Beijing headquarters alone had recruited about 10,000 Nationalist Party members. However, at the same time recruitment in the CCP was stagnant. According to an organization report by the CCP in Guangzhou, there were only some 30 CCP cadres in the city. Prior to its first congress, the Nationalist Party had only managed to set up 12 branches in 12 districts. But after its first congress, it established 9 district committees and 64 branches with over 7780 members. Although the Communists held important positions in 5 district committees and 13 branches, the number of Communist Party members did not increase. Always busy with routine work for the Nationalist Party, the CCP members could not find time to work for their own party. There were over 50 members when the First CCP Congress took place in July 1921. The number tripled, totaling 195, when the Second CCP Congress took place in July 1922, and this number doubled within a year, reaching 432 by June 1923 when the Third CCP Congress was held. However, by the May 1924 expanded Central Executive Committee meeting, the number of Communist Party members had not only not increased but in some regions the number even saw a drastic decline. It was during this same year that the Nationalist Party began its reorganization.

For the Soviet Ministry of Foreign Affairs (MFA), these efforts by the CCP were obviously positive. The Soviets even came to believe that "the Nationalist Party has to depend on the Communist Party because it needs the Communists to organize and take care of the masses. ... The development of the Nationalist Party completely relies on assistance from the Communist Party in all its work." However, it was difficult for the leaders of the Comintern Eastern Department to accept such a sacrifice, which affected the growth of the Communist Party. It advocated that the long debate on whether the working class should become a national revolutionary force under the banner of the Nationalist Party or should be organized under the direct leadership of the Communist Party was to be concluded as soon as possible.

In May 1924, Grigori Voitinsky was dispatched to Shanghai to preside over an expanded CCP Central Executive Committee meeting. He agreed to support Sun Yatsen and to recognize the significance of the First Congress of the Nationalist Party. However, from his perspective the meeting reached rather radical conclusions about the nature of the Nationalist Party and its inner contradictions. First of all, the meeting asserted that the Nationalist Party, as a "bourgeois, nationalist, and democratic political party," naturally tended to seek compromise. Therefore, a struggle between the left and right factions within the party was inevitable. Second, in order to strengthen the left-wing of the Nationalist Party and reduce, or even eliminate, the right-wing forces, the Communist Party should not only avoid the blind expansion of the Nationalist Party but also change its previous practice that overemphasized centralization and unity in the reorganization of the Nationalist Party. This would contribute to an open struggle against the right-wing. Third, since "the industrial working class is the bedrock of our party," the CCP should not help the Nationalist Party organize any unions or allow the union members already organized by the CCP to join the Nationalist Party. Lastly, class struggle had to be introduced into the Nationalist Party because "any compromise of class interests within a democratic party will not augment the momentum of the national liberation movement. Instead, it will reduce it."

It was at this time that conflicts emerged between the Nationalist and Communist parties over negotiations on the establishment of diplomatic relations between China and Soviet Russia, on Outer Mongolia, and on issues related to rights and privileges. Some CCP members, in order to point out the delay in recognizing the USSR by the Beijing government, published articles openly criticizing the Nationalist Party for its unreasonable lack of respect for Outer Mongolia's rights to national self-government. Their position was based on the spirit of the declaration of the Second CCP Congress that called for "respecting the right to self-government of the people along the border and establishing a federation of Chinese republics after Mongolia, Tibet, and the Muslim regions having become self-governing states." Many Nationalist Party members vehemently opposed this Communist position. They not only openly criticized the USSR for entering into negotiations with the Beijing government but also attacked the Communists for defending USSR interests and they demanded that the Communists be harshly punished. Sun Yatsen also openly expressed his disapproval of the Communist position.

The rapid rise in the number of CCP members in the Nationalist Party and their control over the development of Nationalist organizations throughout the nation had already led to resentment by many senior Nationalist Party members who had been displaced during the reorganization. After its expanded meeting in May 1924, the CCP began to demonstrate an increasingly radical attitude toward the Nationalist Party. At the same time, the Soviet government, while expressing its willingness to assist the Nationalist Party, on 31 May signed the *General Agreement on Solutions to the Unresolved Issues Between China and Russia* with the Beijing government, despite the opposition by the Nationalist Party. All this was intolerable to the disgruntled Nationalists.

In June, the Nationalists in Shanghai obtained copies of the *Journal of the Socialist Youth League* and other CCP documents, including the Resolution on the Nationalist Movement and the Nationalist Party adopted at the Third CCP Congress, the Resolution on Comrades Working in the Nationalist Party and Their Attitudes adopted at the First Plenary Session of the Third CCP Congress, and other resolutions passed at the Second National Congress of the Chinese Socialist Youth League and at the expanded CCP Central Executive Committee, and so forth. They immediately took those documents that demonstrated the CCP's organized secret activities in the Nationalist Party to Soviet adviser Borodin. They asked: "What is the Russian attitude toward the Chinese Revolution?" Would it only support the Nationalist Party or would it insist on a "parallel path" by simultaneously assisting the Communist Party? For them, Russia was the root of the problem and the CCP's behavior merely reflected that "Russian policy toward the Chinese Revolution was to manipulate it through admission of the Chinese Communists into the Nationalist Party." In the face of these questions from the Nationalists, Borodin clearly realized that it was impossible to continue concealing the CCP's organized activities within the Nationalist Party. Therefore, he decided to openly share his views with the Nationalists. He told them that from the very beginning relations between the Nationalist and Communist parties had been for "mutual use." "The Nationalist Party used the Communist Party and the Communist Party used the Nationalist Party, but the Nationalist Party reaped more benefits through such 'mutual use.' In the current situation, a 'factionalization of the party,'" he continued, "is inevitable. Since the party Central Executive Committee in reality is unable to serve as the leading center, the emergence of small factions leaning to the left or to the right is only natural. … [and] factionalization may lead the Nationalist Party to its deathbed." However, Borodin believed that "the Nationalist Party has already died. The Nationalist Party is no longer a party. There are Nationalist Party members, but there is no Nationalist Party. Thus, only by admitting new members, such as the Communists, and organizing party groups the competitiveness of the old party members might be promoted and the party resurrected." He said that he hoped that "the competition between the leftists and rightists will generate a central faction that will serve as the core of the party."

The frictions between the Nationalist and the Communist parties over the establishment of diplomatic relations between China and the Soviet Union eventually led to Sun Yatsen's decision to hold the Second Plenary Session of the First Congress of the Nationalist Party in August to discuss the resolution, cosponsored by its Supervisory Committee members, to expel the Communist Party. Although Sun Yatsen did not want to see a split between the two parties and the crisis was temporarily resolved after an "International Liaison Committee" was established, based on a proposal by Borodin to handle relations between the Comintern and the two Chinese parties, the vigilance and even hostility toward the Soviet advisers and the Communist Party could not be suppressed.

The Nationalists' suspicion of the Soviet Union was alleviated somewhat during September and October of 1924 after the rebellion of the Guangzhou Merchant Association and the arrival in Huangpu of the first batch of Soviet weapons. The USSR sent 8000 rifles with bayonets and 4 million rounds of ammunition. This was enough to equip a division, while the students at Huangpu Military Academy could only form three companies with 30 rifles. Together with the large quantity of arms captured from the Guangzhou Merchant Association, the Nationalist Party now had enough weapons to equip not only the first Nationalist Army but also the garrison forces and pickets in Guangzhou. The USSR continued to send a huge number of weapons and munitions to the Nationalists on a number of occasions until the beginning of the Northern Expedition[5] in 1926. The Russian assistance, valued at close to 3 million rubles, included 4000 Japanese rifles with 4 million rounds of ammunition, 14,000 Russian rifles with 8 million rounds of ammunition, 90 various machine guns, and 24 various cannons.

In fact, the funding and loans provided by Moscow to help establish the Huangpu Military Academy, reform the Central Bank, support the reorganization of the Nationalist Party, and provide weapons and ammunition to equip the Nationalist Army made it possible for the Nationalist Party to establish and consolidate its control over Guangzhou under the vicious glare of the numerous warlords in Guangdong, Yunnan, and Guangxi provinces.[6] Sun Yatsen was fully aware of Moscow's contribution. Having failed to obtain any assistance from any other power for many years, Sun had finally found a country that could really help his nation. This was undoubtedly the key reason that he resolutely allied with the Soviet Union.

On 23 October 1924, Feng Yuxiang overthrew the Beijing government that was controlled by the Hebei warlords. He sent a telegram to Sun Yatsen and others, asking them to come to Beijing for the establishment of a national coalition government. Spurred on by Borodin, Sun Yatsen happily agreed. He immediately halted preparations for the Northern Expedition and began a trip north. Having just reached Tianjin, Sun was afflicted with liver disease.

Sun Yatsen's satisfaction with the cooperation with the USSR and his emphasis on future reliance on Soviet assistance was clearly revealed during the last moments of his life. He wrote in his will: "For over forty years I have been devoted to the Nationalist Revolution aimed at freedom and equality in China. Based on my experiences during the past forty years, I now clearly know that if we want to achieve this goal, we must arouse the masses and ally with those nations that treat us as an equal to engage in a joint struggle." In his will, Sun even added a special note for the Soviet government. He wrote that

while suffering from this incurable disease here, I turn my thoughts to you and to the future of my party and nation. … You are the leader of this grand federation of free republics. This grand federation of free republics is the real legacy left by the immortal Lenin for the oppressed nations. What I will leave is the Nationalist Party. I hope that the Nationalist Party will fully collaborate with you to complete its historical work aimed at liberating China and the other nations that have been invaded by the imperialist system. Fate has forced me to leave my cause unfinished and to transfer it to the person who will strictly follow Nationalist Party doctrine and lessons to organize our true comrades. Thus, I have asked the Nationalist Party to continue the work of the national revolutionary movement so that China will free itself from the shackles of semi-colonialism imposed by the imperialists. In order to achieve this goal, I have ordered that the Nationalist Party continue to receive help from you for a long time. I deeply believe that your government will continue to assist our country.

Soviet Intervention and the "20 March" Incident

The Soviet plan to speed up the Chinese Revolution received an unexpected setback with the sudden death of Sun Yatsen. However, the rapid rise of Feng Yuxiang and his National People's Army in the North immediately ignited Moscow's strong desire to directly assist Feng Yuxiang to obtain control over the Beijing government. It is obvious that Japan was causing the greatest concern for the Soviet Union with respect to security in its Far Eastern region. Because the Hebei warlords, compared to the warlords in Anhui and Fengtian, had the worst relations with Japan, Moscow worked very hard to reach a compromise with Hebei warlord Wu Peifu. But without a favorable response from Wu Peifu, Moscow had to pin all its hopes on Sun Yatsen because no matter whether Fengtian warlord Zhang Zuolin or Anhui warlord Duan Qirui controlled the Beijing government, under pressure from Japan they each would adopt a harsher policy toward the Soviet Union. Under such circumstances, the successful mutiny waged by Feng Yuxiang gave Karakhan, Soviet ambassador to China, some new hope.

In early 1925, through Li Dazhao, the CCP leader in the North, and others, Karakhan started to work on Hu Jingyi, commander of the Second Army of the Nationalist Army, to reach an agreement. Hu Jingyi agreed to allow the USSR to send a group of military advisers to work with the Second Army. However, the plan was scrapped because of the sudden death of Hu. Fortunately, at about the same time Borodin succeeded in establishing contacts with Feng Yuxiang and was able to convince him of the benefits of cooperating with the USSR. Feng was willing to partner with the Soviet Union and receive Soviet aid, thus inspiring Karakhan. On 28 April, Karakhan gave a speech to those Soviet military advisers who were about to be sent to assist Feng's troops. Elaborating on Soviet policy toward Feng, Karakhan emphasized that "Feng's army is the cornerstone of the national liberation movement in North China and everything should be done to help make Feng's army stronger and to last longer." Moscow was excited to hear this news. Via Kulun in Outer Mongolia, it immediately sent 18,000 rifles, 90 machine guns, 24 cannons with a huge amount of ammunition, and 10 planes to Feng's army stationed in Zhangjiakou. The China Committee of the Politburo of the All-Union Communist Party (Bolsheviks) (AUCP (b)) engaged in many discussions about the possibility of providing large-scale assistance, totaling 20 million rubles, to Feng Yuxiang's National People's Army.[7] The speed and scale of Soviet assistance to Feng Yuxiang obviously exceeded the assistance to Sun Yatsen and the Nationalist Party. The reason was very simple. Just as Karakhan had stated: "The victory of Fengtian [warlord] Zhang [Zuolin] will be a victory for the conservatives and the imperialists, especially the Japanese, who are a true threat to the Soviet Union. If we are unable to disrupt Zhang, at least he should be weakened. At this point, Feng Yuxiang is Fengtian [warlord] Zhang [Zuolin]'s worse enemy."

On 10 October 1925, warlord Sun Chuanfang of Jiangsu and Zhejiang formed a coalition with the armies from Anhui, Jiangxi, Jiangsu, and Fujian provinces to challenge the Fengtian warlord. Zhili (Hebei province) warlord Wu Peifu broke his silence and announced he would accept support from 14 provinces, making him commander-general of the coalition force against the usurpers. Numerous other anti-Fengtian forces throughout the South spread like a wild fire. In order to take advantage of the situation and bring down the pro-Japanese and anti-Soviet warlord Zhang Zuolin, Soviet diplomats worked with many different forces. While sending his representatives to contact the warlord Sun Chuanfang of Jiangsu and Zhejiang and promising a supply of arms, Karakhan even managed to get close to the wife of Guo Songling, an officer in the Fengtian faction, to convince her to persuade this young and powerful general to revolt. If Feng Yuxiang could take Beijing as well as Hebei province and declare war on Zhang Zuolin, it would not be difficult to bring him down, especially when Guo Songling took the opportunity to stage a mutiny. In order to achieve this goal, the CCP and the Nationalist Party in Beijing, with encouragement by the Soviet diplomats, launched massive demonstrations. The CCP Central Committee (CC) called on "the revolutionary people of the nation, the revolutionary Nationalist Party, and the revolutionary soldiers to immediately join the uprising in Beijing so as to overthrow the treasonous Anfu government, establish a unified national government, and return power to the people."

While Karakhan was making every effort to form a broad anti-Fengtian united front in Beijing, Borodin, taking advantage of the chaotic situation caused by the absence of leadership in the Nationalist Party after the death of Sun Yatsen and the assassination of left-wing leader Liao Zhongkai by right-wing leader Hu Hanmin, was successfully able to exclude the powerful right-leaning leaders Xu Congzhi and Hu Hanmin, and to elevate Wang Jingwei and Jiang Jieshi to the highest political and military positions. This action touched off an anti-Soviet and anti-Communist wave within the Nationalist Party. About one-half of Central Executive Committee and Supervisory Committee members gathered in front of Sun Yatsen's coffin at Biyun Temple, located in the Western Hills near Beijing, to hold a so-called Fourth Plenary Session of the First Congress of the Nationalist Party. They demanded that the

Communists be stripped of Nationalist Party membership and that Borodin be relieved of his position as adviser. In order to maintain the status of the CC of the Nationalist Party in Guangzhou and to win over the wavering Nationalist Party members, Comintern representative Voitinsky and CCP CC leader Chen Duxiu were forced to take steps to console the Nationalist Party members. They proposed limiting the number of CCP members on the Nationalist Party Central Executive Committee to only one-third of the total seats so as to keep the rest of the wavering members on the Central Executive Committee and the Supervisory Committee from joining the "Western Hills Conference Faction." However, the January 1926 Second National Congress of the Nationalist Party revealed that the number of CCP members with powerful positions within the Nationalist Party had actually increased. Aside from keeping the promise to limit the number of CCP members on the Nationalist Party Central Executive Committee and the Supervisory Committee to one-third of the total seats, CCP members held 77 percent of the leading positions in the eight departments and the one office of the Nationalist Party Central Headquarters. The number of CCP members in the National Revolutionary Army reached 100. The directors of the Political Departments of the First, Second, Third, Fourth, and Sixth Armies, the party representatives of all three divisions, and seven of the nine regiments in the First Army directly under Jiang were all CCP members. At the same time, the Soviet advisers were the de facto leaders in almost all the military departments in the Nationalist government. The CCP not only commanded the 2000 armed picketers and 6000 members of the peasant self-defense army but also led about 100,000 organized workers and 600,000 peasants in the Guangdong peasant associations. It is clear that the power of the CCP remained a serious threat to those Nationalist Party members who were still worried about the future of their party.

However, the real power of the Nationalist Party remained in the hands of Wang Jingwei and Jiang Jieshi. Wang Jingwei followed all of Borodin's advice and Jiang, in the eyes of all the Russian military advisers, was a devoted leftist and one of the most revolutionary individuals in Guangzhou.[8] Therefore, both the Russian advisers and the CCP CC were content with the Nationalist Party armies, especially the First Army led by Jiang. They believed that these armies had "reached a high level of political stability and loyalty to the revolutionary Nationalist government," and that there were absolutely no problems. However, shortly after the Second National Congress of the Nationalist Party, an incident on 20 March resulted in an attack on the Soviet advisers and CCP members and then their ultimate expulsion from the party.

There were three direct causes for the "20 March" incident. First, Jiang Jieshi's Northern Expedition plan was resolutely opposed by the Soviet adviser, thus leading to a confrontation. Sun had been intent on carrying out the Northern Expedition so it was seen as a major way to realize Sun's unaccomplished desire. The Northern Expedition plan of the new Nationalist government was originally proposed and completed by former Soviet Chief Military Adviser General Galen (Vasily Konstantinovich Blyukher). As early as the first half of 1925, Galen had come up with an initial draft of a plan, which had been submitted to the CC of the Nationalist Party as well as to Moscow. Having become the military leader of the Nationalist Party in the summer of 1925, Jiang at this time was enjoying rising momentum. His ambition was to move forward with the Northern Expedition plan. However, just as the Nationalist government declared its establishment in Guangzhou and the National Revolutionary Army was officially organized in July 1925, General Galen, Jiang's most trusted adviser, was unexpectedly recalled. In February 1926, Borodin, the chief political adviser who had provided the most support to Jiang during his rise, also suddenly returned to Russia. Kisanka (N. V. Kuybyshev) who assumed the position of chief military adviser, did everything he could to block the Northern Expedition. What Jiang did not know was that Kisanka's attitude actually reflected Moscow's position. Because the war against the Fengtian warlord promoted by Moscow had failed after intervention by the Japanese Kwantung Army, the AUCP (b) CC Politburo became concerned that if the Nationalist Party in Guangzhou were to launch the Northern Expedition, Japan could take the opportunity to hasten its aggression in China's Northeast, threaten the Chinese Eastern Railway, and even force Zhang Zuolin to "declare the independence of Manchuria." Thus, upon hearing of the Nationalist Party's plan to start the Northern Expedition, the director of the Comintern Eastern Department clearly told its representative in China that "we strongly denounce the Northern Expedition."

Second, Borodin, who understood Jiang's personality, was forced to leave Guangzhou and return to Russia when Kisanka and others pushed him out after the Second Congress of the Nationalist Party. Kisanka, as a headstrong and conceited officer, looked down upon the Chinese officers and often ridiculed Jiang Jieshi. Communications between the two became increasingly difficult after they confronted each other regarding the Northern Expedition. Kisanka not only cared little about Jiang's feelings and continued to be condescending and give him long lectures on politics, asserting that if the Chinese Army did not undergo thorough reform, military victories would lead to rule by new warlords. He even indicated that Jiang would become someone like Mustafa Kemal Atatürk in Turkey. Under such circumstances, when Kisanka planned to take one division from the First Army under Jiang to form a new army, Jiang's suspicion that Kisanka was trying to seize his troops and reduce his power was aroused. Jiang responded with a threat to resign from his positions as commander of the First Army, member of the Military Committee, and garrison force commander of Guangzhou so that he could go to the USSR. However, he did not receive any sympathy from Wang Jingwei. Instead, when Jiang presented his proposal to relieve Kisanka, Wang even defended the Russian adviser. All this further intensified Jiang's suspicions and fear. When he accidentally heard that Li Zhilong, the interim director of the Bureau of the Navy and also a CCP member, had ordered the warship "Zhongshan" to sail to Huangpu without his approval, Jiang immediately suspected that it was part of a conspiracy by Wang Jingwei and Kisanka to kidnap him and to send him to the Soviet Union. After long deliberation and some hesitation, Jiang finally chose to stage a mutiny with the First Army under his command.

In the early morning of 20 March, Jiang Jieshi suddenly instructed his troops to implement a curfew in Guangzhou, arrest Li Zhilong and about 50 CCP members in the First National Revolutionary Army, surround the residences of the Soviet advisers in the Eastern Hills and the residences of the Strike Committee of Guangdong and Hong Kong, take all the weapons from the pickets and the security guards for the Soviet advisers, and seize the warship "Zhongshan," which was already back in Guangzhou. Jiang then immediately called a meeting of the Political Committee which adopted a resolution ordering that Kisanka return to the USSR and that all the party representatives in the First Army be replaced. A. S. Bubnov, secretary of the AUCP (b) and director of the Political Department of the Red Army who had been leading a Soviet delegation visiting Guangzhou, agreed that the Soviet military advisers were running too much of the show. Thus, he openly accepted Jiang's demands and removed Kisanka. Impossible to explain the situation or to defend himself, Wang Jingwei had no choice but to hide under the pretext of an illness. Jiang Jieshi, taking advantage of his position as chairman of the Military Committee, pushed to convene the Second Plenary Session of the Second Congress of the Nationalist Party. The plenary session passed the Bill of Party Rectification that had been drafted by Jiang. It clearly provided that CCP members should constitute no more than one-third of the total number of members of the Nationalist Party Central Executive Committee; that the CCP should turn over the list of its members in the Nationalist Party to the chairman of its Central Executive Committee; that the Communists should not participate in any other political organizations and activities except those approved by the Nationalist Party Headquarters; that CCP members should not serve as directors of any departments in Nationalist Party central organizations; that CCP members should not criticize Sun Yatsen or the Three Principles of the People; and that Nationalist Party members were not allowed to join the CCP unless they received approval to withdraw from the Nationalist Party, and so forth.

The meeting of the Second Plenary Session of the Second Congress and adoption of the Bill of Party Rectification not only provided legitimacy to the 20 March mutiny launched by Jiang Jieshi but also allowed Jiang to rapidly rise to become the top military and political strongman holding all power in the Nationalist Party. The biggest catch for Jiang was that thereafter there was no one who could stop him from launching the Northern Expedition. By this time, Feng Yuxiang and Guo Songling had lost their war against the Fengtian warlords and Zhang Zuolin's troops had already entered Beijing. As Manchurian independence was no longer an issue, Moscow ended its opposition to the Nationalist's Party's Northern Expedition.

THE SOVIET ADVISERS AND THE NORTHERN EXPEDITION

The Soviet Union did not directly oppose the Nationalists' attempt to overthrow the Beiyang government and to unify China through military means. In fact, Moscow sent military advisers to China, helped establish the Huangpu Military Academy by providing personnel and funds, provided training for various drills and shooting and tactical exercises, and assigned military advisers to the student army directly participating in the Eastern Expeditions against Chen Jiongming.[9] All this was done in an attempt to help the Nationalist Party train an army that could be victorious. Even when General Pavlov, the chief military adviser, drowned in a military action, Moscow immediately sent General Galen back to China to fill Pavlov's position, clearly indicating the attention Moscow was paying to the military organization and actions of the Nationalist Party.

Under the guidance of the military advisers, the Huangpu Military Academy and the National Revolutionary Army, which was organized later, followed the Soviet model. They appointed party representatives and set up political departments. Based on observations and recommendations from the military advisers, the Nationalist Party selected some promising military and political talent to send to the USSR for further training at Soviet military academies. The Nationalist Party's first army, the First Army of the National Revolutionary Army, was established with help from the student army of the Huangpu Military Academy as well as with the help of the Soviet advisers. With this army, Sun Yatsen and the Nationalist Party no longer had to rely on the local warlords. As the Eastern Expedition forces based on the student army of the Huangpu Military Academy won consecutive victories with the help and command of the Soviet advisers, the sphere of influence of the Nationalist Party gradually expanded from the city of Guangzhou to vast areas in Guangdong and Guangxi provinces. The warlords in these two provinces then all gathered under the banner of the Nationalist Party. With the establishment of the Nationalist government in Guangzhou in the summer of 1925, the National Revolutionary Army quickly grew into seven armies. It was under these circumstances that General Galen proposed and completed the plan to launch the Northern Expedition. The plan stated that "the Northern Expedition should start in the second half of 1926." General Galen believed that the Northern Expedition Army would not only be able to reach the Yangtze River and take Wuhan without too much resistance but also "be able to expand eastward to Shanghai." In a word, "success is undisputable." This is also why from the very beginning Jiang Jieshi was so excited about the Northern Expedition and supported its launch.

The formal beginning of the Northern Expedition of the National Revolutionary Army began on 9 July 1926. Soviet advisers were assigned to almost all the armies and divisions of the Northern Expedition forces to assist the commanders and to strictly follow the battle plan that had been worked out by chief adviser Galen. Galen, who had returned to China based on a request from Jiang, not only personally visited the battlefront but also on several occasions flew to the enemy defense lines to gain firsthand information. Galen depended on a Staff Department composed solely of Soviet officers and specialists as well as a small group of Soviet pilots who conducted reconnaissance and bombing missions against the enemy. It was by following the battle plan that had been designed by Galen that the Northern Expedition Army was able to swiftly take over Hunan and Hubei provinces and then occupy large areas in Jiangxi, Fujian, and Anhui provinces. Even after he turned against the Soviet Union and the Communists, Jiang Jieshi never forgot Galen's contribution and always respected his talents.[10]

The victory of the Northern Expedition also benefited from the participation and support of Feng Yuxiang's National People's Army. Beginning in 1925, Feng had hired Soviet military advisers to train his men. The first group of Soviet military advisers arrived in Zhangjiakou in early May, starting their work in the First National People's Army. One month later, another group of advisers was sent to work in the Second National People's Army. Because Feng's National People's Army was about to engage in a decisive battle with the Fengtian warlords, the Soviet government sent to China Alexander Yegorov, who had served as commander of the Southwest theater which had won numerous victories during the Russian civil war and who after the war served as chief of staff for the Red Army, to assume the position of military attaché so that he could assist Feng's National People's Army from closer proximity. Although such assistance did not help Feng's army achieve a victory, the Soviet government welcomed Feng Yuxiang to Moscow and gave him a large amount of military aid, allowing his National People's Army to be resurrected after its brief collapse. By July 1926, the USSR had provided the National People's Army with 55,857 rifles, 60 guns, 230 machine guns, 18 mortars, and tens of millions of rounds of ammunition. Once the Northern Expedition began, the USSR sent an additional 3500 rifles, 11.5 million rounds of ammunition, three planes, and ten flamethrowers. It was with the generous aid from the USSR and the wholehearted assistance of the Soviet advisers that Feng's army was able to enter Henan from Shanxi, directly threatening Hebei and Shandong provinces that were under the control of the Fengtian warlords. This became an important auxiliary force that helped to achieve the goals of the National Revolutionary Army's Northern Expedition.

The "May Instructions" and the Split Between the Nationalist and Communist Parties

The smooth military progress made by the Northern Expedition allowed Moscow to sing high praises for the Nationalist Army. *Pravda* continuously published articles lauding the National Revolutionary Army, referring to it as a "completely different force from that of the Chinese warlords in terms of its organization and the political consciousness of its soldiers." *Pravda* also stated that it "is a truly people's army," "outstanding and highly respected by the people." Stalin openly concluded that if the revolutions in Europe depended on people's uprisings and riots, the success of the revolution in China would rely on the army because "in China the army of the old regime confronts not unarmed people but armed people represented by the revolutionary army. In China, it is the armed revolution against the armed counterrevolution. This is one of the characteristics and strong points of the Chinese Revolution."

Encouraged by the optimistic moods of Stalin and the AUCP (b) CC, the Seventh Expanded Meeting of the Executive Committee of the Comintern, held at the end of 1926, gave the CCP an even more radical task. It requested that the "CCP should do its best to eventually complete the transition to a non-capitalist revolution," which meant "the establishment of a democratic dictatorship of the proletariat, peasants, and the other exploited classes, and an anti-imperialism and revolutionary government for the transition leading to a non-capitalist (socialist) society." In order to attract peasants to participate in the revolution, the CCP offered their support to take over the governments in the countryside, reduce land rents and tax burdens, confiscate the land owned by warlords, landlords, local tyrants, temples, and churches, and turn over the land to the nation. "The Communists should join the Guangzhou government so as to support the revolutionary left-wing's struggle against the weak and wavering policies of the right-wing," guaranteeing "the nationalization of land, elimination of the foreign concessions, and confiscation of large enterprises, mines, and banks leased to foreign nations," and so forth.

At the end of February or the beginning of March 1927, the CCP CC finally received a copy of the China resolution that had been reached at the Seventh Expanded Meeting of the Executive Committee of the Comintern. Prior to this time, radical revolutionary propaganda had reached the broad masses despite the lack of preparation during the fast-moving Northern Expedition. The worker and peasant movements in Guangdong, Hunan, and Hubei provinces became unruly. In Wuhan alone, over 150 strikes took place within several months after the Northern Expedition Army took over the city. Eager to eliminate poverty and improve their living standards, laborers in all trades competed with one another to hike their demands to such a level that "wages rocketed to a soaring level, workdays were reduced to four hours or less, random arrests took place, courts and prisons were established, transportation was interrupted at will, and factories and shops were confiscated." In Hunan, such radical actions spread to the peasant movement. Capping the rich with "tall hats," forcing them to provide free open meals, engaging in kidnappings, arrests, and killings, banning the raising of pigs and ducks, stopping the shipment of rice and animals, resisting taxes and levees, destroying tax offices, and taking over army food supplies, all this occurred everywhere. In addition, the war seriously affected the economy and trade. As many foreign enterprises were closed, banks shut down, big trade companies declared bankruptcy, and Chinese factories had trouble maintaining normal operations because of the frequent strikes and serious shortage of raw materials. As a result, production gradually became paralyzed, markets withered, the economy became stagnant, and prices skyrocketed. In the face of this situation, the CCP CC took steps to "prevent us from turning too sharply to the left," to limit the anarchist actions, and to oppose the numerous demands by workers and peasants. However, acceptance of the resolution of the Seventh Expanded Meeting of the Executive Committee of the Comintern forced the CCP CC to immediately and drastically change its attitude.

The CCP CC adopted a resolution recognizing that "we made a fundamental mistake in the past by creating an insurmountable gap between the Nationalist Revolution and the proletarian revolution. We assumed that we could only have a Nationalist Revolution today and that any tiny step beyond that would violate the iron law of the revolution. Now we know that we have to break through the limits when making revolution. We should not only win the actual leadership of the proletarian class but we should also establish a democratic dictatorship for the workers, peasants, and other exploited classes so as to place the railways, shipping industry, mines, and large factories under state control. The goal is to march toward socialism." They thus believed that "the Chinese Nationalist Revolution has entered a period of stabilization; it is the right time for the proletarian class to take over the leadership." The CCP CC was confident that "Chinese workers are powerful and revolutionary, and they are capable of shouldering the task of the world revolution." Therefore, the Chinese Revolution must be completed with "one single strike."

Influenced by the resolution reached at the Seventh Expanded Meeting of the Executive Committee of the Comintern, Borodin, the chief Soviet political adviser who had been sent back to China after the 20 March incident, began to help the CCP and the leftists regain control of the Nationalist Party CC but at the same time reduce the power of Jiang Jieshi. The CCP CC also secretly organized forces and was "preparing for a major defensive bloody sacrifice" so as to compete with Jiang Jieshi for control of Shanghai, the most important city in China. However, the AUCP (b) CC, which was always a half-step behind in assessing the revolutionary situation in China, in late March suddenly started to dampen the revolutionary enthusiasm of the CCP CC. It sent consecutive telegrams to the CCP CC, making three requests: first, no armed entry into the foreign concessions should be allowed, so as to prevent a repeat of what had occurred in the foreign concessions in Hankou, which then might lead to concerted intervention by the imperialist countries; second, greater attention should be paid to make better use of the conflict between the leftists and rightists within the Nationalist Party. A direct confrontation with the Nationalist Army should not be rushed and recruitment should remain secret so as to ensure self-protection; third, an armed organization was to be established. No weapons were to be abandoned and all weapons were to be hidden when the balance of power became unfavorable.

Stalin made these requests because he clearly saw the great risk of launching a struggle in Shanghai. Yet he had nowhere to retreat because his China policy faced sharp criticism from Leon Trotsky and Grigori Zinoviev. The danger that Jiang Jieshi might break ties with the CCP provided a strong excuse for Trotsky and others. This situation forced Stalin to focus on class struggle, while remaining unable to alter the existing moderate policy. Stalin openly explained: "The Nationalist Party is a kind of federation—a revolutionary parliament made of leftists, rightists, and Communists. If we are the majority and the rightists are following us, why should we stage a mutiny? Why should we expel the rightists? … At the present time, we still need the rightists. They are capable people who can lead the army in carrying out the anti-imperialist struggle. Jiang Jieshi may not sympathize with the revolution, but he controls the army and can be used in the anti-imperialist struggle." In a speech delivered on 6 April, Stalin famously stated: "We should make the best use of the Nationalist Party. Just like a lemon, it can be thrown away only after being squeezed dry."

However, before the CCP could complete the necessary preparations, on 12 April Jiang Jieshi and the others found an excuse to seize all the weapons from the pickets of the Shanghai General Union. On 18 April, the Nationalists led by Jiang Jieshi set up a separate CC of the Nationalist Party and openly challenged the existing CC of the Nationalist Party and the Nationalist government in Wuhan. At the same time, Jiang began a bloody purge within the party.

After the 12 April incident and the establishment of the Nationalist government in Nanjing, the provinces occupied by the National Revolutionary Army, such as Guangdong, Fujian, Guangxi, Anhui, Zhejiang, Jiangsu, and other provinces in the Southwest, sided with Jiang Jieshi and the Nationalist Party in Nanjing. Zhu Peide in Jiangxi, sandwiched between Nanjing and Wuhan, kept wavering, and only Hubei and Hunan provinces were still controlled by the CCP and under the influence of the left-wing Nationalists. These two provinces had already faced an economic crisis and tense relations with foreign countries due to their radical worker and peasant movements. The situation was exacerbated as water and land transportation was cut off, finances collapsed, and relations among the different forces and even between the army and the worker and peasant movements worsened.

In the second half of May, because of the betrayal of Xia Douyin's troops in Hubei and of Xu Kexiang's army in Hunan, the Wuhan government lost control over much of Hubei and Hunan provinces, further weakening their position. In April, the Beijing government took sudden action against the Soviet embassy, not only arresting and executing a number of Communist and Nationalist Party members, including Li Dazhao, but also publishing numerous secret documents detailing Soviet assistance to the Nationalist Party and to Feng Yuxiang's National People's Army, thus creating tremendous political pressures on both the Nationalists and Feng Yuxiang. As a result, the Wuhan government was forced to announce the firing of Borodin as adviser.

Facing such a serious situation, Borodin and the leaders of the CCP CC in Wuhan tried to reach a compromise so as to escape this dangerous situation. However, Stalin and others began to realize that a split between the Nationalist Party and the CCP was inevitable. In order to deprive Trotsky and the others of an opportunity to prove the failure of the "policy of compromise," Stalin suddenly instructed the Comintern to issue the famous "May Instructions."

While recognizing the need to "fight against overzealous behavior," requesting to "leave the land of the officers and soldiers alone," and making concessions to craftsmen, businessmen, and petty landlords, the May Instructions gave very firm orders. They included strong support for the takeover of the landlords' land at the grassroots levels and doing everything possible to win over the peasants; a change in Nationalist Party membership and admission of new worker and peasant leaders to the Nationalist Party CC; the establishment of the CCP's own army by mobilizing 20,000 CCP members and 50,000 revolutionary workers and peasants in Hubei and Hunan provinces; the setting up of a revolutionary court headed by well-known Nationalists and non-Communists in order to punish the reactionary officers.

Moscow's "May Instructions" not only did not provide any guidelines for the split but also continued to emphasize the necessity of maintaining a united front between the Nationalist and Communist parties. This inevitably tied the hands of the Soviet advisers and the CCP leaders. Many points in the instructions could not be presented to the Nationalist Party CC because they would certainly reinforce a split. Nor could many of the points be implemented at the time. Thus, the CCP CC had no choice but to put the instructions aside and ignore them. Unwilling to give up without a try, M. N. Roy, head of the Comintern delegation who had just arrived in Wuhan, privately showed Wang Jingwei, the Nationalist leader in Wuhan, the telegram from Moscow, hoping to win over Wang's understanding and create an opportunity to gradually implement the instructions. In order to resolve its financial problems and to be able to support the army financially, Wang Jingwei requested a loan of 15 million yuan. However, Moscow only agreed to provide 2 million rubles in aid. Because Moscow did not satisfy his demands, Wang Jingwei did not follow its instructions.

On 22 June, Feng Yuxiang, the only one who could give the Nationalists in Wuhan some hope, openly turned to Jiang Jieshi and the Nationalists in Nanjing. He demanded that the Nationalists in Wuhan send Borodin back to the USSR and adopt a policy that would separate the CCP from the Nationalist Party. Following Feng Yuxiang, Tang Shengzhi, He Jian, and other generals in Hunan openly expressed sympathy for Xu Kexiang and the others, denounced the worker and peasant movements, and attacked the Nationalist Party CC in Wuhan for its continued acceptance of the Communists.

On 8 July 1927, Moscow finally realized that a split was inevitable. It ordered the Communist Party members to withdraw from the Wuhan government in protest. At the same time, it instructed the Communists to unite with the leftists within the Nationalist Party and to convene a new party congress from the bottom up so as to take over leadership of the Nationalist Party.

By this time, Wang Jingwei was forced to disclose to senior Nationalist Party leaders the content of Moscow's "May Instructions." The result was easy to predict. On 15 July, the Nationalist Party CC in Wuhan finalized its policy of parting with the CCP, requiring that all the Communists leave the Nationalist Party and all government offices. With support from the Soviet advisers, the

Communists, who were determined to completely separate themselves from the Nationalists in Wuhan quickly, gathered all the troops under their control and on 1 August began the Nanchang Uprising under the leadership of the "Revolutionary Committee of the Nationalist Party." This action quickly turned the policy of the Nationalist Party authorities in Wuhan from one of separation from the CCP to one of exterminating the CCP. The collaboration between the two parties thus came to a complete halt.

NOTES

1. As for Li Dazhao's admission to the Nationalist Party, Li Yunhan, based on the *Public Relations Journal* of the Nationalist Party's Public Affairs Department, concludes that it took place in early February 1922. According to Li Dazhao's own recollections, however, it occurred during Sun Yatsen's 1922 stay in Shanghai. According to Maring's notes, Li Dazhao went to Shanghai between August and September to attend the meeting at West Lake in Hangzhou that discussed intraparty cooperation with the Nationalist Party. Since Chen Duxiu and the others had joined the Nationalist Party immediately after the meeting, it is reasonable to believe that Li Dazhao was admitted to the Nationalist Party roughly at the same time.
2. According to Maring's notes, it was called the "Reorganization Committee of the Nationalist Party."
3. Among the 25 members of the Central Executive Committee, Tan Pingshan, Li Dazhao, and Yu Shude were CCP members. Among the 17 alternate members of the Central Executive Committee, Shen Dingyi, Lin Zuhan, Mao Zedong, Yu Fangzhou, Qu Qiubai, Han Lingfu, and Zhang Guotao were CCP members.
4. The Standing Committee of the Central Executive Committee consisted of three members. Liao Zhongkai and Dai Jitao were Nationalist Party members and Tan Pingshan was a CCP member.
5. The Northern Expedition was a military campaign launched by the Chinese Nationalist Party against the Beiyang government and other regional warlords in 1926.
6. In addition to the 2 million rubles for assistance that was formally approved in May 1923, Moscow contributed 2.7 million Chinese yuan to the establishment of Huangpu Military Academy, and also provided a 10 million Chinese yuan loan to help stabilize finance in Guangzhou and to establish the Central Bank. See Martin Wilbur, *Sun Yat-sen: Frustrated Patriot* (New York: Columbia University Press, 1976), pp. 148–209.
7. The first batch of weapons finally approved for Feng Yuxiang by the Politburo of the AUCP (b) in October 1925 was about one-quarter of the initially proposed amount.
8. C. Martin Wilbur, *Missionaries of Revolution: Soviet Advisers and Nationalist China, 1920–1927* (Cambridge: Harvard University Press, 1989), pp. 608–9.
9. The Eastern Expeditions of 1925 in Guangdong province, including the campaign against Chen Jiongming's forces in eastern Guangdong in March, the suppression of a revolt by Yunnan and Guangxi forces in June, and a second

campaign against Chen Jiongming in October and November served as "defining moment" trends that would characterize the Nationalist military forces in the following decades.

10. After the Wuhan split, Jiang Jieshi insisted that Galen either remain in his army or be returned to Russia with high honors. After the beginning of the war against Japan, Jiang Jieshi sent repeated requests to the Soviet Union asking that Galen be his chief military adviser.

CHAPTER 3

Moscow and the Soviet Revolution in China

Kuisong Yang

The Soviet Revolution in China began in 1927 and ended in 1936. This period not only marked the closest association between the Chinese Communist Party (CCP) and the Union of Soviet Socialist Republics (USSR) but also presented a historical opportunity that forced the CCP to start moving toward independence and self-reliance.

Prior to this period, the CCP had basically relied on financial assistance from Moscow to carry out its activities. Through the Comintern, the Red Workers' International, the Youth International, and other organizations, Moscow provided fixed monthly operations funds to the CCP as well as to the union and youth league under its leadership.[1] Funding for the CCP, while only about 15,000 Chinese yuan for the entire year of 1921, exceeded the US$ 15,000 per month in 1927. The amount of Soviet financial aid was even greater if its funding for the union, youth league, peasant associations, relief societies, various meetings, temporary organizations, and all kinds of emergencies and rebellions were included. This clearly demonstrates the level of CCP dependence on Moscow during this time. However, as the CCP Red Army gradually took shape and its soviet base areas expanded, the financial reliance of the CCP Central Committee (CC) on Moscow began to decline in 1930. When the Provisional CCP CC completely withdrew from Shanghai and moved to the soviet areas in Jiangxi in early 1933, Soviet financial aid came to a halt. Once the CCP CC was financially self-reliant and no longer dependent on Moscow, changes in their political relations became inevitable.

The changes in relations during the Soviet Revolution are also evident in the shift in the focus of CCP work. After the split between the Nationalist and

K. Yang (✉)
Contemporary China Study Institute, East China Normal University, Shanghai, China
e-mail: yks@vip.sina.com

© The Author(s) 2020
Z. Shen (ed.), *A Short History of Sino-Soviet Relations, 1917–1991*, China Connections, https://doi.org/10.1007/978-981-13-8641-1_3

Communist parties, domestic and external troubles frequently erupted. The USSR openly supported, even with direct intervention by Soviet diplomats, the armed uprisings organized by the CCP. Zhang Xueliang and the Nanjing government intentionally initiated the Chinese Eastern Railroad incident so as to take over the railroad and regain all control and privileges. This either directly or indirectly increased tensions in relations between the Chinese and Soviet governments and eventually led to a complete break in diplomatic relations. Moscow was so determined to support the CCP to start a Russian-style Soviet Revolution that it disregarded the resultant diplomatic damage. From the political guidelines to the formulation of specific documents, from the smuggling of CCP delegates to Moscow to attend a congress to helping the CCP finalize various political resolutions, and from reorganizing the CCP leadership to sending political and military advisers to Shanghai, and even to the soviet areas so as to direct battles from close proximity, Moscow was closely involved in all CCP activities. However, the CCP Revolution directed by Moscow suffered from a series of disastrous defeats before 1930. The Mao Zedong–style rural base areas that were beyond Moscow's plans and experiences displayed a strong vitality. As a result, between the summer and fall of 1930, Stalin made timely adjustments to the existing guidelines, focusing on taking over the major cities, and the authority of the Russian advice was challenged. The focus of the CCP Revolution shifted to the countryside. Russian-style mass uprisings were replaced by military struggles. Although the Soviet Republic of China built after the Russian model eventually was unable to defeat the military campaign launched by the Nationalist Party, Mao Zedong, a native-bred leader who possessed rich guerrilla warfare experience, was able to rise above a large number of CCP leaders who had been trained in the Soviet Union.

CCP Armed Uprisings and the Break in Sino-Soviet Diplomatic Ties

As the Nationalists in Nanjing and Wuhan parted ways with the Communists, the unique scenes of throngs of Russians appearing in the Chinese Army and on Chinese streets disappeared almost overnight. Although Moscow did not give up its efforts to keep its men in China, the Communists were forced to go underground. Was this to be regarded as a complete loss of the 1905 Revolution in Russia or as a temporary setback suffered in July 1917 immediately before the October Revolution? It became a watershed moment used by the Communists to differentiate the revolutionaries from the non-revolutionaries. Stalin refused to recognize that the Chinese Revolution under his guidance had failed. He asserted that the setback in the Chinese Revolution was "similar to the setback suffered by the Bolsheviks in July 1917." The Communists would "return to the streets," at most after a wait slightly longer than that experienced by the Russians between July and October 1917. Therefore, immediately after the Nationalists in Wuhan declared a peaceful parting of ways with the CCP, the Communists, based on the advice of Galen, on 1 August began an armed rebellion in Nanchang, Jiangxi province, with help from its cadres working in the army. But the Nationalist Party Revolutionary Committee swiftly organized a countermeasure. The new young Comintern representative quickly held an emergency meeting of the Provisional CCP CC in Wuhan on 7 August, confirming the new policy of armed uprisings.

From the "1 August" Nanchang uprising to the "9 September" rebellion in southern Hubei, from the Autumn Harvest rebellion in Hunan to the three uprisings in Hailufeng, Guangdong province, to the 11 December rebellion in Guangzhou directed by experts sent by Stalin, these nationwide armed struggles, organized by the CCP CC and aimed at taking over the government, created a gripping movement of rebellions that led the Russians to believe that the success of the revolution was just around the corner. During the Guangzhou uprising, diplomats in the Soviet Consulate in Guangzhou openly worked as military advisers for the Communists. They drove Consulate cars with rebel flags throughout the city as if victory had already been achieved. However, the Guangzhou uprising, lasting only two days, was suppressed by the Nationalist Army. Several Soviet diplomats, as well as thousands of rebels, were brutally killed and their bodies were left to rot on the streets of Guangzhou.

The open support by the Soviet diplomats for the Communist rebellions forced the Nationalists to sever diplomatic ties with the USSR. However, because the Beijing government still existed as the central government of China and the Nationalist government in Nanjing was not recognized by any foreign nations, termination of diplomatic ties was only effective in the areas controlled by the Nationalist Army. However, the failure of the Guangzhou uprising did sober the leaders in Moscow and they decided to shelve their plans for a new uprising. In early 1928, the Comintern and the All-Union Communist Party (Bolsheviks) (AUCP (b)) made great efforts to smuggle about 100 CCP representatives from various locations in China to a suburb of Moscow to attend the only congress in CCP history that was held in a foreign country. There is no doubt that almost all the congress documents were drafted by the Russians or were formulated with the assistance of the Russians. Even the selection of the leaders of the CCP CC strictly followed the preferences of the Russians. At this time, the Russians still believed that there was nothing wrong with the principle of taking over the major cities and engaging in mass rebellions. The problems were caused by the overzealous young CCP leaders who were elected at the 7 August meeting.

Since 1927 Moscow had foreseen a split between the Nationalist and Communist parties as well as a Communist defeat as a result of Chen Duxiu's "rightist capitulationism." The replacement of Chen Duxiu by Qu Qiubai did not bring about any improvement in the situation. For Stalin and others, the fundamental problem was that the CCP leadership was in the hands of petty-bourgeois intellectuals. One of the main reasons that Moscow held the CCP National Congress in the USSR was to make sure that more than one-half of the delegates were revolutionary workers, so that they would elect a new CC in which workers held more than one-half of the seats, and, in turn, the CC would elect a new Politburo with a high ratio of workers. In the end, Moscow believed that Xiang Zhongfa, an old worker and former chairman of the General Union of Hubei Province, met Moscow's criteria. As a result, he became the first and only secretary general in the history of the CCP with a worker background.

Unfortunately, Xiang Zhongfa did not reveal any proletarian insights after his rise to power. Even his working-class background did not guarantee better interactions with the representatives from Moscow. On the contrary, Xiang Zhongfa still had to rely on Li Lisan and other intellectuals to carry out organization and propaganda work. Li Lisan's inclination toward putschism was even stronger than that of Qu Qiubai. He not only strongly advocated a general rebellion throughout the nation but he also asserted that the Chinese Revolution would inevitably lead to intervention by foreign powers, which, in turn, would force the USSR to send troops to China's Northeast. His purpose was to push the world revolution to its final and decisive battle. The representative of the Comintern Far East Bureau in Shanghai vehemently opposed the unyielding decision by the CCP CC to organize a nationwide rebellion. However, Xiang Zhongfa fully supported Li Lisan. He not only slammed on the table in front of the representative of the Far East Bureau but he also wrote to Stalin asking for his intervention. This thoroughly embarrassed the leaders in Moscow. Although they targeted their criticism at Li Lisan, they no longer had any trust in the native worker cadres in China. In order to make sure that Moscow's instructions would be faithfully carried out, Moscow quickly concluded that it could only trust the Chinese students who had been trained in the Soviet Union. Nevertheless, they did not really believe that those young students fresh out of school had many skills. But they did believe that only those students trained in the Soviet Union would understand and carry out Moscow's decisions.

As early as 1921, Moscow began to select appropriate members from the CCP Youth League to be educated in the USSR. The first batch, including Liu Shaoqiu, Ren Bishi, Luo Yinong, Xiao Jingguang, Peng Shuzhi, Bu Shiqi, and others, was sent to study at the Communist University of the Toilers of the East in Moscow. They were followed in 1923 by Liu Bojian, Zhu De, Ren Zhuoyi, Wang Ruofei, Zhao Shiyan, Xiong Xiong, Mu Qing, Fu Lie, and Chen Duxiu's two sons, Chen Yannian and Chen Qiaonian. After 1924, Li Fuchun, Fu Zhong, Li Zhuoran, Deng Xiaoping, and others also had the opportunity to be educated in Moscow. Those who were somewhat more formal students were those 2000 Chinese who entered Sun Yatsen University, which had been established in 1925. A considerable number of those who were admitted to Sun Yatsen University were CCP and Youth League members. Some, including Wang Ming, Bo Gu, Zhang Wentian, Wang Jiaxiang, Shen Zemin, Kai Feng, Xia Xi, Yang Shangkun, Chen Changhao, Li Zhusheng, Sheng Zhongliang, Yu Xiusong, Zhou Dawen, Dong Yixiang, Sun Yefang, and so forth, received a relatively systematic university education. However, these efforts to provide a systematic university education were interrupted by the split between the Nationalist and Communist parties. Most of the CCP members who entered Sun Yatsen University after autumn 1927, including Dong Biwu, Lin Boqu, He Shuheng, Xu Teli, Wu Yuzhang, Ye Jianying, Wu Liangping, and so forth, had been smuggled into the Soviet Union to take refuge. Because of the special role of the military revolution in China, many of these Chinese students engaged in military studies and received training in the operation of radio-transmitters, gathering information, and engaging in espionage. Liu Bocheng, Wang Yifei, Nie Rongzhen, Fu Zhong, Zhu Rui, Chen Geng, Wu Xiuquan, Zuo Quan, Shi Zhe, Zhou Baozhong, Mao Qihua, Xu Zuochao, Chen Changhao, Gu Shunzhang, Li Jianru, and others are among the most famous. As so many people in the CCP received their education in the Soviet Union, it was not difficult for Moscow to select cadres who were 100 percent "Bolshevik" to serve as leaders at various levels of the CCP.

It was only several years after the split between the Nationalist and Communist parties that there was a fundamental change in relations between the CCP and Moscow. The CCP headquarters became increasingly dependent. From the perspective of Moscow, by the Fourth Plenary of the Sixth National Congress in 1931 the CCP CC had made the transition to being "100 percent Bolshevik," under the successive leaderships of Chen Duxiu, Qu Qiubai, and Xiang Zhongfa. This transition was made possible because Wang Ming, Bo Gu, and a large group of students who had studied in the USSR and who were loyal to the Russian Bolsheviks were put in leadership positions in the CCP CC and the Youth League CC immediately after their return to their homeland.

THE CHINESE EASTERN RAILWAY INCIDENT AND "DEFENDING THE SOVIET UNION"

The unique nature of relations between the CCP and the Soviet Union during this period was also clearly evident during the Chinese Eastern Railway incident in 1929.

Because of the Second Northern Expedition launched by the Nationalist government in 1928, the Fengtian army began a massive withdrawal. Japanese officers stationed in the Northeast, who were unhappy with Zhang Zuolin's failure to declare independence of the Northeast as well as by his constant meddling in the affairs west of Shanhaiguan, plotted the Huanggutun incident, killing Zhang Zuolin with a bomb on 4 June. However, Zhang Xueliang, who inherited his father's position, refused to yield to the Japanese treachery. After a long and complicated process, he bravely changed banners and put the Northeast region under the jurisdiction of the Chinese central government.

The banner change in the Northeast did not fundamentally change the situation because of the serious threat from Japan. It was impossible to restore all Chinese rights to the area along the line of the South Manchuria Railway or to retake Lüshun (Port Arthur) from Japan. Nevertheless, taking advantage of the "revolutionary diplomacy" advocated by the Nationalist government in Nanjing in 1929, the young and daring Zhang Xueliang attempted to realize his plan to restore all rights in the Northeast by focusing first on the rights and privileges enjoyed by the Soviet Union in northern Manchuria.

Early in the year, the Northeast government took forceful steps to gain control of the supply of electricity along the Chinese Eastern Railway. Although the USSR initially protested through its consul general in Shenyang and demanded over 1 million yuan to cover its re-location costs, there was no other response. In April, the Northeast government again raised the issue of rights and privileges over the Chinese Eastern Railway. The Soviets made another concession, allowing the Chinese to assume the directorships, which previously had been held by the Russians, of six departments of the Chinese Eastern Railway, including business, engineering, mechanics, services, accounting, and receivables. Emboldened by these early successes, Zhang Xueliang and his associates made some inaccurate assessments in the aftermath.

On 27 May, Zhang Xueliang, accusing the USSR consul general in Harbin of engaging in secret Communist propaganda activities, suddenly sent soldiers and police to search the Consulate and to make a number of arrests. Most people present in the Consulate at the time were attending a meeting. Many of the participants included Russian officials from all the stations along the Chinese Eastern Railway, representatives from the workers' associations in the factories in the Sanshiliupeng area, the heads of the Soviet Aviation Bureau, the Far Eastern Kerosene Bureau, the Far Eastern Commerce Bureau, and other organizations and departments. Although security was part of Zhang Xueliang's consideration, his attempt to secure all rights over the Chinese Eastern Railway was most obvious.

The people's commissioner of foreign affairs of the USSR protested the attack on the Consulate in Harbin and declared that "effective immediately the Soviet government, disregarding the provisions of international law, does not recognize the extraterritorial rights of the Chinese Diplomatic Office in Moscow or the Consulates in other locations in the USSR as provided by international law."

But this action did not intimidate Zhang Xueliang. With encouragement from Jiang Jieshi and the Nationalist government in Nanjing, in the name of the Northeast Executive Commission and other offices, Zhang Xueliang on 10 July declared that China would take back management of the Chinese Eastern Railway because the USSR had violated the Fengtian-Russo agreement that prohibited Communist propaganda in China. On the same day as well as on the next day, the Northeast government dispatched soldiers and police to close down the Soviet Merchant Liner and Trade Company, the National Trade Company, and so forth, and sent anti-Soviet Russians (White Russians) to take over the Departments of Engineering and Mechanics, to force the dismantling of Soviet workers' associations, youth leagues, women's departments, and the children's league, and arrested and deported over 200 Soviet managers, including the Russian director and deputy director of the Chinese Eastern Railway Administrative Bureau.

The USSR initially appeared to be willing to resolve this incident in a peaceful manner. In an ultimatum issued on 13 July, the USSR proposed that meetings were to be held as soon as possible to resolve all outstanding issues involving the Chinese Eastern Railway. However, the Nationalist government in Nanjing was unyielding in its 16 July reply. It claimed that China's action had been an appropriate response to the various organized propaganda activities by the USSR that were aimed at inciting the Chinese people against their own society and government. The purpose of the actions taken by the Northeast authority was to prevent riots and other social disturbances.

Because China disregarded the demand for an immediate release of the arrested Soviet personnel and an end to all illegal actions, on 17 July the Soviet government declared that it would completely sever diplomatic ties with China. It then withdrew all diplomats from its Consulates in Harbin, Qiqihaer, Hailaer, Manzhouli, Heihe, and Suifen River. Soviet employees working for the Chinese Eastern Railway resigned and departed. At the same time, the Red Flag Far East Special Corps was organized to command all military forces in the Soviet Far East. With Galen as commander, it began to threaten the Northeast authority by force, arresting about 1000 Chinese merchants, detaining many Chinese ships, and sending surveillance planes into Chinese territory.

Jiang Jieshi and the Nanjing Nationalist government originally thought their anti-Soviet actions would win support from all the anti-Communist foreign powers. However, to the surprise of the Chinese, the foreign governments were opposed to Chinese efforts to resolve the disputes over rights and privileges through the use of force. As a result, the USSR adopted an even tougher stance against China. It took revenge not only by detaining a large number of Chinese in the USSR and confiscating their property but also by sending troops to harass the border area along China's Northeast. Because Zhang Xueliang was not at all prepared for this Soviet military action, he changed course and sought to seek a settlement. However, the Nanjing government vehemently opposed making any concessions. The Nationalist Party organized many massive anti-Soviet demonstrations aimed at defending the nation's sovereignty. Jiang Jieshi even issued a public statement, claiming that "the top priority of our policy toward Russia is to expose the true color of Soviet Russian aggression. … If Soviet Russia dares to openly undermine world peace and encroach upon our national interests, we will support the government's efforts with our revolutionary spirit, defend our sovereignty, and protect world peace as well as our national interests regardless of the costs."

Finally, after China and the USSR had been engaged in a battle of words for three months, the Tongjiang campaign was launched in the early dawn of 12 October 1929, when the Soviet Army launched a massive attack on Chinese forces in Tongjiang, with 25 planes, 10 worships, and over 40 cannons. Later, over 3000 infantry soldiers and 800 cavalry men joined the action. After some stubborn resistance, the river fleet of the Chinese Navy was almost wiped out.

Five warships, including the Jiangping, Jiang'an, Jiangtai, Lijie, and Dongyi, were sunk, and the Lisui fled back to Fujin with heavy damages. Although 17 officers at ranks lower than regiment commander were killed, soldier casualties reached about 700.[2] By three o'clock in the afternoon, the Soviet Army had occupied the county seat of Tongjiang and the Chinese defense forces had been forced to retreat to Fujin. Because the Soviet forces quickly withdrew after the battle, the Nanjing government believed that within a short period the USSR would not be able to launch another massive attack. Therefore, it refused to make any diplomatic compromises. The Soviet Army then launched another massive two-pronged attack beginning on 17 November. While the Western forces concentrated their attacks on Manzhouli and Zhalainuo'er, the Eastern forces targeted the Suifen River and Mishan county as well as an extension of the bombing to Mudanjiang. Entering over 50 kilometers into Chinese territory, the Eastern forces took over Mishan county and moved to the areas north of Jiamusi and east of Mudanjiang. The Western forces pushed through Manzhouli, Zhalainuo'er, Cuogang, and occupied Hailaer. The Hang Guangdi brigade, part of the Heilongjiang defense forces, was completely wiped out. The brigade commander and all regiment commanders were killed. The Liang Zhongjia brigade, unable to break the siege, was forced to surrender. About 10,000 in the two brigades on the western front were captured. Other losses of personnel and property were impossible to count.[3] The Northeast defense forces on the western front were forced to retreat from Manzhouli and the Mo River line to east of the Hailaer and Xinganling/Boketu line. Zhang Xueliang ordered the troops along the Mo River to protect the merchants and other civilians and to move them to the Neng River so as to keep them close to the food supplies.

The two defeats suffered by the Northeast defense forces caused devastating losses. Despite opposition from Nanjing, Zhang Xueliang was forced to sign an agreement with the Soviet Union. Although the Nanjing government was extremely unhappy with Zhang's actions, Jiang Jieshi reluctantly approved the agreement because of his concern about the rising anti-Jiang movement west of Shanhaiguan. This incident, although beginning as a Chinese effort to recover all its lost rights, ended with heavy military losses, deep suffering among the people, and a huge humiliation for the nation. It also exposed the capabilities of the Northeast Army and the degree of possible intervention by the international community in the Northeast, providing an important source of reference for the Japanese Kwantung Army when it began its outrageous "18 September" incident two years later.

Since the very beginning, the response of the Comintern Far Eastern Bureau to the Chinese Eastern Railway incident was to instruct the CCP CC to publicize the slogan of "defending the Soviet Union with arms" and to organize massive anti–Nationalist Party and pro–Soviet Union demonstrations. The CCP CC responded positively without hesitation. The CCP CC Politburo decided to employ all its propaganda machines, hold a demonstration on 1 August, that is, "Anti-Imperialism Day," and plan a general strike in Shanghai.

Responding to the steps taken by the CCP CC, Chen Duxiu sent a letter criticizing this action. He asserted that "it is not advantageous for us" to "advocate support for the Soviet Union" at this moment. It is too simplistic, he wrote, to assume that "the vast majority of the masses all see the Soviet Union as a friend of the Chinese Revolution." Because of this letter and because of a belief that Chen Duxiu and others were all strongly opposed to the political line of the CCP CC, the CCP CC immediately passed a resolution to expel Chen Duxiu and the others from the party. The CCP CC obviously believed that the views expressed by Chen Duxiu and the others regarding the Chinese Eastern Railway "thoroughly revealed themselves to be wavering opportunists within the party." As for the massive attack by the Soviet Red Army on the Northeast Army in China, the CCP CC insisted that it was a preemptive action forced upon the Soviet Union because an imperialist war against the Soviet Union was imminent and the Nationalist Party had taken the Chinese Eastern Railway by force and had supported the White Russians in their invasion of the Soviet Union. Based on this, it held that "only the liquidationist Chen Duxiu could believe that the peace negotiations between the Soviet Union and Fengtian could have reduced or even eliminated the danger of attacks by the Soviet Union." The party must "intensify its efforts to mobilize the masses for armed struggle and integrate all armed struggles by workers and peasants so as to carry out the task of supporting the Soviet Union with arms and to start a war against the warlords. The ultimate goal is to start a nationwide general rebellion."

Since the Chinese Eastern Railway incident eventually ended with the USSR as victor, the CCP and the Red Army "defense of the Soviet Union with arms" remained mainly in the form of demonstrations and propaganda slogans. No concrete actions were taken.

Following the Soviet Union: The Soviet Republic of China

When the Chinese Eastern Railway incident took place, the CCP CC was still under the leadership of Xiang Zhongfa, who preserved a certain degree of independence. The leadership took the position of "supporting the Soviet Union" on the Chinese Eastern Railway issue not because it blindly followed Moscow but because it shared the same beliefs as almost all Communists at the time. It strongly believed that the world was divided along class lines. Since the Soviet Union was a socialist country, it was the only motherland of the world and the headquarters for the world's Communist parties. Simply put, the existence of Communist parties throughout the world was closely tied to the existence of the Soviet Union. Defending the USSR was thus equivalent to defending the worldwide revolution. Therefore, the existence of the USSR was not only in the interest of all Communists throughout the world but also was a model for all Communist revolutions. In addition to building party organizations in the same format as the Communist Party of the Soviet Union (CPSU) (Bolsheviks), all revolutions in the various countries had to follow the model of the Soviet Revolution.

It was in mid-September 1927 that the CCP displayed the banner of the Soviet Revolution for the first time. Following Comintern instructions, the Comintern representative drafted the Resolution of the Left-Wing Nationalist Party and the Issues of Soviet Slogans, declaring that the Nationalist Party flag had become a symbol of the "bourgeoisie, landlords, and counterrevolutionaries." Therefore, the CCP should not only spread "the Soviet ideology but also should establish soviets in the new high tide of the revolutionary struggle."

In Russian, a "soviet" is a noun meaning "assembly." It had become a special noun simply because it came to denote a committee organized by the striking workers during the 1905 Russian Revolution. According to the revolutionaries, a soviet was a political organization that functioned both as an organizer of strikes and as a self-governing body of workers. Ideal for the Communists to lead the workers fighting against the government, soviets reemerged and became a mechanism in the revolutionary struggle for challenging the legislature and the government during the new revolutionary high tide of 1917. The Bolsheviks eventually used the soviets to lead anti-government rebellions and the soviets became synonymous with the supreme government power apparatus to implement class dictatorship after the victorious revolution.

As a revolutionary mode, a soviet was first applied to the Chinese Revolution in Hailufeng (Haifeng and Lufeng counties) in Guangdong province. Peasant rebels led by Peng Pai called their government a soviet, which was established after their successful rebellion in Hailufeng. However, this was apparently inconsistent with the resolution drafted by the Comintern representative. According to the resolution, "the establishment of soviets are prohibited in small county seats prior to their establishment in central locations, such as Guangzhou and Changsha, which are occupied by revolutionary rebels" so as to make sure that the "true meaning" of proletarian leadership embedded in the soviets is not lost. Thus, what made the Communists, especially the Communists in Moscow, believe that the phase of the Soviet Revolution had finally arrived in China was the Guangzhou rebellion. On 12 December, the second day of the Guangzhou rebellion, the first soviet government in Chinese history whose authority was recognized by Moscow was finally established. Organization of the government, and even official titles, completely copied the USSR model. For example, Su Zhaozheng was appointed chairman of the soviet (Zhang Tailei served as interim chairman in Su's absence), Ye Ting was the commander-in-chief of the Workers-Peasants Red Army, Huang Ping was the people's commissioner of international and foreign affairs, Yang Ying was the people's commissioner of counterrevolutionary extermination, Zhou Wenyong was the people's commissioner of labor, Peng Pai was the people's commissioner of land, Chen Yu was the people's commissioner of justice, He

Lai was the people's commissioner of the economy, and Zhang Tailei was the people's commissioner of the army and navy, and so forth.

However, within two days the Guangzhou rebellion ended in defeat. The consecutive defeats of the urban rebellions, especially the Guangzhou rebellion, forced Stalin to end his experiment of establishing soviet governments in the central cities of China by following the model of the Russian October Revolution. The overthrow of the central cities and the establishment of urban soviets did not take place again until two years later. Taking advantage of participation by Hunan warlord He Jian and his troops in the Central China campaign, Peng Dehuai led the Third Corps of the Red Army to occupy Changsha and to declare the establishment of a Chinese soviet government, with Xiang Zhongfa as president. However, the occupation and the soviet government lasted for only two days. Both ended with the return of He Jian's troops.

In reality, ever since Stalin had permitted the CCP to use the banner of the Soviet Revolution, it had already begun to call the various types of government it had established in small bases in the rural areas as soviets. Only because the CCP CC insisted that the soviets had to be organized by industrial workers in urban centers, it vehemently opposed the *de facto* recognition of peasant governments in the rural areas as real soviets. As a result, the organization of a united soviet government apparatus in all the bases was delayed. Li Lisan, one of the leaders of the CCP CC, until 1930 continued to believe that the soviets had to be established in the cities. No soviets were to be established in the rural areas. In early 1930, based on a demand by the Comintern, the Far East Bureau raised the issue of holding a national soviet congress. However, the CCP CC paid little attention. In the February announcement calling for a soviet congress, the word "region" was intentionally added after the word "soviet" to emphasize that the representatives only represented soviet-type bases. Because of opposition by the Far East Bureau, the CCP CC changed the name of the congress to the "First National Congress of Workers, Peasants, and Soldiers (Soviets)." Yet, it still included a "preparatory committee" as part of the wording to indicate that this congress was not authorized to elect a truly national soviet government. Worrying that the "preparatory committee" might still cause some misunderstanding among the participants at the congress after it convened on 19 May in Shanghai, the CCP CC changed its name to the "Congress of the Soviet Regions." This flip was sharply criticized by the Far East Bureau. On 10 July, the Comintern issued clear instructions that stressed that the organization of a central soviet government should be a top priority for the party and that it was completely possible for a central soviet government to be established in a soviet area where livelihood was sustainable and protection was provided by the Red Army. However, the Comintern's instructions encouraged the CCP CC led by Xiang Zhongfa and Li Lisan to accelerate the launch of large-scale nationwide rebellions aimed at taking over the major cities. Li Lisan insisted that soviets must be established in regions with national significance, such as cities at least the size of Shashi and Yichang in Hubei, and that they should never be established in the countryside. As a result, little progress was made in establishing a unified national soviet central government until Moscow took steps to change the plans of the CCP CC.

In October, the Comintern finally provided a completely new interpretation of the characteristics of the Chinese Soviet Revolution, which was different from the CCP CC's understanding of the model of the Russian October Revolution. Actually, more than five months earlier, Stalin had already told CCP leaders that the Chinese Revolution should take a path different from that of the Russian Revolution, with a greater focus on the development of the Red Army and the base areas. The Comintern later further elaborated on Stalin's views. It pointed out that the Chinese Revolution would not be exactly like the Russian Revolution, which was known for taking over the national government by conquering several major cities. The Chinese Revolution had to take a different path. It "should start a peasant movement and guerrilla warfare in non-soviet areas so as to establish a tight siege on the local cities, the big cities, and the biggest cities. ... We should also organize our own forces within the warlord armies and intensify our work in these armies by ten times. The purpose is to destroy the Nationalist government and to weaken it everywhere. Only in this way will it be possible to prepare for armed uprisings in the large industrial cities and for the occupation of these cities by armed rebel workers and the Red Army."

The Comintern's instructions fundamentally reversed the superstitious attitude of the CCP CC about the role of the working class as well as the impact of the central cities in the Soviet Revolution. After many Chinese students who had been educated in the Soviet Union and who were more faithful to instructions from Moscow were put in leading positions at the Fourth Plenum of the Sixth CCP Congress, the CCP CC followed Comintern instructions and drastically changed the focus of its work. Beginning in February 1931, over 60 percent of cadres and key workers were sent to various rural bases, providing the soviet regions and the Red Army with unprecedented reinforcements.

On 7 November, the Provisional Central Government of the Soviet Republic of China, the unified national soviet central government, was formally established in Ruijin, the capital of the Jiangxi Soviet Region. Mao Zedong was appointed chairman of the Central Executive Committee and of the People's Committee, Zhu De was appointed people's commissioner of the military, Wang Jiaxiang was appointed people's commissioner of foreign affairs, Deng Zihui was appointed people's commissioner of the treasury, Xiang Ying people's commissioner of labor, Qu Qiubai people's commissioner of education, Zhou Yishu people's commissioner of interior affairs, He Shuheng people's commissioner of workers and peasants and director of the Supreme Court, Zhang Guotao people's commissioner of justice, and Deng Fa director of national political security.

Thus, although Stalin still emulated the soviets as the typical format for the Russian Revolution and government, his thinking about the Chinese Revolution was not necessarily more rigid than that of the native CCP leaders.

MILITARY LOSSES UNDER THE SOVIET MILITARY ADVISERS

Although the goal of the Soviet Republic of China was to replace the Republic of China and take the latter's territory as its boundaries, the existence of the Soviet Republic of China as a "state" still depended on its occupation of certain geographic areas. However, it was this kind of situation that brought tremendous frustrations to the soviet base regions and the Red Army that had already faced serious troubles because of the Nationalist military campaigns. The survival of the Communist forces in the provincial border regions of Central and South China was solely the result of China's vast territory and the extreme imbalance in its economic and political development. The remote rural and mountainous regions were not only cut off from the major cities and the major transportation lines but they also existed in a state of self-sufficiency, ideal for armed separation and occupation. Since the beginning of the republic, the warlords had gradually taken over the provinces. Each focused on consolidating his grip over the cities and the major transportation links within his territory, while staying away from the remote border areas with complex topographies. All this allowed for the rise of CCP armed separatism.

Prior to the establishment of the Soviet Republic of China, the Red Army had always regarded the preservation of its own forces as a top priority. It adopted flexible tactics and followed the guidelines of "retreating when the enemy advances, harassing when the enemy camps, attacking when the enemy is exhausted, and pursuing when the enemy retreats." It never stubbornly defended any particular area. At the same time, the Red Army in various regions could easily move around in large areas. It frequently moved across enemy lines in order to allow for its forces to grow. Even in the Central Red Base Area, military maneuvers remained brisk during the first year after the founding of the Soviet Republic of China because the CCP CC had not yet relocated there. Thus, although the Nationalist local authorities launched three military campaigns and Jiang Jieshi commanded a fourth campaign on his own, they won nothing and were soundly defeated by the Red Army which understood the complex topography and could maneuver rapidly. However, the situation drastically changed after the CCP CC retreated from Shanghai to the Central Soviet Region in 1933.

First, most of the leaders on the Provisional CC who retreated to the Central Soviet Region were young students who had returned from the Soviet Union. They did not have any military experience, but they were filled with a sense of mission to defend the Soviet Republic and to begin the final battle against the Nationalist government. Second, Moscow sent to China the military adviser General Manfred Stern, who remained in Shanghai to provide remote command to the CCP. At the same time, Moscow secretly dispatched Otto Braun, a young German who had received his education at a Soviet military academy, to the Central Soviet Area, using the pseudonym Li De, to help Manfred Stern direct the military actions of the Central Red Army. Last, because the Provisional CC comprised young students who had returned from the Soviet Union, it did not trust Mao Zedong or the other founders of the base area and it gave command authority to the young German who only understood military dogma. As a result, the Red Army could no longer rely on flexible and mobile tactics or on its ability to rapidly move back and forth, including fighting behind the enemy lines.

In a strict sense, this was not the situation that Moscow had hoped for. Moscow did not expect the Red Army to fight a battle to defend its own territory in the Central Soviet Area. In referring to the victory won by the Central Soviet Area against the fourth military campaign, Moscow specifically warned the CCP CC that "you should not overestimate the success won by the most recent strategy," and it reminded the CC that "we still are unable to forcefully attack the stationed enemy." Thus, we must "maintain the Red Army's flexibility and mobility, and we should not let the Red Army defend territory at the expense of tremendous casualties. Instead, we should figure out a possible route to retreat ahead of time and be prepared for it." We should "fully utilize a guerrilla warfare strategy that will avoid a disadvantageous confrontation with the enemy's main corps and [we should] adopt tactics that will lure the enemy deep into our territory, separate them, and exhaust them." Forced by the military situation in the spring, Moscow clearly approved that the Red Army in the Hubei, Henan, Anhui Border Region abandon the base area and move to Sichuan and elsewhere. Moscow even reminded the CCP CC that "it is extremely important to expand the soviet bases in Sichuan, southern Shanxi, and, if possible, Xinjiang."

However, Moscow's military principles did not completely translate into the guiding military thoughts of the Soviet military advisers or the leaders of the Provisional CCP CC. The greatest effort made by Li De after his arrival in the Central Soviet Region was to apply the regular military operations that he had learned at military school in the Soviet Union to commandeer the Red Army, which had already become accustomed to guerrilla warfare. After the Nationalist Party launched its fifth military campaign in 1934, Li De, who felt a responsibility to defend the territory, used the familiar regular warfare principles to cope with the Nationalist Army. It was just at this time that Jiang Jieshi learned a lesson from his previous losses and began to pay attention to the coordination of his troops. The troops adopted tactics that focused on building roads and fortresses, while at the same time pushing forward slowly and securely. As a result, the Red Army, which was not good at positional warfare, had to fight passive battles and deal with attrition due to its limited soldiers, weaponry, and ammunition. At the same time, its territory continued to shrink.

Having seen the situation deteriorate in the Central Soviet Region, which was isolated in the south, Moscow, as early as spring 1934, instructed the Provisional CCP CC to consider retreating. By July, the Central Soviet Region was reduced to seven counties. The situation was becoming increasingly dangerous and the Red Army could no longer continue to fight in the region. Following instructions from Moscow, General Manfred Stern first ordered the Seventh Corps of the Red Army to march eastward, as the Northward Resisting-Japan Advance Force, to Fuzhou and then turn north to northeast Jiangxi so as to integrate with the Tenth Army and form the Tenth Corps of the Red Army. Its task was to distract the Nationalist Party troops and to reduce the pressure on the Central Soviet Region by marching into the border region of Zhejiang, Anhui, and Jiangxi provinces and establishing new soviet bases. Later, General Manfred Stern ordered the Sixth Corps of the Red Army in the Hunan and Jiangxi Border Region to break the siege by moving westward so as to establish a guerrilla base in southern Hunan. This was done to prepare for the Central Red Army to break the siege, to settle down in the mountainous area of Hunan, and finally connect with the bases in Sichuan and Shanxi.

By summer, it was impossible to defend the Central Soviet Region. In order to make sure that the tens of thousands of Red Army soldiers and the CC headquarters could safely break the siege, the leaders of the Provisional CCP CC kept its plan strictly confidential. They secretly began preparations for a retreat while pretending that they would continue fighting to the last man. In an evening in mid-October, the CCP CC led 87,000 Red Army soldiers and party and administrative staff members in a secret retreat from the Central Soviet Region, leaving Ruijin and the adjacent towns. They first moved south and then west, while carrying various government, bank, hospital, and press documents on their shoulders or on the backs of horses. As a result, the Soviet Republic of China, an exact copy of the USSR government, ceased to exist on the map of China.

NOTES

1. Financial assistance provided through the Peasant International and Relief International for their counterparts was added after 1926.
2. Another report claimed that three warships of the Northeast Navy were sunk and two more were later lost. Shen Honglie, the navy chief of the Northeast Border Forces, reported that "our army's casualties reached over 500 and navy casualties were about the same."
3. According to Gao Jiyi, director of the Beijing Railroad Bureau, public and private losses in the Northeast exceeded 50 million yuan between the outbreak of the Chinese Eastern Railway incident and this campaign. Based on materials revealed by the Soviets several years ago, between October and November the Soviet Army captured 1334 mid- and high-ranking Chinese officers, 3097 lower-ranking officers, and 14,090 soldiers.

CHAPTER 4

Sino-Soviet Diplomacy Under the Threat of War

Kuisong Yang

The 18 September incident launched by Japanese officers and the Japanese occupation of the three provinces in the Northeast in 1931 seriously interrupted the strategy of the Politburo of the All-Union Communist Party (Bolsheviks) (AUCP (b)) with respect to the Chinese Communist Party (CCP) struggle against the Nationalist Party. The Japanese invasion of Northeast China dragged the Union of Soviet Socialist Republics (USSR), which had always regarded Japan as its most dangerous enemy, into a crisis that likely could end in war with Japan at any time. As a result, the USSR was forced to adjust its policy toward China. At the same time, the rise of Nazism in Germany in 1933 complicated the crisis and made it even more unpredictable. The USSR had to abandon its assistance to the worldwide revolution and to engage in diplomacy with the democratic nations in the West so as to receive assurances for collective security and to prevent a war instigated by the anti-Soviet groups in Germany. It was under the pressure of these multiple crises that the USSR abandoned its policy of isolation and actively began to seek contacts with various foreign governments, including the Nationalist government led by Jiang Jieshi. These moves inevitably affected the policy of the Comintern, whose survival was very much dependent on the USSR. As a result, the formulation and implementation of a new united front policy, including compromises between the CCP and the Nationalist Party, became inevitable.

K. Yang (✉)
Contemporary China Study Institute, East China Normal University,
Shanghai, China
e-mail: yks@vip.sina.com

© The Author(s) 2020
Z. Shen (ed.), *A Short History of Sino-Soviet Relations, 1917–1991*,
China Connections, https://doi.org/10.1007/978-981-13-8641-1_4

The "18 September Incident" and Sino-Soviet Relations

On 18 September 1931, the Japanese Kwantung Army bombed a section of the tracks of the South Manchuria Railway near the city of Mukden, blaming the attack on the Northeast Army, and then took over Fengtian (Shenyang) and began the process of occupying all three provinces in the Northeast.

Two days after the incident, the CCP Central Committee (CC) Politburo declared that the Japanese occupation of the Northeast had three goals. The first was to attack the USSR, the motherland of the proletariats of the world. The second was to loot China and suppress the revolution by Chinese workers and peasants. The last was to start World War II, with the ultimate goal of partitioning China.

Over one month later, on 7 November 1931, the Chinese Soviet Republic,[1] which had been planned by the Soviet Union and the Comintern for a long time, was established. This clearly demonstrated that the incident in the Northeast had not led to an abandonment of class struggle by Moscow or by the Provisional CCP CC. On the contrary, Moscow and the Provisional CCP CC leaders, learning from the experience of the Russian October Revolution, which had taken advantage of the crisis created by the war with Germany and had successfully captured the national government, pinned tremendous hopes on using this opportunity to overthrow Nationalist Party rule.

On 28 January 1932, the Shanghai incident occurred. The Nineteenth Route Army stationed in Shanghai and the Fifth Army sent in as reinforcement put up tough resistance against attacks by the Japanese Navy, winning broad support from Shanghai residents and public media. However, the Politburo of the Provisional CCP CC believed that "the Nationalist warlords and the Chinese bourgeoisie are lackeys of imperialist Japan" and they were "playing various tricks to fool the poor working masses" and using the opportunity to "embezzle donations from the people." It asserted that this was the best time to mobilize the masses for revolution, call upon soldiers to "kill your officers," organize suburban peasants to arm themselves, to take land, and to "carry out guerrilla warfare" so as to "overthrow Nationalist Party rule and establish the people's own government."

Therefore, while the Nationalist troops were bravely resisting the massive attacks by the Japanese Army, the Comintern and the Provisional CCP CC ordered all party organizations in Shanghai to actively initiate mutinies in the war zone. The Provisional CCP CC was instructed to issue public statements to the people of Shanghai, asserting that "the Nationalist Party and the Nineteenth Route Army are scavengers for the imperialists. No matter when, no matter where, no matter which faction, no matter which warlord, the Nationalist Party is the slave of the imperialists. No matter whether it is the Nanjing government or the Guangdong government, or Ma Zhan or Cai Tingkai, they are all the same." The Provisional CCP CC called upon the soldiers on the front "to resist the retreat order by the Nationalist warlords, shoot the officers, and take their guns with them to Zhabei, Wusong, and Nanshi so that they can continue to fight the imperialists to the end." Although disapproving of the slogans targeting Cai Tingkai and other anti-Japanese officers, the Comintern Executive Committee also saw this as an opportunity and instructed the CCP to "establish a Revolutionary Military Committee first in Zhabei, Wusong, Shanghai, and Nanjing, and then in all other major industrial cities, arrest the traitors and high-ranking officers of the Nationalist Army who had surrendered to the Japanese. ... overthrow the rule of the Nationalist government, and establish the revolutionary government of the people."

On 15 April 1932, the Provisional Government of the Chinese Soviet Republic in rural Jiangxi declared war on Japan. The purpose was to call on the masses to "actively pursue the revolutionary war, to take over the urban centers, and to overthrow rule by the Nationalist Party." The provisional government firmly believed that the "overthrow of rule by the Nationalist government" was "a necessary precondition for the smooth development of the national revolutionary war and for the beginning of the fight against Japan."

However, it rapidly became clear that such a policy was impractical. The CCP armed forces soon faced an extremely awkward situation, beginning in the Northeast. Although the Japanese were encroaching upon the three provinces in the Northeast and the main force of the Northeast Army had already moved out of the Northeast, most of the armed forces left behind by the Nationalists and the other political parties continued their resolute resistance. Following the policy of the Provisional CCP CC, the CCP armed forces not only had to simultaneously fight against both Japan and the Nationalist Party, but they also had to attack the Nationalist forces that were fighting the Japanese. As a result, the anti-Japanese CCP guerrilla forces in the Northeast, which were relatively weak, suffered serious setbacks. This situation did not begin to change until September 1932 when the Twelfth Plenum of the Comintern Executive Committee proposed implementing a new policy in Manchuria, that is, to make an effort to unite with all forces that opposed Japan.

Following instructions from the Comintern leaders, the Chinese delegation to the Comintern immediately worked out a new policy aimed at "making the greatest efforts to build a national anti-imperialist united front." It proposed that the CCP in the Northeast should not only establish a united front at the grassroots level but should also collaborate with all other anti-Japanese forces in resisting Japan. It was under the influence of these new instructions that the CCP armed forces devoted to fighting the Japanese in the Northeast began to grow. Beginning as about a dozen guerrilla forces, they evolved into the Northeast People's Revolutionary Army. With six armies, they became the core anti-Japanese forces in the Northeast.

However, with the swift occupation by Japan of the three provinces in the Northeast and especially the establishment of the Manchurian state, the attitude of the USSR began to change. The Soviet Union apparently believed that the Japanese occupation of the three provinces in the Northeast was a "prelude to attacks on the Soviet Union." Since the political and economic center of the USSR had long been focused on Europe and its defense forces in the Far East region, which was close to China's Northeast, were weak, the USSR remained neutral when Japan occupied China's Northeast and established the Manchurian state. Because of this attitude, Moscow continued to support the CCP in its struggle outside of Manchuria against the Nationalist Party, while still refusing to provide any support to the various anti-Japanese forces, including the CCP Army. When a huge number of Chinese troops withdrew into Soviet territory after suffering defeat, they were disarmed and were sent to the Central Asian region, eventually returning to China via Xinjiang. The CCP underground organizations in the Northeast and its anti-Japanese forces were also refused help when they crossed the border to seek support from the USSR Army. In 1933, Feng Yuxiang,[2] with help from the CCP organization in North China, organized the Anti-Japanese Coalition Forces in the Chahar region. When he turned to the Soviet Union for assistance, he too was rejected, leading to the rapid demise of the coalition forces.

In sharp contrast, although there was no mutual trust between the Chinese and Soviet governments, Moscow never ended its assistance to the CCP. However, once Japan invaded the Northeast and posed a severe threat to the security of both nations, the two governments restored diplomatic relations at the end of 1932 in order to distract Japan. It is obvious that because of the threat from Japan, the policy of the USSR toward China inevitably began to change.

CHANGES IN SOVIET FOREIGN POLICY AND ITS RIPPLE EFFECTS

On 30 January 1933, just as the Soviet Union was raising its alert about a possible Japanese invasion, Adolf Hitler, the Nazi Party leader known for his anti-Soviet and anti-Communist positions, obtained control over the national government in Germany and began to establish a fascist system throughout the country. Even the Communist Party of Germany, the largest Communist Party in Europe (excluding that in the Soviet Union), was quickly banned. This situation of facing enemies both in the east and the west led to a realization on the part of Stalin that it was insufficient to guarantee the safety of the USSR simply by depending on the forces of the Comintern and the Communist parties in other countries. Thus, the AUCP (b) began to adjust its foreign policy.

First, aware of Japan's tense relations with the United States and the Chinese Eastern Railway occupied by Japan as a major potential hot spot that could result in diplomatic and military disputes between the two nations, the Soviet government, despite protests from China, openly proposed on 2 May 1933 to sell the Chinese Eastern Railway to Japan. The purpose was to reduce the danger of a confrontation with Japan and to preserve tranquility in the Far East region. Formal negotiations with representatives from the Manchurian state (Manchukuo) began in Tokyo on 26 June.

Second, in order to appease the Chinese government and to make sure that China would not become another source of trouble, the USSR government on 6 August formally informed the Ministry of Foreign Affairs (MFA) of the Nationalist government in Nanjing that it would agree to sign a non-aggression treaty with China. The USSR soon presented China with a draft of a Sino-Russian non-aggression treaty and began formal negotiations with the Nationalist government in Nanjing.

Third, in order to end its political isolation in Europe, in December 1933 the Soviet government presented a formal proposal to establish a collective security system, suggesting that international mutual protection agreements should be signed by nations in the various regions to prevent aggression. The USSR quickly reversed its policy of resistance and applied for entry into the League of Nations.

The adjustments in Soviet foreign policy had a direct impact on the Comintern, forcing it to adjust its former position that had zealously promoted class revolution.

Because the Social Democratic Party of Germany was banned after the fascists came to power, the Socialist Party International (the Socialist Workers' International) took the initiative to propose the formation of an anti-fascist united front among the Socialist and Communist parties. In the face of this situation, the Comintern, despite its resolute opposition to the Social Democratic parties, sent an immediate positive response. Beginning in March 1933, the Comintern tried to establish a united front with the socialist parties in all countries and proclaimed that it would fight with them to achieve world peace. Georgi Dimitrov, the newly appointed general secretary of the Comintern, asserted in July 1934 that "the view that a united front can only be formed at the grassroots level has to be abandoned and the practice of calling the Socialist Party leaders opportunist must come to an end." In the future, the Comintern would "provide Communist parties in all countries guidance on basic policy and issues related to principle," completely altering its universal revolutionary principles and slogans without regard to any of the "characteristics of each nation, party, or organization."

The adjustments in Comintern policy eventually led to the convening of its Seventh Plenum between July and August 1935. The plenum finalized adoption of a new united front policy aimed at achieving peace and protecting the USSR. With this goal in mind, the CCP delegation to the Comintern presented its new policy on a national anti-Japanese united front.

In July 1934, the CCP delegation in Moscow declared for the first time that, in addition to supporting "the banner that only the Soviet Union can save China," the slogan that "the sacred Nationalist war is the only way to save China" should also be endorsed.

In its 3 August letter to the CCP Politburo, the CCP delegation proposed that it must formulate its policy against the current primary enemy of the revolution "based on the international and domestic situations, on the urgent needs of the people, and on how to best take advantage of the enemy's internal contradictions."

On 16 September, the CCP delegation finalized its policy as anti-Japan and anti-Jiang, insisting on "the best use of all anti-Jiang forces, including those warlords in the Nationalist Party."

The CCP delegation provided a detailed explanation of its strategy on 14 November: "It is probably a fact that under current Chinese conditions Jiang Jieshi is the worst enemy of the Chinese people and the Red Army. Thus, any victory by Jiang over the anti-Jiang factions will strengthen Jiang's forces against the Chinese people and the Red Army. For the same reason, any victory by Jiang over the Red Army will reinforce Jiang's forces against the Chinese people and other anti-Jiang factions. ... Therefore, our party should not be a bystander when the anti-Jiang factions launch military actions against Jiang. ... Instead, [we] should take active military actions" to support such a war until such anti-Jiang military actions become part of a national liberation struggle against the Japanese pirates and the Chinese traitors.

The CCP's policy toward the Soviet Revolution was directly affected when the united front strategy aimed at resisting Japan and fighting Jiang became "a method of struggle beneficial to the smooth development of the anti-imperialist revolution and the land revolution as well as to relations with anti-Jiang factions as part of united front relations."

On 3 June 1935, in its instructions to local party organizations in the Northeast, the CCP delegation proposed the formation of a universal anti-Japanese united front. At the Seventh Congress of the Comintern held about one month later, the CCP delegation, on behalf of the CCP, formally presented its plan for an "anti-imperialist people's united front."

The essence of this new policy was to unite everyone, with the exception of Jiang Jieshi, but including members of all parties and organizations, officers and soldiers, and even patriotic and devoted youths in the Nationalist Party and the Blue Shirt society. It proposed that all parties and organizations should select representatives who could form a united anti-Japanese defense government and organize a united Resist Japan Coalition Army so as to both resist Japan and fight Jiang.

Based on this policy, the CCP delegation, in the name of the CCP CC and the Provisional Central Government of the Chinese Soviet Republic, published "A Letter to All Countrymen on Resisting Japan and Saving the Nation" (the so-called 1 August Declaration). Reiterating the resist Japan and oppose Jiang principle, the declaration presented a series of strongly nationalistic slogans, including "fighting for the survival of the nation," "fighting for the independence of the country," and "fighting for territorial integrity."

Because the CCP CC did not have any electronic communications with Moscow during its Long March, the new united front policy proposed by the Comintern and the CCP delegation was not passed on to Moscow in a timely manner. However, news of the policy change was transmitted back to China in bits and pieces as the CCP delegation to the Comintern, led by Wang Ming, repeatedly publicized the new policy via overseas Chinese newspapers, and sent directions in the name of the CCP CC and the Provisional Central Government of the Chinese Soviet Republic via secret channels to the surviving CCP organizations in the areas controlled by the Nationalist Party.

In late November 1935, Zhang Hao (whose original name was Lin Yuying), a liaison sent by the CCP delegation via Outer Mongolia during the Seventh Congress of the Comintern, finally arrived in Baoan less than two months after the CCP CC ended its year-long Long March. Having lost over 90 percent of its troops and all of its base regions, only several thousand soldiers and a few hundred officers were left under the command of the CCP CC. It was at this life-and-death moment that the CCP CC unexpectedly received new Comintern instructions that it should work to build a united front. The CCP quickly regained its political vitality because to a large extent many of its serious defeats in the past had been caused by the radical policy that had abandoned the united front and had imposed self-isolation. Facing constant pursuits, sieges, and frontal attacks by the Nationalist Army, the tragedy of the loss of the southern base regions was bound to be repeated if the rigid Soviet revolutionary strategy were to remain in place. The arrival of the new Comintern policy provided great political flexibility for the CCP and thus dramatically increased the chances of survival for the CCP CC and the Red Army amidst the factional conflicts in the Nationalist Party.

Secret Negotiations on the Sino-Soviet Military Alliance

While the USSR was gradually adjusting its foreign policy, Jiang Jieshi and the Nationalist government were taking the necessary steps to improve relations with the USSR. This was possible because the CCP base regions in the South had been wiped out and the Red Army was no longer a serious threat to Nationalist government rule in Nanjing. Jiang Jieshi no longer worried that the USSR might use the CCP and the Red Army to threaten the government of the Nationalist Party. Therefore, Jiang sent Jiang Tingfu, as his unofficial representative, to the USSR in the autumn of 1934 to determine Moscow's attitude. The USSR cordially received Jiang Tingfu and expressed its willingness to enhance mutual understanding with the Nanjing government. Thus, Jiang Jieshi began to contemplate how to use the USSR to place a check on the Japanese invasion of China.

But something that had long been worrying Jiang Jieshi occurred in early 1935. Ever since the Tanggu Truce was signed in 1933, which allowed the Japanese Army to occupy various passes along the Great Wall, the Japanese Army was gradually encroaching on Hebei and Chahar, intervening in local affairs and propping up puppet governments. Now Japan openly instigated the Northern China Railroad incident and pressured the Nationalist government to sign the He-Umezu Agreement and the Qin-Doihara (Chin-Doihara) Agreement, forcing the Nationalist Party and its Central Army to withdraw from Beiping, Tianjin, and Hebei province and revealing its plans to turn the five provinces in northern China into a second Manchurian state. This situation obviously did not sit well with Jiang Jieshi.

On 4 July, Jiang sent Kong Xiangxi to meet secretly with Dimitry Bogomolov, the Soviet ambassador to China, inquiring whether under current circumstances "the Soviet Union is planning to sign a mutual assistance treaty with China." After Japan increased pressure on China by forcing it to accept the Three Principles of Hirota, Jiang Jieshi secretly met with Ambassador Bogomolov on 18 October to express his desire to sign a secret military agreement with the USSR. About two months later, the Soviet government replied in the affirmative that "the Soviet government does not object to such an agreement and is ready to engage in concrete discussions on the subject with China."

Once the attitude of the Soviet Union became known, Jiang Jieshi could not help but immediately request that the USSR make arrangements so that Deng Wenyi, the military attaché of the Nanjing government in Moscow, could meet on 19 December with General Galen who had been in China in the 1920s working as Jiang's military adviser. He once again made it clear that he would like to collaborate with General Galen. Only two days later, on 21 December, Deng Wenyi returned to Moscow in a hurry. Another two days later, on Christmas eve, Jiang sent his confidant Chen Lifu, alias Li Rongqing, with Russian interpreter Zhang Chong, alias Jiang Huainan, to Moscow via Berlin disguised as staff members of Ceng Tianfang, the Chinese ambassador to Germany. Chen Lifu's responsibility was to negotiate an agreement on military mutual assistance.

However, Jiang insisted on preconditions before he would sign a military mutual assistance agreement with the USSR. He maintained that "Sino-Soviet relations must be built on the foundation of the Sun-Joffe Declaration," that is, the USSR must reiterate its acceptance of the article clearly stating that "Communist organizations, including the Soviet system, should not be applied in China." To be concrete, Jiang Jieshi demanded that the USSR support the establishment of a united China under the leadership of Jiang's government in Nanjing and that the USSR should persuade the CCP to end its activities aimed at overthrowing the Nationalist government. Because of these conditions, Jiang sent Deng Wenyi back to Moscow for further negotiations with the CCP delegation. He ordered Chen Lifu to temporarily stay in Berlin, waiting for the results of the negotiations and then deciding on his next step.

Negotiations between Deng Wenyi and the CCP delegation began on 13 January and continued until 23 January, when both sides finally reached a compromise. They agreed that Pan Hannian would be sent back to China to represent the CCP CC in China in formal negotiations with the Nationalist Party and to seek political solutions to the problems in inter-party relations. This arrangement was approved by Jiang Jieshi. However, on 22 January, a day before Pan Hannian was to set out on his planned trip, Bogomolov met with Jiang Jieshi to discuss the military agreement and the CCP issue. Bogomolov informed Jiang Jieshi that the Soviet government had studied Jiang's proposal and that he hoped the USSR could help persuade the CCP into accepting the unified command of the central government and end its efforts to overthrow the Nationalist government. The Soviet's reply was that if the Nationalist Party wanted to form a united front with the CCP, it had to "negotiate directly with CCP." Of course, the USSR would allow the Nationalist Party and the CCP to conduct negotiations in Moscow. But the USSR did not want to play the role of mediator. The Soviet's refusal to force the CCP to submit to the Nanjing government made Jiang uncomfortable. It is obvious that Jiang believed that the only way to guarantee that the USSR would not support the CCP during the Sino-Soviet cooperation was to have the USSR press the CCP to abandon its policy of overthrowing the Nationalist government by force. The Soviet's refusal to mediate between the Nationalist Party and the CCP meant that the USSR was unwilling to support only the Nationalist government in Nanjing in the future. This inevitably began to sow the seeds of disaster in Sino-Soviet military mutual assistance which was still in the making. Having repeatedly explained his reasoning without receiving any positive response from Bogomolov, Jiang Jieshi sent a telegram to Deng Wenyi, instructing him to halt the negotiations with the CCP delegation.

Although Jiang Jieshi did end contacts with the CCP in Moscow, he had not completely given up hope to find a political solution to the CCP issue. On the one hand, Jiang was looking for Communist contacts inside of China with whom he could negotiate. On the other hand, he was waiting to receive a Soviet response to his proposal. Under these circumstances, although Jiang Jieshi did not send Chen Lifu immediately to the Soviet Union to negotiate a military mutual assistance treaty, he did not recall Chen back to China.

The news about Chen Lifu's trip to Europe to negotiate military assistance with the USSR unexpectedly began to spread among top Nationalist Party officials. Several military and political leaders were opposed to Sino-Soviet cooperation and were very concerned about its impact on the established policy to exterminate the CCP. Hunan warlord He Jian, who was opposed to Sino-Soviet cooperation, came up with the idea of sharing this information with Japan. As a result, Japanese newspapers in Shanghai, including Dōmei News Agency, all openly published reports on Chen Lifu, who was on an undercover trip to the USSR in an attempt to sign a secret treaty. It was just at this time that the Soviet Union and the government of Outer Mongolia signed a mutual military assistance treaty. Hearing this news, the Chinese government voiced its protest. Under such circumstances, for the time being Jiang Jieshi was forced to abandon his plan to form a military alliance with the USSR, and Chen Lifu and his assistants were recalled from Europe.

THE CCP: FROM OPPOSING TO ALLYING WITH JIANG

Because the Soviet government had begun to establish contacts with Jiang Jieshi's Nationalist government in Nanjing and had revealed its intention of discussing mutual military assistance, it would not be difficult to predict the attitude of the Politburo of the AUCP (b) toward the CCP CC's policy of Resisting Japan and Opposing Jiang, which had just been approved by the Seventh Congress of the Comintern. However, because there were no telegram communications between the CCP CC and the Comintern at that time and the CCP delegation was not sensitive enough about this issue, the change in CCP

CC and Comintern policy toward Jiang Jieshi and the Nationalist government in Nanjing did not come about until July 1936.

On 16 June 1936, the CCP CC finally set up a powerful transmitter-receiver and sent its first telegram to the CCP delegation in Moscow. On 2 July, another, even longer, telegram was sent. In these two telegrams, the CCP CC focused on its success in inciting the defection by Zhang Xueliang, the interim commander-in-chief of the Nationalist Party's Northwestern Suppression Headquarters and the Northeast Army. It reported that it had already reached an agreement with Zhang Xueliang that after receiving approval and assistance from the USSR, it would launch the Resist Japan and Oppose Jiang movement in the Northwest, trying to combine Shaanxi, Gansu, Ningxia, Qinghai, and Xinjiang into one region and to establish a Northwestern national defense government as well as a Resist Japan Coalition Army under Zhang's leadership. Given that a rebellion in Guangdong and Guangxi was taking place at this time, the CCP CC requested approval and assistance from the Comintern because it was eager to begin its grand northwestern coalition plan. It also expressed its readiness to admit Zhang Xueliang as a member of the party.

The CCP CC plan was quickly sent to the Comintern and the Politburo of the AUCP (b). It was apparent that China would inevitably face another large-scale civil war if this plan were to be followed and it would be unable to realize Moscow's goal aimed at uniting the whole nation in a war against Japan and reducing the possibility of a Japanese attack on the USSR. Therefore, this plan was immediately rejected by Stalin and others. Georgi Dimitrov, the Comintern general secretary, pointed out at a 23 July meeting that "the current task in China is not to expand the Soviet regions or the Red Army, but to look for opportunities, venues, proper slogans, and proper methods to unite the vast majority of the Chinese people to resist Japan."

On 15 August, Dimitrov sent political instructions to the CCP CC, sharply criticizing continuation of the policy of Resisting Japan and Opposing Jiang. He pointed out that the CCP should support the establishment of a united Democratic Republic of China, the convening of a Chinese National Congress, and the founding of the Chinese National Defense Government based on universal elections. He also instructed that the Soviet regions should be prepared to join the united Democratic Republic of China, participate in the National Congress, and establish democratic systems in their respective territories. Following these instructions, the CCP CC had to quickly readjust its strategy. It immediately came up with a "Draft Agreement Between the Nationalist and Communist Parties on Resisting Japan and Saving the Nation" and prepared to negotiate with the Nationalist government in Nanjing on how to unite and fight Japan together. At the same time, the CCP CC held a self-criticism meeting. It recognized that "since China's arch enemy is now imperialist Japan, it is wrong to treat imperialist Japan and Jiang Jieshi as the same, and the slogan of 'Resisting Japan and Opposing Jiang' is inappropriate."

The 15 August Comintern instructions did change the CCP's policy toward Jiang Jieshi. However, they could not alter the fundamental conditions set by

Jiang Jieshi for a political solution to relations between the Nationalist Party and the CCP. Jiang's conditions required nationwide political and military unification under the Nanjing government, the abandonment of the Soviet Revolution by the Communists, and the reorganization of the government and the army by placing them under the leadership of Jiang Jieshi and the Nanjing government. Jiang's conditions were a world away from the expectations of the Comintern and the CCP. Fortunately, the CCP CC had a rather pragmatic appraisal of the relative power of the two parties. Thus, it did not insist on exaggerated demands and it stated that it was willing to consider making major concessions. It offered to stop all talks and activities aimed at overthrowing the Nationalist government, to allow the Red Army to "accept centralized command and organization" just like all other armies in the nation under the condition that the organization and leadership of the Communist Party members in the Red Army would be retained and the Red Army representatives would be sent to the centralized national military command headquarters led primarily by Nationalist Party members. The core demand was to seek "the formation of a united front under some basic conditions, such as resisting Japan and preserving the Soviet region as well as the Red Army."

However, Moscow was not so pessimistic at the time. On the contrary, it insisted that the CCP CC should not lower its demands so that the party and the Red Army could maintain a favorable position in the rapprochement between the two parties and would not submit to control by the Nationalist Party. Therefore, when the CCP CC reported the extremely difficult conditions of its troops in northern Shaanxi and Gansu provinces, Stalin quickly approved that 550 tons of military materials be sent to the Red Army via Outer Mongolia. It was Moscow's plan to provide materials made it possible for both the Second Corps and the Fourth Corps of the Red Army to move north simultaneously, even after the Fourth Corps had established its own CC. In October 1936, they jointly launched the Ningxia Campaign whose goal was to cross the Yellow River, march north to Suiyuan, move directly to the border with Outer Mongolia, and then pick up aid from the USSR.

While the Second Corps of the Red Army lost its basic fighting capacity and required support and protection from the Central Red Army, the Fourth Corps of the Red Army was unable to end the chase by the Nationalist Army and failed to hold on to the crossing point. Although over 20,000 soldiers of the Red Army managed to safely cross the Yellow River, the main force of the Red Army was left on the east bank of the river and was attacked by the Nationalist Army pursuing from the east and the south. At the same time, the war with Japan began in Suiyuan in early November, making it impossible to receive Soviet aid through that area. Therefore, Moscow decided to deliver aid to the border region between Xinjiang and Gansu. Under these circumstances, tens of thousands of Red Army soldiers and the CCP CC were stuck north of Gansu and east of the Yellow River, unable to cross the river by marching to the west or to remain in the barren counties in northern Gansu waiting for the depletion of its munitions and food. Fighting for its own survival, the CCP CC, on the one hand, had to order the 20,000 Red Army soldiers who had already crossed the Yellow River to stay on the west bank so as to preoccupy the Nationalist troops on both banks of the river. On the other hand, the CCP CC passed a resolution on 8 November, deciding to lead the main force of the Red Army on the east bank of the river to break the siege by moving to the west or the south. It prepared to fight inland for a year so as to break the Nationalist Army's siege on a new Long March.

The departure of the Red Army from Shaanxi and Gansu put Zhang Xueliang, who had formed a close united front with the Red Army, in an extremely difficult position. Members of the Northeast Army led by Zhang, numbering in the hundreds of thousands, had fled their homelands with their families immediately after the "18 September incident" and they had already settled inland for quite a few years. They all depended on Zhang to lead them in a return to their homeland. However, Zhang Xueliang understood that it was impossible to pin his hopes on Jiang Jieshi and the central government to fight his way back to the Northeast. Therefore, Zhang long hoped to receive assistance from the USSR, which was also threatened by Japan. The problem was that Moscow could not forgive Zhang Xueliang or his father, Zhang Zuolin, who on two occasions had deeply hurt the USSR.[3] The Soviet government refused to have anything to do with Zhang Xueliang. However, when Zhang Xueliang and his troops were sent to Shaanxi and Gansu to wipe out the bandits in the Northwest, Zhang secretly established contacts with the Red Army. The CCP CC expressed its willingness to help Zhang form an alliance with the USSR to fight Japan. Both sides also agreed to establish the Northwest National Defense Government as well as the Resist Japan Coalition Army. Under these circumstances, Zhang Xueliang naturally did not want to see the Red Army break the siege and move elsewhere. Thus, upon receiving the secret information from the CCP CC, Zhang sent a reply to the CCP CC earnestly requesting that the CCP and the Red Army stay where they were for about a month so that Zhang could come up with a solution. Zhang then went to Luoyang to meet with Jiang Jieshi, pleading with him to stop fighting the Communists and to lead his troops to Suiyuan to fight the Japanese. Despite numerous pleas, Zhang Xueliang was unable to persuade Jiang, so he decided to burn his bridges. Collaborating with Yang Hucheng and his Seventeenth Route Army, Zhang took advantage of Jiang's arrival in Xi'an to supervise a battle against the Communists and then he launched the Xi'an incident on 12 December. He shocked the entire world by detaining Jiang and his entourage which had arrived to direct the anti-Communist campaign.

The Xi'an incident created a serious crisis that reached the brink of a civil war. Fully aware of this grave danger, the CCP CC made great efforts to seek a peaceful solution. However, having failed numerous times in the past to negotiate with Jiang, the CCP CC had lost all hope of winning over Jiang Jieshi and convincing him to unite with the Communists to fight Japan. Thus, it adopted a policy that sought to organize a Resist Japan Coalition Army and to establish a national "Revolutionary Defense Government" based in Xi'an. It attempted to use two tactics to achieve those goals. One was to encourage the people to demand that the Nanjing government remove Jiang Jieshi from office and turn him over to the people for a public trial. The other was to win sympathy for the Xi'an incident from Jiang's subordinates and the pro-British and pro-American factions in Nanjing.

With respect to the Xi'an incident, from the very beginning Moscow, through the media, had expressed its clear opposition. Although Stalin and the Comintern did not reply immediately to the numerous telegrams from the CCP CC requesting support, the CCP CC did manage to detect from radio broadcasts from Moscow the frustrations caused by the Xi'an incident.

On 17 December, the CCP CC received a reply from Dimitrov. Although the telegram was not fully decoded because of a coding issue, it was not difficult to guess the essence of Dimitrov's message. Thus, when it sent another telegram to the Nationalist Party on 18 December, the CCP CC abandoned its demand for a public trial for Jiang Jieshi and agreed to guarantee Jiang's safety and freedom. At an expanded meeting of the Politburo of the CCP CC held the following day, most participants had begun to realize that the attempt to turn Jiang Jieshi over to the people for a public trial was inappropriate. Another telegram from Dimitrov was received on 20 December, once again confirming Moscow's opposition to the Xi'an incident. Based on this, the CCP CC instructed Zhou Enlai, who had arrived in Xi'an immediately after the incident, to collaborate with Zhang Xueliang and Yang Hucheng in their negotiations with Song Ziwen and Song Meiling, Jiang Jieshi's representatives, so as to peacefully resolve the issue.

In the end, the incident was successfully resolved as the Nationalist Party and the CCP embarked on a road of negotiation and compromise.

Notes

1. The Chinese Soviet Republic, located in the Jiangxi Province, was established in November 1931 by Mao Zedong, General Zhu De and others, and lasted until 1934. Mao was both its state chairman and prime minister. However, it was eventually destroyed by the National Revolutionary Army of the Guomindang in the 1934 encirclement campaigns.
2. Feng Yuxiang was a warlord and leader in Republican China. He spent the early 1930s criticizing Jiang's failure to resist Japanese aggression. On 26 May 1933, Feng Yuxiang became commander-in-chief of the Chahar People's Anti-Japanese Army Alliance. With a claimed strength over 100,000 men, his army drove the Japanese and Manchukuo troops from Chahar Province, but Jiang Jieshi, fearing that the Communists had taken control of the anti-Japanese Army, launched a siege of Feng's army, ultimately leading to Feng's resignation.
3. The two incidents were Zhang Zuolin's search of the USSR embassy and publication of the secret Soviet documents in April 1927, and Zhang Xueliang's search of the USSR Consulate in Harbin and seizure of the Chinese Eastern Railway in 1929.

CHAPTER 5

Sino-Soviet Wartime Cooperation and Conflict

Kuisong Yang

Prior to the outbreak of the Pacific War in 1941, China fought the war against Japan with little international assistance. Only aid from the Union of Soviet Socialist Republics (USSR) helped sustain China's early war efforts. However, Sino-Soviet relations during the anti-Japanese war were marred by the contradictions in their state relations. Support for the Chinese government, as represented by the Nationalist Party, sacrificed, at least partially, the interests of the Chinese Communist Party (CCP). Similarly, providing assistance to the CCP hurt the Nationalist government, which represented national interests at that time. On the one hand, the USSR required that the CCP continue its united front so as to help in the war effort. On the other hand, the USSR both openly and secretly continued to provide assistance to the CCP because it did not want the Nationalist Party to suppress the CCP. The result was that the USSR could neither satisfy the Nationalist Party nor provide sufficient support to the CCP. The consequences quickly became apparent in party and state relations after the outbreak of the Russo-German War.

EARLY SOVIET ASSISTANCE FOR CHINA'S WAR AGAINST JAPAN

Moscow's reaction during the Xi'an incident helped improve Jiang Jieshi's view of the USSR and led to more frequent contacts between the two governments. On 11 March 1937, Jiang Tingfu, Chinese ambassador to the Soviet Union, again proposed to M. M. Litvinov, the people's commissioner of Foreign Affairs, that a Sino-Soviet mutual assistance agreement should be

K. Yang (✉)
Contemporary China Study Institute, East China Normal University,
Shanghai, China
e-mail: yks@vip.sina.com

© The Author(s) 2020
Z. Shen (ed.), *A Short History of Sino-Soviet Relations, 1917–1991*,
China Connections, https://doi.org/10.1007/978-981-13-8641-1_5

signed. Litvinov, however, rejected the proposal and instead suggested there be a Pacific region agreement focusing on China and the USSR, but signed by China, the USSR, the United States, Great Britain, Japan, and other countries. In early April, the Soviet ambassador told the Chinese government that the USSR was willing to provide military assistance to China. Jiang Jieshi not only expressed his gratitude to the Soviet government for its attitude during the Xi'an incident but also promised to do his best to improve bilateral relations. Having noted the positive attitude of the Chinese government, the Soviet government changed its position regarding a mutual assistance treaty. It proposed that the two governments should first begin negotiations on a mutual nonaggression treaty. If a Pacific pact were to be signed, the USSR would also be willing to reconsider a Sino-Soviet mutual assistance agreement. Thus, China and the USSR began concrete discussions on a nonaggression treaty. The treaty was signed on 21 August, immediately after the outbreak of the "7 July incident." The treaty provided that neither side should unilaterally ally with one or more nations to invade the other and if one side were to be invaded by one or more other countries, the other side would not provide any direct or indirect assistance to the third country, take any actions, or sign any agreements that could be used to harm the other side.

Whereas the United States, Great Britain, France, and other countries paid no heed to the Japanese invasion of China and continued to trade military and strategic materials with Japan, the USSR, following the provisions in the nonaggression treaty, immediately prohibited the export of military and strategic materials to Japan and terminated its trade relations with Japan. Thus, at the beginning of China's war against Japan, the only country that stood by China's side and openly provided her with moral, material, and especially military assistance was the USSR, as it also vehemently, without reservation, denounced the Japanese invasion in the domestic media. When Japan requested that foreign nations withdraw their embassies from Nanjing to avoid Japanese air raids, the USSR issued a strong protest through its ambassador in Japan, announcing that the Soviet government would not withdraw its embassy and it furthermore would hold Japan accountable for any and all damages and losses caused by Japanese bombing. General Galen, commander of the Soviet Far East Army, publicly announced that faced with the possibility of a Japanese invasion of China, the USSR, when it was necessary, "would have no choice but to come forward to openly assist China." At the same time, the Soviet government tried, through active diplomatic activities, including collective sanctions, and in various international venues to prevent Japan from expanding its invasion.

In order to obtain Soviet assistance, the Chinese government sent Shen Dexie, a member of the Military Commission, to Moscow to discuss the purchase of weapons and ammunition with Soviet loans. As soon as there were signs of some progress, Jiang Jieshi ordered that Yang Jie, deputy chief of staff of the Military Commission, join the negotiations in Moscow. The two parties quickly signed two loan agreements. They also agreed that, beginning from the end of October, the Soviet government would provide the Chinese government with a US$ 50 million loan, with an annual interest rate of 3 percent, for the purchase of weapons and ammunition (it was publicly announced that the loan was for the purchase of industrial goods and equipment). Within five years, China would repay the loan with tea, leather, cotton, silk, tung oil, animal hairs, and minerals, such as antimony, tin, and tungsten. The second loan, in the same amount, beginning from July 1938, would be used for the same purpose and would be repaid in the same manner. The third loan, starting from July 1939, would amount to US$ 150 million, for the same purpose and with the same interest rate and repayment method.

According to the agreement of both nations, the Soviet Union began to ship the first batch of military material at the end of September 1937. The shipment included 62 heavy bombers, 101 fighter aircraft, 62 aircraft bombers, 82 tanks, 200 anti-tank guns, and some anti-air artillery machine guns and bombs. According to documents published by the Soviet Union, the weapons and ammunition provided by the USSR for China during the early years of the war against Japan (prior to the outbreak of Russo-German War) totaled over 900 planes, 1140 cannons, 82 tanks, over 10,000 machine guns, 50,000 rifles, over 2000 trucks and tractors, over 31,600 bombs, 2,000,000 cannon shells, 2,000,000 hand grenades, 180 million bullets, and so forth. In order to transport this military equipment, the USSR helped China build a highway from Sary-Ozek in the Soviet Union (now in the Republic of Kazakhstan) to Lanzhou via Dihua (now Urumqi) and open an aviation line from Alma-Ata in the Soviet Union to Lanzhou in China. At the same time, the USSR also shipped ammunition and cannons via the sea using ports in the British and French colonies.

In addition to military material, the USSR also sent to China many military advisers and volunteers to assist in the war effort against Japan. At the end of November 1937, the Soviet Union sent M. I. Dratvin, A. I. Cherepanov, K. M. Kachanov, and Vasily Ivanovich Chuikov to China, under the official title of military attachés, to serve as general military advisers to the Nationalist government. By early 1941, there were over 140 such Soviet military advisers in China. They provided many constructive recommendations based on the needs of the Nationalist Army. They also became directly involved in coordinating many important military campaigns, including those in Taierzhuang, Wuhan, Changsha, and Yichang. A Soviet volunteer aviation force began to arrive in China in December 1937. Two bomber squadrons and four fighter plane squadrons, with over 700 pilots and technicians, directly participated in air battles in Wuhan, Yueyang, Hangzhou, Nanchang, Nanning, Guangzhou, and Taipei, and bombed Japanese troops to support the Chinese forces fighting on the ground. The bomber squadron leader and the fighter plane squadron leader both died in the fighting, along with some 200-plus Russians. During this period, Soviet experts helped train as many as 8354 Chinese pilots, navigators, and other aviation technicians.

The significant Soviet assistance to China could not be kept secret from the Japanese. This was one of the reasons behind the strategic debates within the Japanese Army as to whether it should "march south" or "move north." It was apparent that the Soviet assistance to China and the reality of Soviet troops stationed along the border region in the Northeast distracted Japan from its invasion of China and its occupation of Southeast Asia. After two large-scale military confrontations, Japan finally abandoned its war plans to move north and conquer the USSR. These two military confrontations are known as the Zhanggufeng and Nuomenkan (Nomonhan) incidents.

The Zhanggufeng incident took place in the summer of 1938. Located on the east bank of the Tumen River in the Chinese-Korean border region, Zhanggufeng was on high ground, at an elevation of 150 meters in Huichun county of Jilin province. Overlooking Soviet territory across the river, it had some strategic value and thus was guarded by the Japanese Nineteenth Division stationed in Korea. In early July 1938, the Soviet Far Eastern Corps, in order to take control of the east bank of the Tumen River, sent troops to build positions on the west side of the high ground and to confront the Japanese forces that were in close proximity. This eventually led to a military confrontation with the Japanese Army. But Japan was focusing most of its forces on the campaign in Wuhan, so the Japanese Army gathered only a limited number of troops in the Northeast—over 7000 soldiers and 37 cannons. In contrast, the USSR deployed 15,000 troops, 237 cannons, 285 tanks, and 250 planes. The result was the utter defeat of the Japanese Army. The Japanese were forced to propose an end to the battle and to move the defense line to the west bank of the Tumen River, surrendering Zhanggufeng and the surrounding areas on the east bank of the river.

The Nuomenkan incident took place between May and September 1939. Nuomenkan is located east of the Halexin (Halha or Halhin Gol in Russian) River. When Japan invaded China, it used the river as a border, treating west of the river as Outer Mongolia and east of the river as Manchukuo territory. However, the Outer Mongolian Border Army insisted that the Nuomenkan area, east of the Halexin River, was its own territory. In May 1939, the Outer Mongolian Border Calvary was attacked by the Japanese Army while the former was patrolling the Nuomenkan area, thus contributing to a confrontation between the two sides. On 28 May, the Japanese Army sent an infantry regiment to attack Nuomenkan. It was strongly resisted by the Soviet Army, which was comprised of two cavalry regiments, one mechanized infantry battalion, and part of a motorized infantry division. After two days of fierce battles, the Japanese troops were forced to retreat. The Japanese Kwantung Army, on 23 June, sent planes to Tamusk where the Soviet and Mongolian armies were gathered, and in early July it launched ground attacks. This time, the Japanese Army sent three infantry regiments from the Twenty-third Division, an artillery battalion, and the main force of a tank division across the Halexin River in an attempt to destroy the Soviet Red Army and the Outer Mongolian Border Army east of the Halexin River. The Soviet and Outer Mongolian forces responded with the Eleventh Tank Brigade, the Seventh Motorized and Armored Brigade, one regiment from the Thirty-sixth Motorized Infantry Division, and one armored battalion from the Outer Mongolian Border Army. Supported by the air force and artillery firepower, they began a large-scale offensive against the Japanese forces. The Japanese Army, after suffering serious casualties, was once again forced to retreat. On 23 July, the Japanese Army gathered over 80 cannons to launch another round of attacks. However, the result was the same. Unwilling to accept defeat, the Japanese Army organized the Sixth Army on 4 August, with Lieutenant General Michitaro Komatsubara as commander. With the main force of the Twenty-third Division, part of the Seventh Division, the Eighth Border Brigade, and other temporary attachments, the Japanese Army had over 70,000 soldiers, 500 cannons, 182 tanks, and over 300 planes. It was prepared for a prolonged confrontation with the Soviet and Mongolian armies. At the same time, the Soviet and Mongolian armies gathered their forces to form the First Corps. With Georgii Zhukov as commander, it was comprised of the Thirty-sixth Motorized Infantry Division, the Fifty-seventh and Eighty-second Infantry Divisions, the Sixth and Eleventh Tank Brigades, the Seventh, Eighth, and Ninth Motorized Brigades, the Fifth Rifle and Machine Gun Brigade, the Eighth Calvary Brigade, the 212th Airborne Brigade, the Sixth Outer Mongolian Cavalry Brigade, artillery, and other temporary attachments. It had 57,000 soldiers, 498 tanks, 385 armored vehicles, 542 cannons and mortars, 2255 machine guns, 515 planes, and 550,000 tons of munition. After careful preparation for over a month, the Soviet and Outer Mongolian armies launched a three-pronged attack on 20 August. After four days of battle, they had almost wiped out the main force of the Japanese Twenty-third Division.

On 9 September, the Japanese government was forced to send a cease-fire proposal to the USSR through its ambassador in Moscow. By this time, the USSR had already signed the Soviet-German Non-Aggression Pact and Germany had already invaded Poland. According to the secret agreement signed with Germany, the USSR had to send troops to occupy part of Poland. Therefore, the Japanese cease-fire proposal was very desirable. The two sides quickly reached an agreement based on the line that was under actual Soviet control. About nine months later, the USSR held negotiations with Japan on the border between Outer Mongolia and Manchukuo. Japan was again forced to make concessions, allowing the border to be moved about 40 kilometers from the Halexin River into Heilongjiang province and giving 2000 square kilometers of territory to Outer Mongolia.

However, the Soviet assistance did not completely satisfy Jiang Jieshi or the Nationalist government. What Jiang Jieshi most wanted was neither a nonaggression treaty nor Soviet assistance, but rather the signing of a military mutual assistance agreement, which would require that the USSR send troops to help China when the Sino-Japanese war broke out. Unable to foresee the possibility of a massive Japanese invasion, the Nanjing government did not push for negotiations on the mutual assistance agreement after making its initial proposal in April 1937. But after the Sino-Japanese war broke out, it made repeated requests to the USSR, hoping to begin negotiations on such a treaty. However, Nanjing could no longer receive any response from the USSR.[1] After the defeat in Shanghai and the loss of Nanjing, Jiang Jieshi once again raised the issue of a military mutual assistance treaty. He warned the Soviet government that China would be defeated if the USSR refused to send troops to provide assistance. At the same time, Nationalist Party representatives put pressure on their CCP counterparts, asking them to help persuade the USSR to send troops to assist China in the war against Japan. However, the CCP Central Committee (CC) paid no heed to the Nationalists' request. Regardless, it was not until the loss of Wuhan in 1938 that Jiang Jieshi abandoned his efforts to form a military alliance with the USSR. Nevertheless, Moscow never changed its attitude about not intervening in the Sino-Japanese war.[2]

FRUSTRATIONS IN INTERPARTY RELATIONS

Soviet assistance to China's war effort against Japan, while considered unsatisfactory by Jiang Jieshi and his Nationalist Party, also caused frustrations for the CCP CC. However, the frustrations were caused not by Nationalist pressure on the CCP but by the inability of the CCP troops under the leadership of the Nationalist government to receive any share of the huge amount of Soviet assistance to China. Despite all that was provided by the USSR to the Nationalist government, with the approval of Jiang Jieshi the CCP Army only received 120 machine guns and six small anti-tank cannons.

At the beginning of the war against Japan, the CCP Army was in a difficult situation due to its shortage of both soldiers and equipment. There was no doubt that it would be extremely difficult for the CCP Army to survive a total war between China and Japan by relying only on the several hundred thousand yuan it received monthly from the Nationalist government. However, it was impossible to expect that the USSR, under the existing conditions, would bypass the Nationalist government to provide the Communists with weapons and ammunition. This situation created some frustrations among the Communists. However, it is not completely accurate to say that Moscow gave "weapons to the bourgeoisie and books to the proletariat." Although Moscow could not directly send weapons to the CCP CC, it did provide considerable funding at numerous crucial moments.

The most noticeable aid, US$ 500,000 provided by Moscow at the beginning of the war against Japan, was approved by Stalin to help the CCP buy weapons and munitions. Later, in the summer of 1938, when Wang Jiaxiang, a Politburo member of the CCP CC, returned to China, he received US$ 300,000 from Moscow. It is also known that Stalin, based on requests from Zhou Enlai and Dimitrov, the general secretary of the Comintern, decided to provide US$ 300,000 in aid. After the outbreak of the Russo-German War in 1941, Stalin approved another US$ 1,000,000 in aid, based on a request from the CCP CC. Actually, financial and material aid from Moscow arrived intermittently between 1937 and the end of the war. Even after the Comintern was dissolved on 22 May 1943, such aid continued. Although the aid from Moscow was vastly different from the monthly subsidies to the CCP provided by

Moscow in the 1920s and 1930s, Moscow continued to provide financial, and nonmilitary and technical aid to the CCP.

Of course, in the political arena there was greater fostering of the CCP by Moscow during this period. Moscow presented two clear demands to the CCP CC at the very beginning of the war against Japan. One was to make every effort to preserve the fighting capability of the Red Army and to "raise revolutionary vigilance to the maximum level," as the Nationalist Party and the CCP were once again cooperating so that neither the CCP nor the Red Army organizations would be destroyed by Jiang Jieshi due to disintegration, instigation, or espionage. The other was that the Communists should not be afraid of drowning in the sea of the nationalist liberation struggles. Instead, the CCP could learn from the Spanish and French experiences and propose slogans such as "resisting Japan is above everything else," "everything should go through the united front," and "everyone should follow the united front so as to make the Nationalists and the CCP share responsibilities, leadership, and growth." Obviously, this policy helped guide the Chinese Communists, a small and weak force at the beginning of the anti-Japanese war, in maintaining its organizational independence while at the same time also preserving the united front with the Nationalist Party. Moscow's demands effectively checked two trends within the CCP, an overemphasis on either its dependence on the Nationalist Party or its independence even at the risk of confronting the Nationalists.

At about this time, CCP relations with the Comintern still reflected the CCP's subordinate position, with little room for independent political or organizational action. This had a great impact on the formation of the leading core of the CCP CC and the affirmation of its top leaders. During the years in the southern base areas, the top leaders of the CCP CC were basically first nominated by the Comintern representative in China and then approved by Moscow. As a result, Pavel Mif, head of the Comintern Eastern Department, was able to hold the Fourth Plenum of the Sixth National CCP Congress in early January 1931 and to put Wang Ming and other students educated in the Soviet Union in leading positions on the CCP CC. About half a year later, the Comintern representative reorganized the Politburo of the CC that had been elected at the Fourth Plenum of the Sixth National Congress, established a Provisional Politburo, and replaced the general secretary with Bo Gu, another young student in his twenties who had been educated in the USSR. Even after the Provisional CC was forced to relocate to the Central Soviet Region, the vast base area, the huge Red Army, and the massive party organization with over 100,000 members, including a large number of older military and political leaders, because there were no new instructions from the Comintern, were still subject to the leadership and command of several young students who had returned from the USSR with only limited book knowledge. Although senior CCP military and political leaders, after losing numerous battles as well as all the base areas under the leadership of Bo Gu, changed its top leadership at the meeting held in Zunyi during the Long March without guidance or intervention from Moscow. They replaced Bo Gu, who was too young to be a leader, with Luo Fu, another Soviet-educated student (though slightly older). Thus, the effect of Moscow's authority over the CCP was obvious.

The CCP established a highly unified and centralized system because the authority and ability of the party's top leaders were crucial to the survival, development, and future of the party, especially in its complex political struggles as well as in both its civil and foreign wars. After the outbreak of the anti-Japanese war, Moscow, worried about the ability of the CCP leaders to handle the complex political and war situations, sent a large number of senior cadres seasoned with years of policy experience in Moscow, led by Wang Ming, back to China to carry out the Comintern's strategy. Under such circumstances, Wang Ming easily won the support of other party leaders and he replaced Luo Fu as the new *de facto* top leader of the CCP CC. However, when the power struggle within CCP gradually turned in Wang Ming's favor, Moscow did not support either Wang Ming or Luo Fu. Instead, it selected Mao Zedong as the new top leader of the CCP CC. On 14 September 1938, Wang Jiaxiang, who had just returned from Moscow to the CCP CC in Yan'an, delivered instructions from the Comintern and the opinion of Dimitrov that "the CCP Central Committee should be headed by Mao Zedong." Mao Zedong thus became the top CCP leader at the Sixth Plenum of the Sixth National CCP Congress which was held soon thereafter. This, in the words of Mao Zedong "determined the destiny of China."

Moscow was startled as things did not turn out as expected, despite Mao Zedong's initial efforts to carry out the Comintern's strategy and to improve relations between the Nationalist Party and the CCP. Having lost cities as well as land during the war and unable to stop the CCP from developing rapidly behind enemy lines, the Nationalists, at the Fifth Plenum of their Fifth National Congress, adopted a policy to restrain the CCP. This led to constant tensions in interparty relations. Although Dimitrov had tried to persuade Mao Zedong to maintain a cool and moderate attitude toward the Nationalists, during this process Mao refused to sacrifice any interests already won by the CCP. Determined to defeat the Nationalist Party, Mao insisted on "winning unity through struggle" or even through a tit-for-tat struggle. This led to a gradual estrangement and even to confrontation between Moscow and the CCP CC.

Between the end of 1939 and the fall of 1940, many military confrontations occurred between the Nationalist Party and the CCP in the border region between Shaanxi, Gansu, Ningxia, and in the enemy-occupied areas in North and Central China, making interparty relations extremely tense. In order to end the increasing confrontations between the Nationalist and CCP forces caused by the jagged borders and the confusing jurisdictions, the Nationalist Party proposed redrawing the border lines. On 16 July 1940, it requested, in a central government memorandum, that within one month the Eighth Route Army and the New Fourth Army led by the CCP should move to Hebei and Chahar provinces north of the Yellow River and to areas in North Shanxi and North Shandong provinces. It also limited the Eighth Route Army to three armies, six divisions, and five supplementary regiments, and limited the New

Fourth Army to two divisions. The CCP would not be allowed any extra military forces. At this time, the Eighth Route Army and the New Fourth Army already controlled most of the rural areas behind enemy lines in Shanxi, Hebei, Chahar, and Shandong provinces, and it had established bases in Henan, Anhui, and Jiangsu provinces. With the number of its troops already reaching close to 500,000, and with local forces and militia organizations twice that number, it was impossible for the Eighth Route Army and the New Fourth Army to be absorbed in only eight divisions and five regiments or for them to be limited to Hebei, Chahar, northern Shandong, and northern Shanxi. Furthermore, the CCP CC absolutely would not accept that all the guerrilla forces in the areas evacuated by the CCP regular forces were to be handed over to the Nationalist Party.

Having been ignored by the CCP, the Nationalist Party reissued an ultimatum on 19 October, ordering that CCP forces move to the designated areas within one month and threatening them with suspension of their provisions and their soldiers' pay. At the same time, the military command began to draft the Battle Plan for Exterminating the Bandit Armies South of the Yellow River, preparing to launch military attacks if the CCP refused to obey its orders.

Despite suffering repeated defeats in fighting the Japanese, the Nationalist Party under Jiang Jieshi suddenly adopted a tough position toward the CCP and even threatened it with force. This forced Mao Zedong to suspect that Jiang Jieshi was plotting something bigger. After a careful study of the international and the domestic situations, but still unable to figure out what Jiang Jieshi was planning, Mao Zedong came to the conclusion that most likely Jiang was trying to "force our army to areas north of the Yellow River and then to seal off the river so as to exterminate our army with pincer attacks from the Japanese as well as the Nationalist forces."

In order to cope with this serious situation, the CCP CC decided to deploy 150,000 elite troops, launch preemptive attacks, and take the fight to areas behind the invading Nationalist forces, such as Henan and Gansu. In Mao Zedong's words, "if they want to exterminate the Communists, then we must fight against the extermination of the Communists." We should "move to their rear, win a few major victories, and demand the removal of He Yingqing [that is, to purge the bad officials around the emperor] and force the withdrawal of these troops that were attacking the Communists." Of course, Mao was clearly aware that this action would lead to a rupture in relations between the Nationalist and the Communist parties and would be detrimental to the CCP. If by any chance Mao's judgment proved to be incorrect, such a move would "create an everlasting disaster." Thus, Mao wrote a letter to Dimitrov on 4 November requesting instructions. Dimitrov vehemently opposed Mao's plan. Because of his respect for Moscow's opinion and his lack of confidence in his judgment on the collusion between Jiang and Japan, Mao quickly changed his plan and once again began maneuvers with the Nationalist Party. Claiming that the New Fourth Army had failed to move to the North on time and had not followed the route set by the Nationalist Party, in July 1941 the Nationalist forces unexpectedly wiped out the headquarters of the New Fourth Army, with over 7000 officers and soldiers in South Anhui. The Nationalist Party, publicly declaring that the New Fourth Army consisted of rebels, eliminated its unit designation. It is not difficult to imagine how deeply Mao Zedong and the CCP CC were irritated by these actions.

In the face of the South Anhui incident, the Soviet Union, while sharply criticizing the Nationalists' actions, did not end its military assistance. It also continued to ask the CCP to exercise restraint so as to prevent a complete collapse of interparty relations. This forced Mao Zedong to begin to keep a distance from Moscow.

THE RUSSO-GERMAN WAR AND THE REVERSAL OF SINO-SOVIET RELATIONS

While relations between the Nationalist and Communist parties were extremely tense, relations between the USSR and Japan became increasingly delicate. Since the Nuomenkan incident, the Japanese Kwantung Army had increased the number of its infantry divisions to 12, with a total of 350,000 troops. It planned to further expand its forces and to equip them with even better weapons. This meant that at any time the Japanese Kwantung Army would be able to threaten the Soviet Far East and Outer Mongolia. However, at the time the USSR was more concerned about the German threat on the western front. This was not only because the USSR's center of political, economic, cultural, and even industrial activities was located in the western part of the country but also because Germany, after beginning World War II by occupying Poland, had quickly defeated the British and French armies, and had turned Hungary, Romania, Slovakia, and Bulgaria—all countries neighboring the USSR—into subservient states. It was very obvious that after conquering the entire European continent, all that would be left for Germany, aside from attacking the British Isles, would be to conquer the USSR. As Hitler was winning more victories, it was impossible to imagine that the Russo-German Non-Aggression Treaty would be able to restrain the German Army from turning eastward. Thus, the USSR faced an inevitable diplomatic decision—whether it should adjust its policy toward Japan so that it could concentrate its forces on Germany.

Such a policy adjustment toward Japan meant the signing of a treaty of neutrality. The initial proposal for such a treaty came from Japan. Because Japan desperately needed rubber and other strategic materials from the South Pacific, it had already finalized its "strike south" strategy and it wanted to make sure that the USSR would not threaten Manchuria. Therefore, Shigenori Togo, Japanese ambassador to the USSR, proposed, on behalf of the Japanese government, the signing of a Soviet-Japanese Neutrality Pact with the USSR in July 1940. The negotiations were fruitless because of conflicts between the two sides about Sakhalin Island. But in April 1941, after consulting with Germany, the Japanese Foreign Minister gave up all unpractical claims, and the two nations finally signed the Russo-Japanese Neutrality Pact on 13 April. The two sides agreed that "the Soviet Union pledges respect for the territorial integrity and immunity of invasion of Manchukuo; Japan pledges respect for the territorial integrity and immunity of invasion of the People's Republic of Mongolia."

There is no doubt that the signing of the Russo-Japanese Neutrality Pact was an extension of the Soviet diplomatic strategy, as reflected in the Soviet-German Non-Aggression Pact signed with fascist Germany, which was aimed at channeling the danger to the West. If the victims of the Soviet-German Pact were smaller and weaker nations, such as Poland and Finland, the victim of the Soviet-Japanese Treaty was China, which was fighting a lonely battle on its own. In particular, Soviet recognition of Manchukuo was a heavy blow to China's movement to resist Japan, which at the time was facing serious difficulties. Jiang Jieshi, having been complaining about USSR assistance and suspecting its support for an expansion of the CCP, expressed in his diary his anger on the day when the neutrality treaty was signed between the USSR and Japan. He wrote that "although in fact the Russo-Japanese Pact might not affect our war of resistance, the psychological problems that it will create are still beyond description! The origins of my depression and fears, which have appeared during the last two weeks, are unclear. Could they be forewarnings of this Soviet-Japanese pact designed to hurt my country? Alas!"

At this time, Song Ziwen, who had gone to seek assistance in the United States, reported that the US president had approved a loan of US$ 125 million and had "promised to provide China with a US$ 500 million loan for weapons and ammunition." This ignited new hopes for Jiang Jieshi, who began to cast his eyes on the United States and gradually parted ways with the USSR.

Even after the signing of the Russo-Japanese Pact in April 1941, the Soviet government repeatedly sent explanations to the Chinese government, emphasizing that its policy to assist China had not changed. But only two months later Germany rejected the Soviet-German Nonaggression Pact and launched a surprise attack, code-named "Operation Barbarossa," on the USSR. With its vast western territory occupied by the German Army as if with the blink of an eye, the USSR was no longer able continue to provide assistance to China. Except for a very small number of Soviet advisers, most Soviet personnel in China, including those working in an aviation station established by the USSR in Northwest China and those maintaining the strategic road there, quickly withdrew to the USSR.

After the outbreak of the Russo-German War, the problem in Xinjiang had the greatest impact on Sino-Soviet relations. Xinjiang was then ruled by Sheng Shicai who managed to obtain that position by relying on Soviet assistance and support from the pro-Soviet banner. More than once Sheng had requested to join the All-Union Communist Party (Bolsheviks) (AUCP (b)) and he had proposed that Xinjiang be annexed by the USSR. Thus, for a long period, Sheng maintained only very loose contacts with the Nationalist government and Xinjiang was completely under the influence of the USSR. CCP personnel were also well received in Xinjiang. This situation lasted until 1941 when the Russo-German War erupted. Sheng began to befriend the Nationalist government when the USSR had trouble taking care of itself. Sheng first sent his younger brother to meet Jiang in Chongqing. Then he invited Zhu Shaoliang, commander of the Fifth War Zone, and Song Qingling to visit Xinjiang. It was after the outbreak of the Pacific War that Jiang Jieshi for the first time was able to appoint officials in Xinjiang, thus finally placing the province under the jurisdiction of the Chinese government. Sheng Shicai's relations with the USSR began to deteriorate in 1942. Jiang Jieshi took personal actions to force the USSR to withdraw its personnel working in the Xinjiang aircraft factory, the oil field in Dushanzi, the aviation station, and its Red Army garrisoned in Hami. As a result, the Northwest international communications line, an important communication line for China during the early years of the war of resistance, was cut off. At the same time, many CCP personnel working in Xinjiang were arrested and executed. Almost all the successes of the USSR and the CCP that had been achieved through years of diligent work in Xinjiang were lost overnight.

In order to attack Sheng Shicai and create trouble for Jiang Jieshi, the Politburo of the AUCP (b) held a meeting on 4 May 1943 to discuss what measures should be taken to overthrow Sheng Shicai's rule in Xinjiang. With the USSR gradually shifting its offensive in its western front, it decided to groom revolutionary forces among the minority nationalities in Xinjiang, under the cloak of a "National Resurrection Group." The Soviet Union established a special action group led by Major-General Yegnarov of the People's Commissar of Internal Affairs to contact the rebel forces, train and equip them, and smuggle weapons and ammunition into Xinjiang. At the same time, the group carried out revolutionary propaganda work among the minority nationalities and organized a unified "liberation organization" through the Soviet consulates in Xinjiang and underground personnel. The rebel forces of Kazakh herdsmen, led by Osman Batur in the Ashan (Altai Mountains) region, were the first to be recognized and to receive assistance from the Soviet and Outer Mongolian governments. In addition to weapons and equipment, they also received assistance from Soviet and Outer Mongolian military advisers, who helped them rapidly grow into a military force of about 1000 men. Because the entire Altai Mountains region was at war, the Tacheng area, which bordered the Altai Mountains, was also affected. Rebel herdsmen proceeded to attack government forces in Xinjiang. Because it shared borders with the USSR and had a Soviet consulate, the Ili area became a hub for the USSR to support the rebel forces in Xinjiang.

With the massive influx of Nationalist forces, Sheng Shicai quickly lost control over Xinjiang. As a result, in September 1944 he was removed from his positions as provincial governor and garrison commander and he was forced to leave Xinjiang. Yet this did not stop the USSR from plotting an armed rebellion in Xinjiang. One of the important reasons for this was that the USSR had long been trying to annex Tannu Uriankhai (Tang Nu Wu Liang Hai), which was situated north of Xinjiang, northwest of Outer Mongolia, and south of eastern Siberia in the USSR. This region, according to the Burinsky Border Agreement signed by the Qing dynasty and Tsarist Russia in 1727, had been under the jurisdiction of the Qing empire. However, taking advantage of the Second Opium War, Tsarist Russia forced the Qing dynasty to sign three new border agreements, turning over the Amuha River region in western Tannu Uriankhai to Russia. Later, because of the influence of the 1901 Revolution and the declaration of independence by Outer Mongolia, many counties in Tannu Uriankhai also declared independence. Tsarist Russia proceeded to occupy the entire region. Taking advantage of the chaos caused by the October Revolution, the Chinese government managed to regain control over Tannu Uriankhai in 1918. But the Soviet Red Army, under the pretext of exterminating the White Russian Army, quickly reoccupied the region. Instigated by the USSR, Tannu Uriankhai again declared independence in 1921, adopting the new name of the Republic of Tannu Tuva (later changing the name to the People's Republic of Tuva). The USSR immediately extended recognition and established diplomatic relations with the new republic. Many years later, Stalin believed that the time was right for Tannu Uriankhai to be rightfully annexed by the USSR. Thus, in August 1944 the Great Khural of the People's Republic of Tuva passed a declaration, "requesting" that the USSR accept his nation as a republic of the USSR. In October, the Supreme Soviet passed a resolution accepting this "request." "The People's Republic of Tuva" was then changed to "the Soviet Socialist Autonomous Republic of Tuva," becoming part of the Russian Soviet Federated Socialist Republics.

Although the annexation took place during the war, the Soviet government took steps to reduce resistance from China. First, the Soviet government used the rebel forces already mobilized in Xinjiang to launch the "Kongha Rebellion" on 7 October and then took over Kongha county. Immediately thereafter, on 7 November, it organized an even larger rebellion in Yining. This operation was orchestrated by the Soviet consul in Yining who guided the local Uygur "Liberation Organization" in close collaboration with small Soviet forces.

In order to expand the scale and impact of the rebellion, the USSR sent advisory groups from the military and the Ministry of Interior, as well as several army units, to participate in the rebellion. On 12 November, the "Yining Liberation Organization," following the original plan, formally announced the establishment of the "Provisional Government of the Islamic People's Republic of Eastern Turkistan." Elihan Töre, an Islamic teacher, was elected president of the government. The Soviet adviser was the Turk Muhsin. On 5 January 1945, at its fourth meeting the Provisional Government Commission adopted a resolution that announced that the "Eastern Turkistan Islamic People's Republic" had ceded from China and become independent. A "National Army" was quickly organized under the leadership of the Soviet advisers and officers. With support from Soviet aircraft and artillery, the army swiftly occupied most of the areas in Altai, Ili, and Kashgar. Since this rebellion had originated with the slogan of overthrowing Han Chinese oppression, the strong nationalistic sentiments among the rebels inevitably led to massive expulsions and even executions of Han Chinese.

As USSR relations with the Nationalist Party deteriorated, USSR ties with the CCP CC also fell to a new low. Because of its need to deal with the threat from Germany, Moscow urged Mao Zedong not to take extreme measures and completely break relations with the Nationalist Party, even though Moscow was well aware of the Southern Anhui incident that had occurred in January 1941 as well as the heavy losses suffered by the CCP. Nevertheless, without Soviet support, it was impossible for the CCP to retaliate against the Nationalists. In addition, the CCP base areas in North China had suffered from the Japanese Army's all-out retaliation after the Eighth Route Army launched massive attacks on Japanese forces in China in autumn and winter of 1940 (also known as the Battle of the One Hundred Regiments). As the Eighth Route Army was beginning to face an extremely difficult situation, it was incapable of taking any strong military actions against Jiang Jieshi. But this further increased Mao Zedong's distrust and distance from Moscow.

Under these circumstances, the outbreak of the Russo-German War and the USSR's inability to take care of its own interests became catalysts for fundamental changes in Sino-Soviet bilateral relations.

Because of its deep concern about Japan's westward aggression after the outbreak of the Russo-German War, Moscow requested that the CCP CC take active military actions to help the Soviet Union. Mao Zedong's attitude toward such requests was very clear. The Eighth Route Army could only provide strategic, not tactical, assistance. The fundamental principle underlying the Eighth Route Army's response was to be neither reckless nor passive; instead it would engage in prolonged guerrilla warfare. Concretely, it could only help the USSR through assaults and information warfare. Mao Zedong asked Zhou Enlai to tell Zhukov, the Soviet military adviser, that "the gap between us and the enemy in military technology and equipment is too large and we are facing increasing difficulties in manpower, material resources, area, and ammunition. ... Bullets are a rare treasure, averaging twenty for each rifle. Machine guns are in short supply, even cannons are scarce, and there is nowhere to find explosives." Under these circumstances, "our military collaboration might not be a big help. If we take action without considering the sacrifices, it is possible that we will be battered so badly that we will not be able to hold on to the base areas for a long time. This will not be a good thing, no matter how you look at it."

Mao Zedong's passive attitude toward defending the Soviet Union produced discontent in Moscow, but Mao was well aware of this. Thus, only three months after the outbreak of the Russo-German War, Mao held a CCP CC meeting. On the surface, the purpose of the meeting was to discuss the historical causes for the losses suffered by the party, the Red Army, and the base areas after the "18 September" incident in 1931. But the real targets were the party leadership circles led by Wang Ming and Bo Gu who, with their Soviet educations, were greatly influenced as well as deeply trusted by the USSR and the Comintern. As a result of this historical discussion, Wang Ming, Bo Gu, and the others became the targets of criticism. Wang Ming tried to turn the situation around by seriously criticizing Mao Zedong by referring to

Dimitrov's telegram that expressed discontent with Mao's passive attitude toward defending the USSR. However, because Mao Zedong already occupied the top leadership position and the rest of the participants at the meeting had reached a consensus during the prior historical discussion, Wang Ming's efforts to counterattack with the help of external authorities backfired and further exacerbated his position.

Criticism of the historical mistakes made by Wang Ming, Bo Gu, and the others reduced the authority of the Comintern to its lowest point in history. As a result, Moscow was no longer able to intervene in the internal affairs of the CCP CC through its organizational channels. Mao Zedong was not satisfied to merely force the "international faction" of the party into a position of being criticized by the upper echelons of the CC. He wanted to strike while the iron was still hot and dispel any superstition about Wang Ming among the party members. Mao felt this was necessary because most of the cadres were farmers. They worshipped leaders like Wang Ming and others who had received educations and professional training in the USSR, who could recite Marx and Lenin by heart, and "always quoted Greek [and the Soviet] classics." If party members could not eliminate this mentality of blind obedience or really understand that the success of the Chinese Revolution depended on localized Marxism, it would be impossible to completely eliminate the fads of subjectivism and dogmatism. Thus, Mao began a party-wide Rectification Campaign in 1942. His purpose was very clear. He wanted to instill a belief among all party members that Chinese-style Marxism was the only correct ideology that could guide the Chinese Revolution to victory.

About one year after the beginning of the Yan'an Rectification Campaign, on 21 May 1943 Stalin dissolved the Comintern. This step was taken because the USSR desperately wanted the United States and Great Britain to open a second front in Europe; the USSR would need the cooperation of the major powers after the war; and the USSR hoped to prove that it had no intention of inciting Communist parties in other countries to overthrow their governments. In order to convince its allies to trust its sincerity, Soviet diplomats provided concrete explanations and assurances to the leaders of each nation. For example, Alexander Panyushkin, Soviet ambassador to China, assured Jiang Jieshi that the USSR would no longer, not then and not in the future, assist any Communist parties, including the CCP, in any foreign countries after the dissolution of the Comintern.

The dissolution of the Comintern ended the period of history when all Communist parties had to obey orders from one universal command center. This further provided evidence of the correctness of the position that had been adopted by Mao Zedong. Mao openly stated that the Comintern was dissolved because "it could no longer fit the complex and fast-changing situation." The existence of the Comintern as a unified command center for worldwide revolutions, he asserted, was completely unnecessary because a "revolutionary movement cannot be exported or imported." The Communist parties in all nations, he emphasized, had to be more nationalistic.

Without instructions from the Comintern, the CCP's Rectification Campaign proceeded smoothly. However, as the campaign produced a wave of ideological criticism, it led to mutual suspicion and distrust among party comrades. The tense relations with the Nationalist Party and the over-exaggerated enemy threat within the party eventually led to a cadre investigation campaign, which was guided by the CCP CC Social Department and was known for producing "confessions under duress." This forced many party cadres to accept criticism, interrogations, and even imprisonment because they were groundlessly suspected of being "special agents." Although the Comintern had already been dissolved, Dimitrov, the former Comintern general secretary who had paid close attention to the CCP, sent a telegram to Mao Zedong expressing his earnest concern about the CCP's actions and offering indirect criticism.

Of course, all this only further deepened Moscow's extreme distrust of Mao's CCP. Such distrust had already been revealed by the Comintern leaders as early as 1940, when Zhou Enlai went to the USSR for treatment of his injured arm. Moscow was deeply concerned that the CCP had operated in the countryside for too long of a time and that the vast majority of its members were peasants. When Mao adopted an unacceptable stance in defense of the USSR or in its handling of the Soviet-educated leaders within the party, the Soviet leaders began to have fundamental doubts as to whether or not the CCP was truly a Communist Party. Such doubts gradually became public during diplomatic occasions. In his conversation with American Ambassador W. Averell Harriman in June 1944, Stalin commented that "the Chinese Communists are not true Communists, they are the 'man-made margarine-type' Communists." Soviet Foreign Minister Vyacheslav Molotov made a similar comment about the Chinese Communists in a conversation with Patrick J. Hurley, the special envoy of the US president. This is why the top leaders in Moscow had no intention of establishing more direct contacts with Mao Zedong or the CCP CC after the dissolution of the Comintern, except with regard to the transmitter-receiver that earlier had been brought to Yan'an by the Comintern liaison.

THE YALTA SECRET TREATY AND SINO-SOVIET TREATY NEGOTIATIONS

After long preparations, the United States and Great Britain officially opened the second front of the war against fascism in Europe when the Allied expedition forces led by Commander Dwight Eisenhower landed in Normandy, France, in early June 1944. Thereafter, the American, British, and Soviet armies began to attack Germany from the east, west, and south. The Allied nations began the final phase of the war by seeking to smash Nazi Germany in the European theater. The victory of the war in Europe was just around the corner.

As the European theater became increasingly close to victory, the situation in the Pacific War also turned in favor of the Allied forces. In particular, the US island-hopping campaign in the Pacific theater forced the Japanese troops to constantly retreat as the American forces moved even closer to the Japanese home islands. However, the Japanese Army successfully launched a massive offensive, the so-called No. 1 Campaign, also known as the Yu-Xiang-Gui (Henan-Hunan-Guizhou) Campaign, in China in the spring of 1944. Within eight months, the Nationalist troops had lost most of their territory in Henan, Hunan, Guangdong, and Fujian provinces as well as part of Guizhou province. Meanwhile, the Japanese Army was approaching the wartime capital of Chongqing. Thus, even if the American troops began to attack the home islands of Japan, the Japanese Army in mainland China could continue to fight without any intervention by foreign forces. Therefore, the United States had to pin its hopes on the USSR, which could easily join the fight against Japan after the war in Europe had come to an end.

In order to persuade the Soviet Union to participate in the war against Japan, the top leaders of the United States, Britain, and the Soviet Union held an important meeting in February 1945 in Yalta, on the southern coast of the Crimean Peninsula in the USSR, surrounded by the Black Sea. At the meeting, they discussed the important issues that had to be resolved after the war, including issues related to Germany, Poland, and the United Nations. At the same time, they reached a secret agreement on Soviet participation in the war against Japan, the so-called Yalta Agreement. According to this agreement, once the USSR sent its troops to fight Japan, it could maintain the status quo in Outer Mongolia. Second, the privileges enjoyed by imperial Russia prior to the Russo-Japanese War of 1904 would be restored, including the return of the southern part of Sakhalin as well as islands adjacent to the USSR, the internationalization of the commercial port of Dalian to safeguard Soviet interests in the port and to restore the lease of Port Arthur as a Soviet naval base, and the establishment of a Sino-Soviet joint company to manage the Chinese Eastern Railway and the South Manchuria Railway connecting the Soviet Union to Dalian. Third, the Kurile Islands would be returned to the USSR. The Soviet Union pledged that the Soviet Army would enter the war against Japan within two or three months after the war in Europe ended and at the same time it would prepare to sign a Sino-Soviet Friendship Treaty. The US president promised to take steps to persuade Jiang Jieshi to accept the above agreement.

It is worth noting that although the "Nationalist Army" of the Republic of Eastern Turkistan was fighting fierce battles in Xinjiang against forces sent by the Chinese government. Stalin did not even mention this issue. Because China was one of the most prominent members of the allies and Xinjiang was recognized by all the allies as Chinese territory, Soviet support for the separatist forces in Xinjiang obviously could not be made public. In addition, the establishment of a Pan-Turkistan nation on the border of over a dozen Central Asian Soviet republics, home to many minority nationalities, was known for Islamic forces that could upset social stability in the Central Asian region of the USSR. Thus, the Xinjiang issue became an important bargaining chip for Stalin to force the Chinese government to make concessions on various Soviet privileges and interests in China.

In mid-March 1945, President Franklin Roosevelt, in a conversation with Wei Daoming, Chinese ambassador to the United States, revealed the Soviet postwar demands, that is: Outer Mongolia would not be returned to China, the railroads in the Northeast would be jointly managed, and the Soviet Union would have an unconditional long-term lease to Port Arthur. Since Roosevelt did not mention the Yalta Treaty, Jiang initially did not understand why the United States suggested the long-term lease of Port Arthur. Jiang responded that he "would rather see Port Arthur occupied by Russia through force than to recognize Russian privileges in the name of a lease." Jiang even instructed that Wei Daoming should reply to the US government that "the 'foreign concession' is regarded by the people of our nation as the utmost insult, and should be erased from Chinese history."

On 29 April 1945, Patrick J. Hurley, the new American ambassador to China, semi-officially explained the content of the secret agreement reached at Yalta: the South Sakhalin and Kurile Islands would be to the Soviet Union; Korea would be granted independence; Port Arthur would be leased to the Soviet Union; the port of Dalian would be opened as a free port; China and the USSR would equally share the stakes in the Chinese Eastern Railway and the South Manchuria Railway, and the USSR would enjoy special privileges over the two railroads; and the status quo in Outer Mongolia would be maintained. Because the agreement had already been reached among the United States, Great Britain, and the Soviet Union, Jiang Jieshi's attitude changed drastically. On the one hand, he asked Song Ziwen, interim premier who was then in the United States, to request that President Truman help the Chinese government realize its goal that "there will never be privileges on Chinese territory." On the other hand, he asked the Soviet ambassador in China for the Soviet government to "help China restore the territorial integrity and administrative independence of the three provinces in the Northeast." He promised that the Soviet Union would be allowed to use the railroads and ports in the three Northeast provinces and that the two nations could jointly use Port Arthur. However, he clearly stated that Port Arthur absolutely "cannot be leased to the Soviet Union."

However, in his talks with Jiang Jieshi on 12 June, Soviet Ambassador Pietrow opened the conversation by presenting a summary of the five demands from the Soviet government based on the Yalta Agreement. They included the lease of Port Arthur, assurances that the Soviet government would have dominant privileges to the port of Dalian, a joint company to share in the use of the Chinese Eastern Railway would be established, and Outer Mongolia would be recognized as an independent country. Ambassador Pietrow asserted that these five demands were "preconditions" for the Soviet government to agree to negotiate a Sino-Soviet Friendship and Mutual Assistance Agreement.

Under pressure from the US and Soviet governments, a Chinese delegation led by Premier Song Ziwen arrived in Moscow on June 30 to begin bilateral talks with Stalin and Soviet Foreign Minister Molotov on the conditions presented in the secret Yalta Agreement.

Stalin and Song Ziwen held their first formal meeting on 2 July. At the beginning of the negotiations, both sides introduced their arguments about Outer Mongolia. Song Ziwen emphasized that Outer Mongolia was a very important issue for China and he insisted that the agreement should include this issue. However, Stalin asserted, with a somewhat threatening tone, that "the Mongolian people are very eager to achieve national independence and under current circumstances it would be better for China to allow Outer Mongolia to become independent. Otherwise, Outer Mongolia will become a serious unstable element in China's domestic politics because it will unite all Mongols to seek national independence which would put China in a very disadvantageous position." As for the other privileges demanded by the Soviet Union with respect to the three Northeast provinces, Song Ziwen indicated no opposition. The only bargaining on the two sides focused on the length of the lease. Song Ziwen stated that China wanted to limit Soviet usage of Port Arthur and of the Chinese Eastern Railway to 20–25 years, but Stalin insisted that the Soviet Union be allowed use of the port for 40–45 years because of the costs involved in building the bases and other facilities.

Song Ziwen sent several telegrams to Jiang after the meeting with Stalin, presenting several proposals. First, he proposed that use of Port Arthur should be shared by both China and the Soviet Union, but civil authority should belong to China. Second, Dalian should be jointly operated by both China and the Soviet Union. Third, rights to the Chinese Eastern Railway and the South Manchuria Railway should be equally shared. However, Song emphasized that China should absolutely not accept the independence of Outer Mongolia. At most, a high level of autonomy could be granted and the stationing of Soviet troops could be allowed. If Stalin insisted that China should recognize the independence of Outer Mongolia, China would consider ending the negotiations. However, Jiang believed that "the Soviet Union is so determined to have Outer Mongolia that it will not be satisfied with a high level of autonomy or the right to station troops there. If the Soviets are not satisfied, it will not be possible to negotiate on the administrative integrity of the Northeast or of Xinjiang. It will be even tougher to resolve the issue of the Communists. Since Outer Mongolia has already been occupied by the Soviet Union, it will not serve the nation if we suffer real losses just to save faces. If we can sacrifice barren Outer Mongolia for the Northeast, Xinjiang, or the unification of the whole nation," then the great cause of unification can be achieved. Thus, Jiang sent a telegram to Song Ziwen on 7 July, instructing him to make the greatest sacrifice and demonstrate his deepest sincerity. "Outer Mongolia should be allowed to become independent after the war." However, this could only be done on two conditions. "One is the territorial, sovereign, and administrative integrity of the three provinces in the Northeast. The other is that the Soviet Union will never support the CCP or the bandits in Xinjiang."

Despite the instructions from Jiang, in their talks on 7 July Song Ziwen again had a long argument with Stalin about Outer Mongolia. Song insisted that the provision in the Yalta Agreement on the status of Outer Mongolia only required to "maintain the status quo in Outer Mongolia." Thus, China could agree to maintain the status quo, but not formally recognize its independence. However, Stalin asserted that "maintaining the status quo can also be interpreted as recognition of the independence of the People's Republic of Mongolia." Furthermore, the Soviet Union "cannot tolerate leaving Outer Mongolian issues in permanent uncertainty. ... If China insists on its own position," Stalin warned, "then our negotiations will not produce any results." Song firmly held to his position and reaffirmed that "as clearly stated by Jiang Jieshi, China cannot recognize the independence of Outer Mongolia." As a result, Song and Stalin argued throughout the negotiations and parted on bad terms.

It is obvious that there were some differences between Jiang Jieshi's and Song Ziwen's attitudes toward the Outer Mongolian issue. As prime minister and foreign minister, Song Ziwen did not want 1.5 million square kilometers of territory to be given up under his watch. However, Jiang Jieshi was more concerned about unification of the country and consolidation of his regime after the war. After all, since its establishment the Nationalist government had never obtained jurisdiction over the provinces in the Northeast or the Northwest outside of the Great Wall. It thus required assistance from the Soviet Union to exert its rule in those areas. Jiang Jieshi immediately sent a telegram to Stalin after the end of the second round of negotiations and he instructed Song Ziwen to "accurately transmit the contents of the telegram to Stalin without any explanation."

In his telegram Jiang wrote that "after careful deliberation about the common interests shared by our two nations, China agrees to turn Port Arthur into a naval base to be used by both China and the Soviet Union, to declare Dalian a free port, and to accept that the above two arrangements will last for twenty years. In order to allow China to effectively exert its sovereignty and administrative authority over Manchuria, administrative authority over Port Arthur and Dalian will belong to China. The Chinese Eastern Railway and the South Manchuria Railway will be Chinese property, but, the main trunk lines of the two railroads will be jointly operated by the two countries for twenty years." We sincerely hope that the Soviet Union will do its best to help the Chinese government suppress the rebellion in Xinjiang along the Sino-Soviet border so that transportation and trade between our two countries can be quickly restored. We demand that any political, material, or psychological assistance provided by the Soviet Union to China must go through the central government so as to keep the CCP under the unified leadership of the central government. Under these conditions, "the Chinese government agrees" to determine the future of Outer Mongolia through a referendum.

Since Jiang Jieshi had already made his decision, Song Ziwen was left without any other options. However, he still told Stalin that the Soviet Union should understand that a division of any portion of Chinese territory would cause a strong backlash in the national media. He explained that he rejected the independence of Outer Mongolia due to his deep understanding of the extremely strong nationalistic feelings of the Chinese people about territorial sovereignty. If the Chinese government were to recognize the independence of the People's Republic of Mongolia, it would mean that the government was betraying nationalistic sentiments and ignoring public opinion. This would make it very difficult for the government to maintain a solid footing. However, Stalin cared little about Song Ziwen's arguments. He was very satisfied with Jiang Jieshi's concessions. He stated that "with respect to Manchuria we have already issued public statements declaring that we will completely recognize China's sovereignty over Manchuria. As for the CCP, we will not provide support or aid." He was willing to make some concessions on the use of Port Arthur, Dalian, and the Chinese Eastern Railway and South Manchuria Railway for 30 years. As for Xinjiang, Stalin stated that he was not clear about the situation there and did not believe that the weapons used by the rebels came from the USSR. He promised that if the rebels in Xinjiang really tried to win independence and they had used Soviet weapons to achieve that goal, "then they should be exterminated."

There were only two conditions that were unacceptable to Stalin. One was the administrative authority over Port Arthur. Stalin insisted that the administrative leader of Port Arthur must be a Soviet citizen. The other was the claim made by Jiang that the Chinese Eastern Railway and the South Manchuria Railway remained Chinese property. Stalin resented such a claim and emphasized that "these railroads were built by Russians with Russian money." Therefore, he insisted that "we will never agree to immediately hand over management of these railroads to the Chinese." However, he ultimately agreed to accept the proposal that the two railroads could be "jointly managed by the two nations."

The subsequent discussions mainly focused on Port Arthur and the port of Dalian. Jiang Jieshi "first request[ed] that Port Arthur should be jointly used by China and the Soviet Union, since the two nations are allies. Management of their pure military functions should be entrusted to the Soviet Union, while administrative authority should belong to China. In order to allow the two nations to jointly use Port Arthur as a military facility, a Sino-Soviet joint army should be established. Second, Dalian must be a free port and its administrative authority must belong to China. As for the warehouse, transportation, and other operations, they can be settled through business-style negotiations." However, the Soviet side insisted that it was insufficient to only offer Port Arthur to the Soviet forces. The port of Dalian had to be included as part of the Port Arthur military zone and, with the adjacent areas, be turned over to the USSR for management. Based on the secret Yalta Agreement which provided that the USSR should restore the lease of Port Arthur and enjoy privileges in Dalian, Dalian should also be administered by the Soviet Union.

Because Stalin had to go to Germany to attend a meeting of American, British, and Soviet leaders in Potsdam, Sino-Soviet negotiations were postponed until 7 August. But both sides not only continued to argue about administrative authority over Port Arthur and Dalian but also began to dispute the map of the Sino–Outer Mongolian border as provided by the Chinese. Still angry about Soviet annexation of Tannu Uriankhai in 1944, Song Ziwen stressed that the border should be redrawn according to the Chinese map. However, the USSR insisted that the border should be determined by the border posts currently controlled by both sides and the old map should not be used as the basis for the border.

The United States dropped the two atomic bombs on Hiroshima and Nagasaki on 6 and 9 August. On 9 August, the Soviet Army entered China's Northeast. The Japanese emperor openly begged for surrender on 10 August. As the Soviet Army would soon occupy all of the Northeast, time had run out for the Nationalist government to bargain with the Soviet Union.

On 11 August, Jiang Jieshi told Song Ziwen that since "the situation has changed drastically," he was authorized to "make expedient decisions without remote central control" over Outer Mongolia and other unresolved issues. However, Jiang was still very much concerned about the dispute over the Sino-Mongolian border if Outer Mongolia were to be granted independence. He sent a personal letter to Stalin through Jiang Jingguo, who had gone to Moscow with the Chinese delegation for the negotiations. He still hoped that both sides could reach a basic agreement on the Sino-Mongolian border to avoid unnecessary disputes in the future.

On 13 August, Song Ziwen and Foreign Minister Wang Shijie held consecutive meetings with Stalin and Molotov. Making no progress on the Outer Mongolian border issue, China had to accept the Soviet demands. In the morning of 14 August, Wang Shijie sent a telegram to Jiang Jieshi, reporting that "Premier Song and I continued our talks late into the evening. All issues have been resolved and an agreement will be signed today. Outer Mongolia will follow the existing border. The director of the railroads will be a Soviet citizen, but the deputy director and the chairman of the board will be Chinese citizens. A Sino-Soviet Military Committee will be established for Port Arthur." Wang explained that "after repeated negotiations on the Outer Mongolian issue, we feared that we would be unable to achieve the desired results. However, this agreement helps to restore Sino-Soviet relations, reduce the rampant Communist expansion, guarantee the withdrawal of Soviet troops, and limit Soviet privileges in the Northeast. All these are necessary for our future unification and national reconstruction."

THE SOVIET ARMY ENTERS CHINA'S NORTHEAST

On 14 August, the Treaty of Sino-Soviet Friendship and Alliance was officially signed in Moscow. The treaty included four agreements as appendices. These were the Sino-Soviet Agreement on the Changchun Railroad, the Agreement on Dalian, the Agreement on Port Arthur, and the Agreement on Relations Between the Commander-in-Chief of the Soviet Army and the Chinese Government After the Soviet Army Enters China's Three Provinces in the Northeast in This Joint War Against Japan. Based on the above treaty as well as the appended agreements and following a request from the Nationalist government, the Soviet government openly pledged that it "agrees to provide China with moral, military, and other material assistance, and all such assistance will go to the Chinese central government, that is the Nationalist government."

Based on the treaty and the related agreements, China recognized that Outer Mongolia could become independent by a referendum and the current border would be maintained. It also declared that the Chinese Eastern Railway and the South Manchuria Railway (renamed the China-Changchun Railway) would be jointly operated by China and the Soviet Union. However, ownership of the railroads belonged solely to the Chinese government. China agreed to turn Dalian into an international free port. However, China would sign another agreement so that it could lease the designated docks and warehouses in the free port to the USSR. China also agreed to share use of Port Arthur as a naval base. The above agreements on the China-Changchun Railway, Dalian, and Port Arthur would be effective for 30 years.

While the Chinese and Soviet governments were negotiating in Moscow, the CCP CC was holding its Seventh Congress. Aware of the fast-approaching end of the war against Japan, the strong anti-Communist attitude revealed by American Ambassador Hurley, and the inevitable confrontation between the Nationalist Party and the CCP after the war, the Seventh Congress again raised the issue of wiping out imperialism and feudalism. Mao openly warned that "China will become a semi-colony of the United States. This is a new change and high-ranking cadres should focus on studying the United States. We need to be prepared to suffer." However, Mao also strongly believed that once the situation allowed, the Soviet Union would definitely aid the CCP. "International assistance will arrive" after the war. The Soviet Union was the commander-in-chief of the proletarian class for the entire world. Although the Comintern no longer existed, the commander-in-chief was still there. Therefore, Mao proposed that "twenty or thirty brigades, and 150,000 to 200,000 people, should be prepared to leave the military districts and go to Manchuria" so as to collaborate with the Soviet Army in recovering the Northeast and obtaining technology. He stated with excitement that "our existing bases are not solid and lack a foundation. But we will have solid foundation if we have the Northeast." Since the Northeast was the largest heavy industrial base in China, "the Chinese Revolution will have a solid foundation if we can take over the Northeast, even if we lose all the bases that we have." It is obvious, based on past experiences, that the CCP CC knew that the USSR was involved in diplomatic negotiations with the Nationalist government. However, the CCP CC did not believe that such diplomatic agreements would really tie the hands of the USSR or prevent it from assisting the CCP.

Having noted the fast pace of the American campaign and especially the dropping of the atomic bombs on Japan proper, the USSR did not wait for the formal signing of the Sino-Soviet treaty and it launched an all-out attack on the Japanese Kwantung Army in Northeast China in the evening of 8 August 1945. At the time, the Japanese Kwantung Army still had 31 divisions and 13 brigades, with a total force of 970,000. If the affiliated Manchurian and Mongolian forces were included, the combined total force exceeded 1 million. It also had over 5000 cannons and about 2000 planes. Soviet and Outer Mongolian forces had three corps of 13,700,000 men, and over 300,000 men in their naval and air forces. With over 30,000 cannons, 5000 plus tanks and self-propelling artillery, and 5000 fighter planes, they had an absolute advantage, both in terms of manpower and equipment. However, the three provinces in the Northeast occupied territory covering over 1.5 million square kilometers, equivalent to the combined territory of six European countries, such as France, Italy, Spain, Portugal, Switzerland, and Belgium. The theater extended 1500 kilometers from north to south, 1200 kilometers from east to west. The Soviet Army had to launch an attack on the 5000 kilometer front and push 600 to 800 kilometers within three weeks. The challenge of maintaining effective command, communications, collaboration, and fuel and logistic supplies was beyond imagination.

Fighting against the Japanese Kwantung Army was also made difficult by Japan's extremely strong defense systems. The Japanese Kwantung Army had started to build defense systems along the Sino-Soviet border in 1934. By the beginning of the war, it had fortified about 1000 kilometers and constructed over 8000 permanent bunkers. Each fortified area extended between 50 to 100 kilometers wide along the front and 50 kilometers deep. It had three to seven defense networks. Each network comprised three to six support points that coordinated firepower coverage. All the fortresses were newly built, including permanent steel-reinforced cement artillery and machine-gun mounts, steel-roofed bunkers, armored observation posts, firing strongholds built with dirt and wood, infantry bunkers, anti-tank ditches, and barbed wire. All the defense networks were connected by underground tunnels. In the Hutou fortress, 1400 Japanese soldiers in four infantry companies and four artillery companies managed to resist the attacks launched by two Soviet infantry divisions and one tank brigade with strong air support. The Japanese fought until 26 August when their troops were completely wiped out. In the Dongning fortress, 2000 Japanese soldiers in two infantry battalions and two artillery companies withstood the attacks by two Soviet armies. Despite the bombing of over 500 sorties and the continuous shelling of 40 cannons that poured 7000 tons of ammunition, the Soviet troops were unable to take the fortress. The Soviet Army was able to occupy the fortress only after the Japanese Army received order to surrender on 26 August. Throughout the battle, the Japanese suffered only 150 casualties. The Hailaer fortress was defended by one Japanese brigade of 4600 men. The Soviet attack forces gradually increased to two divisions and four artillery regiments, with the assistance of the air force and tanks. However, they were still unable to take the fortress. Japanese casualties totaled about 1600 and Soviet Army casualties totaled over 2000. It was the Japanese tenacious resistance in the fortified areas that not only inflicted heavy casualties on the Soviet troops but also slowed down the Soviet push.

Although the fortified defense by the Japanese Army created a huge obstacle for the Soviet Army, the veteran Soviet troops equipped with overwhelming firepower did have a great military advantage. By 14 August when Japan officially announced its surrender, the USSR had already crushed the resistance by the Kwantung Army, capturing over 600,000 Japanese soldiers and occupying vast areas of China's Northeast.

Notes

1. It is known that Chen Lifu and Wang Chonghui were instructed on 19 and 23 July, respectively, to propose to the Soviet ambassador that negotiations on a mutual assistance treaty should commence immediately. The USSR Foreign Ministry sent a telegram on 31 July, instructing Ambassador Bogomolov not to engage in such negotiations. Bogomolov informed Jiang Jieshi of Moscow's decision on 2 August.

2. In their two conversations with the Soviet ambassador in late August 1938, both Jiang Jieshi and Sun Ke repeatedly expressed their hope that a treaty would be signed to form a military alliance with the USSR. In its 8 September telegram, the USSR reaffirmed that it would not enter the war unless Great Britain and the United States were to join as well or if the League of Nations authorized the Pacific region nations to join. Soviet intervention would legitimatize the Japanese invasion and lead to suspicions among the other powers that the USSR had ambitions to turn China into a Communist country.

CHAPTER 6

China's Civil War and Sino-Soviet and Nationalist-Communist Relations

Kuisong Yang

China after World War II was filled with uncertainty. The American and Soviet influences had a great impact on postwar Chinese history. Eager to maintain a lasting peace with the United States, Stalin made great efforts to avoid causing any trouble in the American sphere of influence. Therefore, when, at the end of the war, the Chinese Communist Party (CCP) Central Committee (CC) attempted to take advantage of the favorable conditions, Stalin intervened, insisting that Mao Zedong should go to Chongqing to negotiate peace with Jiang Jieshi. In reality, Stalin was hoping that the CCP would abandon its arms and fight for its future via a legislative struggle, just as the French had done. However, Mao Zedong did not follow Stalin's advice. He went to Chongqing, but he did not reach any compromise with Jiang Jieshi. Moscow soon realized that without help from the CCP it was almost impossible for the Soviet Union to keep the American forces from entering China's Northeast, which was regarded by the Soviets as their own sphere of influence. The consequence of allowing CCP troops to enter the Northeast was the inevitable extension of the war between the Nationalist Party and the CCP from inside to outside the Great Wall.

K. Yang (✉)
Contemporary China Study Institute, East China Normal University, Shanghai, China
e-mail: yks@vip.sina.com

© The Author(s) 2020
Z. Shen (ed.), *A Short History of Sino-Soviet Relations, 1917–1991*, China Connections, https://doi.org/10.1007/978-981-13-8641-1_6

95

STALIN'S PUSH FOR NATIONALIST-COMMUNIST PEACE NEGOTIATIONS IN CHONGQING

Japan declared its unconditional surrender on 14 August 1945. On the same day, Jiang Jieshi sent a public telegram to Mao Zedong, inviting him to Chongqing to discuss "various important international and domestic issues." On 15 August, President Harry S Truman, on receiving the Japanese surrender, issued "Order No. 1." The order required all Japanese forces in China, except those troops in China's Northeast that were to surrender to the Soviet Army to surrender to President Jiang Jieshi in all of China and north of the seventeenth parallel in Vietnam.[1]

At this time, CCP troops were deployed throughout north, central, even east China along the coast behind enemy lines. It would have been extremely easy for them to take over all the major cities and transportation lines after the Japanese surrender. In sharp contrast, except for some small units in Shandong, Jiangsu, Anhui, and Shanxi, the Nationalist troops, especially the main force of the Central Army, remained in the southwestern provinces, such as Yunnan, Guangxi, Guizhou, and Sichuan—thousands of kilometers away from the major cities along the east coast. Therefore, when Jiang Jieshi suddenly invited Mao Zedong to Chongqing for negotiations, the CCP CC regarded it as "pure deception." The CCP CC, in Zhu De's name, immediately presented six preconditions. It publicly announced that unless "you [Jiang Jieshi] immediately abolish one-party dictatorship, hold a multi-party conference, establish a democratic coalition government," and obtain our approval, "we will reserve our right to speak" on "your government's and its headquarters'" acceptance of the Japanese surrender and all related treaties and agreements. It was after this public announcement that Mao Zedong sent his reply to Jiang Jieshi declaring that "I will consider meeting with you after you have made your opinions public."

At the same time, Mao Zedong ordered CCP forces throughout the country to take over the medium and small cities and towns as well as the nearby major communications lines. He also ordered the immediate deployment of the Eighth Route Army and the New Fourth Army near Beijing, Tianjin, Shanghai, and Nanjing, to smuggle agents into the major cities and try to occupy the cities before the arrival of the Nationalist troops. While the CCP CC was urgently planning the takeover of the major cities, Jiang Jieshi, on the one hand, managed to persuade Albert Wedemeyer, the supreme commander of American forces in China, to transport the Central Army from the southwest to the inland areas, using American warships and planes. On the other hand, Jiang continued to send telegrams to Mao Zedong, asking Mao to "consider the difficulties and dangers faced by the nation, feel the sufferings of the people," and "take the trip [to Chongqing] to work out a grand plan together."

On 20 August, when Jiang Jieshi was sending yet another telegram to Mao Zedong inviting him to Chongqing for negotiations, Stalin, in the name of the Communist Party of the Soviet Union (CPSU) CC, also dispatched a telegram to Mao Zedong and the CCP CC. In it, he emphasized that China should take the road of peaceful development and that Mao should indeed go to Chongqing to negotiate peace with Jiang Jieshi. Otherwise, he claimed China would surely lose half of its population once a civil war began.

Stalin's attitude toward relations between the Nationalist Party and the CCP made Mao extremely unhappy. Mao was eager to strongly resist the prohibition imposed on the CCP by the United States and Jiang Jieshi from taking over the Japanese-occupied areas. However, Mao was also clear that without support from the Union of Soviet Socialist Republics (USSR), or legal status in China, the CCP would have to launch forceful attacks if it wanted to take over the major cities and transportation lines. With their inferior weapons and equipment, it would be impossible for CCP forces to defeat the enemy in the fortified cities or to defend the cities after they were taken. Furthermore, the CCP CC had to maintain good relations with the USSR because it was most important for the CCP CC to send its troops to the Northeast while it was still under Soviet occupation. Only in this way could the CCP rely on the USSR and fundamentally improve its weapons and equipment. Therefore, Mao Zedong had to immediately change his previous orders, instructing that preparations for taking over the major cities be halted. At the same time, the CCP CC decided to make a gesture to Jiang by sending Zhou Enlai to Chongqing in hopes of turning things around. However, three days later, Jiang sent yet another telegram to Mao, insisting that "there are many important issues to be discussed with Monsieur [*xiansheng*]." He asked Mao Zedong and Zhou Enlai to "kindly come together" and he promised to "send planes to pick you up." At the same time, Stalin also sent a telegram, guaranteeing Mao's security while in Chongqing. At this point, Mao Zedong had no choice but to send a reply to Jiang Jieshi on 24 August, stating that he was "most eager to meet with Monsieur and to discuss the grand plan for peaceful reconstruction. Once the plane arrives, Comrade Enlai will immediately fly to Chongqing to present himself before you. This younger brother [Mao] will also go to Chongqing soon thereafter."

On 22 August, the CCP CC came up with an analysis of Soviet efforts to promote peaceful negotiations between the Nationalist Party and the CCP. It warned the entire party that "it is impossible for the Soviet Union to assist us because of the restrictions in the Sino-Soviet treaty and the Soviet desire to maintain peace in the Far East. Jiang Jieshi will take advantage of its legal status to accept the enemy's surrender and the enemy will turn the cities and key transportation lines over to Jiang Jieshi. Under these circumstances, our army should change our strategy. Only several areas should still be taken over and most troops should be positioned so as to threaten the major cities and the vast rural areas, to expand and consolidate the liberated areas, to mobilize the masses for struggle, to focus on training the troops, to prepare to cope with the new situation, and to get ready for a long haul." On the next day, the Politburo of the CCP CC held a meeting during which Mao Zedong stated that he understood the Soviet actions. He pointed out that under the current international conditions, there were obviously serious contradictions and differences between the Soviet Union and the United States, Great Britain, and other countries. Having just ended the Great War, surely no one wanted to see a Third World War take place. If the USSR were to assist the CCP in China, the United States would have to aid Jiang. This would result in the outbreak of another great war, ending any possibility for world peace. Therefore, the Soviet Union and the United States carved out their separate spheres of influence, just as the USSR had done in Europe. The USSR could assist Bulgaria, but it could not aid Greece, which was part of the British sphere of influence. Since the areas inside Shanhaiguan were part of the American sphere of influence, it was more advantageous to the CCP CC that the Soviet Union did not provide aid.

Mao Zedong's analysis was rather accurate. As early as 1944, Stalin had reached a so-called percentages agreement to carve out spheres of influence among the United States, Great Britain, and the Soviet Union after the war. The Soviet Union was allowed to exert influence on its close neighbors and the Eastern European nations, including Poland, Romania, Czechoslovakia, Hungary, Bulgaria, and Yugoslavia. In return, the Soviet Union recognized that the rest of Europe, including Greece and the Balkans, was within the sphere of influence of the United States and Great Britain. This is why the Soviet Union, as Mao Zedong had implied, assisted the Bulgarian Communists but refused to do the same for the Greek Communists. In fact, Stalin's fundamental strategy to handle the Communist forces beyond the Soviet sphere of influence was to ask them to "take the French Road," that is, lay down their weapons and shift to a peaceful legislative struggle. At the end of the war, the guerrillas and militiamen under Communist leadership were the dominant forces in France. However, since Great Britain and the United States only recognized the government of General Charles de Gaulle, the Soviet Union insisted that the French Communists had to collaborate with him. Under Soviet pressure, Maurice Thorez, secretary general of the French Communist Party, broadcast speeches and issued orders, requiring that the military forces led by the French Communist Party be transformed into a regular army, as demanded by the de Gaulle government, and the power of the local governments be transferred to the officials appointed by de Gaulle. The result of these actions was the French Communist Party became the largest political party in the October 1945 elections and four Communists entered the government as ministers. Stalin was very satisfied with the results. He believed, at least for the moment, that this would not only help maintain international peace after the war but would also win support from the United States and Great Britain for Soviet control over the Eastern European nations.

Stalin believed that following the provisions of the Yalta Agreement, China should act accordingly. With the Great Wall as the border, the Northeast beyond the Great Wall was part of the Soviet sphere of influence, whereas the rest of China within the Great Wall was within the sphere of influence of the United States. The Soviet Union only wanted to safeguard its privileges within its own sphere of influence and would never create any trouble on the other side of the Great Wall. It also did not want to see the United States reach beyond the Great Wall. In order to win cooperation from the United States, Stalin did not want the Nationalist Party and the CCP enter into a civil war within the Great Wall. He decided to follow the American plan and support the establishment of a unified Chinese government under the leadership of Jiang Jieshi. It was based on this consideration that Stalin persuaded Mao Zedong to end the armed struggle and go to Chongqing for peace negotiations with Jiang Jieshi. Later, he agreed to allow George Marshall, the special US envoy, to go to China to mediate between the Nationalist Party and the CCP. However, Mao himself would not participate in the negotiations, nor did he agree to include the Northeast of China beyond the Great Wall in any negotiations.

It is not difficult to see that it was due to the intervention by Stalin that the peace talks between Jiang Jieshi and Mao Zedong went smoothly. However, Mao Zedong was not Thorez, the secretary general of the French Communist Party, and China was different from Europe and could not be cut into two halves divided by the Great Wall. Mao Zedong did go to Chongqing to meet with Jiang Jieshi. However, he not only continued to refuse to give up his own army or the base areas controlled by the CCP but he also demanded authorization to take over more areas on both sides of the Great Wall. Thus, the Chongqing talks did not follow the French pattern as Stalin had wished and did not open a door to peace in China.

THE TAKEOVER OF THE NORTHEAST BY THE CCP AND SOVIET ASSISTANCE

Having signed the Sino-Soviet Treaty of Friendship, Alliance, and Mutual Assistance and obtained all the privileges provided in the secret Yalta Agreement after the war, Stalin began to fulfill his promise by pressuring the separatist forces in Xinjiang to hold peace talks with representatives of the Chinese central government. On 14 September 1945, the Soviet consul general was ordered to meet with Zhang Zhizhong, the central government representative sent to Dihua to handle the Yining incident. He assured Zhang that the USSR would help to peacefully resolve the conflict in Xinjiang. On the next day, the Soviet ambassador formally transmitted a message from the Soviet government noting that it was willing to mediate the Xinjiang incident. The negotiations between the two sides began in mid-October 1945 and lasted for about eight months, with the USSR serving as the mediator. The negotiations experienced several ups and downs because there were serious divisions within the "National Army." It was the Soviet Union that took steps to suppress the independence faction and it secretly deported the leader of the independence faction from Xinjiang. A peace agreement was finally signed on 6 June 1946. The "National Army" was regrouped and assigned areas where to be stationed. The Xinjiang Provincial Government was reorganized and accepted the representatives of the "National Army." On 1 July 1946, the Joint Government of Xinjiang Province was established. As the director of the Northwest Regional

Headquarters of the Nationalist government, Zhang Zhizhong concurrently held the position of provincial governor. Ahmatjan Kasimi from the "National Army" and Burhan Shahidia, a Uyghur intellectual, became vice-governors. On the Provincial Government Committee, 41 percent of the seats were held by representatives from the "National Army." The top prefecture and county officials in Kashi, Akesu, and Tulufan were nominated by Ahmatjan Kasimi. Although the "East Turkistan Islamic People's Republic" in Yining was dismantled, the three districts of Ili, Tacheng, and Altay remained autonomous under the "National Army" and the Central Army was prohibited from entering these districts. The "National Army" and its youth organizations were allowed to hold activities and engage in propaganda throughout all of Xinjiang.

Coinciding with the peace talks in Xinjiang, peace negotiations between the Nationalist Party and the CCP within the Great Wall began. In December 1945, George Marshall, the special envoy for the US president, arrived in China to shoulder the task of mediating between the Nationalist Party and the CCP. Because of pressure from the United States and support from the Soviet Union, the Nationalist and Communist parties quickly reached several compromises. Battles within the Great Wall ended, a Political Consultative Conference was held, and a number of important resolutions, including a draft constitution and reorganization of the army, were signed. In early 1946, a new atmosphere of peace and democracy began to emerge in China, showing great potential for a peaceful future. However, the truce within the Great Wall and the prospects for a future peace became a mere illusion when Jiang insisted that only Nationalist government troops, following the Sino-Soviet treaty, had authority to assume sovereignty in the areas beyond the Great Wall, refused to recognize the existence of the CCP troops that had earlier arrived in the Northeast, and excluded the Northeast from the truce agreement signed by the Nationalist Party and the CCP on 10 January.

The precondition for the Soviet Union to support realization of peace within the Great Wall under American leadership was that the United States did not become involved in any affairs beyond the Great Wall. However, from the very beginning the Soviet Union faced two major challenges. One was the ideological ties between the CCP and the CPSU that rendered it impossible for the Soviet Army to refuse to assist the CCP. Immediately after the Soviet Army occupied the Northeast, the CCP troops, taking advantage of the ideological sympathy from the Soviet Army and its need for Chinese troops to maintain order, began to move into the area within the Great Wall. Actually, a special envoy of the Soviet Army went to Yan'an to ask the CCP CC to send representatives to the Northeast so as to help communications. The second challenge was that the United States refused to recognize that there was any provision in the Yalta Agreement prohibiting the Americans from entering the Northeast, and it insisted that an "Open Door" policy should be applied to China's Northeast. Moreover, US marines, who originally did not have any battle assignments in China, suddenly landed in large numbers along the north China coast one month after the war ended in Asia. Although this was done in order to assist the repatriation of Japanese prisoners of war, the American marines directly assisted the Nationalist troops marching toward the Northeast. Greatly alarmed by this new development, the Soviet Army immediately contacted the CCP representative and asked the CCP to send its main forces to the Northeast as soon as possible, even at the expense of all the base areas within the Great Wall if necessary. The purpose was to prevent American and Nationalist troops, with help from the Soviet Army from entering the Northeast. In response, the CCP CC quickly organized over 100,000 troops and hurriedly sent them to the Northeast, thus establishing a large military force in the Northeast. The civil war between the Nationalist and Communist parties was thus expanded to the Northeast region.

As part of its efforts to assume sovereignty over the Northeast, by September 1945 the Nationalist government had already set up a Northeast Headquarters under the Military Commission chairman, with Xiong Shihui as director, and a Northeast Garrison Command, with Du Yuming as commander. It had also divided the Northeast into nine provinces and appointed governors for each province as well as mayors for Harbin and Dalian. However, with the landing of the US marines in north China in late September, negotiations between China and the USSR regarding taking over the Northeast became more complicated. With support from the Soviet Army the CCP troops in the Northeast closed off all land, sea, and air routes entering the Northeast. Under these circumstances, Jiang Jieshi had to take the risk of breaking with the USSR by withdrawing the Northeast Headquarters under the chairman of the Central Military Commission and sending complaints to the United States about Soviet violations of the treaty. At the same time, Jiang ordered the Nationalist Army to launch an all-out attack on Shanhaiguan, which was defended by CCP troops, in an attempt to open the transportation lines leading to the Northeast through the use of force.

The Soviet Army originally planned to complete its withdrawal from the Northeast on 1 December. However, the USSR faced a diplomatic dilemma when the Nationalist government withdrew from its Northeast Headquarters and refused to take over the region. In order to meet its needs for a withdrawal, the Soviet Army had to make some concessions. It agreed to postpone its withdrawal for one to two months, and it promised to begin a withdrawal only after the arrival of the Central Army so it could maintain order. Fulfilling its promises, the Soviet Army forced the CCP troops to remain at least 15 kilometers away from the major cities so as to avoid providing any excuses for the Nationalist Party. The USSR and the Nationalist government also reached an agreement to postpone the final withdrawal of the Soviet Army to 1 February, 1946. The Northeast Headquarters quickly took over Changchun on 22 December, Shenyang on 27 December, and Harbin on 1 January 1946. It controlled Liaobei, Songjiang, and Nengjiang in January. The Nationalist troops soon took over Shanhaiguan and then occupied Suizhong, Xingcheng, and Jinxi. They entered Jinzhou on 26 November 1945, took Xinmin on 12 January 1946, and marched into the Tiexi District of Shenyang on 15 January.

Although the Soviet Union made diplomatic concessions, it did not alter its goals. It insisted that China's Northeast was within its sphere of influence and it absolutely would not allow American meddling. Jiang Jieshi sent his son, Jiang Jingguo, to Moscow at the end of December 1945 and in early January 1946 in an attempt to reach some kind of compromise with the USSR. Stalin's attitude was very clear—he would never allow a third party to enter the Northeast. However, Jiang Jingguo insisted on applying an "Open Door" policy in the Northeast and agreed to allow the USSR only to maintain a dominant position in economic relations. This meant that the Nationalists were determined to allow the Americans and American capital into the Northeast. Stalin obviously would not accept this. He proposed that since the USSR had suffered so much during the war against Japan and most important assets in the Northeast were owned by the Japanese, the USSR would treat them as its war prize. Half of them would be used to compensate for the losses suffered by the Soviet Union. The other half would be used to compensate for the losses suffered by China. Stalin suggested that all key enterprises in the Northeast should be operated jointly as Chinese and Soviet monopolies. Otherwise, the Soviet Army would dispose of them as its war booty.

Actually, in late September 1945, the USSR began to realize that the Americans might enter China's Northeast region. The Soviet Army occupying the Northeast began to remove its machines and equipment from the military enterprises and took all its cash, securities, and precious metals from the bank in the Northeast. On 15 January 1946, Zhang Shenfu and his colleagues, who had been sent by the Northeast Headquarters to take over the Fushun Coal Mines, were killed. On 11 February, the United States and Britain publicized the secret Yalta Agreement, revealing the Soviet plan to obtain privileges in China's Northeast. Angered by this revelation, a nationwide anti-Soviet demonstration was held on 16 February. As Sino-Soviet negotiations on economic cooperation made no progress and the Nationalists' anti-Soviet attitude became increasingly clear, the USSR no longer cared about diplomatic relations. It informed the CCP Northeast Bureau that the Soviet Army would begin to withdraw but would not turn over to the Nationalist government any region south of Shenyang. Thus, the CCP troops could still move about freely. The USSR hoped that the CCP troops would take as much of the Northeast as possible through "massive campaigns."

Because the Soviet Army's withdrawal from southern Manchuria was so sudden, the CCP forces could quickly take over the Andong, Benxi, Liaoyang, Haicheng, Fushun, Tonghua, Tongliao, and Liaoyuan areas. The takeover of most of the industrial areas in southern Manchuria by the Communists worried Jiang Jieshi. He went to Marshall and told him that he was willing to recognize that confrontations between the Nationalist and Communist parties also existed in the Northeast. Thus, he requested that a truce group be sent to the Northeast so as to stop the CCP from going deeper into the areas vacated by the Soviet Army.

As the Northeast truce talks went nowhere, USSR impatience grew. The representative of the Soviet Army repeatedly asked the CCP Northeast Bureau why it treated the Americans so politely and why it allowed the Nationalists to send five armies to the Northeast. The Soviet Army representative emphasized that all the areas vacated by the Soviet Army "including Shenyang and Siping, could be places for major battles, and major battles are expected." The representative insisted that the areas north of Changchun, such as Harbin and so forth, should be placed under solid control and should never be sacrificed. Based on Soviet advice, the CCP CC changed its attitude and firmly decided to "let our troops permanently occupy all of the China Eastern Railroad (including the city of Harbin) and refuse to allow a single Nationalist soldier to enter."

Having realized that its forces were unable to control all of the Northeast, on 20 March the CCP CC proposed a strategic plan whereby the Nationalist Party and the CCP would station their troops in southern and northern Manchuria respectively, with Changchun serving as the point of separation. This plan was supported by the USSR. Based on this plan, the CCP began to collaborate with the Soviet Army to destroy the Beijing Railroad and the Changchun Railroad near Shenyang, to take over the areas east of Jilin city, and to prepare for attacks on Harbin, Qiqihaer, Changchun, and other areas along the railroad line. At the same time, CCP troops were ready to fight against the Nationalist Army in Tieling, Changtu, and Siping to end its move north.

On 1 April Jiang Jieshi publicly stated at the Nationalist Assembly that he would never recognize a "Democratic Coalition Army" or a "democratically elected government," completely shutting the door to a peaceful resolution of the issues in the Northeast. At the same time, the Soviet Union told the CCP Northeast Bureau that the United States used Jiang's takeover of the Northeast to resist the Soviet Union, and Jiang used the United States to fight against the USSR and the CCP. Since the USSR did not want to directly intervene in the Northeast, it hoped that the CCP would do its best to remain in the Northeast and keep it as an unsettled issue. This would push the United States and the Nationalist government into a difficult position. The USSR also informed the CCP that Soviet troops would withdraw from Changchun and from Harbin on 15 April and from Qiqihar on 25 April. It asked the CCP forces to move close to these three cities so that they could take them over after the Soviet withdrawal. Based on this, the CCP CC was determined to stop the Nationalist troops in Siping and Benxi. The Communist forces occupied Changchun, the political capital of the Northeast, on 19 March and took Harbin and Qiqihar soon thereafter. However, the Nationalist troops entering the Northeast at this time were mainly from the Central Army. They were all well-equipped with American weapons and with fighting experience in Burma. They also had greater firepower and battle capacity. In contrast, the CCP forces were put together in a hurry and forced to fight an unfamiliar regular defense battle. Therefore, after about one month, Benxi and Siping were overwhelmed, and soon thereafter Changchun was also lost. It was only because the Nationalist Army had stretched the front too long and the CCP had organized attacks in southern Manchuria, creating a major diversion, that the Nationalist troops did not take advantage of their success and chase the Communist forces across the Songhua River. As a result, the CCP forces were able to establish a solid northern Manchuria base with strong backing from the USSR.

Of course, Jiang Jieshi's intentionally aggressive actions in the Northeast irritated Mao. After the fall of Changchun, Mao decided in June to begin retaliatory campaigns within the Great Wall. Once the CCP began its campaigns in Shandong and elsewhere, the Nationalists took the opportunity to launch its own campaigns against the CCP's central base regions. As a result, the areas that had been under the truce agreement within the Great Wall were once again dragged into a civil war. Once the civil war began, there was no way to stop it.

In June 1946 the nationwide Chinese civil war erupted. Soviet newspapers publicly denounced the Nationalist Party for "quietly serving imperialist Japan by sending its troops to attack the Eighth Route Army" and the United States for instigating and supporting the Chinese civil war. It was clear that the Soviets were on the side of the CCP. In September, about four months after the withdrawal of the Soviet troops from the Northeast, Stalin issued a written statement, urging the United States to withdraw its troops from China. Acting in concert, Andrei Gromyko, Soviet deputy foreign minister, issued a similar statement. Soon thereafter, the Nationalist government signed a Treaty of Friendship, Commerce, and Navigation with the United States, known as the Sino-American Commerce Treaty. The treaty provided that the territories of both nations would be open to each other and commercial ships of each nation would have freedom to sail to all open ports and in all territorial waters of the other. Companies, organizations, and legal persons of one nation could reside, travel, engage in commercial, manufacturing, processing, financial, educational, religious, and philanthropic enterprises in the other nation. They could also purchase as well as maintain real estate and enjoy the same equal rights as native citizens, organizations, and legal persons. Merchandise sold in the other country was to be taxed at the same rate as local merchandise. In theory, this treaty provided equal rights for both nations. However, in reality, such openness provided great advantages for the United States and few pragmatic benefits for China because of the drastically different conditions in the two nations. The drastically different attitudes of the Nationalists toward the United States and the Soviet Union and the inclusion of the Northeast in the list of places completely open to the United States clearly irritated the Soviet Union. When Mao Zedong and Zhu De sent a co-signed congratulatory telegram to Stalin celebrating the 29th anniversary of the October Revolution, Stalin unprecedentedly replied expressing his gratitude. This signaled that the Soviet Union was indicating its resentment of the Nationalist Party in an increasingly public manner.

In a March 1947 speech to Congress, President Harry Truman stated that the United States should provide aid to people in all free countries who were fighting against authoritarian rule. In June, the United States approved the aid program for Europe proposed by Secretary of State George Marshall and began to divide the European countries into free countries eligible for American aid and authoritarian countries ineligible for American aid. In response, the USSR coordinated the activities of the Communist parties in all European countries and prevented the United States from meddling in East European affairs. It also decided to establish the Information Bureau for Communist and Workers' Parties, making public its firm policy of the socialist (democratic) camp confronting the imperialist camp. The actions of the United States and the Soviet Union expanded the increasing estrangement between the two nations into an all-out struggle, thus giving birth to the Soviet-American Cold War.

NOTE

1. "Directive by President Truman to the Supreme Commander for the Allied Powers in Japan (MacArthur)," 15 August 1945, in Department of State, *Foreign Relations of the United States* (cited hereafter as *FRUS*), 1945 (Washington, DC: Government Printing Office, 1946), vol. 7, p. 501.

PART II

Comrades and Brothers, 1948–1959

CHAPTER 7

The Political and Economic Foundations of the Sino-Soviet Alliance, 1948–1949

Zhihua Shen

To understand the origins of the Sino-Soviet alliance, it is necessary to explore the contacts and understandings among the leaders of the Chinese Communist Party (CCP) and the Communist Party of the Soviet Union (CPSU) prior to the formation of the alliance in 1950.[1] From the summer of 1947 to early 1949, after nearly one and half years of informal contacts, a face-to-face formal meeting was scheduled. Endorsed by Soviet leader Joseph Stalin, Politburo member Anastas Mikoyan visited CCP headquarters in Xibaipo from January to February 1949. This was the first step in the formation of an alliance. A CCP delegation, led by Liu Shaoqi, the No. 2 leader in the CCP, secretly visited the Union of Soviet Socialist Republics (USSR) from June to August 1949. When Liu was still in Moscow in late June 1949, Mao announced the CCP policy of "leaning-to-one-side" (i.e., the side of the Soviet Union). The political basis for a Sino-Soviet alliance appeared to be promising.

Prior to the founding of the People's Republic of China (PRC), the only economic relationship between the CCP and the USSR consisted of Soviet economic and technical aid to local CCP governments in Northeast and North China. This economic relationship was a one-way street: the USSR as the supplier and China as the recipient, but it was the foundation for future military and political relations. Meanwhile, the CCP and the USSR disagreed regarding property rights over the Chinese Changchun Railway and utilization of the resources in Northeast China.[2] This was the core issue that the new Sino-Soviet Treaty of Alliance, Friendship, and Mutual Alliance sought to resolve. Mao

Z. Shen (✉)
East China Normal University, Shanghai, China
e-mail: zhaoran@ssap.cn

Z. Shen (ed.), *A Short History of Sino-Soviet Relations, 1917–1991*, China Connections, https://doi.org/10.1007/978-981-13-8641-1_7

hoped the signing of a treaty would establish a legal framework for the alliance. This chapter investigates the historical background, foundation, and basis for the Sino-Soviet alliance from the perspective of each side.

CHANGES IN SOVIET POLICY TOWARD CHINA, 1945–1948

Stalin's postwar China strategy consisted of two goals. The first was to remove Mongolia from Chinese jurisdiction and to secure its independence, thereby creating a broad security zone south of the USSR. The second was to restore the Tsarist Russian sphere of influence in Northeast China to ensure access to an ice-free port in the Pacific. The USSR informed the United States of its first goal at a meeting on 14 December 1944 with Stalin and US ambassador to Moscow, Averell Harriman. At a meeting on 8 February 1945 with President Franklin D. Roosevelt, Stalin secured a US commitment to support him as well as to support the concessions he had obtained in the Yalta Agreement. At the same time, Stalin promised that his postwar China policy would support Jiang Jieshi's Nationalist government and discourage Chinese Communist revolutionary activities.

Working with both sides diplomatically, the United States and the USSR forced the Chinese Nationalist government to accept the Soviet conditions. After the Soviet Army moved into Northeast China, Jiang Jieshi, under duress, finally agreed to sign the "Sino-Soviet Treaty of Friendship and Alliance" for a 30-year term. The USSR and China also signed the "Agreement on the Chinese Changchun Railway," the "Agreement on Dalian [Dairen]," the "Agreement on Lüshun [Port Arthur]," and other related documents.

These agreements guaranteed that the USSR would regain all rights that Tsarist Russia had lost in Northeast China as a result of the 1904–5 Russo-Japanese War. The Chinese Changchun Railway would be jointly owned and operated by China and the USSR, with its director appointed by the USSR. Dalian was declared a free port, with the manager of the port appointed by the USSR. All goods imported and exported through the port of Dalian or transported on the Changchun Railway to or from the USSR were to be free of customs duties, whereas imported and exported goods through the port to China were subject to customs duties. Port Arthur was designated a naval base for joint use, with the chairman of the base appointed by the USSR. The most important civilian administrative personnel in Lüshun city were subject to appointment and removal by Soviet military command authorities. To achieve its goals, Stalin granted assurances to Jiang Jieshi that the CCP would submit to the unified leadership under the Nationalist government. Stalin sought to insure implementation of the guarantees contained in the Yalta Agreement, including restoration of all rights in China that Tsarist Russia had lost as a result of the Russo-Japanese War. For ideological considerations, the Chinese Communists were of little importance in terms of Stalin's handling of relations with the Nationalist government. Thus, how the Soviet Red Army would deal with the Chinese Communist Army in Northeast China was to be decided based entirely on Soviet needs, and CCP policy toward Northeast China evolved in accordance with Soviet attitudes.

Senior CCP leaders Chen Yun, Gao Gang, Zhang Wentian, and others who were on the frontlines in Northeast China realized that the only basis for the Soviet plan was to support Soviet interests. In a 30 November 1945 report to the CCP Central Committee (CC), the Soviets pointed out that their goal was "primarily for the purpose of maintaining peace in the Far East and the world," that is, Soviet policy in the Northeast toward the Nationalists and the Communists was only supplementary to its major goal. Therefore, the CCP would have to prepare for a long-term struggle in the Northeast, and "disabuse our cadres of the notion that … they can pin all their hopes on Soviet assistance."[3] The term "to preserve peace" was merely a way for the CCP to save face. Abandoning the illusion of Soviet assistance indicates that the CCP leadership clearly understood Stalin's Far Eastern policy.

By summer 1948, the Communist offensive had achieved important victories, ushering in an important change in the Chinese situation. Mao Zedong sent a telegram to Stalin during a December 1947 CC meeting, stressing that the Chinese Revolution had reached a turning point. The People's Liberation Army (PLA) had pushed back the general advance of the Nationalist forces and was now entering its offensive phase.

With respect to dealings with the CCP, in May 1948 when discussing with representative plenipotentiary Ivan Kovalev about Mao's telegram asking for assistance, Stalin stated:[4] "Of course we want to give New China all the assistance we can. If socialism succeeds in China, other countries will follow. Then we will know that the global victory of socialism will be assured, and we will not confront any dangers of unexpected events. Therefore, we cannot withhold our financial and other support for the Chinese Communists." Several days later, in a chat with Kovalev on the eve of Kovalev's departure for China, Stalin reiterated this same point.

Actually, the USSR began to provide military assistance to the Chinese Communists in the summer of 1948. In 1947, the volume of trade between Soviet foreign trade organizations and the Northeast Area People's Democratic Authority totaled 93 million rubles. By 1948, it had increased to 151 million rubles. In June 1948, at the invitation of the office of the Northeast Liberated Area People's Democratic Authority, the Soviet government dispatched, under the leadership of Kovalev, a Soviet railway specialist group, including 50 engineers, 52 technicians, and 220 technical personnel and skilled workers, as well as technical equipment and machinery.[5]

With the steady advance toward a victory in the Chinese Communist Revolution, Mao began to pay more attention to relations with the Soviet Union, especially with respect to the foreign policy of New China. The clearest sign of Mao's intent to strengthen relations with the Soviet Union was that, beginning in the spring of 1948, on numerous occasions he asked to visit Moscow, but his trip was repeatedly postponed. In a 14 January 1949 cable, Stalin proposed that the trip be suspended, suggesting, "If you think it is necessary, we can immediately send a Politburo member to Harbin or elsewhere to discuss the relevant issues."[6] On 17 January 1949, Mao replied, "I decided to temporarily postpone [my] trip to Moscow." He did, however, welcome Stalin to send a Soviet Politburo member to visit him at CCP CC headquarters in Xibaipo in late January or early February.

The CCP's drive for a total victory was a momentous event in the growth of the International Communist Movement and it received Stalin's enthusiastic approval. The key question was what would be the policy of New China toward the Soviet Union. This information had to be clear before the USSR would make any fundamental change in its China policy. In order to obtain this critical information, Stalin sent Politburo member Anastas Mikoyan to meet CCP leaders in China.

Mikoyan's Visit to Xibaipo

Mikoyan departed Moscow on 26 January and arrived in Xibaipo on 30 January 1949. He was accompanied by Ivan Kovalev, CPSU representative to the CCP, and Evgenii Kovalev, a CPSU CC interpreter. Before leaving China on 8 February, Mikoyan had held 12 talks with Chinese leaders, mainly Mao and Zhou Enlai, but also Liu Shaoqi, Ren Bishi, and Zhu De. These conversations covered a wide range of topics, including the history of the CCP and the current situation in China. They also included CCP political, economic, military, and foreign policies. Previous research on this topic has relied on the memoirs of two witnesses: Shi Zhe and Ivan Kovalev. Mikoyan's report on his trip, which he drafted in 1960, did not become available until 1995.[7] It basically consists of a summary of his talks from the Soviet perspective. Because Sino-Soviet relations were already in serious trouble at that time, the Chinese contended that Mikoyan's report was biased and one-sided. Citing these documents, many scholars pay too much attention to Sino-Soviet differences. But recently available sources clarify many misunderstandings. After carefully analyzing the 12 memoranda and the many cables in the following months, this author has determined that Sino-Soviet conversations in Xibaipo were actually quite friendly.

During these conversations, CCP leaders demonstrated a pro-Soviet position. In a discussion on CCP history on 3 and 4 February, Mao spoke highly of the CPSU's leadership, guidance, and assistance to the CCP. Given Mao's repeated later accusations regarding Stalin's mistakes, it is impossible to know Mao's true feelings. Nonetheless, it is evident that at least at this time Mao wanted Moscow to know that the CCP was grateful to both the CPSU and to Stalin.

In addition to asking the USSR to provide anti-aircraft guns for urban defense, a loan for economic development (US$ 300 million), silver dollars, paper, and printing ink for curbing inflation, and many other materials, the CCP hoped that the Soviet Union would also send advisers and specialists. At a meeting on 1 February, Zhou Enlai stated, "We would like to ask the Soviet

Union to also provide us with specialists and equipment for the manufacture of arms, and advisers on military reorganization, on military-educational institutions, and rear-guard organization."

The talks on 2 February focused on Sino-Soviet cooperation on industrial development. At a meeting with Mikoyan on 3 February, Liu Shaoqi discussed the issue of China's future industrial development. Another important issue discussed at Xibaipo was CCP relations with the United States and the Western powers. It seems that Stalin did not yet have any opinions on these issues, but the key point was not to provoke the United States. The talks also touched on Sino-Soviet conflicts of interest, especially with respect to Outer Mongolia, Xinjiang, and Northeast China, but these issues were discussed only superficially.[8]

From recently available Russian archival documents, it is apparent that during Mikoyan's visit to China, even though he did not settle any practical issues, the depth of his discussions with Mao, his face-to-face encounters with other CCP leaders, and Stalin's frequent cable exchanges with both Mao and Mikoyan, provided the two sides with an initial understanding of their differences as well as issues of common concern, establishing a foundation for later reciprocal visits by high-level leaders and representing a first step toward the establishment of a future alliance.

After Mikoyan departed Xibaipo, Mao was strongly convinced that to develop and rebuild New China, it was necessary to form an alliance with the Soviet Union. On 16 February, the CCP CC instructed its North China and Northeast Bureaus: The basic policy of foreign trade is to give priority to the needs of the Soviet Union and the new democratic countries in Eastern Europe. To demonstrate the importance of relations with the Soviet Union, in "On the People's Democratic Dictatorship," delivered on 30 June 1949, Mao pointed out: No revolution can be successful without international assistance. "Internationally, we belong to the side of the anti-imperialist front headed by the Soviet Union, and so we can turn only to this side for genuine and friendly help."[9] We must stand with the Soviet Union as allies. When the opportunity presents itself, we will issue a statement to make this clear. Available archival sources demonstrate that contacts between the CCP and the USSR government (and the CPSU) took place frequently after February 1949. The two sides exchanged opinions or responded to the issues discussed during Mikoyan's visit. Andrei Orlov (code name: *Terebin*) originally served as the liaison between Stalin and Mao, mainly by transmitting cables. But he was replaced by Ivan Kovalev as official representative of the CPSU CC to discuss issues directly with the CCP leaders.

Through ongoing consultations, in late May and early June 1949 it became apparent that the CCP and USSR held many of the same views. These included the establishment of a core economic leadership, the strengthening of maritime customs and border troops, acceleration of the establishment of the Central People's Government, and not to publicize Sino-Soviet friendship prior to the formal establishment of diplomatic relations. For the time being, they were not to establish an Eastern Cominform or to seize Hong Kong or Kowloon.

After Mikoyan's trip to Xibaipo, the Soviet Union increased its aid to the CCP. In this regard, the most pressing need was the CCP's request for Soviet advisers and specialists. In a talk with Kovalev on 9 April, Mao "urgently expected Soviet specialists to come to China," so China could make plans "to use their loans rationally. The priority is to restore important units such as industry and railways." When discussing the issue of recapturing the cities, Mao said that it was in fact easier to take cities, especially Shanghai, than it was to run them. Because the CCP had no experience in ruling, Mao was afraid that "the Americans will paralyze the life of the cities." As a result, Mao said, "We have not firmly decided whether to take Shanghai." At last, Mao asked the Soviet Union to send a team of experts "specializing in running cities" before the CCP would attempt to occupy the city. On 3 May, Mao again cabled Stalin and asked him to immediately send Soviet experts because economic reconstruction was the CCP's top priority. On 9 June, Mao yet again cabled Stalin, stating: "We are discussing planning, finance, and a mechanism for organizing economic activities. We have relatively accurate data regarding the necessary number of needed Soviet experts and their specialties." The cable made it clear that China required at least 600 Soviet experts. They were expected to arrive in China in 1949 and in the first half of 1950 to work in sectors such as planning, finance, economic organization, industry, and enterprises. Mao pointed out that the first group of Soviet experts was to include 258 people, who were to arrive in China between June and August. The cable listed the specialties of the more than 600 Soviet experts that China needed. On 12 June, Mao asked Stalin to also send national defense experts.

The closer the CCP came to ruling the country, the more difficult it was for it to manage the economy. Thus, it was in dire need of Soviet assistance. This was the main reason why Mao sent a delegation to the USSR even prior to the founding of the PRC.

Liu Shaoqi's Trip to the Soviet Union

A CCP delegation led by Liu Shaoqi visited the Soviet Union from 26 June to 14 August 1949.[10] For fear of provoking the United States, Stalin asked that the delegation be described in the foreign language press as a Northeast China trade mission led by Gao Gang, Politburo member and head of the CCP Northeast Bureau.[11] The main purpose of the visit was to inform Stalin of the CCP's position on major domestic and international issues. Liu held four formal talks with Stalin. He also had talks on trade issues with Mikoyan and on foreign-policy issues with Soviet Foreign Minister Andrei Vishinski. In addition, the delegation visited Soviet party, government, and other organizations and enterprises to learn how to govern the country after seizing power.

The Soviet Union was well prepared to receive the Chinese delegation. During the first meeting on 27 June, Stalin made it clear that the Chinese would receive what they were requesting. The terms of the US$ 300 million credit were immediately clarified, all of it to be used for the purchase of Soviet goods and equipment at 1 percent interest, which was to be repaid within ten years. Stalin also told the delegation that the USSR was ready to send its first group of experts to China. The Chinese government only had to pay them salaries equivalent to the highest salaries of the best Chinese experts. If necessary, the Soviet government would supplement any difference in their salaries. Stalin also told the Chinese that 15 experts had already been selected to meet the pressing needs in Shanghai. Stalin's generous actions demonstrated that the CPSU intended to form an alliance with the CCP. At the very least, Stalin wanted Mao to believe that this was the case. Liu's visit achieved substantial results, and the CCP responded to Soviet actions in kind.

Due to this visit, the CCP won the trust and support of Moscow. Liu Shaoqi introduced CCP domestic and foreign policies, especially its policy toward the Soviet Union. Stalin revealed that the USSR favored the formation of an alliance, including a cooperative division of labor in the international revolutionary movement. Stalin hoped that China would assume more responsibility to assist the national democratic revolutionary movements in the colonial and semi-colonial countries because China's revolutionary experience could have a great influence and could be assimilated elsewhere. Liu's most important mission was to seek more aid for China's economic development and national defense. In this respect, Stalin basically satisfied all China's needs. The USSR agreed to assist the CCP in building up its navy and air force. During Liu's visit, the two sides also agreed to cooperate on the Xinjiang issue.[12]

In the Sino-Soviet Treaty of 1945, China and the USSR had conflicting interests regarding the Chinese Changchun Railway, Dalian, and Port Arthur.[13] The Mongolian issue was sensitive as well. Although aware of Stalin's definitive attitude, Liu expressed the Chinese view on the issue on behalf of the "democratic parties, students, and workers." The CCP's declared position remained reserved: "The Mongolian people want independence. In accordance with the principle of national self-determination, we should recognize Mongolian independence. If the Mongolian People's Republic is willing to unite with China, we welcome them. Only the Mongolian people have the right to decide." But the talks did not touch on the Mongolian issue, and the CCP and USSR effectively delayed resolution of this controversial issue. During the Moscow talks, Taiwan emerged as another point of contention. From Stalin's perspective, the USSR could assist the CCP in establishing an air force and a navy, but liberation of Taiwan was the CCP's own business.[14]

As revealed by the above, the limits of Chinese and Soviet capabilities to satisfy the other side's requests depended on whether they had similar assessments of global issues and whether cooperation would satisfy their long-term objectives. Because China and the USSR shared a common ideological understanding and similar strategic considerations on international issues, the conclusion of an alliance coincided with their mutual long-term interests. Therefore, Mao and Stalin both worked hard to achieve an understanding and to temporarily set aside any difficult issues. This was the reason for the success of Liu's visit to Moscow, which effectively determined the structure of Sino-Soviet strategic cooperation,[15] and Mao publicly announced his diplomatic policy of "leaning-to-one-side," i.e., the Soviet side.

MAO'S DECLARATION OF THE "LEANING-TO-ONE-SIDE" POLICY

On 1 July 1949, *People's Daily* published Mao's article, "On the People's Democratic Dictatorship," in which he proclaimed his "leaning-to-one-side" policy,[16] whereby New China would side with the USSR in its foreign policy. What prompted Mao to openly declare this policy and what were the results?

Due to errors in the memoirs of those who were involved in Liu Shaoqi's trip to Moscow, previous studies argue that Mao wanted to demonstrate his goodwill so as to pave the way for his Moscow meeting.[17] We can now conclude that the "leaning-to-one-side" statement was a direct outcome of the Stalin–Liu talks on 27 June. Mao had decided on the policy in the previous year. Not only did he make it known within the party on many occasions, he also wanted to ensure that Stalin understood his position. Although Mao's desire to visit Moscow had not been realized, Mikoyan's visit made it possible for the USSR to completely understand the CCP's position. But Stalin's paranoia may have led him to still be unsure about Mao's position, and Moscow itself never had a clear policy.[18] Despite Soviet misgivings, Mao was optimistic about Stalin's attitude after the Stalin–Liu talks on 27 June. Mao learned about the content of the Stalin–Liu talks in the afternoon of 28 June. It was the result he had been expecting, and thus an opportune moment to issue a policy statement. Another reason for Mao's prompt action was his intention to consolidate the success of Liu's visit to the USSR and to further strengthen a move toward a Sino-Soviet alliance. Mao had to temper Stalin's suspicions so that the latter would wholeheartedly support the CCP. One sensitive drawback, however, was CCP contacts with US Ambassador John L. Stuart, beginning in early May 1949.

For two months in mid-1949, American officials saw a potential opportunity to negotiate with the CCP leadership on issues related to the uncertain future of US-China relations. In May and June, Ambassador Stuart held a series of talks in Nanjing with Huang Hua, a high-level CCP foreign affairs official.[19] The CCP attempted to keep the Soviets informed of these talks. Before his meeting on 7 May with Stuart's personal secretary, Philip Fugh, and after his meetings with Fugh on 10 May and with Stuart on 13 May, Huang Hua briefed Andrei Lebowski, first secretary at the Soviet embassy in Nanjing. Mao informed Kovalev about the details of China's contacts with the Americans on 22 May. He declared that the CCP was not interested in the United States.[20] Stalin accepted Mao's position, and thanked the CCP for the information.

In his talks to both the CCP and the CPSU, Mao repeatedly said that he did not seek US recognition of the CCP government. This was his true assessment. He wanted to give the Americans the impression that he paid great attention to this issue, but the purpose was only to dissuade the United States from acting against China. After all, the Chinese Revolution could be affected by US policy, even when victory was so close. On 28 May, the day after Shanghai was captured, Mao issued a cable in the name of the Central Military Commission (CMC), pointing out "recently there are indications that the imperialist countries want to interfere with our revolution. ... [We should] come up with countermeasures." But by remaining in touch with Stuart he gave the impression that the CCP would cooperate with the Americans. Mao was engaging in psychological warfare. After receiving Moscow's consent to continue the talks, the CCP in fact increased contacts with the United States.

Huang Hua notified Andrei Ledovskii, first secretary of the Soviet Embassy in Nanjing, after each meeting with Fugh or Stuart. From Ledovskii's account, Huang tried to convince Moscow that Stuart had initiated the contacts with the CCP. The CCP believed such contacts would contribute to a further understanding of US policy. It would also give the Americans hope of improving relations with the CCP. It is worth noting that Huang told Ledovskii that he had not accepted a letter from Stuart to Mao Zedong. But this episode does not appear either in Stuart's report to the State Department or in Huang Hua's memoirs. In addition, Huang never mentioned to Ledovskii that US Secretary of State Dean Acheson did not support Stuart's trip to Beiping on 1 July.[21] On 2 July, Fugh informed Huang Hua that Acheson had ordered Stuart to rush back to Washington before 25 July, so Stuart was unable to visit Beiping and the contacts between the CCP and the United States came to an end.

Was there a chance in 1949–50 that the CCP and the United States could form a working relationship? Historians have long debated the so-called lost chance.[22] Recently available evidence reveals that there was in fact no possibility for the United States to form any meaningful relationship with the CCP in 1949. Stalin had already displayed his willingness to ally with the CCP prior to US contacts with the CCP in May–June 1949. In addition, Mao had already resolved to lean toward the USSR.[23]

It is obvious that the CCP hoped to give Moscow the impression that Stuart's potential trip to Beiping was based on a US initiative. To demonstrate the CCP's anti-American stance, *People's Daily* published an article exposing a so-called American espionage case in Shenyang. On 24 June, *People's Daily* published another article, denouncing "British and American diplomacy as espionage diplomacy." On 25 June, the CCP Central Committee (CC) cabled its Northeast Bureau, asking it to collect evidence to accuse the US Consulate General in Shenyang of involvement in an espionage case. After announcement of the espionage case, the CCP CC considered deporting the staff in the US Consulate.

When Stalin announced his support of the CCP, Mao became even more determined to lean toward the USSR, and he also became concerned that contacts with the Americans would arouse Stalin's paranoia (Mao's cable of 30 June had already demonstrated such a mentality).[24] Mao thus decided to issue his "leaning-to-one-side" statement. On the same day that Mao approved prohibition of activities by the US Information Agency in China, he also approved of a public trial of US Consul General Angus Ward and his staff. After publication of the US State Department *China White Paper*, Mao published five articles criticizing America's China policy from both historical and current perspectives and he denounced the United States as a dangerous enemy of the Chinese people.[25] Stalin was satisfied with Mao's actions. A CCP CC report on

4 July claimed, "Our policy, in fact, is to lean toward the USSR. If we do not stand with the USSR in opposing the imperialist camp and we try to take a neutralist line, that will be wrong." Mao emphasized, "We hope to receive guidance from Comrade Stalin and the Soviet Communist Party." In response, Stalin indicated his great appreciation. On 6 July, *Pravda* published Mao's article on its front page and also issued a special edition. The journal *Novoe vremia* (New Epoch) also published an article entitled "Mao Zedong on the Foundation of the Chinese People's Democratic Dictatorship."[26]

CONCLUSION

During the second half of the 1940s, Soviet policy toward China was focused on the interests of the USSR rather than the fate of the CCP. Stalin's strategy, which continued until mid-1949, was to steer clear of direct involvement in the Chinese civil war. To avoid providing any evidence of support to the CCP, Stalin put off Mao's repeated requests to visit him in Moscow and he ordered that the Soviet ambassador in Nanjing follow the Nationalist government to Canton in April 1949. Only when a CCP victory was close at hand did Stalin find it necessary to forge a relationship with the Chinese Communists.

During Mikoyan's visit to Xibaipo, CCP leaders and Mikoyan were able to reach some agreements. The USSR was willing to make significant concessions to the Chinese regarding Port Arthur. Through Mikoyan, Stalin admitted that the 1945 agreement was unequal and the USSR was willing to suspend it. He even agreed to immediately withdraw Soviet troops from Lüshun and to renounce any territorial claims to Xinjiang. It was also apparent that the CCP was eager to obtain economic and military aid from the USSR. Mikoyan made promises in several areas, such as Soviet support to help develop an armaments industry and to send Soviet specialists to China. He also agreed to provide weapons and a loan of US$ 300 million. But on sensitive issues, both sides were careful to avoid conflict. Mao pretended not to be aware of Soviet insincerity on the Mongolian issue. The USSR insisted on maintaining the independent status of the Mongolian People's Republic—a Soviet satellite—to which Mao grudgingly yielded. Mikoyan also stated that the Soviets were unwilling to yield on the question of the Chinese Changchun Railway because the USSR did not regard the agreement as unequal.

Liu Shaoqi's mission to Moscow set the stage for the alliance between the USSR and Communist China. The two sides reached agreement on the political, economic, and foreign-policy strategies that New China would pursue. Stalin promised to recognize Communist China once it was established and he offered the preferential credit in the amount of US$ 300 million that the CCP had requested during Mikoyan's visit. Stalin also granted the CCP extensive civilian and military assistance. But substantial differences remained. Stalin refused to provide fighter pilots for the CCP's planned invasion of Taiwan. Stalin also insisted on retaining Soviet privileges in Manchuria and he showed no signs of relinquishing Soviet possession of the Chinese Changchun Railway.

Whether the two sides would sign a new treaty of alliance remained an open question.

At Xibaipo, the CCP and the Soviet leaders clarified their shared ideological concerns. Liu Shaoqi's visit to Moscow demonstrated that the two sides had reached agreement on concrete policies. A political foundation for a Sino-Soviet alliance was thus established, and relations between the USSR and Communist China entered a new phase. Their shared belief in Marxism-Leninism encouraged an alliance, yet it did not eliminate all conflicts of interest between the two sides. This chapter demonstrates that the first consideration for both China and the USSR in the formation of an alliance grew out of national security concerns and concrete economic interests. But due to historical reasons, the two sides encountered conflicts in these areas. Mao and Stalin were both aware that the alliance could not be stabilized without coordination of their diverse national interests. Although at the time both sides attempted to avoid such conflicts of interest, they knew that the conflicts would have to be resolved, and this could only be done at the highest levels of the leadership. In effect, this was the purpose of Mao's trip to Moscow.

NOTES

1. The Soviet Communist Party was called the All-Union Communist Party (Bolsheviks) from 1925 to 1952. It was renamed the Communist Party of the Soviet Union (CPSU) in 1952.
2. In this context, the Chinese Changchun Railway consisted of the Chinese Eastern Railway (from Manzhouli to Harbin to Suifenhe) and the South Manchuria Railway (from Changchun to Dalian).
3. Chen Yun, "Some Suggests Concerning Our Work in Manchuria," 30 November 1945, in *Chen Yun, 1926–1949* (Beijing: Foreign Languages Press, 1988), pp. 214, 216.
4. Ivan Kovalev was minister of transportation during World War II. He was the CPSU CC representative to the CCP from January 1949 to January 1950. He also served as leader of the Soviet experts in China until January 1950 when he was replaced by Ivan Arkhipov.
5. For an analysis of Soviet policies toward China from 1945 to 1948, see Zhihua Shen and Yafeng Xia, *Mao and the Sino-Soviet Partnership, 1945–1959: A New History* (Lanham, MD: Lexington Books, 2015), pp. 12–15.
6. On Mao's numerous requests to visit the USSR, see Shen and Xia, *Mao and the Sino-Soviet Partnership*, pp. 16–20.
7. For reactions to this report, see Sergei Goncharov, John Lewis, and Xue Litai, *Uncertain Partners, Stalin, Mao, and the Korean War* (Stanford, CA: Stanford University Press, 1993), pp. 41–43; Dieter Heinzig, *The Soviet Union and Communist China, 1945–1950: The Arduous Road to the Alliance* (New York: M. E. Sharpe, 2004), pp. 135–36.
8. On the various issues CCP leaders discussed with Mikoyan in Xibaipo, see Shen and Xia, *Mao and the Sino-Soviet Partnership*, pp. 20–27.
9. "On the People's Democratic Dictatorship," 30 June 1949, in *Selected Works of Mao Tse-tung*, vol. 4 (Peking: Foreign Languages Press, 1961), pp. 416–417.

10. The delegation also included CCP CC member Wang Jiaxiang, who was designated as New China's first ambassador to the Soviet Union. See Heinzig, *The Soviet Union and Communist China*, pp. 174–230.

11. Zhihua Shen, *Mao, Stalin and the Korean War: Trilateral Communist Relations in the 1950s*, tr. Neil Silver (London: Routledge, 2012), p. 79.

12. For a detailed analysis, see Shen and Xia, *Mao and the Sino-Soviet Partnership*, pp. 28–30.

13. According to Soviet diplomat Mikhail Kapitsa, "One of the most serious reasons for Stalin's distrust of Mao was Lüshun, Dalian, and the Chinese Changchun Railway." See Goncharov, Lewis, and Xue, *Uncertain Partners, Stalin, Mao, and the Korean War*, p. 67.

14. After the failure of the battle of Jinmen in October 1949, during his visit to Moscow Mao asked the USSR to send a volunteer air force or clandestine forces to assist in attacking Taiwan. Stalin told Mao that the Soviet Union would provide military equipment and advisers, but the Soviet air force and navy could not take part in any military operations. The CCP never again made such a request, but it did ask the USSR to provide air force and naval equipment. For an analysis, see Shen and Xia, *Mao and the Sino-Soviet Partnership*, pp. 30–32.

15. Chen Jian, "The Sino-Soviet Alliance and China's Entry into the Korean War," *Cold War International History Project* (hereafter cited as *CWIHP*) *Working Paper*, no. 2 (1992), p. 15.

16. *Selected Works of Mao Tse-Tung*, vol. 4 (Peking: Foreign Languages Press, 1961), p. 415.

17. For example, Dieter Heinzig notes, "Apparently in order to create a favorable atmosphere for the talks, Mao Zedong published what was up to that time the most decisive public declaration in favor of an alliance with the USSR shortly after the Chinese delegation arrived." See Heinzig, *The Soviet Union and Communist China*, p. 178.

18. A careful reading of Mikoyan's twelve reports during his visit to Xibaipo indicates that Mao asked the CPSU to clearly state its position regarding the CCP, but to no avail. Although he expressed support for some concrete issues, Mikoyan failed to elaborate on the CPSU's comprehensive policy toward the CCP.

19. For details, see Yafeng Xia, *Negotiating with the Enemy: U.S.-China Talks during the Cold War, 1949–1972* (Bloomington: Indiana University Press, 2006), pp. 12–42.

20. For an English account of Huang Hua's contacts with Andrei Ledovskii, see Heinzig, *The Soviet Union and Communist China*, pp. 232–46.

21. Andrei Ledovskii, *Nanjing zhaji* [Random Notes in Nanjing] (unpublished ms.), pp. 47, 52, 54, as cited in Heinzig, *The Soviet Union and Communist China*, pp. 232–45.

22. For the "lost chance" debate in Western scholarship, see Warren I. Cohen, intro., "Symposium: Rethinking the Lost Chance in China," *Diplomatic History*, vol. 21, no. 1 (January 1997), pp. 71–115; John W. Garver, "The Opportunity Costs of Mao's Foreign Policy Choices," *China Journal*, no. 49 (January 2003), pp. 127–36; Chen Jian, "Response: How to Pursue a Critical History of Mao's Foreign Policy," *China Journal*, no. 49 (January 2003), pp. 140–41.

23. Heinzig notes that President Harry S Truman accepted a recommendation from the State Department, the National Security Council, and the Joint Chiefs of

Staff that "it would be about a quarter of a century before Washington would again be able to pursue a successful and active China policy." Heinzig, *The Soviet Union and Communist China*, p. 255.

24. It is a coincidence that the Soviet embassy in China submitted a memorandum on 30 June 1949, titled "U.S. and UK Reactionaries Hope that Bourgeois Nationalism Will Appear in Democratic China." From recently published articles, we can see that US and UK propaganda pay special attention to the inclusion of articles that might arouse nationalistic feelings among the Chinese, especially CCP members. The main purpose is to create enmity between democratic China and the Soviet Union, the CCP, and the CPSU.

25. See, for example, "Farewell, Leighton Stuart," in *Selected Works of Mao Tsetung, vol. 4*, pp. 433–39; "Cast Away Illusions, Prepare for Struggle," 14 August 1949, in ibid., pp. 425–32.

26. Goncharov, Lewis and Xue, *Uncertain Partners*, p. 64.

CHAPTER 8

Conflicts of Interest and Creation of the Alliance Treaty, 1949–1950

Zhihua Shen

Stalin and Mao had different views on how to handle the new Sino-Soviet relationship. Stalin wanted to couch a close relationship within the framework of the Yalta system and to maintain Soviet interests in Northeast China, whereas Mao focused on how to fashion an independent and diplomatic image of New China, how to protect Chinese interests, and how to encourage other political parties (the so-called democratic parties) and the Chinese people to accept the pro-Soviet position of the Chinese Communist Party (CCP). Their differences were epitomized in their debates over whether and how to reach a new alliance treaty. How were the differences between the two sides manifested during the negotiations? Which side made concessions that led to the final agreement? What impact did these talks have on Soviet Far Eastern policy? These questions have been insufficiently studied due to limited access to the historical records. This chapter attempts to answer these questions based on recently declassified Russian archival sources and relevant documents and memoirs published in Chinese.[1]

Mao's Insistence on a New Treaty

Only one month after the establishment of the People's Republic of China (PRC) in October 1949, Mao sent a telegram to Moscow on 8 November 1949 again expressing his wish to visit the Union of Soviet Socialist Republics (USSR), explicitly stating that he would discuss the issue of the 1945 Sino-Soviet treaty. He added that if a new treaty was to be signed, Premier and Foreign Minister Zhou Enlai would go to Moscow. The CCP Central

Z. Shen (✉)
East China Normal University, Shanghai, China
e-mail: zhaoran@ssap.cn

© The Author(s) 2020
Z. Shen (ed.), *A Short History of Sino-Soviet Relations, 1917–1991*,
China Connections, https://doi.org/10.1007/978-981-13-8641-1_8

Committee (CC) cabled Wang Jiaxiang, Chinese ambassador to the USSR, to the same effect. Meanwhile, Kovalev reported to Stalin that Mao had told him that he would like to remain in the USSR and Eastern Europe for three months: the first month for talks with Stalin on the new Sino-Soviet treaty; the second month to visit the Eastern European states; and the third month for recuperation. The Chinese suggested that discussion of the new treaty be at the top of the agenda. Therefore, it was clear that Mao was going to Moscow for the purpose of reaching an alliance with the USSR.

On his arrival at Moscow on 16 December 1949, Mao immediately held official talks with Stalin.[2] However, the first round of talks ended in a deadlock over how to deal with the 1945 treaty. When Mao said that the CCP CC had studied the 1945 treaty after Liu Shaoqi's visit, Stalin cut him short: "The Soviet Union signed this treaty with China in accordance with the Yalta accords," so we have "decided not to change the provisions because any amendment would provide a legal pretext for the United States and Britain to amend the provisions regarding the Kurile Islands and elsewhere." However, Stalin did express a willingness to find a feasible approach to retain the original treaty but also to make revisions. Stalin offered to withdraw Soviet troops from China at the request of the Chinese government. Mao wanted to abolish the agreements immediately, but he was not interested in an immediate withdrawal of the Soviet Army. Stalin made it abundantly clear that the USSR opposed a new treaty.

In an 18 December cable to Liu Shaoqi, Mao stated his understanding of the first round of talks: "The Soviet side does not think it right to change the legitimacy of the original treaty, that the thirty-year Soviet lease of Port Lüshun is to remain valid," but a statement might be issued to the effect that the USSR is willing to withdraw its troops from Port Lüshun. The cable also contained a paragraph that has not been preserved in the Soviet archives. Mao pointed out that the original treaty was no longer significant to the Chinese, but Stalin stressed that it could not be revised during the next two years and he insisted that Zhou Enlai not go to Moscow. Under these circumstances, Mao asked the Politburo to suggest solutions to the problem.

Liu Shaoqi, Zhou Enlai, and Zhu De sent a joint cable on 21 December, expressing the Politburo's opinion that, given the Soviet attitude, "it seems unnecessary" for Zhou to go to Moscow. Mao, however, did not give up. To clarify the Chinese position, on 22 December, Mao asked Kovalev to arrange a meeting with Stalin. He explicitly put forward two options. One was to resolve the problems involved in signing a new Sino-Soviet treaty, in which case Zhou Enlai would go to Moscow for the signing. The alternative was to negotiate all aspects of the treaty but delay the signing for a later date. Although Mao had been hopeful, Stalin did not bring up the topic of the treaty during their two rounds of talks on 24 December.[3]

Mao was disappointed. He angrily told Kovalev that he had only three things to do in Moscow: "to eat, to shit, and to sleep." The Western press suggested that Mao was under house arrest in Moscow, where the atmosphere was tense. Stalin was waiting for Mao to change his position, while Mao was attempting to force Stalin to make concessions. To break the deadlock, Ambassador Wang Jiaxiang suggested that Mao accept an interview with TASS (Tyelyegrafnoe agentstvo Sovetskogo Soyuza).[4] On 1 January 1950, Stalin agreed. It seems that Mao's complaints to Kovalev and his threats to leave had the desired effect on Stalin. Publication of Mao's TASS interview precipitated a shift in Stalin's thinking and Stalin finally acceded to Mao's request to negotiate a new treaty.[5]

On 2 January 1950, Communist Party of the Soviet Union (CPSU) Presidium members Vyacheslav Molotov and Mikoyan went to the dacha where Mao was staying to convey Soviet willingness to sign a new treaty. According to Mao's Security Chief, Wang Dongxing, on 3 January, Mao "was in very high spirits … talking and laughing." The main reason that Stalin conceded was probably the burden of the Cold War, so China's joining of the socialist bloc headed by the USSR was vital to Soviet security in the Far East and to its strategic interests in Asia.

Mao's attitude and behavior undoubtedly added to Stalin's anxieties. Two days earlier, on 1 January, when Nikolai Roshchin, Soviet ambassador to China, visited Mao, Mao declared that he was going "to rest for a week" because he did not feel well, and he canceled a plan to tour the country because "he did not want to visit the factories, to deliver any reports, or make public speeches," and he wanted to return home a month ahead of schedule. But Mao deliberately revealed that China would hold negotiations with Burma and India to establish diplomatic relations, and Britain and other member states of the British Commonwealth "would soon take substantial steps toward recognition of the People's Republic of China."[6] Mao was clearly disappointed with Stalin and he was attempting to exert pressure on Moscow amidst rumors that he was "under house arrest" and that relations between the two countries were strained.[7] In any case, Stalin did not want China to improve relations with any Western country at a time when Sino-Soviet negotiations remained deadlocked.[8] In anticipation of possible changes in the international situation and the threat of better relations between China and the Western powers, Stalin could not afford to let Mao return home empty-handed.[9]

SOVIET DESIGNS FOR THE NEW TREATY

Soviet concessions at this stage, however, remained superficial. Stalin's real objective was to form an alliance with China and at the same time to maintain its interests as embodied in the 1945 treaty. Therefore, the Soviets stepped up preparations for the drafting of a new treaty and the relevant agreements.

The first two drafts by the Soviet Ministry of Foreign Affairs (MFA), prepared from 5 to 9 January, clearly stated that "the agreement on the Chinese Changchun Railway, Lüshun, and Dalian signed on 14 August 1945 will remain valid." Since Stalin had promised to withdraw all Soviet troops from Lüshun naval base after the conclusion of a peace treaty with Japan, the Soviet MFA composed four drafts, with the final version reading: "All Soviet troops now stationed at Lüshun and Dalian will be withdrawn to Soviet territory within two or three years after this treaty enters into force. Withdrawal will begin in 1950." The agreement on Lüshun and Dalian would be revised again after conclusion of a peace treaty with Japan. Another noteworthy change was the name of the treaty, which was changed from the "Treaty of Friendship, Cooperation, and Mutual Assistance" to the "Treaty of Friendship, Alliance, and Mutual Assistance." Mao Zedong used the name "Treaty of Friendship and Alliance" in his talks on 16 December 1949 and 6 January 1950, and Soviet Foreign Minister Andrei Vyshinskii perhaps took this into account when he decided on the final name of the treaty.

To retain some of the content of the old treaty—inter alia, the part concerning Lüshun and Dalian—Vsevolod Duljinevskii, an expert on treaty law in the Soviet MFA, studied international practices and relevant treaties to see if it was possible to retain some of the content. In a memorandum dated 13 January, he suggested to Foreign Minister Vyshinskii, "It is advisable to have the additional clauses retain the provisions of the old treaty; such additional clauses may be written into the text of the new treaty or take the form of a protocol or a special note." Because China had no intention of recovering Port Lüshun in the near future, the strategic interests of the USSR focused on control of the Chinese Changchun Railway and Port Dalian. Therefore, the Soviets attached immense importance to agreement on the railway and Dalian and attempted to treat these as issues separate from the treaty (and the issue of Lüshun). On 16 January, Vyshinskii submitted to Molotov a "Protocol Confirming the Validity of an Agreement on the Chinese Changchun Railway" and a draft "declaration," specifically pointing out that the terms of validity were in strict accordance with the terms stipulated in the agreement on the Chinese Changchun Railway signed in Moscow on 14 August 1945." It was also suggested that the declaration be published in the form of "additional clauses" so that "the signing of this treaty does not affect the respective debts of the two sides in the previous treaty."

On 19 January, the Soviet Ministry of Railways produced a draft agreement on the Chinese Changchun Railway and Port Dalian, which proposed, inter alia, to redefine the composition of the railway assets. This draft stipulated that enterprises along the southern section of the railway (from Harbin to Dalian), which were constructed or reconstructed by the Japanese and previously did not belong to the Chinese Changchun Railway, were to be included in the railway assets. It also exempted all goods required by the Chinese Changchun Railway, and its enterprises and offices, from customs tariffs, special taxes, and all other freight taxes. Additionally, the harbormaster of Port Dalian, though not included in the railway system, had to be a Soviet citizen. At the end of the report to Molotov, Soviet Minister of Transportation B. P. Beshev specifically pointed out that it was because of financial considerations that he put that portion of the railway formerly belonging to the Southern Manchurian Railway Bureau under the assets of the Chinese Changchun Railway, as this section of the railway earned an annual profit of 160 million rubles.

On 21 January, Soviet Deputy Foreign Minister Andrei Gromyko and others submitted to the Council of Ministers a draft resolution and two draft protocols on the Chinese Changchun Railway. The main points included (1) confirmation of the use of the MFA's draft proposals on the Chinese Changchun Railway protocol, which reiterated the validity of the 1945 treaty as the basis for negotiations with the Chinese side; (2) an attempt to reach an agreement with the Chinese government on the issue of joint operation and management of the Chinese Changchun Railway beginning in February 1952; (3) verification of all the items in the Ministry of Transportation's additional draft clauses, with later modifications to be confirmed by the Chinese government; (4) before verifying the assets of the Chinese Changchun Railway, the Soviet side would propose that all fixed assets of the railway be joint Soviet-Chinese assets during the Sino-Soviet negotiations.

By 22 January, special committees presented a total of 12 drafts to Stalin, including the Sino-Soviet Treaty of Friendship, Alliance and Mutual Assistance, the Sino-Soviet protocol on the agreement on Port Arthur and Dalian, the Sino-Soviet protocol on the agreement on the Chinese Changchun Railway, the Sino-Soviet agreement on Soviet loans to China, the protocol on the establishment of a Sino-Soviet aviation and transportation joint-stock company, the protocol on the establishment of a Xinjiang nonferrous metal and rare metal joint-stock company, the Sino-Soviet protocol on goods-for-goods trade and payments, the protocol on Soviet trade with Xinjiang, the protocol on payments to Soviet experts, the Soviet Council of Ministers' resolution on Soviet organizations and Sino-Soviet mixed joint-stock companies' joint management of immovable property in Manchuria and Liaodong Peninsula, and the Soviet Council of Ministers resolution on dispatching Soviet experts and teachers to work in China. The CPSU CC approved the 12th draft. It is noteworthy that these drafts covered all issues that might have come up during negotiations, but they said nothing about the agreement on Lüshun and Dalian or the agreement on the Chinese Changchun Railway. The underlying reason was that the Soviet side did not think it necessary to redraft the two agreements because the original agreement on the Chinese Changchun Railway would remain valid and the agreement on Lüshun and Dalian would not be reconsidered until the conclusion of a peace treaty with Japan. The revisions that were important to the USSR were embodied in the two relevant protocols. Furthermore, Moscow was unwilling to provide the Chinese delegates with an opportunity to discuss the content of these three agreements.

Thus, the USSR prepared all the draft documents for the second round of negotiations, which can be summarized as including the following: the Sino-Soviet Treaty of Friendship, Alliance and Mutual Assistance only established Sino-Soviet alliance relations in principle, without touching on the real interests of each side. On the Chinese Changchun Railway, they reaffirmed that the 1945 treaty would remain in force for 30 years. They then went on to add a new item regarding Sino-Soviet rotation of the administrative positions in the railway administration. There were other provisions, such as verification of assets, exemptions from custom taxes and freight transportation taxes, and rail-way sales taxes, which protected Soviet interests. On Port Arthur and Dalian, the treaty stipulated that Soviet troops would begin to withdraw in 1950, and withdrawal would be completed within two to three years after the treaty entered into force. All other items remained unchanged and would be reexam-ined after the signing of a peace treaty with Japan.

STALIN'S MAJOR CONCESSIONS

On 20 January Zhou Enlai arrived in Moscow as the head of a large Chinese government delegation. He joined the third session of the formal talks between Mao and Stalin on 22 January. Mao and Stalin reached agreement in principle on several issues during the talks: first, the Sino-Soviet treaty would be revised and re-signed; second, the agreement on Lüshun would remain valid until the conclusion of a peace treaty with Japan, when the Soviet troops would be with-drawn; third, the legal validity of the original Chinese Changchun Railway would be maintained, but the contents would be amended; fourth, the USSR would give up its rights to Dalian and Dalian would be restored to the Chinese; and fifth, the leading administrative posts of the Chinese Changchun Railway would be periodically rotated between Chinese and Soviet representatives. Zhou Enlai proposed that the Sino-Soviet investment ratio on the Chinese Changchun Railway be adjusted, increasing the Chinese investment ratio to 51 percent. In addition, the delegation discussed a loan agreement and the Xinjiang trade issue. Mikoyan, Vyshinskii, Zhou Enlai, and Li Fuchun were entrusted with the task of negotiating the details.[10]

The two sides began talks on 23 January and the first item on the agenda was discussion of the draft "Treaty of Friendship, Alliance, and Mutual Assistance Between the People's Republic of China and the Union of Soviet Socialist Republics," as proposed by the Soviet side. The Chinese side submit-ted a revised draft on 24 January. After carefully comparing the two drafts, we find that the revised Chinese draft was not substantially different from the draft originally submitted by the Soviets, except for the order of the paragraphs and the addition of some modifiers. Two rounds of revisions followed, but the dif-ferences were negligible and limited to the wording. This is not difficult to understand since the treaty was primarily aimed at curbing aggression on the part of Japan and its allies, bolstering mutual consultation, and fulfilling com-mon aspirations. The main area of conflict consisted of details regarding the Chinese Changchun Railway, Port Arthur, and Dalian.

To Moscow's dismay, the Chinese suggested a completely different pro-posal. After two days of study, on 26 January the Chinese submitted a draft "Agreement on Lüshun, Dalian, and the Chinese Changchun Railway," pre-pared under the direction of Zhou Enlai. Aside from withdrawing Soviet troops from Lüshun, the Chinese draft rejected almost all the Soviet proposals. This took the Soviets totally by surprise. After receiving the Chinese draft, the Soviet delegates reconsidered the entire document and made numerous revisions.[11]

According to the Russian archives, a new round of negotiations took place from 11 to 13 February. To prevent possible American expansion into Northeast Asia in the event of a Soviet withdrawal and to make up for what the USSR would lose by signing the treaty, the Soviets submitted a new draft agreement that prohibited any leases to foreigners in the Far East region, the Central Asian republics, and Manchuria and Xinjiang. The new draft also prevented the capital of citizens of any third country from becoming either directly or indirectly involved. This is the so-called secret "additional agreement."[12] Because no "foreign country" or "foreign citizen" would have imagined "leasing" USSR territory, it is obvious that this proposed agreement was directed at Manchuria and Xinjiang. According to the Russian archives, at the time Mao voiced no opposition to the additional agreement, but he merely asked for a small textual revision, changing "leasehold" to "the right of leasehold." The Russian archives on the 22 January meeting do not refer to the issue of the "additional agreement," and there is no archival documentation in the currently available Chinese material on this issue. This matter can only be resolved with the release of additional Chinese archival documents.

However, Mao later voiced great unhappiness about the secret "additional agreement." He often referred to Northeast China and Xinjiang as two Soviet "colonies" or "spheres of influence." It was reasonable for Chinese leaders to express unhappiness about this. On the surface, the "additional agreement" seemed fair, but at the time there was no capital of citizens of a "third country" in the Soviet Far East or Central Asia. Therefore, the "additional agreement" in fact restricted China from exercising its sovereignty in Northeast China and Xinjiang.[13] Concerning the other agreements—on mixed joint-stock companies, for example, a subject about which Mao later called (the so-called cooperative issue)—blame should not be placed on the Soviets. As noted, when Mikoyan visited Xibaibo in 1949, Chinese leaders invited the USSR to manage jointly owned and leased companies in China, and during Mao's visit to the USSR, China on its own initiative proposed establishing joint-stock companies in Xinjiang.

The negotiations also touched on issues regarding the signing and announcing of the treaty. Zhou Enlai requested that the signing ceremony be held at 6 p.m., on 14 February, reminding the Soviets that the agreements on trade, aviation, petroleum, and nonferrous metal joint-stock companies were not yet ready for signing. Zhou also told the Soviets that both he and Mao believed that the entire treaty and all the agreements should be formally published.

On 14 February, Liu Shaoqi sent a telegram to Mao stating that the combined meeting of the leaders of the Chinese government and the Chinese People's Political Consultative Conference agreed to the signing of the treaties. That same evening, Stalin and Mao attended the ceremony at the Kremlin to sign the Sino-Soviet Treaty of Friendship, Alliance, and Mutual Assistance. China and the USSR soon published the treaty and the agreements in their respective newspapers. Per the Soviet request, the protocol (to the agreement on the Chinese Changchun Railway, Port Arthur, and Dalian) on supply rights of Soviet troops stationed in Port Arthur and the "additional agreement" were not published. Nevertheless, the conflicts over economic interests had finally been resolved, with the USSR making more substantial concessions.

CONCLUSION

During his trip to the USSR, Mao was able to conclude a new treaty of alliance with the USSR that replaced the 1945 treaty but only after he threatened to return home. In short, Stalin was forced to make concessions in his handling of the economic conflicts with China because he did not want to lose Communist China to the Western bloc. In theory, Mao could have chosen to establish a closer relationship with the West or to have taken a third path. In a supplementary agreement, Stalin declared his willingness to surrender all Soviet rights to the Chinese Changchun Railway and Port Arthur by 1952 at the latest, and administration of Port Dalian was immediately transferred to China. This demonstrated that Stalin had considered the issues in their entirety and acted in such a way so as to include China in a military and political alliance with the socialist bloc led by the USSR. In this way, Soviet strategic interests in the Far East would be assured.

In the early 1950s, the CCP considered the signing of the Sino-Soviet alliance treaty to be a success because it guaranteed both a military alliance with the USSR and direct loans to the PRC. On 20 March 1950, Zhou Enlai, in an internal address to cadres of the Ministry of Foreign Affairs, emphasized that the Sino-Soviet alliance treaty made it less likely that the United States would start a new war of aggression in East Asia. One month later, in a speech to the Sixth Session of the Central People's Government Council, Mao claimed that the victory of the Chinese Revolution had "defeated one enemy, the reactionary forces at home." But the chairman reminded his comrades "there are still reactionaries in the world, that is, the imperialists outside of China." China therefore needed friends. With the forging of the Sino-Soviet alliance, Mao emphasized that China's external position had been strengthened. He further declared, "If the imperialists prepare to attack us, we already have help." To the Chinese Communists, it seemed that the alliance was a realistic choice made against the backdrop of the fierce struggle between the socialist and capitalist camps.

The seeds of the later Sino-Soviet split were planted and grew during the process of the formation of the alliance. After the death of Stalin, Mao began to complain that he had been slighted and treated unequally by Stalin during his visit to the USSR. Yang Kuisong points out that Mao and Zhou, despite all their efforts, were not able to agree on a completely equal treaty and agreement, specifically regarding some concrete issues (i.e., special privileges for the Soviets in Xinjiang and Manchuria). For example, the Soviets asked that the Chinese government pay the Soviet experts in China very high salaries—at least ten times the salaries of their Chinese counterparts. In addition, as a condition for the US$ 300 million low-interest Soviet loans, China had to sell all its surplus industrial raw materials to the USSR.[14] Odd A. Westad has observed, "Uncertain about the long-term viability of a Communist leadership in Beijing, Stalin aimed at getting a treaty that was conducive to Soviet security, rather than an alliance between two Communist-led states."[15]

From an analysis of the negotiation process of the 1950 Sino-Soviet treaty, we can conclude that the signing of Sino-Soviet treaty guaranteed Beijing-Moscow alliance relations and satisfied the essential needs of both China and the USSR. But due to the perceived conflicts of interest between the two sides, the suspicion and resentment between Mao and Stalin grew. Therefore, from the outset the Sino-Soviet alliance existed in a tenuous state. Only because of the outbreak of the Korean War and Mao's decision to send troops to aid Korea under extremely difficult circumstances was the Sino-Soviet alliance ultimately strengthened.

NOTES

1. Russian memoranda on the two principal conversations as well as on the coded telegrams Mao sent back to Beijing can be found in *CWIHP Bulletin*, Issues 6–7 (Winter 1995/1996), pp. 5–9; Shu Guang Zhang and Jian Chen, eds., *Chinese Communist Foreign Policy and the Cold War in Asia: New Documentary Evidence, 1944–1950* (Chicago: Imprint Publications, 1996), pp. 128–42.
2. For a detailed account of Mao's talks with Stalin on 16 December 1949, see Heinzig, *The Soviet Union and Communist China, 1945–1950*, pp. 269–81.
3. Ibid., p. 285.
4. Scholars are still debating who first proposed the idea of an interview with a TASS reporter and who prepared the text for the interview. According to Sergey Radchenko, the interview, including Mao's answers to the questions from the TASS correspondent, was written by Stalin. See H-Diplo roundtable review of Shen, *Mao, Stalin and the Korean War: Trilateral Communist Relations in the 1950s*, at http://www.h-net.org/~diplo/roundtables/PDF/Roundtable-XIV-35.pdf, p. 13. Nevertheless, based on currently available sources, we still do not have a definitive answer to this issue.
5. Current scholarship reveals that discussion of a new treaty was first raised during Mikoyan's visit to China, and it came up again during Liu Shaoqi's visit to the Soviet Union. Before Mao's visit to the Soviet Union, the CCP regarded this as an important task and it notified the Soviet side to this effect. New research has clarified many details. For example, the Soviet side had carefully prepared the text of the treaty before Zhou Enlai's arrival, and the Chinese side did not propose any substantial changes to the text. The key remaining issue to be clarified is the following: why and how did Stalin change his attitude?
6. See Heinzig, *The Soviet Union and Communist China*, pp. 287–90.
7. As soon as Stalin agreed to sign a new treaty, Mao ordered the Chinese Ministry of Foreign Affairs to "delay for a while" a reply to Britain's request to establish diplomatic relations. This reveals Mao's true intentions when referring to the British request to establish diplomatic relations.
8. Goncharov, Lewis, and Xue, *Uncertain Partners*, p. 211.

9. Mao Zedong later commented, "Stalin changed his mind, perhaps due to the help given to us by the Indians and the British."

10. For a detailed account, see Heinzig, *The Soviet Union and Communist China*, pp. 327–37.

11. For Chinese and Soviet bargaining over the terms of the new treaty, see Shen and Xia, *Mao and the Sino-Soviet Partnership*, pp. 53–55.

12. See Heinzig, *The Soviet Union and Communist China*, pp. 348–50.

13. The Chinese side delayed implementation of the additional agreement by taking the first steps only after three years and only with respect to Manchuria. In May 1956, the Soviet government willingly abandoned the "additional agreement." See Heinzig, *The Soviet Union and Communist China*, pp. 350–51.

14. Dieter Heinzig suggests that "There is an indication that the Soviet leadership made a close connection between the delivery of the strategic raw materials and the granting of the credit." See Heinzig, *The Soviet Union and Communist China*, p. 361.

15. Odd A. Westad, *The Global Cold War: Third World Interventions and the Making of Our Times* (Cambridge: Cambridge University Press, 2005), p. 65.

CHAPTER 9

Differences and Cooperation During the Korean War, 1950–1953

Zhihua Shen

The Korean War is one of the most noteworthy events in the history of post–World War II international relations. The conflict determined Cold War–era arrangements throughout Asia. Recently declassified Russian Defense Ministry archives demonstrate that Stalin wavered regarding the dispatch of the Soviet air force for fear of a direct confrontation with US/United Nations (UN) forces. It was 12 days after Chinese troops entered the war that Stalin finally allowed the Soviet air force to provide air cover. Nonetheless, the Union of Soviet Socialist Republics (USSR) thereafter provided comprehensive support to China. During the war, the political, military, diplomatic, and economic dimensions of the Sino-Soviet alliance became apparent. The dispatch of Chinese troops to Korea not only saved the Kim Il-sung regime but also smoothed over Moscow's erroneous policy decisions. In addition, the dispatch of the Chinese troops defended the east gate of the socialist bloc. To a large extent, it also had the effect of influencing Stalin's view of both the Chinese Communist Party (CCP) and Mao Zedong. Thus, the Sino-Soviet alliance safeguarded the gains of the Korean War for the socialist bloc and the war consolidated the political and economic foundation of the Sino-Soviet alliance.

Mao's Eagerness and Stalin's Hesitation to Send Chinese Troops to Korea

The launch of the Korean War was originally the idea of Moscow and Pyongyang. Both Stalin and North Korean leader Kim Il-sung were confident that the United States would not enter the war and they would not need

Z. Shen (✉)
East China Normal University, Shanghai, China
e-mail: zhaoran@ssap.cn

© The Author(s) 2020
Z. Shen (ed.), *A Short History of Sino-Soviet Relations, 1917–1991*,
China Connections, https://doi.org/10.1007/978-981-13-8641-1_9

133

China's help. But they were wrong. To their surprise, within days after the North Korean invasion, the United States immediately declared that it would intervene. The United States soon dispatched air, naval, and land forces to Korea, while simultaneously deploying the Seventh Fleet to the Taiwan Strait to prevent a CCP attack on Taiwan.[1] In principle, Mao was not opposed to national unification by military means, and he understood that Kim was attempting to follow China's example. However, Mao believed that Chinese unification (the CCP taking over Taiwan and Tibet) should have priority over unification of Korea. With the outbreak of the Korean War, the CCP had to abandon its campaign to conquer Taiwan and the offshore islands.

The US/UN entry into the war rapidly resulted in enormous losses to the North Korean military, with its air and naval forces the first to be affected. According to a report by the headquarters of the Soviet Army General Staff, by 3 July 1950—only a few days after the start of hostilities—36 North Korean aircraft and 5 naval vessels had been attacked and destroyed. At this point, Stalin already realized that the war was not going to proceed smoothly. He began to consider how to increase support to North Korea, while insuring that such support would not come directly from Moscow.

Before the war, Soviet assistance mainly focused on training North Korean troops, providing weapons, and drawing up battle plans. Stalin absolutely forbade Soviet forces from crossing the 38th parallel and directly participating in battle. If necessary, he believed that the Chinese Army would provide assistance. Of course, when and how such assistance would be provided would depend on the progress of the war.

Chinese leaders paid careful attention to the possibility of US intervention. On 2 July, Zhou Enlai called in the Soviet ambassador, Nikolai Roshchin, to request that he inform Moscow of the Chinese assessment of the Korean situation. Zhou pointed out that in order to prevent the United States from landing on the peninsula, the North Korean People's Army should rapidly accelerate its drive toward the south, occupy the southern harbors, and station strong defense forces in places such as Inchon. He emphasized that if the Americans crossed the 38th parallel, the Chinese Army, in the guise of volunteers wearing uniforms of the North Korean People's Army, would engage the American forces. To prepare for this eventuality, China would deploy three armies, totaling 120,000 men, to Northeast China. Zhou ended the meeting by inquiring whether the Soviet air force would provide cover for these armies.

All of this was said before any formal decision had been made. China did not formally establish its Northeast Border Defense Force until several days after this meeting, and its troop deployments were not completed before 5 August. Zhou obviously wanted to make Stalin aware that Chinese leaders were willing to assist North Korea. He also wanted Stalin to understand that China expected that the USSR would provide coordinated air cover for the Chinese ground forces.

Stalin responded immediately, wiring back on 5 July: "We think it is correct to concentrate nine Chinese divisions on the Sino-Korean border so that the volunteers can enter North Korea for battle when the enemy crosses the 38th parallel. We will try our best to provide air cover." Eight days later, having received no further information from China, Stalin again asked Roshchin to convey the following message to either Zhou or Mao:

> We are not clear about whether you have decided to deploy nine Chinese divisions along the Sino-Korean border. If you have already made such a decision, we will then prepare to send an air force division equipped with 124 jet fighters to provide cover to these troops. We plan to have our pilots train Chinese pilots for two to three months and then to pass on all the equipment to your pilots. We also plan to have the Shanghai Air Force Division do the same thing.

As these two documents indicate, in order to encourage the Chinese to make a decision and to prepare to dispatch troops to Korea as early as possible, Stalin promised that, in addition to assisting the Chinese in air force training and sending equipment, he would also provide air cover for Chinese troops that "entered North Korea for combat."[2]

US air bombing created a tense situation in Pyongyang, despite the early success of the North Korean ground campaign. On 7 July, Kim met with Soviet ambassador to North Korea, Terentii Shtykov, and requested that Soviet military advisers be deployed to Seoul as soon as possible to participate in the military command of all army groups. If they were not deployed, he warned, the Korean People's Army might face collapse. Kim also said that he was receiving numerous phone calls, all reporting the serious damage inflicted by the US air strikes, including the destruction of railway terminals and bridges. According to Shtykov's observation, this was the first time since the beginning of the war that Kim appeared to be "emotionally upset and somewhat depressed." Stalin then directed his attention to China. On 8 July he instructed Roshchin to request that Mao send representatives to contact the North Koreans.

In fact, China was already making active preparations. While Chinese troops were being deployed in the Northeast, Chinese leaders were also accelerating planning for battle in Korea. On 12–13 July, Zhou told Kim that China would not tolerate US intervention in Korea and the Chinese government was ready to provide, to the best of its ability, all assistance required by North Korea. Meanwhile, China requested that the North Koreans "provide 500 maps of Korea with scales of 1:100,000; 500 maps of Korea with scales of 1:200,000, and 500 maps of Korea with scales of 1:500,000 … and send samples of the North Korea People's Army uniforms as quickly as possible." Kim immediately informed the Soviet ambassador of these requests, asserting: "Now that countries such as the United States have already entered the war on the side of Syngman Rhee, democratic countries such as Czechoslovakia and China should use their armies to assist North Korea." But Shtykov deliberately avoided dealing with this issue.

On 19 July, Kim informed the Soviet embassy of a meeting between his representative in Beijing and Mao, noting that Mao thought the United States would be involved in the war for a long time and would send in more forces.

Mao ended by stating that if North Korea needed help, China "would send its own army to Korea. For this purpose, the Chinese side has already mustered four armies totaling 320,000 men." Kim was keen to discover Moscow's reaction. But even though Shtykov duly asked Moscow for its opinion, Stalin never replied. After raising this question several times, Kim seemed to understand Stalin's thinking—Stalin's reluctance to respond indicated that he had growing doubts about sanctioning such a course.

Shtykov continued to keep Moscow informed about the rapidly changing Korean situation. On 18 July he wrote that the steady advance of the Korean People's Army had activated the southern guerrilla movement, concluding that North Korean leaders and citizens had regained confidence in victory. In August, the Soviet embassy in North Korea submitted another report that reached the same conclusion. It mentioned in passing, however, that the North Korean cadres and masses were now expressing their discontent with the USSR's inability to mobilize its air force in time to prevent US bombing. Based on these optimistic estimates of the war situation, Stalin decided that, for the time being, China did not need to send in its troops. But Mao still seemed keen to do so. Chinese eagerness to dispatch its forces to Korea at a time when victory seemed likely aroused Stalin's suspicions. He thought this would expand China's status and influence in Korea, and in the long run such an outcome would not be to the USSR's advantage.[3]

From 14 to 18 September, Stalin continuously received battlefield reports on the American landing at Inchon, which was fundamentally changing the war situation. On 30 September, Moscow received a report from Shtykov that Seoul was probably already lost, that the road for the main force of the Korean People's Army to retreat north had been blocked, and that communications had been cut off. Kim was worried that the enemy would cross the 38th parallel and that the North Koreans would have no way of rebuilding its army for effective resistance. The Politburo of the Korean Workers' Party discussed the situation and drafted a letter to Stalin asking for air support. It also drafted a letter to Mao, which hinted at asking for help. Lacking in confidence, the North Korean leadership did not know what to do. That same night, Kim sent a letter earnestly requesting that Stalin provide "direct military assistance," and if that was not possible, then to "form an international volunteer army consisting of China and other people's democratic countries."

Facing this emergency situation, Stalin finally gave the green light for Chinese entry into the war. On 1 October, Stalin sent a telegram to Mao informing him that he should intervene with Chinese volunteers, adding that they should begin by organizing defense in the area north of the 38th parallel. Stalin also rather disingenuously stated: "I have not mentioned this to the Korean comrades and do not intend to do so. But I have no doubt that they will be very happy when they hear this."

After Mao received the telegram, he hurriedly drafted a reply the next morning, tentatively agreeing to send troops.[4] After vigorous advocacy by Mao and Peng Dehuai, who was then vice-chairman of the Revolutionary Military

Commission of the Central People's Government, on 5 October, an enlarged meeting of the CCP Politburo adopted a resolution to send troops to Korea. The Chinese People's Volunteers (CPV) command was formally established and the army entered the final prewar preparatory stages.

Although the decision to send troops had already been made, Chinese leaders continued to hesitate. If they had sent troops before the Inchon landing, they could have helped defend the rear areas to ensure the victory of the main force of the Korean People's Army on the front; if the troops had been sent just after the Inchon landing, the Chinese Army could have built a defense line along the 38th parallel to prevent the enemy from continuing to advance north. But now it was too late to do either. By early October, when the main force of the Korean People's Army had practically been wiped out, the opportune moment for China's entry was already lost.

The Chinese Army's weakness was obvious. Roshchin explained to Stalin that Mao's decision to temporarily withhold entry of Chinese troops into the Korean War in his 2 October telegram was based on the grounds that Chinese military equipment was poor and the Chinese Army had no chance to win a war against the Americans. On 7 October, Matveev (a pseudonym for M. V. Zakharov), Stalin's personal representative in North Korea, reported that Interior Minister Pak Il-u had returned from Beijing on 5 October. During his stay in Beijing, Pak Il-u was received by Mao on two occasions as well as by CCP leaders, and they talked at length, sometimes for as long as ten hours. Mao stated that China would do its best to help Korea, but for the time being it would not dispatch troops. Mao's reasons were straightforward: the dispatch of Chinese troops would drag the Soviets into the war, which ultimately would lead to a third world war. Although the Chinese Army was sizable, it did not have modern weapons, an air force, or a navy.

In direct talks with Soviet representatives, Mao was even blunter. On 6 October Mao told Roshchin that he was gratified by the expression employed by Stalin: that the Chinese and Soviets would together fight the Americans. But Mao emphasized that the Chinese Army's technology and equipment were so outdated that it would have to "completely depend on Soviet assistance." During this conversation, Mao "paid special attention to the air force issue," pointing out that in order to send troops, China "must have an air force," so as to protect the Chinese ground forces sent to Korea, to participate in the frontline fighting, and to defend major industrial centers in China. In the end, Mao stated that, in order to report on the situation and to exchange opinions, he would immediately send Zhou Enlai and Lin Biao, a high-ranking Chinese general, to the USSR. As these sources indicate, Stalin undoubtedly knew what Zhou's purpose was even before he headed to the USSR.

On 8 October, Mao informed Kim and Stalin respectively that the CPVs would enter Korea on about 15 October. Everyone seemed relieved that China had decided to send in troops. Kim was beside himself with joy and even went so far as to arrange when, where, and how the Chinese Army would be deployed. But such planning was premature: Stalin was already reconsidering the issue of sending the Soviet air force.

STALIN'S REFUSAL TO PROVIDE AIR COVER FOR THE CHINESE PEOPLE'S VOLUNTEERS

On 11 October, Zhou Enlai and his retinue flew via Moscow to Stalin's summer villa near the Black Sea, where they met with Soviet leaders that same afternoon. Zhou briefed the Soviets on the CCP Politburo's deliberation on the Korean situation and the question of sending troops. He explained that China's dispatch of troops faced major practical difficulties and he emphasized that the Soviets would have to provide weapons, equipment, and air support. Stalin pointed out that he could meet all Chinese needs for military equipment, such as plane, tanks, and artillery. However, the Soviet air force would not be ready for two to two-and-a-half months. After extended discussions, both sides agreed that since neither side was ready, they had to inform Kim to arrange a retreat as soon as possible. After the meeting, Stalin and Zhou sent Mao a joint telegram. Because the air force would not be in a position to provide air cover for the next two months and because it would require at least six months to equip and train the Chinese forces, it would be pointless to attempt to assist Korea. The telegram concluded by stating that Stalin and Zhou awaited Mao's decision.[5]

After receiving the Stalin-Zhou telegram from the Black Sea, Mao deeply contemplated the issue. At 3:30 p.m. on 12 October, when he first read the telegram, his reaction had been: "I agree with your decision." At 10:22 p.m., Mao sent another telegram to inform the Soviets that the Chinese Army had not yet entered Korea and orders had been given to "stop implementation of the plan to enter Korea." Stalin then sent a telegram to Pyongyang to inform Kim the results of the Black Sea meeting and to ask him to organize a retreat.

In fact, Mao was not as resolute as he sounded in his telegram. His actual instruction to Peng Dehuai was "to temporarily suspend implementation of the 9 October order" and "to temporarily delay [the army's] dispatch." He also asked Peng Dehuai and Gao Gang to come to Beijing for consultations. After a Politburo meeting on 13 October, when his comrades fully endorsed the decision to intervene, Mao's policy became clearer. He immediately called in Roshchin and announced that the CCP Central Committee (CC) had decided that "we should help the Koreans." Mao also mentioned that China hoped to pay for the weapons provided by the Soviets by means of a loan.

In a telegram sent to Zhou at 10 p.m. on 13 October, Mao clearly explained the arrangements for China's reconsideration of sending in the army. First, after entering Korea the Chinese Army would only engage in battle with the South Korean army and it would establish bases in order to raise the morale of the troops; Chinese troops would attack American troops only after the arrival of Soviet air volunteers and weapons; Zhou would try to arrange for the Chinese to lease the weapons provided by the Soviets; finally, Zhou would ask the Soviets to send in a volunteer air force within two to two-and-a-half months to support Chinese combat operations. At 3:00 a.m. on 14 October, Mao again sent a telegram to Zhou, reiterating his requests for Soviet assistance, specifically the entry of the Soviet air force.

By this time, Zhou had returned to Moscow and he sent a letter to Stalin conveying Mao's arrangements, mentioning in particular the critical relationship between "the Soviet volunteer air force" and the Chinese volunteers. But Stalin remained suspicious of China's motives. He stated that, even if the Soviet air force was to be sent, it could only operate north of the Yalu River and would not enter Korea to cooperate in military operations with the Chinese volunteers. This poured cold water on the Chinese plan. On 17 October, Mao sent urgent telegrams to Peng Dehuai and Gao Gang, asking them to come to Beijing for consultations and to postpone the date of sending troops. As a result of the meeting on 18 October, it was decided that Chinese troops would nevertheless still be sent into Korea on 19 October.

It was not until 25 October, after the first engagement between the CPVs and UN forces, that Stalin truly believed that the CCP was not a nationalist or "pro-American element."[6] On 29 October, M. V. Zakharov, chief Soviet military adviser in China, informed Zhou that Moscow had agreed that the Soviet air force "is in charge of air defense in Andong," adding that it could fly across the Chinese-Korean border, while also agreeing to move the base from Shenyang to Andong within ten days. On 1 November, the Soviet air force entered the battle over the Yalu River.

Coordination and Unity in Military Strategy

From the CPV entry into Korea to the signing of the Korean ceasefire agreement Mao and Stalin held generally identical views on the conduct of the war and the shifting strategies. On major issues, it was easy for them to coordinate their views, even though their views were not always correct.

After its first two major campaigns since entering the Korean War, the CPV successfully recaptured Pyongyang and pushed the battle line back to the 38th parallel. At this time, there were different internal opinions about whether or not the CPV should continue its successful initiative to launch a third campaign and cross south of the 38th parallel. As chief frontline commander, Peng Dehuai maintained that the CPV was extremely tired, the number of those wounded was continuously increasing, and the troops were in need of rest and reorganization. He also knew that the CPV supply lines were not secured. Most of the troops had no winter clothing and they were running short of ammunition. In addition, medicine and food were in short supply. The situation would only be exacerbated with an advance to the south. Peng thus proposed to launch a third campaign in February and March of the following year (1951). After receiving Peng's telegram, Acting Chief of the General Staff of the People's Liberation Army (PLA), Nie Rongzhen, concurred with Peng's assessment. He thus suggested to Mao that the third campaign be postponed for two months.[7]

The CPV military victory would have secured a favorable position for Beijing to end the war through negotiations if People's Republic of China (PRC) leaders had so desired.[8] But Mao insisted on immediately launching a third campaign and swiftly crossing to the south of the 38th parallel. Stalin and Mao had reached a tacit agreement regarding whether or not the CPV should cross over to the south of the 38th parallel. The Soviet government expressed an attitude of "striking while the iron is hot." On 5 December 1950, the United Nations established a ceasefire group to deal with the Korean issue. On 11 January 1951, the UN General Assembly approved the principles drafted by the ceasefire group, calling for a ceasefire in all of Korea, to be supervised by a UN commission, with a promise that foreign troops would gradually withdraw. A supplementary report provided that, after the ceasefire took effect, the UN General Assembly would organize a conference (with participation by the USSR, the United States, the UK, and the PRC) to deal with Korea, Taiwan, PRC representation at the UN, and other East Asian problems.[9]

In retrospect, this resolution should have provided Beijing with a very favorable opportunity to end the war had it wished to do so. As instructed by Stalin,[10] China instead reacted quickly by rebuffing the UN proposal of "ceasefire first, negotiations second." Zhou Enlai claimed on 17 January 1951 that an initial ceasefire was simply designed "to give the U.S. troops breathing space." Zhou's counterproposal called for a seven-power conference, held in China, to include the PRC, the permanent members of the Security Council (the United States, Britain, the USSR, and France but specifically excluding the Republic of China on Taiwan), plus India and Egypt. The subject of the conference would include the withdrawal of all foreign forces from Korea, the removal of American protective power from Taiwan, and other Far Eastern issues. As a token of good faith, PRC membership in the United Nations would be restored on the first day of the conference.[11]

Under such circumstances, it was impossible for Mao to support Peng Dehuai's request to temporarily suspend the attack. In a telegram to Peng, Mao contended that, if the Chinese Army did not complete the campaign, "it would arouse all kinds of conjectures in the capitalist countries, and all democratic countries would take exception to this position." Although the third campaign achieved limited success, the CPV was obviously spent and weakened. UN forces withdrew in a planned and orderly fashion. Beyond occupying a few (peripheral) territories, the Sino-Korean army was not able to inflict any serious damage on the UN forces. After recapturing Seoul, the CPV was not able to recover from its predicament and could not continue its offensive. On 8 January, Mao recognized the situation and gave Peng Dehuai approval to rest and reorganize.

North Korea and the Soviet military advisers in China strongly opposed Peng's order that the CPV suspend its offensive. Chief Soviet military adviser to China M. V. Zakharov said: "How in the world can an army that has scored a victory not pursue and attack the enemy and then not develop the fruits of its success? This would only give the enemy a respite and it would be committing a grave mistake by losing an opportunity to win a battle." Even after Nie Rongzhen's patient explanation, Zakharov insisted on his opinion. Newly appointed Soviet ambassador to North Korea, V. N. Razuvaev, advocated that the CPV should advance farther south. Kim Il-sung and Pak Hon-yong immediately met with Peng Dehuai and entered into a heated argument. Kim and Pak even lodged a formal complaint against Peng with Mao and Stalin. But Stalin said, "Truth is on Peng Dehuai's side, and Peng is a contemporary strategist." Thus, the conflict between Peng Dehuai and Kim Il-sung was resolved.

In the summer of 1951, the war reached a stalemate along the 38th parallel, and after coordination between Mao and Stalin, Soviet ambassador to the UN Jacob Malik proposed an immediate ceasefire. The failure of a major Communist offensive in late April (the fifth campaign) demonstrated once and for all the inability of the CPV to push the well-equipped US/UN army off the peninsula.[12] Beijing evidently expected to settle the conflict, although not necessarily to reach a ceasefire. After the CPV secured a foothold around the 38th parallel, a peace agreement to restore the status quo seemed advisable to Beijing. As Nie Rongzhen asserted:

> Most of our comrades present ... felt that our forces should stop in the vicinity of the 38th Parallel, which meant a return to the *status quo ante*, would be easily acceptable to all quarters.[13]

Most of the military strategists in Beijing, Nie later recalled, supported this idea. Mao also concurred. A policy of "continuing to fight while negotiating peace [*biantanbianda*]" was thus agreed upon by the central leadership.[14] During Kim Il-sung's visit to Beijing on 3 June, Mao and Zhou persuaded him to accept "restoration of the 38th parallel [as a short-term objective] and a phased withdrawal of all foreign troops [from Korea] through negotiations and a political settlement of Korea's future by peaceful means [as long-term goals]." North Korea was initially opposed to armistice negotiations, but its dependence on China eventually led Kim to agree to an armistice along the 38th parallel.[15]

Mao then requested that Stalin receive Kim Il-sung and Gao Gang. Stalin agreed and Kim and Gao were flown to Moscow in a Soviet jet. After a meeting with Stalin, Kim and Gao reported to Mao on 13 June 1951. Stalin also sent a telegram, stating: "We believe it is a good idea to reach a ceasefire now." Mao wired back to Gao and Kim, hoping that the USSR would contact the United States regarding a ceasefire, to which Stalin agreed. On 23 June, Moscow made a surprise move. Soviet ambassador to the UN Jacob Malik delivered a speech on a UN radio broadcast stating that the Soviet people believed the Korean conflict could come to an end. ... "As a first step, discussions should begin among the parties to negotiate a ceasefire and an armistice that would provide for the mutual withdrawal of all forces from the 38th parallel." Malik, however, said nothing regarding the withdrawal of foreign troops, Taiwan's status, or China's seat at the United Nations.[16] In a further clarification of this statement,

Soviet Deputy Foreign Minister Andrei Gromyko, in a meeting with US Ambassador Alan Kirk on 25 June, confirmed that this was to be a strictly military armistice arranged only by the opposing military commanders, with no provisions regarding political or territorial matters. The broader issues involving the future of Korea could be discussed following the conclusion of an armistice.[17] For Washington, Gromyko's statement appeared to be more positive.

On 30 June, Matthew Ridgway, commander-in-chief of UN forces, issued a formal statement to the Communist commanders in the field proposing a ceasefire. On the same day, Mao sent a telegram to Stalin, stating, "Malik's statement guarantees our initiative in the peace negotiations," and he asked Stalin to personally lead the armistice negotiations. Stalin replied immediately, "It's up to you to lead, Comrade Mao Zedong. The most we can offer is advice on various issues."[18] When Kim Il-sung asked Stalin for negotiation instructions, Stalin told him: "The Korean government must come to an agreement with the Chinese government on the issues raised in the telegram and they must work out the proposals together."[19] Declassified Russian sources reveal that Moscow and Beijing exchanged cables regarding all aspects of the negotiations, and all concrete moves and policy shifts during the talks were reported to and approved by Stalin.

By the second half of 1952, the negotiations at Panmunjom had reached a deadlock over the POW issue. Mao preferred to continue the war and he refused to offer any concessions. But North Korea appeared to be more malleable. Kim Il-sung originally expected to sign an armistice with the United States in May 1952, and in light of the situation, he hoped to arrange economic and political work during the second half of 1952. The POW issue unexpectedly halted the negotiations, "which greatly disappointed the Korean leaders. Kim Il-sung suggested that the Chinese comrades make concessions regarding repatriation of the POWs and make all-out efforts to sign an armistice treaty." In a telegram to Kim Il-sung, Mao said that accepting the enemy's proposals under pressure was equivalent to signing a peace treaty under duress. This would be detrimental to China and North Korea, both politically and militarily. Due to the war, US military forces had become bogged down in the East and they had incurred serious losses at the same time that the construction of socialism in the USSR had been greatly enhanced. These two factors were influencing the development of revolutionary movements throughout the world, thus postponing another world war. Mao pledged that the Chinese people were willing to make all possible efforts to help solve the difficulties faced by the people of North Korea. On the same day, Mao reported this situation to Stalin. On the third day, Stalin sent a telegram with his response: "Your position in the negotiations was completely correct." Stalin personally persuaded Kim Il-sung and indicated his unwavering support for the Chinese position. In sum, from the entry of the Chinese troops into Korea until Stalin's death, Soviet and Chinese leaders, especially Stalin and Mao, were united in their positions and they effectively coordinated their actions.

Initially, Stalin offered aid to the Chinese—air cover, weapons, and other military equipment. But after China's entry into the war, especially after the initial engagement of the CPV with South Korean troops on 25 October, Stalin reversed his policy regarding air cover for the CPV. On 1 November, the Soviet air force, for the first time, threw itself into the battle over the Yalu River. On the same day, MiG-15 fighters of the Belov Air Division flew eight sorties from Shenyang Airport, eight sorties from Anshan Airport, and above Andong-Sinuiju they shot down two US F-82 planes, and anti-aircraft guns also shot down two planes. There were no losses on the Soviet side during this air battle.

During the Korean War, the Chinese Army was able to regroup on a large scale. The following Chinese units were completely re-equipped or reorganized along the lines of the Soviet Army: 56 out of 106 army divisions, 6 tank divisions and an independent tank regiment, 101 (37 centimeter) anti-aircraft gun battalions, 5 field gun divisions and 1 city garrison gun division, 4 searchlight regiments, 9 radar regiments and independent radar battalions, 28 engineer battalions, and 10 divisions of railway corps, signal corps, and anti-chemical warfare corps. By early 1954, China had 28 air force divisions, 5 independent flight regiments, and 3000 plus aircraft, which either had been gifts or had been purchased from the USSR. However, the Chinese navy was not very well developed due to limited funds and technical problems. It was only toward the end of the Korean War that the first Sino-Soviet naval agreement, the "Agreement on Providing Technical Assistance to China for Naval Supplies and Gunship Production" (the June 4th agreement), was signed on 4 June 1953. The military equipment provided by the Soviets was not up to date or advanced, and some of it consisted of US lend-lease surplus goods and materials left over from World War II. Nonetheless, to the Chinese these were advanced weapons, and even more importantly, the USSR was the only country offering China military assistance.[20] Soviet military aid played a vital role in the ability of the CPVs to carry out successful campaigns during the Korean War.[21]

To assist China's economic recovery and development, the USSR provided a large amount of scientific and technological material, primarily via the exchange of books and reference materials and the export of projects and equipment. One of the critical issues that China's economic construction faced was a shortage of science and technology personnel. The dispatch of many Soviet experts and technical personnel to China was necessary for China's recovery. After two Soviet-assisted projects were ratified, the number of Soviet experts arriving in China peaked in 1951 and 1953. According to the Chinese archives, from 1950 to 1953 a total of 1093 Soviet experts worked in China. These Soviet experts helped establish a foundation for modern industrial management. They trained and educated many Chinese in science and technology. The USSR also trained future Chinese experts by accepting Chinese students for study in the USSR and offering internship opportunities for technical cadres. These exchanges took place at a time when China did not have access to any Western technology or expertise, so their importance to Chinese modernization was great.[22]

Conclusion

Had Stalin not changed his mind in early 1950, Kim Il-sung would not have been able to launch the Korean War. Thus, we can conclude that the Korean War was started by Moscow. Stalin wanted Mao to pull out all the stops at the critical moment and he agreed to send the Soviet air force to provide assistance. Suspicious of Mao and the CCP's true intentions, Stalin did not want China to have a hand in Korean affairs before the UN troops crossed the 38th parallel. He also hoped to ensure that the Chinese would not harm Soviet interests in the Far East or intensify the Soviet-US conflict. When the crisis finally erupted and the Chinese entered the war, Stalin reneged on his promise, thus placing China in an awkward situation.

But at this critical moment, Korea could only count on assistance from China. Kim, for his part, did not trust Mao and he was also worried about Stalin's obvious suspicions of Beijing. However, without Moscow's approval, Kim would never have agreed to allow Chinese troops to enter the conflict.

China hoped to dispatch troops to Korea at an earlier date, but this plan was not realized because of Stalin's and Kim's suspicions. For China to send troops, the Soviets would have had to provide weapons and air cover. But neither side fully trusted the other. As the Korean situation worsened, Mao worried that Stalin would go back on his word. At the Black Sea meeting, when Zhou Enlai suggested that China's entry into the war would depend on Soviet air cover, Stalin's suspicions grew.

If Mao had agreed to the decision made at the Black Sea meeting, then not only would all of Korea been occupied by US troops but China's security would have been threatened and the Sino-Soviet alliance would have existed in name only. Taking into consideration the adverse circumstances that China confronted and also the position that China held in the socialist camp, with his back to the wall, Mao decided to risk everything and fight. His decision to enter the war brought China, the USSR, and North Korea together to fight a common enemy. Therefore, China's dispatch of troops was a key step in changing the Sino-Soviet alliance from a superficial alliance to a real one. It was also the precondition for the USSR to send in its air force to assist Korea.

The entry of the Soviet air force into the conflict has always been tangled up with the issue of China's entry into the Korean War. Careful examination of this enormously significant event demonstrates the complicated and subtle relations in the alliance among the Chinese, the Soviets, and the North Koreans. Before China dispatched its troops, Moscow had always been on guard against Beijing, whereas Kim had always been at Stalin's side. But after China sent in its troops, this situation changed fundamentally. China became the main force in the alliance. In numerous subsequent disagreements between Beijing and Pyongyang, Moscow generally supported China—a situation that would last until to the end of the war. The USSR provided China with a large amount of economic aid, thus facilitating China's reconstruction and economic development. This in turn formed the economic foundation for the Sino-Soviet alliance.

When Stalin died in March 1953, the Korean armistice talks were deadlocked. Resorting to military action in Korea was Stalin's last major decision and it was crucial to the international situation. The decision to send Chinese troops to Korea was Mao's first major policy decision after the founding of the PRC, and it had a fundamental impact on the fate of the People's Republic. Sino-Soviet cooperation established a foundation for further growth of the Sino-Soviet alliance. But we should note that Soviet political and economic power, Stalin's prestige in the International Communist Movement and in the CCP, and Stalin's diplomatic skills forced Mao into a passive and subordinate position. For Mao, who contributed so much to the war and to opposing US imperialism, this was a humiliation that he could not long tolerate and it eventually revealed the problems in the Sino-Soviet alliance.

As comrades-in-arms during the Korean War, the Soviets and Chinese created a degree of confidence in each other. Stalin's support for the Chinese during the war was the source of Nikita Khrushchev's steadfast aid to China in the mid-1950s, bringing Sino-Soviet relations to a new stage.

Notes

1. On Soviet estimates of the prewar US position, see Shen, *Mao, Stalin, and the Korean War*, pp. 53–54.
2. Alexandre Y. Mansourov, "Stalin, Mao, Kim, and China's Decision to Enter the Korean War, Sept.16–Oct.15, 1950: New Evidence from the Russian Archives," *CWIHP Bulletin*, Issues 6–7 (Winter 1995/1996), p. 105.
3. For Stalin's hesitation from July to September 1950 about Chinese troops becoming involved in the Korean War, see Shen and Xia, *Mao and the Sino-Soviet Partnership*, pp. 72–77.
4. Because the Russian version of Mao's 2 October cable indicates that the Chinese leaders were not yet ready to send troops to Korea, Alexander Mansourov argues that Chinese leaders might have completely backed away from their original intention of sending troops to Korea by early October 1950. For debate on the authenticity of the Chinese version of Mao's 2 October 1950 cable, see Mansourov, "Stalin, Mao, Kim, and China's Decision to Enter the Korean War," pp. 94–119; Shen Zhihua, "The Discrepancy between the Russian and Chinese Versions of Mao's 2 October 1950 Message to Stalin on Chinese Entry into the Korean War: A Chinese Scholar's Reply," *CWIHP Bulletin*, Issues 8–9 (Winter 1996/97), pp. 237–42. This author concludes that "Mao did not change his goals but rather the tactics he would use to achieve them. Instead of replying directly and positively to Stalin's request, Mao adopted a more indirect and ambiguous response so that he would be able to reconcile his own determination to enter the war with the disagreements still existing among other CCP leaders, while at the same time keeping the door for further communication (and bargaining) with Stalin open" (p. 241).
5. Mansourov, "Stalin, Mao, Kim, and China's Decision to Enter the Korean War," pp. 94–107.
6. "The Communist International and the Chinese Communist Party," July 14 and 15, 1960, in *Selected Works of Zhou Enlai* (Beijing: Foreign Languages Press, 1989), vol. 2, p. 308.

7. Jung-chen Nieh, *Inside the Red Star: The Memoirs of Marshal Nie Rongzhen* (Beijing: New World Press, 1988), p. 640.
8. For a study of the Korean armistice negotiations, see Xia, *Negotiating with the Enemy*, pp. 43–75.
9. For the text of the proposal, see *FRUS*, 1951, vol. 7, p. 64; For the background of the proposal, see William Stueck, *The Korean War: An International History* (Princeton, NJ: Princeton University Press, 1995), pp. 152–54.
10. Ciphered Telegram, Roshchin to USSR Foreign Ministry, 13 January 1951, in *CWIHP Bulletin*, Issues 6–7 (Winter 1995/96), p. 54.
11. "Editorial Note, Chou Enlai to the Acting Secretary General of the UN," 17 January 1951, *FRUS*, 1951, vol. 7, pp. 90–91; Rosemary Foot, *A Substitute for Victory: The Politics of Peacemaking at the Korean Armistice Talks* (Ithaca, NY: Cornell University Press, 1990), p. 30.
12. David Rees, *Korea: The Limited War* (New York: St. Martin's Press, 1964), pp. 225–56.
13. Jung-chen Nieh, *Inside the Red Star*, p. 641.
14. Ibid.
15. William Stueck, *Rethinking the Korean War: A New Diplomatic and Strategic History* (Princeton, NJ: Princeton University Press, 2002), p. 139. In reality, Kim Il-sung had lost much of his power to command the North Korean troops after December 1950 when Chinese and North Korean forces signed an agreement to establish a joint Chinese–North Korean headquarters. This put the commanding power of all Communist forces in Korea into the hands of the Chinese commanders.
16. Editorial Note, "Malik's Radio Address on Korean Ceasefire," 23 June 1951, in *FRUS*, 1951, vol. 7, p. 547; Burton I. Kaufman, *The Korean War: Challenges in Crisis, Credibility, and Command* (Philadelphia: Temple University Press, 1986), p. 191; Stueck, *The Korean War*, p. 208. On the next day, Stalin wrote to Mao, "[Y]ou must always know from Malik's speech that our promise about raising the question of an armistice has already been fulfilled by us. It is possible that the matter of an armistice will move forward." See Ciphered Telegram, Filippov [Stalin] to Mao Zedong, 2 June 1951, *CWIHP Bulletin*, Issues 6–7 (Winter 1995/96), p. 62.
17. Acheson to the Embassy in the USSR, 25 June 1951, *FRUS*, 1951, vol. 7, pp. 553–54; Kirk to the Secretary of State, 26, 27 June 1951, ibid., vol. 7, pp. 555, 560–61; Stueck, *The Korean War*, p. 209; Foot, *A Substitute for Victory*, p. 37.
18. Ciphered Telegram, Mao Zedong to Filippov (Stalin); Filippov (Stalin) to Mao Zedong, 30 June 1951, *CWIHP Bulletin*, Issues 6–7 (Winter 1995/96), pp. 64–65.
19. Ciphered Telegram, Filippov (Stalin) to Razuvaev, with Message for Kim Il-sung, 1 July 1951, in ibid., p. 65.
20. Author's interview with Wang Yazhi from June to September 2001. Wang Yazhi had been Zhou Enlai's military secretary and in the 1950s he served on Peng Dehuai's staff. He was later transferred to the National Science and Technology Commission for Defense.
21. For Soviet military aid to China during the Korean War, see Shen and Xia, *Mao and the Sino-Soviet Partnership*, pp. 85–88.
22. On Soviet economic aid to China during the Korean War, see ibid., pp. 88–91.

CHAPTER 10

Khrushchev's Policy Toward China and the Honeymoon of the Alliance, 1954–1956

Zhihua Shen

Despite Stalin's big-power chauvinism that so troubled Mao, Sino-Soviet mutual assistance and support during the Korean War were a manifestation of the importance of the Sino-Soviet alliance. Diplomatically, the People's Republic of China (PRC) regarded the Union of Soviet Socialist Republics (USSR) as a priority, but the USSR slighted the Chinese both in state-to-state relations and even in party-to-party relations. When the PRC was established in October 1949, Chinese affairs, like Korean, Mongolian, and Japanese affairs, fell under the jurisdiction of the Bureau of East Asian Affairs of the Communist Party of the Soviet Union (CPSU) Central Committee (CC) Foreign Policy Commission.[1]

The Chinese public was generally not supportive of, or even hostile to, the USSR. Violent acts perpetrated by Soviet soldiers, such as the looting and raping of ordinary Chinese citizens after the Soviet Army entered Manchuria in August 1945, engendered great animosity between the two nations. By returning the Chinese Changchun Railway and providing economic aid to China in the early 1950s, the USSR was able to slightly improve the relationship. Nevertheless, during Stalin's later years, the relationship still remained very delicate.

China's involvement in the Korean War greatly enhanced the status and influence of Mao and the Chinese Communist Party (CCP) in the socialist bloc, a change that was clearly felt by Moscow. However, among the new Soviet leaders after Stalin's death, only Nikita Khrushchev really cared about relations with China. Thus, as he ascended to the top position in the Kremlin,

Z. Shen (✉)
East China Normal University, Shanghai, China
e-mail: zhaoran@ssap.cn

© The Author(s) 2020
Z. Shen (ed.), *A Short History of Sino-Soviet Relations, 1917–1991*,
China Connections, https://doi.org/10.1007/978-981-13-8641-1_10

147

Khrushchev began to modify Soviet policy toward China, most conspicuously by increasing aid. This chapter argues that although many people believe that the Sino-Soviet alliance was merely a paper tiger and from the very beginning it was in the process of deteriorating, in fact over the years there was a great degree of cooperation between the two countries, in particular with respect to Soviet economic and technical aid to China.

Khrushchev's Initiative

Khrushchev's first action was to urge the relevant Soviet departments to carry out Soviet-assisted projects in China during its First Five-Year Plan (FYP) period (1953–1957). During talks with Zhou Enlai in August–September 1952, Stalin in principle accepted the requests of the Chinese government and agreed to provide economic assistance during the First FYP period. Specific projects were to be reviewed by the relevant Soviet government departments. The Chinese side proposed large and complicated projects, and it requested designs and products on short notice. However, it was lacking in original documents and basic data. Without much negotiating experience, it was extremely difficult for the Chinese delegation, headed by Li Fuchun, then vice-chairman of the State Planning Commission, and the Soviet delegation, headed by Anastas Mikoyan, to cut a deal.[2] The two sides were able to sign an "Agreement Regarding Soviet Government Aid to the Chinese Government on Developing the National Economy" on 15 May 1953, which provided aid to China to build or rebuild 91 enterprises and to complete 51 Soviet-assisted projects before April 1953, making a total of 141 projects. Li Fuchun reported later, "If we had not had Soviet help during the First FYP period, we could not have achieved such a broad scale and rapidity in economic development. We would have encountered inestimable difficulties."

But there was still a long way to go before the projects could be implemented. Many details were yet to be cleared, and the Soviet side needed to carry out on-the-spot investigations of the projects one by one. The Chinese side also made continuous requests for major additions and revisions to its proposals, thus requiring further negotiations.[3] According to the original plan, the First FYP was to enter into effect in September 1953. But the Sino-Soviet agreement was not yet ready. In early 1954, Mao Zedong issued "a military order," requesting that the State Planning Commission submit a draft FYP within one month after 25 February. When the State Planning Commission asked for an extension, Mao only allowed an additional five days. On 15 April, Chen Yun, vice-premier and chairman of the Finance and Economics Committee of the Government Administration Council, sent Mao a draft that he himself had edited.

Many concrete issues in the Sino-Soviet agreement, however, remained to be resolved. In early April 1954, Zhou Enlai met with Khrushchev in Moscow while Zhou was traveling to the Geneva Conference. Zhou asked Khrushchev to step up Soviet-assisted projects to China. The next day, Khrushchev called in

Mikoyan and K. I. Koval, head of the Department for Economic Liaisons with the People's Democratic Countries, both of whom were in charge of negotiations with the Chinese, to inquire about the negotiation process. They said that they had to "re-evaluate almost all the projects," whereupon Khrushchev asked why the projects could not be implemented. During the discussions, although Koval called the Soviet leader's attention to Soviet limitations to implementing such a large aid program, Khrushchev simply "refused to listen for no reason." Koval's impression was that First Party Secretary Khrushchev was only concerned about the diplomatic implications. Khrushchev was determined to resolve the complicated technical and economic issues that had not been resolved earlier via political means. Khrushchev thus instructed the Soviets to step up negotiations with the Chinese so that the Presidium of the CPSU CC and the Soviet Council of Ministers could examine and approve the draft agreements. Therefore, the atmosphere, pace, and attitude of the Soviets changed dramatically, and many draft agreements were passed. In accordance with a suggestion by Mikoyan, Soviet China specialist Nikolai Fedorenko, in the Ministry of Foreign Affairs, took part in negotiating and drafting several economic agreements.

Khrushchev was quick to respond to Chinese requests for revisions and additions. In July 1954, the Chinese side requested some additions and revisions to the designs and supplies of equipment in the 15 May 1953 Sino-Soviet agreement on Soviet-assisted enterprises. The Chinese also asked the Soviets to help build several new enterprises. Khrushchev agreed immediately, instructing officials "to satisfy the Chinese government's request." The Soviet side not only added an additional 350–400 million rubles for the design and equipment for the new enterprises but also on its own initiative proposed to offer several new military technologies that had not been included in the original agreement. In addition, as a huge gift to mark the Fifth National Day of the PRC, Khrushchev proposed several new aid projects. These included providing additional equipment to the 141 original projects, building 15 new industrial projects, providing 520 million rubles in military loans, transferring to China all Soviet stock in the Sino-Soviet Joint Stock Xinjiang Petroleum Company (established in March 1950), the Xinjiang Nonferrous Metal and Rare Metal Joint Stock Company (established in March 1950), the Civil Aviation Company (established in March 1950), and the Dalian Shipyard (established in July 1951), assisting China in the construction of a railway from Lanzhou to Urumqi to Alma-Ata, organizing through transport via the Sino-Soviet and Sino-Mongolian railway, and withdrawing Soviet troops from Lüshun naval base (including Port Arthur and Dalian) ahead of schedule and returning the base to the Chinese free of charge. Austin Jersild's study helps us understand the broader background of Khrushchev's decision to return the Sino-Soviet joint stock companies and the Lüshun naval base to China. He argues that Stalin's successors "decided 'communism' could not possibly be achieved without a substantial reconciliation with the West, a rapprochement that would allow for easier access to Western technology, industry, and consumer goods."

In this process, the Soviets ended "some of the more abusive practices of the Stalin era."[4]

By 31 May 1955, all Soviet troops had withdrawn from Lüshun naval base, thus ending over half a century of foreign control and domination. This also marked an important event in Sino-Soviet relations. For security and strategic purposes, the Soviet Army had occupied Lüshun and Dalian since 1945. Prior to 1949, this was helpful to the CCP victory in the Chinese civil war. Even after 1949, it was advantageous for the consolidation of CCP power and the safeguarding of security in the Far East. Therefore, the CCP actually had requested that the USSR postpone its withdrawal from the Lüshun naval base. But from the perspective of national sentiment and sovereignty, it was unpleasant to allow foreign troops to be stationed on Chinese territory. Taking this into account, the USSR took the initiative to withdraw its troops from Lüshun ahead of schedule in order to strengthen Sino-Soviet friendship and to consolidate the Sino-Soviet alliance. In response to the Chinese request, the Soviet Army gave the Chinese its installation free of charge, but the Chinese paid for the heavy artillery.[5]

Expanded Economic and Technical Aid to China

In order to assist China to achieve its economic development goals, the USSR dispatched technical advisers and experts to work in China. According to estimates by Li Qiang, vice-minister of the Ministry of Foreign Trade, the number of Soviet experts "more than doubled from 1953 to 1954," and there were even more "from 1954 to 1955." According to a Soviet Foreign Ministry report, the number of Soviet advisers and experts in China was 3113 by the end of 1956, not counting those who had already returned to the USSR upon the expiration of their contracts.[6] One statistic indicates that technical experts increased 46 percent in 1955, 80 percent in 1956, and 62 percent in 1957. After 1957, the number gradually began to decrease. This was the most important period in China's First FYP.

The USSR also provided China with many science and technology reference materials. According to the Sino-Soviet Agreement on Science and Technology Cooperation, aside from the cost of duplication the USSR gave many scientific and technology documents: 31,440 complete sets of documents on technical designs; 3709 sets of basic construction schemes; 12,410 sets of draft sketch maps for machinery and equipment; 2970 complete sets of technical documents; and 11,404 complete sets of departmental technical documents. Annual distribution of these documents totaled 25,896 in 1955; 3359 in 1956; 9837 in 1957; 2678 in 1958; and 10,022 in 1959. In addition, from 1954 to 1957 the USSR offered China 4261 syllabi; 4587 sets of national standards for industrial products; and 221 pieces of sample equipment designed and manufactured for China at preferential prices. During China's First FYP period, 50 percent of all Soviet aid to socialist countries went to China.

Because of Soviet aid, China was able to satisfactorily complete its First FYP. During this period, China's economic construction (total value of social output) increased 11.3 percent every year due to the strong foundation provided by the 156 Soviet-assisted projects. These projects became the first large modern enterprises in China, greatly enhancing China's heavy industry and defense industries, filling in production and technology gaps, and constructing the initial industrial and technological foundation for the national economy. Seventy to eighty percent of the enhanced productivity in basic industry (except the coal and chemical industries) and the defense industries were Soviet-assisted, and some industries were assisted 100 percent by the Soviets. These large enterprises with Soviet assistance imported generally advanced Soviet equipment.

Such a massive aid program was also a major burden on the Soviet economy. According to estimates by Russian scholars, the export value of Soviet-assisted projects totaled 9.4 billion rubles, including 8.4 billion rubles in equipment and 1 billion rubles in technical aid. These funds amounted to 7 percent of the Soviet national income, which could have been used to build 2,680,000 apartments and would have greatly alleviated the housing problem in the USSR. In reality, the Soviets paid a heavy price to assist China's economic development.[7]

A prominent achievement of Soviet aid to China's science and technology development was the formulation of the "Long-term Program for the Development of Science and Technology from 1956 to 1967" (i.e., the "Twelve-year Science Program"). In January 1955, Soviet expert V. A. Kovda, adviser to the president of the Chinese Academy of Science (CAS), drafted "Methods for Planning and Organizing Scientific Research in the People's Republic of China," suggesting that the Chinese side should organize nationwide scientific research. On two separate occasions, 12 February and 7 April, the CAS leadership reported on Kovda's proposal to Zhou Enlai and Vice-Premier Chen Yi, calling it the "National Program Committee for Scientific Research Work." On 22 April, the CCP CC Politburo discussed the CAS report. Liu Shaoqi spoke highly of the report and asked the State Planning Commission and CAS to propose concrete measures for implementation. On 15 September, CAS adopted the "Directives on Formulating the Fifteen-Year Long-term Development Program of the Chinese Academy of Science." From 23 January to 11 February 1956, with the help of Soviet adviser Lazarenko, CAS invited 360 scientists and drafted a long-term scientific development program.

To an even greater extent, the Second FYP depended on Soviet aid, Soviet design plans, and supplies of goods and equipment. The First FYP was drawn up under the guidance of Soviet experts and involved construction of the 156 Soviet-assisted projects. Although China drew up the Second FYP on its own, it still heavily relied on Soviet technical aid. In particular, many of the industrial projects in the Second FYP were actually carried out under Soviet guidance. The Second Plenum of the Seventh CCP Congress decided that

China would seek Soviet advice regarding its Second FYP and it would coordinate the plan with the Soviet Sixth FYP.

In early 1956, the CPSU CC invited the CCP CC to send delegates to attend the Eight-Party Conference of the USSR and the Eastern European countries. The CCP CC decided to send Li Fuchun, vice-premier and chairman of the State Planning Commission, Zhang Wentian, deputy foreign minister, and Huang Kecheng, People's Liberation Army (PLA) chief of the General Staff. In a letter to Mao Zedong, who was then in Hangzhou, Zhou Enlai explained, "It will be beneficial for us to consult with the Soviets on our long-term plans and the dimensions and pace of the Second FYP." On 4 January, Li Fuchun's delegation left for the USSR to inquire about Soviet opinions of China's long-term plans and its Second FYP. The delegation also had two additional tasks: first, to propose another 188 construction projects, which would require assistance from the USSR and the Eastern European countries, and second, to ask for Soviet aid to design a long-term plan for the establishment of China's nuclear industry. Before the delegation's departure, Zhou wrote to Li Fuchun on two occasions and pointed out that the "proposed plans" were to be presented to the USSR and other fraternal parties. "You should pay attention to how they respond." On 6 February, however, when Li Fuchun reported to Zhou on his trip to Moscow, he did not mention the Soviet response to China's Second FYP.

In fact, as early as January 1956, several Soviet experts in China had already raised some tendentious views on China's Second FYP, doubting its projections and seeing them as too radical. While verifying and drawing up a financing plan, Soviet expert Il'in pointed out that, in accordance with Soviet experience, total investment in basic construction should be examined and approved by the Basic Construction Planning Bureau of the State Planning Commission and expenditures should be examined and approved by the Finance Bureau. Il'in argued that the Finance Bureau should be more active. "If expenditures for basic construction and other items are too high, this might lower the people's standard of living." He thought that the comprehensive finance plan of the Second FYP should "have a large finance balance," and should be "carefully examined and verified." Dydinov, director-general of the Soviet Finance Bureau, was more straightforward. He suggested that even though [China] projects a profit of RMB 141.7 billion in its finance plan, this was three times that in the First FYP. "This target is too high." According to Chinese statistics from the FYP of the Petroleum Ministry, "profits would increase eight times while production would only increase five times. This is wrong." In addition, there were no reserve state funds in the financial plan. In the credit plan, the credit fund was accumulated from personal savings without any extra-budgetary funds.

On 6–8 April, Soviet Deputy Prime Minister Mikoyan led a delegation to China. The main purpose of this visit was to acquaint the Chinese side with the Twentieth CPSU Congress and also to discuss Soviet economic aid programs to China. During Mikoyan's visit, the two sides signed two agreements: an agreement on 55 new Soviet-assisted industrial enterprises to China to supplement the existing 156 projects; an agreement to construct a railway from Lanzhou to Almaty in the USSR; and coordinated railway transport along this line beginning in 1960. Neither side discussed the drawing up of China's Second FYP. In May, the Chinese State Planning Commission sent representatives to the USSR to brief the Soviet side on the 188 projects that the Chinese had entrusted the Soviets to design early in the year. The purpose of this trip was to prepare for formal negotiations.

On 18 June, before his departure to the USSR, Li Fuchun met with Soviet adviser-in-chief, Ivan Arkhipov. Arkhipov tactfully pointed out:

> The Second FYP is too large in terms of production and construction. The pace of the increase in industry, agriculture, and basic construction is too high. Thus, it is necessary to study the relevant questions in the following two respects: First, to find out the correct developmental ratios in the national economic departments and the relevant economic sectors; Second, to guarantee a reliable basis in terms of equipment, raw materials, and material and finance resources in the FYP. … The annual investment allocation during the five-year period is uneven.

Arkhipov offered his opinions on every proposal in the plan and he stressed the importance of basing the increase in cash crops on "practicalities."

On 19 June, Li Fuchun led another economic delegation to the USSR to seek Soviet advice on the draft outline of China's Second FYP. The delegation also engaged in negotiations on the Soviet-assisted projects during China's Second FYP period. The Chinese asked for Soviet assistance to design 236 new projects. After several rounds of negotiations, the Soviet side voiced its opinions: the goals of China's Second FYP were too high to be accomplished. The rate of increase was too fast. Investment in basic construction was too high. Material resources were not guaranteed. The Soviet side agreed to assist China design only 217 new projects.

The Soviet leadership also discussed the grand objectives of China's Second FYP. On 27 August, the Presidium of the CPSU held a special meeting to review China's draft Second FYP and Soviet-assisted projects to China. According to the records from the meeting, the majority believed that China's plan was unrealistic. Michael Suslov, Lazar Kaganovich, and Mikhail G. Pervukhin argued that China's "tempo of increase is too fast … the rate of industrialization is unrealistic. … The PRC's Five-year Plan is too high." Regarding aid to China, many felt it would be too much of a burden on the USSR. Georgii Malenkov, then deputy chairman of the Council of Ministers, maintained that the USSR could not assume too much responsibility for China's economic development during its Second FYP period. Khrushchev pointed out, "[We should see] what possibilities remain after satisfying our own needs. We must count on everything to work it out. We should not overextend ourselves at the expense of our own economy." The Presidium meeting approved a letter from the CPSU CC to the CCP CC, entrusting Nikolai Baibakov, chairman of the Soviet State Planning Commission, to transmit it to Li Fuchun, together with the opinions of the Soviet State Planning Commission on China's Second FYP. The letter pointed out that the speed of national economic development in China's draft Second FYP was too fast. Soviet technical aid, especially supplies of equipment, would not be able to arrive before 1960 or even 1961. It seems that Mao's high-speed economic development plan was not only difficult for the responsible State Council officials and departments to accept, it was also beyond Soviet capacity to provide the necessary technical aid.

After about two and half months in the USSR, Li Fuchun returned to Beijing on 3 September. He later reported:

> During the negotiations, the CPSU CC carefully reviewed and checked on our projects. They tried their best, but they could only satisfy half of our requests. This is because we asked them to assist us in too many projects, which comprised a large share of their domestic production. Its supply of raw materials is insufficient. The USSR could not even satisfy its own domestic needs for some equipment.

With emotion, Li later admitted, "Based on these negotiations with the USSR, we could see that our original plan was too rash."

The Chinese took the Soviet advice seriously, and the State Council decided to decrease the targets in the Second FYP. Chairman of the State Construction Commission and later Vice-Premier Bo Yibo recalled, "The Soviet reply played a favorable role in revising the draft Second FYP under the guidance of Premier Zhou, which was soon to be approved by the CCP CC." However, the Soviet reply also forced China to reduce its dependence on Soviet aid. At a State Council Standing Committee meeting, Li Fuchun said, "During the Second FYP period, we should devote ourselves to carrying out a policy of self-reliance. We cannot completely rely on foreign countries. We should enhance new product design to bring old machines and equipment into full play. We should get started and develop gradually, and we should make breakthroughs in technology." The State Council submitted to the CCP CC the "Proposal on the Second FYP for Developing the National Economy (1958–1962) (Revised Draft)" on 9 September. The targets of the revised plan were greatly reduced and therefore they were more realistic.

After several revisions, Mao Zedong approved the State Council proposal on the Second FYP. Mao had been insisting on higher targets, but he acquiesced to the lower targets only after Moscow's attitude had been made clear. On 13 September, Mao wrote on the State Council proposal that had been submitted by Zhou Enlai: "I have read it again one more time. Very good! I made some minor revisions. Please exercise your own discretion!" Mao later added, "Your report is very good. … It is best to say a word or two about the contributions of the Soviets and other experts." Thus, the "Proposal on the Second FYP for Developing the National Economy" was accepted.

SOVIET LOANS AND EXPERTS TO CHINA

The provision of loans was one Soviet method of assisting China. These loans were primarily for the defense industry and military installations. Historians disagree as to the amount of loans the USSR provided to China during the period of Sino-Soviet friendship in the 1950s. Neither the Chinese nor the Soviet governments have published a complete account of Soviet loans to China. According to a Central Intelligence Agency (CIA) report, the USSR provided about US$ 1.3 billion (5.2 billion rubles) in loans to the PRC, US$ 430 million of which was for economic development and the remainder was for military use.[8] Some scholars have argued that the loans totaled about US$ 2.2 billion (8.8 billion rubles), of which US$ 400 million dollars was for military use and the remainder was for industrial construction.[9] Others argue that the loans amounted to about US$ 2.653 billion (about 12 billion rubles).[10] The following is an examination of these inconsistencies based on new data from both Chinese and Russian sources.

Let us first look at the Chinese sources. According to Wang Taiping, ed., *Diplomatic History of the People's Republic of China, 1957–1969*, between 1950 and 1955, the USSR provided 11 loans, or a total of 5.676 billion rubles, to China. Another source, *Capital Construction in Contemporary China*, offers a similar figure: a total of 5.66 billion rubles. A third source, *Foreign Cooperation in Contemporary China*, confirms the 11 loans but provides a more detailed account. "In addition to a loan of US$ 300 million in 1950, China and the USSR signed other agreements for ten loans, with one interest-free loan, and nine loans with a 2 percent interest rate to be paid back within 2–10 years." According to this source, the total was somewhat less: 1.274 billion rubles (about RMB 5.368). What can we learn from these Russian sources? According to *A History of Soviet-Chinese Economic and Trade Relations, 1917–1974*, a Russian source, the total was 6.6117 billion rubles. A comparison of Chinese and Russian sources demonstrates that there is a difference of 935.7 million rubles. According to *The Diary of Yang Shangkun*, actual loans came to 5.676 billion rubles, not 6.6 billion rubles. Yang believed that China received a loan of 986 million rubles from the USSR for the Korean War, not 1.9 billion rubles as indicated by the Soviet sources.

There is an error in the 1951 loans. The newly available sources reveal that the USSR gave China 13 rather than 11 loans in the 1950s. They totaled about 6.6 billion rubles, not 5.676 billion rubles. Chinese sources omit two military loans delivered on 10 April and 12 September 1951. There was no formal agreement for these two loans, and Stalin and Mao personally agreed to them by telegram. Additionally, in March 1961, the USSR proposed that it would offer 1 million tons of grain and 500,000 tons of Cuban sugar as a loan to help alleviate China's famine. The Chinese government agreed to accept the loan of 500,000 tons of sugar, which was equal to about 1.46 billion rubles.

How much of these loans were for economic and military uses respectively? How much of the military loans were related to the Korean War? Based on a variety of sources, I come to the following conclusion: the USSR provided China with a total of 6.288 billion rubles as military loans, which was 95 percent of its total loans to China. The Korean War accounted for about 48 percent of the total military loans, not 60 percent as claimed in Wang Taiping, ed., *Zhonghua renmin gongheguo waijiaoshi, 1957–1969*. The following chart presents additional details (see Table 10.1).

In 1964, China paid off all Soviet loans and interest from the 1950s, one year ahead of schedule. China also paid off the loan credit for Cuban sugar and the entire trade balance, thus eliminating all debt. On 3 December, Foreign Minister Chen Yi announced to Japanese reporters that China had no foreign debts. There are no documents to prove the allegation that the USSR forced China to pay off its debts.

In summer 1948, the USSR had already dispatched a group of technical specialists to the Chinese Communist base area in the Northeast to help repair the railroads. In summer 1949, Liu Shaoqi returned from Moscow with a group of specialists to plan an economic recovery. On the eve of the establishment of the PRC, there were already more than 600 Soviet experts in China. But in July 1960, Moscow recalled all Soviet experts. Few studies have determined how many Soviet experts had been dispatched to China during this period. In several general works, scholars estimate that about 10,000 Soviet experts were sent to China in the 1950s. However, other scholars have pointed out that such estimates are unreliable. It is extremely difficult to come up with a precise figure because, first, the concept of "expert" was never very clearly defined[11] and, second, the statistics were often incomplete. Yet we believe that it is still possible to come up with a reasonable estimate. Based on Chinese and Soviet archival sources, I argue that at the end of 1958, 11,527 experts were working in China's economic, cultural, and educational sectors, of which 89

Table 10.1   Soviet loans to China in the 1950s (100 million) (old rubles)

Sequence	Date	Agreed amount	Actual amount	Military loans (Korean War in brackets)	Economic loans
1	1950.2.14	12	12	12 [12]	
2	1951.2.1	12.35	9.86	9.86 [9.86]	
3	1951.4.10	3.4	3.4	3.4 [3.4]	
4	1951.9.12	6	6	6 [6]	
5	1951.9.15	0.7	0.38		0.38
6	1952.11.9	10.36	10.36	10.36 [about 1]	
7	1953.6.4	6.1	6.1	6.1	
8	1954.1.23	0.035	0.035		0.035
9	1954.6.19	0.088	0.088		0.088
10	1954.10.12	5.2	5.46	5.46	
11	1954.10.12	2.78	2.78		2.78
12	1955.2.28	2.47	2.47	2.47	
13	1955.10.31	7.23	7.23	7.23	
Total		68.713	66.163	62.88 [about 32]	3.283

percent (10,260) were from the USSR. Between 1958 and 1960, the USSR dispatched 915 (1958), 699 (1959), and 410 (1960) industrial and technical experts to China. In comparison, the number of Soviet teachers was much smaller: only 615 between 1948 and 1960. Therefore, from July 1949 to July 1960, more than 12,284 non-military Soviet experts (not including those who went to China to attend meetings or for short-term visits) were dispatched to China. Moreover, a large number of military "advisers" (called "experts" after 1957) were dispatched to China during the same period. According to the Chinese numbers, the Chinese navy employed 3390 Soviet advisers and experts, in addition to experts working in the specialized forces, such as the air force, artillery, and communications. The total number of such experts could easily reach over 10,000.[12] Therefore, the estimated total number of Soviet experts who worked in China at one time or another is over 20,000.

The role of the Soviet experts and advisers was, however, not restricted to economic and technology sectors. In reality, Soviet experts and advisers worked in nearly all Chinese party, government, and military organs during the 1950s. They played a role in establishing rules and regulations in Chinese political and economic systems as well as in other important areas. Soviet experts even assisted in drafting the PRC Constitution. In late March 1954, Ambassador Pavel Yudin reported that Soviet experts working for the Politics and Law Commission under the CCP CC "studied the draft of the PRC Constitution and offered editorial suggestions in response to a request from Peng Zhen. After receiving approvals from the Soviet adviser-in-chief and the ambassador, they transmitted the advice to their Chinese comrades. The Chinese accepted many of their suggestions and modified the draft." When later discussing the draft constitution with Yudin, Mao said, "The Constitution Drafting Committee studied the opinions of the Soviet experts ... and made changes to the draft accordingly." On 26 March, Mao handed the revised draft constitution to Ambassador Yudin and asked him to "transfer it to the CPSU CC for review."

CONCLUSION

Chinese leaders appreciated the Soviet aid. Although after the Twentieth CPSU Congress Mao proposed that China should "use the USSR as a mirror," he was referring to the methods of USSR economic construction. But he did not discuss Sino-Soviet relations. After publication of Mao's "On the Ten Major Relationships,"[13] some cadres and grassroots masses began to question Soviet ideological authority and the relevance of Soviet practical experience. Some even began to show disrespect for the Soviet experts. The Soviet side was well aware of this.[14] But the CCP CC declared that such criticism would not be tolerated. The Propaganda Department of the CCP CC convened a meeting of leading officials in cultural and educational organizations on 20 June 1956. Lu Dingyi, head of the CCP CC Propaganda Department, emphasized that: "It is absolutely necessary to learn from the USSR." If any problems occur in this regard, "It is due to our dogmatism. We should not shirk responsibility and shift the blame to our Soviet comrades." On 16 July, the CCP CC approved and transmitted Lu Dingyi's report. The report asked all units that employed Soviet experts "to study the report of the Central Propaganda Department and to swiftly resolve any issues." On 25 February, the State Council approved and transmitted a document of the State Foreign Experts Bureau stating "It has been our important task in the past, at present, and in the future, to learn from the USSR. While opposing dogmatism, we must not belittle the Soviet experience."

As Stephen Walt points out, "aid can be an effective way to strengthen an ally and thus to protect common or compatible interests."[15] The USSR enhanced the economic capability of the socialist bloc by providing assistance via the experts. The Sino-Soviet relationship in the 1950s was almost entirely one-sided, with the Soviet Union providing security protection and material aid. Nonetheless, China benefited greatly from the Soviet aid program. In fact, Sino-Soviet relations even expanded to the political and diplomatic arenas after the Twentieth CPSU Congress.

NOTES

1. It was only after October 1955 that Chinese affairs were re-assigned to the newly created Bureau of the People's Democratic Countries in the East when the International Department was reshuffled. In May 1957, Chinese affairs were re-assigned to the Department for Liaison with Communist and Workers' Parties in Socialist Countries under the CPSU CC.
2. Early in January 1952, Zhang Wentian, Chinese ambassador to the USSR, cabled Zhou Enlai and Mao Zedong to reveal the problems in the Sino-Soviet economic negotiations: (1) there were no replies to the telegrams sent by the Chinese commercial delegation for a very long time, and (2) the Chinese side constantly changed its requests and was nitpicking.
3. On 17 February 1954, the State Planning Commission asked Zhou Enlai for instructions. The Chinese side planned to ask the Soviet Union to consider some revisions and additions to its technical support for seven Chinese enterprises and industrial parks, such as the Luoyang Ball Bearing Plant and Automobile Factory.
4. Austin Jersild, "The Soviet State as Imperial Scavenger: 'Catch up and Surpass' in the Transnational Socialist Bloc, 1950–1960," *American Historical Review*, vol. 116, no. 1 (February 2011), pp. 116, 114.
5. Nikita Khrushchev, *Khrushchev Remembers: The Last Testament*, tr. Strobe Talbott (Boston: Little, Brown, 1974), pp. 46–47.
6. The report of the National Conference on Reception Work for Foreign Experts on 28 June 1956 estimated that by the end of 1956 the number of experts from the Soviet Union in China would reach about 3500, with 200 experts from other countries.
7. Sergei Goncharenko, "Sino–Soviet Military Cooperation," in Odd A. Westad, ed., *Brothers in Arms: The Rise and Fall of the Sino–Soviet Alliance (1945–1963)*

(Washington, DC: Woodrow Wilson Press and Stanford, CA: Stanford University Press, 1998), p. 160.

8. Reproduced in the National Archives (hereafter cited as NA), RG263, CIA NIE Box 8, NIE 100–3–60, 9 August 1960.

9. Peter Jones and Sian Kevill, comps., *China and the Soviet Union, 1949–84* (Burnt Mill, Harlow, Essex, UK: Longman, 1985), p. 16.

10. Mineo Nakajima, "Foreign Relations: From the Korean War to the Bandung Line," in Roderick MacFarquhar and John Fairbank, ch. eds., *Cambridge History of China, vol. 14: The People's Republic, Part I: The Emergence of Revolutionary China, 1949–1965* (Cambridge: Cambridge University Press, 1987), pp. 282–83.

11. The terminologies require some clarification. Prior to the Polish and Hungarian crises, there were various terms for Soviet aid workers in China. In general, those who worked in administrative, government, or military sectors were called advisers, those who worked in factories and mines were called experts, and those who worked in schools were "professors" or "teachers." In the case of auxiliary personnel, terms such as "technician" (*jishi*) or "sergeant" (*junshi*) were used. On 5 December 1957, the State Council decreed that "expert" (*zhuanjia*) should be the general term applicable to all Soviet aid workers, except for those who had been previously hired specifically as "advisers." On 20 October 1958, the CCP CC and the State Council further instructed that the term "adviser" was to be eliminated and it was to be replaced by the standard term "expert." The "experts" mentioned in this chapter, unless specifically noted, refer to all Soviet aid workers in China. Any estimates of their number are difficult due to the differences in terminology in the original sources.

12. Interviews with Wang Yazhi, June–October 2000.

13. Summed up by Mao Zedong in April 1956, "On the Ten Major Relationships" is an outline of how the PRC would achieve socialist construction of an economic, political, scientific, and cultural Chinese state. It was to be influenced by the Soviet Union but to have Chinese characteristics.

14. For the impact of the Soviet experts in China, see Shen and Xia, *Mao and the Sino–Soviet Partnership*, pp. 110–22.

15. Stephen Walt, *The Origins of Alliances* (Ithaca: Cornell University Press, 1987), p. 225.

CHAPTER 11

The Twentieth CPSU Congress and the Eighth CCP Congress, 1956

Zhihua Shen

Between 1954 and 1955, Sino-Soviet relations appeared to be stable; this was, some would say, the honeymoon of the alliance. But in 1956, at the Twentieth Communist Party of the Soviet Union (CPSU) Congress, Nikita Khrushchev unleashed criticism against Stalin in his so-called secret speech, one of the most shocking and puzzling developments in the International Communist Movement during the Cold War. Many scholars believe that the speech was the trigger for the Sino-Soviet split. In fact, however, there is a much more nuanced story behind this generalization.

The secret speech prompted a series of questions regarding the socialist road, and it had an indirect impact on the evolution of Sino-Soviet relations and Cold War international politics. In Chinese studies of history, evaluations of the Twentieth Congress are still very controversial. In the later Sino-Soviet polemics, the Chinese Communist Party (CCP) Central Committee (CC) argued that it was at the Twentieth Congress that the CPSU "began to renege on Marxism-Leninism in terms of a series of principled issues," in particular, by using the repudiation of Stalin and opposition to the "cult of personality" as a pretext to adopt a "parliamentary road" to socialism. In official Chinese historiography it is claimed that the Sino-Soviet differences originated at the Twentieth Congress.

Until recently, many scholars have continued to believe that the Twentieth CPSU Congress symbolized the emergence of a serious Sino-Soviet rift and was "the first historical turning point in the deterioration of Sino-Soviet

Z. Shen (✉)
East China Normal University, Shanghai, China
e-mail: zhaoran@ssap.cn

© The Author(s) 2020
Z. Shen (ed.), *A Short History of Sino-Soviet Relations, 1917–1991*,
China Connections, https://doi.org/10.1007/978-981-13-8641-1_11

161

relations." Most Western scholars also accept this thesis. For example, historian Lorenz Lüthi argues that "The twentieth congress established the ideological foundation for the disagreements that would rock the Sino-Soviet partnership in the years to come. Most importantly, de-Stalinization threatened to undercut Mao's domestic position."[1] This chapter shows that Mao's attitude was much more complicated and paradoxical than has been previously portrayed.

THE OFFICIAL LINE AND THE ESSENCE OF THE TWENTIETH CPSU CONGRESS

The Twentieth Congress proposed a series of guiding principles, lines, and programs in the international, domestic, and intra-party arenas, representing a dramatic departure from those that Stalin had presided over at the Nineteenth CPSU Congress in 1952. The Twentieth Congress put forward the issue of strengthening collective leadership and opposing a personality cult. This issue was first raised in Khrushchev's report, though he provided a more comprehensive elaboration in his 25 February 1956 report (widely known as the secret speech) entitled "On the Cult of Personality and its Consequences." This speech attracted worldwide attention. To elaborate on the consequences of the personality cult, Khrushchev exposed Stalin's crimes during the Great Purge of the 1930s, his military blunders during World War II, and a multitude of mistakes in his later years.

The de-Stalinization policies that began with the Twentieth Congress provided for the de-Stalinization in the International Communist Movement. De-Stalinization was not a sudden impulse by Khrushchev. It was the common understanding among most of the core CPSU leaders that de-Stalinization gradually developed after Stalin's death, although Vyacheslav Molotov and Lazar Kaganovich were notably reluctant to agree wholeheartedly.

Looking back, we can see that the development of the Cold War interfered with the great power cooperation of the World War II era, forcing Stalin to adjust his foreign policy and security strategy. Demanding conformity, the Union of Soviet Socialist Republics (USSR) imposed the Soviet system on Eastern Europe and established the Cominform.[2] The outbreak of the Berlin crisis in 1948–49 heightened tensions in Europe, and the Korean War expanded Soviet confrontations in Asia. Therefore, the death of Stalin gave Soviet leaders an opportunity to modify the traditional Soviet policy.

The first Soviet attempt to relax international tensions was to persuade the Chinese to find ways to compromise with the United States to end the Korean War. This would be the first collective decision by the new leaders in the Kremlin. One year later, Georgii Malenkov, who succeeded Stalin as chairman of the Council of Ministers, proposed that the USSR advocate "peaceful economic competition" with all capitalist countries, including the United States. This statement differed significantly from Stalin's views on class struggle and violent revolution. Because of internal political struggles, Malenkov was singled out for criticism, which led to his demotion. Even in the face of Malenkov's dismissal, the new Soviet leadership accepted this theoretical framework and logic. Just like Stalin in the 1920s, Khrushchev formed alliances with other party leaders and used the party to manipulate his rivals as well as foreign and domestic policies for his own political purposes and to make allies out of his enemies (Beria, Malenkov, and Molotov) before he ultimately betrayed them.

Thus, the issues proposed at the Twentieth Congress introduced a new era that stressed social development and the importance of the people's livelihood. After Stalin's death, intra-party activities and social development in the USSR presaged conditions for reform. Steps taken by leaders such as Beria and Malenkov reflected the necessity of reform. Therefore, the theoretical prerequisites were already in place. Although the new Soviet leadership, represented by Khrushchev, was politically immature, the new leaders began to reconsider the socialist development model. To be more specific, the Twentieth Congress provided an opportunity for the CPSU to make a fresh start and dispense with the Stalinist model. It also provided a forum for Khrushchev to garner world attention as the new leader of the USSR.[3]

The Impact of the Twentieth Party Congress on Sino-Soviet Relations

To fully understand the impact of the Twentieth Congress on Sino-Soviet relations, the following questions need to be considered. What were the differences between Khrushchev's new policies and China's contemporaneous domestic and foreign policies? What were the differences between the program of the Twentieth CPSU Congress and the program of the Eighth CCP Congress?

The first question deals with peaceful transition. Mao Zedong was obviously dissatisfied with the formulation of the Twentieth Congress. The CCP felt that violent revolution to win political power was a worthy example of the CCP's emulation of the Russian October Revolution and the CCP's invaluable contribution to the world revolutionary process. However, in 1956, Mao and the CCP CC did not publicly raise this issue.[4] Peaceful coexistence, peaceful transition, and peaceful competition were an inseparable trinity in both the theoretical realm and the existing systems. In fact, since the end of the Korean War, from the Geneva Conference in 1954 to the Bandung Conference in 1955, China had been implementing such policies.[5] Thus, the "peaceful policies" proposed at the Twentieth Congress struck a sympathetic chord among the CCP ruling circles. Deputy Foreign Minister Zhang Wentian pointed out at an internal Foreign Ministry meeting on 21 February 1956 that "The view that war is inevitable should be revised. That there are diverse roads to socialism is a reality." Premier and Foreign Minister Zhou Enlai also discussed the issue of peaceful transition, stating on 4 March 1956 at a national conference of professionals in basic construction, labor, and so forth: "International tensions are subsiding. War is not destined to be inevitable. This assessment is correct. When such tremendous changes have taken place in the international situation, peace will be in the hands of the people of the world and thus war can be prevented." At a State Council meeting of cadres on 3 May, when speaking of international relations, Zhou stated, "[We are] for peaceful coexistence. [We should] compare which system is superior and better via peaceful competition and let the people choose." Soon thereafter, *People's Daily* published a series of articles on themes such as "An Important Method for Advocating Peaceful Coexistence" and "The Development of Peaceful Neutrality." In view of such circumstances, Mao withheld any objections he might have had to the notion of peaceful transition, at least for the time being.

With respect to domestic economic policies, Mao's thinking of "the Soviet Union as a mirror" was epitomized in his report "On the Ten Major Relationships." On 25 April 1956, when speaking at an enlarged meeting of the Politburo, Mao summed up China's experience, discussed the ten major relationships in socialist revolution and socialist construction, and set forth his ideas underlying the general line of building socialism with greater, faster, better, and more economical results. "On the Ten Major Relationships" presented an outline on how the People's Republic of China (PRC) would carry out economic, political, scientific, and cultural social construction. The Chinese would be influenced by the Soviet Union, but it would be uniquely Chinese in its characteristics. Mao would not have proposed "socialism with Chinese characteristics" when Stalin was still alive, but the new Soviet leaders also appeared to be breaking away from the Stalinist model as well.

There were many shared concerns in the two countries in terms of the economic policies in Khrushchev's report and the report on the "Sixth Five-Year Plan" by Chairman of the Council of Ministers Nikolai Bulganin and in Mao's elaboration on the ten relationships. Both appear to be adjusting the scale of investment among agriculture, light industry, and heavy industry, modifying the distribution of industry, and improving the people's standard of living. The Soviet embassy in China analyzed Mao's "On the Ten Major Relationships" and came to the following conclusions: The most important items in Mao's proposed ten policies, such as improving the people's welfare and further developing a democratic style of work, are closely related to the resolution passed by the Twentieth CPSU Congress.

However, it is worth noting that neither the CCP nor the CPSU was able to make a complete break from the Stalinist model and to think about socialist development from the perspective of actually reforming the socialist system. In terms of economic construction, China adopted the experience of the Stalin era, especially the experience of the postwar economic reconstruction period. However, Mao believed that China should pay attention to the lessons learned from the shortcomings of the Stalin model. These were the same issues that the new Soviet leaders were pondering after Stalin's death and that were formally raised at the Twentieth Congress. It is important to note that Mao's 1956 so-called exploring China's own road was in essence the Stalinist model. However, by 1957 Mao believed that with his own version of the Stalinist model, China's economy could be better and grow faster than the Soviet model (Mao's understanding of economic issues and the Stalin model was somewhat primitive and superficial). The only difference was that to achieve growth China was attempting to adopt methods that were more suitable to its unique national conditions to achieve growth. Like the Soviet leaders, Mao believed that there was nothing wrong with the principles of the Soviet model—it was only its methods that could sometimes be problematic.

In sum, when the program of the Twentieth Congress was first proposed, the CCP and the CPSU were both exploring issues related to socialist development. There appear to be no "fundamental differences" or "severe ruptures" between the two regarding the program proposed at the Twentieth Congress. The only part of the congress that eventually would lead to any differences of opinion became apparent on the last day of the congress after Khrushchev's secret speech.

The focus of Khrushchev's infamous secret speech was his evaluation of Stalin. His criticism of Stalin had a great impact on the socialist camp as well as on the International Communist Movement. Its effect on Sino-Soviet relations was much more complicated than was generally perceived at the time.

No one doubts that it was Khrushchev who actively pushed to publicize the Stalin issue,[6] but scholars differ in their interpretations of Khrushchev's motives. Some argue that Khrushchev used the issue to attack his political opponents in contending for political supremacy, whereas others believe that he exploited the issue to prevent interference by conservatives and to clear the way for further policy changes. Others feel that Khrushchev was genuinely interested in preserving socialism as a viable model, but a model that would thrive without Stalin's harsh measures. Still others point out that Khrushchev was forced to give the speech simply because the situation demanded it. Despite these various interpretations, one thing is certain: From a longer historical point of view, the swift unraveling of Stalin's crimes prompted a reconsideration of whether the socialist model was still viable. From a realistic point of view, the CPSU's handling of the Stalin issue created ideological confusion in both Soviet society and the socialist camp. It resulted in much resistance as the Soviets advocated new reform policies and a general de-Stalinization.

The hardest hit by the speech was Soviet society. In extensive debates, numerous sharp opinions were raised. Many argued that Stalin, "a person condemned by the state," was stained with the blood of the Communists and "had no right to be buried in Lenin's tomb." Others were even more radical, claiming that Soviet society "has been a highly totalitarian regime" during the last 30 years, worse than "the Spanish inquisition." Some even proposed outlawing the CPSU and burning the Marxist classics. Then again, many contended that it was "unjust" to blame Stalin for all the crimes and the secret speech that "slandered Stalin" was "sheer nonsense" and "Stalin would live forever in history and in the hearts of progressive people." Despite such differences of opinion, the extensive discussions about Stalin caused much confusion. They created a rupture in society because most people who had lived under Stalin's regime had come to revere him.

The reaction of the socialist bloc countries was tense as well. Whereas the Yugoslavs praised the speech, the Communist parties in Western Europe and the United States experienced serious splits. The reaction of the general secretary of the Communist Party of Spain, Dolores Ibarruri, was typical. She recalled, "We feel depressed and heavy-hearted and we are at a loss upon learning those terrible things exposed by the Soviet leaders." In many cases, it seemed that it was not so much the exposure of Stalin's crimes that depressed people as much as the way in which it all came to light. Xinhua News Agency in Moscow summed it up convincingly: The CPSU exposed the Stalin issue without sufficient ideological and organizational preparation. It was spread widely and rapidly, and the CCP failed to provide sufficient explanations afterward. On 8 July 1956, Zhou Enlai told the Yugoslav ambassador to Beijing that it would have been much better for the Stalin issue to have remained within the CPSU. The CCP believed that this would have better served the interests of the worldwide Communist parties.

The response from Eastern Europe was mixed. East German leader Walter Ulbricht could not wait to publish articles praising the CPSU's new spirit. The Albanians publicly agreed with the speech but privately expressed dissatisfaction.[7] The reformers in Poland and Hungary were encouraged, whereas the conservatives were in low spirits. Other Eastern European leaders did not know how to respond. The Asian Communist parties adopted more conservative approaches. The North Korean, Vietnamese, and Indonesian Communist parties restricted any discussion of the personality cult.

In 1956, Soviet leaders confronted a very complicated situation. Stalin had been the embodiment of truth and had been turned into a saint, despite the fact the Soviet people had suffered for many years from his brutal repression. Any theoretical innovation and policy adjustment would have met with strong resistance, but any modification to the Stalinist system would have been impossible if Stalin's personality cult had not been discredited. Because the virus of the personality cult had penetrated every level of Soviet society, any policy alteration had to be gradual to forestall a collapse of the entire society. But due to the surprise nature of Khrushchev's secret speech, pressure from public opinion, and many internal disputes, the CPSU had to slow down and eventually suspend the political thaw. As a result, the 30 June resolution "On the Cult of Personality and its Consequences" retained the main points of Khrushchev's secret speech, but it was greatly toned down. In fact, it emphasized that "it is seriously wrong to conclude that the Soviet system should be modified claiming a cult of personality existed or to look for the origins of the cult of personality in the Soviet system."

MAO'S REACTIONS TO THE ISSUES OF STALIN
AND THE PERSONALITY CULT

The situation in China and the issues China confronted were very different from those in the Soviet Union. The initial CCP response to the Twentieth Congress was quite different from the staunch opposition that the CCP later claimed. The reaction was very contradictory.

After the congress, *People's Daily* printed all the important documents, including Mikoyan's speech, that the CPSU had publicly issued. Before Khrushchev delivered his secret speech, Mikoyan had openly criticized Stalin's abuse of power, his foreign policy errors, and the problems in Stalin's *Short History of the All-Union Communist Party (Bolsheviks)* and *Economic Problems of Socialism in the USSR*.[8] The Chinese *Internal Reference* publication reported commentaries from the Western press on the policy of peaceful coexistence and Mikoyan's speech, with additional news on progress in rehabilitating the political victims of the 1930s. These commentaries provoked intense reactions within Chinese society. According to reports in *Internal Reference*, all cadres, intellectuals, members of the democratic parties, industrialists, and businessmen felt "shocked and perplexed." All sorts of "chaotic ideas and speculations" emerged. Some people even raised doubts about whether the materials had been accurately translated. Most frequently discussed were theoretical issues relating to the evaluations of Stalin and the parliamentary model. There was a universal demand that the CCP CC should offer a clarification.

On 1 March, the Presidium of the CPSU reprinted 150 copies of the secret speech and sent them to the Central Committees of the Communist parties via the overseas Soviet embassies. Vice-Premier Deng Xiaoping, who attended the Twentieth Congress, however, carried his own copy of the speech back from Moscow to Beijing on 3 March. After receiving the text of the secret speech, CCP leaders used a variety of methods to acquaint Chinese citizens with the contents of the Soviet criticism of Stalin. Unlike the North Koreans and Vietnamese, the CCP did not intentionally control the spread of the speech. Instead, CCP authorities orally relayed the text of the secret speech to party members. They also printed a separate edition of the translated Chinese version and distributed it, together with *Reference News* under the masthead: "Internal Publication for Safe-Keeping." Meanwhile, *Reference News* published information on foreign reactions. Although these were internal publications with limited circulation, they were not confidential and thus they spread rapidly. Foreign-language bookstores sold copies of the *Daily Worker*, the American Communist Party newspaper, which published the entire secret speech in English. According to Li Shenzhi, who was then one of Premier Zhou's foreign-affairs secretaries, Mao "did not oppose distributing the content of the secret speech." This seems to indicate that Mao was not worried that de-Stalinization might have serious consequences for Chinese society.

On 3 March, the same day that Deng Xiaoping and Tan Zhenlin returned from Moscow, Mao called a meeting of senior CCP leaders, including Liu Shaoqi, Zhou Enlai, Peng Zhen, Kang Sheng, Nie Rongzhen, and Liu Lantao. At the meeting, Deng reported on the Twentieth Congress. High-level discussions at the congress had focused on the Stalin issue. An enlarged CCP Central Committee Politburo meeting on 11–12 March held that it was highly significant that the congress eliminated the cult of Stalin and exposed his serious mistakes. But CCP leaders maintained that a total repudiation of Stalin was wrong. At a 12 March Politburo meeting, Mao described Khrushchev's secret speech as "first, he lifted the lid; second, he made a blunder." By "lifting the lid," Mao meant that Khrushchev was breaking away from blind faith in Stalin and was implying that each Communist country could do things as it saw fit. By "making a blunder," Mao meant that the CPSU's criticism of Stalin, a man of "great international importance," without prior consultation with other parties was a mistake. The implication was that this "surprise attack" made a mess of the International Communist Movement. Mao also mentioned that he personally held a different opinion on peaceful coexistence, but he did not elaborate on it.

At an enlarged Politburo meeting on 19–24 March, the CCP leadership mainly discussed the mistakes Stalin had made during various periods of Soviet history. Mao proposed his three-seven formula to assess Stalin, stating that Stalin had been 30 percent wrong and 70 percent correct. Mao justified Stalin's mistakes by saying that errors were inevitable because he was the first in history to create a socialist country. In response to the chaotic situation in the socialist camp, the Politburo decided to make the CCP's position known to all. Therefore, the CCP came out in support of the position of the Twentieth Congress, offered a theoretical analysis of the origins of Stalin's mistakes, provided an ideological perspective to Khrushchev's secret speech, and declared its full confidence in socialism.

Following Mao's instructions, *People's Daily* published an editorial entitled "On the Historical Experience of the Dictatorship of the Proletariat," which, personally revised by Mao, was a summary of the Politburo's discussions.[9] The purposes of the article were twofold. First, in view of the ideological chaos in the socialist bloc, the CCP wanted to clearly state its views in hopes of reversing the pessimistic mood among the worldwide Communist parties. Second, the CCP wanted to use its "comprehensive analysis" of the Stalin issue to educate the Chinese people, to assuage their fears, and to reduce any wild speculations. The CCP's article first affirmed the historical achievements of the Twentieth Congress, especially its courage in denouncing Stalin's personality cult; it then presented a comprehensive analysis of the Stalin issue.

The *People's Daily* article, "On the Historical Experience of the Dictatorship of the Proletariat," generated a huge response in the Soviet Union, Eastern Europe, and the International Communist Movement. This was evident in its wide reprinting and the various commentaries in *Pravda*, the Eastern European Communist Party organs, and Communist Party newspapers, as well as in the three reports sent from the Chinese embassy in Moscow to Beijing. For instance, an editorial on 4 April in *Rude Pravo*, the official organ of the Communist Party of Czechoslovakia, pointed out that the *People's Daily* article "thoroughly elaborates on the historical circumstances behind the mistakes associated with Stalin's personality cult in the international revolutionary movement after the birth of the first socialist country. It will help readers in our countries to fully understand the message of the Twentieth Congress of the CPSU."

The CCP was tactfully trying to show, by means of the press, that the CCP was wiser than the CPSU. But in private talks with the Soviets, Mao emphasized that the CCP and the CPSU were in agreement. On 31 March, in "excellent spirits," Mao talked with Soviet Ambassador Yudin for three hours, during which he cited a series of Stalin's erroneous policies toward China. Then he seemed to forgive Stalin for all he had done to China by admitting that Stalin's China policy was "basically right." On Soviet domestic issues, however, Mao regarded Stalin as "a great Marxist-Leninist and an excellent and faithful revolutionary," and he voiced no objections to Stalin's errors that had been mentioned in the secret speech. Available records indicate that in reality Mao differed little from Khrushchev on the Stalin issue. Mao later pointed out that the Twentieth Congress had made a deep impression on him. He said that because the CPSU had taken the initiative to raise the Stalin issue, he and the CCP were also able to think more clearly about many other issues.

On 6 April, Mao and Liu Shaoqi met with Anastas Mikoyan, who had arrived in China to discuss the Stalin issue. Mao told Mikoyan, "The CCP and the CPSU differ somewhat in their opinions. The CCP believes that Stalin's achievements outweigh his mistakes. It is necessary to provide a more comprehensive assessment. We agree on much more than we differ on. It is imperative that we unite to fight our enemies." In a relaxed talk with Ambassador Yudin on 2 May, however, Mao criticized Stalin's mistakes. He praised the courage of the CPSU CC to acutely raise the Stalin issue, and he pointed out that it was necessary to adopt a dialectical attitude in evaluating Stalin by rejecting his negative elements and defending his positive elements. Mao called Stalin a great Marxist-Leninist, despite his many serious mistakes. Mao said that it was not necessary to publicize his mistakes because doing so would be "unfavorable to the revolutionary cause." It was Mao's opinion that the CPSU should not completely repudiate Stalin because in doing so it would risk losing its legitimacy. In the end, Mao once again stressed the importance of the resolution of the Twentieth Congress and the incisive criticism of Stalin. He said that since Stalin's personality cult had already been eliminated, now "we can thoroughly discuss all issues." When mentioning the views of each of the two parties, Mao reported, "We are now in full agreement."

In private, however, Mao was somewhat dissatisfied with Khrushchev's speech. He was not opposed to Khrushchev's criticism of Stalin's personality cult, but he believed that the CPSU "had made serious mistakes in its substance and method of exposing" Stalin. On the substance of the accusations against Khrushchev, Mao told the Polish ambassador on 31 October 1956 that Khrushchev's opposition to the personality cult was "without real substance." Mao felt that it was proper to oppose the personality cult only if the person advocated chauvinism and personal dictatorship. It seems that Mao was not against the cult of personality per se, for less than two years later Mao stated at an expanded session of the Politburo that "there are right and wrong kinds of personality cults. [We should] insist on the right kind of personality cult." Mao felt that it was appropriate to criticize Stalin's personality cult, but in principle it was not appropriate to negate a personality cult. In the final analysis, it appears that Mao, as the leader of the Chinese Revolution and the future of the world revolution, reserved the right to promote his own personality cult.

With regard to the CPSU's method of criticizing Stalin, Mao was unhappy because the CPSU did not beforehand consult with the CCP on an issue of such grave importance. Zhu De, as the head of the CCP delegation to the Twentieth CPSU Congress, had already mentioned this to the CPSU CC functionaries who were accompanying him in Moscow. Later, this criticism reached the foreign diplomats in China. At high-level CCP meetings, senior leaders engaged in endless discussions about the issue. Mao felt that it was the surprise of the CPSU's attack that left the Communist parties totally unprepared and sowed the seeds for ideological confusion. Mao and the CCP also discussed the morality of the Soviet criticism of Stalin. He was distressed that the new Soviet leaders—"those who extolled Stalin to the skies have now in one swoop consigned him to purgatory"[10]—used to praise Stalin to the sky, but now they condemn him to hell. This explains why Mao ultimately accused the new Soviet leaders of lacking "revolutionary morality."[11]

Mao was more concerned about the appearance of an anti-personality cult sentiment in China than in Moscow. Once the Soviets began criticizing Stalin, the Chinese public started to raise disturbing questions. *Internal Reference* reported extensively on the Chinese responses, both from officials and from grassroots society, to the Soviet criticism of the personality cult by officials and grassroots society. Government functionaries in Hebei province asked the following difficult question: "In the past, we praised Stalin's personality cult. But we also composed 'The East is Red' to sing the praises of Chairman Mao. Does that also belong to a personality cult?" People from the industry and business sectors in Guangzhou city said, "In the past, we sometime said, 'Long Live Chairman Mao!' This is not appropriate because it is a feudal practice. It is also a kind of personality cult, which denigrates the collective leadership of the party." Party functionaries in Chongqing raised the question: "Does the Communist Party also follow the rule that 'a new chief brings in new aides'? After the death of Marx and Engels, Kautsky distorted their ideas; after the death of Lenin, Trotsky and Bukharin attacked him; and now that Stalin has recently died, Mikoyan and others have already attacked him. What on earth is happening?" This could not but lead Mao to ponder China's future political situation after his death. But because the Communist world had come out so vociferously against the personality cult, at the time Mao preferred to keep his thoughts to himself.

THE CCP'S REFLECTION ON CHINA'S DEVELOPMENT PATH

In early 1956, the CCP and the CPSU were both rethinking the problems of the Stalinist model. Mao carefully listened to the CPSU's open discussions about the problems under Stalin. Later Zhou Enlai remarked that "Mao Zedong's thinking is a summary of the experiences of the Chinese Revolution and construction, which is based on the experiences and lessons of the CPSU's criticism of Stalin's mistakes." The Twentieth Congress clearly had a big impact on both the CCP and Mao.

After listening to the program of the CPSU's Twentieth Congress, Mao proposed that China should go its own way on the socialist road. Whether Khrushchev intended this or not, Mao interpreted what he heard from Moscow to mean that the Soviets were no longer going to follow the Stalinist model, so why should China?

Instead, Mao proposed using "the USSR as a mirror." According to then Chairman of the State Construction Commission and later Vice-Premier Bo Yibo, this meant looking at the ratios between agriculture, light industry, and heavy industry; the relationship between coastal and inland industries and between the defense and civil industries; the allocation of responsibilities, rights, and interests among the state, collectives, and individuals; and the relationship between the central government and the local governments. Like a mirror, this would reflect the problems in the Stalinist economic system.

With his "mirror" analogy, Mao meant that China should draw lessons from Soviet economic development during the Stalin era, as described at the Twentieth Congress. When Mao talked about the lessons from Stalin's USSR, he was referring to the concrete policies of socialist construction. Mao felt that the CCP and the CPSU were similar in that neither country seriously questioned Stalin's economic model.

Therefore, when Mao proposed that China should follow its own socialist road, he was not considering leading China down a path different from that in the USSR. Mao later explained what he had been thinking in 1956: "Both the Soviet Union and China are socialist countries. Is it possible for us to pursue a faster and better road? Can we adopt a faster, better, and more economic way for socialist construction?" This explains why, in February 1957, Mao proposed that China's industrialization path might differ from that of the Soviet Union. Perhaps China could outpace the USSR in the pursuit of industrialization by increasing steel production—14 million tons of steel within 21 years? This idea foreshadowed the Great Leap Forward and the 1958 national steel-making campaign. Thus, when Mao proposed the policy of "using the USSR as a mirror," he was signaling that he was unwilling to allow China to trail behind the Soviet Union. He wanted China to surpass the USSR.

China adopted many measures of the Stalin era, especially the economic reconstruction policies of the post–World War II era. There was not much new in Mao's "On the Ten Major Relationships," when we compare it with the Soviet reform policies and resolutions of the Twentieth Congress. The problems that the new Soviet leaders had raised at the congress, Mao believed, were the same problems China could observe by looking at the Stalin model as a mirror. Like the Soviet leaders, Mao believed that the Stalinist development model was not wrong, but its method had become problematic.

At the time, neither the CPSU leaders nor the CCP leaders seemed to equate the Stalinist development model with the socialist road. The Stalinist model did not have to be the only path to socialism. They felt that they could pursue socialism by modifying the Stalinist model. Although they understood that the Stalinist version of socialism (characterized by a strong political dictatorship and an overly centralized economic system) was premised on fear, they believed these were exactly the issues that the Twentieth CPSU Congress and the Eighth CCP Congress were attempting to resolve.

Although the Eighth CCP Congress avoided mentioning the term "Mao Zedong Thought," it did not, to the slightest degree, erode the importance of Mao Zedong Thought within the CCP. Judging from his previous instructions on the issue of propagating Mao Zedong Thought, I find that Mao's emphasis was merely on not using the term in public. But he never felt that this was a denial of the importance of Mao Zedong Thought in China. By 1956, Mao's standing in the CCP was at its highest. He faced no challengers within the party. After the Twentieth Congress, opposing the cult of personality had become a banner for all Communist parties, and the CCP could not ignore this banner. Nonetheless, the Eighth CCP Congress handled this issue in a very subtle way. Opposing the personality cult was not the main topic of the Eighth CCP Congress, which was very different from the Twentieth CPSU Congress. Most of the speakers did not even touch on this topic. Liu Shaoqi's political report and Deng Xiaoping's report on amending the party constitution mentioned the issue of the personality cult only in affirming the conclusions of the Twentieth Congress. Deng spoke in defense of the CCP, claiming that "It is right to oppose the personality cult and such criticism must be carried out. But the CCP had noticed this long ago. It is Mao Zedong who is against praising the virtues of a certain individual. [We should] love our leader. This is not a personality cult." He thus tactfully addressed (and avoided) the issue of whether a personality cult actually existed in the CCP.

However, the explanation by the Eighth CCP Congress—that a personality cult did not exist in the CCP—was inaccurate historically. In fact, Mao's cult of personality had begun during the Yan'an Rectification Campaign of the early 1940s. The Yan'an Rectification Campaign established Mao's absolutism, according him full dictatorial power and deifying his role. At the 1945 Seventh CCP Congress, many senior CCP leaders, including Liu Shaoqi, Zhang Wentian, Ren Bishi, Zhou Enlai, Zhu De, and Peng Dehuai, all sang Mao's praises and worshipped him. After the Yan'an Rectification Campaign, the slogan "Long Live Chairman Mao" spread throughout Yan'an.[12] Nevertheless, after Khrushchev's de-Stalinization speech, Mao was passive and unwilling to criticize the personality cult. Thus, when delivering his speech "On the Ten Major Relationships," Mao suddenly said, "In the past, the USSR praised Stalin to the skies. Now Stalin has been condemned to hell. Some people in our country copy Soviet actions." Mao's remarks suggest that he was unwilling to oppose the personality cult; in particular, he was unwilling to see the Chinese oppose a personality cult because if that were the case, he feared his fate would be the same as Stalin's.

CONCLUSION

In 1956, the Soviet Union, China, and many other socialist countries were at a crossroads. Both the USSR and China were beginning to rethink the socialist development model. The Eighth CCP Congress not only coincided with the Twentieth CPSU Congress that was held that same year, but it also corresponded with the Twentieth CPSU Congress in terms of ideas, policies, and development programs. For the CCP, there was no fundamental difference with the CPSU in terms of the political and economic programs announced at the Twentieth Congress, and the congress did not have an immediate negative effect on Sino-Soviet relations.

However, the focus of the Twentieth Congress—de-Stalinization—did ultimately have an effect on Sino-Soviet relations. The open "self-criticism" by the CPSU and the unveiling of Stalin's mistakes lowered the CPSU's prestige and shook its leadership of the socialist camp. The de-Stalinization revelations in the USSR affected CCP internal policies, as reflected in the movement to cut back on use of the words "Mao Zedong Thought" in the press because of their obvious relationship to Stalin's personality cult. But Mao and the CCP also gained from the USSR's revelations. The CCP was able to reach out to help the socialist world work its way out of the ideological chaos that de-Stalinization had thrust upon it. In this process, the CCP gained influence and pride. The two major articles by the CCP CC Politburo that explained the situation in the USSR were translated and sent to Communists throughout the world in this way. Mao felt that he might be able to lead the International Communist Movement, and he also believed that he would be a much more charismatic leader than Khrushchev.

Perhaps these were the seeds of the eventual Sino-Soviet split, since prior to the Twentieth Congress, the CCP followed the CPSU and the CPSU provided substantial economic aid to China. After the congress, the CCP found itself in the situation of being able to assist the CPSU, at least, politically. This occurred in the subsequent political crises in the socialist bloc, namely, the Polish and Hungarian crises of October 1956.

Thereafter, a declaration of equality among the socialist countries, proposed by the Chinese, was adopted on 30 October 1956. This declaration provided new opportunities for Mao. The health of the world socialist movement, according to Mao, was more pressing than the Western belief that Mao was threatened by the criticism of Stalin. This may be why Mao decided to publish "On the Historical Experience of the Dictatorship of the Proletariat." He wanted to reverse the growing pessimism among the fraternal parties, and he also wanted to provide a new way to understand Khrushchev's revelations about Stalin. As others have noted, this may also have been a way for Mao to establish his leadership of the socialist bloc. In any case, there is no question that Mao's reading of the CPSU's program allowed the CCP to find its own road to socialism, while still believing that Stalin's achievements outweighed his mistakes.

NOTES

1. Lorenz M. Lüthi, *The Sino-Soviet Split: Cold War in the Communist World* (Princeton, NJ: Princeton University Press, 2008), p. 46.

2. See Anne Applebaum, *Iron Curtain: The Crushing of Eastern Europe, 1944–1956* (New York: Doubleday, 2012).

3. For details on the Twentieth Congress and the origins of Khrushchev's secret speech, see Shen and Xia, *Mao and the Sino-Soviet Partnership*, pp. 134–41.

4. It was during the Moscow Conference in November 1957 that the CCP stated its different views on peaceful transition, and it was during the Sino-Soviet polemics in September 1963 that the CCP publicly announced its different views on peaceful transition.

5. Whereas the Soviets stressed all-out detente, the Chinese paid more attention to peaceful coexistence with its neighbors.

6. Fedor M. Burlatskii, *Khrushchev and the First Russian Spring: The Era of Khrushchev through the Eyes of his Adviser* (New York: Charles Scribner's Sons, 1988), p. 73.

7. For details, see Elidor Mëhilli, "Defying De-Stalinization: Albania's 1956," *Journal of Cold War Studies*, vol. 13, no. 4 (Fall 2011), pp. 4–56.

8. Roy Medvedev, *Khrushchev: A Biography*, tr. Brian Pearce (Garden City, NY: Anchor Press/Doubleday, 1983), p. 86.

9. A day before formal publication of the article, the CCP CC issued a circular, requesting that "Party committees at every level should organize study sessions among party and youth league members as well as non-party personnel, and should send progress reports on those issues that had been discussed to the CCP Propaganda Department."

10. "On the Ten Major Relationships," 25 April 1956, in *Selected Works of Mao Tsetung*, vol. 5 (Beijing: Foreign Languages Press, 1977), p. 304.

11. "Talks at a Conference of Secretaries of Provincial, Municipal, and Autonomous Region Party Committees," in *Selected Works of Mao Zedong*, vol. 5, p. 354.

12. Gao Hua, *How the Red Sun Rose: The Origins and Development of the Yan'an Rectification Movement*, tr. Stacy Mosher and Guo Jian (Hong Kong: The Chinese University Press of Hong Kong, 2018), pp. 661–705; Daniel Leese, *Mao Cult: Rhetoric and Ritual in China's Cultural Revolution* (Cambridge: Cambridge University Press, 2011), pp. 25–86.

CHAPTER 12

The Polish and Hungarian Crises and CCP Political Support for Khrushchev, 1956–1957

Zhihua Shen

The Twentieth Communist Party of the Soviet Union (CPSU) Congress and the Polish and Hungarian crises further weakened the leadership role of the CPSU. In the process, the status of the Chinese Communist Party (CCP) and of Mao Zedong improved steadily, and the influence of the CCP expanded from Asia to Europe. For a time, the China "whirlwind" was gaining momentum in the socialist bloc, especially in the Union of Soviet Socialist Republics (USSR) and Eastern Europe.

The advance of China's influence in the International Communist Movement was triggered by the publication of two Chinese articles and three visits by Chinese leaders to the USSR and Eastern Europe. Publication of "On the Historical Experience of Proletarian Dictatorship" on 5 April 1956 in the *People's Daily* and "More on the Historical Experience of Proletarian Dictatorship" on 29 December 1956 in the *People's Daily* were perceived as a manifestation of a Marxist-Leninist theoretical accomplishment. The visit of CCP Vice-Chairman Liu Shaoqi and General Secretary Deng Xiaoping to the USSR in October 1956 was the CCP's first attempt to assist the CPSU in handling Eastern European affairs; CCP Chairman Mao Zedong's attendance at the Moscow Conference of World Communist and Workers' Parties in November 1957 (see Part II, Chap. 13) heralded the CCP's equal standing with the CPSU. Premier Zhou Enlai's shuttle diplomacy in January 1957 provided an important link between these two historical events, establishing a solid political and diplomatic foundation for Mao's visit.

Z. Shen (✉)
East China Normal University, Shanghai, China
e-mail: zhaoran@ssap.cn

© The Author(s) 2020
Z. Shen (ed.), *A Short History of Sino-Soviet Relations, 1917–1991*,
China Connections, https://doi.org/10.1007/978-981-13-8641-1_12

CHINA AND THE POLISH AND HUNGARIAN CRISES

In June 1956, a revolt against Soviet control erupted in Poland, but it was eventually defeated by the Polish army. Nevertheless, the Poles gained some concessions from Moscow. Władysław Gomułka, who had been accused of Titoism in the late 1940s, was released from prison, became first secretary of the Polish United Workers' Party, and won the backing of Polish workers against the Soviets. In addition, Poland won control over its own economy, while also remaining loyal to the Warsaw Pact and friendly with the USSR.[1] It has long been assumed that Khrushchev's decision "to suspend further military movements [against Poland] resulted from consultation" with Beijing. Mercy Kuo notes "it seems highly probable and logical that the Chinese had a direct role in diffusing the situation in order for the Poles to make their case against Soviet bullying."[2] But such a view has been refuted by this author, who concludes that China played no role in diffusing the October 1956 Polish crisis. While coping with the 1956 Polish and Hungarian crises, CCP leaders adhered to two principles. First, they seized the opportunity to criticize Stalinism and to join with the Eastern European countries to confront Soviet "big power chauvinism" as well as the abuses of the CPSU. In this way, CCP leaders were stressing the principles of independence and equality in socialist interstate relations, as epitomized, in particular, by China's attitude toward the Polish issue. In essence, it was not so much that the Chinese helped the Soviets resolve the crisis in Poland as they used the crisis to force Soviet leaders to admit their previous mistakes and to issue a general statement on their basic principles governing relations within the socialist bloc. Second, the Chinese leaders focused on coordinating relations between the USSR and its satellites. They emphasized that there should be unity and stability within the socialist camp, and they opposed all measures that deviated from socialism. This was most evident in how Beijing dealt with the 1956 Hungarian crisis.

The 1956 Hungarian Revolution was a spontaneous nationwide revolt against the government of the Hungarian People's Republic (1949–1989) and its Soviet-imposed policies, lasting from 23 October to 10 November 1956. It was the first major threat to Soviet control since USSR forces drove out the Nazis from Eastern Europe at the end of World War II. When the crisis first erupted, the Chinese government had not been closely following events in Hungary. The CCP leadership did not respond to it, even after Soviet troops occupied Budapest. China followed its established principle of listening rather than expressing an opinion when a situation was unclear. Although both the reformers and the conservatives in Hungary looked to China for support, the Chinese ambassador to Hungary, Hao Deqing, criticized the mass movement in Hungary on the grounds that it aimed to overthrow the leadership of the Communist Party. In the face of the unrest, the embassy locked its gates and refused contact with all factions, including its former allies. When officials from the former government led by Mátyás Rákosi sought refuge, Hao Deqing "sent word through his Chinese doorman that they should go to the Soviet embassy instead."[3]

The Chinese government received its first intelligence report about the crisis in Budapest from Moscow. On 21 October, Khrushchev invited the CCP to send a delegation to Moscow for consultation. According to records from the Russian archives and the memoirs of Shi Zhe (Liu Shaoqi's Russian-language interpreter), the delegation arrived in Moscow in the early afternoon of 23 October, and Liu Shaoqi immediately met with Khrushchev. During the meeting, Ernő Gerő telephoned from Budapest to say that he was too busy to go to Moscow for the meeting of the leaders of the socialist countries that was scheduled for 24 October. A short while later, Soviet Defense Minister Marshal Georgii Zhukov telephoned to report that people in Budapest were storming party and government office buildings, that the police were refusing to protect them, and that the national defense army that had been sent in to restore order had already surrendered to the demonstrators. Zhukov added that he had put off Hungarian Defense Minister István Bata, who had telephoned him to plead for Soviet troops to support the Hungarian government, with the excuse that he would need CPSU Central Committee (CC) authorization. About an hour later, when Zhukov telephoned again, Khrushchev told him that the issue of whether or not to send troops at Hungary's request would be decided by the CC Presidium. After briefing Liu, Khrushchev added, "Since you are not familiar with developments in Hungary, and there is no time to consult with you now, I invite you to be present at the Presidium session tomorrow." By then, the decision to send Soviet troops to Budapest had already been taken.

When Liu and his deputy, Deng Xiaoping, attended the meeting of the Presidium on the morning of 24 October, Khrushchev, according to both Russian and Chinese reports, explained that, on orders from the Presidium, late the previous evening, Soviet troops had entered Budapest and order had been restored, with the exception of a few buildings still in the hands of the demonstrators. Khrushchev added that he hoped the Chinese would understand the need for these drastic measures and assured them that the Hungarians had welcomed the Soviet forces. He added that whereas the events in Poland took the form of a dispute within the party, the events in Hungary had to be handled differently because they were a threat to Communist rule; he hoped the Chinese would agree.

In the view of the Chinese, Khrushchev had tried to justify the Soviet military intervention in Hungary after the fact rather than first seeking Chinese approval. In a speech to the Presidium that lasted more than two hours, Liu did not comment explicitly on the events in Hungary. According to a report on his visit to Moscow that he presented at the Second Plenary Session of the Eighth CCP CC on 10 November, after his meeting with Khrushchev, on 23 October, Liu had telephoned Mao. As both lacked detailed knowledge of the Hungarian events, they decided not to comment.

However, the reshuffling of the Hungarian government, which had stalled on 24 October did not restore order: the concessions merely encouraged the militant demonstrators. On 29 October, Khrushchev received a report from the chairman of the KGB (Komitet gosudarstvennoi bezonpasnosti), Ivan A. Serov, and, later in the day, he received a report written jointly by Mikoyan and Suslov, the CPSU's special envoys to Hungary, that stated that the situation was out of control. At the time, Khrushchev was meeting with Liu to discuss how to solve the problems between the USSR and the other Eastern European countries. According to Shi Zhe, after Liu transmitted Mao's advice that the USSR should allow greater political, economic, and military freedoms, the Soviets agreed to draft a declaration on the equality of the USSR and the Eastern European countries, to be adopted the following day.

Khrushchev's recollections match the Chinese sources. According to Khrushchev, during the meeting, which lasted until early the next morning, various solutions to the crisis were considered. Khrushchev relayed to Liu the information reported from Mikoyan and Suslov, both of whom had agreed to resort to the use of force. Later, however, the two both changed their minds. At this crucial juncture, Mao reached the opinion that events in Hungary should be allowed to "go further." The Soviet leaders decided not to resort to the use of force but instead to allow the reconstructed Hungarian government headed by Imre Nagy to settle the crisis.

Meanwhile, the CPSU CC Presidium, following CCP suggestions, on 30 October, discussed the declaration of equality among socialist countries. This implied a willingness to compromise with the Hungarians. According to the minutes of the meeting, Khrushchev arrived during discussion of Mikoyan and Suslov's report and, after summarizing his conversation with Liu the previous night, he recommended adoption of the proposed draft declaration. He also recommended that the withdrawal of Soviet troops stationed in socialist countries should be discussed at the next meeting of the Warsaw Pact.

Toward evening, the Soviets sent Liu a copy of the draft declaration that was similar to his speech on 24 October; some words, even sentences, were identical. The declaration was ratified at 8:00 p.m., with Liu and the Chinese delegation in attendance. Thus, the CCP's proposal for a declaration of equality among the socialist states, made in consideration of the unrest in Poland, led to a decision to peacefully resolve the crisis in Hungary. Thus, the 30 October decision, following two days of indecision, can be partially attributed to CCP influence.[4]

Within hours, the political situation changed dramatically. According to Khrushchev's report to the plenary session of the CPSU CC in June 1957 as well as his memoirs, when he left Liu to return home in the early hours of 30 October, he had decided to forgo armed intervention. New information about the worsening situation in Hungary followed him home, however, and later that morning the Presidium unanimously agreed to send in troops. Owing to the previous notification to China that the USSR would not resort to the use of force, Khrushchev brought all members of the Presidium to the airport on the evening of 31 October to explain the reasons for the change in policy to Liu, who was about to fly home. While waiting to board the plane, the Chinese, according to Khrushchev, unexpectedly agreed to the use of force.[5]

Chinese records of the events contradict Khrushchev's claim that the Soviets made the decision to use force in Hungary on their own. According to Shi Zhe's memoirs, whereas the Soviets sent Mikoyan's report on the deteriorating situation in Hungary to Liu on the morning of 30 October, it was not until 1 November that the Chinese Foreign Ministry received telegrams, dated 29 and 30 October, on the same subject from its embassy in Budapest, reporting on the deteriorating political situation. Owing to the lack of information from the embassy, the developments in Hungary took the Chinese delegation in Moscow by surprise. Throughout the day of 30 October, Liu and Deng discussed the advantages and disadvantages of the withdrawal of Soviet troops versus the use of them to suppress the revolt by force, Liu asked for instructions. Mao replied that both solutions might be discussed with the Soviets, though Mao was inclined to the use of force, provided that action would be postponed until the counterrevolution spread and the people more clearly understood its implications. Thus, that evening the Presidium met with the Chinese delegation at Liu's, not Khrushchev's, request.

According to Chinese sources, in the evening of 31 October, Liu received a telephone call from the CPSU CC, asking the departing Chinese delegation to arrive at the airport an hour earlier than planned to allow time for another meeting with Khrushchev. At the meeting, Khrushchev told Liu that, after a full day of discussion, the Presidium had decided to take the offensive. Liu concurred and then stated that the CCP expected two conditions before Soviet armed intervention: first, an invitation from the Hungarian government and, second, support from the Hungarian masses.[6]

Zhou Enlai's Shuttle Diplomacy and Bloc Unity

After the Polish and Hungarian crises, Khrushchev invited Zhou Enlai to visit Moscow to mediate the conflicts between the Soviets and the leaders of Poland and Hungary. In early January 1957, Zhou led a delegation for about two weeks of shuttle diplomacy in Moscow, Warsaw, and Budapest. The main purpose was to consolidate the socialist camp on a new basis. The so-called new basis referred to modification of the leadership principles in the International Communist Movement, that is, the transition from "the Soviet Union as the head" to "joint Sino-Soviet leadership." The transition was presaged by publication of a *People's Daily* editorial, "More on the Historical Experience of Proletarian Dictatorship," which was the harbinger of Zhou's visit. It would serve as the foundation for the newly emerging unity.

It was in this context that Zhou Enlai began his shuttle diplomacy. Zhou delivered a speech at Moscow airport, stating "The Soviet Union is the firmest standard-bearer of opposing war and colonialism, and a stronghold of maintaining world peace." The Soviet side accorded Zhou a grand reception. *Pravda* editorials highly praised the CCP, Sino-Soviet friendship, and the significance of Zhou's visit. The delegation remained in the USSR from 7 to 10 January.

During this visit, Zhou focused on two issues: first, the importance of supporting the Hungarian government under János Kádár; second, the importance of appealing for unity within the socialist camp. As the Yugoslav ambassador to the USSR, Veljko Mićunović, noted, "China is playing the role of intermediary and is even ready to play the part of arbiter between the USSR and the countries of Eastern Europe, primarily those with which the USSR has been in conflict."[7]

Before the October crises in Eastern Europe, it was rumored that "China, Yugoslavia, and Poland would form an anti-Soviet united front." On the eve of Zhou's visit to the USSR, the Soviet Foreign Ministry proposed to the CPSU CC: to win the understanding of the CCP, it is necessary to let Zhou Enlai know the contents of the ciphered telegrams from the Soviet embassy in Poland; to provide documents to the CCP on the Polish situation; to inform Zhou of the distortions in the Polish press about the Chinese position, in particular, on the Hungarian issue; to instruct the Soviet embassy in Poland to "establish close and direct contacts with the Chinese ambassador" in order to acquire "objective and correct intelligence on the Polish situation"; and to recommend that Konstantin Rokossovsky (a Polish-born Russian citizen and the Soviet-installed Polish defense minister before the crisis) relay the Soviet views on the crisis to Chinese ambassador to the Soviet Union Liu Xiao and Zhou Enlai. Soviet leaders were unhappy to hear Zhou's criticism. They did not contradict Zhou at the meeting, but Khrushchev privately insisted on defending the Soviet position. Mićunović suggested, "It seems as though the Russians are now in favor of recognizing the Chinese as equal partners in the leadership of the socialist camp, even if it is now to the Soviet disadvantage."[8]

Khrushchev did not understand Zhou's stratagem. Although Zhou criticized the Soviet leaders when he was in Moscow, once in Poland (from 11 to 16 January), he made efforts to speak positively about the Soviets. Zhou delivered 21 public speeches and held two private talks with Polish leader Władysław Gomułka. His visit was intended to demonstrate Chinese support for Gomułka's government and to achieve the following goals: to persuade Gomułka to improve relations with the USSR, to stand firm in his revolutionary position and show no difference with the socialist camp on the Hungarian issue, and to unite the whole party to guarantee the direction of socialist development.

When the Sino-Polish communiqué was finally issued, it represented a compromise between all parties. It advocated internationalism and opposed interference in domestic politics, highlighting a common ideology and close contacts among the USSR, China, and Poland, but it did not contain the wording "the socialist camp led by the USSR." It supported the Hungarian government led by Kádár without stating that the Hungarian crisis was a reactionary incident. The communiqué reflected the dual nature of Sino-Polish relations. Mao's basic judgment was that politically and ideologically Gomułka was a rightist and revisionist within the Communist Party and among the people, but he was also a nationalist and he was opposed to Soviet big-party and big-nation chauvinism in foreign policy. Therefore, Gomułka was Mao's target of attack within the CCP's ideological framework and within the party's political indoctrination. Nonetheless, Poland was China's indispensable ally in foreign relations.

The Hungarian government extended an invitation to Zhou Enlai on 30 December 1956. The Chinese did not reply directly, but in response, they invited Hungarian leaders to Moscow for face-to-face talks. At the tripartite talks in Moscow on 8 January 1957, Zhou decided to visit Hungary for one day, as proposed by Khrushchev and at the invitation of János Kádár and Hungarian Minister of State György Marosán. Aside from economic assistance, China and the USSR agreed on the Hungarian issue and fully supported János Kádár's government. Thus, there were no substantive political issues to discuss between the Chinese and the Hungarians.[9] But the significance of Zhou's visit was the fact that Chinese leaders actually appeared in Budapest. As Minister of State Marosán pointed out, this was "invaluable."

The minutes of the talks between Zhou and Kádár indicate that Sino-Hungarian discussions were much more cordial than Sino-Soviet or Sino-Polish discussions. The two sides agreed on almost all issues. On 17 January, Zhou left Budapest for a final three-day stay in Moscow.

Once in Moscow, Zhou gave an account of his travels through Eastern Europe. Due to his visit, he was well acquainted with the political situation in Eastern Europe. Zhou made a concerted effort to influence the CPSU's position. At a meeting on the morning of 18 January, Zhou began to censure the CPSU, thereby annoying Khrushchev. On the Stalin issue, Zhou criticized the CPSU for three reasons. First, the CPSU had failed to offer a comprehensive analysis of the issue; second, the current leaders had not taken personal responsibility for Stalin's mistakes; and third, the CPSU leadership had failed to coordinate with the fraternal parties to handle the issue. Zhou said that the CPSU was bold to expose Stalin, but it could have done a better job, arguing that the current Soviet leaders should not shift all responsibility to Stalin. In Khrushchev's response, he stated that the CCP and the CPSU agreed on Stalin's achievements, but Khrushchev had not elaborated on this in his secret speech. At the time, he believed it was not necessary to consult the fraternal parties on the Stalin issue. Zhou pointed out that the Soviets had interfered in the internal affairs of Poland by moving their troops closer to Warsaw. Khrushchev admitted that this should not have happened, but he denied that it was a mistake. On Soviet-Polish relations, Zhou argued that the Polish people were unwilling to accept the "the Soviet Union as the head because of national disaffection in history mixed with present issues," and Gomułka was trying his best to improve Polish-Hungarian relations. Khrushchev claimed that the Polish people were generally pro-Soviet, and only "certain bad elements" were opposed to the Soviet Union. He denied the accusation of Soviet big-nation chauvinism. Zhou felt that the basic problem of the Soviet leadership was its inclination to always put Soviet interests first. Soviet leaders routinely overstepped their bounds and adopted shortsighted policies. Since they were unsure of their position in the International Communist Movement, they resorted to political and military intimidation to retain control of the socialist bloc. They admitted their mistakes only because circumstances compelled them to do so. But they were not completely convinced that they had made any errors, even though they admitted their mistakes. Most importantly, they did not learn from their mistakes or modify their policies when needed. Thus, it would be necessary to change them with "long-term and patient efforts."[10] Khrushchev was very much offended. He told Mikhail Suslov, a senior member of the CPSU Secretariat and a well-known Marxist ideologue, "Zhou Enlai criticizes us, but we will not accept his lectures!"[11] Reporting to Mao, Mao advised Zhou, "You have tried. If they do not listen, don't mention it again."

Soviet unhappiness with Zhou's lecture was evident at his farewell on the afternoon of 18 January. The atmosphere was rather cool. There were no repeated toasts or rounds of thunderous applause. Bulganin and Zhou Enlai "exchanged conventional toasts." Khrushchev did not say a word. All present felt the tensions. Puzzled Western diplomats did not understand what had occurred,[12] but it was obvious to them that Khrushchev was unhappy. Soviet leaders worded the text of their radio announcement on the joint declaration to their advantage, thus reinforcing the Chinese belief that the new Soviet leaders were intolerant and lacked courage. The Soviet broadcast, in Russian, about the Sino-Soviet joint declaration had been confirmed in advance by the two sides, but the Soviets did not adhere to the agreed-upon text. The most important Soviet change was a different interpretation of intra-bloc relations, deleting the wording "not completely normal."[13]

MAO'S STRONG SUPPORT FOR KHRUSHCHEV

Just as the crisis in Eastern Europe was ending, a much stormier political crisis erupted in the USSR. Once again, Mao provided Khrushchev timely help.

After the Twentieth CPSU Congress, two factions gradually emerged in Soviet leadership circles. Vyacheslav Molotov, Lazar Kaganovich, Kliment Voroshilov, and Georgii Malenkov, who enjoyed a majority in the Presidium, formed an alliance in opposition to Khrushchev. At the 18 June 1957 Presidium meeting, based on a vote of seven to four, the majority harshly criticized Khrushchev and dismissed him from his position of first party secretary. Confronted by this surprise attack, Khrushchev and his supporters, in particular, Suslov and Mikoyan, adopted a dilatory strategy. At the next day's Presidium meeting, Khrushchev delivered a lengthy speech, offering a stern self-criticism. But he secretly asked Defense Minister Georgii Zhukov and KGB Chairman Ivan Serov to move about 200 carefully selected CC members to Moscow on military aircraft. During the eight-day special CC plenary session starting on 22 June, Khrushchev regained the initiative. The CC meeting passed the "Resolution on the Malenkov, Kaganovich, and Molotov Anti-Party Group," expelling them from the CC.

Although Khrushchev was the winner, he was then confronted with great pressure from both within and outside the party. At grassroots-level meetings discussing the CC resolution, the participants were very emotional. Although the majority expressed support for the resolution, many still raised doubts. Khrushchev was aware that he needed the support of other Communist parties, especially the CCP and Mao, in order to consolidate the power of the new CPSU leadership group within the socialist bloc. After the CPSU CC meeting, the USSR immediately briefed the ambassadors from the other socialist countries, especially the personnel at the Chinese embassy. At the same time, the Soviet embassy in China phoned the General Office of the CCP CC, requesting an urgent audience with Mao Zedong. Liu Shaoqi met with Soviet chargé d'affaires Petr Abrasimov in Zhongnanhai, stating that Mao was out of town, but he would still receive a report. Liu reported this development to Mao in the early morning of 3 July. Liu asked if it was possible to leniently treat those old comrades who had made mistakes. On 4 July, *Pravda* published the CPSU CC plenary session resolution and the press communiqué as well as open statements by some socialist parties supporting the resolution. But the majority of the Communist parties, including China, remained silent. At a reception that night, the editor-in-chief of *Pravda* probed Chinese reporters about the reaction in Chinese newspapers. Indeed, China's reaction proved decisive. This can be confirmed from what Chinese students in Moscow had to say. "If Mao Zedong makes no comment, we won't either. Only what Mao Zedong has to say is correct." But Moscow knew nothing about the CCP's views.

Khrushchev was so anxious that he immediately sent Mikoyan to China to seek Mao's opinion. In fact, the CCP CC was concerned as well. On the night of 4 July, a Politburo meeting was in session to study the issue. Although details of the meeting remain unknown, according to Xiao Xiangrong, director of the General Office of the CCP Central Military Commission (CMC), who "relayed the basic principles of the CC" on the following day, "Based on the facts and the right and wrong views of the opposing factions, [the CCP] has decided to support the new CPSU leadership." In the evening of 5 July, Mao met with Mikoyan for eight hours in Hangzhou. After a detailed briefing from Mikoyan, Mao expressed his views: Molotov was attempting to destroy the party leadership due to his psychological state. The handling of the incident by the CPSU was correct, which consolidated party leadership. Some members of the CCP, who previously argued that Molotov and his associates should be allowed to remain in the CPSU CC, changed their minds. Mao pointed out, "[We] should learn a lesson from 'Stalin's purge' in the 1930s, and we should not place too much responsibility on individuals. Solidarity is important."[14] Mao concluded by saying that to some extent the incident had been shocking to the CCP. But the Politburo meeting decided to issue a public statement in support of the CPSU CC resolution.

At a CPSU Presidium meeting, Mikoyan reported that initially the CCP was opposed to expelling Molotov and his associates from the CC, but it eventually agreed. Mikoyan concluded that "our Chinese friends are satisfied with the CPSU CC resolution. … This is very good." The Presidium thus agreed that Mikoyan's mission to China "was useful and necessary." Soon thereafter the

USSR began long-delayed bilateral talks with China on providing nuclear-technology assistance to China and on 15 October signed the "Agreement on New National Defense Technology," symbolizing the beginning of Soviet nuclear-technology assistance to China, and leading to a new stage in Sino-Soviet relations.[15]

Only about four months after "the anti-party incident," another political earthquake occurred within Soviet leadership circles. On 26 October, Khrushchev dismissed Marshal Georgii Zhukov as defense minister. According to newly declassified Russian sources, this was a well-conceived political maneuver by Khrushchev. During the "anti-party" incident in June, utilizing his immense prestige in the army, Zhukov had saved Khrushchev from political demise. But during the incident, Zhukov was reported to have said that, if necessary, he "would call in the army and the people to settle accounts with" the Malenkov-Kaganovich-Molotov group. Khrushchev was thus concerned about the threat that Zhukov might pose to him in the future. Beginning in August, Khrushchev started to plot against Zhukov. He secretly spread rumors and ordered the Presidium, Secretariat, and military officials to collect anti-Zhukov documents. He then sent Zhukov on a 20-day trip to Yugoslavia and Albania. Meeting from 17 to 19 October, the Presidium adopted a resolution on improving political work in the army, and Zhukov's "crime" was described as his attempt to weaken political work in the army and to use the army to intimidate the party. On 22 and 23 October, all Presidium members and high-ranking officers and political commissars in the army were present at a meeting of party activists organized by the Defense Department and Moscow Military District. Zhukov was unaware of these events. After his 20-day visit, Zhukov returned to Moscow at 2:00 p.m. on 26 October. He was driven from the airport to a Presidium meeting. After Zhukov reported on his Balkan trip, the meeting began to criticize his negligence of political work and party leadership in the army. The meeting adopted a resolution that replaced Zhukov with Marshal Rodion Malinovsky as defense minister.[16]

Zhukov was a renowned Soviet general, who enjoyed immense prestige in the army. He was Khrushchev's "savior" during the June incident, and he had recently been elected as a full member of the CPSU Presidium. He had also been awarded a fourth gold medal for Soviet heroes. Thus, his political downfall was difficult to comprehend. Many interpreted his removal as "preparation for his appointment as prime minister in place of Bulganin, who had compromised himself" in the June incident.[17]

Khrushchev was uncertain about this political change. To allay the fuss about such a sudden development, he needed support not only from within the CPSU and the USSR but also from the socialist camp, especially China. Immediately after the CC plenum, the Chinese embassy received a circular from Mikoyan. Mao was quick to respond. He summoned Ambassador Yudin and told him that he was very satisfied with the CPSU's decision to remove Zhukov. Mao said that the CPSU CC had made an important decision, preventing any potential danger that the army would disobey the party. Mao reiterated that he believed that the CPSU resolution on strengthening the role of party organizations in the army and strengthening the absolute obedience of the army to the party was of great significance. Khrushchev was very pleased with Mao's response.

Mao gave Khrushchev timely help, and Khrushchev responded in kind. The Sino-Soviet relationship existed in a cordial status of mutual assistance. Under these circumstances, co-sponsored by the CCP and the CPSU, the Conference of World Communist and Workers' Parties was held in Moscow.

CONCLUSION

Why did Mao, having opposed Soviet armed intervention in Poland, ask Khrushchev to reverse his decision not to send troops into Hungary?[18] In the case of Poland, the goal of both Mao and the CCP CC was to resist Soviet "great-power chauvinism," whereas in the case of Hungary, the goal was the survival of socialism. The key to Mao's shift lies in his interpretation of the events. Mao often talked about the need to "distinguish between enemies and friends." He interpreted the outburst of violence in Budapest, especially the murder of many Communists, as a counter revolutionary incident; that the Nagy government was unable to restore order and was conniving with the demonstrators proved to Mao that Hungary was no longer a socialist country. But the Chinese misinterpreted these events: Nagy's government, however shortsighted and ineffective, never betrayed socialism. Its decision to leave the Warsaw Pact was largely a result of the Soviet armed intervention.

Regarding China's role in the Soviet handling of the Polish and Hungarian crises, we can conclude that the decisions to forgo armed intervention in Poland and to dispatch troops to Hungary on 24 October were taken only by the Soviets. Yet China influenced the subsequent decisions to withdraw the Soviet troops from Budapest and to send them back on 31 October. The CPSU Presidium on 30 October was undecided about whether to take political or military steps in Hungary. At this critical juncture, Mao offered his opinion. Given the choice between withdrawal and intervention, Mao, who leaned toward intervention, preferred to leave the decision to the Soviets. According to Aleksandr Stykalin, before the Presidium meeting of 31 October, the Chinese had notified the Soviets that a meeting of the CCP CC Politburo on 30 October "had pointed to the danger of 'capitalist restoration' in Hungary and it had resolutely opposed the withdrawal of Soviet forces."[19] If Mao had proposed that the Soviets should not send troops to Hungary, or had objected to Soviet armed intervention, as he had in the case of Poland, Khrushchev was unlikely to have ignored his advice. But Mao was the first to openly support armed intervention. This led to renewed discussions at the meeting of the CPSU Presidium on 31 October and to the decision to resolve the Hungarian crisis by force. Thus, China's influence and prestige steadily grew in the USSR and the Eastern European countries after the Polish and Hungarian crises.[20]

Zhou Enlai's shuttle diplomacy seems to have achieved a certain degree of success because it restored some of the shattered unity among the socialist countries and strengthened the socialist bloc for a brief period after the Polish and Hungarian crises (at least up to the Moscow Conference in November 1957). The Western European countries generally believed that Zhou's trip strengthened the socialist bloc led by the USSR and enhanced Sino-Soviet unity. It also helped stabilize the central leadership of the CPSU. Poland remained in the socialist camp and Hungary's revolutionary stance was further confirmed. The conflicts among the members in the socialist bloc had abated.

Zhou's visit also elevated China's influence in the socialist camp.[21] A study by the Central Intelligence Agency (CIA) Sino-Soviet Studies Group notes, "In Soviet slogans since October 1957, only China has been differentiated as to status. China comes first, followed by the other Communist countries in Russian alphabetical order."[22] The CCP attained equal prestige with the CPSU and was a model for other countries. After Zhou's visit, it seemed that China had achieved a leadership role equal to that of the USSR in the socialist camp. As CIA intelligence evaluated, "This intervention marked the coming of age of another colossus—foreshadowed by its 'victory' in the Korean War—and established Mao as the only living exemplar of continuous, successful socialist revolution."[23]

For a short while, two parallel leadership centers coexisted in the International Communist Movement. This new leadership system was further strengthened during Zhou's visit, reaching a peak during the Moscow Conference of World Communist and Workers' Parties in November 1957.

NOTES

1. For an insightful study on Poland in 1956 and East Asia, see Malgorzata K. Gnoinska, "Poland and the Cold War in East and Southeast Asia, 1949–1965," Ph.D. dissertation, George Washington University, 2009, chap. 4.

2. Mercy A. Kuo, *Contending with Contradictions: China's Policy toward Soviet Eastern Europe and the Origins of the Sino-Soviet Split, 1953–1960* (Lanham, MD: Lexington Books, 2001), p. 93; Chen Jian, *Mao's China and the Cold War* (Chapel Hill: University of North Carolina Press, 2001), pp. 146–47.

3. János Radványi, "The Hungarian Revolution and the Hundred Flowers Campaign," *The China Quarterly*, no. 43 (July–Sept. 1970), p. 122.

4. During the Sino-Soviet polemics, the CCP CC accused the Soviet leaders of "adopting a policy of capitulationism at the critical moment when reactionary rebels occupied Budapest and were attempting to abandon socialist Hungary to the reactionaries." Many Chinese scholars still hold this obviously mistaken view.

5. Nikita Khrushchev, *Khrushchev Remembers: The Last Testament*, tr. Strobe Talbott (Boston: Little, Brown, 1974), pp. 418–19.

6. For a comprehensive study of China's role during the Hungarian crisis, see Shen and Xia, *Mao and the Sino-Soviet Partnership*, pp. 168–79.

7. Veljko Mićunović, *Moscow Diary: A Revealing Memoir about the Communist World When Khrushchev Ruled*, tr. David Floyd (Garden City, NY: Doubleday, 1980), p. 189.

8. Ibid., p. 187.
9. One example might help to explain this point: prior to Zhou Enlai's visit to Hungary, Hungary had already drafted a joint communiqué on the talks.
10. Interview with Li Yueran, October 2001 (Li Yueran was a Russian-language interpreter for the CCP CC from 1957 to 1965).
11. Lüthi, *The Sino-Soviet Split*, p. 67.
12. Micunovic, *Moscow Diary*, p. 197.
13. For Zhou Enlai's shuttle diplomacy in early 1957, see Shen and Xia, *Mao and the Sino-Soviet Partnership*, pp. 179–88.
14. Mao was also very worried about a coup in his own court. Thus, he decided to publicly support the CPSU CC resolution. But privately he "believed the Soviet leader had gone too far in purging old party members who had participated in the October Revolution." See Lüthi, *The Sino-Soviet Split*, pp. 73–74.
15. For Soviet aid and restrictions on China's nuclear-weapons program, see Shen and Xia, *Mao and the Sino-Soviet Partnership*, pp. 205–40.
16. At the CC plenum on 28–29 October, Zhukov was relieved of his position on the CPSU CC Presidium.
17. Mićunović, *Moscow Diary*, p. 308.
18. Edward Crankshaw, *The New Cold War* (Baltimore: Penguin Books, 1963), p. 54.
19. See Alexander Stykalin, "The Hungarian Crisis of 1956: The Soviet Role in the Light of New Archival Documents," *Cold War History*, vol. 2, no. 1 (October 2001), p. 137.
20. See Dandan Zhu, *1956: Mao's China and the Hungarian Crisis* (Ithaca, NY: East Asian Program, Cornell University, 2013), esp. pp. 2–3; Dandan Zhu, "The Hungarian Revolution and the Origins of China's Great Leap Politics, 1956–1957," *Cold War History*, vol. 12, no. 3 (2012), pp. 451–72.
21. While we agree with Mercy A. Kuo that "Zhou possessed the political weight to strengthen Chinese influence and propound PRC policy in Eastern Europe," we feel that her assertion that "Zhou's attempt to establish a new paradigm in intra-bloc relations changed the direction and makeup of bloc relations" is overstated. See Kuo, *Contending with Contradictions*, p. 116. We argue that Zhou's achievements were limited and brief.
22. "Soviet Positions on the 'Transition to Communism'—Prior to the Chinese Commune Program, 28 August 1959," Current Intelligence Staff Study, ESAU Documents, IV-59, at https://www.cia.gov/library/readingroom/docs/esau-04.pdf
23. "CIA Senior Research Staff on International Communism, A New Program for International Communism: The Statement of the Moscow Conference of Representatives of Communist and Workers' Parties (December 1960)," 17 February 1961, CIA/SRS-15, https://www.cia.gov/library/readingroom/docs/DOC_0000246535.pdf

CHAPTER 13

Mao, Khrushchev, and the Moscow Conference, 1957

Zhihua Shen

In November 1957, delegates from 64 of the world's Communist parties gathered in Moscow for the largest such gathering ever held. Twelve ruling Communist parties issued a declaration at the end of the meeting, and all 64 parties endorsed a "Peace Manifesto."[1] Scholars have generally assumed that the conference was initiated by the Communist Party of the Soviet Union (CPSU) and supported by the other Communist parties, including the Chinese Communist Party (CCP).[2] But newly declassified archival records and memoirs indicate that the idea of convening the meeting and issuing a joint declaration was proposed by People's Republic of China (PRC) leaders. Moreover, at the preparatory stage and during the conference, Mao Zedong played a vital, indeed indispensable, role.

This chapter examines the preparations for and actual convening of the conference. At the 1957 Moscow Conference, the CCP was on an equal footing with the CPSU, co-leaders of the socialist camp. The Sino-Soviet alliance reached its peak at the end of 1957, and the conference was seen as a prime example of Sino-Soviet collaboration.[3] Shortly after the conference, a rift in the Sino-Soviet alliance emerged and quickly deepened. The main point of contention was over each side's interpretation of the declaration that had been adopted at the conference. Each side accused the other of betraying the Moscow Declaration. Therefore, the Moscow Conference turned out to be a turning point in Sino-Soviet relations.

Z. Shen (✉)
East China Normal University, Shanghai, China
e-mail: zhaoran@ssap.cn

© The Author(s) 2020
Z. Shen (ed.), *A Short History of Sino-Soviet Relations, 1917–1991*,
China Connections, https://doi.org/10.1007/978-981-13-8641-1_13

THE IMPETUS FOR THE CONFERENCE

The dissolution of the Soviet-dominated Communist International (Comintern) in May 1943 was primarily a cosmetic gesture, but it presaged two important changes. First, to bolster the wartime alliance with Great Britain and the United States, Soviet leader Joseph Stalin formally moved away from the strategy of "world revolution." Second, for several years, the world's Communist parties were no longer grouped within a unitary international organization under strict Soviet control. Not until 1947, amid escalating Cold War tensions, did Stalin reestablish a Communist Information Bureau (Cominform) to bind the Communist parties. Unlike the Comintern, however, the Cominform was not comprehensive, consisting of only nine European Communist parties. Moreover, the Cominform lost most of its effectiveness after Stalin broke with Tito and used it to oppose Yugoslavia. By 1952, on the eve of Stalin's death, the Cominform ceased to be an active organization.[4]

Khrushchev's secret speech denouncing Stalin at the Twentieth CPSU Congress in February 1956 held out the prospect of more solid relations among the Communist parties, but, as Mao put it, the speech also "created serious cracks," causing ideological turbulence and organizational disorder in the socialist camp. In both Moscow and Beijing, party leaders were thinking about how to stabilize the situation.

At one time, Mao was interested in the Cominform. When the CCP looked to the Union of Soviet Socialist Republics (USSR) for support during the 1947–49 Chinese civil war, Mao was so enthusiastic about the idea of the Cominform that Soviet leaders believed he was looking to establish a "Cominform in the East." In the spring of 1949, the Communist parties in Burma, Malaya, and Indonesia wrote to the CCP proposing the establishment of a "Cominform in the East," but Mao rejected the proposal because of the ongoing civil war in China. During his visit to the Soviet Union in 1949, Liu Shaoqi suggested that the victorious CCP could join the Cominform, but Stalin replied that such a step was "utterly unnecessary." The Soviet leader claimed that the situation in the East Asian countries was similar to that in China and the CCP instead should consider the establishment of a "coalition of East Asian Communist parties."[5] The outbreak of the Korean War forestalled any move in this direction, and Stalin's death put a de facto end to the Cominform. In 1955, both the USSR and the PRC established formal diplomatic relations with Yugoslavia. Under such circumstances, proposals to set up Comintern-like organizations seemed inappropriate, even on a regional basis. Hence, the CCP rejected the Soviet suggestion.

In April 1956, Mikoyan visited Beijing after his trip to India and Burma. He told Mao that the CPSU hoped that the Communist countries would jointly publish a journal and establish a liaison bureau. But Mao argued against any effort to revive the Cominform: "If we are going to set up a liaison bureau now, it will create fear in the Western countries as well as in countries like India." Mao suggested that instead they "convene a conference to settle issues." The USSR, he added, should host such a meeting: "You convene the conference, and we'll come. A conference can be held as the issues are emerging." The holding of such a conference, Mao contended, would be more effective than establishing organizations and publishing magazines. The lack of Chinese support for a liaison bureau and joint publications essentially doomed Mikoyan's proposal.

Despite these disagreements, Chinese and Soviet leaders agreed on the desirability of formally dissolving the Cominform. On 13 April 1956, the CPSU issued a circular on this issue to all Communist parties, and on 18 April, *Pravda* published a statement indicating that the Cominform and its activities were no longer needed. The organization would be disbanded, and its official journal, *To Strive for Permanent Peace, To Strive for People's Democracy!* would cease publication. The circular stressed, however, that the CPSU and the other Communist parties "will be able to find a new and effective method to coordinate contacts." *People's Daily* immediately published this announcement.

To provide for continued contacts in the wake of the Cominform's dissolution, the CPSU proposed that party leaders "should resolve the issue of the method of contacts among the Communist parties of the socialist countries at a forthcoming meeting." At a session of the Political Consultative Committee of the newly formed Warsaw Treaty Organization, held in Moscow on 22–26 June 1956, Soviet and East European officials further discussed the matter. On 30 June, the CPSU Presidium adopted a "draft resolution on the personality cult and its consequences," attempting to contain the ferment generated by de-Stalinization. With the same goal in mind, Soviet leaders stressed the importance of forging closer ties among Communist parties: "Under the new historical circumstances, international organizations of the working class such as the Comintern and the Cominform have ceased operations. But this does not in the least mean it is no longer important [to maintain] internationalist solidarity and contacts among revolutionary fraternal parties which espouse Marxist-Leninist positions. ... Marxist parties of the working class must, naturally, maintain and strengthen their ideological unity and internationalist fraternal unity." The CPSU and the CCP agreed on this issue, and other Communist parties endorsed their view. General Secretary of the French Communist Party (PCF), Maurice Thorez, indicated in his political report at the Fourteenth PCF Congress that despite the importance of national characteristics, Communist parties must work together to strengthen "the international workers' movement and the solidarity of all Communist parties." Nonetheless, the outbreak of the Polish and Hungarian crises in 1956 temporarily prevented any follow-up.

MAO'S INITIATIVE AND KHRUSHCHEV'S CONSENT

After the upheavals in Poland and Hungary, leaders in both Moscow and Beijing saw an even greater need to strengthen solidarity in the socialist camp. China's role during the crises in Poland and Hungary remains a matter of scholarly dispute, but there is little doubt that Mao and other CCP leaders were worried about the unrest. In the wake of these events, Mao once again decided to promote the convening of a conference of world Communist parties. Soviet leaders, however, were less enthusiastic about such a conference. Zhou Enlai continued to "exchange views with" the CPSU, but he also privately encouraged the League of Communists of Yugoslavia (LCY) to be one of the conveners of the conference.

From Moscow's perspective, the CCP and the LCY were the two most important parties in the socialist bloc after the CPSU. If they were more or less in agreement, the CPSU was ready to accept such a proposal.[6] When the CPSU Presidium discussed the issue on 2 February 1957, Khrushchev mentioned the LCY's reluctance, and he said that the CPSU should not seem unduly enthusiastic when notifying other parties about the conference. The CPSU might initiate bilateral consultations with other parties and consult with the CCP regarding the timing. The CPSU Presidium authorized Politburo member Mikhail Suslov and Foreign Minister Dmitri Shepilov to draft a letter to the CCP. On 7 February, the CPSU Presidium approved a letter to the CCP, agreeing to Mao's proposal for a world Communist conference. The letter indicated that the CCP should prepare to chair the conference and to consult with the CPSU about preparations for a gathering in late March or early April 1957.

Chinese leaders were caught off guard when the CPSU suggested that the CCP should convene the conference. Leaders in Moscow were not aware that the CCP had proposed that the CCP and LCY be joint conveners. The letter from the CPSU Presidium said that "according to the known agreement," the CCP should oversee the preparatory work. Wang Jiaxiang, the head of the CCP's International Liaison Department, sought clarification. Chinese officials concluded that the telephone conversation between Zhou in Moscow and Peng Dehuai in Beijing had been bugged. Mao felt that under the circumstances, the CCP would have to decline. In response, the CCP stated that China was not prepared to sponsor the conference, and the conference should be convened by the CPSU. The Chinese also stressed that such a conference should be carefully organized and must not be rushed.

About four months later, the CPSU once again urged the CCP to agree to a conference of world Communist parties. The CPSU proposed holding a secret meeting in July and recommended that no formal agenda be set in advance so that the participants could decide on the procedures for the conference, as was preferred by the LCY. The CCP agreed but suggested that prior consultations be held to learn the views of the other parties. The Chinese wanted the final declaration only to include points that were unanimously accepted. Because the final document would be politicized throughout the world, the CCP proposed circulating a draft document before the conference so that it could be revised and agreed upon. Such preparations would take longer and would be more troublesome, but the CCP believed the extra effort would be worthwhile.

In addition to the extra time required for preparations, the proposal was delayed by the latest round of internal political maneuvering in Moscow. In his struggle against the "Malenkov, Kaganovich, and Molotov Anti-party Group," in summer 1957 Mao provided Khrushchev with timely help, much to the latter's relief. Khrushchev realized that he could not delay a world Communist conference any longer if he wanted to retain the support of the CCP. On 9 July, Soviet chargé d'affaires, Petr Abrasimov, again met with Liu Shaoqi, relaying the CPSU's proposal for a conference of ruling Communist parties to be held in the near future. Liu replied on behalf of the CCP that it was necessary to reach a consensus about such a conference, to consult with the other ruling parties in advance, and to come up with a mutually agreed-upon document. Khrushchev was reassured, and the CPSU began actively preparing for the conference.

Soviet-Yugoslav relations had been strained by the Polish and Hungarian crises. To gauge Tito's view of the proposal for a world Communist conference, the CPSU sent a high-level delegation to Yugoslavia. On 18 August 1957, the two CPSU officials who oversaw relations with foreign Communist parties—Boris Ponomarev and Yuri Andropov—sent a cable from Belgrade, indicating that they had spoken with Edvard Kardelj, Aleksandar Ranković, and other top Yugoslav officials. The LCY Executive Committee had decided not to attend the conference or to sign any joint declaration, ostensibly because doing so would complicate the international situation for Yugoslavia. The CPSU Presidium met the same day and decided to send the draft declaration to former member states of the Cominform and, in particular, to ask the Soviet ambassador in Poland to report to Polish leader Władysław Gomułka. The CPSU Presidium also decided that if all these parties consented, the conference would be held even if the LCY did not attend. On the next day, Soviet leaders sent a formal invitation to Mao to visit the USSR to take part in the 40th anniversary celebration of the Bolshevik Revolution and to attend the international conference of Communist parties. Soviet leaders assured Mao that the CPSU would send all the conference documents to the CCP for comment. Mao gladly accepted the invitation. In early September 1957, the CCP announced that Mao would lead the Chinese delegation to Moscow. This announcement was intended to signal that important meetings would be held during the celebration and that the CCP hoped all parties would "send their top people to Moscow."[7] On 6 and 10 October, enlarged meetings of the CCP Politburo discussed the forthcoming Chinese delegation to Moscow.

On 22 October, Zhou Enlai gave the Soviet embassy in Beijing a list of CCP officials who would take part in the Moscow Conference and the dates of their travel. The main issue that still needed to be resolved was the draft declaration, which had not yet been confirmed by the CCP. It was not until 28 October that the Soviet ambassador, Pavel Yudin, transmitted Khrushchev's private invitation to Mao Zedong and the draft declaration to the CCP. Yudin said that the draft declaration had been sent to the LCY for advice but that the LCY leaders had refused to accept it. The CCP General Office arranged to have the draft declaration translated into Chinese and distributed to CCP experts. One of those who reviewed it, Hu Qiaomu, said that it had to be revised.[8]

On the evening of 29 October, Mao met with Yudin and reported that the CCP Politburo had carefully discussed the Moscow Conference documents sent by the CPSU. He said that the draft required extensive editing, but that the main content could be retained. Regarding the transition to socialism in some capitalist countries, Mao argued that the declaration should mention two possibilities: peaceful and non-peaceful transition. Regarding the social democratic parties, Mao wanted to raise the issue in a more categorical way. "Not only should we stress the issue of uniting with the right-wing socialist parties, we should also find wording to include capitalist democratic forces and progressive forces as well as socialist parties." Referring to the Anti-party Group, Mao hoped that their names would not be singled out in the declaration. Finally, Mao said that the CCP could see three options if Yugoslavia or Poland (or both) refused to sign the declaration. One option would be to adopt the declaration even if one or two delegations opposed it. Mao preferred to issue a declaration, and he said that the abstention of one or two parties would not cause "great chaos under heaven." A second option would be to issue a brief communiqué mentioning only those issues that could be accepted unanimously. A third option would be to issue a joint CCP-CPSU statement. Mao asked Yudin to relay his views to Khrushchev and the CPSU Presidium.

On 30 October, Liu Shaoqi chaired a CCP Politburo meeting that reviewed the draft declaration. The assembled officials believed that Mao should go to Moscow earlier than planned and bring with him a document for the Soviet side to review. The CCP Politburo also approved a Standing Committee resolution, establishing the principles for the CCP delegation. On 2 November, the CPSU Presidium discussed Yudin's summary of his talks with Mao. The Presidium favored Mao's first option rather than the option of a brief communiqué. Even if the LCY would not sign the declaration, the conference could still issue a comprehensive declaration, perhaps combined with a joint Sino-Soviet statement. The CPSU Presidium directed Mikhail Suslov to oversee revisions to the document and to take into account the CCP's views. Suslov was supposed to transmit the revised document to the Presidium as soon as possible. The need for prompt action was underscored later in the day when a large Chinese delegation led by Mao arrived in Moscow.

Mao's Efforts to Ensure a Successful Conference

Both the CCP and the CPSU believed that a world Communist conference would strengthen unity in the socialist camp. The CCP Politburo, at its meeting on 30 October, unanimously endorsed Mao's goal of using the Moscow Conference as a display of unity. The guiding principle for the Chinese delegation was "first to protect the CPSU but second to criticize it." Chinese leaders wanted "to seek unity through struggle, to reach unanimity through consultation, and to seek common ground while preserving differences." The CCP's emphasis on unity meant that the Chinese leaders had to handle CCP-CPSU relations well in order to avoid inflaming Soviet-Polish relations and to mediate Yugoslavia's relations with the socialist camp. Three key issues shaped Beijing's relations with Moscow: first, Sino-Soviet disagreements about the viability of a peaceful transition to socialism; second, the Polish leaders' reluctance to endorse the description of the USSR as the "leader" of the Communist world; and third, the LCY's refusal to attend the conference and to sign the declaration.[9] The trick was to produce a declaration that would be acceptable to all sides.

The drafting of a broadly acceptable declaration dominated the proceedings of the conference. After the Chinese delegation arrived in Moscow, Khrushchev met with Mao, who said, "I have come earlier than planned to come up with a good declaration. We have prepared a draft for your reference." On 3 November, the CCP and the CPSU started to discuss the proposed declaration. Mao stressed the importance of discussing the document with everyone. "It is only a formality to convene a conference," he added. Khrushchev said that all the parties had agreed to adopt a declaration and that Polish leader Władysław Gomułka was willing to sign it. Khrushchev also noted that the Soviet draft was being revised to consider the CCP's advice, including the point about not mentioning Malenkov, Kaganovich, and Molotov. Mao responded that the Chinese side agreed with more than 90 percent of the original Soviet document, and he suggested that the CCP and CPSU should jointly revise the declaration.

After the CCP and CPSU delegations worked on revising the draft for about a week, on 11 November, the CCP Politburo approved the draft declaration and authorized the delegation to prepare a final version. On 12 November, the CPSU Presidium approved the draft declaration and instructed Suslov to discuss a final version with the CCP. Meanwhile, the CPSU and the CCP agreed that the delegations from the capitalist countries should not attend the meeting of the ruling Communist parties on 14 November, lest they face problems when they returned home. Soviet and Chinese leaders also agreed that a meeting of all 64 Communist parties would be held after the meeting of the ruling parties. A Peace Manifesto for the latter meeting would be drafted by the CPSU and the Polish United Workers' Party.

On the question of moving from capitalism to socialism, the final draft included two major amendments based on CCP views: first, while mentioning the possibility of a peaceful road to power (the word "transition" was not used), it also affirmed the possibility of a non-peaceful road, stressing that the nature of "the road to socialism in each individual country depends on actual historical circumstances." Second, although the draft referred to parliamentary politics, it also emphasized the desirability of a broad mass struggle that would destroy reactionary resistance and create the essential conditions for achieving a socialist revolution. The CCP sent its secret memorandum only to the CPSU and did not disclose it at the plenary session. Indeed, the existence of the memorandum did not become public until the 1963 Sino-Soviet polemics. However, the content of the memorandum did not differ from the declaration, except for the addition of two points: first, the possibility of a peaceful transition should not be overemphasized, and, second, despite the benefits of a united front with the left-wing socialists, Communists "must not blur the principled boundary with the socialist parties over the issue of a socialist revolution."

The main reason for the CCP's insistence on a different view was to empha-size its own experience in seizing power through violent means and revolution-ary struggle. In contrast, the CPSU's formulation reflected the general line of the Twentieth CPSU Congress. CCP leaders believed that if the Soviet view was accepted at the international Communist conference, this would augur a new era in the International Communist Movement and cast doubts on the revolutionary experiences of the CCP. This was a serious sign of Sino-Soviet differences in the 1957 Moscow Declaration. On the surface, the CCP delega-tion was bickering about the wording of peaceful transition. But in fact, it was unwilling to mention the Twentieth CPSU Congress in the declaration.[10] For Sino-Soviet unity, Mao made compromises and concessions.[11] However, the quest for common ground while reserving differences sowed the seeds for the later Sino-Soviet polemics.

During the Moscow Conference, the most conspicuous issue that Mao dis-cussed both in his public speeches and in his private talks was the role of the Soviet leadership in the socialist camp. A series of events, beginning with the Twentieth CPSU Congress, had shaken the position of the CPSU. The CCP acknowledged that the USSR was the home of Vladimir Lenin, the first social-ist country, and the long-time leader of the International Communist Movement. To strengthen unity in the socialist camp, the priority was to safe-guard the prestige of the CPSU and confirm that the USSR was the "leader" of the socialist world. In his heart, Mao regarded Khrushchev as politically immature and lacking in Marxist-Leninist thinking, and he was dismayed that Khrushchev had "created serious fissures" in the International Communist Movement. But to safeguard unity in the socialist camp, Mao decided it was essential to uphold the leadership role of the USSR in the socialist camp. When discussing Sino-Soviet relations in early 1957, Mao said:

> There is no big problem in Sino-Soviet relations. Although there are some prob-lems, we are much closer now than earlier. These problems stem from historical habits and different ways of thinking and handling issues. [We should] be patient and work out our differences. [We should] talk to each other and consult with each other whenever there is an outstanding issue. It is necessary to convene meetings. The new situation will force them to change, and they have already adjusted. If they adjust gradually, we are in no hurry. We should help them. Contradictions exist, and we should seek common ground while reserving our differences. We can resolve our differences in the future.

Even when discussing the leadership of the USSR, Mao was staking out a special place for the CCP. In his defense of the prestige of the USSR, he was projecting himself as the mentor and guide of the International Communist Movement.

Although the phrase "the socialist camp under the leadership of the USSR" continued to appear in Chinese newspapers, many socialist countries had ceased using it after the Polish and Hungarian crises. Even the CPSU was considering abandoning the expression "the socialist camp led by the USSR" in order to relax tensions among the socialist countries.[12] At the behest of the CPSU Presidium, the original Soviet draft declaration deleted all references to "the socialist camp led by the USSR." Khrushchev had pointed out that the inclusion of such phrases in an international declaration might be interpreted as an effort to restore the CPSU's domination over the other Communist parties and to abandon the new type of relationship based on equality and cooperation. The CPSU was surprised to find the phrase "the USSR as the leader" in the CCP's draft declaration. Khrushchev suggested "the USSR and China as the leaders," but Mao said it would be inappropriate: "Although the relationship between fraternal parties is based on equality, we cannot claim equality with you on this issue. We are still far behind. We cannot assume responsibility if both our countries are leaders."[13]

The Polish, Yugoslav, and Italian parties objected to the phrase "the USSR as the leader." Delegates from the other parties remained silent, although some apparently agreed with the objections. Mao sought to persuade both the CPSU and the other parties to accept the phrase. Despite Mao's appeal, agreement remained elusive. After the draft declaration was handed out on 11 November, the CPSU and CCP delegations received a number of complaints, the most important of which came from the Polish delegation. An editorial committee was formed to revise the draft. The committee met for the entire day on 15 November and engaged in a heated debate. The Polish delegation continued to oppose singling out the USSR as the "leader" of the socialist world and spoke against including references to "U.S. imperialism" and "the U.S. imperialist aggression clique." During a break late in the afternoon, Deng Xiaoping reported the impasse to Mao, who decided to visit the Polish delegation for a face-to-face discussion with Gomułka.

According to the record of this meeting, Mao's attempts to persuade had some effect. But Chinese interpreter Li Yueran believed that Gomułka was extremely reluctant to accept Mao's position. Yang Shangkun, another participant in the talks with Gomułka, was more upbeat: "It has become better. The views of both sides are now closer. It might be possible to come to an agreement tomorrow." After the meeting with Gomułka, Mao met with Khrushchev and Suslov during the night to relay Gomułka's opinions and to discuss the agenda for the meeting on the following day.

The editorial committee met in the morning of 16 November to complete the drafting process. Suslov reported on the revision of the draft declaration during the afternoon's plenary session. Mao then spoke in support of the draft:

I consider our declaration to be a good one. We have used a good method to achieve our goal—the method of consultation. It is one that maintains both principle and flexibility. Indeed, it is an integration of both principle and flexibility. An atmosphere for consultation has been created, one that would not have been possible in Stalin's later years. ... This declaration is correct. It contains no element of revisionism or opportunism.

Under Mao's influence, all the assembled leaders, including Gomułka, spoke in favor of the declaration. The plenary session adopted the draft and asked the editorial committee to make one last amendment.[14] The final declaration referred to "the socialist camp led by the USSR" without mentioning the "convener of the conference"—wording that represented a compromise by all sides.

Mao's success in obtaining approval for the USSR's leadership status was mitigated somewhat by the way he stated the issue, especially in his offhand speech on 18 November. In this speech, he used a Chinese proverb to explain why every bloc needs a head: "A snake without a head cannot proceed." This figure of speech was awkward for the delegates from the Western countries, where a snake is not a propitious sign. Mao also said that the USSR, as the most powerful of the socialist countries, was the only conceivable head of the social-ist camp at the time. China, he added, was a big country politically but "small economically," and therefore, it was not qualified to be the leader. But he then invoked another Chinese proverb to stress that the USSR would need help: "An able fellow needs the help of three others, a fence needs the support of three stakes. You, Comrade Khrushchev, even though you are a beautiful lotus, you, too, need the leaves to set you off." According to this logic, the USSR was the head because it alone could assume responsibility, but once China's econ-omy developed, China could be the head of the socialist camp. Two years later, when Soviet and Chinese leaders quarreled, Khrushchev protested: "Only you can accuse us, but we are not even allowed to criticize you. Although you talk about 'the socialist camp under the leadership of the USSR,' you in fact do not have the slightest respect for the opinions of the CPSU." Khrushchev later came to realize that "if all parties acknowledge one party as the head, then the head can be replaced. A head today, another head tomorrow. We believe that the Chinese are preparing to be the future head."[15]

Khrushchev's suspicions were well founded. The influence of the CCP and of Mao in the socialist bloc had been elevated since the Twentieth CPSU Congress and the Polish and Hungarian crises. Mao's advice about how to handle contradictions among the people received warm praise from the other Communist parties. Under these circumstances, CCP members increasingly came to believe that the Chinese party should replace the CPSU as leader of the socialist bloc. Mao had argued that the Chinese economy was not powerful enough, and for the time being, China could not directly assume a leadership role, but Mao was instrumental in establishing the principle that the socialist bloc should have a leader.[16]

The LCY played an influential role during the Moscow Conference, despite the delicate relationship between the LCY and the socialist camp. After Stalin's death, Khrushchev had apologized to Yugoslav leader Josip B. Tito and made efforts to improve Soviet-Yugoslav relations, encouraging other East bloc parties to do the same. Although Mao did not trust Tito and Edvard Kardelj, and he believed that Yugoslavia was still a "capitalist country," China and Yugoslavia established diplomatic relations in March 1955 and also restored ties between their Communist parties. In September 1956, the LCY sent a delegation to attend the Eighth CCP Congress. During a meeting with the Yugoslav delegation, Mao criticized Stalin's "big-nation and big-party chauvinism," claiming that Stalin treated him as a semi-Tito who was sympathetic to the LCY.

When the Yugoslav delegation led by Kardelj and Aleksandar Ranković arrived in Moscow on 5 November, the Soviet reception was low key, and at the next day's formal meeting between the CPSU and the LCY, the atmosphere was tense. Khrushchev announced that an international Communist conference would be held in Moscow, and they had already decided to issue a joint declaration, even if Yugoslavia refused to sign it. Khrushchev accused the LCY of accepting US aid, thus violating the spirit of international proletarian solidarity. He insisted that the LCY was responsible for the current tensions in Soviet-Yugoslav relations. In response, Kardelj upheld Yugoslavia's non-alliance policy and stressed that the division of the world into blocs would increase the risk of a third world war. The LCY, he said, advocated dissolution of the two opposing blocs, renunciation of war, and pursuit of peaceful coexistence. Each country, he declared, should have the right to choose its own road of social development. He argued that Yugoslavia's acceptance of US aid was the direct result of Soviet hostility. The meeting turned out to be unpleasant, as Khrushchev, with no alternative strategy, resorted to insults.[17]

Mao's attitude toward the LCY was more tolerant. He neither criticized Yugoslavia's position nor tried to pressure Kardelj to sign the declaration. Although Mao had no contacts with the Yugoslav delegation during the conference, he spoke warmly about the LCY during his extemporaneous speech on 18 November, singling out the Yugoslav delegation when speaking about unity. Mao said:

> I am also glad that the Yugoslav comrades signed the second declaration. The fact is that they signed the Peace Manifesto of the sixty-odd parties. What does this signify? It signifies unity. They did not sign the twelve-country declaration. Therefore, of the thirteen [Communist] countries, one is missing. They say they would have found it difficult. But I maintain that this is also acceptable. We cannot coerce people. If Yugoslavia is unwilling to sign it, let us leave it at that. In another couple of years, I think they will be able to sign a different declaration.

The Yugoslav delegation seemed happy. During a break, Kardelj went up to Mao and said that he was very satisfied with the Chinese comrades' understanding and he was grateful to Mao for his speech. This was one of the few positive moments for the Yugoslav delegation during the Moscow Conference, and it allowed Mao to express his views to the LCY.

In confronting other differences that arose during the Moscow Conference, the CCP consistently advocated "seeking common ground while respecting differences." For example, when the Italian party was reluctant to go along with the provision that "the main danger at present is revisionism," the CCP added the following language to the declaration: "As far as each Communist party is concerned, each has the right to identify what the main danger is at any given time." Similarly, the CPSU's insistence on starting an international Communist publication provoked opposition. The compromise was that such a publication would not be a forum for criticism of any party.[18] Mao actively assisted in the preparation of a joint document that was compatible with the goal of "seeking common ground while respecting differences."

In the end, however, the final results were unclear. The 1957 Moscow Declaration had no binding effect, and it contained many ambiguities. Thereafter, each party went its own way and cited the declaration whenever conflicts arose with other parties. The document ended up being a mere scrap of paper.

Mao's Central Role at the Moscow Conference

Mao's proposal to hold the Moscow Conference was prompted by the USSR's declining ability to impose its will on the world Communist movement in the wake of Stalin's death and the turmoil stirred up by the Twentieth CPSU Congress.[19] The CCP attached great importance to the conference and put considerable effort into it.[20]

From the outset, Mao was the most visible figure at the conference, and the CCP delegation was accorded special treatment. Khrushchev sent two senior officials—Pyotr Pospelov of the CPSU Secretariat and Deputy Foreign Minister Nikolai Fedorenko—to prepare a warm welcoming ceremony in Irkutsk, the CCP delegation's first stopping point in the USSR. But before his departure, Mao had requested that the Soviet side not arrange a large-scale welcoming ceremony in Irkutsk, saying that he and Song Qingling could not be in an open car because of the cold weather and he would wait until his arrival at Moscow airport before delivering his remarks.[21] Thus, it was not necessary to organize a welcoming ceremony while on their way to Moscow. Khrushchev acted accordingly. The reception in Irkutsk was very brief. After arriving in Moscow, Mao and his chief aides stayed at the Kremlin (with two villas on the city outskirts as backup), unlike all the other guests who stayed at villas on the outskirts of Moscow. Khrushchev told Mao that CCP leaders would be staying "very close to the meeting hall" in rooms that "connect with St. George's Hall [the meeting place] through a corridor. It is very convenient." Mao would "stay in a tsar's palace. We have chosen the best room for you."

Mao's public appearances in Moscow were followed with great interest. Yang Shangkun recalled that at the ceremony marking the October Revolution, everyone stood up to salute Mao when he walked on to the stage. Both at the beginning and the end of Mao's speeches, he received standing ovations. When delegates from other parties spoke, the audience applauded without standing up. During the celebration at Red Square, contingents of marchers called out Mao's name to show respect. After the procession, people ran up to Mao, cheering. "According to the Soviet comrades," Yang wrote, "this is unprecedented."

Mao's subsequent speech at the conference also attracted the attention of many interested parties. Each guest read aloud from a prepared text, and a Russian translation was distributed to the audience. Only Mao made three extemporaneous speeches. In particular, at the conference's plenary session on 18 November, all speakers delivered their speeches standing behind a platform. Only Mao remained seated while speaking.[22]

One of the most memorable aspects of Mao's 1957 visit to Moscow was his extemporaneous speech on 18 November during which he put forth several propositions that attracted the attention of, and in some cases baffled, the other participants.[23] Mao began his speech by proclaiming a slogan that was quickly embraced by others in the Soviet bloc: "The east wind prevails over the west wind." As he put it:

> It is my view that the international situation has now reached a new turning point. There are two winds in the world today, the east wind and the west wind. There is a Chinese saying, "Either the east wind prevails over the west wind or the west wind prevails over the east wind." It is characteristic of the situation today; I believe that the east wind is prevailing over the west wind. The forces of socialism are overwhelmingly superior to the forces of imperialism.

To bolster his case, Mao cited ten events: World War II, the Chinese Revolution, the Korean War, the Indochina War, the Suez crisis, the crisis in Syria, the launch of Sputnik 1 and 2, the British withdrawal from Asia and Africa, the Dutch withdrawal from Indonesia, and the French withdrawal from northern Africa. These events, he argued, indicated a clear trend: "Our skies are all bright, but those of the West are darkened by clouds." During private exchanges, Khrushchev repeatedly expressed his disapproval of Mao's conclusion. He believed that the USSR was temporarily ahead of the United States in terms of military and some scientific programs but that "we should not underrate the U.S. potential, especially its tremendous strength in science." Gomułka, in a conversation with Mao, noted: "After the USSR launched the two Sputniks, the capitalist countries admitted that they are behind. But it is wrong to believe that they will never achieve such feats. I believe they will soon have things such as rockets." Gomułka pointed out that the issue was "which strategy we should adopt under the current circumstances." He believed that "our policy should make the situation less sharp." In contrast, Mao's original intention of proposing "the east wind prevails over the west wind" was to stress that socialism no longer had to worry about international confrontations.

Another aspect of Mao's speech that attracted immediate attention was his discussion of the internal struggle within the CPSU. When speaking about unity, Mao inserted the following comment about the ouster of Molotov:

> I endorsed the solution of the CPSU CC on the Molotov question. That was a struggle of opposites. The facts proved that unity could not be achieved and that the two sides were mutually exclusive. The Molotov clique took the opportunity to attack at a time when Comrade Khrushchev was abroad and unprepared.

However, even though they waged a surprise attack, our Comrade Khrushchev is no fool. He is a smart person who immediately mobilized his troops and waged a victorious counterattack. That struggle was one between two lines—one erroneous line and one relatively correct line.

Mao's intention was to endorse the removal of the Anti-party Group, to support Khrushchev, and to exhort the CPSU to make allowances for previously loyal comrades who had committed mistakes. But, for two reasons, his remarks prompted negative responses: First, Mao had privately urged the CPSU not to "mention the names of Molotov and his associates," but then he publicly raised the matter. Thus, Soviet leaders were bound to question his intentions. Second, Mao depicted the anti-party affair as a "two-line struggle," a largely unfamiliar term that—at least after translation—was understood by many to refer to two cliques within the CPSU leadership.

Yet another point in Mao's speech that provoked confusion was his boasting that China would overtake Great Britain within 15 years. Speaking on 18 November, Mao declared:

> Comrade Khrushchev has told us that the USSR can overtake the United States in fifteen years. I can also tell you that in fifteen years we may have caught up with or overtaken Great Britain. After talking twice to Comrades Pollitt and Gollan and asking them about the situation in their countries, I find out that at present Great Britain produces 20 million tons of steel annually and in another fifteen years it may produce 30 million tons of steel annually. Well, what about China? In another fifteen years we might produce 40 million tons annually. Will this not amount to overtaking Great Britain?

Not many people in the audience took Mao's boasting too seriously. What did it amount to if the only measure was the production of crude steel? Khrushchev's timetable for catching up with the United States was challenged by Soviet economists and by members of the CPSU Presidium.[24] Mao's speech sounded the first clarion call for China's 1958 mass steel production movement. More importantly, behind the slogan of overtaking Great Britain and catching up with the United States, Mao was talking about surpassing the USSR. Only in this way could China assert true leadership of the socialist bloc.

The most controversial point in Mao's speech was his speculation about nuclear war and its consequences. After the CCP delegation returned to China, Khrushchev attended a reception hosted by the Chinese embassy in Moscow on 27 November and expressed dissatisfaction with Mao's remarks. According to Khrushchev's recollections, "Except for the one outburst led by [Madame] Sun Yatsen, the audience was dead silent." After the meeting, many delegates responded strongly. Antonín Novotný, the first secretary of the Communist Party of Czechoslovakia, complained: "Mao Zedong says he is prepared to lose 300 million people out of a total population of 600 million. What about us? We have only twelve million people in Czechoslovakia." Gomułka similarly "expressed his indignation in no uncertain terms."[25] Another participant,

Shmuel Mikunis, secretary general of the Israeli Communist Party, recalled that Mao's "favorite theme, to which he kept returning, was World War III. He regards this as an inevitable event, for which one must be ready at any moment. I would even go so far as to say that he lives and thinks in terms of this war, as though it has already begun."[26]

It was not difficult for Chinese officials to understand Mao's speech. But the main problem with the speech was that—because it was extemporaneous—the translation was imperfect; an unfortunate circumstance made even more so by the fact that the speech broached such a sensitive topic in the presence of European delegates. Furthermore, misunderstandings under these circumstances were inevitable. Mao purposefully used such irritating language to elaborate on his own thinking, and the European delegates did not understand Mao's philosophical approach. In fact, they took him quite literally. A day after returning to Beijing, when briefing members of the CCP Politburo Standing Committee, Mao deemed the conference to be generally successful. The 12-party declaration was a good one, he said, and everyone was satisfied. But two issues were not included in the declaration: (1) peaceful coexistence and (2) relations with the social democratic parties. Mao said that the five principles of peaceful coexistence were surely right, but the CPSU was surely wrong to regard peaceful coexistence as its overarching foreign-policy guideline. In the International Communist Movement, the general principle had to be more than peaceful coexistence. It had to include providing support to world revolution and proletarian internationalism. Support for world revolution naturally raised the question of how to treat war, especially nuclear war. The Twentieth CPSU Congress had proposed a transition to communism through peace rather than war. Mao had always been against the view that nuclear war would destroy humanity. At an intra-party meeting after returning from Moscow, Mao discussed the topic of nuclear war even more thoroughly:

> Be prepared for a big war; the imperialist maniacs may drop atomic bombs. Only a little more than 10 million people died during World War I, more than 30 million people died during World War II. If an atomic war is fought, [we have] no experience. The best is that one-half the population will survive. The second best is that one-third of the population will survive. Out of the world's population of 2.7 billion, 900 million will survive. It is easier to get things done with 900 million people, a good trade for the end of imperialism and permanent world peace. Thus, if an atomic war breaks out, it will not necessarily be bad; it will be both a bad thing and good.

In a footnote to Mao's remarks, Deng Xiaoping said that the Twentieth CPSU Congress "refers only to peace, not war; this is no good. It states that war is not inevitable, but it does not say how to deal with war once it occurs. The Moscow Declaration [of 1957] resolved this issue, and this is what Chairman Mao spoke about in Moscow." Such differences between the sides would steadily increase over the next decade.

CONCLUSION

The 1957 Moscow Conference was a joint Sino-Soviet effort to establish a mechanism for resolving intra-bloc issues and for bolstering the International Communist Movement. In effect, Khrushchev was attempting to reestablish an international organization to coordinate the activities of the Communist parties around the world. Mao understood Khrushchev's position, but he resented Moscow's domination of the International Communist Movement and, after Stalin, he was unwilling to accept another "overlord." Hence, he proposed a conference as an alternative to a new Cominform. Khrushchev initially disliked the CCP's proposal, but in the wake of the Polish and Hungarian crises, he finally accepted Mao's suggestion. By this point, both the CCP and the CPSU valued the role of Yugoslavia, and they therefore attempted to enlist the LCY to improve their own status. But Tito wanted to preserve Yugoslavia's independence and policy of non-alliance, and he was not about to join the socialist bloc.

When China and the USSR agreed to serve as joint sponsors of the conference, Mao argued that the key was to reach unanimous approval of the conference document. The resultant declaration was a product of Sino-Soviet coordination and compromise. The CPSU accepted almost all the CCP's revisions, and the CCP tacitly approved inclusion of the program of the Twentieth CPSU Congress. The special courtesies Mao received and his assertiveness in Moscow seemed to indicate the CCP's newfound confidence. Mao's emphasis on the leadership role of the Soviet Union, his open comments on the intra-party struggle, and his boasting about overtaking Great Britain and catching up with the United States all indicated his aspiration to compete with the Soviet Union for leadership of the International Communist Movement.

Both the Soviet Union and China regarded the Moscow Conference as a success. Immediately after the conference, the CPSU organized party members and activists throughout the USSR to study the conference documents. This was accompanied by more than a month of continuous coverage about the conference in the press. At a December 1957 plenum, the CPSU CC expressed satisfaction that "the most important issues of principle and theory in modern international development of the Twentieth CPSU Congress have received the full support of the fraternal parties. This testifies to the ideological consensus and unity in the International Communist Movement." At the time, the CCP was preoccupied with Mao's "anti-rightist movement" and thus did not organize extensive study sessions. But the Eighth CCP Congress proclaimed that "the Moscow Conference of the World Communist and Workers' Parties and the two adopted declarations have opened a new era in the modern International Communist Movement, which immensely inspires all peaceful, democratic, and progressive forces in the world."

The Moscow Conference marked the peak in the Sino-Soviet alliance, but it was also, in some sense, a turning point in the relationship. The sticking point was not the Sino-Soviet differences per se, which were not unusual between allies. Under normal circumstances, the notion of "seeking common ground while respecting differences" would have made perfect sense. But even though the Sino-Soviet alliance in 1957 was still in a honeymoon phase, the issue at stake—the question of who would lead the International Communist Movement—was far from normal. Khrushchev had consolidated his position after the ouster of the Anti-party Group, and bountiful harvests in the USSR had augured steady economic progress. The launch of the two Sputnik satellites and the successful trial voyage of the first Soviet nuclear submarine presaged a rapid increase in Soviet military capability. The CCP, for its part, had gained prestige after the Twentieth CPSU Congress. Mao believed that he was much more refined theoretically than Khrushchev, and many CCP leaders shared this view. At the Moscow Conference, Mao reaffirmed the CPSU's leadership role in the socialist bloc, but thereafter he increasingly sought to challenge it. Before long, Sino-Soviet differences could no longer be resolved through "seeking common ground while preserving differences."

Against the backdrop of the Cold War, was imperialism better dealt with through relaxation or through confrontation? Which country's economy grew faster, and which model of development manifested the superiority of socialism? Both the PRC and the USSR were striving to find answers to these questions. In so doing, each country sought to demonstrate its own credentials to lead the International Communist Movement. Merely a year after the end of the Moscow Conference, these latent differences intensified, sparking a bitter Sino-Soviet schism. Therefore, even though the Moscow Conference underscored the confrontation between East and West, it also became a turning point in relations within the Communist bloc.

NOTES

1. Of the 68 parties that attended the conference, 4 (including the American Communist Party) made no public appearance for fear of persecution back home. Although 81 parties attended the Moscow Conference in November 1960, Mao Zedong was not present because of growing tensions with Moscow. Soviet and Chinese officials at the 1960 meeting could present only a facade of unity to the outside world. Hence, the 1960 Moscow Conference cannot be compared to the 1957 conference.
2. This view has been continuously recycled in the Chinese literature. See Lüthi, *The Sino-Soviet Split*, p. 75.
3. The Sino-Soviet relationship was at its friendliest stage (the "honeymoon period") from October 1954 to late 1957. This periodization differs from the traditional view in Chinese academic circles.
4. Stalin proposed the idea of convening a meeting of the Cominform in early 1951 and designated Italian Communist Party General Secretary Palmiro Togliatti as general secretary. But Togliatti declined, and no such conference was ever held.
5. Goncharov, Lewis, and Xue, *Uncertain Partners, Stalin*, pp. 71–73, 232–33; for a recent study on the Asian Cominform, see Zhihua Shen and Yafeng Xia, "Leadership Transfer in the Asian Revolution: Mao Zedong and the Asian Cominform," *Cold War History*, vol. 14, no. 2 (May 2014), pp. 195–214.

6. The Chinese Foreign Ministry reported that China's role in Soviet foreign relations became much more important after the Polish and Hungarian crises. The USSR adopted "a series of new approaches to strengthen Sino-Soviet friendship."

7. Mićunović, *Moscow Diary*, p. 294.

8. Hu Qiaomu had been Mao's political secretary since 1941 and was at that time director of China's Information Agency and deputy head of the CCP Propaganda Department. He was also the chief drafter of many important CCP documents.

9. For a detailed discussion of these three points, see Shen and Xia, *Mao and the Sino-Soviet Partnership*, pp. 249–62.

10. The CCP opposed the following wording in the draft declaration: "The Twentieth CPSU Congress creatively developed Marxism. The Eighth CCP Congress and the Congresses of the French Communist Party and the Italian Communist Party also showed loyalty to Marxism." The CCP insisted it was unnecessary to mention the Eighth CCP Congress. The congress of an individual party was its own business and required no approval by the international conference.

11. At the Moscow Conference in November 1960, the most controversial issue between the CCP and the CPSU was whether to mention the Twentieth CPSU Congress in the conference declaration.

12. Mićunović, *Moscow Diary*, pp. 191–92.

13. Khrushchev, *Khrushchev Remembers*, p. 254. According to reports from the Chinese embassy in the USSR, the formulation "the socialist camp under the leadership of the USSR and China" first appeared in the USSR in February 1955 after Khrushchev's visit to China in February 1954.

14. Gomułka pointed out in his speech at the plenary session on 17 November that to recognize "the USSR as the head" was simply recognizing the historical reality.

15. Khrushchev, *Khrushchev Remembers*, p. 254.

16. Later, during the Sino-Soviet polemics, the CCP CC argued that the reference to Moscow's leadership role "means only that the CPSU undertakes more responsibilities and obligations."

17. Edvard Kardelj, *Reminiscences: The Struggle for Recognition and Independence in the New Yugoslavia, 1944–1957* (London: Blond and Briggs, with Summerfield Press, 1982); Mićunović, *Moscow Diary*, pp. 314–18.

18. On 31 January 1958, Soviet leaders asked for Beijing's views on the prospect of starting a theoretical journal for the International Communist Movement. The CPSU suggested that the journal be a joint publication of all parties to publicize Marxism-Leninism and to exchange experiences. The CCP concurred. The resulting journal, *Problems of Peace and Socialism*, was published in Prague in 34 languages from 1958 to 1991 and distributed to 145 countries.

19. The International Communist Movement subsequently held several conferences to try to resolve the problems. Major conferences included the December 1960 Moscow Conference, the March 1965 Moscow Conference, and the June 1969 Moscow Conference.

20. In a reflection of Mao's attention to the conference, the Chinese side prepared 396 separate gifts for Mao to take to the USSR. The gifts for the Soviet leaders occupied almost an entire railway car.

21. Song Qingling was the widow of Sun Yatsen, the founding father of modern China. She was then a vice-president of the PRC.

22. Mao explained that he once suffered from cerebral anemia and he felt great discomfort when speaking while standing.

23. On Mao's 18 November speech, see Shen and Xia, *Sino-Soviet Partnership*, pp. 263–70.

24. Medvedev, *Khrushchev*, pp. 115–16.

25. Khrushchev, *Khrushchev Remembers*, p. 255.

26. *Vremya i my* (Tel Aviv), no. 48 (1979), pp. 164–65, quoted in Medvedev, *Khrushchev*, p. 122.

CHAPTER 14

Differences Over Domestic and Foreign Policies, 1957–1959

Zhihua Shen

When Mao Zedong proposed to "take the USSR as an object lesson" after the Twentieth Communist Party of the Soviet Union (CPSU) Congress, he meant that China should develop on the socialist road faster than the Union of Soviet Socialist Republics (USSR). When, at the 1957 Moscow Conference, Mao insisted that "the Soviet Union [act] as the head" of the socialist bloc, he humbly stated that China was a small country economically. Therefore, he insisted, it was impossible for China to lead the socialist camp. Nevertheless, at the time, Mao was preparing China for significant economic development. When Nikita Khrushchev put forward the slogan of overtaking the United States within 15 years, Mao certainly did not want to lag behind.

In 1958, Mao proposed that economically China would overtake the United Kingdom within 15 years. In fact, his inner goal was to surpass the USSR in terms of the pace of socialist construction. For this reason, he was considering the possibility of taking steps different from those of the USSR so that China would enter Communist society ahead of the USSR. Mao soon implemented the Great Leap Forward and the People's Communes Movement. But Khrushchev's criticism of the People's Communes reflected a serious Sino-Soviet difference on domestic policy that Mao could not tolerate. The Chinese Communist Party (CCP) decided to publicly criticize Moscow, thus creating a critical turning point in the history of the Sino-Soviet alliance.

Sino-Soviet solidarity began to decline in 1958. During the first half of the year, there were mutual Sino-Soviet expectations for closer collaboration. But

Z. Shen (✉)
East China Normal University, Shanghai, China
e-mail: zhaoran@ssap.cn

© The Author(s) 2020
Z. Shen (ed.), *A Short History of Sino-Soviet Relations, 1917–1991*,
China Connections, https://doi.org/10.1007/978-981-13-8641-1_14

209

several incidents, such as the dispute over a joint long-wave radio station, a "joint submarine fleet," and the People's Republic of China's (PRC) shelling of Jinmen, eventually resulted in Khrushchev's decision to renege on the Sino-Soviet agreement and to suspend shipments to China of a sample nuclear bomb and related technical materials. The Soviet declaration of neutrality with respect to the 1959 Sino-Indian border conflict exacerbated the situation, as the alliance rapidly approached a complete collapse.

CONTROVERSIES OVER THE GREAT LEAP FORWARD AND THE PEOPLE'S COMMUNE MOVEMENT

Mao had long dreamed of a great leap forward in China's economic development for rapid entry into Communist society. In March 1955, at the National CCP Congress, Mao declared that China "would catch up with and surpass the most powerful capitalist countries in several dozen years." In October, at the Sixth Plenum of the Seventh CCP Congress, Mao stated that China would construct a socialist society within 15 years, and China would catch up with the United States within 50–75 years. On 13 November, in keeping with Mao's thinking, an editorial in *People's Daily*, using the term "Great Leap Forward," pointed out that after achieving the collectivization of agriculture, "we have a foundation and now we must achieve a 'great leap forward' in production." On 2 December 1957, at the Eighth National Congress of the All-China Trade Unions, Liu Shaoqi, Mao's second in command, also declared the goal of surpassing Britain and catching up with the United States. Thereafter, the slogan of "surpassing Britain and catching up with the United States" became an important motivation for the Great Leap Forward.

The CCP was vigorously pursuing the goal of surpassing Great Britain and catching up with the United States in 1955–56 to demonstrate the superiority of the socialist system. But the goal of the Great Leap Forward promoted by Mao in 1958–59 was to catch up with and surpass the USSR and to demonstrate that China's economic developmental model was superior to that of the USSR. It appears that the purpose of Mao's embrace of the idea of leaping forward was to outdo the USSR. After returning from Moscow in November 1957, Mao had become impatient. He complained to his staff, "Is economic construction in peacetime more difficult than defeating Jiang Jieshi's army of eight million strong? I don't buy that!" At a meeting with Soviet Ambassador Pavel Yudin in February 1958, Mao spoke about the difficulties the USSR faced as the first socialist country, claiming, "The key difference between you [the USSR] and China and other socialist countries is that you do not have a predecessor." Mao said that the USSR should have been able to accomplish in about 25–30 years what would normally take 40 years, but he implied that China could develop faster. At the March 1958 meeting in Chengdu, Mao spoke about the grave consequences of following Stalin's repression of the Chinese Revolution. He was fully confident of China's going its own way in the future. He pointed out, "If, in eighteen years, we can equal what they have done in the past forty years, it will naturally be all right, and we should do precisely that. For there are more of us, and the political conditions are different, too: we are livelier! —and there is more Leninism. ... The speed of construction is a thing that exists objectively. Everything which, objectively and subjectively, is capable of achievement, we must endeavor to achieve by going all out, aiming high, and producing greater, faster, better, and more economical results." Mao also berated those who were suspicious of the Great Leap Forward, saying "Those people are unaware that the mainstream of Marxism has now shifted to the East." With truth within his grasp and sophisticated skills in mobilizing the masses, Mao felt that China's pace to surpass the most powerful capitalist countries would naturally accelerate.

To catch up with the USSR, Mao not only needed an increase in productivity but he also needed a faster change in the relations of production so that China could enter Communist society ahead of schedule. As early as the beginning of 1958, he had conceived of an ideal blueprint to achieve this goal. In March and April, he spoke with Liu Shaoqi and Chen Boda, director of the central Policy Research Office, about the "merging of townships and cooperatives" and the establishment of People's Communes. The CCP central leadership formally suggested changing "smaller cooperatives into larger cooperatives" (*xiaoshe bian dashe*). On 1 July, Chen Boda at Peking University gave a talk entitled "Under the Banner of Mao Zedong," in which, for the first time, he publicized Mao's master plan for Chinese society in the future: "Our direction is to gradually and orderly merge 'industry, agriculture, commerce and trade, education and culture, and the people's militia' into a large commune, which will constitute the basic unit of our society." The talk was immediately published in *Red Flag*, the CCP's theoretical journal. In early August, as he inspected communes in Henan and Shandong provinces, Mao noted "the People's Communes are good," after which communes began to spread rapidly throughout the country. At the time, many CCP party members believed firmly that in both theory and practice the country could expedite the pace of productivity by continuously changing the relations of production and raising the level of public ownership. The People's Communes, which were a result of the Great Leap Forward, could promote an even greater leap toward communism. Soviet diplomat Aleksei Brezhnev agreed that the Great Leap Forward was a "profound conceptual vision," but he sarcastically commented that it also "reflected the utter economic illiteracy" of the CCP leadership.[1]

In Mao's view, not only would China surpass the USSR in economic development, it would also surpass the USSR in modifying the relations of production. At the Zhengzhou Conference in November 1958, after reading Stalin's *Economic Problems of Socialism in the USSR*, Mao, Liu Shaoqi, and Deng Xiaoping discussed the transition to Communist society, comparing the situation in China with that in the USSR. Mao stated, "What does it mean to be successful in building socialism? What is the [nature of the] transition to communism? We should give a definition." Referring to China, Mao stated resolutely:

"Work really hard for three years, keep going for another twelve years, and we will make the transition to communism within fifteen years. We will not publicize this goal, but we must pursue it." Comparing China with the USSR, Mao said that Stalin only fulfilled the first transition, from collective ownership to ownership by the whole people. Regarding the second transition, from distribution according to work to distribution according to one's needs, the USSR was only boasting: "One hears footsteps without seeing anyone coming down the stairs." In China, "we have begun to make the second transition: people don't have to pay for meals." "The collective farms in the USSR only engage in agriculture, not in industry; they sow a wide acreage but they reap meager harvests, so it is no wonder that the USSR cannot make the transition to communism." In contrast, Mao stated, the People's Communes are the product of economic development and the 1958 Great Leap Forward. They are the product of two transitions. At present, we are making the transition from socialism to communism, that is, from socialist collective ownership to ownership by the whole people. We will make the transition from socialist ownership by the whole people to Communist ownership by the whole people. The communes are the best grassroots unit for a Communist social structure. Mao concluded that China had found the correct path to communism:

> Stalin did not find an appropriate way to make the transition from collective to public ownership and then from socialism to communism. He did not find the right solution. Now we have the People's Communes, which will accelerate our socialist construction and will be the best way for the countryside to make the transition from collective ownership to public ownership, and then from socialism to communism.

By the end of 1958, Mao not only firmly believed that by means of the Great Leap Forward and the People's Commune Movement the CCP had found the right path to achieve communism earlier than the USSR. Mao quipped, "We can do it faster. It seems that our mass line makes it easier to get things done. ... The USSR has been building socialism for forty-one years, and it did not make the transition to socialism within twelve years. It is panicking because it is already behind us." In Mao's view, China could surpass the USSR in economic development and show to the whole of mankind an accelerated path to communism. Once this program was accepted and supported by every ally, especially the USSR, the CCP would assume leadership of the socialist camp.[2]

In general, Soviet leaders were in favor of the Great Leap Forward. During his visit to China in the summer of 1958, Khrushchev said, "We experienced Russians were surprised at the plans put forward by our Chinese comrades. If you can accomplish your entire plan, about which we have no doubt, this will greatly shock your Asian neighbors." Perhaps Khrushchev was speaking insincerely, but he did not say anything negative. A study by the Sino-Soviet Studies Group of the Central Intelligence Agency (CIA) notes, "as late as June 1958 Khrushchev bestowed an unusual accolade on the Chinese party for its 'enormous contribution to the theory and practice of the socialist revolution.'" Thus, at least up to the summer of 1959, Soviet leaders appear to have supported the Leap, praising the enthusiasm of the Chinese people in building socialism. However, although the Soviets reacted to the Leap with enthusiasm, there were only descriptive reports about it in the Soviet press rather than significant commentaries. This shows that the CPSU leaders had adopted a very cautious position regarding China's internal policies.

It has been argued that the USSR refused to provide the urgently needed technical and economic assistance to China because it opposed the Great Leap Forward.[3] However, recent archival sources prove otherwise. The USSR assisted in publicity about the Great Leap. Almost all Soviet economic districts took production orders from China, several thousand enterprises took Chinese orders, and more than 100 Soviet units assisted China in product designs. In those factories and workshops manufacturing equipment for China, wall posters proclaimed "fulfilling orders from People's China ahead of schedule." Soviet enterprises were well prepared to fulfill orders for key construction projects, such as Baotou Iron and Steel, the Sanmenxia Key Water Control Project, the Fengman Hydroelectric Power Station, and the Beijing Heat and Power Station. In fact, Soviet-assisted projects during the Great Leap outnumbered earlier Soviet-assisted projects. According to statistics from the State Planning Commission, prior to 1959, the USSR assisted a total of 113 projects. But after 1959, in addition to the already agreed-upon projects, the USSR promised to assist China in building 125 new enterprises in accordance with agreements signed on 8 August 1958 and 7 February 1959. Although there were cases in which the Soviets were unwilling to increase the supply of goods or were late in delivery, these were mainly due to technical reasons, not political considerations. In his report to the Second Plenum of the Eighth CCP Congress in May 1958, Li Qiang, deputy minister of foreign trade, admitted that the Chinese side often changed project plans and contracts at will and this had created difficulties for the USSR.

The initial Soviet reaction to the People's Commune Movement was more cautious. At first, the Soviets considered the People's Commune Movement a novelty, and observers sought more concrete information. After the Chinese press reported that the issue had been discussed at the Beidaihe meeting, the Soviet embassy in Beijing on 22 August suggested that "China and the USSR [should] exchange views on how to further develop the socialist system in the countryside." According to the Beijing Municipal Committee of the Chinese Youth League, a visiting Moscow youth delegation in September showed great interest in the People's Communes and sought more information about them. In May 1959, the Soviet-China Friendship Association reported a similar interest in the People's Communes by other visiting Soviet delegations.

Nonetheless, the Soviet press gave little coverage to the People's Commune Movement due to caution on the part of the leadership. On 6 September 1958, Yuri Andropov, head of the Department for Liaison with Communist and Workers' Parties in Socialist Countries, submitted a report to the Central

Committee (CC) on the People's Commune Movement. Referring to how the USSR should react, the report stated that since the CCP attaches great importance to this organizational structure, "We should, in the spirit of Soviet-Chinese friendship, introduce this subject in our press using reports published in China." At the same time, however, the report also proposed further research.

After careful study, the CPSU CC felt that the CCP had committed mistakes of radicalism and rash advance. But for the sake of maintaining cordial relations, it would make no comment. A Politburo study group presented two clumsy alternatives:

> On the one hand, if we praise the People's Communes for the sake of maintaining good relations, we will deceive the international workers' movement; on the other hand, if we preserve the truth and criticize [the movement] as a case of a 'leftist' policy, we will widen the differences between the two parties.

Therefore, the CPSU central leadership decided that it was better "not to mention this issue, that is, neither praising nor criticizing the People's Commune Movement for the sake of maintaining stable relations." This suggestion was approved by the CPSU Politburo. Thus, for a long time, there were no commentaries on the People's Communes in the Soviet press.

The first time a Soviet leader spoke about the People's Communes was on 30 November 1958, when Khrushchev held a meeting with Polish leader Władysław Gomułka. Official Polish documents reveal Khrushchev's dislike of the People's Communes. He said, "The Chinese are organizing communes. There were communes in our country thirty years ago. We are tired of them. For the Chinese, let them try. They will gain experience after causing serious harm." Yet, at that time, the content of this talk was kept secret. Later, it was rumored in the West that the Soviet leader was expressing different opinions in private about the People's Communes. After the Twenty-first CPSU Congress, Khrushchev stated, "Society cannot jump from capitalism to communism without experiencing socialist development. ... It is wrong to believe that Communist society will suddenly arrive. ... Egalitarianism does not mean a transition to communism. Rather it only damages the reputation of communism." It was obvious that Khrushchev was criticizing the Chinese.[4] Although the Soviet press later denied this, it is clear that when Khrushchev publicly criticized the idea of a rapid transition to communism, he was indirectly criticizing the Chinese People's Communes.

Six months later, Khrushchev finally publicly stated what he thought of the People's Communes. During a mass rally in Poland on 18 July 1959, he recalled the mistakes in setting up communes in the USSR in the 1920s, stating:

> Someone once made the following argument, "Now that we are striving for communism, let us set up communes." ... It seems that at the time many did not understand what communism is and how to build it. ... Although communes were established, there was a lack of both the material prerequisites and the politi-

cal conditions, that is, the peasants' political consciousness. The result was that everyone wanted to lead a better life, but no one wanted to do more for public projects.

Khrushchev concluded that the communes were not workable, thus justifying the Soviet collective farms. Unlike the report of the Twenty-first CPSU Congress, this talk did not mention China, and its tone was more tolerant; therefore, it should not have elicited a strong reaction. When Polish newspapers published the talk, the part about the communes was deleted. But *Pravda* published the speech in full. This was an extremely poorly timed decision because the CCP leadership meeting in Lushan was taking place at that time. Mao was indignant about Defense Minister Peng Dehuai's frank admonition of policy blunders. Khrushchev's speech further antagonized Mao, who decided to attack Khrushchev publicly.[5]

Within the CCP, two different assessments of the economic situation in 1958 provided the backdrop for the 1959 meeting in Lushan. It is no wonder that a personal letter from Peng Dehuai stirred up a hornet's nest. Mao was determined to attack those who dared to criticize his great experiment in building communism. On 16 July, Mao ordered that Peng's letter be distributed to those attending the meeting. Still angry, he read another two reports revealing complaints by grassroots cadres about the Great Leap Forward and the People's Commune Movement. The reports complained that having the whole population produce steel had led to "more loss than gain," "a waste of money and energy," and it was a political rather than an economic move. They also stated that "the People's Communes are not superior. They are an artificial product … prompted by an impulse." Then came a report from the Foreign Ministry, indicating a widespread belief among cadres in the USSR that China had encountered difficulties and that the CCP had made mistakes. Mao distributed these materials without any comment. On 28 July, Khrushchev's remarks in Poland about the People's Communes were sent to Lushan. There was no way Mao could tolerate Soviet leaders joining the debate and siding with the "rightists" in the CCP.

On the next day, Mao gave instructions that all these materials be distributed to the participants at the meeting, saying "I ask all comrades to look into whether or not the communes that failed in the USSR are identical to our communes and to predict whether or not our communes will fail. … What is consistent with history can never fail and can never be stopped artificially." It appears that this still did not satisfy Mao. On 1 August, he had these materials also delivered to Wang Jiaxiang, director of the CCP's International Liaison Department, with a note:

> I wrote a few words to refute Khrushchev. In the future, I will write articles to publicize the advantages of the People's Communes. Khrushchev and the like oppose us for three policies—the policy of letting one hundred flowers bloom, the People's Communes, and the Great Leap Forward—or at least they are having

doubts about them. I think they are now in a passive position while we are in a very active one. What do you think? ... We should be prepared to declare war with the entire world, including opponents and skeptics within our own party, on account of these three objections.

It seems that at that point, Mao not only linked Peng with Khrushchev but was determined to launch an attack on Khrushchev and to allow the clashes between China and the USSR to come out in the open.

CONTROVERSIES OVER THE PROPOSED LONG-WAVE RADIO STATION AND THE "JOINT FLEET"

After the Moscow Conference, Sino-Soviet friendship entered a period of unprecedented prosperity. The two countries closely cooperated diplomatically, and the economic and political relationships both expanded significantly. It seemed that the respective leaders agreed on the unity of the socialist bloc. It was in this atmosphere that a long-wave radio station and a joint submarine fleet were proposed. In Khrushchev's opinion, it was natural to raise these issues. By the end of 1957, one problem that the Chinese navy faced was how to develop new technology to upgrade its existing fleet, whereas the Soviets were trying to make better use of their Pacific fleet. The needs of both countries were the driving force behind their expanding military cooperation.

Both the USSR and the PRC desired to set up a long-wave radio station, yet how to go about it remained unresolved. On 18 April, in a letter to Peng Dehuai, Soviet Defense Minister Rodion Malinovsky suggested establishing a 1000 kilowatt long-wave transmitter and a long-range receiver in southern China. He said the total expense would be 110 million rubles, of which 70 million rubles would be paid by the USSR and 40 million rubles by the PRC. After construction, the two installations would be used jointly. On 24 April, Mao instructed the relevant parties to reply as follows: the PRC agrees to set up the installation on Chinese territory, but it alone will be responsible for all expenses and will be the sole owner of the installation. In accordance with Mao's proposal, at the 152nd meeting of the CCP Central Military Commission (CMC) held on 10 May, Peng Dehuai said that the long-wave radio station should be built solely with Chinese funds; Peng also said that the station could offer intelligence to the USSR during peacetime, and the USSR could send representatives to the station during times of war. However, under no circumstances would the USSR be allowed to establish military facilities on Chinese territory. On 23 May, the CMC met again to ensure that the PRC would not establish a joint long-wave radio station. On 4 June, Peng informed the top Soviet military adviser in China of its decision.

On 12 June, Peng officially answered Malinovsky, reaffirming the Chinese government's position and suggesting that the two countries sign an agreement. On 28 June, assistant director of the Department of Naval Communication Forces, Letvensky, led a group of six Soviet specialists to China, bringing with them a draft agreement. The USSR still insisted on jointly constructing a long-wave radio station and sharing the costs. Discussions between Soviet and Chinese leaders went in circles without reaching any agreement. On 21 July, Peng wrote another letter to Malinovsky, reaffirming the PRC's principle of establishing a long-wave radio station on its own: "We welcome the Soviet specialists' offer of aid and advice on technical aspects of the project. Regarding the funds needed for the project, the PRC alone will assume responsibility."

On 21 July 1958, Ambassador Yudin requested a meeting with Mao, saying he had something very urgent to report. During the meeting, Yudin explained that since the United States was their common enemy, if war were to break out in the future, Khrushchev wished to discuss the possibility of establishing a joint fleet with his Chinese comrades, possibly including Vietnam as well. He hoped that the CCP CC would dispatch Zhou Enlai and Peng Dehuai to Moscow to discuss the issue in detail. Mao immediately pointed out that although the PRC requested Soviet aid, it had never considered the possibility of setting up a "cooperative." After Yudin completed his report, Mao seized on the issue of the "joint fleet," asking again and again: is setting up a "cooperative" a prerequisite for Soviet aid? Otherwise, will the Soviets refuse to help [China]? Yudin repeatedly explained that it was only a suggestion, and the Soviets wanted to invite their Chinese comrades for further discussions. But Mao insisted that the first task was clarification of the guiding principle: whether this would be joint cooperation or unilateral Soviet aid. If the USSR was reluctant to offer aid, the PRC could abandon the plan to develop nuclear submarines.

At 11 a.m. the next morning, Mao summoned Yudin and others to Zhongnanhai for a discussion with all Politburo members in Beijing, whereupon Mao stressed that his statements represented the opinions of all Chinese leaders. Mao was obviously well prepared and asked his staff to record the conversation on a mini-recorder.[6] According to the records of the conversations, which now have been officially published in China, Mao restated the PRC's rejection of a "joint fleet" and declared that China was withdrawing its request for Soviet aid. Mao vented his long pent-up grievances toward the Soviet leaders, especially Stalin, by using this episode as a pretext to criticize the USSR. Although Mao repeatedly stated that it was a question of "one finger to nine fingers," meaning that the PRC and the USSR were in agreement on almost all issues, what impressed the Soviets was "Mao's torrential outpouring of condemnation in a steady flow for the entire day. … All the issues were actually related to Sino-Soviet national and party relations." The Soviets were "greatly depressed," realizing that "they had absolutely no understanding of Chinese policy and they had overestimated the importance of ideology and had underestimated the difference between the national interests of the two countries."

Yudin and his staff returned to their embassy and discussed the situation through the night, finally concluding that Mao opposed a naval fleet built jointly by the USSR and China. Yudin immediately drafted a report to the CPSU CC and delivered it early the next morning. Khrushchev and Defense

Minister Malinovsky arrived in Beijing for a secret visit from 31 July to 3 August. Between 5:00 p.m. and 9:00 p.m. on 31 July, Mao and Khrushchev held a meeting in Huairen Hall in Zhongnanhai. During their conversation, Khrushchev first gave a long, drawn-out explanation for the initial Soviet proposal concerning the submarine fleet. Khrushchev firmly denied that the USSR had used words such as a "combined fleet" or a "joint fleet." He maintained that it was Yudin who misconstrued the Soviet meaning, and the entire episode was "a misunderstanding." Khrushchev again expressed that ownership would surely belong to the PRC, but since the USSR would use it, it was reasonable to share in the expense of the project, perhaps in the form of loans. Mao obstinately refused Soviet loans, and even threatened to abandon the project if the USSR insisted. Their talks ended at this.[7]

The atmosphere of the meeting was tense and Mao was impolite, but he was not as rude as he had been to Yudin. After all, Khrushchev was coming to offer an explanation and to admit "mistakes." Moreover, Khrushchev exonerated himself by implying that Yudin was responsible for all the mistakes, which may have had something to do with Yudin's sudden stroke and absence from their talks. Khrushchev evidently felt that the long-wave radio station and joint fleet had caused such fierce responses from the Chinese leadership that they might influence the entirety of the relationship. He therefore had no other choice but to find a scapegoat, and in early 1959, Yudin was relieved of his ambassadorship. From the evidence above, however, it seems Yudin actually did not misconstrue Khrushchev's intent. At most, his mistake was in not completely changing his words after discovering Mao's opposition; with his feeble explanation, he only further angered Mao.

From the evidence above, we can conclude that the Soviet leaders had no ill intent, but the way they raised the proposal was too direct and they did not consider the nationalistic sentiments among the Chinese. From this perspective, it was Mao who overreacted, although it is understandable that from a nationalist perspective, Mao, a leader of a country that had experienced so much humiliation, felt slighted by the Soviet proposal. As an ally of the USSR and the supreme leader of his country, he was quick to take offense. Mao's overreaction, although indicative of his personality, seems to have been a function of his fear of a change in the direction of developments in Sino-Soviet relations, and it was an indication of his volatile psyche. For a long time, Mao had been dissatisfied with Stalin's chauvinism and the PRC's unequal status vis-à-vis the USSR. But the PRC's status had improved considerably after the Korean War, especially after Stalin's death. And the time when the CPSU could arbitrarily dictate events had long passed, and the CCP had become an equal. The situation in 1957 was completely different from that in 1950 when Mao first visited the USSR. Under such circumstances, Mao would no longer tolerate Khrushchev if he were to act like Stalin. Although Mao repeatedly stated that "the USSR is the leader of the socialist camp," in reality, the situation had changed to such an extent that "the leader" had to consult with the CCP on all issues.

The crisis finally passed. The PRC obtained its desired aid, and Khrushchev was satisfied that the matter had been resolved as a result of his visit. In his report to the Presidium of the CPSU CC, he stated, "The visit was useful [and] the talks were frank." The Presidium agreed that "this was a productive visit." The assertion that the incident caused the collapse of the relationship is far-fetched. This was only distorted later during the Sino-Soviet polemics.[8] But why was Mao Zedong so agitated with a proposal by its supposed ally? This was a product of Mao's strong personality. However, if we link Khrushchev's visit to Beijing and the PRC's bombardment of Jinmen in late August, we cannot but think that Mao really had another purpose.

The communiqué published after Mao and Khrushchev's talks states: "The two sides spoke in an extremely sincere and friendly atmosphere. We fully discussed the urgent and significant issues in the current international situation, the issue of advancing and strengthening the friendship, alliance, and mutual aid in Sino-Soviet relations, and jointly striving to peacefully resolve international problems and to defend world peace. A consensus was reached on all issues." These words, however, did not erase the bad but hidden feelings of both leaders regarding the incident. Sino-Soviet relations deteriorated further when the PRC bombed Jinmen without notifying the USSR in advance.[9]

INTENSE CONFLICTS OVER THE SHELLING OF JINMEN

Barely three weeks after Khrushchev left China, the PRC bombed Jinmen on 23 August. As a result, US Secretary of State John F. Dulles believed that the CCP's military action was "probably agreed upon at the recent meeting between Khrushchev and Mao."[10] In response to journalists, Chinese Nationalist leader in Taiwan Jiang Jieshi stated that this action was surely "the outcome of the meeting between the two bandits—Khrushchev and Mao in Beiping."

During periods of military action, Mao wanted his enemies to be aware of Sino-Soviet solidarity. But the PRC's military actions were a big surprise to Moscow. Beijing's refusal to notify Moscow violated Article 4 of the alliance treaty, which clearly stated: "Both High Contracting Parties will consult each other in regard to all important international questions affecting the common interests of the USSR and China, being guided by the interests of the consolidation of peace and universal security."[11] Moscow was furious at Mao's "surprise attack." Mikhail Kapitsa, then acting director-general of the Far East Bureau of the Soviet Foreign Ministry, who accompanied Foreign Minister Andrei Gromyko to China during the crisis, recalled "The Chinese were then our allies, and they had an obligation both as allies and as fellow Communists to keep us informed of their intentions. The American Pacific Fleet was steaming toward Taiwan. Yet the Chinese rashly went ahead with their shelling without any consultation."[12] After only three days of intensive shelling did the Chinese Foreign Ministry transmit a brief notice to Moscow, stating that liberation of the offshore islands was an internal Chinese affair and the United

States might not become involved in the conflict. Within about a week, as Moscow was still unaware of the situation, it only issued news stories to support the PRC's military action in principle. On 4 September, the US government issued the "Xingang Statement," declaring that it was the responsibility of the United States to defend Taiwan against aggression, and the US Congress had authorized the president to use military force to guarantee the security of Jinmen, Mazu, and the other offshore islands. Indirectly, the White House even threatened a nuclear war.[13]

By this time, the USSR had decided to send Foreign Minister Andrei Gromyko to China on a fact-finding mission. Gromyko met with both Mao and Zhou. The Chinese side explained, "The military action was designed neither to take over Jinmen nor to liberate Taiwan." The Soviets agreed with the Chinese tactics. The memoirs of Chinese and Soviet participants differ as to whether Mao had asked for Soviet nuclear protection. Gromyko recalled, "The general drift of Mao's attitude was that there should be no giving in to the Americans and that we should act on the principle of meeting force with force." Mao advised that the USSR should not take any military action against the Americans during the first stage and should let them "penetrate deep" into China. "Only when the Americans are in the central provinces should you give them everything you've got."[14] Gromyko was implying that in the event of war Mao wanted the USSR to use nuclear weapons against the Americans. Yan Mingfu, Mao's interpreter, recalled, "Mao said, 'Why should we be afraid of an atomic bomb? We don't have an atomic bomb now but will have one in the future. We don't have one yet, but you do.'" Mao also said, "Our policy is that we will bear all consequences of a war by ourselves, [and we] will not drag the USSR into the water. …" It seems that Gromyko was overemphasizing Mao's request for Soviet nuclear protection. Gromyko was carrying a draft letter to Eisenhower that was to be reviewed by the Chinese. After Chinese modifications, Moscow handed the letter over to the US chargé d'affaires in Moscow. The letter claimed that the USSR "would do everything to defend the security of both states."[15]

Mao's crisis management avoided direct military confrontation with the United States. Had the United States become directly involved in the conflict, China would have tried its best to alleviate the crisis. But outwardly, China would not give the impression of weakness.[16] Of course, it was necessary to demonstrate the strength of the Sino-Soviet alliance and to continue to receive Soviet aid. But what Mao wanted was deterrence or to prevent things from becoming worse even if it could not deter US involvement. Thus, it was imperative that the Soviet leaders become involved. In the end, Mao was satisfied with Khrushchev's letter to Eisenhower.[17]

As an ally, the USSR should have been consulted regarding the PRC's military actions prior to the shelling, but the USSR still had to take responsibility for later actions. Khrushchev was annoyed and unaware of Mao's thinking. Thus, he was justified in feeling that there was a general weakening in Sino-Soviet relations, and in retaliation, he decided to rescind the October 1957 promise to deliver a model atomic bomb to China by June 1959.[18]

The Sino-Indian Border Clashes and Soviet Neutrality

On 25 August 1959, Chinese and Indian border garrisons clashed at Longju, a point north of the McMahon Line along the eastern section of the Sino-Indian border. Two Indian soldiers were reportedly killed. On 27 August, Indian troops withdrew from Longju to south of the McMahon Line. After the incident, a new wave of anti-Chinese activities spread throughout India. By political and diplomatic means, as well as public opinion, India was attempting to pressure China to make concessions. Thereafter, changing from his milder attitude, Nehru then openly accused the Chinese of "invading" India's northeast border and of failing to honor its promise to Burma and India regarding the McMahon Line.[19] Nehru stressed that in order to begin border negotiations, China had to accept the McMahon Line. Mao and his colleagues were prepared for anti-Chinese sentiment in India and in the West, but they were taken aback to learn of the Soviet policy of neutrality and to hear Soviet accusations against the Chinese. Although the Chinese side made several attempts to prevent the USSR from releasing a TASS (Tyelyegrafnoe agentstvo Sovetskogo Soyuza) statement, it was issued at 7:00 p.m. on 9 September (Moscow time), a day earlier than originally scheduled. It expressed "regret" over the Sino-Indian border incident and in effect declared "neutrality" on the Sino-Indian border conflict.

Why did Moscow wish to release a statement on the Sino-Indian border conflict against Chinese will? Khrushchev later recalled that the USSR was eager to state its position because it did not agree with Chinese actions. Kapitsa recalled that Khrushchev wanted to create a good atmosphere for his forthcoming visit to the United States and he was furious about the border clash. Gromyko too wanted to create "a good tone" for Khrushchev's visit to the United States.

The CCP CC was very disappointed with Moscow's statement. On 13 September, the Chinese replied to the USSR, criticizing the Soviet government for "accommodating and compromising on important matters of principle" and accusing the TASS statement of "exposing Sino-Soviet differences about the Sino-Indian border conflict." As he delivered the Chinese letter, Chinese Foreign Minister Chen Yi said, "The TASS statement is very disadvantageous to China. But many in India, the United States, and the UK welcome it."

Therefore, Moscow's policy of neutrality was mainly for tactical considerations. In appearance, Sino-Soviet differences focused on how to deal with Indian Prime Minister Jawaharlal Nehru. In principle, there were no differences between Chinese and Soviet leaders in terms of their view of Nehru and the Indian government. The real difference was about the forthcoming US-Soviet summit. The USSR insisted that the exchange of visits between American and Soviet leaders was "presently the most important international issue. ... If Soviet-American relations steadily move toward peaceful coexistence, it will have a great positive impact on the international situation. It will contribute to the consolidation of world peace." Moscow promptly relayed information regarding Khrushchev's US visit to Beijing. From the Soviet perspective, the Chinese attacks belittled the importance of the Sino-Soviet summit. In CCP CC internal discussions, it was argued that "in order to accommodate the needs of the U.S. administration," on 20 June 1959, Khrushchev suspended nuclear aid to China prior to his trip to the United States and declared Soviet neutrality with respect to the Sino-Indian border conflict. This "demonstrates that he harbors malicious intentions toward China while making a trip to the United States." Many years later, Zhou Enlai was still arguing that the Soviet declaration of neutrality was Khrushchev's gift to Washington in exchange for his visit. But it was difficult for the Chinese to speak out at the time because of the sensitivity of the issue. China had to openly show its support for a relaxation of international tensions. Although Mao could not tolerate Khrushchev's trip to the United States, there was nothing he could do about it.[20]

After his trip to the United States, Khrushchev rushed to Beijing to participate in the ceremony marking the tenth anniversary of the founding of the PRC. As he disembarked from his plane, he never expected that the Chinese leaders would seize the occasion to severely criticize him. On 2 October, Khrushchev had "a strained, fuming meeting" with Mao and other Chinese leaders.[21] When Khrushchev attempted to persuade the Chinese to improve relations with the United States by lessening tensions in the Taiwan Strait and releasing the detained Americans in China, Zhou Enlai rejected this request, stating that Taiwan was an internal Chinese affair. On the Sino-Indian border conflict, Khrushchev censured the Chinese action that had forced Nehru into "a very difficult position," and he stated: "If you will allow me to say what is not permitted for a guest to say, the events in Tibet are your fault." When Mao responded by bringing up the TASS statement, Khrushchev retorted, "Do you really want us to approve of your conflict with India? That would be stupid on our part."[22] Foreign Minister Chen Yi argued that Nehru was an agent of US imperialism and that as a Communist country, the USSR was obligated to support China.[23] Chen Yi and Mao accused Khrushchev of opportunism. An agitated Khrushchev noted, "What a pretty situation we have: on the one hand, you use the formula of the USSR; on the other hand, you do not let me say a word."[24] The meeting ended on a bad note.[25]

Khrushchev was obviously offended. The next day, he sent Gromyko to inform Chen Yi that he had to return to the USSR ahead of schedule due to an emergency. All previously scheduled visits to other Chinese cities had to be canceled.[26] It has been argued that the meeting between Chinese and Soviet leaders in October 1959 was a critical turning point in Sino-Soviet relations. The meeting neither resolved any issues nor reached any mutual understanding.[27] In actuality, there was no emergency for Khrushchev to deal with in Moscow. He thus made a detour to Siberia and Vladivostok. On 6 October, Khrushchev spoke at a mass rally, stating that "it is unwise to long for war and to be prepared to fight like a bellicose rooster." Many believe that Khrushchev was criticizing Chinese foreign policy in general and attacking Mao in particular. The report attracted the attention of Mao, who ordered it to be circulated to Liu Shaoqi, Zhou Enlai, Chen Yi, and Peng Zhen, among other top Chinese leaders. Mao asked them to "read it within two days" and to "think it over" in preparation for a meeting with him.

CONCLUSION

Against this backdrop, China and the USSR were turning against each other and relations were deteriorating. The Taiwan Strait crisis of 1958 demonstrated Sino-Soviet differences over major foreign policy issues, after which Khrushchev decided to teach the CCP a lesson. A CIA study in June 1960 states that "the ideological pretension that Communist China was leading the bloc in an accelerated march to communism and the theoretical rationale for the commune as a 'creative development' of Marxism-Leninism posed a fundamental challenge which Moscow could ill afford to ignore." The Soviet attitude toward the People's Communes indicated Sino-Soviet differences in domestic policies, which Mao could no longer tolerate, so he resolved to criticize Moscow. According to the Soviet and East European advisers in China, "Mao is even worse than a 'Chinese Tito,' as his vision for the future is reminiscent of the distance from agrarian China to the future socialist world."[28]

Although both Mao and Khrushchev recognized that China and the USSR had fundamental common interests and their alliance was of great importance, each also thought that the other's mistakes had to be corrected. Mao intended to be the standard-bearer for the world's socialist countries, specifically, to catch up with and overtake capitalism and imperialism and to make China a leading example in the International Communist Movement. However, Moscow took this theoretically based attack as a challenge to the socialist bloc under the leadership of the USSR.

Khrushchev had reasons for not impulsively reneging on the agreement regarding nuclear assistance to China. In Moscow's view, "Taking serious military-political action in the area of Taiwan at the end of August, our Chinese friends, basing their position on the assumption that a solution to the Taiwan issue was solely a Chinese domestic affair, did not beforehand inform the Soviet government of their plans."[29] A furious Khrushchev repeatedly told Mao that although the Taiwan issue was China's internal affair, it was a matter that affected their entire relationship. As allies, China and the USSR were expected to coordinate policies on matter of such importance. In face-to-face talks, Khrushchev complained to Mao that the USSR was not kept informed about what China would do from day to day. In his view, China's behavior was an insult to all its allies. More importantly, China's foreign policy during the Taiwan Strait crisis demonstrated that China had deviated from the principle of peaceful coexistence, as articulated in the 1957 Moscow Declaration. But Mao believed that increased international tensions were fundamentally unfavorable to the common interests of the socialist bloc. As Mao stated: "I think we can loudly proclaim to people all over the world that tensions are rather detrimental to Western countries, to the United States as well. ... Take our country, for example; all our country has been mobilized by now, and if some 30 to 40 million people hold demonstrations and assemblies for Middle East events, this time (during the Taiwan Strait Crisis), at least 300 million people will be out there, and they will be educated and tempered."[30] Whereas Moscow was pursuing detente in international relations, Mao was creating further tensions. Hence, in consideration of Mao's proposition at the Moscow Conference that "the east wind prevails over the west wind" and his unconventional remarks on nuclear war, Khrushchev became worried about what Mao would do with nuclear weapons. When he resolved to renege on the Sino-Soviet agreement on new technology for national defense, Khrushchev had few doubts about the ultimate effect of his decision on the Sino-Soviet alliance.

The bombardment of Jinmen demonstrated Sino-Soviet differences in foreign policy, and Khrushchev was determined to force China to modify its policies by suspending nuclear assistance. One month later, Soviet criticism of the People's Communes Movement reflected differences in domestic policy. At that point, Mao could no longer tolerate Khrushchev's attitude and decided to adopt a policy of criticizing Moscow.

Superficially, Sino-Soviet differences in 1959–1960 were a result of the Sino-Indian border conflict. But the real cause was the debate about improving Soviet relations with the United States. Khrushchev maintained that the purpose of China's heavy-handed policy toward India was to destroy the Soviet-American summit and to obstruct progress toward a relaxation of tensions. But in Mao's view, the Sino-Indian conflict was only a minor issue. The core issue was the Soviet policy of lessening tensions with the United States. The purpose of Moscow's policy of neutrality in the Sino-Indian conflict was to guarantee the success of the US-Soviet summit. Thinking about their common enemy, China and the USSR were reluctant to criticize one another's policy toward United States, so instead they disagreed over policy toward India.

On the one hand, Mao needed the socialist bloc, and even wanted to lead it, but he knew that without the USSR, the socialist bloc would not exist. On the other hand, it was necessary to take a clear-cut stand on major matters of principle because only those who had true Marxism on their side were qualified to lead the socialist bloc. Therefore, Mao decided to argue with the CPSU about theories of revolution and war, believing that he could overcome any objections. After October 1959, both countries began releasing propaganda about the correctness of their respective policies. *Soviet-Chinese Friendship* reprinted articles from the Soviet press that obviously contradicted the position of the CCP.[31] China retaliated in kind.[32]

NOTES

1. Lüthi, *The Sino-Soviet Split*, p. 90.
2. On Mao's utopian economic plan to overtake the Soviet Union, see Shen and Xia, *Mao and the Sino-Soviet Partnership*, pp. 284–90.
3. Medvedev, *Khrushchev*, pp. 143–44.

4. A research report on the Twenty-first CPSU Congress by the US State Department points out that Khrushchev's remark on the communes was the Soviet response to the Chinese challenge to Moscow's ideological leadership. See Intelligence Report, No. 7982, Recent Developments in Sino-Soviet Relations, 27 March 1959, MF2510409-0169, Main Library of the University of Hong Kong.

5. For Soviet attitudes toward the Great Leap Forward and the People's Commune Movement, see Shen and Xia, *Mao and the Sino-Soviet Partnership*, pp. 290–95.

6. But due to a lack of technical skills, Mao's staff failed to record Mao's second conversation with Yudin.

7. The records of the conversations between Mao and Khrushchev on 31 July and 3 August 1958 were in the private collection of Soviet military historian Dmitri Volkogonov and have now been collected in the US Library of Congress. Volkogonov collected a large amount of literature on Soviet history. According to an agreement with Volkogonov, the United States declassified his collection in 2002. Vladislav Zubok compiled and published two versions; the version in English is in *CWIHP Bulletin*, Issues 12–13 (Fall/Winter 2001), pp. 250–62.

8. Mao Zedong later joined in the criticism of the Soviet Union. On 22 May 1963, he spoke with Victor Wilcox, general secretary of the New Zealand Communist Party, about Khrushchev's 1958 visit to China. Mao said that the purpose of Khrushchev's visit had been the "joint fleet" issue. But Mao claimed that he had reached an agreement with Khrushchev regarding the long-wave radio station.

9. For a detailed analysis of the Sino-Soviet disputes over the proposed long-wave radio station and the "joint fleet," see Shen and Xia, *Mao and the Sino-Soviet Partnership*, pp. 308–21.

10. Memorandum of Conversation, 3 September 1958, *FRUS*, 1958–1960, vol. 19, p. 126.

11. Treaty text, in Harold Hinton, ed., *The People's Republic of China, 1949–1979: A Documentary Survey* (Lanham, MD: Rowman & Littlefield, 1980), vol. 1, p. 124; Lüthi, *The Sino-Soviet Split*, p. 99.

12. Telegram from Beijing to Washington, 6 July 1974, National Archives (College Park, MD), cited in Michael Share, "From Ideological Foe to Uncertain Friend: Soviet Relations with Taiwan, 1943–1982," *Cold War History*, vol. 3, no. 2 (2003), p. 9.

13. "White House Press Release," 9/4/1958, *FRUS*, 1958–1960, vol. 19, pp. 135–36.

14. Andrei Gromyko, *Memoirs* (New York: Doubleday, 1990), p. 251.

15. "Telegram from the Embassy in the Soviet Union to the Department of State," 9/7/1958, *FRUS*, 1958–1960, vol. 19, pp. 145–53; Lüthi, *The Sino-Soviet Split*, pp. 102–3.

16. The CCP CC had decided to give up the goal of liberating Jinmen, but in 6 September propaganda material, it still retained slogans such as "[We] must liberate Jinmen and Mazu" and "[We] must liberate Taiwan."

17. For the Soviet reaction to the PRC's shelling of Jinmen, see Shen and Xia, *Mao and the Sino-Soviet Partnership*, pp. 321–28.

18. Khrushchev, *Khrushchev Remembers*, p. 269. See also Jay Taylor, *The Generalissimo: Chiang Kai-shek and the Struggle for Modern China* (Cambridge, MA: Belknap Press of Harvard University Press, 2009), pp. 501–2.

19. In their talks from 31 December 1956 to 1 January 1957, during Zhou's visit to India, Zhou Enlai and Nehru discussed the McMahon Line. Zhou said, "[A]lthough the question is still undecided and it is unfair to us, we still feel that there is no better way than to recognize this Line." See Mushirul Hasan, ed., *Selected Works of Jawaharlal Nehru*, series II, vol. 36 (1 December 1956–21 February 1957) (New Delhi: Jawaharlal Nehru Memorial Fund, 2009), pp. 583–603.

20. A Russian scholar has wrongly affirmed that Mao changed his stand toward Khrushchev's trip to the United States due to the TASS statement of neutrality.

21. Dong Wang, "The Quarrelling Brothers: New Chinese Archives and a Reappraisal of the Sino-Soviet Split, 1959–1962," *CWIHP Working Paper*, no. 49 (2006), p. 24.

22. "Record of Conversation of Comrade Khrushchev N. S. with CC CCP Chairman Mao Zedong ...," 2 October 1959, APRF, copy on Reel 17, Volkogonov Collection, Library of Congress, Washington, DC. For an English translation, see http://digitalarchive.wilsoncenter.org/document/118883

23. Roderick MacFarquhar, *The Origins of the Cultural Revolution, vol. 2: The Great Leap Forward, 1958–1960* (New York: Columbia University Press, 1983), p. 261.

24. "Discussion between N. S. Khrushchev and Mao Zedong," 2 October 1959, APRF, f. 52, op. 1, d. 499, Il. 1–33. For an English translation, see http://digitalarchive.wilsoncenter.org/document/112088

25. Lüthi, *The Sino-Soviet Split*, pp. 146–50.

26. Ivan Arkhipov, *Memoirs of Sino-Soviet Relations* (author's personal collection); author's interview with Igor A. Rogachev, 22 July 2011.

27. Chen Jian, "The Tibetan Rebellion of 1959 and China's Changing Relations with India and the Soviet Union," *Journal of Cold War Studies*, vol. 8, no. 3 (Summer 2006), pp. 54–101.

28. Austin Jersild, *The Sino-Soviet Alliance: An International History* (Chapel Hill: University of North Carolina Press, 2014), p. 155.

29. RGANI, f. 5, op. 49, d. 134, p. 84, cited in Vladislav Zubok and Constantine Pleshakov, *Inside the Kremlin's Cold War: From Stalin to Khrushchev* (Cambridge, MA: Harvard University Press, 1996), p. 223.

30. "The U.S. Imperialists Are Caught in Their Own Noose," 8 September 1958, in *Mao Zedong on Diplomacy* (Beijing: Foreign Languages Press, 1998), p. 272.

31. In 1957, the Soviets decided to publish a Chinese-language weekly about the Soviet Union for a Chinese audience in response to "the accelerating cultural misunderstandings of the late 1950s" between the two countries. *Sino-Soviet Friendship* was edited in Moscow, published in Beijing, and distributed in China. See Jersild, *The Sino-Soviet Alliance*, pp. 184–96.

32. The Chinese began to publish the *Friendship Daily* newspaper (in Russian) in 1955, first as a daily in 1955 and then as a weekly in July 1957. *Friendship Daily*, reporting on developments in China and the Soviet Union, was edited in Beijing, and published and distributed primarily in the USSR for a Soviet audience. As Sino-Soviet relations deteriorated in the early 1960s, the two publications were transformed from serving as a "window of friendship" to being on the "forefront of the polemics," disseminating the political viewpoints of each government. Consequently, both publications, *Friendship Daily* and *Soviet-Chinese Friendship*, were forced to shut down in September 1960.

PART III

From Split to Confrontation, 1959–1978

CHAPTER 15

Open Struggles and a Temporary Truce, 1959–1961

Danhui Li

Differences between the Chinese Communist Party (CCP) and the Communist Party of the Soviet Union (CPSU) in the late 1950s over both foreign policy—China's bombardment of Jinmen in 1958 and the border clashes with India in 1959—and domestic policy—the Great Leap Forward and the People's Commune Movement—provoked an increasingly contentious ideological dispute: which party, the CCP or the CPSU, represented orthodox Marxism? Which party was capable of guiding the International Communist Movement in the right direction? And which party should be the leader of the movement? After the November 1957 Moscow Declaration, the CCP moved toward the left, whereas the CPSU moved toward the right.

After the Twenty-first CPSU Congress in February 1959, CPSU propaganda stressed the importance of avoiding war and the establishment of peaceful coexistence and a peaceful transition to socialism. Conversely, after the onset of the Great Leap Forward, CCP propaganda stressed the inevitability of war, the likely transition to socialism via armed struggle, and the impossibility of peaceful coexistence with the imperialists. Each party stressed the parts of the Moscow Declaration that suited it, but each claimed to want to maintain the Communist bloc. After heated and emotional debates in October 1959,[1] each side demanded that the other should admit its mistakes. The only remaining question was the following: which party would ultimately reveal the existence of their differences, and when and by what means?

This chapter explores the emergence of the evolution of the Sino-Soviet split from late 1959 to late 1961, the evolution of ostensible convergences in

D. Li (✉)
World History Institute, East China Normal University, Shanghai, China
e-mail: lidanhui0601@vip.163.com

© The Author(s) 2020
Z. Shen (ed.), *A Short History of Sino-Soviet Relations, 1917–1991*,
China Connections, https://doi.org/10.1007/978-981-13-8641-1_15

foreign policy, the background to the CCP concessions in terms of foreign and domestic policy interactions, and the temporary detente in relations. The period between the quarrels at the Sino-Soviet summit in October 1959 and the Twenty-second CPSU Congress in October 1961 was critical to the evolution of Sino-Soviet relations. It provided both parties an opportunity to achieve a new unity. The ideological compromises devised at the 1960 Moscow Conference, albeit limited, might have lasted longer had the CCP and the CPSU seized the opportunity and had the CCP proved flexible rather than unyielding in the ideological struggle. Had Sino-Soviet party-to-party relations stabilized, the Union of the Soviet Socialist Republics (USSR) and China might have continued to be partners rather than antagonists.

Two Rounds of Contestation in the Name of Unity

As late as spring 1960, both the CCP and the CPSU regarded the maintenance of Sino-Soviet unity as their foremost goal. Although each claimed to apply the principles of Marxism-Leninism, each defined the principles in different terms. In December 1959, Mikhail Suslov, a senior member of the Secretariat of the CPSU Central Committee (CC) and a well-known Marxist ideologue, reported to a CPSU CC plenary session, "We should uphold the position our party deems correct. We must make all efforts to overcome the difficulties in our relations on the condition of adhering to our principles."

During the same month, Liu Shaoqi, vice-chairman of the CCP CC and president of the PRC, stated at a CCP CC work conference: "We should be serious and sincere in dealing with Sino-Soviet relations. We must be firm in principle, but flexible in tactics." Similarly, at a Politburo Standing Committee meeting in Hangzhou from 4 to 6 December, Mao Zedong noted that Nikita Khrushchev, first secretary of the CPSU, had two choices: "The first is further deterioration in his overall policy orientation, and the second is changing for the better. But we should remain confident that his mistakes will eventually be rectified." In the following January, Mao told an enlarged meeting of the Politburo, "Although Khrushchev has his shortcomings, we should help him. We should make efforts to win him over."

As both the CCP and the CPSU claimed to hold the correct theoretical position, each expected the other to compromise. Thus, China tried to use its leverage to push the USSR to shift its ideological stance. Making use of policy differences toward India and the occasion of the commemoration of Lenin's birthday in the early 1960s, China engaged in two rounds of contestation with the USSR in the name of unity.

The first occasion arose from a disagreement over the Sino-Indian border conflict. On 19 January 1960, Premier Zhou Enlai, at a meeting with Stepan Chervonenko, Soviet ambassador to China, asked Chervonenko to convey China's view that the 1959 Sino-Indian border conflict had been instigated solely by India. He added that China hoped that Khrushchev, who was about to visit India, would not show any interest in mediating the Sino-Indian conflict. When the CPSU replied on 22 January that the USSR would continue "strictly observing neutrality,"[2] Zhou, taken by surprise, told Chervonenko that for one Communist country to remain neutral when another was being bullied by a capitalist country was not only unprecedented but also tantamount to being partial to India. When Chervonenko explained that he had misused the term "neutrality" when verbally conveying the CPSU's instructions, Zhou replied that "eliminating the word [neutrality]" will not reassure China. In the Chinese view, a declaration of neutrality and an expression of regret over the Sino-Soviet border dispute, which was published by TASS in September 1959, revealed not only the true position of the USSR but, for the first time, the existence of a Sino-Soviet disagreement.[3] Given the disagreements between Mao and Khrushchev in Beijing in October 1959, the CCP expected that the CPSU would attempt to placate it by standing by China in its dispute with India. Several months later, China asked the USSR to indicate a more obvious signal of alignment with China, challenging the Soviet policy of neutrality.

On 8 January 1960, Khrushchev warned Mao that during the next 18 months, the USSR planned to unilaterally reduce its armed forces by some 1.2 million troops. On the next day, in a foreign ministry report, Zhou Enlai wrote: "After Khrushchev makes his suggestion about disarmament by all world parliaments at the Fourth Session of the Supreme Soviet on 14 January, the Chinese National People's Congress (NPC) will pass a resolution supporting disarmament [on the one hand], but also [on the other hand] it will formally declare that China will not bear any responsibility [for the outcome], as China was not involved [in the decision]." But when, on Mao's instructions, Wu Xiuquan, a vice-director of CCP's International Liaison Department (ILD) who was also a member of the CCP CC, asked Chervonenko to relay China's views to Khrushchev, Wu only mentioned support for disarmament. He failed to mention China's refusal to be responsible for the outcome. On 1 February, in a letter to Khrushchev agreeing to attend the conference of the Warsaw Pact countries which was to be held in Moscow in February, Mao argued that the conference should try to diffuse international tensions, expose the goals of the bellicose imperialists, and promote the global desire for peace. Mao did not disclose that China would agree to take responsibility for disarmament only if it were to formally participate in the decisions.

China sent Kang Sheng, an alternative member of the CCP CC Politburo; ambassador to Moscow Liu Xiao, who was also a member of the CCP CC; and Wu Xiuquan to attend the conference as observers. China's purpose in attending this conference was to spell out its views on Khrushchev's policies of peaceful coexistence and disarmament in front of Moscow's East European allies. On 4 February, in a speech along the lines previously approved by the CC, Kang Sheng told the conference that international tensions had lessened "because the east wind prevails over the west wind." He continued:

As the U.S. imperialists, who are enemies of the Chinese people, adopt a policy of excluding our country from international affairs, the Chinese government must declare to the entire world: all international agreements on disarmament and other agreements made without the formal participation of the PRC and without the endorsement by its representatives will not be binding on China.

Kang was obliquely warning the USSR not to agree to disarm on China's behalf. The USSR believed that the reason the CCP published Kang Sheng's speech in its party organ, *People's Daily*, intended to show that the CCP intentionally wanted to reveal to the Western world information about the Sino-Soviet disputes and what had been discussed at internal meetings of the socialist bloc.[4]

Khrushchev's visit to the United States in September 1959 had been portrayed in the USSR as "a turning point in Soviet-American relations," as "open[ing] a new epoch in international affairs," and as "a new period in the evolution of world peace." Keen to promote the CPSU's policy of detente and frustrated by the CCP's refusal to cooperate, at the meeting's closing banquet on 4 February, Khrushchev obliquely attacked Mao, saying that if an old man was not wise, he was as useless as a pair of old worn-out galoshes that had been discarded in a corner.[5]

Khrushchev's rude insult was taken very seriously by the Chinese. He had not only criticized China's foreign and domestic policies but he had also specifically directed his criticism at China's supreme leader. This touched on Mao's paranoia and provoked swift and direct retaliation by China. On 6 February, *People's Daily* published the text of Kang's speech, entitled "Comrade Kang Sheng Talks about the Current International Situation at the Political Consultative Committee Conference of the Warsaw Treaty Member Countries." In response, Pyotr Pospelov, an alternate member of the CPSU Presidium and a leading member of the CPSU CC Secretariat, issued a statement on behalf of the CPSU CC, criticizing China's foreign and domestic policies and attributing China's dispute with India to its aggressive nationalism.

The Soviets did not publish Khrushchev's or Pospelov's remarks. Nor did the outside world learned of the details in Kang's speech until it was published in the *People's Daily*. By then, the speech had not only attracted the attention of the outside world but it had also offended the Soviets for revealing the Sino-Soviet dispute to the Western world.[6]

The dispute over foreign policy issues arose from China's suspicions of Khrushchev's partiality for Indian Prime Minister Jawaharlal Nehru during his visit to India. To some extent, this dispute was a vehicle to vent China's anger about the TASS statement in 1959. Therefore, it was not a dispute about a common program of the International Communist Movement. The Chinese demand that the USSR should remain in step with China in terms of foreign policy and Soviet criticism of China's foreign and domestic policies at the bloc conference were both acts of interfering in each other's internal affairs. They were also a reflection of the contradiction between bloc interests and the interests of each member state. For China, the purpose of this dispute was intended to upset Khrushchev, reminding him not to forget his proletarian brothers-in-arms and allies, as he was currying favor with capitalist Nehru. In order to achieve the goal of helping Khrushchev and of winning him over to China's correct line, it was necessary that China initiate an ideological struggle. Thus, the anniversary of Lenin's birth on 22 April 1960 gave the CCP an opportunity to attempt to bring Khrushchev back on the correct ideological path.

The criticisms that Khrushchev and other Soviet leaders launched against Chinese policies and against Mao spurred the CCP to actively publicize its own views so as to curb Khrushchev's move toward revisionism. After Mao, on 22 February 1960, told a meeting of the Politburo Standing Committee to issue a counterattack against Khrushchev, the Politburo in early March decided to publish a series of articles that elaborated upon Lenin's views on issues of the era, war and peace, and proletarian revolution and dictatorship. At four meetings held in February, the CCP CC Secretariat had already discussed the contents of three articles: an editorial in *Red Flag* drafted by Chen Boda, a leading CCP ideologue and vice-director of the CC Propaganda Department; a report by Lu Dingyi, director of the CCP CC Propaganda Department and an alternate member of the Politburo; and an editorial in the *People's Daily* drafted by Hu Qiaomu, vice-director of the Propaganda Department. On 10 and 16 February, Mao read and revised the first article. Thus, the CCP CC used the commemoration of Lenin's birth as an opportunity to issue a counterattack in the media against the CPSU.[7]

In actuality, via newspapers and magazines or conferences, the CCP and the CPSU were openly expressing each other's views on important theories as well as on domestic and foreign policies. In reality, this is what brought the Sino-Soviet split out into the open, giving the Western world a glimpse of the dispute from public statements. After 1960, the ideological Sino-Soviet polemics on the commemoration of Lenin's birthday made the Sino-Soviet rupture more noticeable. Nonetheless, this debate did never directly reveal the other party by name. The CCP was a challenger, implicating that Khrushchev was a revisionist. The CPSU felt obligated to take steps to buttress its control over the member states of the Warsaw Pact. The Chinese articles, which either directly or indirectly criticized the CPSU's application of the theory and tactics of Leninism, were translated into foreign languages and circulated in Bulgaria, Romania, Czechoslovakia, the German Democratic Republic, the Democratic People's Republic of Korea (DPRK), and even the capitalist countries. "We can see," explained Frol Kozlov, a member of the CPSU Presidium, on 13 July 1960, "that the Chinese comrades want to become the leader and guide of the International Communist Movement by attempting to prove that Chinese views are the only [true] views of Marxism-Leninism." Whereas the CCP and the CPSU appeared to disagree about which party properly applied Marxism-Leninism, the dispute arose due to political as well as ideological reasons: the CCP claimed that China, rather than the USSR, was better suited to lead the socialist bloc and to ensure that the World Communist and Workers' parties proceed in the right direction.

Khrushchev had once warned anyone who tried to sow discord between the USSR and China: "Don't try to find a crack in a place without a crack." It would not be found, "as they will not see their own ears." After this round of contestation was brought before the public, all the Communist parties agreed that the struggle against revisionism was more than an anti-Yugoslav struggle. Once the CCP's articles were in print, "it seemed there were two centers and two opinions." Even the Western world had become aware of the Sino-Soviet differences. According to State Department China specialist, Allen S. Whiting, publication of these three articles was "the first clear manifestation of the depth and seriousness of the long-accumulating antagonism."[8] To the West, however, the implications of "the divergence of opinions between the dragon and the bear" remained unclear. Perhaps they only disagreed over tactics.

Through two rounds of contestation with the CPSU, the CCP took its first step toward compelling Khrushchev and the CPSU to remain in step with CCP policies. One accidental interlude, that is, the U-2 spy plane incident, tilted the scale of Sino-Soviet unity toward the CCP. At that time, Mao saw the possibility of Khrushchev moving closer to the ideological positions of the CCP.

Interactions in the Wake of the U-2 Spy Plane Incident

China's ideological challenge to the USSR was intended to warn Khrushchev not to make concessions to the imperialists at the four-power summit meeting between the United States, the USSR, the UK, and France, to be held in Paris in May 1960 to discuss Berlin. US President Dwight Eisenhower did Mao a great service when, on 1 May, two weeks before the summit, a US U-2 spy plane was brought down over Soviet territory and its pilot, Captain Francis Gary Powers, admitted to spying.[9] At the Fifth Session of the Fifth Supreme Soviet on 5 May, Khrushchev accused the United States of invading Soviet airspace and warned the Western ambassadors in the audience that the USSR, having established a missile command, had the capability to respond.

US aircraft had often invaded Soviet airspace. But the downing of a spy plane, just at the juncture of heated Sino-Soviet debates over theoretical issues and on the eve of the Paris summit, placed Khrushchev, who had been preaching detente with the West, in a dilemma. On the one hand, he wished to avoid a crisis with the United States; on the other, he may have worried that the conservatives within the CPSU would seize the opportunity to undermine him. To protect his status in the International Communist Movement, he had to respond to the claim in the Chinese media that the imperialists were immutable by taking a tough line against the United States.

On 16 May, at the preliminary session of the four-power summit, Khrushchev denounced the US invasion of Soviet airspace as bellicosity, and he demanded that Eisenhower punish the responsible officials. When Eisenhower only offered not to resume U-2 flights during the remainder of his administration, the summit meeting was suspended. At a press conference in Paris, on 18 May, Khrushchev warned that the USSR would not only shoot down US spy planes but would also destroy their bases. However, he also added that if the United States "stopped provoking the socialist countries in the next six to eight months, then we will meet with our partners to discuss and resolve the international issues." Khrushchev did not wish to wreck the summit.[10]

Mao and the other CCP leaders were excited by the sudden and intensified international situation caused by the spy plane incident and Khrushchev's changing position. They came to see the possibility of Khrushchev moving closer to the Chinese position as a result of Chinese pressure. During this period, *Internal Reference* reprinted many foreign media comments on China's impact on Khrushchev's decisions that reflected the likes and dislikes of the CCP. *Internal Reference* also indicated that CCP leaders and Mao paid special attention to China's ideological pressure on Khrushchev and the CPSU CC. Nonetheless, Mao soon calmly noted the other side of the issue even before the end of the propaganda campaign, and he offered the following two opinions:

First, Mao believed that Khrushchev altered his position not because he was willing to but only because he was forced to do so by the Chinese government. Second, Mao, seeing Khrushchev as unpredictable but persuadable, reopened the debate over ideology. Mao's attitude led to the formation of CCP CC policies at the Beijing Conference of the World Federation of Trade Unions (WFTU). China wanted to exert more pressure on the USSR and to prevent Khrushchev from moving toward the right.

CONTENTION AT THE WFTU CONFERENCE IN BEIJING

The CCP had endorsed the 1957 Moscow Declaration of 12 ruling parties in socialist countries—based on the decision at the Twentieth CPSU Congress and the Peace Manifesto signed by delegates of 64 Communist and Workers' parties (including the League of Communists of Yugoslavia [LCY]), which more closely reflected Khrushchev's views. The CCP thereby accepted the program of the Twentieth CPSU Congress as the guiding principle of the International Communist Movement. With the widening gap in Sino-Soviet thinking, posture, and policies, neither side was willing to abandon its respective views and each side was eager to win over the other side. By any calculation, it was only a matter of time before the CCP would challenge the CPSU's control over the majority of the members in socialist international organizations. From the perspective of the CCP, China's radical slogans and programs for the revolutionary parties and social groups in favor of armed struggle in Asia, Africa, and Latin America were more attractive than the cautious Soviet strategy. Thus, making use of the anti-imperialist and anti-American situation in the wake of the U-2 incident, the CCP tried to open up a second front in these organizations as part of its struggle with the CPSU. Its declared goal was unity through criticism.[11]

The 11th meeting of the General Council of the WFTU, one of the most important meetings of front organizations in the International Communist Movement, held in Beijing from 5 to 9 June 1960, was attended by 64 delegations from 58 countries. Prior to the opening of the meeting, China and the USSR debated what issues were to be included in the general report of the Secretariat of the WFTU. The Chinese delegation noted that the report contained major mistakes on at least six topics, such as war and peace, the National Liberation Movement, and the general crisis of capitalism. Furthermore, it was wrong to refer to China's Great Leap Forward and the People's Communes with quotation marks. This was an indication of an unfriendly attitude toward the Chinese people.

At a meeting on 1 June with Liu Ningyi, head of the Chinese delegation, head of the Soviet delegation and WFTU vice-president Viktor Grishin replied that the use of quotation marks was merely correct Russian usage. The next day, at a meeting of trade union delegates from 12 socialist countries, China was accused of a "left-wing infantile disorder." After the Secretariat revised the report on 3 and 4 June, the Chinese, although still describing parts of the report as "erroneous," agreed to allow it to be discussed at the meeting of the General Council.[12] Liu Ningyi stated that the CCP, out of respect for the views of the majority, would not repeat its criticism at the plenary sessions.

At the opening plenary session on 5 June, Marcel Boula, a leading member of the Secretariat, delivered a report on behalf of WFTU President Louis Saillant of France. Grishin spoke in the afternoon. Their speeches touched on the invasion of Soviet airspace by the U-2, the threat from US imperialism to world peace, and the likelihood of a third world war. But the Chinese delegates, who heard what seemed to them to be a program aimed at promoting peaceful coexistence, peaceful competition, and peaceful transition, accused the CPSU of trying to impose its erroneous views on the international democratic organizations and attempting to alter the correct line.

In anticipation of open disagreement at the plenary sessions, the CCP CC invited over 40 trade union leaders from 17 Communist and Workers' parties to an evening dinner meeting on 5 June,[13] hosted by Liu Shaoqi, Zhou Enlai, and Deng Xiaoping, and the Chinese asked that the guests report their views on the CCP's views of the international situation to their respective CCs. When, after the dinner, Deng elaborated on the CCP's views, the Soviets at the meeting accused him of "Trotskyism" and of imposing his own views on others. After reluctantly listening to Deng's discussion of the first issue, "On Our Era," Grishin immediately raised objections. He rejected Deng's explanation, and he was the first to leave the meeting, even though Liu and Zhou both requested that he remain. The delegates from the East European countries soon followed. Therefore, the meeting was brought to an end.[14]

Owing to the Soviets' intransigence, the Chinese failed to modify the draft report. The Chinese believed it was impossible to come to an agreement with the Soviets behind closed doors. To promote their own program, they publicized CCP views among the delegates from the other countries.[15] To carry out this policy, Zhou Enlai gave a banquet in honor of all delegates and delivered a speech on 6 June. He said that peace "depends on the people's struggle against the imperialists. ... Peace will never come if [you] beg the imperialists for it. ... [As] the bellicose nature of the imperialists will never change ... [we should] resolutely expose the disguises of the modern revisionist traitors." On the following day, the *People's Daily* printed a special edition on "anti-imperialism," "anti-modern revisionism," and "anti-colonialism."

To elaborate on Chinese views, on 8 June, Liu Changsheng, a Chinese delegate and vice-chairman of the All-China Federation of Trade Unions, told a meeting of the General Council of the WFTU that the assumption that war could be avoided was wrong: "We proposed peaceful coexistence between the socialist and capitalist countries. But the imperialists headed by the United States insist on a Cold War policy of arms expansion and war preparations. ... We should resolutely oppose the imperialist Cold War policy ... engaging in a tit-for-tat struggle. ... Only in this way can we prevent the Cold War from evolving into hot war." Liu Changsheng showed that China's views were different from those included in the general report that had been delivered at the meeting. The speech, loudly applauded, was seconded by many delegates from Asia, Africa, and Latin America.[16]

Meanwhile, the Chinese and Soviet delegates on the editorial committee that was responsible for drafting the conference's general resolution and a resolution on anti-colonialism also engaged in a fierce tit-for-tat struggle. The Chinese argued that the "peaceful road is not relevant. Don't beg the capitalists for peace!" The Chinese presented motions in support of Algeria's struggle for national independence, the struggle for liberation in Africa, and aid to Cuba. The Secretariat, paralyzed by the disagreements, first proposed to adjourn the General Council meeting in favor of holding a meeting of all delegates. After the Chinese efforts, the Secretariat eventually rescinded the proposal to adjourn. The Soviet delegates agreed: "Divergent points will not be included." After sustained haggling, an agreement was reached on 9 June, which, according to the Chinese, "is much better than what we expected."[17] In his report to the CCP CC, Liu Ningyi claimed that, for the first time, the Trade Union Movement agreed to resist semi-revisionism.[18]

The Chinese had tried to put leverage on Khrushchev to change course by winning the backing of the Asian, African, and Latin American countries that were fighting their own wars of national liberation. At the WFTU meeting, in an open report by a non-party organization to the outside world, China, for the first time, publicly stated that it disagreed with the USSR over both ideology and policies, thus bringing the Sino-Soviet split to the attention of the international Communist organizations.

Naturally, the Soviets resented being criticized in front of the WFTU, a non-Communist organization. They argued that the disagreements between the CCP and the CPSU would be exploited by the capitalists and imperialists to undermine the International Communist Movement and the working classes in their struggle for peace and socialism. However, when the Communist members of the General Council of the WFTU refused to support China, CCP leaders adopted even more divisive tactics. At meetings attended by both Communists and non-party members, the CCP criticized the approaches of the CPSU and the other fraternal parties on all substantive issues—the issue of the transition from capitalism to socialism, peaceful coexistence with the capitalist countries, and peaceful competition between socialism and capitalism.[19] Thus, the Sino-Soviet dispute ceased to be merely a disagreement among the

Communists. The US Central Intelligence Agency and other agencies soon learned about the Sino-Soviet disagreements at the WFTU meeting in Beijing.[20]

The Chinese tactics at the WFTU Conference and the support they won from the Asian, African, and Latin American delegates created a dilemma for Khrushchev. He either had to move closer to the Chinese position or had to face the charge of splittism at meetings of international socialist organizations. Moscow obviously felt the pressure and attempted to avoid the issue. China's offensive tactics at the WFTU Conference explain the counterattack launched by the Soviets and their East European allies at the June Conference of Communist and Workers' Parties of the Socialist Bloc, held in Bucharest two weeks later. As Suslov noted, the Bucharest Conference was called to reverse the results of the WFTU Conference at Beijing.

A Tit-for-Tat Struggle at the 1960 Bucharest Conference

On 2 June, prior to the WFTU Conference, the CPSU CC invited the leaders of the ruling parties of the socialist countries to meet in Bucharest later in the month during the Third Congress of the Romanian Workers' Party. The meeting was to discuss the international situation after the summit in Paris and to "exchange views in order to settle on our common policy." All the parties accepted the invitation, with the exception of the CCP. Mao came to understand that CCP pressure had been the deciding factor in changing Khrushchev's position after the U-2 incident. Mao thus had decided to publicize the CCP's ideology and its disagreement with the CPSU in a bid to seize leadership of the International Communist Movement.

On 5 June, at a meeting with Kang Sheng and other CCP officials, Mao proposed the convening of a Conference of World Communist and Workers' Parties on 7 November, rather than in June as proposed by the Soviets: "We are busy in June and we are unable to attend." If the Soviets agreed, the CCP would send a delegation to Moscow in August to draft the conference documents with the Soviets. Two days later, on 7 June, the CPSU CC notified the CCP that the Conference of Delegates from Communist and Workers' Parties in the Socialist Bloc and the Political Consultative Conference of the member states of the Warsaw Pact, scheduled for June, would be postponed. On 10 June, the CCP CC replied: "We completely agree to postpone the two conferences," but the CCP CC suggested that the Conference of Communist and Workers' Parties should be enlarged to include the entire world. As at the 1957 Moscow Conference, however, only the 12 ruling parties were to sign and issue the final declaration. An editorial commission was to be established to prepare the draft declaration before the conference. The CPSU agreed to this proposal. But a new circular to all fraternal parties from the CPSU, relaying the deliberations between the CPSU and the CCP, stated that discussions on international issues would not be excluded at the Bucharest Conference on the condition that no resolution would be issued. All the fraternal parties agreed to this. This foreshadowed the forthcoming struggle at Bucharest.

After the Sino-Soviet struggle at the WFTU Beijing Conference, the Chinese paid special attention to propaganda in the Soviet media, and they were prepared for a possible Soviet counterattack. At an enlarged Politburo meeting held in Shanghai on 14–18 June, Mao read a report which stated that articles in the Soviet media commemorating publication of Lenin's article, "Left-wing Communism: An Infantile Disorder," represented a counterattack against China, and the purpose was to undermine the CCP's influence by labeling it "modern left-wing opportunism." Mao believed the Soviets were trying to discredit the views expressed in the three Chinese articles commemorating Lenin's birth.

On 16 June, Peng Zhen, the CCP's deputy secretary general led a delegation to attend the Congress of the Romanian Workers' Party to "persuade" Khrushchev and the CPSU to rectify their mistakes. Prior to their departure from Beijing, Mao instructed the Chinese delegation to "persist in unity, but also to uphold principles. … to argue on the basis of reason, but also to leave a little leeway." While on the way to Bucharest, Peng engaged in almost nine hours of discussions in Moscow with Frol Kozlov, a member of the CPSU Presidium, who told Peng that in order to forestall any disagreement in Bucharest, Khrushchev wished to "persuade" the Chinese to admit that they had made mistakes at the WFTU Beijing Conference. Kozlov posed the following question, "How can you seek anti-Soviet allies?" The Soviets again referred not only to the likelihood of war, the nature of imperialism, and the viability of peaceful coexistence, and they also criticized China's domestic policies, such as "Let a hundred flowers bloom and let a hundred schools of thought contend," and the General Line of the International Communist Movement. In addition to answering these questions, the Chinese repeated their objections to the Soviet assessment of Stalin, peaceful transition, and the decisions taken at the Twentieth CPSU Congress. Attempts at mutual persuasion resulted in confrontation, and nothing substantial was agreed upon.

Khrushchev had assumed that the Communist and Workers' parties throughout the world would treat the 1957 Moscow Declaration as an agreed-upon program that had settled outstanding issues. The CCP, in contrast, claimed that many issues remained to be settled. For this reason, the CCP ignored the principles in the 1957 Moscow Declaration and the Peace Manifesto. In doing so, the CCP was confronting not only the CPSU but also the other Communist parties, whereas the CPSU was counting on support from the other socialist parties at the Bucharest Conference. During their meeting, "Kozlov repeatedly waved a thick document under Peng's nose," and when Peng Zhen asked what it was, Kozlov replied: "We will discuss this after we arrive in Bucharest." It turned out to be "a 68-page Soviet condemnation of Chinese policies."[21] As a result, the CCP delegation predicted that Khrushchev would most probably call a meeting of the fraternal parties during the Third Congress of the Romanian Workers' Party to criticize the CCP. After further intelligence gathering, Liu Xiao flew to Shanghai to report to Mao and Liu Shaoqi on this new development. Mao and the CCP CC decided not to compromise—"[We will have to] respond again. Nothing more than destruction." The CCP CC would adhere to its position.

The Conference of Communist and Workers' Parties of the Socialist Bloc and the Conference of Delegates from the Communist and Workers' Parties of 51 Nations (generally known as the Bucharest Conference) were held in succession in Bucharest from 24 to 26 June. The central topic of discussion at both conferences was the CCP's erroneous views of world affairs and the strategies and tactics of the International Communist Movement. The Soviets admitted that the exchange of views was prearranged.

During the conference, led by the CPSU delegation, the CCP came under attack from all sides. Peng Zhen maintained a posture of "glorious isolation" and argued vehemently, sparing no effort in his counterattack on his opponents. Both sides spoke with biting sarcasm, hurting each other's feelings and pride. According to the Soviet delegates, the Chinese delegates definitely had an opportunity to explain the CCP's views. In spite of this opportunity, Peng delivered three speeches, but he did not answer any of the questions asked by the other delegates. He only repeated—so he said—what Mao had told him to say. He made the accusation that the CPSU's memorandum was all "slander and libel against the CCP." But Peng also acknowledged that he had not read the entire memorandum.

At the Conference of Communist and Workers' Parties, several fraternal parties proposed that the conference should issue a communiqué, and this proposal was endorsed almost unanimously. Thus, whether or not the CPSU was manipulating behind the scenes, Khrushchev was able to create a dilemma for the CCP: The CCP had the choice of either submitting and signing the communiqué or admitting to charges of sectarianism and splittism. The communiqué highlighted the ideas in the 1957 Moscow Declaration and Peace Manifesto, which supported the positions of the CPSU—the possibility of avoiding war, peaceful transition to socialism, and the pursuit of peace as the primary duty of all Communist parties. Thus, the CPSU was taking revenge against the CCP for what had occurred at the WFTU Beijing Conference. The conference also authorized the CPSU to call a conference of world Communist and Workers' parties in the coming autumn. Therefore, in Bucharest, Khrushchev once again regained the initiative from Mao in the International Communist Movement.

At this point, the CCP CC could not opt for "destruction," and it preferred not to become an adversary of the other fraternal parties. The CCP did not want to split with the CPSU, and it still "attempted to leave some leeway and to give him [Khrushchev] a helping hand." On 24 June, the CCP CC in Beijing instructed the CCP delegation to sign the communiqué. At the same time, on 26 June, the CCP CC instructed the Chinese delegation to distribute a written statement that criticized Khrushchev by name, accusing him of violating the Sino-Soviet agreement prior to the conference, of using the draft communiqué to launch a surprise attack on the CCP, of tarnishing the prestige of the CCP in the International Communist Movement, and of rudeness in imposing his will on others. The statement declared that the CCP would not yield to errone-ous anti–Marxist-Leninist arguments. For the first time, the CCP criticized Khrushchev by name, while, at the same time, it still tried to play down the significance of its criticism.

The CCP's uncompromising attitude provoked Khrushchev to use eco-nomic leverage. On 16 July, the Soviet government notified the Chinese gov-ernment that it had unilaterally decided to recall all Soviet experts posted in China. On 25 July, it announced that the recall would take place between 28 July and 1 September, and it turned down a CCP request to reconsider.[22] At the time, there were 1390 Soviet experts working in China. In addition to the recall, Moscow also "tore up 343 contracts and supplementary contracts con-cerning the experts, and scrapped 257 projects on scientific and technical coop-eration."[23] Thus, the Sino-Soviet disagreement over ideology expanded into a disagreement over state-to-state relations. Both Sino-Soviet party-to-party and state-to-state relations were on the verge of collapse. A split in the Sino-Soviet bloc appeared imminent.

Toward a Temporary Detente

In 1960, China faced both a domestic crisis and a deteriorating security envi-ronment. The Great Leap Forward had caused "three bitter years" of severe economic crises from 1959 to 1961, with probably more than 20 million peo-ple starving to death due to the failure of Mao's bid for self-reliance.[24] Even before the withdrawal of the Soviet experts, Mao and his associates had been forced to reorient their development strategy. The withdrawal of the Soviet experts in July 1960 worsened China's already dire economic conditions.

At the same time, China attempted to reduce international pressures. Its relations with India were hardly cordial after the border conflicts in 1959, the US military was increasingly involved in Indochina, the Nationalists on Taiwan were frequently carrying out small-scale raids along China's southeast coast, and Jiang Jieshi was even threatening to "mount a [large-scale] counterattack against the mainland." China faced rivals both north and south.

The economic recession and the external challenges, which were worrying to senior CCP leaders, led to calls for a comprehensive review of China's for-eign policy. A Politburo Standing Committee meeting, held from 7 to 17 January 1960 and chaired by Mao, decided that "strenuous and active efforts should be made to open up new prospects in China's foreign relations." In establishing his priorities, Mao stated: "The resolution of international issues will be determined by the work we can achieve domestically. The defeat of revisionism depends not only on politics but also on the economy." Zhou Enlai later added that "unity [with the CPSU] is a priority. … Criticism or struggle may not be valid. Unity requires patience and time."

Mao thus defined the struggle with Khrushchev as a "contradiction" among the people. It was possible to reach unity through criticism. The CCP CC sanctioned a 24-Chinese-word policy: "Uphold principle and attack later; uphold struggle and leave leeway; uphold unity and oppose splittism," with the aim of achieving Sino-Soviet unity. Pragmatists such as Liu Shaoqi, Zhou Enlai, and Deng Xiaoping regarded national security as more important than ideology. They recognized that China required Soviet help not only to learn from the Soviet experience of building a socialist society but also because cordial relations with the USSR would reduce the threat from the United States and the Jiang Jieshi clique. Thus, an improvement in relations with the USSR was of strategic importance. The threat from the imperialist enemy forced the CCP to make ideological concessions to buttress rather than to undermine its partnership with the CPSU.

Before the conference of 81 Communist parties in November 1960, the CCP and the CPSU met twice at Moscow in an attempt to heal the rift in world communism. Deng Xiaoping, in Moscow between 17 and 22 September to meet with Suslov, for tactical reasons deliberately tested Khrushchev by reciting a long list of Chinese grievances, including Stalin's violation of Chinese sovereignty in the Sino-Soviet Treaty of February 1950 and the Soviet proposal for a long-wave radio station and a "joint fleet" in 1958.[25]

Liu Shaoqi and Deng Xiaoping led the Chinese delegation to attend the Moscow Conference of Communist and Workers' Parties, which opened on 5 November 1960. When Khrushchev, on 10 November, made a speech criticizing the CCP in the presence of the delegates from 81 countries, Deng, on instructions from the CCP Politburo, accused Khrushchev of "big-nation" chauvinism and of being the "father party." His speech, which provoked an uproar, seemed likely to break up the conference, until a "petition" organized by Ho Chi Minh, chairman of the Vietnamese Workers' Party, asked that the Soviets and the Chinese try to avoid a split.[26]

To break the deadlock, Liu Shaoqi tried to engineer a compromise to serve as a new basis for Sino-Soviet relations. After repeated consultations, the two parties eventually reached an agreement: the final statement would echo the 1957 Moscow Declaration regarding the evaluation of the Twentieth CPSU Congress; it would eliminate the charge of sectarianism but it would CCP views on peaceful coexistence, peaceful transition, peaceful competition, and so on, and soften the wording about nationalism and sectarianism. Liu and Khrushchev also agreed not to quarrel in public: every issue was to first be discussed between the CCP and the CPSU, then to be discussed with other Communist parties, and only then be brought before a plenary session.

After the Moscow Conference in November 1960 and Liu's state visit to the USSR in early December, Sino-Soviet relations showed some signs of relaxation.[27] Not only Liu but also other CCP leaders showed a willingness to tolerate the views of the CPSU. Due to China's domestic economic predicament, Mao was forced to consider China's relationship with the Soviet Union from a pragmatic perspective. For this reason, Mao decided to suspend the ideological debates with the USSR and to settle on concessionary policies. His attitude made it possible for Liu and other CCP leaders to make relevant compromises, thus avoiding a premature split in the International Communist Movement.[28]

In sum, beginning in early 1960, the CCP made an effort to force Khrushchev to move closer in the direction of CCP policies, and to some extent Khrushchev did so. But after late 1960, there was a reversal, as CCP policies moved closer to those of the CPSU, and their respective views began to merge. This laid a foundation for a temporary Sino-Soviet detente.[29]

The Sino-Soviet detente lasted from late summer 1960 to late autumn 1961. During this period, the Chinese ceased to publish ideological articles on Sino-Soviet differences.[30] In terms of politics and diplomacy, the CCP adopted a policy of self-restraint and compromise with respect to the Soviet-Albanian disputes. The two countries also cooperated to reach a peaceful resolution of the Laotian crisis. During the Berlin crisis of 1961, China supported the position of the Soviets and the Warsaw Pact countries in terms of signing a peace treaty with Germany. As Deng Xiaoping noted, "Sino-Soviet relations developed smoothly after the Moscow Conference. China and the USSR have established very good cooperation in the international arena." Such cooperation extended to military affairs, national defense, economics, and science and technology.

According to Foreign Minister Chen Yi, the adjustment of the CCP's position vis-à-vis that of the USSR consisted of "toleration in major respects," a so-called revolutionary compromise and reconciliation, and thus it could only be "transitional." The underlying cause of the Sino-Soviet differences remained unresolved, rendering the detente fragile. Although Sino-Soviet relations could not develop once the ideological differences between the two emerged, they could maintain a detente when the two countries suspended or toned down their ideological struggle to focus on their common interests.[31]

CONCLUSION

A careful examination of the history of Sino-Soviet relations from late 1959 to late 1961 reveals that after their heated and emotional debates in October 1959, Chinese and Soviet leaders harbored good intentions to achieve a new unity. But such intentions were fragile because of the realization that the new unity was conditional. Each side upheld the correctness of its position and each side believed that the other side should soften its ideological position. Because they each treated the issue as a matter of major principle, neither was willing to compromise on ideological grounds. According to Mao, the CCP should be proactive in influencing the CPSU and assisting Khrushchev. Thus, a new round of contradictions and conflicts emerged in Sino-Soviet relations. The CCP first brought the Sino-Soviet differences into the open to the international socialist organizations at the WFTU Beijing Conference. The Soviets surely felt betrayed by this Chinese challenge. In response, Khrushchev organized a joint attack on the Chinese delegation at the Bucharest Conference.

Due to his personal frustrations, Khrushchev unilaterally decided to recall all Soviet experts from China, expanding the Sino-Soviet dispute from ideology to state-to-state relations.[32]

Confronted with a serious economic recession in the wake of the Great Leap Forward, Mao was willing to compromise with the USSR, emphasizing practical interests and suspending the ideological debates, but also standing up to Soviet pressures. Simultaneously, the content and rhetoric of CCP foreign policy and propaganda were moving closer to that of the CPSU, thus reaching a temporary detente in Sino-Soviet relations.

It was against Mao's nature to compromise with the USSR. To make long-term concessions to Khrushchev on ideological issues was too much for Mao to tolerate. Any concessions were only made on the basis of weighing the advantages and disadvantages of the Chinese situation. This was a matter of utilitarianism; therefore, it did not eliminate the deeper roots in the Sino-Soviet split. The two Moscow conferences (in 1957 and 1960) created two authorities in the International Communist Movement, thus coming into conflict with the traditional idea of one authority. According to Mao, the Soviet revisionists should no longer guide the International Communist Movement, as the focal points of the revolution had shifted to Asia, Africa, and Latin America, and instead, the CCP should assume responsibility for leading the International Communist Movement. Mao's ambitions could no longer tolerate the program of the Twentieth CPSU Congress, and the Sino-Soviet detente proved to be only transient. The subsequent Sino-Soviet polemics resulted in an ideological and emotional rupture between the two parties, and a split in their organizational relations was only a matter of time.

NOTES

1. For the quarrels at the Sino-Soviet summit in October 1959, see Shen and Xia, *Mao and the Sino-Soviet Partnership*, chap. 10.
2. See Lüthi, *The Sino-Soviet Split*, p. 115.
3. On 13 September 1959, Chinese Foreign Minister Chen Yi presented the Soviets with a letter of protest, pointing out that the "TASS announcement reveals to the public Sino-Soviet differences regarding the Sino-Indian border clashes. This only grieves our friends and gladdens our enemies." At the November 1960 Moscow Conference and in the talks among the Sino-Soviet parties in July 1963, Deng Xiaoping explicitly pointed out that the TASS declaration of 9 September 1959 revealed publicly for the first time the Sino-Soviet differences. For Deng's talk at the November 1960 Moscow Conference, see Peter Jones and Siân Kevill, comps., *China and the Soviet Union, 1949–84* (Burnt Mill, Harlow, Essex, UK: Longman, 1985), pp. 21–22.
4. Interview with Yan Mingfu, by Shen Zhihua and Li Danhui, March 1998.
5. Interview with Yan Mingfu by Shen Zhihua and Li Danhui, March 1998.
6. Interview with Yan Mingfu by Shen Zhihua and Li Danhui, March 1998; *Tokyo News*, 13 March 1960; *The Times*, 17 April 1960.

7. For analysis of Sino-Soviet disputes over the commemoration of Lenin's birth, see Danhui Li and Yafeng Xia, *Mao and the Sino-Soviet Split, 1959–1973* (Lanham, MD: Lexington Books, 2018), pp. 6–10.
8. Allen S. Whiting, "A Brief History," in Clement J. Zablocki, ed., *Sino-Soviet Rivalry: Implications for U.S. Policy* (New York: Frederick A. Praeger, 1966), pp. 10–11.
9. For the U-2 incident, see Michael R. Beschloss, *Mayday: Eisenhower, Khrushchev and the U-2 Affair* (New York: Harper & Row, 1986), pp. 121–22, 173, 372.
10. I argue that the collapse of the Paris Summit was due to two reasons: the arrogance of the US government and Chinese pressure. Khrushchev was forced to play tough because of Eisenhower's noncooperative stance after the downing of the U-2 plane.
11. Lüthi, *The Sino-Soviet Split*, p. 167.
12. Interview with Zhu Tingguang by Shen Zhihua and Li Danhui, 5 June 2002. Zhu was chief of the International Propaganda Division of the CCP CC Propaganda Department. He was heavily involved in the Sino-Soviet polemics. The author has not seen the text of the general report of the eleventh meeting of the WFTU General Council.
13. According to Russian records, it was the CCP Politburo members who invited nearly 40 foreign trade union leaders (who were Communist Party members) for dinner and discussion.
14. Interview with Zhu Tingguang by Shen Zhihua and Li Danhui, 5 June 2002.
15. Interview with Zhu Tingguang by Shen Zhihua and Li Danhui, 5 June 2002.
16. The conclusion that the Chinese won broad support for their position at the WFTU meeting from the Asian, African, and Latin American delegates is based on a *People's Daily* report; Interview with Zhu Tingguang by Shen Zhihua and Li Danhui, 5 June 2002.
17. Interview with Zhu Tingguang by Shen Zhihua and Li Danhui, 5 June 2002.
18. Interview with Zhu Tingguang by Shen Zhihua and Li Danhui, 5 June 2002. Liu Ningyi, who was then chairman of the All-China Federation of Trade Unions, does not refer to this meeting in his memoirs.
19. Oleg Borisovich Borisov and Boris Trofimovich Kolosov, *Soviet-Chinese Relations, 1945–1970* (Bloomington: Indiana University Press, 1975).
20. Memo, "Sino-Soviet Relations," 9 August 1960, National Security Archives, Washington, DC, US Fiche 64, Item 255, NIE 100-3-60; memo, "Authority and Control in the Communist Movement," 8 August 1961, National Security Archives. Washington, DC, U.S., Fiche 84, Item 318, NIE 10-61.
21. Lüthi, *The Sino-Soviet Split*, pp. 169–70.
22. Ibid., p. 175.
23. John Gittings, *Survey of the Sino-Soviet Dispute* (New York: Oxford University Press, 1968), p. 139.
24. Jonathan D. Spence, *The Search for Modern China* (New York: Norton, 1991), p. 583; Philip Short, *Mao: A Life* (New York: Henry Holt, 1999), p. 505; Edwin E. Moise claims that "the total number of deaths seems to have been at least 16 million more than there would have been during three years of normal food supply." See Edwin Moise, *Modern China, A History* (London: Longman, 2nd ed., 1994), p. 142.
25. "Memorandum of Conversation between the CCP Delegation and the CPSU Delegation," *CWIHP Bulletin*, Issue 10 (March 1998), pp. 172–73.

26. Lüthi, *The Sino-Soviet Split*, pp. 188–91.
27. Liu Shaoqi led a high-level Chinese delegation, including four Politburo members and two alternate Politburo members, to attend the Moscow Conference. For a discussion of the Moscow Conference, see Dong Wang, "The Quarrelling Brothers: New Chinese Archives and a Reappraisal of the Sino-Soviet Split, 1959–1962," *CWIHP Working Paper*, no. 49 (7 July 2011), at https://www.wilsoncenter.org/publication/the-quarrelling-brothers-new-chinese-archives-and-reappraisal-the-sino-soviet-split-1959
28. When speaking about Chinese concessions at the 1960 Moscow Conference, Chen Yi later stated that "the Party Center and Chairman Mao made the decision. Members of the party delegation did a great job."
29. For analysis, see Li and Xia, *Mao and the Sino-Soviet Split*, pp. 24–30.
30. From "The Diary of S. V. Chervonenko: Transcripts of the Conversations (Excerpts) With the General Secretary of the CC CCP Deng Xiaoping, 1 March 1962," *CWIHP Bulletin*, Issue 10 (March 1998), p. 175.
31. Niu Jun, "1962: The Eve of the Left Turn in China's Foreign Policy," *CWIHP Working Paper*, no. 48 (October 2005).
32. See Austin Jersild, "The Soviet State as Imperial Scavenger: 'Catch up and Surpass' in the Transnational Socialist Bloc, 1950–1960," *American Historical Review*, vol. 116, no. 1 (February 2011), p. 130.

CHAPTER 16

The Collapse of Party Relations and the Deterioration of State Relations, October 1961–July 1964

Danhui Li

This chapter attempts to offer a multicausal interpretation of the most critical period in the Sino-Soviet split—from the Twenty-second Communist Party of the Soviet Union (CPSU) Congress in October 1961, when the Chinese Communist Party (CCP) began to call the CPSU a revisionist party, to July 1964, when the CCP published its ninth commentary and CCP-CPSU party relations were suspended. The chapter demonstrates that neither a "conflict of national interests" nor a "conflict of ideology" can fully explain the schism between Beijing and Moscow. A conflict of national interests was the result, not the cause, of the Sino-Soviet split. The Sino-Soviet struggle over ideology was only for the sake of appearances. Competition over the interpretation of Marxism-Leninism in fact was a struggle for leadership of the International Communist Movement. Only when a party had the authority to interpret Marxism-Leninism could it be considered the legitimate leader of the movement. The unwillingness of either China or the Union of Soviet Socialist Republics (USSR) to compromise on the issue of leadership of the wider International Communist Movement precipitated the rupture in the Sino-Soviet alliance.

D. Li (✉)
World History Institute, East China Normal University, Shanghai, China
e-mail: lidanhui0601@vip.163.com

© The Author(s) 2020
Z. Shen (ed.), *A Short History of Sino-Soviet Relations, 1917–1991*,
China Connections, https://doi.org/10.1007/978-981-13-8641-1_16

Open Strife and Veiled Struggle at the Twenty-Second CPSU Congress

Albania and Yugoslavia are Balkan countries with close historical ties. The Albanian Communist Party was established under the direct guidance of the Yugoslav party in 1941. It was renamed the Party of Labor of Albania in 1948. When Yugoslavia was expelled from the Communist Information Bureau (the Cominform) in 1948, Albanian Communist leader Enver Hoxha joined Moscow in condemning Belgrade.[1] Thereafter, Soviet-Albanian relations remained friendly for a considerable period. When the Warsaw Pact was formed in 1955, Albania was a founding member, and the Soviet naval station in Vlorë, Albania, served as an important Warsaw Pact base. But when, under Nikita Khrushchev, Soviet policy toward Yugoslavia in the mid-1950s was modified, the leaders of the Albanian party became upset. Their relations with the USSR soured, and the Albanians turned to the CCP. At the Bucharest Conference in June 1960 and the Moscow Conference of World Communist and Workers' Parties in November 1960, the Albanian party became the CCP's strongest supporter vis-à-vis the USSR.[2] At the Fourth Congress of the Party of Labor of Albania in February 1961, with a high-level Soviet delegation in attendance, Enver Hoxha accused Khrushchev of being a revisionist and a dictator. At the March 1961 session of the Political Consultative Committee of the Warsaw Pact, Khrushchev decried Albania's unfriendly attitude toward the Soviet forces in Vlorë. As the Soviet-Albanian relationship soured, Khrushchev halted economic aid and withdrew the Soviet naval forces from Vlorë.

At this point, the CCP still valued its relationship with the USSR, which had improved since Khrushchev's quarrel with his Chinese hosts in October 1959, and hence, the CCP was reluctant to sacrifice its newly achieved detente with the USSR for the sake of defending Albania. Therefore, the CCP adopted a two-pronged strategy. On the one hand, it tried to "take into consideration the importance of unity with Albania" and "not to make Albania feel that it was getting a cold shoulder from China because of the improvement in Sino-Soviet relations"; on the other hand, China "would not attempt to meet all the needs of Albania." Thus, China adopted a cautious attitude, attempting to maintain a neutral position and making efforts to mediate in the Soviet-Albanian quarrel.

Meanwhile, the CCP and the CPSU remained in close contact. In January 1961, the CPSU Central Committee (CC) adopted a resolution to convene the Twenty-second CPSU Congress so that Khrushchev could establish a new party program. In February, Soviet Ambassador Stepan Chervonenko relayed this news to Liu Shaoqi. On 24 July, a week before the 112-page draft CPSU program was formally released, Chervonenko handed a copy in Russian, with a Chinese translation, to Peng Zhen, deputy general secretary of the CCP CC, and to Yang Shangkun, director of the General Office of the CCP CC.

The new program included peaceful coexistence, peaceful transition, and peaceful competition—which had also been on the agenda of the Twentieth Congress—and proposed the new concepts of "a state of the entire people" (the USSR) and "a party of the entire people" (the CPSU). These notions effectively put an end to the dogma of domestic class struggle and dictatorship of the proletariat. From the CCP's perspective, the document represented "a milestone in the formation of [CPSU] revisionism." Several months earlier, at the June 1960 Conference of the World Federation of Trade Unions in Beijing, when the CCP learned that Khrushchev was working on a new program, the Chinese delegates had attacked the program of the Twentieth Congress in hopes of "preventing Khrushchev from falling into a revisionist quagmire." It turned out that not only was the CCP unable to "save" Khrushchev but also the CCP had to set aside its differences with the CPSU and make compromises in fall 1960 to reach a temporary detente. Because the new CPSU program, which the CCP regarded as revisionist, was to be the guiding principle for world communism, Chinese leaders had no choice but to reopen the ideological struggle with the CPSU. Defending the Albanian party was just the starting point.

In August 1961, Chinese Ambassador Liu Xiao attended a meeting of party leaders of the Warsaw Pact member states as an observer. Under instructions from Beijing, Liu Xiao objected to the exclusion of the Albanian delegation from the conference and called for the decision to be reversed, but Khrushchev rejected Liu's proposal. This incident clouded the Sino-Soviet detente, but the CCP did not change its policy. Although Mao and his associates held a negative view of the new CPSU program, they did not make their opinions public before the convening of the Twenty-second Congress.

On 9 September 1961, the Soviet chargé d'affaires in Beijing, Nikolai Sudarikov, told Foreign Minister Chen Yi that the lack of commentaries in the Chinese press about the new CPSU program was causing foreign missions in Beijing to believe that the CCP opposed the program. Chen Yi denied the accusation, noting, "We have published the entire document and we have also issued it as a separate edition." Chen claimed that CCP leaders were preoccupied with domestic agricultural and provincial issues and had not found time to study the document in any detail. In fact, the CCP had published both the new CPSU draft program and the former program without comment. According to an East German analysis, this "was intended to create the impression that there were some contradictions between the two programs."[3]

Chen Yi's explanation was only an excuse. From 23 August to 16 September, a CCP CC work conference met in Lushan to review industrial and agricultural issues. The attendees also frequently discussed the new CPSU party program. According to Mao and his associates, Khrushchev's concepts of "a state of the entire people" and "a party of the entire people" were open challenges to proletarian dictatorship. The CPSU was on the verge of degenerating into a bourgeois party from a proletarian party and into a revisionist party from a Marxist party. But at this point, CCP leaders were still attempting to avoid an ideological struggle. Mao was willing to compromise so as not to undermine his principles.

To maintain firm in principle and flexible in tactics, Mao and his colleagues adopted a roundabout way of reacting to the Twenty-second Congress. The CCP CC avoided open criticism of the CPSU program prior to, during, and after the conference, but it took a firm stand in defending the Party of Labor of Albania, thus implicitly revealing its displeasure with the CPSU program. Khrushchev seems to have had a similar strategy, using the party congress to attack the Albanian party by name, while in essence really attacking the CCP. These reactions demonstrated that their initial mutual reactions were intended to prolong the Sino-Soviet detente, while they engaged in a veiled struggle.

At a late September meeting with Chervonenko, Deng Xiaoping made a final effort, to no avail, to mediate Soviet-Albanian relations.[4] Before departing for Moscow, Zhou Enlai told Ho Chi Minh and other Vietnamese leaders, "We are going to attend the Twenty-second Congress of the CPSU and to congratulate them. ... But we are also going to emphasize the importance of unity and anti-imperialism."

The Twenty-second CPSU Congress was held in Moscow from 17 to 31 October 1961. In his formal report, Khrushchev elaborated on the issue of "a state of the entire people" and "a party of the entire people," and he condemned Stalin and criticized Enver Hoxha by name. In a speech on 19 October, Zhou Enlai reiterated the well-known Chinese positions on international issues and declared: "It is the international obligation of all Communists to safeguard the unity of the socialist bloc. It is not a Marxist-Leninist position to expose differences among fraternal parties in front of the enemy." Zhou's speech won some applause, but not from Khrushchev or the other Soviet leaders on the rostrum.

On the following day, at an enlarged CCP CC Politburo meeting, Deng Xiaoping presented the decision of the Politburo Standing Committee regarding the Twenty-second Congress. Although no documents from the meeting have yet come to light, the actions by the CCP delegation suggest that the Politburo had decided on a policy of flexibility and restraint, using both hard and soft tactics. In Beijing, the *People's Daily* published excerpts of Khrushchev's report and the full text of Zhou Enlai's speech. It thus paid attention to the CPSU report, but it also reiterated the CCP's emphasis on unity. In Moscow, the Chinese demonstrated their opposition to Khrushchev's criticism of Stalin. On 21 October, the Chinese delegation led by Zhou Enlai paid homage to Vladimir Lenin and Joseph Stalin by placing wreaths at their tombs. The wreath for Stalin read: "To J. V. Stalin, a great Marxist-Leninist."

On the following day, Zhou Enlai spoke with Soviet leaders Khrushchev, Frol Kozlov, Anastas Mikoyan, and Yuri Andropov for more than nine hours. Zhou explained the CCP's position on Soviet-Albanian relations, the Twentieth CPSU Congress, the congress' evaluation of Stalin, and the anti-party incident of June 1957 (when Georgy Malenkov, Lazar Kaganovich, and Vyacheslav Molotov were purged after failing to oust Khrushchev). Zhou did not directly criticize the CPSU program, and he avoided a face-to-face debate over ideological issues. In his meetings with Communist party leaders Ho Chi Minh and

Le Duan of Vietnam and Kim Il-sung of North Korea, Zhou criticized Khrushchev's handling of the Party of Labor of Albania, but he did not refer to the report and the new party program of the Twenty-second Congress.

Meanwhile, the CPSU attempted to moderate its confrontation with the CCP over the Albanian issue. On the one hand, Khrushchev bluntly stated: "In the past we needed your help very much. At that time, the opinion of the CCP mattered to us. But now the situation is different." On the other hand, he also wanted to maintain solidarity with the CCP. He invited the CCP delegation for lunch during the recess on 22 October, but he avoided discussing politics.

When referring to the Soviet Party Congress, Zhou called for reliance on proletarian internationalism to resolve differences among fraternal parties, alluding to the CPSU's heavy-handed tactics in dealing with the Albanian party. Zhou's speech was denounced by several delegates to the congress. On 23 October, after Khrushchev publicly criticized the Party of Labor of Albania, Zhou left Moscow in protest. Upon Zhou's return to Beijing, Mao went to the airport to greet him, thus highlighting the political implications of his return and demonstrating Mao's displeasure with the new CPSU program. The Soviet chargé d'affaires, Nikolai Sudarikov, reported that Mao seldom appeared in public and almost never personally went to the airport. By greeting Zhou at the airport, Mao was indicating his strong support of Zhou's performance at the Twenty-second Congress and giving Zhou's early return special meaning.

On 26 October, the *People's Daily* published a condemnation of Khrushchev that had been issued by the Party of Labor of Albania six days earlier. In his concluding remarks on 27 October, Khrushchev had declared, "We share the anxiety expressed by our Chinese friends and appreciate their concern for greater unity. ... If the Chinese comrades wish to make efforts toward normalizing relations between the Party of Labor of Albania and the fraternal parties, the CCP is most able to contribute to resolving this problem." Khrushchev then challenged Beijing's leaders regarding the issue of peaceful coexistence and the nature of imperialism, implying that the CCP's policy was one of an "irredeemable dogmatist." Three days later, at a CCP CC Politburo Standing Committee meeting, Mao decided to protest the Soviet accusations but without publishing any critical articles. Peng Zhen, who was acting head of the Chinese delegation after Zhou Enlai's departure, instructed Ambassador Liu Xiao to maintain friendly relations with the USSR because "Sino-Soviet relations are changing and there is still [a possibility for us to] improve relations."

In China, the CCP launched a propaganda campaign to condemn the Twenty-second Congress and its program. This became a new point of contention in Sino-Soviet relations. At a meeting of central government staff on 9–10 November, Zhou emphatically stated, "The CCP differs from the CPSU over issues of principle. In the ideological struggles between the CCP and the CPSU, there is the question of 'who triumphs over whom?' The CCP will never renounce its position. ... The PRC will never yield to the USSR and will always rely on its own strength to build socialism." On the following day, Mao commented on foreign media reports that supported the Chinese position:

"Revisionists attempt to isolate China, but who, in fact, has been isolated? Revisionists separate themselves from the masses and fall into isolation. We (the so-called dogmatists) have won the support of the masses."

After information regarding the Twenty-second CPSU Congress was publicly released in China, the Albanian issue and the Soviet party program were widely discussed among ordinary Chinese. When the *People's Daily* published Hoxha's anti-Soviet report, Yuri Andropov, head of the Department for Liaison with Communist and Workers' Parties of the Socialist Bloc, called in Ambassador Liu Xiao to condemn the Chinese publication. As a result, the Sino-Soviet detente was thrown into disarray. Because they did not want to make a complete break with the USSR, CCP leaders and the People's Republic of China (PRC) Foreign Ministry issued numerous directives to bring the situation under control. On 17 November, the CCP CC issued a directive on Soviet-Albanian relations. Regarding Hoxha's report, the directive stated, "At present, we should not express our opinion." Regarding Soviet-Albanian relations, the directive affirmed, "We should defend the correct views and stance of the Party of Labor of Albania." However, it proscribed large-scale mass parades and debates on the issue. On 26 November, the Foreign Ministry issued directives on the Twenty-second Congress to its overseas missions, instructing Chinese diplomats to strictly follow Zhou's speech at the congress when answering questions from diplomats of fraternal parties. The Foreign Ministry advised: "If someone dares to start a debate, it must be forcefully refuted. Do not become entangled in it." In December, when the USSR severed relations with Albania, China continued to provide Albania with political, economic, and military aid. However, CCP leaders reaffirmed the 26 November directive of the PRC Foreign Ministry, ordering central and local government officials not to take any initiative to discuss Soviet-Albanian relations when meeting foreigners.

On 22 February 1962, the CPSU CC wrote to the CCP CC, accusing Chinese newspapers of supporting "Albania's anti-Lenin activities." On 1 March, Ambassador Chervonenko handed Deng Xiaoping a letter, proposing to improve relations with Albania and to set aside Sino-Soviet differences. After reading the letter, Deng said, "In the end, the large party should take the initiative on such issues. Issues of prestige do not exist for a large party and a large country. … Your letter calls for solidarity, and that is good."[5] Chervonenko agreed with Deng and hoped that the issues between the two parties would not prevent them from achieving unity. But when officials in Beijing called for an international conference of the Communist parties to resolve the issues raised in the Soviet letter, Soviet leaders rejected the idea. They insisted that the Party of Labor of Albania should abandon its position as a precondition for an international conference. On 26 April 1962, the PRC Foreign Ministry instructed its embassy in Moscow that the CCP had adopted a policy of "relaxation matching relaxation" in its relations with the USSR. The Sino-Soviet relationship had reached a stalemate—tensions mixed with relaxation.

MAO'S INTRANSIGENCE

Against the background of deteriorating Sino-Soviet relations, changes were taking place in Soviet policy toward China's Xinjiang region. Rather than cooperating with the Chinese on the repatriation of Soviet nationals as had been done in the past, Soviet Consulate officers began actively exhorting residents to depart. In the early 1960s, local ethnic minorities fled to the USSR by the thousands, with the total number reaching 61,361 by late May 1962. Most had been recruited by the Association of Soviet Nationals. This exodus is known as the "Tacheng Incident in the Ili region" (or the "Ita Incident"). Traditional problems between states (border disputes, repatriation of nationals, etc.)—problems that the socialist alliance supposedly had made irrelevant—had returned with a vengeance and intensified steadily by the end of the decade.

Although the Ita Incident was related to the worsening of Sino-Soviet relations after the Twenty-second Congress, there is no evidence, despite insistence by Chinese leaders, that CPSU leaders directly engineered the incident. Nevertheless, it had a serious effect on Sino-Soviet state-to-state relations, and it also affected Chinese leaders' thinking about national security interests. It led to Mao's perception of Sino-Soviet relations as "contradictions between the enemy and us" and was a major factor in his push for a complete break.

China's economic situation was catastrophic in the wake of the Great Leap Forward, the People's Commune Movement, and more than three years of disastrous economic policies. In devising its policy toward the USSR, Mao was forced to reconsider China's immediate interests: first to relieve the economic hardships and then to resolve the differences of principle with Khrushchev. Not only did the CCP make major concessions to the CPSU at the Moscow Conference in 1960, but the CCP also tolerated the new CPSU program. But these compromises were not welcomed by Mao. After the Twenty-second Congress, he claimed: "We adhere to Marxism and stand on the side of 95 percent of the people. We are not isolated. ... I feel depressed because we have committed mistakes in the last few years. ..." But Mao still believed the fundamental policies of the CCP, including those during the Great Leap Forward, were basically correct. While agreeing to a few adjustments, Mao would not tolerate any questioning of the validity of the policies pursued by the CCP since 1958. This was Mao's psychological line of defense; while acknowledging his mistakes, he reacted strongly to any attempts to change direction.

To carry out the economic adjustments and rectify the mistakes of the Great Leap Forward, in his report to the 7000 Cadres Conference in early 1962, Liu Shaoqi tactfully criticized the policies of the Great Leap, declaring: "Natural disasters account for 30 percent of the problem, and mistakes in our work account for 70 percent."[6] Mao rejected this view, arguing: "The aim of the Great Leap Forward is to demonstrate that China can develop faster than the USSR and China's developmental road is better than the Soviet road. The purpose of the People's Commune Movement is to provide the socialist bloc countries with a better and more direct road to communism." Mao thus attributed differing opinions within the party to class struggle, claiming that a "new rightist view is emerging within the party." At the conference, Mao voiced his concerns about this trend: "The revisionists want to overthrow us. If we do not pay attention to and struggle against [revisionism], within a few years, or in several scores of years at the most, China will become a fascist dictatorship." Mao began to change his foreign policy of moderation and his conciliatory stance toward the USSR. By seeking a break with the USSR, he believed that he would eliminate any possible Soviet allies within his domestic opponents.

In a supplementary speech on foreign policy, Liu Shaoqi stated: "Comrade Mao Zedong has pointed out that in order to fulfill our international obligations, it is essential that we do a good job at home. ... We should mainly pay attention to domestic issues." Liu advocated restraint and moderation in Chinese foreign policy. Wang Jiaxiang, director of the CCP's International Liaison Department (ILD), was also concerned about China's radical and "leftist" diplomatic trends. He thought it was imperative that the ILD offer new perspectives on China's international strategy.[7]

Under Wang Jiaxiang's guidance, the ILD prepared several documents related to China's overall strategic direction and foreign policymaking, matters unrelated to the work of the ILD. Wang, together with two deputies, Liu Ningyi and Wu Xiuquan, decided to employ the method of "a newsletter within the party," writing directly to Zhou Enlai, Deng Xiaoping, and Chen Yi, the frontline leaders in charge of foreign relations.[8] The first letter was sent on 27 February 1962 and the second was sent on 31 March 1962. In these newsletters, Wang argued that the propaganda banners of peace and anti-imperialism should be appropriately balanced. If China were only to emphasize anti-imperialism, the peaceful nature of its foreign policy would be weakened. With the strategic aim of achieving a long-lasting, peaceful international environment that would enable China to build socialism and accelerate its economic development, Wang suggested that the PRC should issue a statement proclaiming that Chinese foreign policy had always been a policy of peace. Wang also discussed tactical issues related to foreign policy. With regard to policy toward the USSR, he suggested that China should try to prevent Khrushchev from reaching a compromise with the United States and isolating China. Thus, at the meetings of the international Communist parties, Wang argued: "It is not appropriate for us to take the lead. Due to the domestic situation, it is inappropriate for us to push forward in foreign affairs." He wanted to avoid provoking disputes with Moscow. If the USSR were to instigate disputes, China would initiate a united front with the fraternal parties and seek common ground with the USSR while also reserving differences and adhering to the principle of not imposing its opinions on others.

Wang's proposal was poorly timed. For Mao, the detente with the USSR was only temporary, and the underlying cause of the Sino-Soviet differences remained unresolved. Mao felt that the positions in Wang's proposal were similar to the views of Khrushchev. At the Beidaihe Work Conference, held from 25

July to 24 August 1962, Mao delivered a speech on class, international and domestic politics, and contradictions. In accordance with Mao's views, the CCP CC called for a new approach to the international situation. As Kang Sheng, an alternate Politburo member and Mao's "anti-revisionist fighter," put it in November 1962: "A Marxist-Leninist leftist contingent has taken shape and is developing. CCP influence is growing day by day. Mao Zedong Thought is becoming the banner of the world revolutionary people. This clearly shows that the United States represents imperialism, Khrushchev represents revisionism, and Mao Zedong represents Marxism. In the international situation, the east wind is prevailing over the west wind."

On 14 September 1962, at a meeting of the East China group (so named because its delegates were from the East China region) to prepare for a CCP CC plenum, Foreign Minister Chen Yi was the first to call Wang Jiaxiang's proposal the "three reconciliations and one reduction," that is, reconciling with the imperialists (the United States), the revisionists (the USSR), and the reactionary (Indian Prime Minister Jawaharlal) Nehru and reducing aid to the struggles of the people of Asia, Africa, and Latin America. Thus, the positions of both Chen Yi and Wang Jiaxiang were at odds with China's foreign policy position in 1962.

At the Tenth Plenum of the Eighth Party Congress, held 24–27 September 1962, Mao made a political comeback, after having retreated to the CCP's "second line" in the wake of the disastrous Great Leap. He alleged that Wang Jiaxiang's approach represented a revisionist foreign policy, echoing Chen Yi's disparagement of the "three reconciliations and one reduction."[9] Mao maintained that the agricultural policy of Deng Zihui, head of the CCP's Rural Work Department who had encouraged farmers to work for their own interests, was revisionist. He condemned the united front policy of Li Weihan, head of the CCP CC's United Front Work Department, as "caving in to the capitalists." He emphasized "class struggle," denouncing contrary views within the party leadership as "right opportunism" and a reflection of revisionism.[10]

Another incident also contributed to Mao's vigilance. Peng Dehuai, who had been commander-in-chief of the Chinese People's Volunteers (CPV) during the Korean War and minister of defense in the 1950s, criticized Mao's radical economic policy during the Great Leap. Thereafter, Mao retaliated at the summer 1959 Lushan Conference and purged Peng for seeming to echo Khrushchev's criticism of the Great Leap and the People's Commune Movement.[11] In June 1962, Peng sent Mao a written statement of 80,000 words, pleading for a reevaluation of his case.[12] Still wary of Peng, Mao regarded him as a challenge to his absolute leadership and thus denounced him as a revisionist within the CCP. Peng's request for rehabilitation hit a raw nerve with Mao with respect to CPSU interference in CCP internal affairs. He declared that support for Peng's rehabilitation was a wind of reversing correct verdicts. Meanwhile, Mao disparaged those who attempted to reassess the economic situation in 1962, referring to them as winds of excessive pessimism, and he also denounced support for the agricultural family responsibility system as a wind of individual farming. Mao connected these two winds to Khrushchev's criticism of the Great Leap and the People's Commune Movement. As Lorenz Lüthi notes, "This linguistic modification allowed the Chairman to place any domestic critic under the category of revisionism."[13] Mao claimed that "foreign and domestic revisionists were colluding" to oppose China. He believed that any questioning of policy blunders was as threatening to him as was Peng's alleged connivance with Khrushchev in 1959 to attempt to overthrow Mao. Thereafter, Peng was criticized at the Tenth Plenum of the Eighth Party Congress for attacking the party and collaborating with China's enemies.

Thus, from May to June 1961, the CCP held numerous conferences to rectify mistakes and adjust policies as well as to prevent a further deterioration in agriculture and industry. But these rectification measures challenged Mao's original policies and were more than he could tolerate. Although he admitted that he and the CCP had made mistakes during the Great Leap and the People's Commune Movement, he maintained that this was the price China had to pay in order to embark on a more efficient path of economic development and construction of socialism, which ultimately would expedite the introduction of communism into China and prove that Mao was wiser and better qualified than Khrushchev to be the leader of the socialist bloc. From the Beidaihe Conference in July to the Tenth Plenum of the Eighth CCP Congress in September 1962, China's domestic winds were once again reversed. Mao raised the issue of class struggle and suspended the rectification of leftism. He linked divergent views within the party and the so-called three winds to Khrushchev, attempting to unearth the international background to this phenomenon. The result was a modification of the pragmatic foreign policy principles China had adopted since the second half of 1960. Niu Jun views 1962 as "the eve of the 'left turn' in PRC foreign policy" and a precursor to the Sino-Soviet polemics.[14] But Mao was really more concerned about his personal power and personal standing than he was about ideology. He was only using ideological correctness to defend his policy decisions and to attack both real and imagined enemies. China and the USSR soon entered a new round of diplomatic struggles.

Less than one month after the Tenth Plenum of the Eighth Congress, both the Cuban missile crisis and the Sino-Indian border war erupted almost simultaneously. In an attempt to manage these crises, at first the CCP and CPSU attempted to cooperate, but then they clashed.[15]

Sino-Soviet frictions during the Cuban missile crisis and the Sino-Indian border conflict reflected the divergent diplomatic strategies and policies of the two parties. CCP's perceptions of the USSR underwent fundamental changes, and Sino-Soviet contradictions that had emerged since 1960 led Chinese leaders to increasingly view the bilateral relationship as one between "the enemy and us"—between revisionism and Marxism and between the capitalist class and the proletariat. "Because the nature of the state-to-state relationship has changed, the USSR attempts to subvert China over territory, independence, and sovereignty. The USSR has become a 'bad brother and a revisionist brother.'" Khrushchev, based on the CCP's depiction, was a "traitor" and a "mouthpiece of the bourgeoisie."

As perceptions changed, so did China's policy toward the USSR. Rather than invoking the 24-word Chinese guiding principles of 1960, which sought to achieve Sino-Soviet unity, CCP leaders now emphasized struggle and taking an initiative. They vowed that they would use both revolutionary and Marxist tactics to counter reactionary and revisionist tactics, and they would "not be afraid of Sino-Soviet relations moving toward the edge of a precipice."

As Chinese foreign policy continued to move to the left, an internal CCP document stated:

> The Chairman told us, "From now on, and within 50 to 100 years, there will be an era of great transformation and victory for the world socialist movement." In such an era, we must engage in new struggles. Lacking sufficient understanding of this new situation, numerous comrades advocate the "three reconciliations and one reduction." This is because they do not have a good command of the Chairman's aforementioned speech.

In addition to the leftward turn in Chinese foreign policy, the formation of leftist contingents in the International Communist Movement was another important factor contributing to the qualitative change in CCP perceptions of the CPSU. As the leaders in Beijing saw it, more Communist parties supported the CCP's view and "Mao Zedong Thought" than they supported the CPSU. CCP leaders believed the time had come to assume leadership in the International Communist Movement, and the resultant dispute with Moscow spawned the great polemics.

FRATERNAL PARTY CONGRESSES IN THE FOUR EASTERN EUROPEAN COUNTRIES AND THE ONSET OF THE GREAT POLEMICS

As the CCP was preparing to use Khrushchev's concessions with the United States over the Cuban missile crisis to launch a new wave of attacks against US imperialism, which was, in essence, against Soviet revisionism for its alleged "selling us out and supporting Nehru" in the Sino-Indian border war of 1962, Khrushchev began to persuade the Eastern European parties to prepare for a new round of struggle with the CCP. These new rounds took place during the four Eastern European Communist Party congresses, held successively from early November 1962 through January 1963: the Eighth Congress of the Bulgarian Communist Party (5–14 November 1962), the Eighth Congress of the Hungarian Socialist Workers' Party (20–24 November 1962), the Twelfth Congress of the Communist Party of Czechoslovakia (4–13 December 1962), and the Sixth Congress of the Socialist Unity Party (SED) of Germany (15–21 January 1963). Wu Xiuquan, vice-director of the ILD, with the portfolio for liaison with Communist and Workers' Parties in the Socialist Bloc, led a Chinese delegation to attend all four congresses. Mikhail Suslov, Otto Kuusinen, Leonid Brezhnev, and Khrushchev, respectively, led the four CPSU delegations.

At the Bulgarian and Hungarian party congresses, there were many open attacks on the Party of Labor of Albania, along with veiled attacks on the CCP. At the Bulgarian Party Congress, over 20 out of the 64 parties in attendance attacked the Albanian party. At the Hungarian Party Congress, over 30 out of the 60 parties in attendance attacked the Albanian party. In their reports, both János Kádár, the Hungarian leader, and Otto Kuusinen, the head of the CPSU delegation, attacked the CCP by innuendo. Some delegates even attacked the CCP by name. The CCP CC posited that the Hungarian Party Congress was held under the guidance of the CPSU, which was organizing the anti-China activities. This constituted a new round of attacks on the CCP by the revisionists. The CCP CC instructed the Chinese delegates to use a reception in the evening of 24 November to rebut its critics and to make three major points: the deterioration in relations between the USSR and Albania was attributable to the CPSU; the current anti-China chorus was being directed by the CPSU; and party congresses should be an occasion for promoting unity rather than fomenting splits. A CCP telegram instructed Wu Xiuquan "not to name the USSR" in his speech because the Soviet delegate had not named the CCP in his attack. Wu responded at the reception accordingly, which aroused strong protests from the delegates of the fraternal parties, but he later earned praise from the CCP leadership.

When the CCP delegation arrived at Prague on 3 December, Leonid Brezhnev, head of the CPSU delegation, was already there with a large contingent. On the next day, Antonín Novotný, First Secretary of the Communist Party of Czechoslovakia (KSČ), accused the Albanians—that is, the Chinese—of egging on the Cubans to a nuclear war, and he attacked unnamed "dogmatists, sectarians, and nationalists" who supported the Albanians. In his address to the congress, Brezhnev condemned the Party of Labor of Albania as self-proclaimed Marxists, attempting to drag humankind into a nuclear war. The CCP regarded this as an order to mobilize against China. Thereafter, there was an unremitting drumbeat of criticism of the Albanians and their Chinese allies from both Czechoslovak and foreign speakers. The Chinese delegation compiled a list of over 60 fraternal delegations, of which 50 attacked the Albanians by name and, among these, 20 attacked the CCP by name. These numbers were even higher than those at the Bulgarian and Hungarian party congresses, thus constituting a peak in anti-China activities. The Czechoslovak party, the host, was now at the forefront of the anti-Chinese and anti-Albanian forces. In his address to the congress, Wu Xiuquan attacked Soviet foreign policy, defending Chinese positions and accusing the host party of allowing its congress to be abused by attacks on other parties. Wu was frequently interrupted by banging, trampling, hushing, and shouting. Subsequent speakers at the congress publicly attacked the CCP and the Chinese delegation.

After receiving a report from the Chinese delegation in Prague, on 7 December, Liu Shaoqi chaired a Politburo Standing Committee meeting to assess the situation. The meeting decided that China had to fight back against the anti-Albanian and anti-Chinese activities at the East European party congresses. It instructed the Chinese delegation to issue a special statement, to uphold its principles, and to strike only after the enemy had struck. It also decided to publish several articles to rebut the attacks on the CCP by the East European parties, the first of which was the attack by the Czechoslovak Party Congress. Mao consented to the Politburo Standing Committee's decision. On 8 December, before the end of Novotný's closing address, Wu Xiuquan handed a "Statement of the Chinese Delegation" to the executive chair of the congress, which Novotný proceeded angrily to read to the congress. The statement criticized the congress' attack on the Party of Labor of Albania and the CCP, and censured the "unusual manners [such] as shouting and hissing" that had been displayed. The CCP CC later issued a circular, stating:

> The anti-China clamors at the congresses of the Italian Communist Party and the Communist Party of Czechoslovakia were doubtless guided by Moscow.[16] They demonstrated further steps by modern revisionists to split the International Communist Movement. The Cuban missile crisis exposed the true color of the modern revisionists. They are very unpopular and want to use anti-China tactics to divert attention. This is a two-line struggle in the International Communist Movement. It is an on-going struggle.

On 14 December, the *People's Daily* published a selection of Novotný's and other delegates' anti-China remarks. On the following day, it issued a long editorial entitled: "Workers of All Countries Unite, Oppose Our Common Enemy." The editorial stated that there was an adverse current, which was anti-Marxism-Leninism, and anti-Chinese and anti other Marxist-Leninist parties, and it was disrupting unity in the International Communist Movement. It pointed out that the Bulgarian, Hungarian, Italian, and Czechoslovak party congresses, which had been held during the preceding month, "unfortunately turned into arenas for attacking fraternal parties. This reached a peak at the Italian, and Czechoslovak party congresses." Mao personally edited the *People's Daily* article and finalized the title. In Mao's view, what had occurred at the Bulgarian, Hungarian, and Czechoslovak party congresses constituted a so-called encircle-and-destroy-campaign between the CPSU and the CCP. Publication of the *People's Daily* editorial on 15 December indicated the beginning of the open polemics between the CCP and the Soviet bloc.

After the Bucharest Congress, the Moscow Conference of 1960, and the Twenty-second CPSU Congress, the CCP felt it no longer had to set aside differences and play down the ideological struggle. On 18 December, the CCP CC issued the "Circular on Carrying Out Anti-Revisionist Education Work Inside and Outside the Party." The circular asserted that under the guidance of Khrushchev, revisionists were unable to restrain themselves from attacking the CCP at the four East European party congresses. It stated, "From now on, we should conduct anti-modern revisionist propaganda work within the entire party and army under our control." From late December 1962 to 8 March 1963, the Chinese published six related articles, responding to the criticism and attacks voiced at the East European party congresses. These constitute the so-called seven polemical articles. Although the seven articles did not openly criticize the CPSU by name, the target of their attacks was indeed the CPSU leadership. As Mao and Liu Shaoqi stated at CCP CC Politburo Standing Committee meetings on 7 and 8 March, "In these articles, we are elaborating on our views and aiming at the views of the CPSU. ... From our perspective, open polemics have many advantages. They are defensive in form but offensive in essence. They expose the true colors of modern revisionism." In response, on 7 January 1963, *Pravda* published an editorial that censured the CCP, although not by name, for assuming the position of Lenin and imposing its own socialist prescription on the fraternal parties, thereby splitting the International Communist Movement.

The Sixth Congress of the SED was convened from 15 to 21 January 1963 in East Berlin. Khrushchev led a large CPSU delegation to the meeting. The East Germans had devised tough measures to prevent dissident foreign voices from being heard. Only delegations led by the first secretaries of fraternal parties had a right to deliver oral fraternal greetings; others would have to be content with presenting their greetings in writing and having them published in the local press. Realizing that this would provoke an enormous row if it were to be strictly followed, the East Germans excused China and Czechoslovakia from this rule. But the other parties had to be content with regional spokesmen: the Cubans spoke for Latin America, and the Japanese spoke for Asia. This meant that pro-China parties, such as North Korea and Indonesia, could not speak, and their pro-China messages could not be published in the East German press. Worse still, in his opening report on 15 January, East German party leader Walter Ulbricht blamed the Chinese for abandoning peaceful coexistence on the Sino-Indian border.

On the following day, Khrushchev gave a partially conciliatory speech in view of China's counter-campaign against "encirclement." He proposed that future public interparty debates should cease, that within their own ranks, parties should desist from criticizing fraternal parties, and that the Albanians should abandon their mistaken viewpoints and return to the fraternal socialist family. The East Germans immediately supported this "correct advice" and demanded to know the response of the Chinese delegation. Wu Xiuquan asked Beijing for instructions. On 17 January, the CCP Secretariat discussed Khrushchev's speech and decided "to change our address [to the congress] ... adopt a magnanimous attitude, advocate unity, oppose false unity, and expose the trick of the so-called termination of public disputes." On 18 January, Wu Xiuquan delivered the CCP's address to the congress, attacking Yugoslavia by describing it as a "Tito clique" and a "special squad of American imperialism in the realization of Tito's counterrevolutionary global strategy."[17] Provoked by Wu Xiuquan's criticism of Yugoslavia, whose representatives were in attendance at the congress, the East German chairman repeatedly tried to cut Wu's speech short by ringing his bell, but Wu read on. The East German delegates then tried to drown him out with shouts and whistles, stamping their feet and banging on their desks.[18] In protest, the Chinese delegation walked out of the

conference hall during the singing of the "Internationale" at the closing ceremony. In a reply from the CCP CC to the SED CC on 27 March, the Chinese
justified this act by stating, "You should know that your singing with the traitors was a grave 'political' act."[19]

After the CCP delegation returned home, the CCP concluded that
Khrushchev was organizing "a new peak in revisionist attacks on Albania and
China." To maintain pressure on the CPSU, Mao approved that on 27 January
1963, the *People's Daily* would publish an article entitled: "Let Us Unite on
the Basis of the Moscow Declaration and Moscow Statement" (the fourth of
the seven polemics). The article accused the East German congress of "crude
attacks … against the Chinese Communist Party," and it condemned its "bra-
zen attempts, which were in open violation of the Moscow Declaration [1957]
and the Moscow Statement [1960] … to reverse the verdict passed on by the
Tito clique of Marxist-Leninist renegades." It blamed the CPSU of starting the
current ideological dispute at its Twenty-second Congress, and it accused the
CPSU of pushing the International Communist Movement "to the precipice"
of a split.

On 10 February 1963, *Pravda* published an editorial refuting a 27 January
1963 *People's Daily* article that condemned the League of Yugoslav Communists
and proposed the convening of a new international conference and the suspension of the open polemics. On 21 February, the CPSU CC sent a letter to the
CCP CC calling for a suspension of the polemics and for joint planning of an
international conference of the Communist parties. The letter claimed that
Sino-Soviet disagreements have been "artificially inflated and exacerbated,"
and they can be "explained by different conditions in which this or that detach-
ment of the International Communist Movement is working."[20] According to
Sergey Radchenko, the letter demonstrated that Khrushchev "still thought he
could resolve the China problem."[21] In another letter to the CCP on 30 March,
the CPSU proposed "drawing up a General Line of the International
Communist Movement to fit the fundamental tasks of our time." Because
"peaceful coexistence," "peaceful competition," and "peaceful transition" had
been affirmed as the common program of international communism at the two
Moscow conferences, Khrushchev's intention was to have this common program accepted as a "general line" at a fraternal party conference. This was the
minimum to which the CCP could agree. The CCP reacted vigorously. On 14
June, the CCP replied to the CPSU letter with an article entitled: "A Proposal
Concerning the General Line of the International Communist Movement"
(published in the *People's Daily* on 20 July). The CCP proposed very different
ideas regarding the General Line of the International Communist Movement,
steadfastly defending the 1957 Moscow Declaration and the 1960 Moscow
Statement. The CCP took a big step toward claiming leadership of the
International Communist Movement from the CPSU.

Khrushchev attempted to counter the CCP criticism of his handling of the
Cuban missile crisis and Moscow's position on the Sino-Indian border war.
However, the attacks on the CCP, guided by Moscow at the four East European

party congresses and the Twelfth Congress of the Italian Communist Party (2–8 December 1962), provoked the CCP into engaging in open ideological polemics with the CPSU. Although 42 parties publicly accused the CCP at the five fraternal party congresses, this was fewer than those at the Moscow Conference of 1960. More leftist groups among the fraternal parties stood up to speak on behalf of the Party of Labor of Albania and the CCP, thus enhancing the CCP's confidence in continuing to engage in the polemics. Thus, the five European party congresses provided a platform for the CCP to engage in the polemics, and they also represented a turning point in the formal inception of the polemics. As a January 1963 CCP circular pointed out, "Modern revisionists' attacks on our party will not weaken us to the slightest extent. On the contrary, they will offer us the right to counterattack and censure them. Open polemics are to our advantage." Thereafter, Poland, Hungary, East Germany, Czechoslovakia, and Bulgaria became the main allies of the CPSU in the ideological polemics with the CCP. China's relations with these five East European countries rapidly deteriorated.

THE FORMATION OF LEFTIST CONTINGENTS IN THE INTERNATIONAL COMMUNIST MOVEMENT

At the June 1960 Bucharest Conference when Khrushchev opposed the Chinese delegation, only the Albanian, Indonesian, and Japanese Communist parties supported the CCP. At the Conference of World Communist and Workers' Parties in 1960, China attracted more supporters. Ten Communist parties, including those of North Korea, North Vietnam, Albania, Indonesia, Japan, Burma, Malaya, Thailand, Australia, and New Zealand, endorsed the CCP's anti-revisionist program. After the Twenty-second CPSU Congress, pro-Chinese leftist parties spread from Asia to Latin America, Western Europe, and North America. CCP leaders were especially pleased when the Italian Communist Party (leftist) and the French Communist Party (leftist) published articles entitled: "Long Live Leninism," echoing the CCP's 1960 article. The leftist Communists worked with the CCP to use Mao Zedong's and Liu Shaoqi's articles as theoretical weapons in their struggles against revisionism.

Mao and his associates were greatly encouraged by the new trend in world communism, and they attributed it to the CCP's anti-revisionist position under the guidance of Mao Zedong since 1956. A CCP internal document stated: "Mao Zedong Thought is becoming the theoretical weapon of all Marxists and Leninists … and the banner of the International Communist Movement." At the Tenth Plenum of the CCP's Eighth Party Congress, on 26 September 1962, Zhou Enlai declared: "Marxist truth and the center of the world revolution are shifting from Moscow to Beijing."

Thereafter, CCP's ambitions to be the leader of the world revolution continued to grow. This raised the issue of who were the real Marxist-Leninists and who were the real leaders. An internal CCP document claimed, "Chinese revolutionary practice has proved that only our Chairman Mao can develop

Marxism-Leninism. ... Khrushchev discarded Marxism-Leninism after the Twentieth CPSU Congress. We are the ones who have raised high the banner of Marxism and Leninism since the 1957 Moscow Declaration." For this reason, the anti-revisionist struggles of the people of the world have to be guided not only by Marxism-Leninism but also by Mao Zedong Thought. At the National Foreign Affairs Conference in November 1962, Chinese leaders formally raised "the issue of jockeying with the revisionists for the leadership position in the international struggle." They also stipulated concrete measures for achieving this goal: concentrating on anti-US imperialism and assisting the national liberation movements.

After setting out to vie for leadership of the International Communist Movement against the USSR, the Chinese devised the following agenda: to divide the world into three—imperialism, revisionism, and Marxism-Leninism—and to promote Mao Zedong as the leader of the world revolution. Accordingly, the CCP took an active and offensive position in its struggle against Khrushchev's revisionism. Chinese leaders came to regard the issue of whether to "struggle" or to "reconcile" with Khrushchev as a matter of whether or not "[the CCP] upholds Marxism-Leninism, is revolutionary, and remains a proletarian party." Mao connected the struggle with Khrushchev to domestic issues, claiming, "The struggle with revisionism is not only an international issue but also a domestic issue."

The new agenda also stipulated that the CCP would "actively support the development of leftists in order to strengthen the Marxist-Leninist contingents." The CCP would enhance its contacts with leftist parties and would reject accusations of "interfering in their internal affairs ... and splitting their parties or engaging in factionalism." Furthermore, the CCP would strengthen its work in Asia, Africa, and Latin America to consolidate regional international organizations and to bolster the leftist leadership, and it would also provide a distinctive Marxist-Leninist program for guiding the world revolution. The CCP labeled the program of the Twenty-second CPSU Congress "a comprehensive manifestation of revisionism" and it openly opposed it as the common program of world communism. The Chinese emphasized the virtues of Mao Zedong Thought and formulated a common program for the International Communist Movement. Based on Mao's instructions, the CCP would "attempt to break through the revisionist ring of encirclement, gradually establish an independent banner, make Beijing the center of international activities, and put on a rival show to challenge imperialism and revisionism."

By this time, neither the CCP nor the CPSU was willing or able to make any substantive concessions. In the CPSU's view, any concession would indicate abdication of its leadership of the International Communist Movement. From the CCP's perspective, any concession meant surrendering to revisionism and this would preclude a bid for leadership of the International Communist Movement.

From July to October 1963, the USSR published many articles and editorials attacking the CCP. In response, from 6 September to 12 December, the *People's Daily* and *Red Flag* published six lead articles denouncing CPSU theories and policies. These six articles constituted the first of the "Nine Commentaries on the CPSU's Open Letter" that intensified the Sino-Soviet ideological polemics.[22]

The CCP leaders were full of a fighting spirit, condemning the CPSU both in speech and in writing. In an early January 1964 CCP CC Politburo Standing Committee meeting, Liu Shaoqi stressed that "one of the reasons why we cannot suspend the polemics right now is that many leftist parties have been mobilized, are enjoying the polemics, and are preparing to censure the CPSU."

CONCLUSION

For two years, from fall 1959 through mid-1961, the CCP and the CPSU tried to restore their relations that had been damaged by their heated quarrel in October 1959. A fragile detente was achieved, but it only lasted from late summer 1960 to late autumn 1961. In October 1961, the Twenty-second CPSU Congress adopted a new program that declared that the USSR was "a state of the entire people" and the CPSU was "a party of the entire people." In response, the CCP launched a new wave of propaganda decrying the new CPSU program. In March 1962, when the CCP proposed a new international Communist conference to resolve their ideological differences, the CPSU demanded that the Albanian leaders abandon their position. Although a new international conference did not take place, the two sides attempted to halt the deterioration in their relations. Sino-Soviet relations reached a stalemated truce, with warmer spells alternating with cooler phases. But the Ita Incident (see above) in spring 1962 affected the thinking of Chinese leaders about national security interests and accelerated Mao's determination to break with the USSR.

China's domestic political developments further complicated Mao's policy toward the USSR. To rectify the leftist errors in China's domestic policy since the Great Leap Forward, several Chinese leaders began to question the validity of the CCP's overall domestic and foreign policy principles. Wang Jiaxiang advocated a moderate foreign policy and a relaxation of tensions with the USSR. But Mao reacted forcefully to those who differed with him over concrete policy issues, denouncing them as accomplices of Khrushchev and excoriating them as revisionists. This leftward turn in Chinese foreign policy in the fall of 1962 was closely related to China's domestic political developments, rendering Sino-Soviet relations even more problematic.

The CCP soon clashed with the CPSU over concrete diplomatic issues. At the height of the Cuban missile crisis, the CCP supported Khrushchev's confrontation with the United States in hopes that Moscow would support China in its border conflict with India. But after the USSR decided to remove its nuclear missiles from Cuba, the CCP accused Khrushchev of "adventurism and capitulation." Because the CPSU expressed serious reservations about Chinese policy during the 1962 Sino-Indian border war, Beijing regarded the USSR as "a bad revisionist brother."

The CCP-CPSU struggles over foreign policy strategies in 1962 were not fundamentally different from their struggles in 1958 and 1959. But Mao and his colleagues now believed that the Soviet leaders were revisionists, and Mao became even more determined to compete with the USSR for a leadership role in the International Communist Movement. At a foreign affairs work conference on 13 November 1962, Chen Yi told the audience: "In today's world, only our Chairman Mao is able to develop Marxism-Leninism. The practice of the Chinese Revolution fully proves this. [The Soviet] revisionists cannot match our Chairman." Chen Yi declared that "the center of the world revolution has moved to our country." He further claimed that the struggle between the world revolution and revisionism should be guided not only by Marxism but also by Mao Zedong Thought.

In addition to the correlation between China's domestic and foreign policies, the leftward turn in China's foreign policy and the formation of an international leftist contingent were important factors in the CCP's decision to engage the CPSU in ideological polemics. During the Sino-Soviet ideological debates, the East European Communist and Workers' parties sided with Moscow as their relations with Beijing deteriorated. The failure of the Sino-Soviet party talks in July 1963 demonstrated that a breakdown in Sino-Soviet party relations was already inevitable. By means of the subsequent polemics, the CCP intended to present itself as the champion of true Marxism-Leninism and the natural leader of world communism. The fraying of CCP-CPSU ideological and emotional connections was soon followed by a breakdown of CCP-CPSU organizational relations.

NOTES

1. Leonid Gibianskii, "The Origins of the Soviet-Yugoslav Split," in Norman Naimark and Leonid Gibianskii, eds., *The Establishment of Communist Regimes in Eastern Europe* (Boulder, CO: Westview Press, 1997), pp. 291–312; Jeronim Perović, "The Tito-Stalin Split: A Reassessment in Light of New Evidence," *Journal of Cold War Studies*, vol. 9, no. 2 (Spring 2007), pp. 32–63; Mark Kramer, "Stalin, the Split with Yugoslavia, and Soviet–East European Efforts to Reassert Control, 1948–1953," in Mark Kramer and Vít Smetana, eds., *Imposing, Maintaining, and Tearing Down the Iron Curtain: The Cold War and East-Central Europe, 1945–1989* (Lanham, MD: Rowman & Littlefield, 2013), pp. 97–123.

2. For Albanian archives on Sino-Albanian relations and the Sino-Soviet split, see Ana Lalaj, Christian Ostermann, and Ryan Gage, eds., "'Albania is not Cuba': Sino-Albanian Summits and the Sino-Soviet Split," *CWIHP Bulletin*, Issue 16 (Fall 2007/Winter 2008), pp. 183–340.

3. Lüthi, *The Sino-Soviet Split*, p. 206.

4. "The Diary of S.V. Chervonenko: Transcripts of the Conversations (Excerpts) With the General Secretary of the CC CCP Deng Xiaoping," 1 March 1962, *CWIHP Bulletin*, Issue 10 (March 1998), p. 174.

5. Ibid.

6. "Cause of the Present Economic Difficulties and Methods for Overcoming Them," 31 May 1961, in *Selected Works of Liu Shaoqi*, vol. 2 (Beijing: Foreign Languages Press, 1991), p. 315; "Speech at an Enlarged Working Conference of the Central Committee of the Party," 27 January 1962, in ibid., p. 398.

7. For a study of Wang Jiaxiang's 1962 foreign policy suggestions, see Yafeng Xia, "Wang Jiaxiang: New China's First Ambassador and the First Director of the International Liaison Department of the CCP," *American Journal of Chinese Studies*, vol. 16, no. 2 (October 2009), pp. 147–53.

8. In early 1962, in the wake of the disastrous Great Leap Forward, Mao resigned from the first line of responsibility in PRC affairs, leaving day-to-day operations to his senior associates—Liu Shaoqi, Zhou Enlai, and Deng Xiaoping. On the second line, Mao focused on policymaking and theoretical research.

9. When Wang Jiaxiang learned that Mao did not like his idea, he hurried to make a self-criticism and give up without a fight. See Xia, "Wang Jiaxiang," pp. 148–49, n. 48.

10. Ibid., pp. 150–53.

11. Shen and Xia, *Mao and the Sino-Soviet Partnership*, pp. 297–98.

12. At the 7000 Cadres Conference in early 1962, Liu Shaoqi once again blamed Peng Dehuai, accusing him of "having illicit relations with the USSR." Liu Shaoqi's accusation prompted Peng Dehuai to write to the CCP CC, asking for a reevaluation of his case. Nevertheless, Liu had made it clear that the rehabilitation of cadres excluded Peng Dehuai.

13. Lüthi, *The Sino-Soviet Split*, p. 222.

14. Niu Jun, "1962: The Eve of the Left Turn in China's Foreign Policy," *CWIHP Working Paper*, no. 48 (October 2005), p. 36.

15. For how the CCP and CPSU managed their relations during the Cuban missile crisis and the Sino-Indian border war of 1962, see Li and Xia, *Mao and the Sino-Soviet Split*, pp. 63–67.

16. At the Tenth Congress of the Italian Communist Party in December 1962, General Secretary Palmiro Togliatti and Soviet delegate Frol Kozlov censured the Chinese and defended Khrushchev's record in Cuba. They also criticized the Chinese for the Sino-Indian border conflict. The Chinese delegate, Zhao Yimin, responded by attacking Tito (read Khrushchev). Lüthi notes, "Almost all delegates of the Italian party congress denounced Zhao's speech." For details, see Lüthi, *The Sino-Soviet Split*, p. 230; Radchenko, *Two Suns in the Heavens*, p. 43.

17. "Note from the First Secretary of the SED CC, Walter Ulbricht, to the Chairman of the Communist Party of China, Mao Zedong, on the Chinese Delegation's Behavior at the Sixth SED Party Congress," Berlin, 12 February 1963, Stiftung Archiv der Parteien und Massenorganisationen der DDR im Bundesarchiv, ZPA JIV 2/202/284, cited in W. Meissner, *Die DDR und China 1945–1990: Politik - Wirtschaft - Kultur. Eine Quellensammlung* (Oldenbourg: Wissenschaftsverlag GmbH, 1995), p. 138.

18. Wu Xiuquan recalled that it was the Germans who tried to stop him.

19. "Response from the CCP CC to the SED CC Concerning the Events at the Sixth SED Party Congress to the CC of the Socialist Unity Party of Germany," Beijing, 27 March 1963, Stiftung Archiv der Parteien und Massenorganisationen der DDR im Bundesarchiv, ZPA NL 182/1222, cited in Meissner, *Die DDR und China 1945–1990*, p. 140.

20. "Letter of the Central Committee of the CPSU to the Central Committee of the CCP," *Peking Review*, no. 12 (22 March 1963), p. 9.

21. Radchenko, *Two Suns in the Heavens*, p. 47.

22. William E. Griffith, ed., *The Sino-Soviet Rift* (Cambridge, MA: MIT Press, 1964).

CHAPTER 17

Mao's Changing Perceptions of Internal Disturbances and External Threats, Mid-1963 to the End of 1964

Danhui Li

The polemics led to a breakdown in Sino-Soviet party-to-party relations. Because state relations among the socialist countries depended on close party relations, it is not surprising that the rift in party relations led to the collapse of state relations. Starting from mid-1964, Mao modified China's foreign and defense strategies and adjusted China's domestic economic and political directions. In light of his real, or imagined, views of internal disturbances and external threats, Chinese foreign policy moved from anti-imperialism to anti-imperialism *and* anti-revisionism. In this respect, Mao made two major decisions. First, the target of China's national defense strategy would be transformed from countering the United States to countering both the United States and the Union of Soviet Socialist Republics (USSR); second, Mao began to contemplate the launching of a political revolution (i.e., the Cultural Revolution). Thus, at the same time, the USSR became an imaginary enemy of China, and for the USSR China had become an expansionist power coveting Soviet territory. As a result, each side sought to strengthen its military defense.

Mao's Changing Security and Strategic Thinking

The Soviet 7600-kilometer-long border runs along China's northeast and northwest. China's northern neighbor, the Soviets' close ally, Mongolia, which has a 4677-kilometer border with China, is protected by the USSR. When the

D. Li (✉)
World History Institute, East China Normal University, Shanghai, China
e-mail: lidanhui0601@vip.163.com

Z. Shen (ed.), *A Short History of Sino-Soviet Relations, 1917–1991*,
China Connections, https://doi.org/10.1007/978-981-13-8641-1_17

Sino-Soviet relationship was flourishing, this situation along the northern frontier assured China's security. But when the Chinese Communist Party (CCP) split with the Communist Party of the Soviet Union (CPSU) and state relations deteriorated, the border became a sensitive matter.

After China clashed with the USSR at Bozaige Pass in Xinjiang in August 1960, sporadic border conflicts continued to occur. In March 1963, a *People's Daily* editorial stated that the 1858 Treaty of Aigun (Aihui), the 1860 Sino-Russian Treaty of Peking, and the 1881 Treaty of Ili (as it is called in Chinese or the Treaty of St. Petersburg as it is called in English, which ended the Ili crisis) were unequal treaties imposed on the Chinese government by the Tsarist government.[1] The USSR was concerned about Chinese interpretations of these earlier treaties. In Moscow's view, by using the charged phrase "unequal treaties" China was coveting Soviet territory. In response, according to Chinese sources, beginning in early 1963 Moscow enhanced its military and security strength along the border. It also increased military aid and redeployed its troops in Mongolia.[2] In July, the USSR signed the "Agreement on Soviet Aid to Mongolia for Enhancing its Defense along its Southern Border" and then proceeded to send prospecting teams to areas along the Mongolian railway and to the provinces to the east to prepare an area for the staging of troops. After touring the Sino-Soviet border in Northeast China, Minister of Public Security Xie Fuzhi reported to the CCP Central Committee (CC). He claimed that the Khrushchev clique had increased its military forces along the Sino-Soviet border. Along certain parts of the border, the number of Soviet troops had doubled.[3] As he paid close attention to the situation in the Far East, Khrushchev began to consider extending the operational area of the Warsaw Pact from Europe to Asia. On 10 July 1963, in a letter to Polish leader Władysław Gomułka, Khrushchev supported Mongolia's application to join the Warsaw Pact. In reality, Soviet efforts to strengthen ties with Mongolia were meant to target China.[4] On 15 July, Mongolian leader Yumjaagiin Tsedenbal issued a formal request to join the Warsaw Pact, but his request was rejected due to opposition by the Polish and Romanian governments on the grounds that "an initiative with regard to Mongolia might in a certain sense play into the hands of the People's Republic of China (PRC) and could be used to blame our side for carrying the dispute into the area of military alliances and moving down the path of dividing the [socialist] camp along military lines."[5]

The CCP Central Military Commission (CMC) held a conference on Sino-Soviet and Sino-Mongolian border defense in September and October 1963. The conference reconfirmed the guiding principles of CCP CC border defense: "Neither advance forward nor retreat; Do not take the initiative to stir up trouble; Strike only after the other side attacks first." The conference also proposed that "[We] have to be militarily prepared to deal with possible border conflicts provoked by the revisionists." It is worth noting that in 1963, six years before the conflicts on Zhenbao Island, the Chinese already perceived the Soviets to be a military threat.

Sino-Mongolian relations continued to deteriorate. In August 1963 Mongolian leader Yumjaagiin Tsedenbal published an article critical of China in *Pravda* and on 4 September, in a talk with journalists in Moscow, he condemned China directly. In December, the Fifth Plenum of the Fourteenth CC of the Mongolian People's Revolutionary Party adopted a resolution entitled "On the CCP Leadership's Splittism in the International Communist Movement and the Position of the Mongolian People's Revolutionary Party," as anti-China propaganda reached a new high in Mongolia.

From February to August 1964, China and the USSR held negotiations on border issues, but they failed to reach agreement. During this period, the USSR reportedly greatly reinforced its military presence along the border. According to Chinese reconnaissance, beginning in July 1964 the USSR increased its troops and installations along the western section of the Sino-Soviet border. These troops engaged in frequent maneuvers, and senior officers increased their visits to the area. The year 1964 represented a turning point in the escalation of tensions along the Sino-Soviet border. These developments led Mao to regard the USSR as a major threat to Chinese national security.

In February 1964 Mao told North Korean leader Kim Il-sung that it was possible that the USSR would start a war with China if the Soviet Union failed to subdue it by other means. At a CCP CC work conference held between 15 May and 17 June, Mao shifted the goal of China's Third Five-year Plan from resolving the issue of "food, clothing, and daily necessities" to war preparedness. He proposed the Third Front construction program and the establishment of military industry in every province.[6] When explaining the division of the Third Front area, Zhou Enlai opined, "The Northwest and the Northeast are the first front of defense against revisionism. ... The Third Front of Defense (TFD) consists of Qinghai, southern Shaanxi, southern Gansu, and Panzhihua in Sichuan." It is worth noting that the US escalation of the Vietnam War during the summer of 1964 might have contributed to Mao's thinking regarding the TFD. Thus, the TFD was not merely meant to oppose the revisionists.

Referring to his new strategy, at the June CMC War Planning Conference and the CCP CC Work Conference, Mao negated the *Beiding nanfang* defense strategy (putting up strong resistance against a US and Japanese invasion from East and Northeast China, while allowing Jiang Jieshi's and US troops into China from Southeast China), which had been proposed by Lin Biao in 1962. Since the 1950s, China's defense strategy had been directed against the United States, and the main area of an expected attack was along the southeast coast or along the Sino-Indian border in the west and southwest. From the 1950s to the early 1960s, China's main industrial enterprises and infrastructure were located in Northeast and North China, whereas the area south of Shanghai was intended to be relinquished in time of war. The *Beiding nanfang* depended on the existence of a strong Sino-Soviet alliance in which China could depend on the USSR for its defense. By 1964, however, Mao realized that China could no longer rely on the USSR. After losing Soviet support, Mao believed that it might be impossible to resist an enemy invasion from the north if the United States and Japan were to attack from the Northeast. He then ordered large cities such as Beijing and Tianjin to be on military alert and to prepare for war.

It is clear that Mao was focusing on a military defense strategy from the perspective of how the USSR would affect China's national security. At that time, Defense Minister Lin Biao was unaware of Mao's new thinking. Upon hearing the briefing by Yang Chengwu (deputy chief of the General Staff of the People's Liberation Army [PLA]) on Mao's speeches on strategic defense, Lin became very agitated after linking this to Mao's other talks regarding vigilance against Khrushchev-type people within the CCP. Lin was worried that he would be unable to keep pace with Mao in recognizing the USSR as a threat to China's national security. The differences between their thinking reflected Mao's new consideration of China's security strategy vis-à-vis the USSR. At a CCP CC Politburo meeting in July 1964, Mao said: "Do not pay attention only to the east and not to the north, and do not only pay attention to imperialism and not revisionism. We must prepare for war on both fronts." This was the first time Mao formally raised the issue of preparedness for a potential defensive war against the USSR.[7]

On 10 July, at a meeting with visiting delegates from the Japanese Socialist Party, Mao opined that "the Soviet Union occupies too much land. ..." He stated:

> About a hundred years ago, the area east of Baikal, including Khabarovsk, Vladivostok, and Kamchatka, became Russian territory, We have not yet presented a bill for this list. ... Outer Mongolia is much larger than the Kurile Islands. We once asked the Soviets to return Outer Mongolia to us. They turned us down. ... They are attempting to place Xinjiang and Heilongjiang under their jurisdiction, and they have increased their military forces along the border.[8]

On the following day, the Japanese visitors revealed the content of Mao's talk to journalists in Hong Kong. On 13 July, Japan's three leading newspapers (*Asahi Shimbun, Yomiuri Shimbun,* and *Mainichi Shimbun*) reported in length on Mao's support of the Japanese position on the Kurile Islands and the articles claimed that Mao supported the return of the islands to Japan.[9] On 1 August, *Asahi Shimbun* and *Yomiuri Shimbun* published the content of Zhou Enlai's talks with members of the Japanese Socialist Party, in which he stated that China had consistently supported the Japanese request to recover lost territory.

Mao's first open discussion on the Sino-Soviet border issue produced a strong reaction in the USSR. On 2 September, *Pravda* reprinted Mao's conversation with the Japanese Socialist Party delegation, together with a long editorial entitled "On Mao Zedong's Conversation with Members of the Japanese Socialist Party." The editorial strongly condemned Mao's conversation with the Japanese, which "exposed the Chinese leader's aim and position that he had not dared to reveal earlier." Mao's viewpoint was "to re-allot territory ... which would lead to very dangerous consequences." The article expressed "its resolute condemnation of the Chinese leader's expansionist view."[10] On 15 September, in a meeting with a visiting Japanese parliamentary delegation, Khrushchev acrimoniously responded to Mao, "The Russian Tsars launched many plundering wars. … The Chinese emperors were by no means inferior. … They conquered Mongolia, Tibet, and Xinjiang. … If anyone dares to impose war on us, we will spare no effort to fight them. We own sufficient weaponry. … If aggressors dare to launch a war, they are doomed to perish."

Khrushchev's strident language and unyielding position surprised Mao. In meetings with foreign visitors, Mao had often asked, "Will Khrushchev attack us? … Will he send troops to conquer Xinjiang, Heilongjiang, or even Inner Mongolia?" Although Mao still believed that a massive Soviet invasion of China was unlikely, in his view the Soviet threat was more real and imminent than the American threat. He unequivocally stated, "We should be prepared." Mao was considering another modification of China's defense strategy vis-à-vis the USSR.

From September to November 1964, a panel from the Headquarters of the General Staff of the PLA reconnoitered important regions in the North, Northeast, and Northwest, paying particular attention to the routes used by Soviet troops to launch attacks on Japanese forces during World War II and to areas of the former Japanese fortifications.[11] Meanwhile, China also began to strengthen its defenses along the western sector of the Sino-Soviet border. In an intelligence report, the Ili Military Command, which was regarded as "an anti-revisionist outpost," proposed to "focus on the anti-revisionist struggle and to coordinate with anti-imperialism, to gather and sort out information regarding current Soviet and Mongolian military movements, to be constantly on the alert to a surprise attack by the enemy and any emergency, and to remain vigilant of any earlier attempt by the enemy." During the first half of 1964, the Xinjiang Military Command submitted to the Headquarters of the General Staff several documents, including "War Preparedness and the Sino-Soviet Border Preparatory Plan" and the "War Plan for the Sino-Soviet Border."

Khrushchev's sudden fall from power in October 1964 provided Chinese leaders with an opportunity to improve Sino-Soviet relations (see below). However, their efforts failed, and a complete rupture and dissolution of the Sino-Soviet alliance was only a matter of time. This provided an impetus for China to prepare for war. China's starting point for modifying its foreign strategy was not only to defend itself against the United States but also to designate the TFD areas as strategic bases for defense against both the USSR and the United States. In the early 1960s, as China adopted its anti-imperialist and anti-revisionist policy, which was called "fighting with two fists," anti-revisionism was mainly an ideological struggle. However, as anti-revisionism became wedded to China's national security strategy, China adopted the "fighting with two fists" policy as its military defense principle and prepared for a two-front war against both the United States and the USSR.

When the Vietnam War escalated in early 1965, through diplomatic signaling China and the United States reached a tacit agreement that neither would cross the 17th parallel.[12] In Mao's view, the United States no longer constituted the main threat to China's security—a greater threat came from the USSR. In April and May, based on a series of important instructions by Mao on strategic issues, the CMC convened several meetings to redesign China's strategic battle plans. It was decided that national defense work in the "Three Norths"— China's North, Northeast, and Northwest regions—would be strengthened, along with that in the southeastern region, all of which were identified as China's main strategic regions.[13] Thus, ironically, at the height of the Vietnam War, the focus of China's military defense shifted from the south against the US to the north against the USSR.

Mao's assessment of the Soviet threat and his reconsideration of China's defense strategy against the USSR re-affirmed his notion that the USSR had turned to be a capitalist state and the CPSU was a bourgeois and fascist party. Importantly, this assessment also affected China's domestic political situation. Mao felt it was necessary to link the current domestic situation and consolidation of proletarian dictatorship with the influence of Soviet revisionism. He was on the alert against Soviet collusion with subversive forces within China and he sought connections between his domestic rivals and the USSR. This provided him with a theoretical and practical basis for an emphasis on class struggle within China. With the USSR as a perceived imaginary enemy to China's national security, it was easy for Mao to launch a political campaign to eliminate so-called agents of Soviet revisionism within the CCP. In Mao's view, the only way to prevent revisionists from usurping the highest positions in the CCP was a political revolution, that is, the Great Proletarian Cultural Revolution.

Anti-revisionist Struggles at Home

In combating Soviet revisionism, Mao claimed that his theories reflected Marxist orthodoxy and that the CCP's general and specific policies represented the right direction for the International Communist Movement, thus making China the center of the world proletarian revolution, with the CCP as its leader. But in 1965, Mao began paying more attention to the influence of revisionism within the CCP and China's socialist road. From an ideological perspective, according to Mao the danger of revisionist subversion was much more serious than the danger of peaceful transformation.

At the Tenth Plenum of the Eighth CCP Congress in September 1962, Mao again raised the issue of class struggle, producing a reversal in China's domestic political winds. He stated: "From today on, we must speak about class struggle every year and every month. We must speak about it at the plenary sessions of the CC and at the party congresses. In this way, we will have a much more clear-headed Marxist-Leninist line." The linking of domestic issues with international revisionism was Mao's approach to analyze the political situation within the CCP. He was constantly reminding the entire party of the danger that China might change its political color. In early 1963, Li Fuchun, director of the State Planning Commission, submitted to the CCP CC "the essentials regarding compiling a long-term plan" in relation to the Third Five-year Plan.

Li emphasized the production of food, clothing, and daily necessities and a reduction of investment in national defense and advanced military technology. The purpose of this development strategy was to further recover and adjust the national economy. The majority of CCP CC leaders supported such a strategy. But Mao regarded this approach as busying people with economic construction without resolving the fundamental political issues and thus threatening China's future political direction. Although Mao eventually consented to this development strategy, his emphasis on economic interests and construction differed greatly from his emphasis on political development.

In May 1963, Mao presided over an enlarged Politburo Standing Committee meeting in Hangzhou, the topic of which was opposing revisionism from abroad and guarding against revisionism at home. The meeting adopted the *Draft Decision on Certain Problems in Our Present Rural Work*, which stressed class struggle and guarding against revisionism. The decision stated: "Serious class struggle exists in Chinese society, and in many communes and production brigades. The leadership has fallen into the hands of landlords and rich farmers. ... If we do not engage in class struggle and production and scientific experiments, within a short while our Marxist party will turn into a revisionist party, and China will change its political color."

By early 1964 Mao's concerns had increased, with a more concrete assessment of the severity of China's domestic class struggle. According to Mao, the emergence of revisionism in the USSR was the outcome of domestic capitalism, aristocratic workers, rich peasants, and international imperialism. The USSR was dominated by revisionists, and capitalists had already taken over political power. In his numerous conversations with visiting foreign delegations, Mao claimed that there were about 35 million landlords and capitalists in China and a small number of people in factories and party and government organizations who favored the revisionists and imperialists. But Mao's assessment that there were revisionists within the CCP was much more serious. It was possible that China would become a revisionist country if Chinese leaders did not remain vigilant.

In accordance with this thinking, it was imperative that the CCP shift its focus from economic development to class struggle and to guarding against revisionism. To achieve such a strategic transformation, favorable conditions had to be created to sway public opinion. By 1964, Mao's perception of the existence of revisionism in China was obvious. He therefore became determined to shift his primary focus from opposing and condemning international revisionism to launching a domestic class struggle to insure China's correct political direction.[14]

From Mao's perspective, the real threat to proletarian dictatorship was the emergence of revisionism within the CCP CC. On 14 January 1965, under Mao's direct supervision, the CCP CC Politburo stipulated "Several Issues Raised in the Socialist Education Movement in the Countryside" (also known as the "23 articles"), introducing the concept of "those people in positions of authority within the party who take the capitalist road." Mao repeatedly warned against "the emergence of revisionism in the party center" and "Chinese Khrushchevs who are still nestling beside us." The document which stated "The focus of this campaign is to punish the capitalist roaders in power within the party" soon became the guiding document for the "Four Cleanups" Movement. The target of the struggle was clear.[15] Ironically, Liu Shaoqi and Deng Xiaoping, who shared Mao's view of Khrushchev, wholeheartedly supported Mao in the Sino-Soviet polemics, and actively participated in the battle against Soviet revisionism, were soon to became Mao's targets of struggle and Chinese "Khrushchevs."

The Sino-Soviet polemics laid the theoretical, public opinion, and political foundations for the unfolding of the Great Cultural Revolution. From the perspective of China's domestic politics, the Sino-Soviet polemics were carried out against the backdrop of the rapid development of "leftism" and guided by the enlargement of class struggle. Meanwhile, the Socialist Education Movement was carried out domestically for the purpose of guarding against revisionism by the formation of "continuous revolution under the proletarian dictatorship." Mao's basis for the Great Proletarian Cultural Revolution rested on two factors—the "23 articles" from the Socialist Education Movement and the "15 principles" from the ninth polemic. Thus, the Sino-Soviet polemics (opposing revisionism internationally) and the Socialist Education Movement (guarding against revisionism domestically) were wheels on the same bicycle, moving in concert to drag China into the abyss of the Cultural Revolution.

By early 1965, Mao had established the groundwork for launching a political revolution and consolidating his political power. But he still needed an incident to justify such a launch.[16] While the Khrushchev clique was becoming an imaginary enemy, the Sino-Soviet border negotiations were making progress and it seemed likely that an agreement would be reached. Soviet concessions would have likely brought about a new detente in Sino-Soviet relations. Therefore, the results of the Sino-Soviet border negotiations were complicating overall Sino-Soviet relations.

THE FIRST ROUND OF NEGOTIATIONS OVER THE BORDER ISSUE

The Sino-Soviet border negotiations began against the backdrop of heated ideological polemics and increasing tensions as well as outright border conflicts. The CCP's seventh polemic, titled "The Leaders of the CPSU are the Greatest Splitters of Our Times," published on 4 February 1964, condemned Khrushchev as the "chief representative of modern revisionism."[17] In reaction, on 12 February, the Presidium of the CPSU CC sent a letter to fraternal parties (excluding China), calling for "collective measures" and a "most resolute rebuff" against CCP factional activities. On 14 February, Mikhail Suslov "delivered a 150-page-long report that condemned from all possible angles and perspectives the factional activities of the Chinese leadership with reference to nationalism, great-power chauvinism, petit-bourgeois mentality, Trotskyite leanings, and Mao's personality cult." The CPSU planned to use the report "as the basis for public action against China."[18] It was in this atmosphere that a Chinese delegation headed by Vice-Foreign Minister Zeng Yongquan and a Soviet delegation headed by General Pavel Zyrianov met in Beijing on 25 February 1964 to begin border talks. From that point until 15 August 1964, they held 8 plenary sessions, more than 10 meetings of the heads of the delegations, and more than 30 meetings of advisers and experts.

Mao remained well informed about the negotiations as Zhou Enlai directly guided the activities of the Chinese negotiating team. The Chinese negotiators reported directly to Zhou on general principles as well as on specific actions. Zhou would then ask for Mao's instructions on important issues. The Chinese negotiating principles were the following: to reaffirm that the treaties between the Tsarist government and the Qing government were unequal; in order to keep the negotiations moving along, China would agree to negotiate on the basis of the previous treaties to resolve border issues; China would not attempt to recover territories lost to Russia in the aforementioned treaties, but the USSR should unconditionally return to China those territories that belonged to China according to those treaties but were later forcibly taken by the Russian and Soviet governments; and finally, China expected to reach a negotiated settlement over specific trouble spots along the disputed sections of the border.

Mao set what he expected to be the minimum objective for the Chinese negotiators: the issue of the "unequal treaties" had to be raised, and if the USSR admitted the existence of the "unequal treaties," China would forsake the 35,000 square kilometers of disputed territory.[19] Mao hoped to use the negotiations to temporarily ease tensions along the border and to ensure a smooth launch of his long-planned political revolution. According to Mao's calculation, it would be impossible for the USSR to accept the idea of "unequal treaties," but Mao intended to use the issue as China's starting point in its negotiation with the USSR. The purpose was to demonstrate to the Chinese people that he was defending Chinese national interests. He did not really care whether there would be a successful resolution of the border issue. As a CIA intelligence report points out, "Khrushchev calculated correctly that Mao was more interested in depicting him as a new imperialist Tsar than in acquiring Soviet-held land. Mao's land claim was indeed part of the bitter political feud, and Mao's main goal was to extract a political surrender, rather than small territorial concessions, as the price for a final settlement."[20] It is no wonder that the USSR reacted so strongly to China's "unequal treaties" thesis.

Indeed, Mao's conversation on 10 July torpedoed the negotiation process and resulted in an acceleration of the already tense situation in Sino-Soviet relations. As the Chinese and Soviet delegations were working toward a concrete solution to the problems along the eastern sector of the border, China faced three options: first, to set aside the "unequal treaties," ownership of Heixiazi Island, and to reach an agreement to resolve the border problems in the eastern sector; second, to continue the current stalemate but to allow the negotiations to continue; and third, to pressure the Soviets to acknowledge the "unequal treaties." Mao Zedong chose the third option.

In a conversation with foreign visitors in September and October, Mao said that he did not really want those territories to be returned. He only wanted it to be mentioned that the treaties had been unequal. China is now "taking the offensive ... making idle talk" in order to make "Khrushchev a little tense. ... Its goal is to obtain a reasonable ... boundary treaty." Mao's argument was inappropriate. When the negotiation teams were about to reach a draft agreement regarding the eastern sector of the border, it was unnecessary to make "Khrushchev a little tense." To raise the territorial claims at this juncture only served to provoke Khrushchev and bring the border negotiations to a screeching halt. In our view, Mao intentionally torpedoed the talks.

In view of Mao's bottom line for negotiations, that is, "if the Soviet Union acknowledges the unequal treaties, we will forgo the disputed territory," Mao's true intention was to negotiate with the Soviets in order to relieve tensions rather than to resolve the border problems. He was interested in continuing the talks but not in solving the problems.[21] To launch his great political revolution, Mao could not lessen the diplomatic pressure on Khrushchev. He could not allow a gradual improvement in Sino-Soviet relations through border negotiations. The Soviet government, which relied on international law to resolve border conflicts, could therefore not accept Mao's terms. But members of the Chinese negotiation team failed to fully grasp Mao's bottom line, so Mao soon became dissatisfied with the Chinese negotiators, who played down the ideological struggles and turned their attention to resolving concrete issues. Mao held that Liu Shaoqi and Zhou Enlai were attempting to reconcile with the Soviet revisionists. (At the beginning of the Cultural Revolution, Zeng Yongquan was purged for being close to Liu Shaoqi.) Based on his July declaration of territorial claims, Mao was putting those central government officials who preferred to compromise with the USSR on notice. He needed the Sino-Soviet tensions to stir up the moral indignation of the masses so that they would vigorously participate in Mao's forthcoming political movement.

The USSR strengthened its military cooperation with Mongolia after China proposed the "unequal treaties" issue. With the breakdown of the border negotiations in 1964, Moscow also increased its military forces in the Far East to counter China's ambitions to recover its lost territory. Khrushchev's removal from office seemed to offer the new Soviet leadership with an opportunity to improve Sino-Soviet relations. But because Mao's real intention was to force the new Soviet leaders to change their course, Zhou Enlai's mission to Moscow failed and the Sino-Soviet alliance completely collapsed (see the next section).[22] With the further deterioration of Sino-Soviet relations, the prospects for an agreement on the eastern sector of the border became hopeless.

KHRUSHCHEV'S FALL AND ZHOU ENLAI'S TROUBLED VISIT TO MOSCOW

At 12 a.m. on 16 October 1964, Soviet Ambassador Chervonenko urgently called on Wu Xiuquan, vice-director of the CCP CC International Liaison Department (ILD), to notify him of the CPSU CC's decision to remove

Khrushchev from office. He also handed Wu a letter from the CPSU to the CCP stating that the CPSU would continue the programs of the Twentieth, Twenty-first, and Twenty-second Party Congresses. In the Chinese view, this meant a continuation of Khrushchev's policies. The CPSU would work for unity in the International Communist Movement. Mao and other senior leaders were immediately apprised of the situation. On the same day, the *People's Daily* published the news about Khrushchev's fall. Beginning on 15 October, Mao chaired almost daily Politburo Standing Committee meetings to assess the effects of Khrushchev's fall. He claimed that Khrushchev's forced resignation had much to do with the ideological polemics. The CCP's nine polemics supposedly exposed the true color of Khrushchev's revisionism and forced him into an indefensible position. The decision by the October plenary session of the CPSU confirmed Mao's March prediction that Khrushchev would fall. Mao estimated that the Soviet leadership might experience some changes. There were three possibilities. "First, [the CPSU] will turn from revisionism to Marxism-Leninism, [but] at present this possibility is very small; second, [the situation] may become worse than it was under Khrushchev, but this possibility is also not very great; third ... [the CPSU] might still pursue a revisionist line, but in doing so its policy might change. The probability of this occurring is rather high." Mao's initial policy was to wait and see what changes would occur and, in the meantime, to praise the CPSU's decision to relieve Khrushchev of duty.[23]

After receiving the CPSU's circular, Mao instructed that a congratulatory letter, jointly signed by Mao, Liu Shaoqi, Zhu De, and Zhou Enlai, be sent to the new first secretary of the CPSU CC, Leonid Brezhnev, the new Soviet premier, Aleksei Kosygin, and chairman of the Presidium of the Supreme Soviet, Anastas Mikoyan. This was not merely a courtesy letter but a rather substantial political document issued at a critical juncture in Sino-Soviet relations. The congratulatory letter, with a warm and friendly attitude, was delivered to Chervonenko on the same day, the Central People's Radio Station broadcast it in the evening, and the *People's Daily* published it on the following day.[24]

On 19 October, after assuming the post of first party secretary of the CPSU CC, Brezhnev delivered a public speech in Moscow's Red Square. He declared that the CPSU would continue the lines of the Twentieth, Twenty-first, and Twenty-second Congresses. These were "the sole and unshakable lines of the CPSU and of the Soviet government in the past, at present, and in the future." The speech explicitly demonstrated to Brezhnev's compatriots that the new CPSU CC leadership would continue to follow the path established by Khrushchev. On the next day, *Pravda* published Brezhnev's speech. Nonetheless, there were signs of changes toward the "left" in numerous *Pravda* articles and speeches given by Soviet leaders, including Brezhnev and Kosygin. These changes emphasized the imperialist threat to peace, the need to strengthen national defense, and the need to provide more support to the anti-imperialist and anti-colonial struggles. As the CPSU suspended its anti-China propaganda, the CCP stopped publishing polemical articles and articles by leftist fraternal parties that condemned Khrushchev. The CCP also expressed the hope that relations with the CPSU would improve.[25] The USSR also ended discussions on a specific timetable for the conference of fraternal parties. These new developments seemed to indicate to the Chinese leadership that the uncertain elements in the fundamental policy of the new Soviet leaders would pose uncertainties for the evolution of Sino-Soviet relations. After waiting ten days, Mao decided to take the initiative. At a Politburo Standing Committee meeting on 27 October, he proposed sending a high-level Chinese delegation (led by Zhou Enlai and Vice-Premier Marshal He Long) to Moscow to attend the celebrations on the anniversary of the October Revolution. The CCP adopted a policy of "first pushing and second observing" in order to influence the new CPSU leaders to move closer to the CCP position.

The Chinese delegation led by Zhou Enlai and He Long arrived in Moscow on the evening of 5 November. An upbeat Kosygin met Zhou at the airport. Yu Zhan notes that Soviet security personnel rudely interrupted Soviet citizens' conversations with members of the Chinese delegation. On 6 November, Brezhnev politely rejected Zhou's last-minute request to give a public speech, which had been prepared beforehand, calling for "the Chinese and Soviet parties to unite on the basis of Marxism-Leninism and proletarian internationalism." These seemed to be ill omens for the coming negotiations.

On 7 November, Soviet leaders hosted a reception in the Kremlin for the members of the visiting Communist delegation and for the diplomatic community. During the banquet, Soviet Defense Minister Rodion Malinovskii, who was obviously drunk, made an anti-US war-mongering remark, which upset US Ambassador Foy D. Kohler. Zhou Enlai and members of the Chinese delegation walked over to Malinovskii to congratulate him on his "wonderful anti-imperialist toast."[26] Malinovskii told Zhou, "I do not want any Mao or Khrushchev to hamper us. ... The Soviet and Chinese people want happiness, and we will not allow any Maos or Khrushchevs to put obstacles in our way." As US journalists were present, Zhou could not tolerate such a provocation, so he simply walked away. Other Soviet marshals also came over, and the Chinese interpreters heard Malinovskii yelling, "We already did away with Khrushchev, now you should get rid of Mao." Malinovskii then turned to He Long, cursing both Stalin and Mao. Speaking to the Chinese, Soviet Marshal Matvei V. Zakharov uttered "to everything there is a season."[27]

The Chinese delegation soon left the reception and returned to the embassy. Zhou and his colleagues, in reviewing the entire episode, believed that it had not been accidental. It represented an intolerable insult to the Chinese people, state, party, and leader Mao Zedong. The Chinese believed that the Soviets were brazenly inciting the overthrow of the Chinese party and its leader. On the evening of 7 November, the CCP CC received an urgent cable from the Chinese delegation, reporting on the incident. The Chinese delegation proposed to lodge a formal protest with the CPSU CC and asked for instructions regarding further responses.

On the morning of 8 November, Mao chaired a CCP CC Politburo Standing Committee meeting to discuss the cable. Mao said, "Now this is to our advantage. We seized their mistake. We should use this to take the offensive. Don't put it aside for future discussion!" Mao asked Deng Xiaoping to respond to the Chinese delegation with a request to lodge a formal protest and to demand a formal response from the CPSU. The Chinese delegation was instructed to take the offensive, condemning the new CPSU leadership for disrupting unity and carrying on "Khrushchevism without Khrushchev." The CCP would not suspend the open polemics unless the CPSU admitted its mistakes and they reached an agreement. Evidently, Mao was attempting to use this incident to pressure the CPSU to change its course and to move closer to the CCP.

After receiving the instructions from the CCP CC, Zhou lodged a formal protest with CPSU leaders Brezhnev, Kosygin, and Mikoyan, who were having dinner with the Chinese delegation at the Chinese ambassador's residence on 8 November. Zhou claimed that the issue was not simply the behavior of Malinovskii. Many in the Soviet leadership held the same opinion. Zhou accused the Soviets of trying to incite the overthrow of Mao Zedong. Zhou warned the Soviet leaders that such an approach would not only worsen Sino-Soviet relations but also would be fruitless. Zhou stated that the differences in Sino-Soviet basic principles should not and could not be attributed to a struggle between Mao and Khrushchev.

Brezhnev and Kosygin attempted to gloss things over in order to stay on good terms with the Chinese. On behalf of the CPSU CC, Brezhnev apologized for Malinovskii's blunder. Brezhnev explained that Malinovskii was not a member or an alternate member of the Presidium, had only spoken nonsense while drunk, and had nothing to do with the position of the CPSU CC. The phrase "to everything there is a season" was only intended to refer to Khrushchev. Brezhnev persuaded Zhou to trust the CPSU leadership and invited the CCP delegation to Moscow to improve relations between the two parties. Zhou dismissed the explanation and insisted "Drunken people speak the truth." He stated that the Chinese delegation reserved the right to revisit the issue in the future. As Lorenz Lüthi has suggested, "Malinovskii's tactless remark indicated that it was not only the Chairman who had personalized Sino-Soviet discord, but officials on the Soviet side as well."[28]

Since Mao had determined that the new Soviet leadership was carrying out "Khrushchevism without Khrushchev," he wanted the Chinese delegation to utilize the Soviet "blunder" to take the offensive. In the end, Zhou stated that he would seriously consider Brezhnev's and the Presidium's explanations and he proposed a toast to CCP-CPSU solidarity. In reality, Zhou had very little room in order to maneuver to salvage the upcoming negotiations that now appeared to be a lost cause.

Indeed, Mao in Beijing had control over the Chinese delegation's activities, and Zhou had little flexibility. Mao adopted a policy of aggressive "pushing," which limited the negotiations to irrational political debates. Thus, they could not achieve any concrete results. They failed because the Chinese delegation insisted on modifying the CPSU program, which had been defined as the General Line of the International Communist Movement, and also by rejecting the convening of a new international fraternal party conference. Indeed, perhaps Mao was never really interested in anything concrete. As he put it later, "It is imperative to seek out the CPSU's intention. It is not surprising that we could not reach agreement. It is enough that we got a little bit of information." Mao achieved partial success. China discovered Moscow's bottom line for restoring relations with China. In doing so, China also revealed to the world its intention of upholding the unity of the International Communist Movement. Through consultations with the other fraternal parties in Moscow, the CCP delegation reiterated its position that the decision to convene an international conference of fraternal parties, which had been reached when Khrushchev was still in power, was illegal due to the lack of consultation with the other fraternal parties.[29] The CCP intended to undercut the CPSU's efforts to convene this conference and to make the CPSU the culprit in dividing the International Communist Movement.[30]

When Zhou and his delegation arrived in Beijing from Moscow on the afternoon of 14 November, a large contingent of senior Chinese leaders, including Mao and Liu Shaoqi, met them at the airport. This reception was identical to the one given to the last CCP delegation that had returned from negotiations in Moscow in July 1963. It was a political show of unity and strength by the CCP. The *People's Daily* issued the news about the Sino-Soviet negotiations but it did not report any substantive achievements. In such a manner, Mao was continuing to demonstrate his determination to break with the CPSU.

After the Chinese delegation left Moscow on 14 November, *Problems of Peace and Socialism*, a publication of the World Communist and Workers' parties but dominated by the CPSU, released its November issue. Under the heading "Reports by Communist Party Newspapers on the International Communist Party Conference," it published documents and speeches by those parties that supported the convening of the conference as well many articles openly condemning the CCP. The CPSU was thereby announcing the failure to reach a Sino-Soviet detente.

After consulting with Zhou, Mao ordered that the convening of a conference of fraternal parties should be blocked. China would refuse to participate and would condemn the conference if it were to be held. Furthermore, China could not be compelled to end the polemics. Mao ordered that an article be published on Khrushchev's fall, indicating the failure of Khrushchev's line.

On 16 November, the CPSU CC held a plenary session to adjust the new leadership core. The former cast of characters from the Khrushchev era was retained and all the newly elected members had been supporters of the Khrushchev line. The CPSU CC was demonstrating its firm and unshakable determination to follow the former party line. But Brezhnev also expressed his enduring interest in improving relations with the CCP. He urged the adoption of a more flexible policy to deal with China in the future. The CPSU would continue to debate the CCP, but it would avoid intensifying conflicts with the Chinese people.

The CCP acted swiftly. On 21 November, *Red Flag* issued an editorial, entitled "Why Did Khrushchev Fall?" It listed 12 evil deeds by Khrushchev to prove that his fall represented the bankruptcy and failure of modern revisionism. China thus launched a new round of polemics. The CPSU responded in kind. On 6 December, *Pravda* published an editorial, alluding to the CCP's criticism of the "all people's state" as defending "the cult of personality." The CPSU-CCP polemics had international implications and the USSR would not revert to the policies of the Stalin era.

The truce between China and the USSR, which lasted for one month, had ended. CCP-CPSU relations returned to ideological polemics. Although the CCP upheld the banner of developing Sino-Soviet state-to-state relations, it continued to expose the new CPSU leadership in party-to-party relations. The CCP gave up any effort to reconcile with the CPSU. The complete collapse of the Sino-Soviet alliance and the official split of the International Communist Movement were imminent.

CONCLUSION

From 1960 to 1964, China and the USSR intensely debated the basics of Marxist theory. During the first two years, this was a debate within the socialist bloc, and it was an attempt to persuade the other side to admit its mistakes and to remain in the bloc. It demonstrated that although the Sino-Soviet relationship had significantly deteriorated, the split was not yet final in the minds of many of the participants at the time. By late 1962, however, the CCP began to see Sino-Soviet differences as a contradiction with an enemy, and it launched its ideological polemics. The purpose was to defeat and excommunicate the other side from the movement. Thus CCP-CPSU party relations collapsed. Meanwhile, due to national security concerns, in 1964 Mao modified China's foreign and defense strategies, and the USSR, along with the United States, became one of the two main enemies threatening China's national security. The USSR saw China as expansionist, coveting Soviet territory as the Sino-Soviet border negotiations reached a stalemate in August 1964. Indeed, the Sino-Soviet alliance had already collapsed by mid-1964.

The year 1964 was critical to the Sino-Soviet alliance. With the collapse of party relations, Sino-Soviet relations were on a collision course. As the USSR was amassing troops along the Sino-Soviet and Sino-Mongolian borders, Mao's perception of the Soviet threat to China's national security was growing. Mao made the fateful decision to shift China's foreign and defense policy from opposing US imperialism to opposing both US imperialism and Soviet revisionism. Mao used the USSR, and specifically Khrushchev, as a scapegoat, claiming that they represented a serious threat to China's national security, as the USSR became China's "imaginary enemy." Mao linked his international strategy with China's domestic politics. In his view, the USSR had already become a capitalist and fascist country that was attempting to infiltrate China to carry out subversive activities. It was thus necessary to launch a political revolution in order to rout out Soviet agents in China.

Mao personally supervised the Sino-Soviet border negotiations. For Mao, these negotiations were only for tactical purposes, and he was not interested in resolving the border dispute. When it seemed that the two sides were about to reach an agreement on the eastern sector of the border, Mao publicly raised the "territorial claims," thus sabotaging the talks. Lorenz Lüthi notes that Mao's "[E]xcessive demands on the Soviet Far East were his preferred method of making Khrushchev uneasy."[31] To the Soviets, this "evoked historical memories of Russia's uneasy relationship with the East, marked by conquests by nomadic tribes." In Khrushchev's imagination, the Sino-Soviet split had changed from a power struggle "into a kind of clash of cultures and civilizations."[32]

The Sino-Soviet border negotiations were a turning point in Sino-Soviet relations. Previously, the struggle between the two countries was mainly for ideological domination, but now conflicts over national security and the military complicated the ideological struggle. To a certain extent, the foundation of Sino-Soviet relations had changed, shifting from emphasizing internationalism and a world Communist ideology to a focus on national interests.

Khrushchev's fall seemed to offer an opportunity for a CCP-CPSU reconciliation. As Sergey Radchenko has put it, "Brezhnev's 'collective leadership' blamed the split on Khrushchev's rude and careless actions and initially emphasized common ideology as a good reason for the two sides to reach an agreement."[33] The new Soviet leaders, Brezhnev and Kosygin, were eager to repair relations with the Chinese, but Mao's aggressive efforts to force the Soviet leaders to move closer to the Chinese position destroyed any hopes of reconciliation. In a sense, the Malinovskii incident served only to accelerate the final showdown.

NOTES

1. Sarah Paine, *Imperial Rivals: China, Russia, and Their Disputed Frontier, 1858–1924* (Armonk, NY: M. E. Sharpe, 1996), pp. 3, 28–29, 96, 328, 352.
2. Soviet troops had withdrawn from Mongolia in the 1950s.
3. Sergey Radchenko disputes this point. He writes, "Mongolia's leader Yumjaagiin Tsedenbal requested the presence of Soviet troops in December 1965, and the new Soviet-Mongolian Treaty, signed in January 1966, provided for such a contingency, but Moscow was not in a hurry to send troops to a foreign country and it was only after the threat of war with China increased considerably in February 1967 that the decision was taken to station what would become the 39th Soviet Army in Mongolia," See Radchenko, *Two Suns in the Heavens*, pp. 189–90.
4. On the Mongolian request to be admitted to the Warsaw Pact, see "Mongolian Request for Admission to the Warsaw Pact," 15 July 1963, Parallel History Project on Cooperative Security (cited hereafter as PHP), at http://www.php. isn.ethz.ch/collections/
5. "Polish Foreign Minister Memorandum Regarding Mongolia's Possible Accession to the Warsaw Treaty," 20 July 1963, in PHP, at http://www.php. isn.ethz.ch/collections/

6. For detailed studies on the construction of the Third Front, see Barry Naughton, "The Third Front: Defence Industrialization in Chinese Interior," *The China Quarterly*, no. 115 (September 1988), pp. 351–86; Lorenz Lüthi, "The Vietnam War and China's Third-Line Defense Planning Before the Cultural Revolution, 1964–1966," *Journal of Cold War Studies*, vol. 10, no. 1 (Winter 2008), pp. 26–51.

7. Wang Zhongchun, "The Soviet Factor in Sino-American Normalization, 1969–1976," in William C. Kirby, Robert Ross, and Gong Li, eds., *Normalization of U.S.-China Relations* (Cambridge, MA: Harvard University Asia Center, 2005).

8. Mao had been referring to the disputed southern Kurile Islands between the USSR and Japan since the end of World War II. In Japan, this is known as the North Territories dispute.

9. *Asahi Shimbun, Yomiuri Shimbun*, and *Mainichi Shimbun*, 13 July 1964.

10. Dennis J. Doolin, *Territorial Claims in the Sino-Soviet Conflict: Documents and Analysis* (Stanford, CA: Hoover Institution on War, Revolution, and Peace, 1965), pp. 47–57.

11. Wang, "The Soviet Factor in Sino-American Normalization, 1969–1976."

12. James Hershberg and Chen Jian, "Informing the Enemy: Sino-American 'Signaling' and the Vietnam War, 1965," in Priscilla Roberts, *Behind the Bamboo Curtain: China, Vietnam, and the World Beyond Asia* (Washington DC and Stanford CA: Woodrow Wilson Center Press and Stanford University Press, 2006), pp. 193–258.

13. Wang, "The Soviet Factor in Sino-American Normalization, 1969–1976."

14. See Li and Xia, *Mao and the Sino-Soviet Split*, pp. 100–102.

15. According to Chen Boda, who assisted Mao in drafting the document; by that time Mao had already decided to purge Liu Shaoqi.

16. For detailed descriptions of Mao's schemes to begin a political revolution, see Roderick MacFarquhar and Michael Schoenhals, *Mao's Last Revolution* (Cambridge, MA: The Belknap Press of Harvard University Press, 2006), pp. 14–31; Alexander V. Pantsov, with Steven I. Levine, *Deng Xiaoping: A Revolutionary Life* (New York: Oxford University Press, 2015), pp. 237–45.

17. *Peking Review*, no. 6 (7 February 1964), p. 10.

18. Radchenko, *Two Suns in the Heavens*, pp. 95–96.

19. Interview with Li Fenglin, former Chinese ambassador to the USSR, 24 March 2006.

20. CIA Intelligence Report, "The Evolution of Soviet Policy in the Sino-Soviet Border Dispute," ESAU XLV/70, 27 April 1970, at https://www.cia.gov/library/readingroom/docs/esau-44.pdf

21. He Fang, who was a Soviet specialist in the Foreign Ministry in the 1960s, confirmed this argument via an oral interview with the author. The author gratefully acknowledges his input.

22. Li and Xia, *Mao and the Sino-Soviet Split*, pp. 103–10.

23. In addition, when Chervonenko told Wu Xiuquan about Khrushchev's fall, based on Wu's response Chervonenko felt that the Chinese side had already received the information from another channel.

24. The congratulatory letter stated that China "is pleased with each progress the Great Soviet Union has made in its development … wishes the continuous development of an unbreakable fraternal friendship between the Chinese and Soviet people."

25. Chervonenko reported to Moscow that Peng Zhen had said at the Beijing Municipal CCP Party Committee meeting of activists that Chinese leaders planned to take an initiative to improve relations with the USSR. Zhou Enlai expressed the same wish to the visiting Japanese socialists.
26. Georgii Arbatov, *The System: An Insider's Life in Soviet Politics* (New York: Times Books, 1992), p. 109.
27. Ibid., pp. 109–10; Interview with Yan Mingfu by Li Danhui, 24 September 2007.
28. Lüthi, *The Sino-Soviet Split*, pp. 291–92.
29. While in Moscow, the Chinese delegation had met with numerous fraternal party delegations.
30. For a detailed discussion, see Li and Xia, *Mao and the Sino-Soviet Split*, pp. 110–19.
31. Lüthi, *The Sino-Soviet Split*, p. 300.
32. Radchenko, *Two Suns in the Heavens*, p. 119.
33. Ibid., pp. 162–63.

CHAPTER 18

The Schism in the International Communist Movement and the Collapse of the Alliance, 1965

Danhui Li

By 1965 the Chinese Communist Party (CCP) and Communist Party of the Soviet Union (CPSU) had entered a new phase in their conflict, centering around the March 1965 Moscow Conference and the issue of aid to Vietnam. This again reflected competition over leadership in the International Communist Movement. The conference also signaled an official split in the movement. In March 1966, the CCP Central Committee (CC) rejected an invitation to attend the Twenty-third CPSU Congress, and thus the organizational relationship between the CCP and the CPSU completely collapsed. The latter issue was related to rivalry over Vietnam. Because China could not tolerate Soviet influence in Vietnam, it thus attempted to limit Soviet aid to Vietnam. China and the Union of Soviet Socialist Republics (USSR) constantly clashed over the transport of Soviet supplies to Vietnam through China. Starting from 1965, the USSR shifted its policy of "hands-off" (*tuoshen*) to "lending a hand" (*chashou*) and continuously increased its aid to Vietnam, especially military aid. As Soviet-Vietnamese relations grew closer, Beijing grew more worried. Meanwhile, after their split, China and the USSR both engaged in intense competition for prestige and influence in the Third World. But China had suffered two crushing blows by the fall of 1965: the destruction of its closest and most important non-bloc party—the Communist Party of Indonesia (PKI)—and its abandonment of the Second Bandung Conference in November due to China's inability to secure the exclusion of the USSR from participation.

D. Li (✉)
World History Institute, East China Normal University, Shanghai, China
e-mail: lidanhui0601@vip.163.com

© The Author(s) 2020
Z. Shen (ed.), *A Short History of Sino-Soviet Relations, 1917–1991*,
China Connections, https://doi.org/10.1007/978-981-13-8641-1_18

THE MARCH 1965 MOSCOW CONFERENCE AND THE RIFT IN THE INTERNATIONAL COMMUNIST MOVEMENT

By the mid-1960s, Mao Zedong was arguing, "The majority of the more than 100 Communist parties in the world no longer believes in Marxism-Leninism." He opined that only about ten parties were on the side of the leftists. But with the evolution of the Sino-Soviet ideological polemics, there were followers of Mao in many parties in the International Communist Movement. Because Mao united with the leftists in the world's Communist and Workers' parties, relied on the left-leaning political parties, and supported revolutionary struggles and world revolution, the CCP increasingly came to be regarded as the center of world communism. With the growth of the leftist contingent and the formation of a new bloc, the International Communist Movement was clearly split. Under such circumstances, Mao was determined to go his own way. In his view, because the CPSU and many other parties had become revisionists, the CCP would have to lead the left-leaning parties to struggle against the imperialists in Asia, Africa, and Latin America. Therefore, the CCP began to formally challenge the CPSU's leadership of the International Communist Movement. It also attempted to shift the blame for the split in the movement on Moscow.

In a letter dated 29 February 1964, in reply to a Soviet proposal of 29 November 1963 regarding the convening of an international conference, the Chinese rejected the idea, advocating instead a conference of 17 fraternal parties (including Albania) to prepare for an international conference of the world Communist parties to be held in fall 1964. In a subsequent letter dated 7 May, the Chinese opposed a Soviet 7 March proposal to expand membership of the preparatory committee, that is, to include all 26 parties on the editorial board of the 1960 Moscow Statement.

In a letter dated 15 June, the CPSU CC responded by castigating the CCP, stressing, "It has been proved that the General Line of the International Communist Movement as defined in the Moscow Declaration (1957) and the Moscow Statement (1960) is correct. In view of the changing international situation, it is time to call a new international conference to supplement and develop the ideas in the 1957 declaration and the 1960 statement, and to analyze and resolve new issues." Thus, the CPSU argued that the CCP's proposal to postpone the conference was unacceptable. The CPSU felt that the CCP's true intention was to form a clique that would be obedient to Beijing in order to expand its supporters and to create a favorable situation for itself at future conferences. The CPSU's 15 June letter also criticized the CCP for making participation at the conference an issue for promoting division and resolutely opposing the CCP leaders' aspirations for special status in the International Communist Movement.

Whether or not the CCP's aim of postponing the international conference was to win over more supporters, the CPSU's comment presented it as a fact: If the international conference were to be held in accordance with the CPSU's wishes, in view of the numbers of CPSU and CCP supporters, the CPSU program would remain the General Line of the International Communist Movement. In Mao's opinion, such a conference would replicate the history of condemnation of the CCP, even adopting "collective measures" to expel the CCP. Mao could not tolerate such a development. Because he had decided to break with Moscow and to make a fresh start in the International Communist Movement, he formulated a specific strategy to achieve his goal. "We need to prod him [Khrushchev] into convening the conference and goad him into accepting blame for the open split." Mao soon instructed the CCP CC to reply to the CPSU's letter of 15 June. He personally edited the reply dated 28 July, inserting the following paragraph:

> Because you have made up your mind to convene the meeting, you have to do it. If you don't, your word will not count and you will have made yourself into a laughingstock. You have no way to back down. ... If you don't proceed with the meeting, other people will say that you have followed the advice of the Chinese and the other Marxist-Leninist parties. You will thus lose face. But if you convene the meeting, you will end up in a hopeless situation.

Khrushchev was hot tempered and easily irritated. Two days later, the reply of the CPSU CC pointed out that the 1957 Moscow Conference had adopted a resolution to entrust the CPSU to call a conference of world Communist and Workers' parties in consultation with the fraternal parties. The CPSU notified the CCP that a meeting of the editorial board of 26 fraternal parties would be convened on 15 December, regardless of the absence of any party. Provoked by Mao, Khrushchev was determined to convene the meeting. The CPSU continued to state that the purpose of the meeting was not to condemn or excommunicate any party from the International Communist Movement or from the socialist bloc but rather to find common ground, to unite all parties, and to seek a solution to differences. In the CCP's opinion, the main issue was no longer to resolve differences but rather to dismiss the Khrushchev revisionists from the International Communist Movement. The CCP immediately rejected the CPSU's proposal. On 19 August, Mao again called a meeting of CCP leaders to discuss the issue. All participants agreed that even if the CCP and the Party of Labor of Albania were the only two dissenters, the CCP would still refuse to participate in the 26-party preparatory meeting. Mao said, "Our party is adopting such a firm position so that the left-leaning fraternal parties will be even firmer."

After Khrushchev's fall in October 1964, Mao took the initiative to propose contacts with the new Soviet leadership. He sent a Chinese delegation to Moscow for talks with the CPSU CC. Taking advantage of the changes in the leadership, Mao attempted to force the new Soviet leaders to negate Khrushchev's line and program. Trying to take the initiative to achieve new unity, Mao also freed the CCP from blame for splitting the International Communist Movement. But the Malinovskii incident and the CCP's insistence on complete self-abasement by the CPSU foiled any efforts to improve relations. From Mao's perspective, the CCP's attempt to bring the CPSU closer to China was not primarily aimed at reconciliation but rather it was a last-ditch effort to continue on the traditional road of the International Communist Movement. If the new Soviet leaders were to abandon Khrushchev's policies and to accept the CCP's program as the guiding program of the International Communist Movement, then the CCP would guide the movement along the correct path, as defined by Mao. Otherwise, the CCP would withdraw from the International Communist Movement and go its own way to lead the people in Asia, Africa, and Latin America in their revolutionary struggles.

Against the backdrop of Zhou Enlai's strong opposition to the convening of an international conference of fraternal parties and efforts by the Chinese media to block any information regarding the failed party talks,[1] Soviet leader Leonid Brezhnev was trapped in the same dilemma as Khrushchev had been: If the CPSU called off the conference, it would lose much of its authority and prestige as the leader of world communism. If the CPSU insisted on holding the conference, then it would enrage the CCP, which might unite with several small parties to boycott the conference. This would lead to an open rift in the International Communist Movement. The only solution seemed to be to continue with the conference, but to play down its tone, signifying to the CCP that the rift was not fatal. CPSU leaders decided to postpone the 26-party editorial board meeting, originally scheduled for 15 December 1964, to 1 March 1965. They suggested changing the meeting into a consultative conference, with the delegates not having any responsibility for drafting a new international document or for setting a date for a future conference. The purpose of the conference was consultation, appealing to the fraternal parties for unity in the International Communist Movement and strengthening joint anti-imperialist actions ("unity of action"). The CPSU first discussed the new format with five East European parties, that is, the Bulgarian, Hungarian, Polish, East German, and Czechoslovak parties, then sought the endorsement of Australian and nine other Communist parties. The Cuban, Italian, and British Communist parties also agreed to attend the conference. The Vietnamese Workers' Party announced that it "did not see anything wrong with the meeting," but still it refused to attend. The Korean Workers' Party also refused to participate, and the Romanian Communist Party did not express any clear interest in attending. As the convener of an international conference, the CPSU made sufficient efforts to consult with the fraternal parties in a consultative and equal manner in order to avoid an open split within the International Communist Movement.[2]

On 27 November, when Ambassador Chervonenko delivered to Vice-Foreign Minister Liu Xiao the CPSU letter of 24 November addressed to the CCP CC regarding postponement of the meeting, it appeared to be an ultimatum. In responding to the Soviet view that the decision to convene the conference was not at the insistence of the CPSU but was the result of consultation with other fraternal parties, Liu Xiao and Wang Li, vice-director of the International Liaison Department (ILD), accused the new Soviet leaders of imposing their views on fraternal parties and continuing Khrushchev's divisive policy. On the following day, at a Politburo Standing Committee meeting,

Mao said, "They want to have the meeting, let them have it. We look forward to it. Let them fall into the abyss and dig their own graves."

The CCP did not respond to the CPSU's compromising posture, continuing to forcefully oppose the convening of a conference of fraternal parties. To avoid further provoking the CCP and to avoid responsibility for splitting the International Communist Movement, the CPSU had a difficult time in coming up with an effective policy to promote a January 1965 international conference of world Communist and Workers' parties. The CPSU CC Presidium believed that the CCP was exerting pressure on the CPSU, attempting to "force us to reconsider the principal foundation of our foreign and domestic policies," "to achieve complete normalization of political relations between our two countries, and to gradually adjust our ideological and political differences as the main direction of our political relations with China." Thus, the CPSU CC adopted a resolution, "On Measures for Normalization of Soviet-Chinese Relations," proposing that the CPSU would "carry out a series of measures to seize the initiative and gradually improve relations with the CCP, and achieve normalization in Soviet-Chinese relations within five to seven months." However, to pin the burden of splitting the International Communist Movement on the CCP, the CPSU would "take measured initiatives" in communications, talks, and meetings and would "propose concrete suggestions for improving cooperation in the economy and science and technology and to achieve normalization in state-to-state relations." If the CCP turned down all these suggestions, "it would demonstrate to the International Communist Movement that the CCP leaders are responsible for deepening the disagreements in the International Communist Movement." The International Department of the CPSU CC also proposed that the USSR and China should "hold a summit either in Beijing or Moscow in January/February 1965," which is "an important step" toward normalization of Soviet-Chinese relations. Preparing for the anticipated Soviet-Chinese summit, the CPSU Presidium carefully deliberated different options and came up with several Soviet responses to possible Chinese queries. The CPSU CC and the Soviet government were to stress: "It is now important to discuss measures for improving Soviet-Chinese government-to-government relations." At this point, the CPSU CC continued to try to persuade the CCP to attend the March fraternal parties' conference by putting aside CPSU-CCP disagreements and improving Soviet-Chinese government-to-government relations. While waving an olive branch to the CCP, the CPSU did not intend to forsake its principles. As Brezhnev pointed out, the USSR "will seek to improve relations with China, but this will not be done by making unwanted compromises."

In early February 1965, Chairman of the Council of Ministers Aleksei Kosygin stopped by in Beijing on two occasions while on his way to and from Vietnam. Zhou Enlai held talks with Kosygin, making a final effort to avoid a rift in the International Communist Movement. On 11 February, Mao told Kosygin that Zhou Enlai and Chen Yi had urged him [Kosygin] not to convene a conference on 1 March, but "I am personally in favor of the convening of this conference"; otherwise, the authority of the CPSU will be undermined. Mao vowed to continue along the anti-revisionism and anti-dogmatism path for 10,000 years. On the fraternal parties' conference, Mao unequivocally stated, "If you want us to attend the conference, you have to declare that your 14 July 1963 letter and your February 1964 expanded plenum of the CPSU CC were erroneous. Get rid of them. We oppose your program. … We are attacking the Twentieth and Twenty-second CPSU congresses." Mao insisted that it was not the proper time to hold an international conference of fraternal parties because the contentious issues had not all been fully debated. It should be postponed for 8–10 years. Kosygin suggested that both sides "put aside issues on which they could not reach agreement." In this way, they could achieve unity and improve bilateral relations. Mao responded, "We shall meet and contact each other, but we are not considering diplomacy."[3] A contemporaneous Central Intelligence Agency (CIA) study pointed out that "the Mao-Kosygin interview played an important role in clearing the way for the March meeting in Moscow. It served to clarify matters for any members of the Soviet leadership who may still have had illusions about the degree of Chinese intransigence."[4] In Brezhnev's opinion, Mao's statement demonstrated the CCP's demand that all fraternal parties accept the CCP's 25 points on the General Line of the International Communist Movement proposed in June 1963 as well as its determination to contend with the CPSU for leadership of the International Communist Movement. It also blocked the CPSU's intention to set aside differences and to achieve normalization of bilateral state-to-state relations, thus destroying the CPSU's illusion that it could improve relations with the CCP.

As the United States was escalating the war in Vietnam, the consultative conference of world Communist and Workers' parties was being held in Moscow from 1 to 5 March. Among the 26 invited parties, only 19 attended. The Communist parties of China, Albania, Vietnam, Indonesia, North Korea, Romania, and Japan refused to attend. Disagreements soon emerged even among the parties attending the conference. Some asked the CPSU to immediately reconcile with the CCP, whereas others censured the CPSU for adopting a wavering attitude. When discussing the draft communiqué, the Italian Communist Party maintained that it should only mention the creation of favorable conditions for a future international conference. The British Communist Party held that the most important condition for an international conference was that the CPSU and the CCP hold joint meetings and achieve normalization. The Italian delegates had reservations about any mention of the 1957 Moscow Declaration and the 1960 Moscow Statement in the final communiqué as some principles in these documents were already outdated. As Sergey Radchenko writes, the conference "showed that the International Communist Movement had not yet made up its mind to follow Beijing or Moscow."[5]

The conference produced two documents: a declaration on the Vietnamese incident[6] and a conference communiqué. In view of the current international situation and the anti-imperialist struggle, the participants unanimously supported the Vietnamese people, the Vietnamese Workers' Party, and the

National Liberation Front of South Vietnam. The communiqué pointed out that "it is necessary to unite in the struggle for a common goal even if there are major differences in the political line and major theoretical and practical issues." It advocated "the suspension of unfriendly and humiliating open polemics against fraternal parties ... and opposition to interference in the affairs of other parties." It urged a cessation of open polemics by collective efforts and meetings among the parties.

For CPSU leaders, the basic result of the conference was that the participants were committed to strengthening the unity of the International Communist Movement on the basis of the 1957 Moscow Declaration and the 1960 Moscow Statement. The CPSU thus believed it was still possible to protect its position of leadership in the International Communist Movement. However, "The outcome of the Moscow meeting clearly showed the CPSU that, for the time being, a world Communist conference remained impossible, as it had been for Khrushchev, to organize without unacceptable defections and political losses."[7] But for the CCP, the conference created numerous unfavorable factors affecting its prestige and status in the International Communist Movement. First, the conference was held at a time when the United States was escalating the war in Vietnam. It produced a document promoting assistance to Vietnam and countering the United States. The CPSU thus took the initiative to uphold the banner of anti-imperialism and to assist national liberation movements and people's revolution. This placed the CCP in an awkward situation. It had two options: to submit to the leadership of the CPSU or to continue the ideological polemics, which would weaken its image as the anti-imperialist flag bearer. Second, to stipulate a proposal for strengthening unity and offering concrete measures. Moscow was thus able to assume the banner of promoting unity in the International Communist Movement. The CCP was forced into a passive position and had to assume the burden of having a poor reputation because of violations of its previously accepted common program and the splitting of the International Communist Movement. The CCP reacted vehemently, condemning the March Moscow Conference as "illegal and divisive."

Less than 24 hours after publication of the declaration on the Vietnamese incident, and while the Soviet government was still negotiating with the Vietnamese government on concrete measures for aid, on 4 March 1965, Asian, African, and Latin American students in Moscow, along with Soviet students, held demonstrations in front of the US embassy protesting its imperialist military invasion of Vietnam. Students clashed with Soviet police and several were arrested and injured. One Chinese student was arrested, more than 30 were injured, and 9 were hospitalized. On 5 March, the Chinese embassy lodged a formal protest with the Soviet Foreign Ministry. The *People's Daily* reported on the entire incident as well as on the Chinese note of protest.[8] Lorenz Lüthi argues that the attack was very likely organized and supported by Chinese authorities and designed to damage the international reputation of the USSR, while deflecting from the Chinese government any attempts to limit or obstruct Soviet military aid to North Vietnam.[9] Making use of the incident, the

CCP accused the USSR of persecuting students and slavishly offering an apology to the US imperialists. The Foreign Affairs Office of the State Council issued a circular, stating two positions: first, the conference was the one that Khrushchev had originally planned; second, the conference was illegal and the CCP would not recognize it. Because the CPSU unilaterally decided to convene the meeting, it would have to bear the consequences.

On 12 March, *Pravda* published an editorial entitled "An Important Step toward the Unity of World Communism," which highly praised the March Moscow Conference. On the same day, the Soviet Foreign Ministry presented a note to the Chinese government regarding demonstrations near the Soviet embassy in Beijing. On 16 March, Ambassador Chervonenko made an appointment to meet with Yu Zhan, director-general of the Foreign Ministry's Department of Soviet and East European Affairs. He stated: "China's demonstrations are not at all helping the anti-imperialist cause." In the face of the CPSU propaganda, China stepped up its counterattack. On 23 March, the *People's Daily* published an article, personally edited by Mao, entitled "On the Divisive Moscow Conference." The article emphatically pointed out that the March Conference "is an important step in splitting the International Communist Movement. ... The two-line struggle in the International Communist Movement has reached a new stage." The CCP proposed conditions for achieving a new unity within the International Communist Movement: the CPSU had to openly admit that the decision to convene the March Conference was wrong; that Khrushchev revisionism, great power chauvinism, and splittism were wrong; that the revisionist programs of the Twentieth and Twenty-second congresses were wrong; that the CPSU's anti-China, anti-Albania, and anti-Japanese Communist Party positions were wrong; and the CPSU should promise not to make the mistakes of Khrushchev's revisionism. Otherwise, the CCP would continue its polemics. The purpose of the CCP attack was not only to negate the CPSU program as the guiding principles of the International Communist Movement but also to negate Soviet domestic policies. The CCP requested that the CPSU admit that its party program and principles were wrong. Only when it slapped its own face could the CPSU aspire to a new unity in the International Communist Movement.

While Moscow regarded the March Conference as a great contribution to the unity of the International Communist Movement, the CCP's intransigent attitude and fierce attack on the new CPSU leadership represented an implicit ultimatum. Three days later, at the March CPSU plenum, Mikhail Suslov condemned the CCP as completely unreasonable. Suslov stated: "They ask our party to admit that the programs established at the Twentieth, Twenty-first, and Twenty-second congresses are erroneous. They have insulted fraternal parties with aggressive language and have charged them as 'revisionists,' 'traitors,' and 'double-dealers.' This can only be regarded as a new anti-Soviet and anti-world communism Cold War." The CPSU and its supporters could hardly accept the CCP's terms for unity.

The March Conference signified the official split in the International Communist Movement. As Zhou Enlai pointed out, "The March Conference was a blank wall set up by the CPSU for our two parties." Afterward, the leftist contingent led by the CCP engaged in an ideological contest against the CPSU. The CCP never again participated in any international conferences organized by the CPSU.

By April 1965, China's policy turned farther left, emphasizing that China's foreign policy consisted of three principles: anti-imperialism; supporting world revolution; and peaceful coexistence, equality, and cooperation among the socialist countries. Anti-imperialism and supporting world revolution became the central thesis in Chinese diplomacy. During a meeting with Ambassador Chervonenko, who was about to leave his post, Liu Shaoqi stated that the foundation for Sino-Soviet unity was China's three foreign policy principles. Liu Shaoqi warned the Soviet ambassador, "If you don't change the general line of your foreign policy, it will be very difficult for us to cooperate in international affairs." At a meeting with the new Soviet ambassador, Sergey Lapin, who was presenting his credentials, Liu Shaoqi reiterated, "We differ on political, theoretical, and principle issues. We are no longer afraid that you will undermine us in our economic relations. ... Since we differ in terms of both line and policy, it will be very difficult for us to improve our relations."

One year later, the CCP CC rejected a CPSU invitation to attend the Twenty-third CPSU Congress to be held on 22 March 1966.[10] The organizational relationship between the CCP and the CPSU broke down completely and they parted company, each going its own way. This was a devastating blow to the socialist bloc. As Western media reported, "The Communists speak loudly of 'unity,' but there is no more unity and no prospect of unity."

As the CPSU told the participants at the March Conference that China had attempted to block any Soviet military aid to Vietnam passing through Chinese territory and Suslov accused the Chinese of rejecting unity of action in aiding Vietnam, Moscow and Beijing began to clash over opposition to US aid for Vietnam. Whereas the Vietnamese believed that the priority for the International Communist Movement was to unite to counter US military involvement in Vietnam, China focused on the struggle with the Soviet revisionists and argued that the condition for a successful anti-imperialist struggle was "to continue to expose the true color of the modern revisionists." With the increase in Soviet aid to Vietnam, the Vietnamese Workers' Party straddled the Sino-Soviet confrontation in order to acquire aid from both sides. It agreed to the convening of the conference, while at the same time appeasing China by refusing to send delegates. Nonetheless, it gradually moved away from the Chinese position. China could not tolerate the Soviets usurping the anti-imperialist banner or allowing the Vietnamese to move closer to Moscow and to lose its southern barrier. As China and the USSR were engaged in ideological contention over the March Moscow Conference, they were also struggling over the issue of aid to support the Vietnamese War of Resistance against US military involvement and support for the South Vietnamese government.

CONTRADICTIONS AND CONFLICTS IN THE JOINT ACTION
TO AID NORTH VIETNAM

In Moscow's view, "the Vietnam War was the final and most powerful argument for Moscow and Beijing to put aside their disagreements and to make joint efforts to help a 'fraternal' country under attack."[11] Beijing was concerned about the effects massive Soviet aid would have on Soviet-Vietnamese relations and Sino-Vietnamese relations. In Beijing's view, Brezhnev's domestic and foreign policies were "worse than Khrushchev's." Chinese leaders believed that when Khrushchev was in power, the USSR was unable to separate Vietnam from China because Soviet aid to Vietnam was minimal. From Beijing's perspective, the USSR now had ulterior motives in increasing aid to Vietnam. As Zhou Enlai told Vietnamese leaders, "We are constantly concerned about the revisionists standing between us." Chinese leaders thus repeatedly warned the Vietnamese leaders that Soviet aid was insincere and that the aim was first to isolate China, second to control Vietnam, and third to engage in subversive activities. The Soviets intended to make trouble for both China and Vietnam. Therefore, it was better for Vietnam not to accept Soviet aid.[12] As Thomas Christensen puts it, "Mao still viewed Vietnam largely as an opportunity for him and his party to gain prestige in the International Communist Movement at the expense of the Soviet Union."[13]

The deterioration of Sino-Soviet relations and Mao's determination to eliminate revisionists within the CCP blocked any meaningful Sino-Soviet cooperation to aid Vietnam. In February 1965, Kosygin visited Beijing on his way to Vietnam. In a conversation with Zhou Enlai, he discussed the issue of concerted action on the Vietnam issue. Kosygin later relayed this to the Vietnamese. Thus, the Soviets felt that "we are in agreement [with the Chinese] on this issue." When Kosygin mentioned this to Mao, Mao said, "It is the Americans who compel us to do this." After the March 1965 Moscow Conference, the CPSU CC and the Council of Ministers of the USSR wrote to the CCP CC and the State Council of China proposing a tripartite summit of Vietnam, China, and the USSR in an attempt to set aside differences and adopt joint actions. The Soviets asked, "When the enemies are at the gate of Vietnam … why cannot the representatives of the three socialist countries, China, Vietnam, and the USSR, get together to discuss joint actions to support the Vietnamese people's violent struggle?" The CCP replied in July, rejecting the proposal and accusing the CPSU: "Your so-called 'joint action' is to ask the fraternal parties to take orders from you—'the father party'— and 'the fraternal parties' and 'the fraternal countries' to serve as tools in your plan to dominate the world under the Soviet-U.S. collaboration." The Chinese denounced past Soviet diplomatic activities regarding negotiations over Vietnam, charging the USSR with continuing to collude with the United States and insisting that a tripartite meeting would harm the Democratic Republic of Vietnam (DRV). They thus rejected joint action of any kind with the Soviets.[14]

In late February 1966, a Japanese Communist Party (JCP) delegation visited China. The JCP delegation was in China for a total of 35 days (9–17 February, 28 February–11 March, 21 March–4 April). In between, it visited North Vietnam and North Korea. The purpose of the Japanese mission was to promote a socialist united front against US imperialist aggression in Indochina. The draft communiqué of the Japanese and Chinese leaders (including Liu Shaoqi and Zhou Enlai) did not mention the USSR by name, but it proposed to establish an anti-imperialist international united front, including the USSR, to take joint actions in assisting Vietnam. Mao told Miyamoto Kenji, JCP general secretary, "The CPSU welcomes your attitude, but we don't." Mao negated Miyamoto's view that it was possible to take joint action with mass organizations under the leadership of the CPSU, even if they [China] rejected joint action with the CPSU leadership.[15] According to a CIA intelligence report, Mao "demanded new changes in the joint communiqué already agreed upon (apparently to insert direct attacks on the Soviets). When Miyamoto would not yield on either point, Mao tore up the communiqué and tongue-lashed Chou [Zhou Enlai]—in front of Miyamoto—for having agreed to it."[16] In Mao's view, China would definitely not take joint action with the Soviet revisionists, for Mao believed that "[J]oint action with the Soviet Union in foreign affairs would hamper" his struggle at home.[17] The visit of the JCP delegation to China became a turning point in JCP-CCP relations. Six months after the trip, the JCP-CCP dispute erupted into a bitter, public fight. The CCP took definite anti-JCP actions in Japan and refused to send a delegation to attend the Tenth JCP Congress which opened on 24 October.[18]

The Sino-Soviet rivalry affected the war in Vietnam in two important ways. First, Sino-Soviet competition actually increased North Vietnam's military power and, second, because of Chinese pressure on the Vietnamese and Chinese criticism of the Soviets, "the Soviets were first unable and then unwilling to push Hanoi into negotiations with Washington before 1968."[19] Although differences of geography necessitated different Soviet and Chinese approaches to aiding Vietnam and countering the United States, in practice they had to cooperate in various ways, leading to contradictions and conflicts. Between 1965 and 1969, China and the USSR engaged in a series of hostile, and sometimes even fierce, confrontations. These were evident mainly in disputes over military aid and its transport.

China and the USSR collaborated passively in aiding Vietnam in the mid- and late 1960s. But they frequently quarreled. China emphasized the importance of planning the transport of Soviet aid to Vietnam, while the USSR stressed the special circumstances and demanded special treatment. The conflicts were due to various factors, such as China's strong anti-Sovietism, Soviet bureaucratism and low work efficiency, the Soviet wooing of the Vietnamese, and China's intention to prevent Vietnam from leaning too close to the USSR. Some Soviet practices disrupted China's overall transportation planning, but these would not have become major irritants if the two countries had still maintained friendly relations. However, during a period of hostility, both

China and the USSR made use of the transport issue to support their respective positions.[20]

However, since the mid-1960s, Hanoi had relied more heavily on Soviet military aid than it had relied on Chinese aid, and Moscow also assisted Hanoi in its dialogue with the West. Chinese leaders became increasingly concerned that Vietnam would dominate any postwar alliance with the USSR. By the early 1970s, the Vietnamese Communists believed that China would eventually betray Vietnam in its search for rapprochement with the United States.[21] Thus, Hanoi's relationship with Moscow grew closer.

When the Vietnam War entered its last phase in the early 1970s, China helped North Vietnam transport the supplies it requested in preparation for a future attack. At the same time, China and the USSR had reopened border negotiations in October 1969, so their conflicts were intensifying. Nevertheless, disputes still occasionally flared, China and the USSR generally followed the principle of cooperating to assist Vietnam.

SINO-SOVIET COMPETITION IN THE THIRD WORLD

In the mid- and late 1950s, China divided the world into imperialist, socialist, and nationalist countries. One important aspect of China's foreign policy was to win over and unite with the nationalist countries in Asia, Africa, and Latin America, to expand its anti-US united front, and to isolate and strike against the imperialist bloc headed by the United States. Because China and most countries in Asia, Africa, and Latin America shared similar problems as a result of imperialism and colonialism, they faced the same challenges. Thus, supporting the national liberation struggles in Asia, Africa, and Latin America and developing friendly relations with the newly independent nations in these areas became one of China's diplomatic priorities. By providing aid, China attempted to facilitate the development of independent national economies in these countries, to gradually lessen their reliance on the imperialists, and to strengthen forces for world peace. In the late 1950s, China still respected the USSR as head of the socialist bloc and still coordinated its Third World policies with the USSR. Moscow "saw the increasing Chinese presence in the developing world as a positive factor in the international competition between the capitalist and socialist systems."[22] But the Sino-Soviet split in the early 1960s changed this cooperative relationship.

With the deterioration of Sino-Soviet relations in the late 1950s and early 1960s, the CCP and the CPSU both set their propaganda machines in motion, elaborating on their respective views regarding the nature of the contemporary era, anti-imperialism, anti-colonialism, and the national liberation movements and revealing their political orientations to the Third World countries. In foreign policy, the USSR emphasized peaceful coexistence and detente with the West. Moscow advocated a "non-capitalist path of development," arguing that assisting the Asian, African, and Latin American countries was an important task of the world socialist system so that the Third World countries could disengage from colonial and semi-colonial status by peaceful competition with the capitalist system. Newly independent nationalist countries could choose socialism, escape the capitalist developmental stage, and follow the non-capitalist road. The CCP accused the CPSU of being the defender of neo-colonialism, and it stressed the importance of struggle with the imperialists and colonialists for national liberation and independence in Asia, Africa, and Latin America.

Mao turned China's domestic and foreign policies farther left at the Tenth Plenum of the Eighth CCP Congress in August/September 1962. At a national foreign affairs conference in early 1963, the CCP unambiguously stated its plan to compete for leadership in the Third World. By the end of the year, the CCP had defined the Sino-Soviet relationship as a contradiction between the people and the enemy.

In June 1963, the CCP CC proposed its 25 points regarding the General Line of the International Communist Movement. Together with the CCP's theoretical debates with the CPSU in July, the 25 points revealed the formation of a CCP theoretical framework: they detached the national liberation movements from the CPSU world socialist system; they defined the national liberation movements as the first step in the world revolution, that is, a bourgeois-democratic revolution, whose task was to overthrow imperialism and capitalism; and they asserted that a bourgeois-democratic revolution had to be accomplished before proletarian dictatorship and a socialist system could be established. During this initial stage of world revolution, bourgeois leaders of the national revolution could become leaders of the national liberation movements. But national capitalist regimes, under the control and influence of capitalism, could not transcend the capitalist stage and directly enter the socialist revolution. Proletarian parties in nationalist countries could only seize political power through violence and establish socialism through violence. The CCP proposal expanded the scope of the International Communist Movement, making China's revolutionary experience a universal model for Third World national liberation movements. It thus established a theoretical foundation for Mao's ambition to lead the Third World.[23]

From September 1963 to mid-1964, Mao proposed the concept of two intermediate zones. According to Mao, most countries in Asia, Africa, and Latin America were in the first intermediate zone and could be China's direct allies. Mao claimed that former colonial powers, such as England, France, Belgium, Holland, West Germany, and Japan, were in the second intermediate zone and could be "indirect allies of the people." China's diplomatic strategy was to rely on the countries in the first intermediate zone, to win over the countries in the second intermediate zone, and to struggle against the US imperialists and the Soviet revisionists. In January 1964 Mao for the first time referred to China as a "Third World" country. He thus detached China from the socialist bloc and provided a theoretical basis for establishing China as the leader of the Third World.[24] At the beginning of the Cultural Revolution, the CCP further proposed, "We must oppose modern revisionism in order to carry out the struggle against imperialism." On National Day in October 1966, the CCP CC formally put forward the slogan, "Down with modern revisionism centered around the Soviet revisionist leadership clique!" thereby linking the USSR with the United States as China's enemy. The CCP attempted to place the Third World countries in opposition to the USSR and to undermine Moscow's theoretical basis as leader of the Third World.

To compete with Moscow for leadership in the Third World, Beijing firmly supported seizing political power through violence, especially for the Communist Party of Burma, the Malayan Communist Party, the Communist Party of Thailand, and the guerrilla war chiefs in the small Latin American countries. This sharply contrasted with Moscow's advocacy of "peaceful coexistence and economic competition."[25] China's tactics and propaganda won many converts among the Asian and African countries. In a number of cases, it seems that Beijing was successful in seizing leadership of the "national liberation struggle." The chairman of the Indonesia Committee of Supporters of Peace explained to "the editor in chief of *Pravda* that 'you need to know that the countries of Asia and Africa are on the side of China because its position is closer to theirs; they think that national independence must be achieved with force, even with all-out war.'"[26]

China also strengthened political, economic, and diplomatic activities in the newly independent countries. For instance, "Chinese aid pledges in 1963–1964 totaled US$ 266.3 million to nine African countries, as opposed to only US$ 72.2 million to six countries in the years prior to 1963, not including military aid."[27] To improve China's public profile and diplomatic impact, Premier Zhou Enlai and Foreign Minister Chen Yi toured ten African countries in late 1963 and early 1964, including the United Arab Republic,[28] Algeria, Morocco, Tunisia, Ghana, Mali, Guinea, Sudan, Ethiopia, and Somalia. At a farewell banquet in Accra on 15 January 1964, Zhou put forth China's eight principles of foreign aid, emphasizing aid based on mutual benefit and equality, respect for sovereignty, no-interest credits, provision of top-quality equipment, training of local technical cadres, and living standards for Chinese experts not to exceed those of their local counterparts. It thus announced China's full-scale entry into competition with the USSR and the United States.[29] China's foreign-aid practices, such as the living standards for Chinese experts were not to exceed those of their local counterparts, had already been positively received. In March 1960, a Nepalese paper noted "because of the differences in personnel costs, Chinese aid is 'more than the aid of other friendly countries' and 'shows how aid from developed countries to underdeveloped countries should be.'"[30]

China supported left splinter factions within the world Communist and Workers' parties. The CCP lent its support to minor factions with anti-Soviet revisionist orientations, though they might not even have had Marxist-Leninist programs or organizations. In particular, the CCP had great influence on the PKI. On 5 August 1965, a PKI delegation led by Secretary General D. N. Aidit visited Beijing. The advice offered by Mao and the CCP to the PKI had a strong influence on Aidit's decision to become involved in the 30 September coup, which ended disastrously for the PKI.[31] As Jeremy Friedman notes, the People's Republic of China (PRC) "had lost its closest ally, the fifth most populous country in the world with the largest nonruling Communist Party, one that had openly declared an alliance with Beijing and one on which the PRC had hoped to underpin the building of an Afro-Asian–Latin American power structure."[32] From Moscow's perspective, this proved the correctness of the CPSU program. Brezhnev pointed out, "The main reason why the members of the PKI had to pay such a high price is because the PKI leaders had deviated from the General Line of the International Communist Movement." The CPSU CC thus blamed the Maoists for the destruction of the PKI. Mao, however, argued that the Indonesian revolution had not yet ended. He claimed that Indonesian reactionaries provoked the PKI to follow the Chinese revolutionary path of encircling the cities from the rural areas and engaging in armed struggle. He asserted that the experience of the PKI would prove the correctness of Mao Zedong Thought and the errors of Soviet revisionism.

The theme of the Moscow Conference in March 1965 was to call on all socialist countries and all Communist and Workers' parties of the world to unite in joint action to support Vietnam's war against the United States. The CCP's rejection of joint action in Vietnam put it in a passive and awkward position, planting the seeds for later Sino-Vietnamese discord. But Mao decided to make a fresh start in leading the left-leaning political parties in the International Communist Movement. Meanwhile, he attempted to exclude the USSR from Afro-Asian affairs. Both China and the USSR wanted to make use of the escalation of the Vietnam War to cast Vietnam's War of Resistance against the United States as a useful example of the correct nature of their respective stances. Beijing and Moscow competed for leadership of world revolution via struggle over the convening of the Second Afro-Asian Conference.

During the preparatory period for the Second Afro-Asian Conference from April 1964 to October 1965, in view of China's challenge to Soviet leadership in the Third World, Moscow actively lobbied for its inclusion. Beijing firmly opposed Moscow's participation. For Mao, the main purpose of China's participation in the Second Afro-Asian Conference was to unite the political left with middle elements. According to Mao, the middle elements were in the majority in the Afro-Asian countries and China should expose Moscow's face of "fake anti-imperialism and true traitor" in order to unite with the middle elements and isolate the USSR. In Mao's opinion, if China could win over the support of the political left, which made up 30 percent of the total population, and unite with the majority of the middle elements, victory would belong to the political left. Mao even conceived of the idea of holding a conference of the Afro-Asian political left and middle elements.

According to Soviet Foreign Ministry statistics of May 1965, of the 50-plus countries that planned to participate in the Second Afro-Asian Conference, about 24–26 supported Soviet participation, but the number was increasing. In other words, about half of the participants supported the inclusion of the USSR. Many leaders in the Afro-Asian countries through their media emphasized that Soviet participation would enhance the significance of the conference and be conducive to their common anti-imperialist, anti-colonial, and anti–neo-colonial cause. The Soviet role was widely recognized not only because of its geographical location but also due to its standing in the revolutionary and liberation struggles. *Pravda* declared that the Afro-Asian countries regarded Soviet participation of vital importance and they would not defer to those who opposed a USSR presence at the conference. Thus, China decided to withdraw from the Second Afro-Asian Conference due to its rigid and inflexible policy of excluding Soviet participation. This led to the indefinite suspension of the conference and an open split among the Afro-Asian countries.[33]

CONCLUSION

To win over the Third World countries, the Soviet leadership under Brezhnev modified the CPSU line and program under Khrushchev and became more aggressive in the ideological arena. The basic tone of Moscow's foreign policy turned toward anti-imperialism and anti-colonialism, thus moving closer to the CCP's tone. Due to the escalation of war in Vietnam in 1964, the convening of the Moscow Conference in March 1965, and the struggle over the convening of the Second Afro-Asian Conference, Beijing and Moscow both became anti-imperialist centers of the world revolution. But the situation was not to the advantage of Vietnam's War of Resistance against the United States. China's intransigence over unity of action damaged its revolutionary credentials and planted the seeds for later Sino-Vietnamese discord. The Soviets outsmarted the Chinese, enhancing their prestige at the March Moscow Conference and during the preparatory stage of the Second Afro-Asian conference. Therefore, Moscow regained its leadership position in the promotion of world revolution. In 1965 China suffered a series of failures in its foreign policy—its refusal to attend the Moscow Conference in March marked a formal split in the International Communist Movement; Beijing lost an important ally when the PKI was purged in September; and CCP opposition to Soviet participation in the Second Afro-Asian Conference caused an open split among the African and Asian countries. Thereafter, China could only lead a small number of radical left-leaning groups in the anti-imperialist and anti-colonial movements, thus dampening Mao's aspirations to lead the world revolution.

From the mid- to late 1960s, China and the USSR cooperated passively in providing support to Vietnam but there were constant disputes due to poor communications. China emphasized the importance of observing agreed-upon plans when it shipped aid to Vietnam, whereas the USSR maintained that unusual circumstances required unusual solutions. A variety of factors, including China's strong anti-Soviet bias, inefficiencies in the Soviet bureaucracy, Soviet dissatisfaction with China, Soviet efforts to win North Vietnam loyalty, and China's attempts to prevent Vietnam from leaning toward the USSR, gave rise to Sino-Soviet discord. Soviet behavior undoubtedly had a negative impact upon China's plans to ship supplies to Vietnam. Whether or not it was initially intended, both China and the USSR seized any opportunity to oppose and spar with the other. Even so, in these years their quarrels did not seriously affect their support for Vietnam and their opposition to America's war efforts in Vietnam.

NOTES

1. In its no. 21–22 issue of 1964, *Red Flag* published an editorial entitled "Why Did Khrushchev Step Down?" Thereafter, *People's Daily* reprinted a number of articles and speeches by fraternal parties on Khrushchev's removal, criticism of modern revisionism, and queries on the convening of an international conference.

2. For a contemporaneous study, see CIA Intelligence Report, "The Sino-Soviet Struggle in the World Communist Movement Since Khrushchev's Fall," Part I, September 1967, ESAU 34, pp. 15–35, CIA unclassified documents, https://archive.org/stream/ESAU-CIA/The%20Sino-Soviet%20Struggle%20in%20the%20World%20Communist%20Movement%20Since%20Khrushchev%27s%20Fall%20%28Part%201%29#mode/2up

3. For an English translation of Mao's conversation with Kosygin on 11 February 1965, see "Memorandum of Conversation, A. N. Kosygin and Mao Zedong," in Radchenko, *Two Suns in the Heavens*, pp. 227–34.

4. CIA Intelligence Report, "The Sino-Soviet Struggle in the World Communist Movement Since Khrushchev's Fall," Part I, p. 118.

5. Radchenko, *Two Suns in the Heavens*, p. 157.

6. The declaration censured American military intervention in Vietnam and expressed support for the Vietnamese people, the Vietnamese Workers' Party, and the National Front for the Liberation of South Vietnam, which were fighting against imperialist aggression.

7. CIA Intelligence Report, "The Sino-Soviet Struggle in the World Communist Movement Since Khrushchev's Fall," Part I, p. 122.

8. Radchenko, *Two Suns in the Heavens*, pp. 149–50.

9. Lorenz Lüthi, "The Origins of Proletarian Diplomacy: The Chinese Attack on the American Embassy in the Soviet Union, 4 March 1965," *Cold War History*, vol. 9, no. 3 (August 2009), pp. 411–16.

10. For details, see Radchenko, *Two Suns in the Heavens*, pp. 166–71.

11. Ibid., p. 163.

12. "Zhou Enlai and Pham Van Dong, 9 October 1965," and "Zhou Enlai and Le Duan, 23 March 1966," in Odd Arne Westad, Chen Jian, Stein Toonesson, Nguyen Vu Tung, and James Hershberg, eds., "77 Conversations between Chinese and Foreign Leaders on the Wars in Indochina, 1964–1977," *CWIHP Working Paper*, no. 22, pp. 89–90, 93–94.

13. Thomas Christensen, *Worse than a Monolith: Alliance Politics and Problems of Coercive Diplomacy in Asia* (Princeton, NJ: Princeton University Press, 2011), p. 184.

14. CIA Intelligence Report, "The Sino-Soviet Struggle in the World Communist Movement Since Khrushchev's Fall," Part III, September 1967, ESAU 36, p. xviii, https://archive.org/stream/ESAU-CIA/The%20Sino-Soviet%20Struggle%20in%20the%20World%20Communist%20Movement%20Since%20Khrushchev%27s%20Fall%20%28Part%203%29#mode/2up

15. Lüthi, *The Sino-Soviet Split*, p. 335.

16. CIA Intelligence Report, "The Sino-Soviet Struggle in the World Communist Movement Since Khrushchev's Fall," Part II, September 1967, ESAU 35, pp. 94–95, https://archive.org/stream/ESAU-CIA/The%20Sino-Soviet%20Struggle%20in%20the%20World%20Communist%20Movement%20Since%20Khrushchev%27s%20Fall%20%28Part%202%29#mode/2up

17. Radchenko, *Two Suns in the Heavens*, p. 155.
18. CIA Intelligence Report, "The Disintegration of Japanese Communist Relations with Peking," December 1966, ESAU 33, pp. 30–38, https://archive.org/stream/ESAU-CIA/The%20Disintegration%20of%20Japanese%20Communist%20Relations%20with%20Peking#mode/2up
19. Christensen, *Worse than a Monolith*, p. 182.
20. For a detailed analysis of Sino-Soviet disputes on military aid and its transport to Vietnam, see Li and Xia, *Mao and the Sino-Soviet Split*, pp. 202–12.
21. Qiang Zhai, *China and the Vietnam Wars, 1950–1975* (Chapel Hill: University of North Carolina Press, 2000), pp. 217–19.
22. AVPRF f.0100 o.48, p. 203 Por. 37, d. KI–722, 201, cited in Jeremy Friedman, "Soviet Policy in the Developing World and the Chinese Challenge in the 1960s," *Cold War History*, vol. 10, no. 2 (May 2010), p. 257.
23. Friedman, *Shadow Cold War*, pp. 31–32, 62–63.
24. Yafeng Xia, "Mao Zedong," in Steven Casey and Jonathan Wright, eds., *Mental Maps in the Early Cold War* (Houndsmill, Basingstoke, Hampshire, UK: Palgrave Macmillan, 2011), pp. 168–69.
25. Friedman, *Shadow Cold War*, p. 13.
26. Cited in Friedman, "Soviet Policy in the Developing World," p. 261.
27. Friedman, *Shadow Cold War*, p. 119.
28. The United Arab Republic was a short-lived political union, from 1958 to 1961, between Egypt and Syria. Egypt continued to be officially known as the United Arab Republic until 1971.
29. Friedman, *Shadow Cold War*, pp. 117–18.
30. Cited in Friedman, "Soviet Policy in the Developing World," p. 258.
31. Chinese sources reveal that Mao and other CCP leaders encouraged Aidit to take up arms to seize political power in Indonesia.
32. Friedman, *Shadow Cold War*, p. 142.
33. For an analysis of Sino-Soviet competition in the Third World, see Li and Xia, *Mao and the Sino-Soviet Split*, pp. 213–19.

CHAPTER 19

The Breakdown of State Relations and the Sino-Soviet Military Confrontation, 1966–1973

Danhui Li

During the Great Proletarian Cultural Revolution, officially launched in May 1966, the Soviet Union was systematically demonized and Chinese public discussions were strongly anti-Soviet. After the breakdown of the first round of border negotiations in 1964, the border issue became politicized, as territorial disputes became a new source of military conflicts and bargaining chips for the leaders in both countries, affecting the fate of their bilateral relations. The Sino-Soviet border conflicts gradually escalated. The outbreak of armed conflicts on Zhenbao Island (Damansky Island in Russian) on the Ussuri River in March 1969 brought the two countries to the brink of a major war, and the Sino-Soviet alliance no longer existed. The threat of war from the Soviet Union forced Mao to modify China's diplomatic strategy from confronting the United States to seeking reconciliation with Washington. After President Richard Nixon's historic trip to China in February 1972, Mao was contemplating a quasi-alliance with the United States.

THE CULTURAL REVOLUTION AND THE STRONG ANTI-SOVIET FERVOR

In early 1966, the Communist Party of the Soviet Union (CPSU) Central Committee (CC) began to prepare for the convening of the Twenty-third CPSU Congress. At the CPSU CC plenum on 19 February 1966, Brezhnev proposed that the Twenty-third CPSU Congress would not debate or criticize Chinese Communist Party (CCP) leaders because all CPSU members were in

D. Li (✉)
World History Institute, East China Normal University, Shanghai, China
e-mail: lidanhui0601@vip.163.com

© The Author(s) 2020
Z. Shen (ed.), *A Short History of Sino-Soviet Relations, 1917–1991*,
China Connections, https://doi.org/10.1007/978-981-13-8641-1_19

agreement with the CPSU's restrained and moderate policy to deal with the CCP. After the plenum, Brezhnev wrote to Mao and the CCP CC, inviting the CCP to send a guest delegation to attend the Twenty-third CPSU Congress. In view of the CCP's refusal to attend the March 1965 Moscow Conference, its boycott of the CPSU's appeal for joint action to aid Vietnam and resist the United States, and the intense ideological struggles between the CCP and the CPSU, the CPSU was attempting to reach some sort of compromise.

Mao Zedong, who at the time was contemplating a political revolution at home, was unwilling to accept the CPSU's olive branch. In his letter to the CCP CC regarding the CPSU's invitation, Mao treated the CPSU with utter contempt, ignoring any basic diplomatic etiquette. He pinned the epithet of "blackleg" on the CPSU, saying, "A group of blacklegs have a meeting. Why should we send them a congratulatory letter? We will send them a letter in reply, briefly stating our reason for not attending." On 18 March, a Politburo Standing Committee meeting deliberated the issue of whether or not the CCP should send a delegation to attend the CPSU Congress. It approved Mao's idea of not attending and not sending a congratulatory letter.

On 20 March, the CCP CC issued a circular indicating that it would not send a delegation to attend the Twenty-third CPSU Congress and not send a congratulatory letter. On 22 March, the CCP CC sent a reply to the CPSU CC, combatively declaring, "The CPSU CC is walking farther and farther on the road of revisionism, splittism, and great power chauvinism. You are colluding with the U.S. imperialists, attempting to establish an anti-China, anti-people, anti-national liberation movement, and an anti-Marxist-Leninist 'holy alliance.' Under such circumstances, how can you expect the CCP, which you regard as an enemy, to attend such a conference?"

The Soviet leadership under Brezhnev, who had attempted to improve relations with China, felt a bit embarrassed at the CCP's refusal. CPSU leaders felt that the CCP's refusal to attend the congress was a formal step to draw a clear distinction with the CPSU in the International Communist Movement. It was a new stage in the CCP's nationalistic agenda. The purpose of the upcoming "Great Proletarian Cultural Revolution," which Mao was advocating, was in essence to strengthen anti-Sovietism. CCP leaders were increasingly connecting their fate with anti-Sovietism. Meanwhile, the CPSU CC was attempting to adopt an uncompromising position, uniting with the majority of the world's Communist and Workers' parties to resist CCP influence.

Thus, 86 Communist and Workers' parties attended the Twenty-third CPSU Congress, held in Moscow from 29 March to 8 April 1966. In view of the CCP's intransigence, the Soviet leaders "narrowed Chinese policy to a simple manifestation of 'nationalism.'"[1] At the congress, Brezhnev insinuated that the CCP's "departures from Marxism-Leninism, both to the left and to the right, become particularly dangerous ... when they are combined with the manifestation of nationalism, whether it is in the form of great power chauvinism, hegemonism, or some tendency toward national isolation and separateness." But he continued to wave an olive branch, stating that the CPSU "is ready for a meeting with the CCP at the highest levels to reassess our differences in order to seek a solution on the basis of Marxism-Leninism."[2]

Attendance by the Korean Workers' Party and the Vietnamese Workers' Party at the Twenty-third CPSU Congress demonstrated that these two parties were no longer yielding to the CCP's position in the Sino-Soviet split. It also indicated that they were moving closer to the CPSU's position.[3] The Twenty-third Congress again demonstrated that the majority of world Communist and Workers' parties were united with the CPSU. To counter the potential effect of the Soviet party congress, the CCP CC issued a special propaganda circular, stating, "They talked about improving relations with China at the congress, which was an utter lie to cheat the people of the world. ... The CPSU insists on revisionism, splittism, and playing the game of phony unity. ... It was thus completely right for the CCP not to send a delegation to attend the congress." Full of fighting spirit, Mao and the CCP lifted the curtain of anti-Sovietism in the Great Proletarian Cultural Revolution. When the Cultural Revolution officially began in May 1966, Foreign Minister Chen Yi told foreign reporters that "the Soviet Union is among the most dangerous friends, without which China would feel safer."

On 16 May 1966, a CCP CC Politburo expanded meeting issued the CCP CC "Notification" (also called the "May 16 Notification"), which was personally revised by Mao. It stated: "[T]hose representatives of the bourgeoisie who have sneaked into the party, the government, the army and various cultural circles are a bunch of counterrevolutionaries. Once conditions are ripe, they will seize political power and turn the dictatorship of the proletariat into a dictatorship of the bourgeoisie. ... persons like Khrushchev, for example, who are still nestling beside us."[4]

In the Communiqué of the Eleventh Plenary Session of the Eighth Central Committee of the Communist Party of China, adopted on 12 August 1966, the CCP announced: "Our Party's public criticisms of Khrushchev revisionism over the last few years have been entirely correct and necessary. ... it is imperative to oppose modern revisionism. There is no middle road whatsoever in the struggle between Marxism and Leninism and modern revisionism. A clear line of demarcation must be drawn in dealing with the modern revisionist groups within the CPSU. ..."[5] The CCP unequivocally kicked the Soviet "revisionist clique" out of the international united front of anti-US imperialists and their lackeys. Thus, the CCP severed all connections with the CPSU, linking the major theme for launching the Cultural Revolution with the objective of anti-Sovietism. Mao's ultimate goal of launching the Cultural Revolution was "opposing revisionism." "Opposing revisionism" was to fight against Soviet revisionism, and "guarding against revisionism" was to prevent Khrushchev-type careerists and schemers from usurping supreme party and state power.

From 1967 to 1969, on behalf of the common cause of anti-revisionism, anti-imperialism, and anti-colonialism, leaders of international leftist groups and leftist leaders of nationalist countries made pilgrimages to China and felt honored to be granted an audience with Mao. During these meetings, Mao was repeatedly revered as the leader of the Third World and "the great revolutionary of our times." Beyond all doubt, the pilgrimages of world leftist leaders further prompted Mao to lead an independent international force to counter the CPSU. The illusion that the Chinese Revolution was the model of the world revolution and Beijing was the sacred place of this revolution propelled Mao and the revolutionary spirit and anti-Soviet fervor of the Chinese masses.[6]

Confronted with the CCP CC's uncompromising position, the CPSU responded in kind on 31 August 1966, stating that the Eleventh Plenum of the Eighth CCP CC had "completed the procedure in favor of using the anti-Soviet line as official CCP policy." It declared that the CCP's stance was designed to "split the International Communist Movement, to split the socialist big family, and to weaken the anti-imperialist front." This was the first open statement against China after Brezhnev had come to power. Soviet newspapers and periodicals soon published many articles censuring the Cultural Revolution, thus escalating the Sino-Soviet ideological struggle.

Meanwhile, the CPSU made serious efforts to bring in line the East European–Central European Communist states (including East Germany, Poland, Czechoslovakia, Bulgaria, and Hungary) and to take joint action against China's anti-Soviet stance. At the CPSU plenum in December 1966, Brezhnev thoroughly criticized China's "Great Cultural Revolution" and attacked Mao by name, stating "the great power ambition and anti-Soviet policy of Mao Zedong and his clique have entered a new phase. … The Cultural Revolution of the Chinese leadership poses a threat to socialist solidarity and the entire Communist movement." The Soviet Union planned to unite with over 60 Communist and Workers' parties to hold a new international conference, attempting to take collective measures against the CCP's new policy. The CPSU's December plenum passed a resolution on Soviet foreign policy and Sino-Soviet relations, calling to expose the Chinese leadership's anti-Leninism, great power chauvinism, and nationalism.

Beijing was determined to match Moscow in this new round of ideological polemics. On 13 December 1966, *Red Flag* (no. 15) published a long article entitled "The Dictatorship of the Proletarian and the Great Proletarian Cultural Revolution," which for the first time systematically explained China's Cultural Revolution. It asserted that the "China's great proletarian cultural revolution, unparalleled in history, has sounded the death knell of imperialism and modern revisionism." *Red Flag* singled out the new Soviet leaders, Brezhnev, Kosygin, and Aleksandr Shelepin, for attack, claiming that they were worse than Khrushchev.[7]

In China's foreign propaganda, Mao Zedong Thought was depicted as the third milestone in the history of Marxism. In early November 1967, Mao commented on a major *People's Daily* polemical editorial, "To Advance Forward Along the Road Opened Up by the October Socialist Revolution." Mao approved the editorial, asserting, "This article will deal a blow to the Soviet revisionists." The article labeled the Soviet leadership under Brezhnev and Kosygin "the center of modern counterrevolutionary revisionism and another headquarters of world reactionaries" and it formed a new "Holy Alliance" with "all the most reactionary forces in the world against communism, against the people, against revolution and against China."[8] The article was full of bitter and abusive denunciations of the CPSU.

After the beginning of the Cultural Revolution, especially during the "Red August" of the Red Guard movement, anti-Soviet mass incidents occurred throughout China. The Soviet embassy in China, the embodiment of Soviet state power, became the target of Red Guards and "revolutionary masses."[9] On 22 August 1966, Soviet embassy councilor Aleksei Brezhnev and his colleagues were departing the embassy to participate in an airport send-off ceremony for Zambian Vice-President Reuben C. Kamanga when they noticed a huge portrait of Mao Zedong sitting on a pile of stones near the embassy compound. Brezhnev and his colleagues were asked to get out of their car to "walk past Mao's portrait with their heads bowed." After negotiations, Brezhnev and his colleagues were allowed to leave for the airport. Arriving at the airport, Brezhnev asked the Vietnamese ambassador to notify Foreign Minister Chen Yi of this incident. But after being apprised, Chen Yi and Zhou Enlai did not take any action to address the incident. The Soviet foreign minister soon lodged a protest with the Chinese foreign minister, but to no avail. Foreign diplomats, in particular Soviet diplomats, experienced great hardships in their working and living conditions in Beijing.

With the Cultural Revolution in full swing, all Chinese colleges and universities "suspended classes to make revolution" in order to concentrate every ounce of energy on the Cultural Revolution. On 20 September, the Chinese Ministry of Higher Education informed the Soviet embassy that classes for foreign students would be suspended for one year because it was not possible to hold classes only for foreign students. Furthermore, all Soviet students were to depart China within 10–15 days. On 7 October, the Union of Soviet Socialist Republics (USSR) Ministry of Higher Education notified the Chinese embassy that based on the principle of reciprocity, the Soviet Union intended to suspend the education of all Chinese students and expected them to return to China by October. This was a normal diplomatic practice, but the Chinese Foreign Minister presented the Soviet embassy in Beijing a note of protest on 22 October, stating this "unjustifiable decision" was further worsening relations between the two countries.[10] A new wave of demonstrations and harassment of Soviet diplomats erupted in October 1966 and lasted until early 1967. Chinese students in the Soviet Union clashed with the Soviet police while laying wreaths at Lenin's and Stalin's mausoleums. On 25 January 1967, a group of 69 Chinese students, returning to China from France and Finland via Moscow, went to Red Square to lay wreaths at the Lenin Mausoleum. As they were nearing the mausoleum, they started to read out quotations from Mao's little red book, shouting loudly, "Down with Modern Revisionism!" Soviet police tried to push the students out of the square, but according to Chinese reports, over 30 Chinese students were injured, with 4 seriously wounded and 1 left in critical condition.[11] The Chinese government reacted forcefully to the

Red Square incident. On 26 January, Foreign Minister Chen Yi issued a hostile statement against the Soviet government and its leadership. On the same day, Zhou Enlai and Chen Yi, on behalf of the CCP CC, the State Council, Chairman Mao, and Lin Biao, sent a personal telegram of "warm regards" to the students. From the evening of 26 January to 11 February, about one million people demonstrated in front of the Soviet embassy in Beijing. The Red Guards demanded that the Soviet diplomats come out of the embassy "to bow their heads" and "admit their mistakes." Unlike the Red Guard siege of the Soviet embassy in August 1966, the Chinese government strongly and publicly supported the demonstrators. In the wake of the nationwide struggle over political power, the supposedly grassroots anti-Soviet campaign escalated. Telephone connections between the Soviet embassy and the Chinese Foreign Ministry were cut off, and entry and exit to the Soviet embassy were blocked. In a word, the Soviet embassy was besieged.[12]

On 2 February 1967, the Chinese Foreign Ministry notified the Soviet embassy that "beginning from this moment, personnel in your embassy are not allowed to leave the compound. Otherwise, their safety cannot be guaranteed." The Soviet leadership decided to evacuate its nonessential personnel and dependents from China, but the departing Soviet personnel faced a difficult ordeal on their way to the airport when they were confronted by Red Guards. After nearly three weeks of massive anti-Soviet demonstrations, China and the Soviet Union were on the verge of breaking diplomatic relations. On 5 February, in a meeting with Red Guard representatives from Xi'an, Foreign Minister Chen Yi said, "The problems with the Soviet Union may develop further. Perhaps diplomatic relations will be broken off. Perhaps there will be a war. Your place [Xi'an], as well as the Northeast and Inner Mongolia, will be the forward posts."

Soviet leaders felt that war was imminent. On 4 February, the CPSU Politburo passed several resolutions. Moscow decided to station troops along the Sino-Mongolia border. But the Soviet leadership made a farsighted decision to remain in Beijing as long as it could. A Central Intelligence Agency (CIA) document explains:

> The Soviets were well aware why the Chinese might wish to force them out, and the Chinese were well aware why the Soviets were determined to stay. A formal break in diplomatic relations would serve as a legal pretext to sever permanently the Soviet land and air transportation routes across China, and thereby present the USSR with the unpleasant dilemma of either accepting an end to their military aid to North Vietnam—an unthinkable political disaster—or shipping their sensitive military equipment to the DRV by sea and running the terrible risk of a renewal of their 1962 confrontation with the United States Navy.[13]

The embassy siege temporarily ended on 11 February, but the propaganda battle continued with greater intensity. Beginning in February 1967, *Pravda* issued a series of articles that vehemently attacked Mao and his policies.[14]

Meanwhile, Moscow was eager to take organizational and collective measures to shore up support for the CPSU and "to try to isolate the CCP virus." At the CPSU CC plenum in December 1966, Brezhnev said, "To convene a Conference of World Communist and Workers' Parties has become a practical problem. … We will not permit the CCP leaders and other parties to obstruct the convening of such a conference." Beginning in early 1967, Moscow made a concerted effort to hold an international conference of world Communist and Workers' parties, which it had been trying to organize since 1964. The CPSU hoped to convene such a conference in November 1967 on the 50th anniversary of the October Revolution. As a CIA intelligence study reported:

> The November ceremonies … present a fortuitous and unique opportunity to the CPSU: an accidental circumstance providing the CPSU, at just the moment when the Chinese have virtually withdrawn from the movement, with a legitimate occasion for an impressive display of the CPSU's historic credentials to lead the movement and a complete roster of parties obliged to be present.[15]

But this world Communist conference did not take place. To struggle against China and Maoism on an international scale, Soviet leaders stepped up efforts to organize a group of "like-minded fraternal parties that could collectively deal with Beijing." This is the origin of the Interkit—the International on China—"a series of meetings held interchangeably in the different capitals of the socialist bloc," beginning in December 1967 when Oleg Rakhmanin, the Soviet Union's leading China specialist and first vice-director of the Department for Liaison with Communist and Workers' Parties in the Socialist Bloc, hosted in Moscow a delegation of heads and vice-heads of central party International Departments from the East European socialist countries and Mongolia to coordinate China policy. One of the items on the agenda was to "exchange opinions regarding further counteractions to the Mao-group policy as well as regarding coordination of research efforts and exchanges of information in this field." The Chinese translated the Interkit as "China International" (*duihua guoji*).[16]

The Soviet Union was sensitive to and vigilant of China's uncompromising stand and strong nationwide anti-Sovietism. A report of the Far East Department of the Soviet Foreign Ministry in July 1966 argued that China's refusal to attend the Twenty-third CPSU Congress demonstrated that China's foreign policy objectives were undergoing substantial changes. Based on its unwavering anti-Soviet policy, China was attempting to expand its contacts with the West. By revising its former slogan, "The United States is the main enemy," China formally announced that the Soviet Union was as hostile as the United States. To struggle against imperialism headed by the United States and to struggle against "modern revisionism" centered in the Soviet Union were China's "two indivisible tasks." At the CPSU plenum in December 1966, Brezhnev said, "While opposing the CPSU and our country, Mao Zedong seems to have extended an olive branch to the Americans to make them understand that China and the United States now have a basis for close contacts."

On the eve of the anniversary of the October Revolution in 1968, the CCP CC stipulated that China would no longer send a congratulatory letter to the CPSU on the anniversary; China would send only 20 cadres at the level of director-general or below in government ministries to attend the October Revolution reception at the Soviet embassy in Beijing. The CCP CC International Liaison Department (ILD) would not send any representatives. By then, the CCP and the CPSU had broken off all contacts.

CLASHES ON ZHENBAO ISLAND AND MILITARY CONFRONTATION

In January 1966, the Soviet Union signed a 20-year Treaty of Friendship, Cooperation, and Mutual Assistance with Mongolia. According to Chinese sources, the Soviet Union began to send mechanized troops to Mongolia in March 1966. But Sergey Radchenko shows that the Soviet Union did not send troops to Mongolia until February 1967.[17] The Sino-Mongolian border, a stretch of 4500 kilometers, constituted a military threat to China's North, Northeast, and Northwest. The distance from Erenhot, on the Sino-Mongolian border, to Beijing, via Zhangjiakou, is only about 560 kilometers. Much of the terrain is level enough to be accessible by mechanized troops and tanks. Soviet doctrine held that its army groups could extend more than 700 kilometers within ten to fourteen days. Intercontinental missiles deployed deep inside Soviet territory and intermediate-range missiles stationed near the Chinese border could attack any location in China.[18]

In view of the reinforcement of Soviet troops along the Sino-Soviet border, Mao and other Chinese leaders felt further pressure from the Soviet military. They thus laid out a war-preparedness plan. On 16 March 1966, at a meeting of the CCP CC Northern Bureau, Zhou Enlai pointed out: "North China might be the target of enemy attacks and thus should be the main battle-ground. ... To be more specific, it is necessary to establish a system of war preparedness in North China." In late March, during his meeting with Japanese Communist Party leader Miyamoto Kenji, Mao briefly mentioned that China was prepared for US attacks on its east coast—in Shanghai, Guangzhou, Qingdao, and Tianjin. He then focused on possible attacks from the Soviet Union, noting that China was "prepared for attacks by revisionists—invasions of Manchuria, China's three Northeast provinces, Xinjiang ... and then Beijing."

The Soviet invasion of Czechoslovakia in August 1968 and the Soviet occupation of a socialist country within six hours had a serious effect on China. China reacted to the Soviet invasion with alarm, mainly because it believed "that the Brezhnev doctrine could apply to China as well as to Eastern Europe."[19] To a large extent, the Soviet invasion of Czechoslovakia prompted Mao's decision to change China's foreign policy strategy. This established the ideological, social, psychological, and logical foundation for Mao's transformation of China's foreign and strategic policies in the early 1970s.

Meanwhile, the Sino-Soviet border clashes escalated. According to Chinese sources, from October 1964 to March 1969, there were 4189 border incidents—one and one-half times more than those that took place between 1960 and 1964. Along the eastern sector of the Sino-Soviet border, intense conflicts occurred on Wubalao Island on the Heilong River and on Qiliqin and Zhenbao Islands on the Ussuri River. Zhenbao Island soon became the focal point of the border conflicts. From 1966 to early 1968, conflicts escalated from pushing and shoving Soviet soldiers to attacking Chinese border personnel with clubs. By late 1968 and early 1969, Soviet border troops frequently transported armed Soviet soldiers to Zhenbao Island to engage with Chinese frontier guards. On 7 February 1969, according to Chinese sources, Soviet soldiers fired at a Chinese patrol party, thus further deteriorating tensions along the Sino-Soviet border.

Beijing had several options to resolve the Sino-Soviet border clashes. The first possibility was to adopt a position of restraint and to maintain the status quo. Chinese soldiers would only enter the island to engage the Soviets in political and diplomatic struggles and would make efforts to avoid violent confrontations with the Soviet Union; the second possibility was to restrain the level of fighting and to avoid an expansion of the war; and the third possibility was to strike against any Soviet troops that attempted to prevent Chinese soldiers from landing on the islands regardless if there were to be violent conflicts. In the ultra-leftist atmosphere of the Cultural Revolution and the nationwide "anti-revisionist" and anti-Soviet campaigns, Mao opted for the third plan, that is, to fight against the Soviet Union with armed force. The remaining issue to be decided was to choose an opportunity and a locality. Under such circumstances, plans for a "counteroffensive" on Zhenbao Island were proposed.

In January 1969, a Soviet tank on Qiliqin Island killed four Chinese residents. On 24 January 1969, the Central Military Commission (CMC) cabled the Shenyang and Beijing Military Regions, instructing Chinese frontier troops to choose an opportune time and location to fight back, but "to fight back only when there is a good chance of winning." The CMC stressed that the battle on the frontier was mainly a matter of political and diplomatic struggles. Therefore, every act of frontier defense was to consider the overall situation and strictly follow the rule of asking for instructions from and reporting to superiors.

It is quite possible that Mao wanted to interfere with the Soviet leadership of the International Communist Movement. From 17 to 22 March 1969, the preparatory meeting of the world Communist and Workers' parties was to be held in Moscow. It was decided that the World Communist and Workers' Parties Conference would be postponed to 5 June. In the wake of the Soviet invasion of Czechoslovakia, Moscow had to call a new Conference of World Communist and Workers' Parties to ensure unity, to engage in joint actions against imperialism, and to establish the CPSU's program as the general agenda for the International Communist Movement. Meanwhile, with the further deterioration of Sino-Soviet relations, the Soviet Union wanted to use the platform of a new international conference to organize criticism of the CCP, to remove the centrifugal tendency toward the CPSU in international communism, and to isolate the CCP and other leftist organizations.

Mao was very much aware of the CPSU's objective in organizing the Conference of World Communist and Workers' Parties. He wanted to utilize the Zhenbao Island conflict to show that the Soviet Union had not only invaded Czechoslovakia but it had also created military conflicts along the Sino-Soviet border. Mao believed that this would reveal the true color of Soviet "social imperialism," and it would also prove that the policy of strengthening unity and joint action against imperialism proposed by the Soviet Union was deceptive. Mao wanted to undermine the conference.

By late February, the CCP CC approved the battle plan of the Heilongjiang Provincial Military District to strike Soviet troops on Zhenbao Island. The first military conflict between China and the Soviet Union broke out on Zhenbao Island on 2 March.[20] By 15 March, fighting was becoming increasingly tense. On 17 March, the Soviet Army once again dispatched tanks and infantry troops to the island in an attempt to haul back its bombed tanks, but they were forced to retreat under intense Chinese fire. Both sides suffered casualties in the course of three battles on the island. According to presently available Chinese sources, China suffered 29 deaths and 62 injuries in these three battles. An assessment by the Foundation for Strategic Research, the Headquarters of the People's Liberation Army (PLA) General Staff reported that Soviet casualties (both dead and wounded) reached about 250. The same report stated that Russia, after disintegration of the former USSR, generally agreed that there were 58 dead and 94 wounded on Zhenbao Island.

After the Zhenbao Island incident, the Soviet Union responded swiftly. First, Moscow lodged a strong protest against China; second, on 7 March, the director-general of the Information Department of the Soviet Foreign Ministry and the deputy commander of the Soviet Frontier Defense Army held a press conference, elaborating on the conflict on 2 March; third, Soviet leaders called on the Soviet public to demonstrate against the Chinese; fourth, on 11 March, the Soviet ambassador to West Germany issued a formal complaint against China with respect to the Sino-Soviet border clashes. He intended to alert the West to new developments in Sino-Soviet relations; fifth, on 17 March, the Soviet Union called on member states of the Warsaw Pact to condemn China's invasion of the Soviet Union, requesting that the East European countries send troops to sensitive areas along the Sino-Soviet border to deal with the Chinese through collective measures; sixth, on 15 March, when reporting on the border conflicts, Moscow Radio continuously proclaimed the power of the Soviet nuclear missiles and the ineffectiveness of China's nuclear power, thus posing a nuclear threat against China; seventh, the Soviet Union proposed the concept of an Asian collective security system. On 29 May, a *Pravda* editorial condemned China for making trouble in Asia and asked several Southeast Asian countries to establish a "collective security" organization. On 5–17 June, Moscow was finally able to hold an International Conference of 75 Communist and Workers' Parties, which was less than the 81 parties that had attended in 1960. Fourteen parties did not attend, including, most significantly, the Vietnamese and North Korean parties, although in this case the

Cuban party did attend. Brezhnev pointed out that the Chinese leaders "have shifted from a policy of criticizing peaceful coexistence to engineering violent conflicts." The conference openly condemned the anti-Soviet and anti-socialist policy of Mao and his clique. It unequivocally confirmed the CPSU's leadership role in the International Communist Movement and the CPSU's general line. For the first time, Brezhnev formally proposed the establishment of an "Asian collective security system." His intention was to contain Chinese expansionism in Asia.

China also wanted to publicize the incident. First, after the incident, massive demonstrations against the alleged Soviet incursion into Chinese territory took place all over China. In less than ten days, from 4 to 12 March, more than 400 million people had participated. The *People's Daily* and *Liberation Daily* published editorials entitled "Down with the New Tsar!" identifying the Soviet leadership with the former rulers of the Russian empire.[21]

Second, at the meeting of the "Central Cultural Revolution Small Group" on 15 March 1969, after being informed of the war situation on Zhenbao Island, Mao opined, "Let it [the Soviet Union] in, and we can then mobilize the people. ... We will gain mastery by striking only after the enemy has struck. ... Let the enemy have an upper hand and occupy Mudan River. Foreigners will know about it." After reading a report on the Zhenbao Island incident, Mao said that the Sino-Soviet conflict "poses a new issue for the United States." Mao opined that the Sino-Soviet split made it possible for the United States to shift from fighting two and a, half wars to fighting one and a half wars. The United States would modify its foreign and defense policies in accordance with the changing Sino-Soviet relations. After the Ninth Party Congress, Mao authorized Zhou Enlai to make arrangements for four marshals, Chen Yi, Ye Jianying, Xu Xiangqian, and Nie Rongzhen, to engage in a joint study of the international situation.[22] In mid-May, Zhou Enlai, following Mao's instructions, asked the four marshals to "pay attention to" international affairs. He urged them to meet "two to three times each month" to discuss "important issues" related to international security and to provide the CC with their opinions.

The marshals in the study group believed it was unlikely that the Soviet Union would wage a large-scale war against China. They emphasized, however, the need for Beijing to be prepared for a worst-case scenario. Within this context, Chen Yi and Ye Jianying contended that in order for China to be ready for a major confrontation with the Soviet Union, "the American card" should be played. In a written report entitled "Our Views about the Current Situation," which was completed on 17 September, the marshals pointed out that "although Moscow intends to wage a war of aggression against China" and "has made war deployments," the Soviet leadership "cannot reach a final decision because of political considerations." The marshals proposed that, in addition to waging "a tit-for-tat struggle against both the United States and the Soviet Union," China should use, the "negotiations as a means to fight against them." They suggested that perhaps the Sino-American ambassadorial talks should be resumed "when the timing is proper."[23]

The Ninth CCP Congress was held in Beijing from 1 to 24 April 1969. In his political report to the congress, which had been approved by Mao, Lin Biao, China's defense minister and Mao's designated successor, stressed the danger of launching an aggressive war by the US imperialists and the Soviet revisionists. He called for a united front of all people to fight against "our common enemy," claiming, "We will not attack unless we are attacked; If we are attacked, we will certainly counterattack."[24] The purpose of the report was to highlight the Sino-Soviet conflict on Zhenbao Island and to warn the United States that Sino-Soviet relations were teetering on the brink of war, thereby alerting Washington that the Soviet Union was China's main enemy, and China would not take any initiative to provoke a war with the United States in Indochina.

Third, China was combat-ready for war with the Soviet Union. Lin Biao's report emphasized that it was necessary for China to be prepared to fight the US imperialists and the Soviet revisionists in both conventional and nuclear warfare. At the First Plenum of the Ninth CCP Congress on 28 April, Mao declared that China should "be prepared for war."[25]

Fourth, China declined to respond to the Soviet request for negotiations, which gave Mao time to publicize the seriousness of the tensions in Sino-Soviet relations. On 21 March, Chairman of the Council of Ministers Alexei Kosygin attempted to talk to Mao and Zhou Enlai via the Sino-Soviet hotline, but he was turned down by the telephone operator. In the early hours of 22 April, Li Lianqing, deputy director-general of the Soviet and East European Department of the Foreign Ministry, informed the Soviets: "In view of the present situation in Sino-Soviet relations, it is inappropriate to talk over the phone. If the Soviet government has anything to say, it should be proposed through diplomatic channels." Several days later, on 29 April, the Soviet government issued a statement proposing "to resume the talks that began in Beijing in 1964." But the Chinese failed to reply. On 11 April, the Soviet government again proposed negotiations in Moscow. On 14 April, the Chinese government notified the Soviets that "We will respond to your request. Please hold your horses!" But the Chinese government did not respond until 24 May, declaring that "China has always maintained that border issues should be resolved via negotiations." On 26 July, when the Soviet Union again proposed holding high-level talks, the Chinese did not respond.

China's procrastination in responding to the Soviet requests, along with its anti-Soviet stance and preparations for war, encouraged Soviet hardliners. Soviet leaders were extremely suspicious of Beijing's motives. They believed that Mao hoped to seek assistance from the West, and they accused China of colluding with imperialists such as the United States. Out of concern for the prospects of a Sino-American rapprochement, Soviet leaders attempted to pressure Beijing to agree to negotiations.

The Soviet Union thus adopted two measures: First, it heightened the nuclear threat against China. On 14 July, *Izvestiya* published an article by Marshal Matvei Zakharov, who had been chief of staff of the Transbaikal Front during World War II and had helped plan the invasion of Manchuria. The article stated that "Soviet experience in smashing Japan's Kwantung Army convincingly and explicitly demonstrated that any attempt to invade the Soviet Far East frontier and its ally—the Mongolian People's Republic—will be doomed to scandalous failure." On 28 August, *Pravda* published an editorial, stating, "If war breaks out under the current situation, no continent will survive the catastrophe of modern and destructive weapons and missiles." According to Henry Kissinger, assistant to the US President for national security affairs, Soviet leaders even considered carrying out a preemptive nuclear strike against China.[26] Second, the USSR forcefully retaliated against China. On 13 August, more than 300 Soviet soldiers, armed with two aircraft, dozens of tanks, and armored vehicles, invaded the Tielieketi region of Xinjiang's Yumin County, eliminating a platoon of over 30 Chinese soldiers.

Under such circumstances, China took two steps: first, after the Tielieketi incident, Mao realized that it was possible that war might break out on a larger scale. On 28 August, with Mao's approval, a CCP CC directive asked the people and troops along the border to prepare for war. China thus entered a period of high-level war preparedness. Second, Beijing attempted to lower the level of military tensions along the Sino-Soviet border area. After all, China's publicity concerning the Zhenbao Island incident was more for political rather than for military purposes. The political implications of the Zhenbao Island incident were much more important than the military implication. It was to China's advantage to attempt to stabilize Sino-Soviet relations that were on the brink of war. Chinese leaders were looking to avoid a two-front war and to retain a certain degree of security in the face of the aggressive Soviet threat. Obviously, they also wanted to reduce the danger of Soviet-American collusion. Most importantly, Zhou intended to utilize the occasion to promote US interests by expediting the Sino-American rapprochement process, which was slowly moving ahead via mutual signaling.[27] Therefore, China accepted the Soviet proposal to hold a high-level meeting.

On 11 September, after some complications,[28] Kosygin was able to hold a talk with Zhou Enlai at the Beijing airport, reaching a four-point provisional agreement on preserving the status quo along the border, withdrawing forces from both sides of the disputed areas, avoiding any confrontation along the border in the future and beginning consultations among the border authorities regarding the disputes. Zhou declared that "China has no territorial pretensions with regard to the Soviet Union." During the meeting, Zhou also raised the issue of Soviet intentions to carry out a "surgical operation" against China's nuclear facilities, and he stated that if this were to occur, it would constitute an invasion of China and China would fight to the end. According to an informational memorandum that the Soviets handed to the East German leadership about the Kosygin-Zhou meeting, the Soviet Union "declared the provocative nature of the contrived imperialist propaganda to the effect that the Soviet Union is allegedly preparing a preventive strike on China."[29] Kosygin proposed normalizing relations in the areas of railway and air communications and high-frequency telephone links, establishing and developing bilateral economic ties and expanding trade relations, and signing a trade protocol. He also proposed establishing a method for economic cooperation during the current Five-year Plan period (1971–1975) and the exchange of ambassadors. Zhou said that he would report these proposals to the CCP CC Politburo. On behalf of the Soviet government, Kosygin asked Zhou to convey to Mao his wish to achieve normalization of relations. But during the meeting, Zhou tried to avoid any "closeness" or "friendliness" with the Soviets. Zhou obviously had the potential Sino-American rapprochement in mind, and he did not want to send Washington the wrong message.[30]

Based on the oral agreement between the two premiers and the Soviet leaders' pressing desire to improve relations with China, Chinese leaders seemed to conclude that their Soviet counterparts did not wish to exacerbate the situation. They were temporarily relieved, but thereafter Beijing's attitude quickly hardened. Soon after Kosygin was on his flight from Beijing, at 7:00 p.m. on 11 September, the Chinese Foreign Ministry phoned and notified the Soviet embassy in Beijing that the Chinese wanted to make changes to that day's news coverage on the meeting between the two premiers. The Chinese insisted on deleting the phrase "the meeting was constructive and held in an atmosphere of frankness." When the Soviet chargé d'affaires, Aleksei Elizavetin, asked Vice-Foreign Minister Qiao Guanhua about the reason for the change, Qiao hinted that the decision had been made by the top leader, and even the premier could not make any decision on this issue.[31] The Chinese thus failed to act on Kosygin's proposal regarding improving relations between the two countries.

The Soviet Union became even more concerned about a possible Chinese preemptive nuclear strike against the Soviet Union after the Kosygin–Zhou Enlai meeting. Moscow decided to continue to place pressure on Beijing by way of attempting to pose a nuclear threat. On 16 September, Victor Louis published an article in *The Evening News* (London). In the West, many believed that Louis was authorized to reveal Moscow's views on the thorniest of issues. The article reported on two new trends in Moscow's policy toward China: first, Moscow was discussing the option of attacking China's nuclear facilities at Lop Nur; second, Moscow was scheming to establish an alternative CCP leadership with the alleged purpose of "saving socialism" in China. He argued that such a threat had become quite practical in the wake of the Soviet invasion of Czechoslovakia.

Two days later, Beijing responded to Moscow's threat. Zhou Enlai wrote to Kosygin, proposing that China and the Soviet Union should both assume joint responsibility for not resorting to force and for not using nuclear weapons to attack the other side. On 26 September, Kosygin delivered a confidential letter to Zhou, proposing that both sides "strictly observe the Sino-Soviet demarcation line in the air." He also proposed the signing of a special Sino-Soviet nonaggression and non-use-of-force treaty. This was the equivalent of a Soviet pledge of non-use of nuclear weapons against China and of no large-scale attack against China during periods of high tensions. Although the letter did not mention the four points reached at the Kosygin-Zhou airport meeting, Kosygin reported that Moscow had instructed Soviet border troops to maintain the status quo and to avoid use of military force. Meanwhile, China and the Soviet Union agreed to hold talks on border issues at the vice-foreign–ministerial level in Beijing, starting on 20 October. By entering into border negotiations with Moscow, Beijing was attempting to create the impression that should Washington remain uncompromising in its talks with the PRC regarding a Sino-American rapprochement, at any moment there might be a breakthrough in Sino-Soviet relations.

The oral agreement from the airport meeting and the pledge in Kosygin's confidential letter could not dispel the real pressure from the one million Soviet troops deployed along the Sino-Soviet border. In particular, it could hardly eliminate the shadow of the veiled Soviet threat to strike against China's nuclear facilities and to sponsor an anti-Mao regime in China. Even though Sino-Soviet border negotiations were scheduled, many within the CCP were worried about a surprise Soviet attack against China and were suspicious that the negotiations were being used as a smoke screen. Mao clearly overreacted to the possibility of war between China and the Soviet Union. Thus, on the one hand, Mao and CCP leaders waved an olive branch to Moscow in the hopes of alleviating tensions. On 1 October, Mao told Ch'oe Yong-gŏn, president of the Presidium of the Supreme People's Assembly of the Democratic People's Republic of Korea (DPRK), "The United States is pleased with the Sino-Soviet split. We don't want war." Mao attempted to transmit to Moscow via the North Koreans his wishes for a relaxation of tensions along the Sino-Soviet border. On 6 October, the CCP CC Politburo discussed, and Mao approved, Zhou Enlai's letter to Kosygin. The letter stressed that China and the Soviet Union should reach agreement regarding maintaining the status quo along the border and avoiding violent conflicts after the beginning of border negotiations. It also pointed out that the relaxation of tensions along the border and the border negotiations would be conducive to the resolution of the issues between the two countries. Zhou's response once again reiterated that both sides "pledge not to use nuclear weapons against the other." On the other hand, Beijing implemented a contingency plan in order to avoid falling into a passive position. Prior to the beginning of the Sino-Soviet border negotiations, many party and state leaders, as well as government units, cadres, and their families, were sent out of Beijing to various provinces. On 17 October, Lin Biao dictated the "Urgent Directive Regarding Strengthening Combat Readiness to Prevent a Surprise Attack by the Enemy." On the following day, PLA Chief of the General Staff Huang Yongsheng issued the directive to the 11 military regions, the PLA navy and air force, and the Beijing Garrison under the heading "Vice-Chairman Lin's Order No. 1." The Chinese Army entered into emergency combat readiness, and all units reached a first degree of combat readiness. Soldiers and residents along the border remained on the alert. Sino-Soviet relations thus faced a state of intense hostility. The Sino-Soviet Treaty of Friendship, Alliance and Mutual Assistance had become a mere scrap of paper.

MAO'S STRATEGIC CHOICE AND THE US-CHINA QUASI-ALLIANCE

The war scare gave Chinese leaders sufficient incentive, both strategically and psychologically, to reconsider their long-standing confrontation with the United States.[32] The perception of an extremely grave threat from the Soviet Union pushed Mao to break with the existing China policy framework.[33] Most scholars now agree that China's alignment with the United States was the result of the Sino-Soviet border conflicts rather than a motive for a "counterattack."

When Richard Nixon entered office in January 1969, the US strategic position was on the wane. In Asia, the Vietnam quagmire was revealing that America had been seriously weakened. Nixon was determined to enhance the US position in world affairs. In order to do so, he made the withdrawal of US forces from Vietnam a top priority. He thought one of the best ways to bring an end to the war was by improving relations with China.[34]

After over two years of secret and delicate diplomacy between Beijing and Washington, Henry Kissinger made two trips to Beijing, in July and October 1971. Explaining US concerns about Soviet foreign policy, Kissinger promised that the Nixon White House would inform Chinese leaders of any US-Soviet arrangement that might affect Chinese interests. This was a significant move since Washington only grants this privilege to its close allies. Kissinger's secret visit to Beijing in July resulted in immediate dividends for the Nixon Administration in terms of dealing with Moscow. The Kremlin was so anxious to forestall the US-China rapprochement that it began to reorient its strategy of confrontation with the United States. The Soviet ambassador to Washington, Anatoly Dobrynin, was suddenly eager to set a date for a Nixon-Brezhnev summit, and Soviet negotiators reached agreement regarding Western access to Berlin, quieting another crisis point between the two superpowers.[35] Kissinger's triangular diplomacy seemed to be working. Obviously, the Soviets were concerned about the US-China rapprochement as it would strongly influence the strategic balance in world affairs.[36]

President Nixon made his historic trip to Beijing in February 1972. The Soviet Union, which was one of the principal subjects covered extensively during Kissinger's two visits to Beijing in 1971, was also central to discussions during Nixon's trip. At the beginning of his first meeting with Zhou Enlai on 22 February, Nixon promised that Kissinger would brief Chinese officials about what Nixon termed "sensitive information" and that Kissinger would also brief them after the US talks with the Soviet Union.[37] US records confirm that on the following day, in a three-hour meeting with Vice-Foreign Minister Qiao Guanhua, with Marshal Ye Jianying, vice-chairman of the CMC in attendance, Kissinger told the Chinese about Soviet military deployments against China and about the state of negotiations between Washington and Moscow.[38]

Nixon's handwritten notes for his meeting with Zhou show that he made a series of points and assurances about the USSR:

Russia:

1. Maintain balance of power—
2. Restrain their expansion (if our interests are involved)
3. Try to reduce tension between us
4. Not make them irritated at you—
5. Make no deals with them we don't offer to you—
6. Will inform you on all deals[39]

The talking points for Nixon-Kissinger's briefing to the Chinese on the "sensitive" information regarding the Soviet Union indicate that America had two basic objectives in discussing the Soviet issue with Chinese leaders. First, America planned to exploit Chinese worries about the Soviet Union to win Chinese assistance with respect to other issues. Kissinger had earlier suggested that Nixon should draw a clear picture of the Soviet encirclement of China and tell the Chinese that the United States would try to help divert Soviet pressure on the PRC. Kissinger advised Nixon to avoid mentioning that the PRC required US protection. The PRC could express contempt for the USSR, but it would never admit fear. As realists, in Kissinger's judgment, the Chinese would appreciate the counterweight the United States could provide in Asia and elsewhere. Second, Nixon should assure Chinese leaders that the United States would not choose sides in the Sino-Soviet dispute. The United States would not collude with Moscow against China, and at the same time, China would have no veto on US dealings with Moscow. There can be no doubt that Nixon and Kissinger believed that the successful US-China summit in Beijing would have a favorable impact on the American position vis-à-vis the Soviet Union.[40]

Based on their presentation, Nixon and Kissinger both attempted to prepare China for the possibility of Soviet-American agreements on arms control and to ease any lingering Chinese fears that the United States and the Soviet Union would collude against China. Nixon and Kissinger addressed China's fear of a Soviet invasion by declaring that the United States would, at least within limits, seek to end Soviet expansionism. In the meantime, they gave China an incentive to go along with improvements in Soviet-American relations: The United States would offer China whatever it gave to the Soviets.[41]

In response, Zhou explained China's four-point policy toward the Soviet Union. First, China would not provoke the USSR; second, should the Soviets invade Chinese territory, China would fight back; third, the Chinese meant what they said; and fourth, if the Soviets launched air attacks against China, the Chinese would fight back. Nixon assured Zhou that it was not in US interests to see the Soviet Union and China at war, as war between major powers could not be contained.[42]

At the end of Nixon's trip, China and the United States signed the Shanghai Communiqué, signifying a rapprochement in US-China relations. Nixon and Kissinger aspired to utilize China to balance the Soviet threat, as did Mao and

Zhou. Without forming an anti-Soviet alliance, American and Chinese leaders reached a tacit agreement on "opposing international [Soviet] hegemony."[43] In effect, Nixon's high-profile summit meetings in February 1972 with Chinese leaders replicated Kissinger's earlier visits to Beijing in July and October 1971. Determined to move ahead but firm on the principal issues, the leaders of both sides proved to be worthy negotiating partners. At the core of US-China summit diplomacy, there was a common concern about the Soviet threat. This was the beginning of Sino-Soviet-US triangular diplomacy during the later stages of the Cold War.

Mao, however, was not a consistent strategic planner. He still vacillated between promoting world revolution and seeking detente with the US "imperialists." He was uncomfortable psychologically and hesitant when, in the early 1970s, he moved from his hardline anti-American policy to a more conciliatory approach. This switch was due to his perceived threat from the USSR and the lack of momentum in a hoped-for world revolution. Yet it seems that China received instant gratification from its reconciliation policy with the United States. Mao, who was accustomed to the strategy of "defeating enemies one by one" in military and united front work, was obviously excited. He put forth a new concept. He was thinking of utilizing Sino-American common concerns about Soviet expansionism to establish a geopolitical complex of countries that he termed a "strategic line," extending from Europe, Turkey, Iran, and Pakistan to China, Japan, and the United States. This geopolitical complex also included many countries outside the line that "opposed the Soviet Union, irrespective of their ideological positions."[44]

During his meeting with Henry Kissinger on 17 February 1973, Mao proposed this new plan for the first time. He said, "We were enemies in the past, but now we are friends." Not only did the Soviet threat to Europe and Asia exist, but it was growing. Mao proposed his strategy of establishing "a horizontal line"—"the US, Japan, [China], Pakistan, Iran, Turkey, and Europe"—in order to "commonly deal with a bastard [the Soviet Union]." During a later meeting with Japanese Foreign Minister Masayoshi Ōhira in early January 1974, Mao proposed the concept of "a big terrain," referring to those countries adjacent to the "horizontal line."[45] In May 1973, in an effort to work toward the establishment of formal diplomatic relations, the United States and the PRC established the United States Liaison Office in Beijing and a counterpart PRC office in Washington.

However, Mao's strategic design of "aligning with the United States to oppose the Soviets," "a horizontal line," and "a big terrain" were not realistic goals. Mao was disheartened to see the frequency of US-Soviet summits resulting in positive outcomes.[46] During Kissinger's sixth visit to China (his first as secretary of state) from 10 to 14 November 1973 and during a meeting on 12 November, Mao came to realize that the United States was in a very advantageous position and was no longer in dire need of the China card after its exit from the Vietnam quagmire. Mao began his conversation with Kissinger by discussing the Soviet threat to China. Kissinger seized the opportunity to emphasize a possible Soviet attack on China and declared that the United States would not allow a violation of China's security. Mao, a man with a strong sense of self-respect, felt he was being forced into a defensive position, and as a result, he was resentful and humiliated.[47]

Although Mao did not get the kind of cooperation he envisioned from the United States in order to counter the Soviet Union, after Nixon's historic trip, Kissinger defined US-China relations as "a kind of quasi-alliance." This grew out of understandings from Kissinger's conversations with Mao and Zhou in 1973. As Kissinger put it, "From then on, Beijing no longer sought to constrain or check the projection of American power—as it had before President Nixon's visit. Instead, China's avowed goal became to enlist the United States as a counterweight to the "polar bear" by means of an explicit strategic design."[48] Jeremy Friedman concurs, noting that Chinese policy in the 1970s was "clearly focused on building the broadest possible base of support, and the widest front of Third World unity, to oppose Soviet hegemony."[49]

CONCLUSION

Starting from mid-1964, Mao refocused China's foreign strategy from anti-US imperialism to both anti-US imperialism and anti-Soviet revisionism. In China's domestic affairs, Mao paid more attention to prevention of a repeat of Khrushchev's revisionism in China than to the possibility of a strategy of US peaceful evolution against China. Opposing revisionism (abroad) and guarding against revisionism (at home) became the ultimate objectives of Mao's Cultural Revolution. In dealing with other parties and countries, the CCP treated all fraternal parties and countries that did not support China's current policy as revisionist parties and members of a Khrushchev clique. Thus, during the first three years of the Cultural Revolution, China adopted an ultra-leftist foreign policy, hitting out in all directions and carrying out an anti-imperialist and anti-revisionist revolutionary diplomacy.

Confronted with the Soviet encirclement of China, with a huge Soviet force deployed along the Sino-Soviet border, and with collective measures by the Soviet bloc against China, Beijing felt a serious threat from Moscow. In the wake of the Zhenbao Island incident and the Soviet nuclear threat, Mao came to see the Soviet Union as China's No. 1 security threat. In Mao's view, the Soviet "social imperialists" had replaced the US imperialists as the No. 1 enemy of China and the people of the world. He thus resorted to his united front strategy—reconciling with the United States in order to form a worldwide anti-Soviet united front. On the diplomatic front, Chinese diplomacy returned to normalcy. Beginning in 1970, China improved relations with all countries with which it had existing diplomatic relations, except for the Soviet Union, India, and Indonesia. In addition, 11 countries established formal diplomatic relations with China during the period between 1968 and July 1971, that is, before Kissinger's secret trip to Beijing. These changes laid a solid foundation for the Sino-American rapprochement.

As the United States and China were earnestly working toward reconciliation from 1969 to 1972, China and the Soviet Union were engaging in border negotiations. The two sides fiercely debated and quarreled about the nature of the Chinese-Russian historical treaties, whether they should sign a new state treaty or a provisional agreement, and whether there were disputed areas between the two countries. Both China and the Soviet Union had divergent strategic intents, and thus, they were working at cross-purposes. The Soviet Union insisted on signing a new state-to-state treaty premised on the non-use of force, linking non-use of nuclear weapons with improved bilateral relations. At the negotiation table, Moscow played the nuclear weapons card. The Soviet Union intended to relax tensions with China in order to slow down and undermine the Sino-American rapprochement. For China, the signing of a provisional agreement would restrain the Soviet Union from attacking China, especially with nuclear weapons. More importantly, playing the Soviet card would be to China's advantage in terms of Beijing's rapprochement talks with Washington. In the discussions after each session of the Sino-Soviet border talks, Zhou Enlai would first ask about the US responses and reactions to the talks, not about the talks per se.[50] Moscow believed that Beijing was using the Sino-Soviet border talks as a chip in its strategic relations with the US imperialists. Whether China would up the ante or reduce the stakes in this political transaction depended on the changes in the international political situation.

In sum, with changes in China's diplomatic strategy, the Soviet-American Cold War system underwent subtle changes, in both Asia and globally. In the 1950s, China and the Soviet Union had formed an alliance, and China was at the forefront of the anti-US policy in Asia. When the Sino-Soviet split took place in the 1960s, China adjusted its foreign policy in an attempt to join forces with the United States to counter the Soviet Union. As Henry Kissinger notes, "In fact, throughout the 1970s, Beijing was more in favor of the United States acting robustly against Soviet designs than much of the American public or Congress."[51]

Arguably, had China adopted a more flexible strategy in managing its triangular relations with both Washington and Moscow, Beijing would have had much greater leverage and would have gained a more favorable strategic status in great power relations. But Beijing's intention to turn the Sino-American relationship into an anti-Soviet tool dispelled any concerns in Washington about a possible Sino-Soviet rapprochement, weakened China's ability to use the Soviet chip in dealing with the United States, aggravated China's relations with Vietnam, and consolidated the Soviet-Vietnamese alliance. China's intense anti-Soviet position thus deepened the Sino-Soviet Cold War.

Notes

1. Radchenko, *Two Suns in the Heavens*, p. 171.
2. CIA Intelligence Report, "The Sino-Soviet Struggle in the World Communist Movement Since Khrushchev's Fall," Part III, September 1967, ESAU 36, pp. 26–27. http://www.foia.cia.gov/cpe.asp

3. Under strong Chinese pressure, the Japanese Communist Party (JCP) did not attend the Twenty-third CPSU Congress. The Party of Labor of Albania also refused to attend.
4. "Circular of the Central Committee of the Communist Party of China on the Great Proletarian Cultural Revolution," 16 May 1966. https://www.marxists.org/subject/china/documents/cpc/cc_gpcr.htm
5. *Peking Review* 9, no. 34 (19 August 1966): 4–8.
6. For a factual account of Sino-Soviet relations during the Cultural Revolution, see Jones and Siân Kevill, comps., *China and the Soviet Union, 1949–84*, pp. 73–86.
7. *Peking Review* 9, no. 52 (23 December 1966): 18–23.
8. *To Advance Along the Road Opened Up by the October Socialist Revolution* (Peking: Foreign Languages Press, 1967), pp. 13, 15.
9. For the Red Guard siege of the Soviet embassy, attacks on Soviet personnel in China, and Moscow's responses, see Radchenko, *Two Suns in the Heavens*, pp. 177–98; For anti-Sovietism in China during the Cultural Revolution, based primarily on Chinese sources, see Li Mingjiang, *Mao's China and the Sino-Soviet Split: Ideological Dilemma* (London: Routledge, 2012), pp. 136–50.
10. The struggle over the suspension of school for students in both countries occurred after the first Red Guard siege of the Soviet embassy in August 1966.
11. For details, see Radchenko, *Two Suns in the Heavens*, pp. 188–89; Li, *Mao's China and the Sino-Soviet Split*, pp. 138–39.
12. Radchenko, *Two Suns in the Heavens*, pp. 188–89; Li, *Mao's China and the Sino-Soviet Split*, pp. 139–40.
13. CIA Intelligence Report, "The Sino-Soviet Struggle in the World Communist Movement Since Khrushchev's Fall," Part I, September 1967, ESAU 34, pp. 46–47, CIA unclassified documents, https://archive.org/stream/ESAU-CIA/The%20Sino-Soviet%20Struggle%20in%20the%20World%20Communist%20Movement%20Since%20Khrushchev%27s%20Fall%20%28Part%201%29#mode/2up
14. Jones and Kevill, eds., *China and the Soviet Union*, pp. 81–82.
15. CIA Intelligence Report, "The Sino-Soviet Struggle in the World Communist Movement since Khrushchev's Fall," Part III, September 1967, ESAU 36, p. 90. CIA unclassified documents, https://archive.org/stream/ESAU-CIA/The%20Sino-Soviet%20Struggle%20in%20the%20World%20Communist%20Movement%20Since%20Khrushchev%27s%20Fall%20%28Part%203%29#mode/2up
16. For a recent study on the Interkit, see James Hershberg, Sergey Radchenko, Péter Vámos, and David Wolff, "The Interkit Story: A Window into the Final Decades of the Sino-Soviet Relationship," *CWIHP Working Paper*, no. 63 (February 2011), pp. 8, 10, 11–12. The Interkit continued until 1986.
17. Radchenko, *Two Suns in the Heavens*, pp. 189–90.
18. Wang, "The Soviet Factor in Sino-American Normalization, 1969–1976."
19. Elizabeth Wishnick, *Mending Fences: The Evolution of Moscow's China Policy from Brezhnev to Yeltsin* (Seattle: University of Washington Press, 2001), p. 32.
20. For studies on the March 1969 Zhenbao Island incident, see Neville Maxwell, "The Chinese Account of the 1969 Fighting at Chenbao," *China Quarterly*, no. 56 (Oct.–Dec. 1973), pp. 730–39; Lyle Goldstein, "Return to Zhenbao Island: Who Started Shooting and Why It Matters," *China Quarterly*, no. 168 (Dec. 2001), pp. 985–97.

21. https://apps.dtic.mil/dtic/tr/fulltext/u2/a083370.pdf

22. Mao first asked the four marshals to study international issues on 19 February 1969. In the afternoon of 1 March 1969, the marshals held their first seminar in the Zhongnanhai leadership compound.

23. "Report by Four Chinese Marshals, Chen Yi, Ye Jianying, Nie Rongzhen, and Xu Xiangqian, to the Central Committee, 'Our Views about the Current Situation' (Excerpt)," 17 September 1969, Wilson Center History and Public Policy Program Digital Archive. https://digitalarchive.wilsoncenter.org/document/117154.pdf?v=7ac377d7a2546d86b46f11693f4ea7b

24. Lin Biao, "Report to the Ninth National Congress of the Communist Party of China, delivered on 1 April and adopted on 14 April 1969. https://www.marxists.org/reference/archive/lin-biao/1969/04/01.htm

25. Mao Zedong, "Talk at the First Plenum of the Ninth Central Committee of the Chinese Communist Party," 28 April 1969. https://www.marxists.org/reference/archive/mao/selected-works/volume-9/mswv9_83.htm

26. See Henry Kissinger, *The White House Years* (Boston: Little, Brown, 1979), p. 183. In the latter half of the year, the Western press also reported rumors of Soviet plans to strike at China's nuclear base.

27. Xia, *Negotiating with the Enemy*, pp. 141–45.

28. Western media suspected that Kosygin planned to meet with Zhou Enlai at Ho Chi Minh's funeral in early September 1969. But the Chinese delegation led by Zhou to express condolences arrived on 4 September and left the same day. Thus, Zhou intentionally avoided meeting with Kosygin in Hanoi. Chinese sources denied such speculation. After arriving in Hanoi on 6 September, through the Chinese embassy in Vietnam, Kosygin asked to meet with Zhou Enlai in Beijing on his way back to Moscow. However, Kosygin did not receive a Chinese invitation until he was already in Dushanbe, in the Tadzhikistan Republic of the USSR on 11 September.

29. Christian Ostermann, "New Evidence on the Sino-Soviet Border Dispute," *CWIHP Bulletin,* Issue 6–7 (Winter 1995/1996), pp. 192–93.

30. Gao Wenqian, *Zhou Enlai: The Last Perfect Revolutionary*, tr. Peter Rand and Lawrence R. Sullivan (New York: Public Affairs, 2007), pp. 7–8.

31. Ostermann, "New Evidence on the Sino-Soviet Border Dispute," p. 193.

32. For studies that analyze the relationship between the Sino-Soviet border clash and the Sino-American rapprochement, see Kuisong Yang, "The Sino-Soviet Border Clash of 1969: From Zhenbao Island to Sino-American Rapprochement," *Cold War History*, vol. 1, no. 1 (August 2000), pp. 21–52; William Burr, "Sino-American Relations, 1969: Sino-Soviet Border Conflict and Steps Toward Rapprochement," *Cold War History*, vol. 1, no. 3 (April 2001), pp. 73–112.

33. See Yafeng Xia, "Chinese Elite Politics and Sino-American Rapprochement, January 1969–February 1972," *Journal of Cold War Studies*, vol. 8, no. 4 (Fall 2006), p. 8.

34. Xia, *Negotiating with the Enemy*, p. 159.

35. The Quadripartite Agreement on Berlin was signed on 3 September 1971 by the Soviet Union, the United States, Great Britain, and France. See Anatoly F. Dobrynin, *In Confidence: Moscow's Ambassador to America's Six Cold War Presidents (1962–1986)* (New York: Times Books, 1995), p. 233. For the significance of this agreement to the Soviet leadership, see Robert M. Gates, *From the Shadows: The Ultimate Insider's Story of Five Presidents and How They Won the Cold War* (New York: Simon & Schuster, 1997), p. 44.

36. Mr. and Mrs. Strober's interview with Winston Lord, in Deborah H. and Gerald S. Strober, *The Nixon Presidency: An Oral History of the Era* (Washington DC: Brassey's, 2003), p. 130.
37. Nixon-Chou Talks (Soviet Union, 22 February 1972), p. 10, box 848, National Security Council File (cited hereafter as NSCF), Nixon Presidential Materials Project, National Archives (cited hereafter as NA).
38. Qiao (Guanhua)-Kissinger Talks (23 February 1972, 9:35 a.m. –12:34 p.m.), box 92, HAK Office Files, NSCF.
39. "Nixon's Notes, 22 February 1972," folder 1, box 7, President's Personal Files, WHSF, Nixon Presidential Materials Project. On the previous day, Nixon and Zhou Enlai held one "plenary" session, which William Rogers and other State Department officials were permitted to attend. The private sessions included Kissinger, but not any State Department officials.
40. "The President Briefing Paper for the China Trip"—The Soviet Union, pp. 5, 7, folder 4, box 847, NSCF.
41. Nixon-Chou Talks (Soviet Union, 23 February 1972), pp. 21, 36–39, folder 6, box 848, NSCF.
42. Ibid., pp. 3, 20.
43. For a study of the US-China rapprochement, see Xia, *Negotiating with the Enemy*, esp. pp. 189–212.
44. For details, see Kuisong Yang and Yafeng Xia, "Vacillating between Revolution and Detente: Mao's Changing Psyche and Policy toward the U.S., 1969–1976," *Diplomatic History*, vol. 34, no. 2 (April 2010), pp. 395–423.
45. William Burr, ed., *The Kissinger Transcripts: The Top Secret Talks with Beijing and Moscow* (New York: New Press, 1998), pp. 83–101. In the published English minutes, which were supplied by the Chinese, there is no mention of "China," but the word is in the Chinese record.
46. Gao, *Zhou Enlai: The Last Perfect Revolutionary*.
47. Burr, *The Kissinger Transcripts*, pp. 183–84.
48. Henry Kissinger, *On China* (New York: Penguin Press, 2011), p. 276.
49. Friedman, *Shadow Cold War*, p. 200.
50. Shen Zhihua and Zhang Yue's interview with Wang Jinqing, 29 September 2000. Wang was a member of the Chinese border negotiating team with the Soviet Union in the 1970s, and later Chinese ambassador to the Soviet Union.
51. Kissinger, *On China*, p. 277.

PART IV

The Road to "Normalization," 1979–1991

The normalization of Sino-Soviet relations took a completely different path from that of Sino-US relations. Whereas the latter was a matter of recognizing the other side as a legitimate representative of the state and of establishing diplomatic relations, diplomatic relations between the People's Republic of China (PRC) and the Union of Soviet Socialist Republics (USSR) were established early on and were never suspended. Therefore, the so-called normalization was to find a premise, acceptable to both sides, upon which a normal relationship between the two countries would rest. It had to be sustainable and positioned in the middle of a spectrum, with alliance at one end and confrontation at the other. Whether and how such a position could be found and maintained depended on whether the two sides could reach a consensus on the guiding principles for their bilateral relations.

From the onset, the Sino-Soviet relationship was essentially a relationship between two new states born amidst chaos and revolution. The founding of the PRC opened a new chapter in that relationship. From the beginning of the Sino-Soviet alliance, there were three guidelines that operated simultaneously in the Sino-Soviet relationship: general norms that guided relations among modern states; the so-called socialist ideals and the spirit of proletarian internationalism; and the leader, that is, the Communist Party of the Soviet Union (CPSU), and the led, that is, the CCP. Based on these complicated guidelines, the two countries determined that interparty relations were to be the core of their interstate relationship. With friendly relations between the two countries, other historical issues were utterly neglected by the leaders of both sides. As a result, bilateral relations gradually spiraled downward to a low point consisting of border disputes and resultant military confrontations. The two countries thus had to come up with a new foundation for their bilateral relations; both the process and the outcome of this search eventually achieved the consequent "normalization."

As an historical process, normalization was affected by various complex factors, among which three were particularly crucial. These were the history of Sino-Soviet relations, the domestic politics of the two countries, and the triangular strategic relationship among the PRC, the USSR, and the United States. Together, these factors constituted the intricate background from which the trajectory and the end result of normalization of Sino-Soviet relations can be traced and analyzed. It is imperative to sort out the history of Sino-Soviet relations, the domestic politics of the two countries, and the "strategic triangle" among the PRC, the USSR, and the United States in order to understand the causes, incentives, background, and characteristics of Sino-Soviet normalization, which simultaneously proceeded in parallel with competition between the two countries at both the regional and global levels. The consequences of this process not only brought about normalization between the two countries but also produced profound changes in strategic relations in East Asia and the world. Its lasting impact can still be felt in the post–Cold War era.

CHAPTER 20

The Issue of "Normalization"

Jun Niu

The Genesis of "Normalization"

The relaxation of Sino-Soviet relations began in the spring of 1979 when the two sides began talks on terminating the 1950 "Sino-Soviet Treaty of Friendship, Alliance and Mutual Assistance." However, proposals by the two sides for normalization of relations can be traced back much earlier. Long before 1979 Chinese and Soviet leaders had realized, however vaguely, the necessity of separating their inter-state relations from their inter-party relations and the importance of maintaining a normal state-to-state relationship.

It was during the Polish and Hungarian incidents in the fall of 1956 that the Chinese government officially put forward the "Five Principles of Peaceful Coexistence" as the foundation of inter-socialist-state relations, including Sino-Soviet relations. On 1 November 1956, in a statement in support of the Soviet "Proclamation on Developing and Further Strengthening the Friendship and Cooperation between the Soviet Union and the Other Socialist States," Beijing made it clear that "all socialist countries are independent and sovereign states," and "it is even more important for the mutual relations among the socialist countries to be based on the five principles."

In view of the special circumstances and the later Chinese approach to handling Sino-Soviet relations, it is significant that the Chinese leaders raised the issue that the socialist countries were "independent and sovereign states," even though they still perceived inter-state relations to exist within the framework of the socialist camp and proletarian internationalism. According to their thinking, as a guideline for inter-socialist-state relations, the "Five Principles of Peaceful Coexistence" could not be separated from proletarian internationalism.

J. Niu (✉)
School of International Studies, Beijing University, Beijing, China
e-mail: niujunpku@gmail.com

© The Author(s) 2020
Z. Shen (ed.), *A Short History of Sino-Soviet Relations, 1917–1991*,
China Connections, https://doi.org/10.1007/978-981-13-8641-1_20

329

It should be pointed out that this guideline was not intended to refer exclusively to Sino-Soviet relations, and relations between the two countries at that time were fundamentally different from their relations in the 1970s.

Based on currently available materials, the first reference to the concept of "normalization" of Sino-Soviet relations was made during a meeting between Chinese Premier Zhou Enlai and Soviet Prime Minister Kosygin at Beijing Airport on 11 September 1969. According to the recollections of Kudashev, a Soviet interpreter, as well as recently declassified official Soviet minutes of the meeting, it was Kosygin who took the initiative and proposed that "[we] should find a way to normalize the relationship between our two countries" and "it is necessary to take every step possible to normalize Sino-Soviet relations." Currently available information is found in the *Chronicle of the Life of Zhou Enlai*, compiled by the Party Literature Research Center under the Chinese Communist Party (CCP) Central Committee (CC). According to this book, at the meeting Zhou said: "Sino-Soviet disagreements over theories and principles should not affect state relations between our two countries and should not obstruct the normalization of our bilateral relationship." Confirmation of who first raised the issue of normalization must await declassification of the Chinese minutes of the meeting. It is nevertheless quite clear that the two sides achieved a certain consensus, even though the party relationship had been irrevocably damaged, that efforts should be made to maintain normal state relations. As a result, the Soviet and Chinese prime ministers agreed to hold talks about the border disputes, to restore trade relations, and to re-assume ambassadorial appointments.

The Soviet leaders' assessments of this meeting remain unknown. According to indirect sources, Kosygin hoped to take a positive view of the Chinese position. The Chinese records reveal that the Chinese leadership also regarded the meeting as an important positive event. Two days after the meeting, Zhou reported to Mao Zedong that "such governmental contacts between China and the Soviet Union are unprecedented." Mao, endorsing Zhou's report, concurred with Zhou's judgment. Thereafter, on 18 September, as instructed by Mao and the Politburo, Zhou sent a letter to Kosygin proposing a settlement of the Sino-Soviet border disputes. At the time, Beijing was ready to issue a government statement based on the possible response from the Soviet side. Although the two sides may have had different interpretations of the situation, there was no question that at the very least the meeting between Zhou and Kosygin had led the leaders of the two countries to begin to consider the issue of normalization of relations.

However, the consensus reached by the two prime ministers soon proved difficult to be put into action. In his reply to Zhou's letter, Kosygin only raised the issue of "normalizing the border situation." At the same time, China still engaged in comprehensive war preparations against a potential large-scale invasion by the Union of Soviet Socialist Republics (USSR). Nevertheless, the idea of normalizing Sino-Soviet inter-state relations and the follow-up steps put forward by the Zhou-Kosygin meeting were significant. Under pressure due to the military conflicts along the border, the leaders were very much inclined to find a suitable way to separate inter-party relations from inter-state relations.

Undoubtedly, the crisis caused by the border clashes gave rise to discussions of normalization at the Zhou-Kosygin meeting. Nevertheless, even at the onset of the Sino-Soviet ideological polemics, efforts had been made to separate party relations from state relations, lest the ideological conflicts would seriously affect state relations. In fact, during the early years of the Sino-Soviet polemics, both sides attempted to promote normal state relations. In this regard, the Chinese leadership may have engaged in such deliberations earlier and more carefully, making greater efforts than the Soviet side, notwithstanding that its position underwent some drastic changes. This is because if the ideological discords were to have a negative impact on state relations, China would likely be the loser.

Early in 1960, the CCP CC decided "to strive to postpone the split between the Chinese and Soviet parties and states." Clearly, Chinese leaders were already aware of the difference between inter-party and inter-state relations and they acted accordingly. On 16 July 1960, the USSR imposed sanctions and recalled all Soviet experts stationed in China. The action extended the ideological discord between the two parties to the field of inter-state relations. In communicating with the Soviet government, Chinese leaders expressed a desire to maintain normal relations and they proposed to hold government negotiations over the contentious bilateral economic and trade relations. Such efforts constituted a first attempt by the Chinese side to prevent the Sino-Soviet ideological discord from spilling over into inter-state relations. Consequently, in 1961 Sino-Soviet economic and trade relations continued to grow, and the two sides reached agreements on repayment schedules for Chinese trade debts and Soviet interests in China. In addition, the two sides concluded several new agreements on economic cooperation and also reached a five-year agreement on science and technology cooperation.

Between February and August 1964, the Chinese and Soviet governments engaged in negotiations on the border issues. This represented yet another effort to manage state relations even as party relations were deteriorating. In spite of high tensions between the two sides, they still managed to reach a preliminary agreement over demarcation of 4200 kilometers of the 4280 kilometers along the eastern section of the Sino-Soviet border. In this respect, the two sides either drafted some working group agreements or reached some oral understandings. It was only due to the domestic turmoil in each of the countries that the negotiations did not resume after the adjournment of the negotiations in August 1964.

In February 1965, Kosygin passed through Beijing on two occasions during visits to Vietnam, during which he held several talks with Mao, Zhou, and other Chinese leaders. Based on various sources, the talks covered a wide range of issues, including the inter-party ideological dispute, bilateral cooperation to aid Vietnamese resistance against the United States, support for the newly independent African countries, and other bilateral issues. It is noteworthy that during these talks Chinese leaders brought up the idea of separating inter-party relations from inter-state relations. As indicated in one of Zhou's reports to Mao, Chinese leaders hoped to leave some room for future improvements in state relations. After the talks, however, as Sino-Soviet inter-party relations completely broke down, inter-state relations deteriorated rapidly as well. Nevertheless, without such efforts by each side to preserve normal state relations even as party relations were fracturing, the idea of "normalization" would never have been raised at the Zhou-Kosygin meeting at Beijing Airport in September 1969, nor would the steps to stabilize bilateral relations entail the idea of normalization. In view of some positive developments in Sino-Soviet relations after this September 1969 meeting, Soviet leaders came to believe that "some signs of normalization" are appearing in Sino-Soviet relations and the Soviet side will "strive to normalize relations with the PRC."

In sum, the idea of "normalization of Sino-Soviet relations" emerged from the course of the Sino-Soviet split, and later, after the complete breakdown of bilateral relations, it became a common goal pursued by both sides. Discussions about "normalization of Sino-Soviet relations" took place in the discourse of each country's foreign policy, and from the very beginning such discussions conformed with their respective domestic politics.

Interactions During Confrontation

As indicated in Part III, the border clashes in the spring and summer of 1969 resulted in escalating tensions and hostilities in Sino-Soviet relations. The two sides not only intensified their mutual criticism and accusations in terms of the ideological polemics but they also came to view each other as strategic threats to their respective national security. This was particularly notable on the Chinese side which, as a result, made fundamental adjustments to its national security strategy. On the one hand, the Soviet Union was perceived to be the source of the next world war and the principal and most dangerous threat to China's national security. Between February 1973 and January 1974, Mao successively devised his so-called "horizontal line and a big terrain," also known as the "international united front against hegemony." On the other hand, China achieved a historic reconciliation with the United States, which in turn introduced the Sino-Soviet-US strategic triangle into the international politics of the Cold War. As China's Soviet policy became more entangled in the Cold War, Chinese leaders were more inclined to approach Sino-Soviet relations from the perspective of a global balance of power rather than from the perspective of bilateral relations.

During this period, Chinese policy toward the USSR continued its rhetoric on the normalization of Sino-Soviet relations. According to several speeches by Soviet leaders, as early as the 1970s the Chinese proposed that the two countries base their respective relations "on the foundation of the Five Principles of Peaceful Coexistence." In August 1973, the CCP held its Tenth National Party Congress. In the section of the political report to the congress on the international situation and Chinese foreign policy, the Chinese highlighted the danger of Soviet hegemony, while also stating that "the Sino-Soviet controversy on matters of principle should not hinder the normalization of relations between the two states on the basis of the Five Principles of Peaceful Coexistence."[1] For the first time, the guiding principles for normalization of Sino-Soviet relations were written into a high-level CCP document. In view of later developments, this statement in the report to the CCP Tenth National Congress assumed great significance. It clearly indicated that Chinese leaders had come to realize that the future normalization of Sino-Soviet relations could only be based on general norms of international relations and bilateral relations could never be restored to the level of the 1950s. The statement represented an unequivocal expression of future Sino-Soviet relations.

During the same period, Soviet policy toward China pursued two trends. One was to continue to put political and military pressure on China, such as increasing Soviet military deployments in East Asia, proposing to form an "Asian collective security system," and concluding a series of treaties of friendship, which were very similar to military alliances, with countries such as Vietnam and Afghanistan. In addition, Moscow worked to sow discord between China on the one hand and the United States and Japan on the other in order to prevent these countries from establishing an anti-Soviet strategic alliance. The Soviet Union put pressure on the United States and Japan by issuing incessant press attacks on Chinese foreign policy in an attempt to drive a wedge between Sino-American strategic cooperation and to prevent Japan from actively seeking the development of Sino-Japanese relations.

At the same time, Soviet leaders, like their counterparts in Beijing, concluded that normal Sino-Soviet relations had to be based on a footing that was quite different from that of the Sino-Soviet alliance in the 1950s. Nevertheless, Soviet leaders still held on to the possibility that there could be an even closer relationship between the two countries. At the Twenty-fourth Communist Party of the Soviet Union (CPSU) National Congress in March 1971, as well as at some other major party meetings, Soviet leaders made it clear that the Soviet government "not only wants to make all-out efforts to promote normalization of Sino-Soviet relations but also wants to work for the restoration of friendly neighborly relations between the two countries." At about that time, the Soviet side took several initiatives to propose measures to relax tensions and improve bilateral relations. The Chinese side rejected these proposals on the grounds that the Soviet government should first carry out the September 1969 understanding that had been reached during the Zhou-Kosygin meeting.

Pinning their hopes on the notion that after "normalization on the basis of the Five Principles of Peaceful Coexistence," Sino-Soviet relations could develop "even further," Soviet leaders launched a new diplomatic offensive to improve Sino-Soviet relations based on the opportunities presented by the deaths of Zhou Enlai and Mao Zedong in January and September 1976, respectively. It is particularly noteworthy that when Mao died in the early morning of 9 September, the Soviet government immediately released the news without any comment. At the same time, the CPSU CC sent its condolences to the CCP. These steps were widely viewed as attempts by the Soviets to improve relations with China. On 13 September, Foreign Minister Andrei Gromyko and other Soviet officials visited the Chinese embassy in Moscow to offer their condolences. The event was reported by the Soviet press, and thereafter criticism of China in the press ended for a while. As indicated in a later speech by Brezhnev, it is possible that the Soviet leaders expected that Mao's death would introduce changes to China's domestic politics and possible shifts in its foreign policy, tipping the scales toward the Soviet Union and hence providing an opportunity to improve Sino-Soviet relations. In this speech, Brezhnev said: "Currently China is going through a complicated period. To some extent, the situation may affect the current position of the Chinese leadership."

However, the efforts by Soviet leaders failed to elicit the desired responses from the Chinese side. The CCP CC refused to accept the Soviet telegram of condolence. It also returned telegrams of condolence from those Communist parties that were deemed to be "revisionist" followers of the USSR. The new Chinese leaders took every opportunity to reiterate their determination to continue Mao's foreign policy, including its position that the Soviet Union was a source of war and its policy of opposing Soviet hegemony through an anti-Soviet international united front. In August 1977, the political report to the Eleventh CCP National Congress asserted: "The two powers, the Soviet Union and the United States, are the source of a new world war, and Soviet socialist imperialism in particular presents the greater danger. ..." We are "confronted with threats and aggression by imperialism, and especially by social-imperialism. The Soviet revisionists are bent on subjugating our country and we must be prepared for war. ..."[2] On 1 November, the *People's Daily* published an editorial on Mao's "theory of the three worlds." At this crucial political turning point, the Chinese article reaffirmed the correctness of Chinese foreign policy during the last several years of Mao's life, vouching that the new leadership was determined to continue to follow this policy. As noted above, initially the "three worlds" theory was directly associated with the establishment of an anti-Soviet international united front. Dismayed by the responses from the new Chinese leadership, beginning in the spring of 1977, Soviet leaders continued their criticism of China and the Soviet news media resumed its attacks on China.

On 3 November 1978, the Soviet and Vietnamese governments signed the "Soviet-Vietnamese Treaty of Friendship and Cooperation" and concluded a military alliance. The USSR played a crucial role in inciting Vietnam to seek regional domination and, in particular, to launch the war against Cambodia. On 25 November 1978, Vietnam established a puppet Cambodian government and immediately thereafter invaded Cambodia. On 1 January 1979, the Vietnamese Army took over Phnom Penh, the Cambodian capital. The Soviet-Vietnamese strategic partnership was forged with the clear intention of aiming at China, and, naturally, China was alarmed. Soviet support of Vietnam intensified the existing discord between China and Vietnam over bilateral and regional issues, particularly over Vietnam's invasion of Cambodia. Eventually the Chinese government decided to launch a military attack on Vietnam, which was also intended to roll back Soviet expansionism in Southeast Asia and to encourage other states to resist Soviet expansionism.

On 17 February 1979, Chinese troops began an offensive against Vietnam from Longzhou and Jingxi in Guangxi province and from Hekou and Jinping in Yunnan province. The Chinese government issued a statement declaring that the military offensive against Vietnam was aimed at Soviet expansionism in Southeast Asia. "The collusion between big Soviet hegemony and small Vietnam hegemony in their aggression and expansionism is the root cause for the collapse of peace in Indochina and the endangerment of security and stability in Southeast Asia." The USSR condemned the Chinese attack while also increasing military activities along the Sino-Soviet border. The hostile atmosphere between China and the USSR increased significantly.

THE BEGINNING OF RECONCILIATION

Soon after China ended its war against Vietnam, Sino-Soviet relations experienced some major changes. The Chinese and Soviet governments finally began formal negotiations, albeit at a low level, regarding the expiration of the "Sino-Soviet Treaty of Friendship, Alliance and Mutual Assistance," which had been signed by the two governments on 14 February 1950 for a term of 30 years. The treaty stipulated that negotiations regarding renewal of the treaty would begin one year prior to expiration of the treaty, which was set for 11 April 1980. Based on available information, both sides seriously considered the future of the treaty and hoped to use this opportunity to ease tensions between the two sides.

It would be overly simplistic to conclude that the Soviets neither wanted the treaty to be terminated nor did they anticipate a Chinese proposal for terminating the treaty. It is more likely that Moscow merely did not want to take the initiative to end the treaty. In an interview with *Time* magazine of the United States on 22 January 1979, Brezhnev expressed the view that "now and again statements heard from Peking alleging that the Sino-Soviet Treaty of Friendship, Alliance and Mutual Assistance concluded in 1950 has lost all significance." As far as the Soviet government was concerned: "We shall never tear up on our own will a document which epitomizes friendship between the people of the USSR and China." It was possible that Moscow was posturing to take the diplomatic high ground; on the one hand, it left room to ease Sino-Soviet relations and, on the other hand, it wanted to avoid any responsibility if the relations further deteriorated.

The reaction by the Chinese side was more complicated—due very much to the transformations taking place both inside and outside of China. At the time, China was actively promoting the establishment of an anti-Soviet international united front. As a result, extending the treaty of alliance with the Soviet Union would contradict Chinese foreign policy. For example, in July 1978 when

China and Japan resumed long-overdue negotiations on the peace treaty, the most controversial issue was China's insistence on including in the treaty an anti-hegemony clause. This issue had caused the suspension of negotiations for two years after 1976 and it inevitably once again became the focus in the new round of negotiations. At the time, China still insisted on the inclusion of the clause. According to diplomatic memoirs, in order to persuade the Japanese side to accept the Chinese position, when talking to Japanese Foreign Minister Sunao Sonoda on 9 August, Chinese Foreign Minister Huang Hua said that upon expiration, the Sino-Soviet Treaty of Friendship would be abrogated. Sonoda's face allegedly immediately "broke into a big smile."[3] On 10 August, Deng Xiaoping told Sonoda that the Chinese side would "make a formal announcement on the abrogation of the treaty when the time arrives."[4] Obviously, from the perspective of the Chinese leaders, termination of the Sino-Soviet treaty was both a logical choice and a requirement for expedient foreign policy considerations.

After the Third Plenary Session of the Eleventh CCP CC and a wave of ideological emancipation, China experienced a period of unprecedented dynamic growth of new ideas and new thinking, which led to reflections and discussions on both domestic and foreign policies, including Sino-Soviet relations. According to the memoirs of some Chinese diplomats, at the time the Sino-Soviet Friendship Treaty elicited many internal discussions. After some debate, the Chinese embassy in the Soviet Union took the view that the normalization of relations with the United States and Japan had rendered the military alliance with the Soviet Union obsolete. However, judged from the fact that Moscow did not take any military action during the Sino-Vietnamese War, the treaty did indeed play a restraining role. Hence, from an overall perspective, the most reliable approach was to replace the former treaty with a new one. This would not only avoid any turmoil after the Sino-Soviet military alliance was dissolved but it would also contribute to stability along China's borders and strengthen China's position in the Sino-Soviet-U.S. strategic triangle. The embassy suggested that China and the Soviet Union should hold diplomatic negotiations regarding bilateral relations to reach a new accord. Ma Xusheng, the counselor in the embassy at the time, reported the proposals to the MFA and he was left with the impression that the MFA shared the embassy's views. Nevertheless, it should be noted that these recollections are insufficient to provide a complete picture of Chinese decision-making at the time.

It is possible that after such internal deliberations, the MFA submitted its "Request for Instructions Regarding Not Renewing the Sino-Soviet Treaty of Friendship, Alliance and Mutual Assistance," which was approved by Deng Xiaoping on 24 March 1979. In early April, Deng further instructed that the Sino-Soviet treaty, which existed in name only, should not be extended. However, to resolve the outstanding issues between the two countries and to improve bilateral relations, Deng suggested that the two sides should hold negotiations and conclude a new accord.[5] On 3 April, Huang Hua met Soviet Ambassador Ilya Shcherbakov to inform him of the notice by the Chinese government regarding not to extend the treaty. The notice stated that the Sino-Soviet treaty had played a historical role in promoting Sino-Soviet friendship and in maintaining peace in the region. Nevertheless, in view of the sweeping changes taking place in the world as well as the Sino-Soviet split, the treaty existed in name only, and hence the Chinese government had decided to terminate it. It proposed that in order to reach a new accord the two sides had to negotiate the outstanding issues and seek to improve bilateral relations. To avoid any uproar about the ending of the treaty, Huang told Shcherbakov that the Chinese side would not at that time release the Chinese government note revealing that the Sino-Soviet treaty would not be renewed upon its expiration.[6] On the same day at their meeting, the Seventh Session of the Standing Committee of the Fifth National People's Congress adopted a resolution that stipulated that the Sino-Soviet Treaty of Friendship, Alliance and Mutual Assistance "will not be extended upon expiration."

On the next day, Moscow issued a statement accusing China of taking "a well-planned road of further complicating and undermining Sino-Soviet relations" and insisting that China bore "all responsibility" for the ending of the treaty. During the following days, the major Soviet news media began a wave of propaganda denouncing China. However, on 7 April, three days after China's announcement of termination of the treaty, Soviet Foreign Minister Andrei Gromyko met the Chinese ambassador to the Soviet Union, Wang Youping, and handed him the Soviet reply. It stated that the Soviet government agreed to negotiations and asked that the Chinese side let the Soviets know the topics of the negotiations and the goals that the Chinese side expected to achieve. This reversal in the Soviet position did not come as a sudden change. It is highly unlikely that Moscow did not anticipate the possibility that the Chinese would terminate the treaty. Furthermore, the Soviet side had long been advocating negotiating with the Chinese. In fact, in both January 1971 and June 1973 the Soviet government had proposed to Beijing that the two sides should conclude a treaty on the non-use of military force and a non-aggression treaty. On 24 February 1978, the Supreme Soviet sent a letter to the Chinese National People's Congress, proposing that the two countries issue a statement of principles on the norms for bilateral relations and hold talks at an "appropriate high level" to achieve them. It also suggested an exchange of visits by the two congressional bodies. At the time, the Chinese side had rejected both these proposals. But with the termination of the friendship treaty, the conclusion of a new treaty was unavoidable, handing the Soviet side the most welcome opportunity that it had been waiting for.

On 5 May, in a meeting with Soviet Ambassador Shcherbakov, Chinese Vice-Foreign Minister Yu Zhan presented a Chinese memorandum on the possible topics and purpose of the proposed negotiations. The memorandum proposed the following goals: the setting of norms for bilateral relations, removing the obstacles to normalizing state-to-state relations, promoting exchanges in the areas of trade, science and technology, culture, and so forth, signing new agreements based on the results of the negotiations, and the holding of border talks.

The Chinese proposals reflected the inclinations of the Chinese government at the time, that is, to formulate guidelines for relations between the two countries and to begin talks on normalization. On 4 June, Moscow agreed to begin negotiations and suggested talks at the vice-ministerial level to be held in Moscow in July and August. The Soviet side suggested that the two sides draw up documents to govern bilateral relations and present the main contents of the documents.

The Chinese government accepted the Soviet suggestion on talks to be held in Moscow. Unlike in the past, the Chinese side no longer demanded that resolution of the border issue be a precondition for the holding of talks. The fact that the Chinese dropped this precondition and agreed to hold talks first in Moscow clearly indicated a Chinese policy shift. Only several months earlier, in its reply to the letter from the Supreme Soviet, China had still insisted that a relaxation of tensions and the holding of negotiations depended on Soviet implementation of the understanding that had been reached at the airport by the Chinese and Soviet prime ministers in 1969 and on the conclusion of agreements on alleviating border tensions and resolving border issues, including the withdrawal of Soviet forces from Mongolia. This new position was closer to that of the Soviets, and the two sides now appeared to share some common ground. The Chinese objective at the time was probably to resolve the principles for bilateral relations and to confirm them with formal treaties, which, in many ways, overlapped with Soviet intentions.

On 24 June, the Chinese government appointed Chinese Ambassador Wang Youping as head of the Chinese negotiating delegation and formed a Sino-Soviet State Relations Negotiation Office. The Chinese delegation was instructed to draft several documents: a draft agreement on bilateral relations, a draft agreement on maintaining the status quo on the border to prevent military clashes and to negotiate other border issues, and proposals and opinions regarding general exchanges between the two countries. In view of the discussions by the foreign policy apparatus and the work of the delegation, preparations on the Chinese side were initially carried out along the lines of establishing and reaching agreement on the principles for bilateral relations. In August, the MFA completed its "Report on Negotiating Sino-Soviet State-to-State Relations." The specific content of the report has yet to be made public. However, Deng Xiaoping wrote the following comment: "Better to discuss this with the Politburo." Obviously, Deng was not satisfied with the MFA's plan and he wanted further deliberations.

On 29 August, with all leading members present, the CCP Politburo convened a special meeting to discuss the negotiations with the Soviet Union. Hua Guofeng presided over the discussions and Deng made a key speech, pointing out that the Chinese goal was to remove the Soviet threat to Chinese national security rather than to discuss principles for normalization of bilateral relations. China would not improve relations while the Soviet Army was still bearing down along the Chinese border. Specifically, the USSR had to withdraw its forces from Mongolia and end its support of the Vietnamese invasion of

Cambodia. The two sides were to make a commitment not to station their military forces or to establish military bases in neighboring countries and not to use neighboring countries to threaten each other. The approach to the negotiations was not to seek hasty results, and flexibility on the part of the Chinese would depend on the progress of the negotiations. The exact decisions adopted at this Politburo meeting remain unknown. Nevertheless, based on Deng's political status and the later evolution of Chinese policies, it is safe to say that, as demonstrated in Deng's speech, Chinese leaders had decided to shift the purpose of the negotiations from establishing principles for state relations and related agreements to eliminating the Soviet threat to Chinese national security. This shift reflected Chinese leaders' determination to continue pursuing an international anti-Soviet united front. This significant policy change, as embodied in Deng's words, not only became the guiding strategy for future negotiations but also constituted the key factor that would determine the course of Sino-Soviet normalization in the years to come.

As discussed previously, the foreign policy apparatus intended to use the termination of the Sino-Soviet treaty as an opportunity to promote negotiations on normalization and to achieve tangible results. The Chinese leadership appeared to support negotiations on state relations for they shared the view that any improvement in Sino-Soviet relations was in line with the transformation of China's national strategy. However, the top leaders ultimately decided that removal of the Soviet threat to Chinese national security was China's top priority. At the same time, they also wanted to avoid any negative impact on the stability and development of Sino-US relations by appearing to hastily reconcile with the USSR. After all, it was their conviction that only Sino-US strategic cooperation would bring China strategic benefits, including security and economic advantages. As for the Soviet Union, it not only posed a threat to China but also it could only provide China with limited economic and other assistance.

One event is worth noting. On 27 August, Deng Xiaoping held talks with American Vice-President Mondale and the next day they signed two agreements, one on Sino-US cultural exchanges and one on Sino-US cooperation in hydraulic power and resource utilization. Deng highly praised the agreements and was convinced that there was bright future for political, economic, and scientific-cultural cooperation and exchanges between China and the United States. Such progress in Sino-US relations may have had an impact on Deng's consideration of China's relations with the Soviet Union and the Politburo resolution reached the following day. During a meeting with President Nixon before the beginning of the Sino-Soviet negotiations, Deng informed the Americans of the guiding principles of the Chinese negotiations. According to Deng, the precondition for Sino-Soviet negotiations was to remove the obstacles to bilateral relations, namely Soviet "expansionism and hegemony" that involved not only border issues. The Soviet Union had deployed one million troops along the border and posed a real threat to China. Deng also briefed the Americans about the proposals that the Chinese side was going to raise during the Sino-Soviet negotiations. In so doing, Deng apparently hoped to deflect any negative repercussions from the Sino-Soviet negotiations on strategic cooperation between China and the United States.

In March 1979, Deng's speech at a CCP meeting on theoretical work reflected the thinking of Chinese leaders about Chinese foreign policy at the time. Deng said, "It is now even clearer to everyone how brilliant and far-sighted was the strategy of differentiating the three worlds formulated by Comrade Mao Zedong in the evening of his life. It is also clearer how brilliant and far-sighted were his policy decisions on this issue, namely, that China should side with the third-world countries and strengthen its unity with them, try to win over the second-world countries for a concerted effort against hegemonism, and establish normal diplomatic relations with the United States and Japan. This strategic principle and these policies have been invaluable in rallying the world's people to oppose hegemonism, changing the world political balance, frustrating Soviet hegemonists' arrogant plan to isolate China internationally, improving China's international environment, and heightening China's international prestige."[7] Under this guidance, the handling of Sino-Soviet relations unavoidably assumed certain characteristics and limits. During the meeting, other ideas were also floated about, such as "playing the Soviet card properly is necessary" and "[relations with the Soviet Union] can be relaxed from time to time if it is required," but these ideas were not included in the meeting briefs.

Sino-Soviet negotiations at the vice-ministerial level officially began in Moscow on 17 October. Following the original plan, the Soviet side put forward a draft of a "Declaration on the Principles for Mutual Relations" and suggested that the draft be deliberated. However, the Chinese side introduced its own "Proposals for Improving Sino-Soviet Relations" and demanded that first the Soviet military threat to China must be removed. This included a reduction in Soviet military forces in the areas adjacent to China to the pre-1964 level; the withdrawal of troops and equipment stationed in Mongolia; and the end of Soviet support for the Vietnamese invasion of Cambodia as well as an end to the expansion of Soviet economic and trade relations. In making resolution of the border issues a priority, the Chinese side took the view that the existence of the Sino-Soviet Treaty of Alliance in the past did not stop the clashes between the two countries nor did it end the Soviet threat. For this reason, it was necessary for the USSR to take real action to remove the threat to China and thus to prove that a new treaty would be meaningful. The Soviet side contended that the USSR had no intention of threatening China. The Sino-Soviet negotiations were not to exceed bilateral relations or to involve third countries, namely the troops stationed in Mongolia and the Vietnamese invasion of Cambodia. Each side held to its respective position during the following talks, and after six sessions they still could not reach any agreement. At the end of the sixth session, on 3 December, the two sides agreed to move the talks to Beijing in the spring of 1980.

On 27 December 1979, the Soviet Army invaded Afghanistan. On 31 December, Chinese Vice-Foreign Minister Zhang Haifeng lodged a protest against the invasion with Soviet Ambassador Shcherbakov and postponed the vice-ministerial talks. On 20 January 1980, the Chinese MFA spokesman formally announced that the Soviet invasion of China's close neighbor, Afghanistan, placed a new obstacle on the course of normalizing Sino-Soviet relations. As a result, it was inappropriate to continue the Sino-Soviet negotiations. The negotiations were thus suspended.

NOTES

1. Chou En-lai, "Report to the Tenth National Congress of the Communist Party of China," delivered 24 August 1973 and adopted on 28 August 1973, in *Peking Review* 16, nos. 35–36 (7 September 1973): 17–25, at p. 23.
2. Hua Guofeng, "Political Report to the Eleventh National Congress of the Communist Party of China," delivered on 12 August 1977 and adopted on 18 August 1977, *Peking Review* 20, no. 35 (26 August 1977): 23–57, at p. 43, 53.
3. In Huang Hua's *Memoirs* (Beijing: Foreign Languages Press, 2008), pp. 228–30, Huang Hua does not mention that Brezhnev raised the issue of abrogation of the Sino-Soviet treaty.
4. Huang, *Memoirs*, p. 327.
5. Ibid., p. 294.
6. Ibid., p. 496.
7. Deng Xiaoping, "Uphold the Four Cardinal Principles," 30 March 1979, *Selected Works of Deng Xiaoping 1975–1982* (Beijing: Foreign Languages Press, 1984), p. 168.

CHAPTER 21

Embarking on "Normalization"

Jun Niu

BREZHNEV'S SPEECH IN TASHKENT

Although the Sino-Soviet vice-ministerial negotiations were suspended after the Soviet invasion of Afghanistan, the door for exchanges between the two countries continued to open wider and visits at all levels began to increase. Sergey Tikhvinsky, the well-known China scholar and vice-president of the Sino-Soviet Friendship Association, and Mikhail Kapitsa, director of the First Far East Department of the Soviet Ministry of Foreign Affairs (MFA), visited Beijing and met with their counterparts in Chinese research institutes and governmental organizations. Some Soviet scholars from the Soviet Academy of Sciences visited Northeast China. China also made reciprocal visits to the Soviet Union. There were increased contacts between the Chinese embassy and the Soviet MFA. These exchanges certainly helped bring about a better understanding and better policymaking on both sides. In particular, this was occurring at the time when the Chinese government and universities had just started to resume Soviet studies and to restore those research institutes that had been abolished during the Cultural Revolution. The increase in the number of exchanges with the Union of Soviet Socialist Republics (USSR) not only facilitated further exchanges but also prepared the two sides to take future actions when opportunities would present themselves based on rational judgment. In addition, some transaction negotiations between the two sides produced satisfactory results. By February–March 1982, sensitive international public opinion observers began to notice that there was a conspicuous increase in exchanges between China and the Soviet Union. Both sides were exploring ways to improve bilateral relations, but the Soviet side was becoming more active in taking initiatives.

J. Niu (✉)
School of International Studies, Beijing University, Beijing, China
e-mail: niujunpku@gmail.com

© The Author(s) 2020   343
Z. Shen (ed.), *A Short History of Sino-Soviet Relations, 1917–1991*,
China Connections, https://doi.org/10.1007/978-981-13-8641-1_21

On 24 March 1982, Brezhnev delivered a speech on Soviet policy in Asia at a medal-awarding ceremony held in the Central Asian city of Tashkent.[1] In his speech, he touched on Soviet policy toward China, India, and Japan. The China part of the speech was recognized by international opinion at the time as the most positive signal thus far indicating Soviet intentions to improve Sino-Soviet relations. The first part of the speech emphasized Soviet recognition of China as a socialist country, indicating that the main Soviet concern was the type of policies that China was pursuing, not about its domestic politics. In contrast with Soviet statements in the past, the core message of Brezhnev's speech was that the USSR no longer placed its hopes for better relations with Beijing on the possibility of internal changes in China.

The second part of Brezhnev's speech was about the Taiwan issue, which undoubtedly was aimed at the Sino-US negotiations over the US sale of arms to Taiwan at the time. In April 1979, in its commentary on the Taiwan Relations Act that had just been passed by the US Congress, Moscow denounced the Americans for practicing a "two-Chinas policy" and criticized the Chinese government for abandoning its own fundamental principles on the issue. It is worth noting that with respect to US-Taiwan relations, China was also attacked by its old comrade-in-arms, Albania, which condemned Beijing's position as "deceiving the Chinese people." There was no question that Brezhnev seized the right moment to expound upon Soviet adherence to the principle of one China during the period of Sino-US tensions over Taiwan and to let the Chinese government know that with regard to Taiwan, which was the most sensitive and troublesome issue in Sino-US relations, the Soviet position should be taken into consideration and could be helpful to China.

The third part of the speech, regarding resolution of the border issues, was a response to long-time Chinese concerns and indicated Soviet willingness to engage in negotiations about the border. On 24 March, perhaps to emphasize Soviet sincerity to resolve the border issues, Soviet First Foreign Minister Leonid Ilichev gave an interview to a Reuters reporter in which he repeated the same proposal on border negotiations that had been mentioned in Brezhnev's speech. He announced that as the head of the Soviet delegation on border negotiations, he was "ready to hold border negotiations immediately."

The fourth part of the speech concerned the guiding principles for negotiations on Sino-Soviet state relations. Brezhnev adhered to existing Soviet policy about no preconditions and no involvement of any third party; hence, the talks were to be strictly limited bilateral relations.

Brezhnev's speech indicated that the Soviet side had abandoned its previous position that the goal of negotiations was to achieve agreement on the principles of bilateral relations. Instead, the new orientation was to "reach agreement on steps for improving Sino-Soviet relations." The agreement could include political, economic, and cultural aspects of bilateral relations. Moscow obviously hoped that by taking a flexible attitude toward negotiations, it could ease the tensions between the Soviet Union and China sooner rather than later. Moscow also became more realistic on the issue of state relations and abandoned its previous position of aggressively pushing for an agreement. It was willing to reach agreements and to restore cooperation in non-political areas, such as trade, science and technology, and culture. Moscow clearly realized that even if the two sides could not find common ground on strategic issues, they could, and should, relax tensions and develop bilateral relations.

After Brezhnev's speech, the Soviet and East European press urged the Chinese government to take the Soviet gestures seriously. This signaled that the Soviet leadership indeed wanted Beijing to take notice that Soviet leaders had never before broached the issue of improving relations with China. Nevertheless, the background to Brezhnev's speech clearly revealed two characteristics of the Soviet policy adjustment toward China. First, the USSR had no intention of giving up its strategy of establishing regional domination. Second, unlike the issue of maintaining the superiority of Soviet strategic armaments in Europe, adjustment of its China policy was not a top priority on the Soviet agenda. The adjustment was also not the result of any major domestic policy shift in the Soviet Union. These two features determined Moscow's limitations with regard to improving relations with China.

Opening the Gates of Normalization

According to the *Chronicle of the Life of Deng Xiaoping* and Qian Qichen's autobiography, either on 24 March, the same day as Brezhnev's speech, or on the next day, 25 March, Deng called upon the MFA to issue a response to the speech.[2] By the account of then Foreign Minister Huang Hua, the previous night the MFA had already held internal deliberations on the speech. On 25 March, Huang Hua delivered a personal report to Deng, and Deng instructed the MFA to issue an immediate public response. Deng wanted the response to be short and precise, and properly balanced. It was to make principled rebuttals of any attacks but to maintain flexibility and keep the door open.[3] Accordingly, Qian Qichen issued a brief statement at an MFA press conference, announcing that the Chinese government had "noticed" Brezhnev's speech on Sino-Soviet relations and stating that China "pays more attention to the actual actions of the Soviet Union." Huang Hua believed this was China's "initial reaction," as masterminded by Deng Xiaoping.

The sequence of China's reactions orchestrated by Deng Xiaoping is the key to fully understanding the responses of the Chinese decision-making apparatus to Brezhnev's speech. According to Qian Qichen's memoirs, it appears that the foreign policy apparatus did not react or take any actions in response to Brezhnev's speech prior to Deng's instructions. However, Huang Hua's memoirs discuss in some detail the internal deliberations by the MFA and make it clear that Deng's decision was taken after the official MFA report. Since both Qian Qichen and Huang Hua were participants in the deliberations, further investigations are necessary to ascertain the accuracy of these events.

According to Huang Hua's account, the MFA's analysis held that Moscow was compelled to make a policy adjustment toward China. The relevant factors included the unfavorable Soviet position in the Sino-Soviet-US strategic triangle, the intensified Soviet-US military confrontation in the form of an armaments race, economic difficulties at home, and so on. Brezhnev's speech was merely a friendly gesture, and based only on the speech it is difficult to know the true intentions of the USSR. Nevertheless, the speech contained something positive, and the MFA suggested that China should seize the opportunity to ease tensions and to gradually normalize relations. This would benefit China in two respects: it would improve China's international environment and it would increase room for China to maneuver within Sino-Soviet-US triangular relations.[4] Obviously, the foreign policy establishment was quite proactive in promoting normalization of Sino-Soviet relations and had thoughtfully considered the diplomatic ramifications.

Deng's decision taken after the MFA report was probably preliminary and intentionally exploratory, thus permitting future latitude. As the highest decision maker with overall responsibility, Deng very likely placed different priorities on China's various strategic needs. In the afternoon of 16 April, Deng asked the visiting Romanian Communist Party Secretary, Nicolai Ceauşescu, to deliver a message to Brezhnev, stating that China attached great importance to actual actions, which could be discussions on issues such as Cambodia and Afghanistan, or the withdrawal of the USSR Army from the Sino-Soviet border or Mongolia. Without such actions, China would not be convinced. This was the earliest expression of what later became the so-called "removal of the 'three major obstacles'" proposed by the Chinese. It suggests that even before formal discussions by Chinese decision makers on normalization of Sino-Soviet relations began, Deng had already entertained some clear ideas and had communicated them to the Soviet side.

One characteristic of the Chinese decision-making system should be noted. Even though the supreme decision makers and the government apparatus shared the same goals of relaxing tensions and normalizing relations between China and the Soviet Union, they differed in terms of their considerations and approaches. On the one hand, the latter, for whatever reasons, was more concerned with various issues concerning bilateral relations at the state level. The former, on the other hand, focused on fundamentally improving China's security environment and its strategic global position. Answers to the question of whether or when to normalize relations had to serve national strategic security purposes and the international united front against Soviet hegemony. Ultimately, China's strategic concerns had to be reasonably and effectively met. Deng's conversation with Ceauşescu signaled a certain flexibility: the "three major obstacles" could be resolved one by one.

As had occurred many times in the past, once again Chinese foreign policy was shifting, this time it was its policy toward the Soviet Union, mainly due to the tremendous political changes occurring at home rather than due to any outside forces. The national development strategy proclaimed by the Chinese Communist Party (CCP) Central Committee (CC), focusing on economic development and the policy of reform and opening, led to successive changes in various aspects of Chinese foreign policy. In a word, the transformation of China's national development strategy, not a change in the external environment, was the primary driving force behind the fundamental shift in Chinese foreign policy during this period.

However, factors such as the influence of long-held foreign policies, especially those involving major issues, were equally significant. Foreign policy had to be compatible with the national development strategy, but, at the same time, fundamental foreign policy issues would carry the same weight. Following the consistent theoretical logic and patterns adopted by Chinese leaders, if they could not reasonably and persuasively prove some basic concepts, such as "era," "situation," "structure," "relative strength," or the "guiding foreign-policy principles," and frame and implement policies accordingly, the grand strategy of reform and opening could not be adopted and win wide support. At the very least, it would have been much more difficult than what eventually transpired.

As revealed by the trajectory of Chinese foreign policy, changes wrought mainly by domestic policy shifts more often than not experienced a period of delay and their impact were not immediately reflected in every aspect of Chinese foreign policy. In addition, the foreign policy of the new era occurred on the heels of the extreme leftist foreign policy of the Cultural Revolution. Despite the new political line endorsed by the Third Plenary Session of the Eleventh CCP CC, the development of a new foreign policy had to wait for the leftist mistakes to be corrected and for things to be set on the right track. Therefore, the shift in Chinese foreign policy took place slowly and lagged far behind the sea changes in domestic policy. Changes in China's foreign policy perceptions took place even more slowly, and policy toward the Soviet Union was perhaps the last to change.

At the Third Plenary Session of the Eleventh CC in late 1978, the CCP leadership made the major decision to focus government work on economic construction. The decision had vital ramifications on foreign policy changes. These changes were obvious in at least two areas. First, Chinese leaders had to determine whether there would be a relatively long peaceful and stable international environment. In fact, based on the political report of the Eleventh CCP National Congress and later commentaries by China's official news media, Chinese leaders were convinced that the danger of a major war clearly continued to exist. During the war against Vietnam in February 1979, Chinese leaders lowered their concern about the Soviet threat due to accurate intelligence and the fact that the Soviet military did not take any hostile actions during the war. Nevertheless, after the Soviet invasion of Afghanistan, Chinese anxieties about the USSR quickly intensified.

Thereafter, Chinese leaders had to answer a second question: if they presumed the existence of a danger of war and a threat to peace, could they construct a safe environment and an international relationship that was compatible with China's development strategy? In the 1970s, Chinese leaders drew the conclusion that world wars and major foreign invasions were unavoidable and threats of war were always imminent. The tensions between China and the

USSR and the deep concerns about Soviet threats were the reasons behind such a conclusion. The long and large-scale war preparations in China at the time were geared toward the possibility of a Soviet invasion.

Embedded views often cause people's perceptions to lag behind reality. Until the late 1970s and the early 1980s, Chinese leaders held the view that it was both necessary and feasible to secure a period of peace by carrying out appropriate foreign policies so that the economy could develop. The result was a paradox in China's foreign policy: on the one hand, Beijing insisted that China's modernization required a peaceful and stable international environment, and on the other, Chinese perceptions of the international situation became increasingly alarmist, envisaging an increased Soviet threat and even a possible Soviet invasion. As a result, for a time after the Third Plenary Session of the Eleventh CC, Chinese leaders continued to unswervingly pursue the anti-hegemony international united front of the Mao period. At a CCP CC meeting held in January 1980, Deng proposed three paramount missions for the 1980s: anti-hegemony, reunification, and economic development. Hegemony referred to none other than the Soviet Union.[5] After the war with Vietnam, China took a series of major actions, such as joining the American-led boycott of the Moscow Olympics and conducting massive military exercises in northern China to build up its international anti-Soviet front.

It is also possible that China's choice of a modernization model was the reason for the delays in changes to China's Soviet policy. Historically, one of the major rationales for China's policy of "leaning to one side" after the establishment of the People's Republic of China (PRC) was the idea that China should embrace the Soviet development model. In retrospect, at the Third Plenary Session of the Eleventh CC, Chinese leaders reversed this 1949 decision and began a new long march of reforms aimed at negating the Soviet model. This decision was made in accordance with both historical experiences as well as current events. In light of information obtained thus far, the large number of Chinese delegations sent abroad in the summer of 1978 played a key role in this policy change. The most significant delegation, led by Vice-Premier Gu Mu, was the visit to five West European countries from 2 May to 5 June 1978. Upon its return, the delegation prepared a detailed report and presented it to the CC. On 30 June, Gu Mu gave an account of the delegation's findings to the Politburo and later to Deng Xiaoping himself. The details of these meetings have yet to become available. But, as far as China's Soviet policy is concerned, one crucial consequence of the meetings was the establishment of a new direction, that is, to learn from the West. As soon as Chinese leaders decided to promote modernization, it became apparent that Sino-Soviet relations did not occupy a prominent place on their agenda.

Nevertheless, the new direction of learning from the West had a rather complicated impact on Sino-Soviet relations. On the one hand, it indeed deflected attention from Chinese leaders, but, on the other, it removed a huge obstacle to reformulating China's Soviet policy and provided a logical rationale for improving Sino-Soviet relations. Determined to learn from the West in the course of modernizing China, Chinese leaders inevitably reexamined China's past development experiences, from which they drew a negative conclusion. Concurrent with the nationwide debate over the "criterion of truth," the Chinese media began to discuss diverse "socialist models." The main thrust of the discussions was that there was no single, universal model for socialist development and China did not monopolize so-called true socialism. China could not use its own model to judge the nature and policies of other countries or to label others with a certain "ism." Such reasoning was extended to Sino-Soviet relations and it fundamentally challenged the legitimacy of China's ideological disputes with the Soviet Union. It signified that Chinese leaders could no longer treat ideological differences as a component of Sino-Soviet relations, and it would be even more difficult for them to use ideology to obstruct any improvement in Sino-Soviet relations.

Two key issues, national security and development strategy, determined the course and timetable for the transformation of China's Soviet policies. In general, shifts in domestic politics obviously impelled Beijing to reconsider Sino-Soviet relations, but it is possible that for a while Chinese leaders simply did not pay sufficient attention to this issue. It is very likely that it was not until 1981, when Sino-US relations suffered a series of setbacks after Reagan's election, that Chinese leaders began to consider adjusting policy toward the Soviet Union. Even then, the degree of adjustment was directly affected by the handling of Sino-US relations.

The shift in Chinese leaders' views on war and external threats corresponded to the changes in China's relations with the United States and the Soviet Union, especially the latter. In the early 1970s, the key factor that redirected Sino-US relations from confrontation to rapprochement was their common interest in dealing with Soviet expansionism and ending the Indochina war. In the following years, China pursued normalization of relations with the United States as a major foreign policy goal.

In the spring of 1978, the Carter administration finally took the step of normalizing Sino-US relations, and on 5 July 1978, the two countries began secret negotiations. On 1 January 1979, the two countries formally established diplomatic relations. Looking back at history, if it were not for their common need to stop Soviet expansionism, it would have been more difficult for China and the United States to normalize relations and to develop close ties within such short time. Nevertheless, cooperation on international security issues did not eliminate the fundamental differences between China and the United States. In April 1979, not long after the establishment of formal diplomatic relations, the US Congress passed the Taiwan Relations Act. Chinese leaders reacted strongly to this move. They equated the Taiwan Relations Act with "actually negating the political foundation for normalization of Sino-U.S. relations." Consequently, Deng warned the United States that the act must not set a precedent.

In 1981, soon after he entered the White House, Reagan announced a so-called dual-track China policy. Under this policy, his administration would continue to develop Sino-US relations and, in accordance with the Taiwan Relations Act, it would sell arms to Taiwan, including advanced FX fighters. This stance caused a serious jolt to Sino-US relations and convinced Beijing that Sino-US relations were facing a severe test. CCP leaders decided to take a series of actions to halt such a regression in US policy on the Taiwan issue. Beijing canceled planned visits by Chinese military leaders to the United States and openly denounced the Reagan administration for interfering in China's domestic affairs. Deng Xiaoping personally delivered a warning to the United States.[6] Beijing was ready to take further steps if necessary, including lowering the level of diplomatic relations with the United States. At the same time, China clashed with the United States on many other issues as well.

After the establishment of diplomatic relations, disagreements, particularly antagonism over Taiwan, between the two countries led Chinese leaders in early 1981 to distance China from the United States and to readjust its triangular strategy regarding relations with the United States and the Soviet Union. On 11 January, Deng read the MFA report "Instructions on Our Countermoves to Reagan's Strengthening of Ties with Taiwan." The content of the report has yet to be made public, but it is likely that it was not in line with Deng's thinking. On the report, Deng wrote, "let the Politburo hold a formal discussion," asserting that at the time "the most pressing issue is that Taiwan officials will take part in Reagan's inauguration, for which the MFA should take up the matter with [the United States] and make counter plans." Some indirect evidence reveals that on the same day, Deng met with senior MFA officials and discussed countermoves against the Reagan government. In these conversations, Deng expressed three important actions: first, to strike back at the Reagan administration's challenge over the Taiwan issue because anything less would tarnish China's status and reputation; second, to prepare for a regression in Sino-US relations to their pre-1972 level, but each of China's steps had to be appropriate and well thought out; and third, despite the twists and turns, to continue the goal of maintaining normal and stable Sino-US relations. On 16 January, the Politburo held a meeting to discuss Sino-US relations. Judging from the measures adopted by the Chinese government thereafter, it appears that Deng's view prevailed.

As Chinese leaders were prepared to have a showdown with the Americans, they also assessed China's position in the Sino-Soviet-US triangle. The key factor in Deng's determination to pursue a hard line for the sake of stabilizing Sino-US relations was that Chinese leaders perceived the Soviet threat to be less serious than before. The following question was posed: "If Sino-U.S. relations are to deteriorate, how much more aggressive can the Soviet Union become?" The implication was that the Soviet threat to China's national security had decreased so much that China no longer had to rely on the United States to balance its concerns. As a result, China could afford to take a firmer stance regarding the reversal by the Reagan administration. At a 23 January Politburo meeting on foreign policy, Deng suggested that it was necessary to have a serious discussion on how to assess the international situation, how to make a judgment about the Third World, and how to deal with the United States and the USSR.

Judging from the available information, Chinese leaders spent quite some time discussing foreign policy. The resultant views on policy toward the Soviet Union were rather complicated. On the one hand, Chinese leaders maintained that it was necessary to ease Sino-Soviet relations, but, on the other, they were also concerned that if a turnaround were to come about too quickly, China might lose more than it would gain. On 11 February, at another Politburo meeting on foreign policy, Deng pointed out that China's diplomatic strategy of establishing a united front against hegemony should not be changed. China could hold talks with the Soviet Union on trade and border issues. Yet, as long as there was no major development in Soviet policy (such as Soviet withdrawal from Afghanistan), negotiations on state relations should not be resumed. Deng insisted that a pivotal principle was involved here and any change would be detrimental to the fundamental framework of Chinese diplomacy. At a meeting of the Politburo Standing Committee on 13 June, Deng elaborated further on Sino-US relations: China must employ a "policy of brinkmanship" and be prepared for, not afraid of, a regression in Sino-US relations. This was the only way to make the Americans more cautious and for China to achieve positive results, that is, to maintain, or to further develop, Sino-US relations. By selecting such a "brinksmanship policy" in its confrontation with the Reagan administration, Beijing's goal was to eventually achieve a stable and even closer relationship with the United States.

Between the summer of 1981 and the summer of 1982, China and the United States held negotiations on the issue of arms sales to Taiwan. At this crucial moment, as the Sino-US confrontation over Taiwan was escalating and a contest of wills was underway, Brezhnev delivered his 24 March speech. Deng wanted the Chinese government to make a swift response. It is possible that Deng intended to utilize the relaxation of Sino-Soviet relations to put pressure on the United States. In his memoirs, Qian Qichen, in discussing the background to Deng's decision, believes that because of the "new progress" achieved in the Sino-US negotiations on Taiwan arms sales and the fact that "a new framework for Sino-U.S. relations was basically established," China was able to issue a rapid and positive response to Brezhnev's speech. However, in reality, China and the United States did not achieve any progress in their negotiations over Taiwan arms sales. Qian's memoirs may overstretch the timeline, but it signifies that during that summer when Beijing decided to take major steps to improve Sino-Soviet relations, the main reason behind this decision was the Chinese belief that stable Sino-US relations would be conducive to normalization of Sino-Soviet relations.[7] This reflects the thinking of Chinese leaders that normalization of Sino-Soviet relations could strengthen China's bargaining position with the United States. In the meantime, China did not want to let the USSR take advantage of the troubles between China and the United States and hence gain an upper hand in its negotiations with China. Such maneuvering marked a profound change in Chinese leaders' world outlook.

At the founding of the PRC, one key justification for the CCP to ally with the Soviet Union was China's confrontation with the United States. In the fall of 1969 when Mao Zedong decided to relax Sino-US relations, he was very concerned about the perceived Soviet threat. It is possible that he even viewed a tense Sino-Soviet relationship as a necessary precondition for a relaxation in Sino-US relations. At the end of 1978 when Deng Xiaoping was determined to conclude Sino-US negotiations on establishing diplomatic relations, he believed that in order to fend off the Soviet threat, it was necessary to normalize Sino-US relations without delay.[8] During his visit to the United States in January 1979, Deng openly denounced Soviet foreign policy time and again, and he once more called for an international united front against hegemony. History reveals that, for a very long time, Chinese leaders were convinced that China could not simultaneously maintain good relations with the two superpowers that were engaged in a Cold War confrontation. Precisely because of this long-held view, as Chinese leaders embarked on the road of normalizing Sino-Soviet relations, they also underscored the beginning of a gradual transformation of the Chinese strategic outlook that had been formed under the influence of the Cold War.

On 14 July 1982, when Sino-US negotiations were winding down, Deng called a meeting at his home to discuss Sino-Soviet relations. The impetus for the meeting occurred on 13 July when the American side put forward a plan to resolve the issue of arm sales to Taiwan. At the meeting, Chinese leaders held the view that a final decision had to be made and it was time to conclude the negotiations with the Americans. When some meeting participants noted that relations with the Soviet Union should also be improved, Deng concurred. He said that China should strive for a "major improvement" in Sino-Soviet relations, but such an improvement had to be conditional. Deng summed up the three points he had raised during his conversation with Ceaușescu as the "three major obstacles" that the Soviet Union had to take an initiative to resolve: withdrawal of its armed forces from the Sino-Soviet border areas and from the People's Republic of Mongolia, withdrawal from Afghanistan, and pressuring Vietnam to withdraw from Cambodia. It would be acceptable to the Chinese side if the Soviet side could accomplish only one of these obstacles. Deng's proposal was supported by those present at the meeting. Deng also suggested that the MFA send Yu Hongliang, director of the Department of Soviet and East European Affairs, to Moscow to "inspect the work of the embassy," but actually the purpose of his visit was to pass this message directly on to the Soviets. The 14 July meeting became a milestone in the Chinese leaders' decision to begin to promote normalization of Sino-Soviet relations.

Deng obviously had started to consider how to simultaneously maintain Sino-Soviet and Sino-US relations from a new perspective. After Chinese and US representatives signed the 17 August communiqué on arms sales to Taiwan, Chinese leaders believed that China now had all the prerequisites to deal with Sino-Soviet relations. On 10 August, a week before the signing of the communiqué, Yu Hongliang, Chinese ambassador to the Soviet Union, had traveled to Moscow, carrying with him the talking points drafted by the MFA.

According to both Huang Hua and Qian Qichen, the talking points had been personally approved by Deng and contained two major issues: first, China recognized that the moment had arrived to take some concrete actions to improve Sino-Soviet relations; second, China suggested that the Soviet side could begin by persuading Vietnam to withdraw its military forces from Cambodia, or by dealing with other issues affecting Sino-Soviet relations, such as reducing its armed forces along the border. The two sides should also find a way, acceptable to both, to withdraw Soviet forces from Mongolia and, at the same time, to seek a reasonable solution to the situation in Afghanistan.[9] Soon after his arrival in Moscow, Yu invited Soviet Vice-Foreign Minister Leonid Ilichev to a meeting at the Chinese embassy. At the meeting with Ilichev, who was accompanied by Mikhail Kapitsa, director of the First Far East Department, Yu delivered the Chinese message almost word for word from the talking points. This was the first official direct presentation by China to the USSR on a solution to the "three major obstacles."

Ilichev indicated that he would have to ask for instructions for the Soviet response. Yu then continued his journey to Poland. On his return, he met once again with Ilichev, and Ilichev told him that he had reported the contents of their conversation to Soviet leaders, and the Soviet government would issue an official response. It is not clear how the Soviet leaders reached its decision, but the result was positive. On 20 August, Viktor Maltsev, Soviet first vice-foreign minister, met the interim Chinese chargé d'affaires, Ma Xusheng, and delivered a memorandum with the official Soviet reply. The Soviet side indicated that it was willing to negotiate with China at any time, in any location, and at any level in order to "remove any obstacles to normalization of relations." After he received this reply, Deng immediately decided to resume Sino-Soviet negotiations, which had been suspended for more than two years. The two sides reached an agreement that political consultations regarding normalization of bilateral relations would be conducted by special envoys at the vice-ministerial level. On 5 October, negotiations were held in Beijing, thus inaugurating the course of normalization of Sino-Soviet relations.

On 18 September, on a private train, Deng Xiaoping held a one-on-one meeting with Kim Il Sung during which Deng discussed four issues regarding Sino-Soviet relations. First, the goal of Sino-Soviet contacts was to normalize bilateral relations. Second, the Chinese proposal to remove the "three major obstacles" was prompted by the Soviet threat to Chinese security, and the Soviets could first remove any one of these obstacles to indicate their sincerity. Third, Sino-Soviet negotiations would take a long time, and negotiations at the vice-ministerial level would be unable to settle the real problems anytime soon. Fourth, China was in a more advantageous position than the Soviet Union, and the Soviet leaders were anxious to achieve results because for them "things are more difficult." This perception led Chinese leaders to impose strict controls on the progress in Sino-Soviet relations, hoping not to give the impression that they were overanxious to improve the relationship.

The Stalemate in Political Negotiations

Sino-Soviet political negotiations between the respective vice-foreign ministers began in Beijing on 5 October 1982. By June 1988, the two sides had held 12 rounds of "marathon" negotiations.

The first round, held in Beijing, lasted for 21 days. During that period, the two sides had six meetings. From an analytical perspective, this round was particularly important. During the meetings, the two sides unequivocally explained their respective positions and principles. Despite serious differences, both sides wanted the negotiations to serve as a forum to seek normalization. The meetings not only provided an opportunity for each side to better understand the other's position but also provided a platform on which the two sides could control the course of normalization and from time to time even improve their respective strategic positions.

The Chinese envoy was Qian Qichen, then vice-minister of the MFA, and the Soviet side was represented by Leonid Ilichev, Soviet vice-foreign minister in charge of African affairs at the time. Ilichev had gained experience in dealing with the Chinese due to his more than ten years of negotiating with senior Chinese diplomats, such as Qiao Guanhua, Han Nianlong, Yu Zhan, Wang Youping, and others. He had a good grasp of the issues and of the complexities involved in Sino-Soviet relations. But, at the same time, as a professional diplomat in a bureaucratic setting, Ilichev seemed to lack a certain sensitivity for important new information and was overcautious to a fault.

According to Qian Qichen's memoirs, by following Deng's instruction to "not make a drastic turnaround" and to "not rush to achieve results," the Chinese side established the following guideline for the negotiations: "keeping the overall strategic perspective in mind and adhering to the principles." At the time, the Chinese clearly already had a plan for demanding that the Soviets take real steps to remove their threat to China. When Deng said that the Soviets could "start with one thing," the Chinese meant that the Soviets should "stop supporting the Vietnamese invasion and press Vietnam to withdraw from Cambodia."[10]

The guideline for the Chinese delegation during the first round of political consultations signified the final formation of Chinese policy on the normalization of relations with the Soviet Union. The policy as a whole encompassed the following: first, the goal of normalization of Sino-Soviet relations was to advance China's strategic interests; second, China's strategic interests in this particular respect were to eliminate Soviet threats to China and to alleviate the tensions China faced in its border areas, which could be realized by steps such as resolution of the Indochina issue, namely Vietnamese withdrawal from Cambodia; third, due to the consideration that stabilizing and improving Sino-US relations outweighed normalization of Sino-Soviet relations and the perception that China had strategic advantages over the Soviet Union, China was not in any hurry to bring about rapid results.

Decision-making on the Soviet side remains unknown. The most important question is whether the abovementioned conversations between Deng and Ceauşescu in April and between Deng and Kim Il Sung in September were passed on to the Soviet leaders before the beginning of the Sino-Soviet negotiations. Since Romania and North Korea belonged to the Soviet camp and maintained good relations with the USSR, it would be inconceivable that Ceauşescu and Kim did not pass on Deng's words to the Soviet leaders, especially in the case of Ceauşescu who had been playing an important role in delivering messages to the two superpowers on behalf of China. Chinese leaders counted on Ceauşescu. When they spoke with him, there was usually a special purpose. Of course, we still need archival confirmation. If Soviet leaders were informed of the content of Deng's conversations, it is reasonable to assume that their unhurried position in the negotiations was in reaction to Deng's position. Ilichev's position and attitude during the talks indicated that the thinking of Soviet leaders at the time did not exceed the scope of Brezhnev's 24 March speech.

During the negotiations, some major differences between Chinese and Soviet attitudes toward the normalization issue became apparent. China, preoccupied with its concern about national strategy, insisted on holding the negotiations in its quest to achieve a preset strategic goal, that is, gradual and complete removal of the Soviet threat to Chinese security. Therefore, normalization of Sino-Soviet relations could only be achieved on the basis of mutual trust at the strategic level.

The Soviet side wanted to improve bilateral relations through negotiations in order to reduce the pressures it faced in Asia. It had no desire to make fundamental adjustments to its already existing strategic positions, nor did it have any intention of reducing its military pressure on China. The Soviet side would have been content with some sort of improvement in bilateral relations. The Soviet definition of "normalization" was to reach agreement on the principles for bilateral relations and then to sign a diplomatic document based on these principles. In fact, ever since Brezhnev's 24 March speech, there had been much discord on the Soviet side and the Soviets were unable to reach a consensus on its China policy. Not until a 9 September Soviet Politburo meeting on foreign policy did Brezhnev clarify the guiding policy for Soviet negotiations as "to explore the possibilities of removing unnecessary tensions and prejudices in Sino-Soviet relations."

The differences between the two sides were fully apparent in their political consultations and prevented the negotiations from making any real progress. On 5 October, the two sides began their first round of consultations. Qian Qichen focused his attention on removing the "three major obstacles." He stressed that normalization required that the two countries make joint efforts and take real actions in order to eliminate those serious obstacles that prevented the normal development of bilateral relations. He set forth the Chinese demand on prioritizing issues in the negotiations by pointing out that since it would be difficult to remove all the obstacles between the two countries at once, forcing the Vietnamese to withdraw from Cambodia could serve as a starting point. First, the selection of this issue as a priority was attributed to its crucial importance to peace in the region. Second, it was only required that the Soviets to assert their influence. So far, there is no available information about the Chinese internal discussions over why the Chinese established Vietnamese withdrawal from Cambodia as the first step in the first round of negotiations.

In contrast, Ilichev insisted on the Soviet's repeated stand that, first, there should be no "preconditions" attached to an improvement in Sino-Soviet relations; second, normalization of Sino-Soviet relations should not be detrimental to the "interests of any third country"; and third, the Soviet Union had never "threatened China." Time and again, he emphasized that the Soviet side wanted to improve bilateral relations and to continue past practices. He proposed to jointly draft a document on the Sino-Soviet state relationship or to first reach an agreement on improving and developing economic, trade, science, and cultural relations.

The marked differences often caused sharp exchanges and intense interactions between the two sides. However, since both sides intended to continue talking, outside of the meetings they tried to maintain a less tense mood. The Chinese side arranged sightseeing trips for the Soviet delegation and created opportunities for more relaxed private exchanges. Qian Qichen took the occasion to reaffirm to his counterpart that it was China's true desire to work for normalization of bilateral relations. He further explained that the message Yu Hongliang had delivered in August contained important new elements, which expounded upon the seriousness the Chinese side attached to making real efforts to improve Sino-Soviet relations. For example, on the issue of reducing military forces along the border, the Chinese wording implied that both sides should shoulder responsibility for withdrawal from the border area. With respect to Indochina, the Chinese wording only required that Moscow facilitate a Vietnamese withdrawal from Cambodia, and it did not involve other aspects of their relationship. Ilichev responded by reiterating the Soviet position on these issues without adding any new ideas.[11]

After six meetings, the first round of political talks concluded on 21 October. To show that the Chinese side attached great importance to the negotiations as well as to an improvement in Sino-Soviet relations, Chinese Foreign Minister Huang Hua met Ilichev on 24 October. The latter took the opportunity to reinforce the Soviet positions, whereas, as usual, Huang rejected them one by one and once again asked that Moscow carry out one or two things to eliminate the "obstacles."[12] Although the two sides engaged in a fierce battle of words during the negotiations and failed to reach common ground on any issue, Beijing still held a positive view of the negotiations. It recognized that by having a frank exchange of views and, consequently, achieving a better understanding of each other's stands, the two sides could make positive progress.

The second round of talks, held in Moscow in March 1983, followed the same pattern of continuous arguments without any real progress. By the eighth round of negotiations in April 1986, the two sides had not been able to break the deadlock regarding the issue of removing the "three major obstacles." At the same time, neither side wanted to suspend the already lengthy and futile talks. They each displayed a tenacious political will to keep the talks going as a means to continue a dialogue. If one considers the lack of progress in the negotiations and the ongoing Sino-Soviet confrontations on regional and global issues, continuation of the negotiations surely reflected the full determination of the two sides to improve relations.

The impasse during the protracted negotiations was caused by profound reasons on each side. From the very beginning, the Soviet Union refused to discuss security and global strategy. Every step in the Chinese proposal about removing the "three major obstacles" touched upon Soviet overall policy, and particularly upon its policy in Southeast Asia. As long as there was no fundamental foreign policy shift in Moscow, which actually would also require major domestic policy changes, it would be very difficult for the USSR to take any real steps. Without support from an overall foreign policy adjustment and incentives from domestic policy changes, Soviet policy toward China was seriously constrained by the political situation in Moscow. During these years, the Soviet top leadership faced numerous turnovers due to health issues. Brezhnev died on 19 November 1982, soon after the conclusion of the first round of consultations. It is very likely that after his 24 March speech, Brezhnev's health halted any further readjustment to Moscow's China policy.

As discussed above, the decision by the Chinese leaders to improve Sino-Soviet relations was adopted in conjunction with the idea of "keeping a distance from the United States" and was directly linked to the Sino-Soviet-US strategic triangle. Undoubtedly, it was due to a distrust of the United States that Chinese leaders intended to maintain a distance from the United States. The Chinese goal was not to be taken advantage of strategically. Nevertheless, the reality was that even though the Cold War between the United States and the USSR was intensifying at the time, Sino-US relations were not affected by Chinese efforts to improve relations with Moscow. After a period of ups and downs, in the fall of 1983, Sino-US relations stabilized. During the first half of 1984, Chinese and American leaders exchanged visits. Thereafter, there was marked progress in cooperation in various fields.

To what extent did the improvement in Sino-US relations during this period affect the course of Sino-Soviet normalization? This question merits careful study. For instance, when visiting the United States in January 1984, Chinese Premier Zhao Ziyang told President Reagan that China was talking with the Soviet Union; however, he noted that it was unlikely that there would be any significant improvements in Sino-Soviet relations. In a joint interview with five American television networks, Premier Zhao noted that China would not adopt an equidistant policy in its relations with the United States and the Soviet Union. In Beijing, on 22 February, when meeting with a delegation from the Center for Strategic and International Studies led by Zbigniew Brzezinski, in answering a question from Brzezinski, Zhao said that if there were to be any changes in China's international strategy, they would mainly be caused by

America's policy toward Taiwan. Deng also made it clear that as neighbors China and the Soviet Union would "make some improvements and develop their relations," but "Sino-Soviet relations will not see any drastic changes" unless the Soviet Union takes steps to remove the "three major obstacles."

Clearly, any progress in Sino-US relations would strengthen China's position in its negotiations with the Soviet Union. In the meantime, such progress could also block any improvements in Sino-Soviet relations, even to the point of reducing China's desire to make any major changes in their relations. It is possible that Chinese leaders had concluded that for China to continue to improve relations with the Soviet Union, it would be necessary for it to maintain or even to raise its preconditions. After all, China still referred to Soviet foreign policy as hegemony, and anti-hegemony remained a major goal of China's foreign policy. Chinese leaders still viewed Soviet military deployments and actions in Asia as direct and serious threats to Chinese security. This view remained unchanged.

Funeral Diplomacy and Its Influence

The deadlock in the political talks did not bring Sino-Soviet relations to a complete standstill. With a relatively stable domestic situation, the Chinese leadership took more initiatives than the Soviets to improve bilateral relations. When the Soviet political situation became more complicated after the successive deaths of Soviet leaders, Chinese efforts became the principal driving force behind any improvement in relations.

On 10 November 1982, the Soviet government announced the death of Leonid Brezhnev. The Chinese side immediately decided to use the occasion to improve Sino-Soviet relations. There was a precedent in the history of Sino-Soviet relations that one side tried to use the occasion of the death of an important leader in the other country to break a stalemate between the two countries. As noted, when Mao Zedong and other Chinese leaders died in 1976, the Soviet Union tried to improve relations with China by offering condolences and taking part in funeral activities. However, on these occasions, China did not reciprocate. Upon hearing of Brezhnev's death, the CCP CC immediately sent a telegram to Moscow to offer its condolences and also sent a wreath to the Soviet embassy in Beijing. The MFA suggested that Ulanfu, vice-chairman of the Standing Committee of the National People's Congress, and Foreign Minister Huang Hua personally offer condolences at the Soviet embassy and take the opportunity to convey the Chinese desire for normalization of bilateral relations.[13] In comparison with the Soviet reaction after the death of Mao, the Chinese responses, although similar, were more positive. The MFA's suggestion was approved and implemented. The Soviet side expressed its appreciation and Soviet media issued positive reports on the Chinese gestures.

These initial efforts by the Chinese were exploratory. It is likely that, encouraged by the friendly exchanges between the two sides, Chinese leaders decided to take further action. After the Soviet government announced, at the end of a three-day period of national mourning (from 12 to 15 November), a state funeral for Brezhnev would be held on 15 November, Beijing decided to send a delegation headed by Foreign Minister Huang Hua to attend the funeral. The delegation included director of the Department of Soviet and Eastern European Affairs Ma Xusheng, vice-director of the Department of Soviet and Eastern European Affairs Wang Jinqing, and Li Fenglin, director of the Office for Sino-Soviet Negotiations. Before their trip, the MFA submitted the following guidelines for the delegation: first, an improvement in Sino-Soviet relations was the central theme of the mission, and the Chinese side should not be the first to raise the issue of disputes, nor should it make any direct reference to the "three major obstacles" or hold any formal talks. Second, the delegation should only issue positive comments about Brezhnev and confirm the Chinese appreciation of Brezhnev's repeatedly expressed desire to improve relations with China. Third, the delegation should emphasize China's sincere desire to improve relations between the two countries as well as China's realistic attitude and approach for a gradual normalization. Fourth, Chinese condolences should highlight the traditional friendship between the two countries. Fifth, the delegation should extend congratulations to the new leaders and convey greetings from the Chinese leaders. Sixth, any reference to inter-party relations or to the activities of other countries in the Soviet camp should be avoided.[14] The CCP CC endorsed the MFA's proposal.

To ensure that the Chinese delegation would arrive in Moscow for the funeral on time, the Chinese government dispatched a chartered plane on 14 November. Such an arrangement is a telling example of how much importance the Chinese side attached to this diplomatic mission. In the evening of 13 November, Foreign Minister Huang Hua telephoned Deng to report on their preparations and itinerary, and to ask for further instructions. During their telephone conversation, Deng added some new points and revisions to the MFA guidelines for the delegation. As directed by Deng, the delegation would express, first, China's hope that the two sides would make joint efforts to eliminate any obstacles in the bilateral relations; second, China should take an initiative to call on Soviet Foreign Minister Gromyko for a frank dialogue; third, the delegation should call on Andropov, the new general secretary of the Communist Party of the Soviet Union (CPSU), to express the hope that the new Soviet leadership would make efforts to improve Sino-Soviet relations. In addition, Deng suggested that in order for the Soviet public to understand and pay attention to the significance of the visit by the Chinese delegation, Chinese Foreign Minister Huang Hua should broadcast the Chinese position directly to the public by accepting an interview from the Xinhua News Agency.[15] This would also prevent any possible deviations by the Chinese delegation from the stipulations set by Beijing.

Deng's considerations behind these instructions remain unclear. However, they attest to Deng's persistence in upholding the principle of removing the "three major obstacles." Obviously, he wanted Foreign Minister Huang Hua to present China's stand accurately and explicitly in Moscow and to avoid losing focus amidst all the ceremonial functions. This raises two possibilities about Deng's additional instructions. One is that the proposal by the MFA, approved by the CC, had not been personally blessed by Deng. The second possibility is that after the initial exploration into making the condolence call, Deng had decided to become more proactive in promoting normalization by using the opportunity of attending the funeral in Moscow. The second possibility is more likely. This once again is indicative of Deng's insistence on paying attention to strategic considerations when making decisions about normalization. Deng would never allow any diplomatic protocol or perfunctory exchange to hijack the real issues in the course of normalization.

The Chinese delegation departed Beijing on the early morning of 14 November. Soon thereafter, Deng made another decision. He instructed the Xinhua News Agency to run a short assessment of Brezhnev that should consist of neither criticism or simple praise.[16] If Qian Qichen's memory is accurate, in comparison to the MFA proposal, Deng's instructions indicated increased criticism of the Soviet Union under Brezhnev. In following Deng's directive, in the name of Foreign Minister Huang Hua, Hu Qiaomu drafted a statement, which was published on the same day. While reflecting the points contained in the MFA proposal, the statement briefly reviewed the history of Sino-Soviet relations, launching a veiled criticism of the Soviet Union under Brezhnev, while expressing hope that the new Soviet leadership would renew efforts to improve bilateral relations. Additionally, unlike the MFA proposal, the statement unequivocally raised the issue of the "three major obstacles."

Soon after Huang Hua arrived in Moscow, he was immediately informed by the Chinese ambassador, Yang Shouzheng, that a most urgent telegram from the CC was waiting for him. As soon as he read the telegram and the Xinhua News Agency's statement, Huang immediately recognized the differences between the Xinhua News Agency's statement and the MFA proposal. The telegram instructed Huang Hua that his presentation should make two changes to the original proposal and should be consistent with the principles expressed in the Xinhua statement. One change instructed Huang Hua, in his capacity as foreign minister, to request a meeting with Gromyko in an effort to hold political talks at the ministerial level. This would immediately raise the Sino-Soviet political negotiations from the vice-ministerial to the ministerial level. The second change was that during his meeting with Andropov, Huang was to clearly convey that the Chinese side had high hopes for the new Soviet leadership and was willing to deal with the new leaders.[17] This urgent telegram signified the completeness of the guiding principles for China's "funeral diplomacy." It also set the tone for Huang's visit to Moscow and indicated that the Chinese side sought to use "funeral diplomacy" to achieve positive results in Sino-Soviet relations.

All the memoirs and reports from the Chinese side suggest that the Soviets responded positively to the Chinese "funeral diplomacy" and accorded the Chinese delegation a "warm and friendly" reception. The Soviet press widely reported on the Chinese activities and informed the Soviet public of the Chinese intention to improve relations. After the funeral, in a break with the ceremonial protocol for heads of foreign delegations, Andropov granted

Huang Hua more time, thus giving Huang an opportunity to pass on the Chinese leaders' wishes to improve bilateral relations. For whatever reason, Huang Hua was not able to obtain another private meeting with Andropov, thus rendering the one meeting between the two even more significant. After the meeting, the Soviet side went through the Chinese message word by word with Huang Hua to confirm the accuracy of its content. All these actions reflected the response of the new Soviet leadership to China's "funeral diplomacy" and the seriousness of Moscow's wish to improve relations.

Huang Hua's most important progress in Moscow occurred during his formal meeting with Soviet Foreign Minister Gromyko. On the afternoon of 16 November, the foreign ministers of the two countries met for the first time in 20 years, and the meeting lasted for one hour and a half. Huang later recalled that for a while he had thought that this meeting could break the impasse between the two sides, an expectation more optimistic than the original prediction that the Chinese delegation would not achieve any real breakthrough. Huang's optimistic expectations may have been a reflection of Gromyko's positive tone. During their meeting, Huang reaffirmed China's requirement that the Soviets remove the "three major obstacles," but he omitted that the Soviet Union could start by persuading Vietnam to withdraw from Cambodia. He was hoping that Gromyko would make a gesture on the issue of withdrawing Soviet military forces from the border. However, Gromyko completely ruled out the possibility of discussing a Vietnamese withdrawal from Cambodia, nor and furthermore he did not express any willingness to withdraw Soviet troops from the border, even though he did say that the Soviet Union would make all possible efforts within its jurisdiction to improve bilateral relations. He stressed that China and the Soviet Union should start from noncontroversial issues, such as trade, economic cooperation, and cultural exchanges. Foreign Minister Huang Hua took the position that such bilateral exchanges could be arranged gradually, but they would not have a significant impact on normalization of relations.[18] In the end, the talks did not achieve any results that could be defined by the Chinese side as real progress, but they produced a more favorable atmosphere for promoting better relations.

It is worth noting that there are some differences between Huang Hua's and Qian Qichen's descriptions of the evolving Chinese policy. According to Qian Qichen, in the message delivered by Yu Hongliang on his trip to Moscow in August 1982, the Chinese side had already suggested that, in the removal of the "three major obstacles," the Soviet Union could "start from persuading Vietnam to withdraw from Cambodia or from other issues affecting bilateral relations, such as reducing its military forces along the Sino-Soviet border."[19] During the first meeting of the vice-foreign ministers, Qian explicitly told the Soviet side that the Soviet Union could start by persuading Vietnam to withdraw from Cambodia. In private with the Soviet side, he explained in some detail that it was essential to start from this issue because Vietnamese expansionism in Indochina was destroying regional peace and stability, and thereby increasing China's concern about its own security. In addition, this would be more realistic as well as easier for the Soviet side to implement since the withdrawal only involved the Vietnamese troops in Cambodia, unlike the issue of withdrawing Soviet troops elsewhere. Qian emphasized that Vietnamese withdrawal was "a key step" toward realizing normalization, but he did not elaborate on how the Chinese side would react if the Soviet side agreed to take this step. Based on Qian's recollections, it can be assumed that this proposal must have been part of the negotiation plan prepared for the Chinese delegation and must have been approved by Chinese leaders.[20]

Yet, in Huang Hua's account of Yu Hongliang's message, he did not mention Vietnamese withdrawal from Cambodia. Furthermore, regarding "funeral diplomacy," he recalls that in his talks with Gromyko, the Chinese side did not propose any concrete steps, but he was hoping the Soviet side would make a move to withdraw its forces from the border.[21] Ma Xusheng, who participated in the talks as a member of the Chinese delegation, seconded Huang's version of events. According to Ma, both Huang and Gromyko stressed the importance of Sino-Soviet relations, and Huang claimed that if any one of the "'three major obstacles' was removed, relations would move one step forward." Ma considered the above statement by Huang to be "the first time the Chinese had a more flexible Chinese attitude" about the removal of the "three major obstacles." Ma's testimony, as a long-time participant in Sino-Soviet negotiations, is useful reference, but it is unclear which part of Huang's statement he thought to be a "flexible attitude": removal of any one of the three obstacles or moving the relationship a step forward. After all, during the political talks, the Chinese side had never spelled out how China would reciprocate a Soviet move to remove the "three major obstacles." These participants' accounts indicate that during the vice-ministerial political talks in October 1982, the Chinese suggestion that the Soviets persuade the Vietnamese to withdraw from Cambodia was not a decision based on overall strategic considerations. Clarification of this point is essential to understand China's future policy adjustments.

No matter how the Chinese "funeral diplomacy" is evaluated, the commitment on both sides to improve bilateral relations is beyond any doubt. Chinese leaders at the highest level supervised the entire decision-making process for the "funeral diplomacy." In some important events, they personally took a hand in the operations. Soviet leaders reciprocated the Chinese leaders' sentiments and regarded the occasion as an opportunity to improve Sino-Soviet relations. Gromyko received instructions from Andropov prior to his talks with Huang Hua, and he told Huang Hua that he was speaking on behalf of Andropov when he stated that the Soviet Union wanted to improve Sino-Soviet relations. Although the two sides did not make any progress in resolving their strategic differences, the leaders of the two countries gained a better understanding of the other side's intentions to improve relations. This newly found mutual trust played an important role in the eventual improvement of Sino-Soviet relations. In fact, Sino-Soviet relations soon underwent some marked changes. In particular, Soviet policy gradually began to change.

The new Soviet leadership first adopted measures, albeit limited, to remove some of the Chinese strategic concerns, mainly in two respects. The first concerned security. Although the Soviet Union did not take actions to remove the "three major obstacles," it did not take any actions to escalate tensions. Second, the Soviet side made some symbolic gestures.

In the spring of 1983, the Soviet Union and the United States began a new round of negotiations on the reduction of intermediate-range missiles deployed in Europe. The international news media noted that China was paying close attention to these negotiations. China was concerned that once the Soviet Union reached an agreement with the United States, it would re-deploy intermediate-range missiles to the east of the Ural Mountains, thus putting more military pressure on China.[22] On 26 August, Andropov told *Pravda* that if the Soviet Union and the United States reached an agreement that was acceptable to both sides, the Soviet Union would reduce the missiles deployed in Europe and those missiles would be destroyed and not be re-deployed in other regions. This was to let the Chinese know that they did not have any reason to worry. Undoubtedly, this statement by Andropov played a positive role in alleviating Chinese concerns. The Chinese side expressed approval about this part of the interview: "In comparison with the previous Soviet stand insisting on moving the missiles from Europe to East Asia, this is a step forward."

In the same interview with *Pravda*, Andropov also discussed Sino-Soviet relations. He asserted that "certain positive trends have appeared" between the two countries, and the two sides can do a lot more in "further expanding trade, economic, and scientific cooperation as well as cultural and sports exchanges." On the issue of the "three major obstacles," Andropov said, "we still have some substantial differences with China on certain international issues and in our relations with other countries. Nevertheless, it is our firm belief that arrangements for Sino-Soviet relations should not harm any third country."

The *People's Daily* published excerpts of Andropov's interview on 28 August. This unusual move clearly indicated the importance Chinese leaders attached to the interview. However, the *People's Daily* did not publish the part of the interview on the "three major obstacles" and only summarized it as: "In the interview, Andropov did not mention the obstacles that exist in Sino-Soviet relations and still insisted on the so-called 'no harm to a third country' in considering Sino-Soviet relations." Deng Xiaoping, in a meeting with Senator Harry Jackson on 27 August, took a very negative position regarding this part of Andropov's interview, stating that Andropov's comment about Sino-Soviet negotiations not affecting "any third country" was tantamount to "negating the premise behind Sino-Soviet negotiations."

Chinese signals were neither clear nor consistent. On 2 September, Chinese President Li Xiannian, in a welcoming speech to Jordanian King Hussein, lauded Andropov for his expressed wish to improve Sino-Soviet relations. At the same time, President Li pointed out that "there are still some obstacles on the road to normalization." This was the first open response by a Chinese leader to Andropov's interview. TASS and major Soviet newspapers reported on Li's speech. It is quite possible that the Chinese government announced this official stand as a precursor for the forthcoming visit of Soviet Vice-Foreign Minister Kapitsa.

Kapitsa visited China from 8 to 16 September. The official explanation for the visit was that Kapitsa was preparing for the third round of the vice-ministerial political talks. This was the first time in 20 years that the Chinese government had officially invited a Soviet vice-minister to visit China. In view of his activities in Beijing and his farewell speech at the airport, Kapitsa's mission was very likely intended to explore the possibility of advancing Sino-Soviet relations on behalf of the new Soviet leadership, thus exceeding the scope of merely preparing for political talks. At the very least, this visit confirmed for both sides their mutual interest in promoting better relations. In a conversation with Kim Il Sung on 24 September, Deng made a major revision to his comment on Andropov's interview during the previous month. Deng alleged that Andropov had changed the Soviet stance regarding "a third country" in the matter of removing the "three major obstacles," from "not involving a third country" to "not harming a third country."

During this period, the level of political contacts between the two countries was steadily upgraded. After the formal talks between the two foreign ministers during Brezhnev's funeral, the two governments began to consider raising the level of contacts. One of the plans at the time was for the Chinese government to invite the first vice-chairman of the Council of Ministers of the Soviet Union, Ivan Arkhipov, to visit China. However, before Arkhipov could make this visit, the political situation in the Soviet Union took another turn when Andropov died on 9 February 1984. The Chinese government had known about Andropov's illness for some time and decided to send Vice-Premier Wan Li to attend Andropov's funeral. This decision once again raised the level of political exchanges between the two countries.

During his visit for the funeral, Wan Li held a long talk with Arkhipov, first vice-chairman of the Council of Ministers. This was the first meeting in 20 years between the two countries at the vice-premier level. The new Soviet leader Chernenko sent out a clear signal that the Soviets desired better relations. Through the Chinese embassy, the Soviets inquired whether Wan Li wished to meet Chernenko. Wan Li's reply was "a guest must suit the convenience of the host," which was interpreted by the Soviet side that the Chinese had no intention of meeting Chernenko, and consequently there was no follow-up. Higher-level contacts between the two countries could have been achieved the previous year, but owing to the misjudgment by the Chinese in their decision-making and execution, the opportunity was lost. Before the trip, Deng instructed the Chinese delegation not to initiate any meeting with the new Soviet leaders, but if the Soviet side proposed a meeting, then the delegation could accept the invitation and listen to what they had to say. In contrast to the more proactive orientation of the Huang Hua mission to Brezhnev's funeral, this time the Chinese appeared to be more cautious. On the one hand, this cautiousness may be due to the fact that the Chinese were less familiar with Chernenko, who had experience in handling European affairs but had never visited Asia. Chinese leaders had had very little contact with him and held the opinion that he was a mediocre leader and in poor health, hence "a transitional figure with no great potential." On the other hand, Beijing's cautiousness may also have reflected the Chinese leaders' thinking about how to proceed with Sino-Soviet normalization. In the previous month, the Chinese premier had just completed a visit to the United States, and China and the United States were in the middle of preparing for President Reagan's forthcoming April visit. Under these circumstances, it would be logical for Chinese leaders to attempt to control the speed of Sino-Soviet normalization.

From 21 to 29 December 1984, Ivan Arkhipov, first vice-chairman of the Council of Ministers of the Soviet Union, visited China and held talks with senior Chinese leaders. On 28 December, China and the Soviet Union signed three important documents—the Accord on Economic and Technical Cooperation, the Accord on Scientific Technological Cooperation, and the Accord on Establishing a Sino-Soviet Committee on Economic, Trade, and Science and Technology Cooperation. The two sides also agreed to negotiate a long-term trade agreement. In September 1984, the foreign ministers of the two countries, Wu Xueqian and Andrei Gromyko, held formal talks during the meeting of the United Nations General Assembly. Even though the meeting did not touch on any fundamental issues, it nevertheless inaugurated the third round of Sino-Soviet political negotiations. Beginning from this meeting, the foreign ministers of the two countries regularly met at the United Nations (UN), which served as a mechanism for maintaining contacts.

Another significant development occurred in 1983 when China began to improve and develop relations with the Eastern European countries, such as Poland, Hungry, Czechoslovakia, and Bulgaria. In 1986, Erich Honecker, the leader of the German Democratic Republic, and Wojciech Jaruzelski, the leader of Poland, visited China in succession, marking an overall improvement in China's relations with the Eastern European countries. It is possible that the Soviet Union anticipated that improved relations between China and the Eastern European countries could have a favorable impact on China's policy toward the Soviet Union.[23]

After the summer of 1982, the slowly evolving Sino-Soviet political relations created a favorable atmosphere for relaxation and improvements in bilateral relations. As China's reform and opening policy forged ahead, Beijing had a huge need to develop relations with the USSR in various other areas. In no time, this stimulated the restoration and development of exchanges and cooperation in trade, economics, science and technology, and culture between the two countries. During Arkhipov's second visit to China to attend the first session of the Sino-Soviet Committee on Economic, Trade, and Scientific and Technology Cooperation in March 1986, the two sides signed a Summary of the First Session of the Sino-Soviet Committee on Economic, Trade, and Science and Technology Cooperation and the Sino-Soviet Protocol on Conditions for Exchanging Engineering and Technical Personnel. These agreements promoted the further development of Sino-Soviet economic and trade relations. A major development in connection with the overall progress in economic and trade relations was the resumption and development of regional trade between Northeast China and the eastern border regions of the Soviet Union. In greeting the relaxation of bilateral relations and the strong demand for opening up border trade in the Northeast, which had undergone significant reforms, the Chinese leadership was more willing to support the development of border trade between the two countries.

In retrospect, Sino-Soviet bilateral relations, in the form of economic, scientific and technological, cultural, and personnel exchanges, were quickly restored and gained momentum after 1983. The stalemate in the political and strategic security arenas did not hinder the development of trade and economic cooperation. On the contrary, increasing cooperation between the two countries in other areas actually accentuated the stagnant and irrational political relations and hence created pressure for an effective solution to the political dilemmas between China and the USSR.

NOTES

1. Xinhua, "On Leonid Brezhnev's Speech in Tashkent," 26 March 1982, in *FBIS-China*, 29 March 1982, p. C1.
2. Qian Qichen, *Ten Episodes in China's Diplomacy* (New York: HarperCollins, 2005), p. 2.
3. Huang Hua, Memoirs (Beijing: Foreign Languages Press, 2008), p. 499.
4. Ibid.
5. Deng Xiaoping, "The Present Situation and the Tasks Before Us," 16 January 1980, *Selected Works of Deng Xiaoping 1975–1982* (Beijing: Foreign Languages Press, 1984), pp. 224–25.
6. Deng Xiaoping, "Our Principled Position on the Development of Sino-American Relations," 4 January 1981, at https://dengxiaopingworks.wordpress.com/2013/02/25/our-principled-position-on-the-development-of-sino-u-s-relations/. Accessed 7 January 2019.
7. Qian, *Ten Episodes in China's Diplomacy*, pp. 3–4.
8. "Message to Compatriots on Taiwan," 1 January 1977, *Beijing Review* 22, no 1 (5 January 1979): 16–17.
9. Huang, *Memoirs*, p. 501; Qian Qichen, *Ten Episodes in China's Diplomacy*, pp. 5–6.
10. Qian, *Ten Episodes in China's Diplomacy*, p. 11.
11. Ibid., pp. 7–12.
12. Huang, *Memoirs*, pp. 502–503.
13. Ibid., p. 504.
14. Ibid., p. 505.
15. Ibid., p. 506.
16. Qian, *Ten Episodes in China's Diplomacy*, p. 14.
17. Huang, *Memoirs*, p. 509.
18. Ibid., pp. 514–15.
19. Qian, *Ten Episodes in China's Diplomacy*, pp. 5–7.
20. Ibid., pp. 9–10.
21. Huang, *Memoirs*, pp. 512–16.
22. *New York Times*, 2 March 1983.
23. "China-Eastern Europe Relations," in Wilson Center Digital Archive: International History Declassified, at https://digitalarchive.wilsoncenter.org/collection/501/china-eastern-europe-relations. Accessed 13 January 2019.

CHAPTER 22

The Turning Point in "Normalization"

Jun Niu

Breaking the Political Deadlock

In the fall of 1985, the Chinese leadership made a major decision on the so-called three major obstacles, turning the period into a landmark year on the path to Sino-Soviet normalization. Based on indirect documentary evidence recently published in China, it was in the spring of 1985 that Deng Xiaoping once again began to pay attention to this issue. On 18 April, when talking with former British Prime Minister Edward Heath, Deng indicated that in order to remove the "three major obstacles," the Soviets should first persuade Vietnam to withdraw its troops from Cambodia. Deng reasoned that "it should be relatively easy and less costly for the Soviets to get the Vietnamese out of Cambodia." This was the first time that Deng had expressed such an idea.

As discussed earlier, the Chinese side had put forward this proposal during the first round of political talks at the vice-ministerial level. Later, in bilateral discussions at various levels, the Chinese side again mentioned this idea, though phrased differently. This seems to indicate that initially the idea was not necessarily finalized nor did it constitute a strategic priority. When Deng discussed the "three major obstacles," he put a priority on the massive deployment of Soviet troops along the Sino-Soviet and Sino-Mongolian borders. Although suggesting that the Soviet side might take steps to remove the "three major obstacles," Deng did not indicate that a certain order had to be followed. Therefore, when Deng spoke about this to Heath, the thinking of the Chinese leadership must have changed. Of course, these deductions from indirect evidence cannot be verified until the relevant archives are declassified.

J. Niu (✉)
School of International Studies, Beijing University, Beijing, China
e-mail: niujunpku@gmail.com

© The Author(s) 2020
Z. Shen (ed.), *A Short History of Sino-Soviet Relations, 1917–1991*,
China Connections, https://doi.org/10.1007/978-981-13-8641-1_22

367

In March 1985, Mikhail Gorbachev became the new Soviet leader. At the conference of the Communist Party of the Soviet Union (CPSU) Central Committee (CC) where he was elected party general secretary, Gorbachev indicated that the Soviet Union hoped to "significantly improve our relations with the PRC and it is also our view that as long as the two sides are willing, this can be done." The Chinese side reacted quickly by sending Vice-Premier Li Peng to Moscow to attend the funeral of Gorbachev's predecessor, Konstantin Chernenko. The Chinese leadership decided that at a proper time, Li Peng should talk to Gorbachev. According to Li Peng's diary, on the evening of 12 March, on his way from the airport to his hotel, Li told Igor Rogachev, chief of the First Far East Department of the Soviet Ministry of Foreign Affairs (MFA), that he had an important message for the Soviet leadership.

In the afternoon of 14 March, Li met with Gorbachev and other Soviet leaders. During their conversation, Gorbachev suggested that any improvement in Sino-Soviet relations should not be limited to economics; rather, political relations should be discussed as well. He also proposed elevating the bilateral dialogue to a higher level. Li replied that even though the two countries were no longer allies, they could become good neighbors and good friends. Other Chinese participants later recalled that Gorbachev also expressed his hope for a "major improvement" in Sino-Soviet relations. Li Peng wrote in his diary that this meeting did not produce any substantive consensus. Actually, in contrast to the talks by his predecessors, there is nothing worth mentioning about Gorbachev's talks with Li except the meeting itself, which can be interpreted as a continuation from the Yuri Andropov period of a proactive policy toward China. Subsequent developments reveal that not only did the China policy toward the Union of Soviet Socialist Republics (USSR) not undergo any major changes but the Chinese side did not make any new moves toward the USSR. Based on the timeline, Deng's conversation with Heath in April may be seen as a response to Gorbachev's gesture in hoping for a better relationship.

It was in the fall of the same year that Chinese leaders finally took a meaningful step. On 9 October, Deng asked Romanian President Nicolae Ceauşescu, who was visiting China, to carry an oral message to Gorbachev: regarding the issue of the "three major obstacles," if a credible understanding could be reached by the two sides about a Vietnamese withdrawal from Cambodia, he personally or General Secretary Hu Yaobang would agree to hold a summit meeting with Gorbachev. Deng said that he would even be willing to go to Moscow to meet with Gorbachev. Deng's message indicated two important changes in Chinese policy. First, Soviet persuasion of the Vietnamese to withdraw from Cambodia was now directly linked to Sino-Soviet normalization. Second, a favorable Soviet decision to settle the issue of the Vietnamese invasion of Cambodia would be rewarded with a visit to Moscow by the Chinese top leader. A first Sino-Soviet summit in 30 years would be desirable to any politician with an ambition for greatness and, given his personality, especially someone like Gorbachev.

In making a Vietnamese withdrawal from Cambodia the first and even the sole precondition for Sino-Soviet normalization, the Chinese leadership demonstrated its eagerness to pacify China's southern frontiers. This is also evidence of Beijing's conviction at the time that the Soviet military presence along China's borders with Mongolia and the Soviet Union was no longer a threat to Chinese security. At the very least, Chinese leaders no longer believed that the Soviets wished to invade China. Therefore, from the perspective of Chinese security, the "Soviet threat" had been downgraded.

By arranging visits by Chinese and Soviet leaders as a symbol of Sino-Soviet normalization, Deng provided Gorbachev with a concrete and desirable reward. Gorbachev's position as the new Soviet leader would be significantly consolidated if he were to accomplish a meaningful improvement in Sino-Soviet relations. Simply put, Deng's message to Gorbachev actually reduced the "three major obstacles" to just one obstacle, that is, Soviet willingness to put pressure on Vietnam to withdraw from Cambodia. This obvious and major change in the Chinese position indicates that the Chinese leaders intentionally hoped to use the issue of Sino-Soviet normalization to end the conflict in Indochina.

The reason for such a drastic shift in Chinese policy requires a careful explanation. As Sino-Soviet relations were steadily improving, the Chinese leadership felt it was necessary to stress the political significance of normalization to avert any marginalization of its strategic concerns over the issue of the "three major obstacles." Gorbachev's wish to improve bilateral relations was certainly a factor. Nevertheless, the most important stimulus behind Beijing's resolution to take steps to readjust its Soviet policy came from within China. These included the evolution of China's economic development strategy and especially the leap in the Chinese leaders' thinking about important international issues at the time. Since 1978, the Chinese leadership had carefully deliberated these issues and, by the summer of 1985, the cumulative result of such deliberations was a sea change in policy.

In the mid-1980s, Deng put forward the view that peace and development were the two major themes in the world.[1] This was a drastic departure from Beijing's understanding of the characteristics of the "times," negating the official view about the issue of "the times" long held by the Chinese Communist Party (CCP). In connection to this cognitive change and in the wake of the downsizing of the administrative structure of the People's Liberation Army (PLA) in 1983, in the spring and summer of 1984 the Chinese leadership began to consider implementing a plan to reduce the size of the PLA by about one million troops. On 1 November, when announcing this decision at a meeting of the CCP Central Military Commission (CMC), Deng outlined the newly formed view that a "world war could not possibly break out in our times."

Between 23 May and 6 June 1985, the CMC called an enlarged meeting to discuss implementation of the plan to cut one million troops. In view of the content and scale of the meeting, preparations probably had begun before March 1985, the month when Gorbachev took power. The meeting adopted three vitally significant decisions: (1) construction of national defense would defer to the needs of economic construction, meaning that the portion of military expenses in the state budget would be further reduced; (2) one million PLA troops would be cut; and (3) the orientation of the anti-Soviet international united front in Chinese foreign policy would be dropped, and the idea of a "Sino-Soviet-U.S. strategic triangle" would no longer serve as the basis of China's foreign policy making.

During the meeting, Deng explained some of the new conclusions reached by Chinese leaders during the past several years. These conclusions, along with the decisions taken at the meeting, would have an impact on China's Soviet policy in the years to come. When speaking with some officials on 4 June, Deng pointed out that after careful observations and deliberations, China's policy making had accomplished "two important transformations." The first transformation was to "change the old view that the danger of war was imminent." These words can also be reasonably extended to an understanding that the Soviet threat was not as serious as previously perceived. The second transformation was to abandon the policy of an anti-Soviet international united front and to approach Chinese foreign policy making from the framework of a "Sino-Soviet-U.S. strategic triangle."[2]

Deng's talk at the meeting was a profoundly significant historical event which marked China's withdrawal from the Cold War. Ever since China's fundamental shift in its strategy at the Third Plenary Session of the Eleventh CC, Chinese foreign policy had been caught in a contradiction between two goals. As was said at the time, Chinese foreign policy must at once "serve the strategy of dispersing the present threat and opposing hegemonism as well as the strategic goal of creating a peaceful and stable international environment for the realization of modernization." Thereafter, Chinese leaders repeatedly made statements to international society, including the USSR, that China had already abandoned its anti-Soviet international united front as the strategic goal of its foreign policy, and it hoped to improve relations with the USSR based on a pluralistic global political order. For example, during his visit to Moscow to attend Chernenko's funeral, Li Peng unequivocally told Soviet leaders that China had "changed" its anti-Soviet international united front policy. This would give China more "room to maneuver." When meeting with Austrian President Rudolf Kirchschläger, Deng admitted that in his later years, Mao Zedong's judgments about the international situation "were not without flaws."

Another noteworthy development at the time was that the Chinese leadership had basically completed its modernization plan that aimed to bring China to the level of a moderately developed country by the middle of the twenty-first century. To achieve this goal, Deng said that "China would need a long period of peace to realize their full modernization."[3] Very likely, this consideration about the future played a key role in Deng's determination to make fundamental changes to China's national security strategy and its foreign policy. It represented a fundamental paradigm shift, and, as shown by later developments, it could not but have a significant impact on the deliberations by the Chinese leadership on Sino-Soviet relations.

Aside from these changes within China, the evolution of Sino-US relations and the changes taking place in Indochina were also important factors. First, the transformation and development of Sino-US relations during this period had some complicated effects. In January and April 1984, the leaders of the two countries exchanged state visits. Chinese leaders took advantage of these high-level exchanges to push the US government to make further commitments regarding the Taiwan question, hoping to create a more relaxed political atmosphere for further development of Sino-American relations. After President Reagan visited China from 16 April to 1 May, the Sino-US relationship entered a period of comprehensive growth. In particular, military cooperation between the two countries made unprecedented progress. As Qian Qichen reasons in his memoir, stable growth in Sino-US relations would convince Chinese leaders that China was in a favorable strategic position and would be able to more actively and confidently pursue Sino-Soviet normalization.[4]

However, the actual influence of Sino-US relations on the way in which Beijing handled its relations with the USSR is not quite so simple. Chinese leaders did indeed believe that stabilization and the rapid expansion of Sino-American relations would create favorable conditions for dealing with the Soviets. They became confident that China could more actively take an initiative in dealing with the USSR. Yet the growth of Sino-American relations also put strains on how Beijing dealt with the Soviets, and it also necessitated unhurried policies. In reality, Chinese leaders mainly sought strategic benefits from Sino-Soviet normalization because the Soviets could not offer much for China's economic development. Thus, a rushed settlement with the Soviets would risk damaging Sino-US relations. This is why Chinese leaders repeatedly explained to the Americans that Sino-Soviet relations could not possibly be reversed to the situation in the 1950s; China would never again forge an alliance with the Soviet Union, and China was not attempting to balancing between the United States and the Soviet Union.

The reorientation of Chinese foreign policy in the summer of 1985 also reflected a readjustment of Beijing's Indochina policy. The main purpose of the policy readjustment was to "pacify the southern frontier," aiming to end the Vietnamese invasion of Cambodia as quickly as possible and to restore peace and stability in the region. This goal was consistent with the needs of China's economic development strategy. China could not possibly make an all-out effort to pursue its modernization goals, while risking being dragged into an endless war in Indochina. The strategic idea behind "pacifying the southern frontier" was directly related to Chinese leaders' attitude toward the "three major obstacles." In asking Ceaușescu to convey his oral massage to Gorbachev, Deng was attempting to show Beijing's eagerness to swiftly resolve the Indochina problem. After all, the border conflicts between China and Vietnam were continuing. This situation not only interfered with Chinese economic development but also, because of the complexity of the Cambodian issue, put China in a position that could only damage its international prestige.

China was not alone in making policy readjustments. In the summer of 1985, the situation in Indochina also changed significantly. Vietnam was suffering from serious economic and other difficulties because of its war in Cambodia. Vietnamese leaders began to express a willingness to settle the Cambodian issue via diplomatic and political means. The international press at the time was rather pessimistic about economic and political conditions in Vietnam, suggesting that its invasion of Cambodia had already made Vietnam "the poorest country" in the world. Even before the death of General Secretary Le Duan in 1986, the Vietnamese Communist Party CC had begun to reexamine and criticize Le Duan's economic policies. Serious grievances and contradictions were obviously on the rise inside the Vietnamese Communist Party. The dead end in Cambodia, compounded by the improvement in Sino-Soviet relations, compelled Vietnamese leaders to publicly consider relaxing relations with China.

On 25 March 1985, Vietnam issued a five-point proposal for a political settlement of the Cambodian issue. Although not a real breakthrough, the proposal nevertheless contained some new expressions on the key issue of a Vietnamese military departure from Cambodia. At the time, all countries concerned appraised the proposal negatively for failing to make any breakthrough. However, it is noteworthy that the Vietnamese made the proposal two weeks after Chernenko's death. The real significance of the proposal was possibly to make a gesture to the new Soviet leaders. During the second half of June, Le Duan visited Moscow to solidify relations with the new Soviet leaders. At a welcoming banquet, Gorbachev went so far as to say that the Soviet Union and Vietnam both wanted to normalize relations with China, believing that this would contribute to regional and world peace. Willingly or not, Le Duan also expressed the hope that the "traditional friendship and normal neighborly relationship" between Vietnam and China would be restored. Information available does not reveal what role the Soviets played in encouraging Le Duan to make this statement on Sino-Vietnamese relations. At a press conference on 28 June, a spokesperson for the Soviet MFA stated that during their talks, the Soviet and Vietnamese leaders "touched upon the issue of Sino-Soviet relations," and they had agreed that normalization of Sino-Soviet and Sino-Vietnamese relations "will help enhance peace in Asia and international security." Le Duan's visit concluded with a Soviet-Vietnamese communiqué that expressed a similar idea. However, it is reasonable to assume that Gorbachev expected that the Vietnamese leaders would not fall out of step with Moscow in dealing with China.

All these developments indicate that Deng's oral message of 9 October was not a simple negotiating tactic. At the very least, Deng carefully deliberated the issues, including making some significant readjustments to his strategic considerations. In dealing with the USSR, Chinese leaders began to shift their focus from removal of the so-called Soviet threat to Chinese security to an all-out effort to settle the Indochina issue. By improving its relationship with the USSR, China was seeking to improve its strategic interests in Indochina, which included a complete thwarting of Vietnamese expansionist ambitions and creating favorable conditions for eliminating tensions in the region. This clearly demonstrates that in its normalization efforts with Moscow, Beijing had already narrowed its main objective to tangible and regional strategic interests.

Objectively, the logic for China to utilize Sino-Soviet normalization to force a Vietnamese withdrawal from Cambodia was the extremely complex and difficult Cambodian issue. The problems that China would have to deal with regarding political arrangements in Cambodia after a Vietnamese withdrawal would come not only from the USSR and Vietnam. Such linkages reflected Beijing's consideration of its strategic interests. Among a range of factors affecting Sino-Soviet normalization, the Cambodian issue became increasingly important, even to the point of determining the progress in Sino-Soviet normalization. Yet Moscow did not have absolute control over the Cambodian situation. Therefore, Beijing had to decide to what extent Soviet efforts on this issue would be acceptable for the Chinese to agree to a Sino-Soviet summit and, at the same time, to still leave room for Beijing's future maneuvering. It also depended on the Chinese leaders' evaluation of the problem at different times.

CHANGE OF POLICY IN MOSCOW

As recorded in the *Chronicle of the Life of Deng Xiaoping*, during a meeting in Bulgaria on 22 October, Ceauşescu delivered Deng's message to Gorbachev, and Gorbachev promised to give it serious consideration. Due to the situation in Sino-Soviet relations at the time, Beijing could not have immediately learned of this development. It is also possible that even if Chinese leaders had received this information, they would not have been satisfied with Gorbachev's noncommittal response. In an interview published in the 4 November issue of *Time* magazine, Deng discussed the solution to the "three major obstacles" in a certain order.[5] Very likely because of such an open reaction by the Chinese leadership, two days later the Soviet government informed Beijing that Deng's message had been received.[6] Soon thereafter, the Soviets suggested that a summit meeting should be held in a certain location in the Far East. The way in which Moscow responded to Deng's message and Beijing's continuation of its stance on the "three major obstacles" seem to indicate that Gorbachev was not yet ready to take substantial steps to improve relations with China.

On 23 December 1985, Li Peng passed through Moscow after a visit to Europe. The Soviet side proposed an impromptu meeting between Gorbachev and Li. Since such a meeting had not been planned, Li Peng asked for instructions from Beijing. Li Peng himself was inclined to accept the Soviet proposal, but the MFA was rather passive about the meeting. Finally, General Secretary Hu Yaobang gave a green light for a courtesy call. In an afternoon meeting on the same day, Gorbachev first told Li that he had received Deng's message and he had returned a positive reply. He then outlined Soviet policy toward China, which Li summarized in two points: first, the USSR would continue its efforts to seek normalization with China, and second, the Soviet government hoped to "stand on the same frontline" with China in international affairs. In response, Li clarified the Chinese attitude, saying that China wanted to develop friendly relations with Western countries and could not possibly forge a united front with the Soviet Union. He pointed out that the key to improved Sino-Soviet relations at the time was resolution of the Cambodian issue and that "all problems between the two countries can be discussed if the Soviet Union will press Vietnam to withdraw its troops from Cambodia." The two sides once again clearly failed to reach a consensus on a settlement of the Cambodian issue.

From the perspective of the characteristics and process of Chinese decision-making, the aftermath of Li's unplanned summit was not necessarily all positive. Based on Deng's consistent decision-making style, he presumably would not support such an impromptu move, which potentially could lead to a derailment of China's Soviet policy. After all, if the summit could be arranged so easily, it could have an unforeseen consequence of shifting China's strategic focus and easing the pressure on the USSR. What happened thereafter reveals that Moscow overstated the meeting, immediately attracting international attention and speculation. The Chinese response was swift and unequivocal. Chinese Foreign Minister Wu Xueqian soon issued a public statement: "Since the existing obstacles between the two countries have yet to be removed, there has not been any substantial improvement in Sino-Soviet political relations."

During his meeting with Li Peng, Gorbachev disclosed that he was not in a position to take major actions to improve bilateral relations due to the tremendous difficulties he faced at home. Some Chinese participants at the meeting later recalled that during the two-hour meeting, Gorbachev mainly talked about two issues: improvement of Sino-Soviet relations and domestic reforms in the Soviet Union. He "spent a considerable amount of time discussing the situation in the Soviet Union" and the difficulties that the reforms had encountered. In examining his remarks, it can be assumed that Gorbachev was seeking to tell the Chinese that he sincerely wanted to improve bilateral relations (or possibly that he favored holding a summit with Chinese leaders), but at the time he was preoccupied with domestic issues. The conclusion that Chinese drew from their understanding of Gorbachev's talk was that domestic conditions in the USSR were not quite ready for a change in Soviet policy toward China. In his July visit to the United States, Li Peng shared his impression of Gorbachev with Vice-President Bush, stating that whether Gorbachev was capable of "consolidating his power" awaited further observation.

In February 1986, the CPSU held its Twenty-seventh Congress. In his political report, Gorbachev indicated that the Soviet Army would leave Afghanistan. With respect to Sino-Soviet relations, he merely reiterated the goal of seeking bilateral improvements without taking any new initiatives. In the wake of the Soviet party congress, the CCP CC called a meeting to evaluate its substance. At this meeting, Li Peng suggested that the USSR had only taken a small step in improving Sino-Soviet relations and it had not accepted Chinese conditions for resolving the Indochina question. As Qian Qichen remembers, at this time the political discussions between China and the Soviet Union had not made any substantial progress in resolving the "three major obstacles." Nevertheless, the Twenty-seventh CPSU Congress was important for the later reorientation of Soviet policy toward China. Gorbachev's power was consolidated and his reform measures were endorsed. Such developments proved to be vitally important for the changes in Soviet foreign policy in the years to come.

Soon after the Soviet party congress, the situation in Indochina changed dramatically. In particular, Vietnam issued a timetable to remove its troops from Cambodia. On 4 March, Polish newspapers published an interview with Nguyễn Dy Niên, first vice-foreign minister of Vietnam. Nguyễn revealed that Vietnamese troops would leave Cambodia before 1990, or even earlier, regardless of the continued presence of some remnants of the Pol Pot regime. This was the first time since its invasion of Cambodia that the Vietnamese government unofficially set a timetable for its military departure without predicating it on elimination of the Khmer Rouge. Furthermore, on 10 March, the Vietnamese MFA issued a "Memorandum on China's Hostile Anti-Vietnamese Policy," accusing China of ignoring Vietnam's stated position that it "will withdraw all its troops from Cambodia by 1990 or even earlier if a political settlement can be reached." The Vietnamese authorities thereby formally declared a timetable for their military departure. Soon thereafter, the foreign ministry of the Heng Samrin regime in Cambodia indicated that a political settlement of the Cambodian issue could be reached within two years at the most. The connection between the Twenty-seventh CPSU Congress and the change in Vietnamese policy requires careful exploration, which may help fully evaluate Gorbachev's China policy in particular and his foreign policy in general. However, this must await further declassification of the Soviet archives.

The various sides immediately responded positively to the change in Vietnamese policy. Representatives from the three sides of the Coalition Government of Democratic Kampuchea (CGDK) held a meeting in Beijing and produced an "eight-point proposal" for a political settlement of the Cambodian issue. The most important item was the proposal for direct Vietnamese-CGDK negotiations on the issue of a Vietnamese withdrawal. According to this proposal, the withdrawal could be implemented in two phases: the first phase would lead to talks between the CGDK and the Heng Samrin regime, and completion of the second phase would result in a quadrilateral coalition government headed by Prince Sihanouk. Thus, the post-Vietnam political arrangement in Cambodia would not exclude the regime currently supported by Hanoi. It is, of course, unimaginable that the CGDK could have made such a landmark decision without Beijing's endorsement. On 18 March, the same day that the CGDK put forward its eight points, Hu Yaobang met with CGDK leaders. Hu hailed the eight points as an expression of "not only the interests of the entire Cambodian nation but also a far-sighted orientation for eliminating the hotspots of war in Southeast Asia and enhancing peace and stability in the region." Therefore, "it is also a very generous proposal that is mindful of the interests of the Vietnamese people." Hu Yaobang's comments openly committed Beijing to accepting the CGDK proposal.

At the same meeting, Hu Yaobang also spoke about Sino-Vietnamese relations. He pledged that China did not harbor any "bad ideas" toward Vietnam, and "as long as Vietnamese troops leave Cambodia, the traditional friendship between China and Vietnam can be restored." This can be understood as an indication that Beijing would be willing to participate in the process of settling the Cambodian issue according to the CGDK proposal, including making contacts with Vietnam and improving relations with Vietnam in the future. On 22 April, the 25th anniversary of the establishment of Sino-Laos diplomatic relations, the Chinese government took an initiative to improve relations with Laos. This improvement would thereafter assume some momentum. In June 1988, the two governments restored diplomatic relations at the ambassadorial level and normalized bilateral relations. Therefore, the spring of 1986 represented a starting point for a general relaxation of the Indochina situation.

These developments constituted the basic background for a readjustment of Soviet policy toward China. On 28 July 1988, in a speech in Vladivostok, Gorbachev spoke at some length about Sino-Soviet relations. Regarding the question of the Soviet military presence in Mongolia, Gorbachev stated that "Soviet and Mongolian leaders are considering withdrawing a considerable portion of Soviet troops from Mongolia." He also indicated a desire to develop cooperation with China in various areas, an understanding and respect for China's domestic policies, and a willingness to negotiate with China regarding the border disputes along the Amur River to support the principle that "the border line follow the main tributary of the river." In implying a willingness to consider a reduction of Soviet forces along the Chinese border, he asserted that the "Soviet Union regards it extremely significant to reduce the armed forces and conventional weapons in Asia to a reasonable size," and "is willing to discuss with the PRC concrete steps to downsize the army." Regarding Cambodia, Gorbachev admitted that the Khmer people had suffered enormously and, like many other issues in Southeast Asia, the future "depended on normalization of Sino-Vietnamese relations." He also indicated that the USSR would be "willing to withdraw its troops from Afghanistan upon a request from the Afghan government." Indeed, these points answered nearly all of Beijing's concerns.

Soon after Gorbachev's speech, the USSR began to implement its promises regarding a military withdrawal from Mongolia and Afghanistan. Yet Moscow did not take any meaningful steps to press the Vietnamese to leave Cambodia. Gorbachev's speech clearly indicated that Moscow was unwilling to continue its support of Vietnam's endless war in Cambodia, which had cost the USSR both economically and politically. However, despite the Chinese suggestion, Moscow did not want to pressure Hanoi. In treating the situation in Cambodia as a regional issue, Gorbachev said that a solution depended on normalization of Sino-Vietnamese relations. This policy choice on the part of the Soviets involved careful calculations in Moscow. On the one hand, the Soviet leadership was not yet ready, and actually unable, to cajole Hanoi into withdrawing its troops from Cambodia. On the other hand, given the importance that Beijing attached to the Cambodian issue, the Soviets wanted to at least show a positive attitude toward improving Sino-Soviet relations. In April of that year, at the eighth round of the Sino-Soviet political talks at the vice-ministerial level, the Soviet side had suggested that the Cambodian issue could be regarded as a regional conflict and a solution could be discussed with China. Gorbachev's speech followed the same logic whereby the Cambodian issue was a regional conflict, and its resolution involved the major countries directly involved, that is, China and Vietnam.

While appreciating Gorbachev's sincerity about improving Sino-Soviet relations, Chinese leaders believed that his speech obscured the core issues in the bilateral discord and did not completely satisfy China's geostrategic concerns. In a word, the priority in China's geostrategic concerns was no longer the "massive Soviet troops amassed along the border," but a Vietnamese withdrawal from Cambodia and a thorough elimination of the origins of the tensions in Indochina. In the Chinese view, any improvement in Sino-Soviet relations had to also enhance China's strategic interests in Indochina. Just at this time, the death of General Secretary Le Duan strengthened China's position. On 13 August, Chinese Foreign Minister Wu Xueqian summoned the Soviet chargé d'affaires and relayed China's unhappiness that Gorbachev had overlooked the issue of a Vietnamese withdrawal from Cambodia, which was the central point in Deng's message delivered via Ceauşescu.[7] On 2 September, during an interview with American journalist Mike Wallace, Deng professed that if the USSR could urge Vietnam to "take solid steps" in the direction of withdrawing from Vietnam, he would be willing to meet with Gorbachev.[8] At about the same time, the leaders of the CGDK made an official visit to China and held a cabinet meeting in Beijing. The meeting proclaimed that the CGDK would insist that the Vietnamese accepted its eight-point proposal as the basis for negotiations. The Chinese government immediately expressed support for this position.

By the summer of 1986, Sino-Soviet relations had turned for the better. With the exception of the Cambodian issue, the two sides had reached agreement on all other issues. In particular, the Soviet side had already begun to remove two of the "three major obstacles" named by the Chinese. As a superpower that had to deal with complex issues in the Asia-Pacific region and in the world, the USSR took these steps not merely out of consideration of the Chinese factor. Nevertheless, such policy steps contributed to confidence-building between Beijing and Moscow and further relaxed Chinese anxieties about a "Soviet threat." As Chinese leaders became more confident, they became more proactive in promoting improvements in Sino-Soviet relations and even more willing to make concessions on certain issues.

Removal of the Last Obstacle

In February 1987, Sino-Soviet relations took a major step forward during the first round of border negotiations held in Moscow. After Gorbachev's Vladivostok speech, the Chinese side immediately agreed to reopen the border

negotiations. In August 1986, Foreign Minister Wu Xueqian had already proposed to the Soviet side that the talks, which had been suspended for nine years,
be resumed. In September, during a United Nations (UN) conference, the foreign ministers of the two countries reached agreement on resuming the border
talks in Moscow during the following February. Thus, in February 1987,
Chinese Vice-Foreign Minister Qian Qichen and his Soviet counterpart, Igor
Rogachev, led their respective delegations in the border negotiations. The Soviet
side showed a positive attitude toward the talks. Mikhail Kapitsa, director of the
Institute of Oriental Studies of the Soviet Academy of Sciences, said on a Soviet
television program that a settlement of the Sino-Soviet border dispute was
"extremely important" for bringing the two sides closer with respect to issues
such as Cambodia and Afghanistan. The border talks began in a friendly and
pragmatic atmosphere, and neither side wanted to bog down the talks over historical grievances. They agreed to first untangle the eastern border disputes.
Treaties and international conventions demarcating the boundaries would be
used, and the agreements reached by the two sides in 1964 would remain in
effect. Thereafter, the border talks alternated between being held in Beijing and
in Moscow. Agreements were reached on the demarcation of most of the eastern border and also on the principles for demarcating the western border.[9]

In May, the Soviet position on the Cambodian issue began to show signs of
change. On 13 May, in concluding the tenth round of Sino-Soviet political
discussions, Soviet Vice-Foreign Minister Rogachev reiterated Gorbachev's
position that the Cambodian issue would be discussed with China as a regional
rather than a bilateral issue. He nevertheless indicated that the USSR was ready
to "provide whatever assistance possible for a settlement of the Cambodian
situation." Meanwhile, he said that the Khmer Rouge should not be included
in a future political settlement; this was not only a Soviet condition but also an
international desire. One day earlier, Gorbachev had met with Bulgarian leader
Todor Zhivkov who brought yet another message from the Chinese leadership.
On 23 May, when talking with *L'Unità*, the organ of the Italian Communist
Party, Gorbachev expressed his new thinking on foreign affairs. For the first
time, he discussed the Cambodian issue as part of Sino-Soviet normalization,
suggesting that both sides should pay attention to the Cambodian issue and a
resolution could only be achieved through political means.

There were obvious reciprocal interactions between Soviet and Chinese
leaders, and Gorbachev's talk was a response to a Chinese message. In early
May, when Zhivkov visited China, Chinese Premier Zhao Ziyang asked him to
convey to Gorbachev the following message: a Vietnamese withdrawal is the
key to resolving the Cambodian question; Cambodian domestic politics after a
Vietnamese departure will have to be decided upon by the Cambodian people
themselves; and although not supporting any faction to monopolize political
power, China hoped that Prince Sihanouk could head a coalition government.
In indicating that China would not support the Khmer Rouge to control
Cambodia after a Vietnamese withdrawal, the Chinese leadership was
responding positively to Soviet and international concerns. When speaking

with Zhivkov, Deng said that mutual misgivings between the Chinese and Soviet parties "should be written off with one stroke and all matters should be forward-looking." On 11 May, Deng asked visiting UN Secretary General Pérez de Cuéllar to deliver a Chinese proposal to the Vietnamese: (1) Cambodian domestic politics and any individual's mistakes could not justify aggression against Cambodia, and Vietnam must withdraw its troops from Cambodia and end the war; (2) after a Vietnamese withdrawal, the four sides in Cambodia should decide the future of their country; (3) China would support a quadrilateral coalition government under Prince Sihanouk and did not want the Khmer Rouge to take power; and (4) Sino-Vietnamese relations could be normalized only after the Cambodian issue was settled. Beijing thus clearly indicated the extent to which it was willing to compromise over Cambodia.

The change in Soviet foreign policy had more profound origins than merely interactions with China. It was a consequence of Gorbachev's "new diplomatic thinking." After the Twenty-seventh CPSU Congress, Gorbachev's leading position became increasingly solidified, which enabled him to put forward, in the name of his "new thinking," systematic ideas for reforms, including new perspectives on world politics and new conceptions of Soviet foreign policy. Guided by such "new thinking," Gorbachev carried out a large-scale foreign policy readjustment and a reshuffling of personnel in the MFA. By 1986, these readjustments had been largely completed. As a result of these changes, in 1987 the world witnessed a relaxation and continued improvement in Soviet-US relations, a Soviet-US agreement on mid-range missiles, which was approved by the Supreme Soviet, the Geneva Accords on settlement of the situation in Afghanistan, reached by the United States, the Soviet Union, and other countries, as well as Soviet-US discussions over settlement of the Cambodian issue in talks on regional conflicts.

However, these policy readjustments intensified the existing disagreements between Moscow and Hanoi. The Soviet media began to publicly indicate its discontent. In early August, both *Pravda* and *Izvestia* openly criticized the Vietnamese government for failing to use Soviet assistance more effectively and for the unsatisfactory situation in Soviet-Vietnamese trade. Under these circumstances, there were sufficient incentives to bring about a change in the Soviet position on Cambodia. Information provided by the MFA reveals that it was from this point on that the Soviet government began to seek a serious political resolution to the situation in Cambodia and a way out of the Indochina conflict.

Yet Gorbachev in his Vladivostok speech had already announced the priority of Soviet policy in the Asia-Pacific region, that is, Soviet departure from Afghanistan before considering the Cambodian issue. The reason was simple: the situation in Afghanistan was much more serious for the Soviet Union than the situation in Cambodia, and it could be decided by Moscow alone. Therefore, although the Soviets repeatedly professed their position toward Cambodia, they were slow in taking any real action. At the time, Vietnam insisted on linking its withdrawal from Cambodia with denying the Khmer Rouge any position in a new Cambodian government. Moscow was unable, or unwilling, to persuade Hanoi to de-link the two issues. On 16 November, when receiving a delegation from the Japanese Social Democratic Party led by Takako Doi, Deng once again said that if the Soviet Union was willing to act on the Cambodian issue, he would be willing to meet with Gorbachev in any location in the Soviet Union. On 27 November, in his meeting with Zambian leader Kenneth Kaunda, who was on friendly terms with Beijing, Gorbachev told his guest that he had noted Deng's conversation with the Japanese delegation and he was looking forward to meeting with Deng in Beijing, Moscow, or any other location. Yet Gorbachev insisted that the Chinese should not establish any "preconditions." This was the first time that Gorbachev openly responded to the Chinese suggestion for a summit meeting.

The Soviets, however, did not take meaningful steps in such a direction until after the Geneva agreement regarding Afghanistan was reached among the Soviet Union, the United States, Pakistan, and Afghanistan in April 1988. At the time, the United States appeared to be coordinating with China and urging Moscow to act. On 24 May, before going to Moscow to meet Gorbachev, President Reagan publicly demanded that Vietnam provide a "timetable for a rapid withdrawal from Cambodia." He urged the Soviet government to play an active role in promoting a Vietnamese withdrawal from Cambodia, and he indicated that he would discuss this issue with Soviet leaders during his visit.

On 23 May, Soviet Foreign Minister Eduard Shevardnadze told his Vietnamese counterpart, Nguyen Co Thach, that the USSR was ready to work with all sides concerned on the Cambodian question and contribute to its resolution. Two days later, the Vietnamese government announced that 50,000 troops would leave Cambodia in June, and the remaining troops would be commanded by Phnom Penh before leaving at the end of 1990. On the following day, Igor Rogachev remarked that the Vietnamese decision on a partial military withdrawal would be an important item on the agenda of the 12th round of Sino-Soviet political discussions. On 29 May, the Soviet government issued a statement that praised the Vietnamese decision as a "significant and constructive contribution" and reiterated Soviet willingness to work with the countries concerned to find a solution.

According to Qian Qichen's recollections, at that time the Soviet side regarded settlement of the Afghan question as a model for foreign troops to leave Cambodia. It is probably because of this clear Soviet gesture that Beijing thought that conditions for resolving the Cambodian issue were ripe. In early June, at a UN conference in New York, Foreign Minister Shevardnadze met with Qian Qichen and suggested the holding of Sino-Soviet discussions on the Cambodian issue.[10] From 13 June to 20 June, the 12th round of the Sino-Soviet vice-ministerial discussions were held in Moscow. At the end of this round, it was announced that there would be no more talks. After 12 rounds of discussions at the vice-foreign–ministerial level, the two sides had settled most of the outstanding issues concerning normalization of bilateral relations, and thus these discussions were no longer necessary. Instead, the two sides agreed to hold special talks on the Cambodian issue at the vice-ministerial level to remove the last "obstacle" to normalization of bilateral relations. This announcement indicated that there was only one minor issue remaining between Beijing and Moscow.

During the UN conference, the Chinese delegation probably sensed that not only did the countries concerned insist on a Vietnamese withdrawal from Cambodia but also that the Khmer Rouge would not be in charge of the country after a Vietnamese departure. On 1 July, the Chinese MFA issued a four-point statement to clarify its attitude toward the Cambodian issue. The statement included complete and swift Vietnamese withdrawal from Cambodia, a quadrilateral coalition government headed by Prince Sihanouk, international supervision of the Vietnamese withdrawal and of the peace in Cambodia, and Chinese participation in international guarantees for Cambodia's independence, neutrality, and nonalignment. The next day, Li Peng gave his first interview to foreign journalists after becoming Chinese premier. He basically reiterated China's attitude toward Sino-Soviet relations and the four-point statement of the MFA, indicating that a meeting between the Chinese and Soviet foreign ministers would depend on the results of the discussions at the vice-ministerial level. At this point, the Chinese side clearly stated that it did not support the Khmer Rouge's control of the Cambodian government after the withdrawal of Vietnam nor did it support the Khmer Rouge leaders, who were widely opposed by the international community, to participate in the Cambodian coalition government.

Between 27 and 31 August, Chinese and Soviet vice-foreign ministers held their first round of discussions on the Cambodian issue. Some results were achieved, but the Chinese were less satisfied than the Soviets. On 1 September, Qian Qichen told Rogachev that the two sides had found some common ground, but there were still differences over certain important issues. A similar assessment was also made by a spokesperson of the Chinese MFA. The Chinese gesture was intended to press the Soviets to move more rapidly, but the achievements of the talks were actually greater than the Chinese were willing to publicly admit. On 2 September, Rogachev publicly remarked that the Soviet government wanted the Vietnamese to withdraw completely from Cambodia by the following year and hoped that this would have a positive impact on Sino-Soviet relations. This remark seems to reveal that Sino-Soviet disagreements at the time were limited to a timetable for a Vietnamese withdrawal since Beijing wanted a complete withdrawal before 1990. As revealed in Li Peng's diaries, in July Hanoi informed the Chinese government that Vietnamese troops would begin to leave Cambodia at the end of 1989. Moscow was apparently willing to address this discrepancy in the timetable. When informing his Vietnamese counterpart of the Sino-Soviet discussions, Rogachev probably told the Vietnamese about the Chinese position on a timetable and the Soviet attitude. At the time, the Vietnamese obviously did not appear to be receptive to the Chinese position.

The Soviets and Chinese also reached a consensus to separate the Cambodian issue into "internal" and "external" aspects and to find respective solutions. This represented an important step forward. Thus far, the Vietnamese had insisted on linking their departure from Cambodia with the exclusion of the Khmer Rouge from a new coalition government, and the Soviets had also insisted that after a Vietnamese departure, Prince Sihanouk would only be the head of a temporary nongovernmental body. In this way, the current pro-Vietnamese Phnom Penh regime would remain, and the chance that the Khmer Rouge would be part of a new government would be reduced. Rogachev's remarks indicated that for the moment, the Chinese and Soviet sides could not yet settle this difference. Their purpose of the agreement on dealing with the internal and external aspects of the Cambodian question was to de-link the Vietnamese withdrawal from a new Cambodian government, and therefore represented an effort to break the deadlock. At the time, however, Moscow did not go very far in meeting the Chinese position. For instance, a Soviet-Vietnamese joint communiqué dated 24 September still held that a Vietnamese withdrawal and elimination of the Khmer Rouge threat were two "related key issues."

On 16 September, Gorbachev, in a speech in Krasnoyarsk, made two important points with respect to Sino-Soviet relations. First, the vice-foreign–ministerial discussions had improved mutual understanding about the Cambodian question, and preparations for a Sino-Soviet summit could begin immediately. Second, he formally suggested for the first time that direct Sino-Vietnamese negotiations over Cambodia should be held, expecting that such negotiations would "play an important role in improving the Asian situation." This shows that, on the one hand, the USSR hoped to accelerate the negotiation process for a Sino-Soviet summit, and, on the other hand, the USSR hoped to break the deadlock by promoting direct negotiations between China and Vietnam. This represents a significant development in Soviet foreign policy and is one of the reasons that the Chinese positively appraised Gorbachev's speech. Soon after the Krasnoyarsk speech, Beijing accepted Moscow's invitation for Foreign Minister Qian Qichen to visit the Soviet Union. On 28 September, the Soviet MFA issued the news about scheduled mutual visits by the Chinese and Soviet foreign ministers, which were to begin with Qian's visit to Moscow.

On 9 October, a special high-level meeting was called to discuss a Vietnamese withdrawal as the goal of Qian's visit. It determined that if the Vietnamese agreed to withdraw their troops in 1989, then Beijing would agree to hold a summit meeting with Soviet leaders. In other words, in terms of normalization of Sino-Soviet relations, Cambodian domestic politics after a Vietnamese withdrawal was no longer a focal point of the foreign ministers' meetings and would not be an issue blocking a Sino-Soviet summit. One month later, another meeting of Chinese leaders decided on the concrete details for meetings of the top leaders. The main task of Qian Qichen's 1–3 December visit to Moscow was to "make preparations for the Sino-Soviet summit."[11] All of these changes clearly demonstrate that the Chinese side was taking a more positive attitude toward a summit and this decision had been taken even before the meeting of the foreign ministers. What led Chinese leaders to accelerate the process for a summit may have been related to broader issues, but a more definitive answer must await further declassification of the archives.

The foreign ministers' meeting covered two topics. One was arrangements for the Sino-Soviet summit. It seems that the Soviet side did not want the Cambodian issue to further delay the summit, but Moscow also had to take care of its relationship with Vietnam. In fact, it would have been very difficult for the Soviet Union to make a final decision for the Vietnamese. As recalled by Qian Qichen, in his meeting with Gorbachev, the Soviet leader took the lead and expressed his wish to visit Beijing, and Qian personally extended an invitation for Gorbachev to visit China in 1989. The two sides agreed that the summit would be held during the first half of the year. At the foreign ministers' meeting, the two sides reached an agreement on the schedule for the Vietnamese withdrawal from Cambodia. The Soviet side repeated Gorbachev's suggestion at Krasnoyarsk that China and Vietnam should negotiate directly to finalize the timetable for a withdrawal of Vietnamese troops, but it would take place no later than the end of 1989. The foreign ministers' meeting concluded with "joint minutes" that embodied the mutual understandings between the two sides. These included an early and just political settlement of the Cambodian issue and for Vietnam to begin pulling out from Cambodia between June and December 1989.[12]

Soon after the foreign ministers' meeting, the Vietnamese MFA phoned the Chinese embassy to arrange a meeting with the Chinese ambassador. On 15 December, Chinese Ambassador Li Shichun visited the Vietnamese MFA and received a letter signed by Vietnamese Foreign Minister Nguyen Co Thach to be delivered to Qian Qichen. The letter contained a proposal that before March 1989, the foreign ministers of the two countries should meet in Beijing. The Chinese reply arrived on 23 December, suggesting that a Vietnamese vice-foreign minister visit Beijing without delay to discuss the Cambodian issue. Thus, direct Sino-Vietnamese negotiations were on the agendas of both governments. The above analysis indicates that it is very likely that behind the scenes the USSR was placing pressure on the Vietnamese. The positive response by the Chinese side is, of course, related to both the progress in the foreign ministers' talks and the level of trust established between the two countries.

Direct Sino-Vietnamese negotiations undoubtedly would not only have a positive impact on a political settlement of the Cambodian issue but would also decrease Chinese pressure on Moscow. On 6 January 1989, the Vietnamese government announced that all Vietnamese troops would leave Cambodia no later than September of that year. In mid-January, Vietnamese First Vice-Foreign Minister Dinh Nho Liem secretly visited Beijing. During his visit, Vietnam clearly promised that according to the framework agreement for resolving the Cambodian issue, the Vietnamese Army would withdraw from Cambodia by the end of September 1989, and the Chinese side accepted this timetable. Although the two sides still had some differences on political issues, the facts show that the differences had no substantive impact on a Sino-Soviet summit.

On 2 February, Soviet Foreign Minister Shevardnadze visited Beijing to make preparations for the summit, including arranging the time for Gorbachev's visit, establishing the principles for bilateral relations in the years to come, and exchanging opinions on border negotiations and confidence-building on the two sides. On 4 February, Deng met with Shevardnadze who delivered a letter from Gorbachev. In his letter Gorbachev expressed a desire to hold a summit meeting with Chinese leaders, pointing out that normalization of Sino-Soviet relations had reached a critical juncture and that the two sides could find ways to resolve their differences.

At the foreign ministers' meetings, the core issue was the Cambodian issue. The Chinese side continued to use the summit to press the Soviets to make a commitment to resolve the Cambodian issue. After some twists and turns, on 6 February the two sides issued parallel statements on settlement of the Cambodian issue and announced that Gorbachev would visit China from 15 May to 18 May. Judging from the content of the statements, the two sides still had some differences on how to solve the Cambodian issue. Yet, as revealed by later developments, even if Beijing and Moscow had completely agreed, the Cambodian issue was too complicated to be settled smoothly.

"NORMALIZATION"

Between 15 May and 18 May 1989, with an invitation from Chinese President Yang Shangkun, Gorbachev made an official visit to China and held talks with Chinese government and party leaders, such as Zhao Ziyang, Li Peng, and Yang Shangkun, during which they achieved a consensus on all aspects of their bilateral relations. The visit marked comprehensive normalization of party and state relations between the two countries.

However, the most significant event during Gorbachev's visit was his meeting with Deng Xiaoping on 16 May. Deng's paramount policy-making position necessitated the decision on the Chinese side would be made at the highest level. Hence, at the beginning of the meeting Deng announced normalization of Sino-Soviet relations. The content of their meeting is only partially published in the third volume of the *Selected Writings of Deng Xiaoping*. The core of Deng's talk on the occasion was to "put the past behind and open up a new era." He believed that the Sino-Soviet ideological disputes of the past did not have much substantive significance and that the most important issues for China were dignity and security. In other words, future Sino-Soviet relations were to be constructed on a nonthreatening foundation of mutual respect. He was confident that there was enormous room for growth of bilateral relations. It was essential for both sides to "do more practical things and indulge in less empty talk."[13] According to Gorbachev's recollections, he did not raise any objections to Deng's points. In a sense, he gave a nod to the guiding role Deng played in this historic event.

On 18 May, the two sides issued a Sino-Soviet joint communiqué, which included 18 articles. Article 2 states that "the two sides agree that the Sino-

Soviet high-level meeting symbolizes the normalization of relations between the two countries." Article 3 clearly stipulates that Sino-Soviet relations will be premised on the famous "five principles of peaceful coexistence." These would pave the way for stable growth of Sino-Soviet relations in the years to come and would facilitate a smooth transition in the bilateral relationship after the fall of the USSR. The other contents of the communiqué covered concrete issues in Sino-Soviet relations at the time. They were arranged in an order to show that cooperation between the two countries to resolve the Cambodian issue remained a top priority. This illustrates the importance of building strategic mutual trust in relations between the major powers. Strategic mutual trust could serve as the basis for the powers to deal with issues of common concern. In this respect, whether or not there were immediate results at times could be less important.

During the next two years, the two governments fully restored relations and established exchanges in the political, economic and trade, military and security, and cultural, science, and education areas. They also continued mutual high-level visits. For instance, from 23 to 26 April 1990, Chinese Premier Li Peng visited the Soviet Union. The six agreements concluded during Li's visit, covering bilateral cooperation in a range of economic, scientific, security, financial, and border issues, indicated substantial progress in the bilateral relationship.

From 15 May to 19 May 1991, CCP General Secretary and President of the People's Republic of China (PRC) Jiang Zemin visited the Soviet Union. Jiang's visit was the second summit between the two countries after Gorbachev's visit two years earlier, and it was also Jiang's first meeting with Soviet leaders since he assumed the top position in the CCP. At the time, the domestic situation in the Soviet Union was tumultuous, but Jiang did not touch upon the subject during his visit. The joint communiqué issued by the two governments reiterates the five principles of peaceful coexistence, especially the principle of noninterference in each other's internal affairs. It states that the existence of different views and approaches in handling internal affairs should not hinder the normal development of bilateral relations. During Jiang's visit, the two governments held extensive discussions. The most important achievement was the signing by the two foreign ministers of the "Agreement on the Eastern Section of the Boundary between the People's Republic of China and the Union of Soviet Socialist Republics," which finalized a treaty based on the consensus reached during the Sino-Soviet border negotiations. In view of the tortuous history of Sino-Soviet relations, this treaty is illustrative of the historic significance of the summit. It shows that normal and stable Sino-Soviet relations could provide a solid foundation and driving force for the settlement of any historical problems, regardless of how complicated they might be.

Three months after Jiang's visit, the "19 August incident" took place in the Soviet Union. Soon thereafter, the three Baltic republics, Estonia, Latvia, and Lithuania, took the lead in announcing their independence, followed by similar announcements by the other republics of the Soviet Union. On 12 December 1991, with the exception of the three Baltic states and Georgia, the 11 other former members of the USSR established the Commonwealth of Independent States. Four days later, in a televised speech, Gorbachev announced his resignation as president of the USSR. With the final disintegration of the USSR, Sino-Soviet relations also became history.

NOTES

1. Deng Xiaoping, "Peace and Development are the Two Outstanding Issues in the World Today," 4 March 1985, in *Selected Works of Deng Xiaoping, vol. 3 (1982–1992)* (Beijing: Foreign Languages Press, 1994), p. 111.
2. Deng Xiaoping, "Speech at an Enlarged Meeting of the Military Commission of the Central Committee of the Communist Party of China," 4 June 1985, in *Selected Works of Deng Xiaoping, vol. 3*, pp. 131–33.
3. "The Chinese Need a Long Period of Peace to Realize their Full Modernization," in Jimmy Carter, *Keeping Faith: Memoirs of a President* (New York: Bantam Books, 1982), p. 209.
4. Qian, *Ten Episodes in China's Diplomacy*, pp. 1–32.
5. "An Interview with Deng Xiaoping," *Time* 126(18): 4 November 1985 pp. 30–42, at p. 40.
6. Qian, *Ten Episodes in China's Diplomacy*, p. 18.
7. Ibid., pp. 19–20.
8. Deng Xiaoping, "Replies to the American TV Correspondent Mike Wallace," 2 September 1986, in *Selected Works of Deng Xiaoping, vol. 3*, p. 170.
9. Qian, *Ten Episodes in China's Diplomacy*, p. 19.
10. Ibid., pp. 37–38.
11. Ibid., p. 23.
12. Ibid., pp. 24–26.
13. Deng Xiaoping, "Let Us Put the Past Behind Us and Open Up a New Era," 16 May 1989, in *Selected Works of Deng Xiaoping, vol. 3*, pp. 300–304.

Further Reading

Bernstein, Thomas P. and Hua-Yu Li, eds. *China Learns from the Soviet Union, 1949–Present*. Lanham, MD: Lexington Books, 2010.

Dittmer, Lowell. *Sino-Soviet Normalization and its International Implications, 1945–1990*. Seattle: University of Washington Press, 1992.

Elleman, Bruce A. *Diplomacy and Deception: The Secret History of Sino-Soviet Diplomatic Relations, 1917–1927*. Armonk, NY: M.E. Sharpe, 1997.

Friedman, Jeremy. *Shadow Cold War: The Sino-Soviet Competition for the Third World*. Chapel Hill: University of North Carolina Press, 2015.

Garver, John. *Chinese-Soviet Relations, 1937–1945*. Oxford: Oxford University Press, 1988.

Griffith, William E. *Albania and the Sino-Soviet Rift*. Cambridge, MA: MIT Press, 1963.

Griffith, William E. *Sino-Soviet Relations, 1964–1965*. Cambridge, MA: MIT Press, 1967.

Griffith, William E. *The Sino-Soviet Rifts, Analysed and Documented*. London: Allen and Unwin, 1964.

Heinzig, Dieter. *The Soviet Union and Communist China 1945–1950: The Arduous Road to the Alliance*. Armonk, NY: M.E. Sharpe, 2004.

Jersild, Austin. *The Sino-Soviet Alliance: An International History*. Chapel Hill: University of North Carolina Press, 2014.

Jones, Peter and Sian Kevill, eds. *China and the Soviet Union, 1949–1984*. London: Longman, 1985.

Kaple, Deborah A. *Dream of a Red Factory: The Legacy of High Stalinism in China*. Oxford: Oxford University Press, 1994.

Kuo, Mercy A. *Contending with Contradictions: China's Policy toward Soviet Eastern Europe and the Origins of the Sino-Soviet Split, 1953–1960*. Lanham, MD: Lexington Books, 2001.

Li, Danhui and Yafeng Xia. *Mao and the Sino-Soviet Split, 1959–1973: A New History*. Lanham, MD: Lexington Books, 2018.

Lüthi, Lorenz. *The Sino-Soviet Split: Cold War in the Communist World*. Princeton, NJ: Princeton University Press, 2008.

Radchenko, Sergey. *Two Suns in the Heavens: The Sino-Soviet Struggle for Supremacy, 1962–1967*. Washington, DC: Woodrow Wilson Center Press and Stanford: Stanford University Press, 2009.

© The Author(s) 2020   387
Z. Shen (ed.), *A Short History of Sino-Soviet Relations, 1917–1991*,
China Connections, https://doi.org/10.1007/978-981-13-8641-1

Radchenko, Sergey. *Unwanted Visionaries: The Soviet Failure in Asia at the End of the Cold War*. Oxford: Oxford University Press, 2014.

Robinson, Thomas. "China Confronts the Soviet Union: Warfare and Diplomacy on China's Inner Asian Frontiers. Pp. 218–301, in Roderick MacFarquhar and John K. Fairbank, eds. *The Cambridge History of China, vol. 15: The People's Republic of China, Part II, Revolutions within the Chinese Revolution, 1966–1982*. Cambridge: Cambridge University Press, 1991.

Shen, Zhihua and Yafeng Xia. *Mao and the Sino-Soviet Partnership, 1945–1959: A New History*. Lanham, MD: Lexington Books, 2015.

Westad, Odd Arne, ed. *Brothers in Arms: The Rise and Fall of the Sino-Soviet Alliance, 1945–1963*. Washington, DC: Woodrow Wilson Center Press and Stanford: Stanford University Press, 2009.

Westad, Odd Arne. *The Global Cold War: Third World Interventions and the Making of Our Times*. Cambridge: Cambridge University Press, 2007.

Whiting, Allen S. "The Sino-Soviet Split." Pp. 478–542, in Roderick MacFarquhar and John K. Fairbank, eds. *The Cambridge History of China, vol. 14: The People's Republic of China, Part I, The Emergence of Revolutionary China, 1949–1965*. Cambridge: Cambridge University Press, 1987,

Zagoria, Donald. *The Sino-Soviet Conflict, 1956–1961*. Princeton, NJ: Princeton University Press, 1962.

Zhang, Shuguang. *Economic Cold War: America's Embargo against China and the Sino-Soviet Alliance*. Washington, DC: Woodrow Wilson Center Press and Stanford: Stanford University Press, 2001.

INDEX[1]

A

Abrasimov, Petr, 183, 193
Accord on Economic and Technical Cooperation, 365
Accord on Establishing a Sino-Soviet Committee on Economic, Trade, and Science and Technology Cooperation, 365
Accord on Scientific Technological Cooperation, 365
Adventurism, 264
Afghanistan, 333, 340, 341, 343, 346, 347, 351–353, 374, 376, 378–380
  USSR invasion of, 347
Africa, 201, 235, 237, 244, 255, 263, 286, 288, 296–298
  Zhou Enlai and, 288
Afro-Asian political left, 299
Agreement between the Provincial Government of the Three Eastern Provinces of the Republic of China and the Government of the Soviet Socialist Federation (Feng-Russian Agreement), 14
Agreement on Dalian, 90, 110
Agreement on Lüshun, Dalian, and the Chinese Changchun Railway, 128
"Agreement on New National Defense Technology," 184

Agreement on Port Arthur, 90, 127
Agreement on Providing Technical Assistance to China for Naval Supplies and Gunship Production, 143
Agreement on Relations between the Commander-in-Chief of the Soviet Army and the Chinese Government After the Soviet Army Enters China's Three Provinces in the Northeast in this Joint War against Japan, 90
Agreement on the Chinese Changchun Railway, 110, 125–127, 129
Agreement Regarding Soviet Government Aid to the Chinese Government on Developing the National Economy, 148
Agricultural family responsibility system, 255
Aidit, D. N., 298, 302n31
Air communications, 315
Albania
  CCP and, 248, 251, 252, 258, 259, 261, 262, 287, 290
  after China and, 290
  Communist Party of, 248
  Khrushchev and, 248, 250, 251, 261, 262, 287, 292
  Soviet-Albanian relations, 248
  See also Party of Labor of Albania

[1] Note: Page numbers followed by 'n' refer to notes.

© The Author(s) 2020
Z. Shen (ed.), *A Short History of Sino-Soviet Relations, 1917–1991*,
China Connections, https://doi.org/10.1007/978-981-13-8641-1

All-China Federation of Trade Unions, 210, 237, 245n18
Allied nations, 84
All-Union Communist Party (Bolsheviks) (AUCP b)
 CC Politburo of, 28
 China Committee of Politburo of, 26
 Comintern and, 28, 32, 41
 foreign policy of, 32, 33, 58
 optimistic mood of, 32
 Politburo of, 28, 36n7, 55, 63, 64, 80
Altai Mountains region, 80
Ambassadors, 14, 183, 234, 316
Anarchists, 4, 8
 CCP parting ways with, 8, 33
Andropov, Yuri, 193, 213, 250, 252, 368
 Huang Hua and, 359–362
 three major obstacles and, 363, 364
Anti-aircraft guns, 112, 143
Anti-colonial struggles, 277
Anti-imperialism, 46, 236, 250, 254, 267, 271, 293, 296, 299, 300
Anti-Imperialism Day, 46
Anti-Japanese Coalition Forces, 58
Anti-Japanese war, 69, 75, 76
Anti-Party Group, 182, 192
Anti-rightist movement, 204
Aristocratic workers, 273
Arkhipov, Ivan, 119n4, 153, 226n26, 364, 365
Assemblies (soviets), 224
Atatürk, Mustafa Kemal, 28
AUCP b, see All-Union Communist Party (Bolsheviks)
Austrian-Hungarian empire, 4
Autumn Harvest rebellion, 41

B
Baibakov, Nikolai, 153
Balkans, 98, 184, 248
Bandung Conference, 163, 285
Baotou Iron and Steel, 213
Basic Construction Planning Bureau, 152
Bata, István, 177
Battle Plan for Exterminating the Bandit Armies South of the Yellow River, 77
Batur, Osman, 80
Beidaihe Work Conference, 254

"Beiding nanfang" defense strategy, 269
Beijing
 border negotiations with Moscow, 29, 131, 142, 144, 167, 168, 192–194, 213, 221, 317
 Feng Yuxiang mutiny, 15, 25, 26
 Indochina and, 372, 376
 Kissinger secret trip to, 321
 Kosygin and, 289, 294, 315, 316, 330
 lowering military tensions along Sino-Soviet border, 315
 Moscow pressure on, 125, 383
 Pyongyang and, 144
 Soviet leadership in, 299, 308, 345
 threat from Moscow, 377
 USSR and, 12, 22, 41, 131, 176, 217, 219, 226n32, 231, 235
 WFTU Beijing Conference, 239, 240, 243
Beijing Heat and Power Station, 213
Beiyang government
 foreign affairs of, 11
 representative plenipotentiary appointed by, 12
 sovereignty and, 11, 12
 State Affairs Meeting, 13
Berlin crisis, 162, 243
Big-power chauvinism, 147
Bilateral aid, 331
Bilateral economic ties, 316
Bilateral relations
 development of, 316, 333, 355, 365, 366, 369, 385
 Gorbachev and, 368, 374, 384
 improvement in, 365
 normalization of, 15, 290, 330, 338, 353, 356, 380, 381
 obstacles to, 339
 relaxation of, 365
Black Sea meeting, 138, 144
Blue Shirt society, 60
Bo Gu, 42, 43, 75, 82, 83
Bo Yibo, 154, 171
Bogomolov, Dimitry, 61–63, 93n1
Bolshevik Revolution, 20, 193
Bolsheviks, 3, 4, 20, 40, 43, 48, 193
Borodin, Mikhail, 18, 20, 23–28, 33–35
Boula, Marcel, 236
Bourgeois-democratic revolution, 297

Boxer Indemnity, 13, 14
Braun, Otto, 51
Brezhnev, Aleksei, 211
Brezhnev, Leonid, 257, 282, 288, 289,
    294, 299, 300, 303, 306, 307, 309,
    310, 313, 334, 335, 343–346, 351,
    355, 357–360, 364
  on CCP, 279, 280, 290, 304, 358
  death of, 341n3, 345, 358–360, 364
  on Great Proletarian Cultural
    Revolution, 306
  Huang Hua, and, 341n3, 364
  interest in improving relations with
    CCP, 280
  leadership of, 211, 258, 277, 279,
    290, 300
  relations with China and, 289, 304,
    345, 358, 359
  speech on Soviet policy in Asia, 344
  Taiwan and, 258, 344, 351
  Time (magazine) interview with, 335
  24 March speech, 351
  Xinhua News Agency and, 360
  Zhou Enlai and, 277–279, 307
British Communist Party, 290
Bubnov, A. S., 29
Bucharest Conference of Communist and
    Workers' Parties of Socialist
    Countries, 238–241, 262
  Khrushchev and, 243, 248
Bulganin, Nikolai, 164, 182, 184
Bulgaria, 78, 98, 233, 262, 306, 365, 373
  Communist Party, 257
Bureaucratism, 295
Burinsky Border Agreement, 80
Burma, 103, 125, 190, 221, 262, 298
Bush, George H. W., 374

C
Cai Tingkai, 56, 57
Cambodia
  coalition government, 381
  Khmer Rouge, 375, 378, 379, 381, 382
  Vietnam and, 334, 335, 339, 340,
    352–354, 361, 367, 369, 372,
    375, 376, 379, 380
*Capital Construction in Contemporary
    China*, 155

Capitalism
  advanced nations of Europe, 7
  capitalist class, 20, 256
  crisis of, 235
  domestic, 273
  move to socialism from, 194, 195
  stage of, 18n2
Carter, Jimmy, 349
CAS, *see* Chinese Academy of Science
CCP, *see* Chinese Communist Party
CCP CC, *see* Chinese Communist Party
    Central Committee
Ceauşescu, Nicolai, 346, 352, 355, 368,
    371, 373, 377
  Deng Xiaoping and, 346, 355, 368,
    371, 373, 377
Ceng Tianfang, 62
Central Asia, 129
Central Asian Soviet republics, 85
Central Cultural Revolution Small
    Group, 313
Central Intelligence Agency (CIA),
    155, 186, 212, 223, 238, 275,
    290, 295, 308
Central Military Commission (CMC),
    116, 183, 216, 268, 269, 272, 311,
    318, 369
Central People's Government
    Council, 130
Central People's Radio Station, 277
Central Red Base Area, 51
Central Soviet Area, 51, 52
  Red Army in, 10–12, 16–18, 47, 52,
    64, 65, 72, 81, 110
Central Soviet Region, 51–53, 75
CGDK, *see* Coalition Government of
    Democratic Kampuchea
Chahar People's Anti-Japanese Army,
    67n2
Changchun, 9, 101, 103, 104, 119n2
Changchun Railway
  control of, 126
  goods required by, 126
  legal validity of, 128
  Sino-Soviet investment ratio, 128
Changsha, 8, 48, 49, 71
Chen Duxiu, 7, 20, 27, 36n1, 41–43, 47
Chen Jiongming, 30, 36–37n9
Chen Lifu, 62, 63, 93n1

Chen Yi, 151, 156, 221–223, 243,
    244n3, 249, 254, 255, 265, 289,
    298, 305, 307, 308, 313
    Red Guards and, 307, 308
    on USSR, 156, 221, 222, 243
    Ye Jianying and, 313
Chen Yu, 48
Chen Yun, 111, 148
Cherepanov, A. I., 71
Chernenko, Konstantin, 364, 368,
    370, 372
Chervonenko, Stepan, 230, 231, 248,
    250, 252, 276, 277, 283n23,
    284n25, 288, 292, 293
    Deng Xiaoping and, 250, 252
    Liu Xiao and, 288
    Wu Xiuquan and, 276, 283n23
    Yu Zhan and, 292
China
    Albania and, 248, 252, 261, 290
    alignment with U.S., 318
    anti-imperialism and, 236, 250, 254,
        267, 271, 293, 296, 299, 305
    anti-Soviet international united front,
        334, 335, 370
    Army emergency combat readiness,
        314, 317
    assistance from USSR, 64, 66, 152
    Brezhnev, L., relations with, 257, 258,
        278–280, 282, 288–290, 294,
        299, 303, 304, 306, 334, 335,
        344–346, 351, 355, 357–360, 364
    Chinese Eastern Railway and, 8–14,
        18n1, 28, 43–47, 53n3, 58, 67n3,
        85–89, 91, 119n2
    on danger of Soviet hegemony, 333
    decision-making system, 346
    domestic affairs of, 223, 264, 321, 350
    economic development of, 115, 144,
        150, 151, 153, 209–212, 254,
        256, 273, 346, 348, 369, 371
    external position of, 130
    foreign-aid policies of, 298
    foreign policy of, 111; leftward turn in,
        257, 264, 265; reorientation of,
        371; ultra-leftist, 321
    four-point policy toward USSR, 319
    funeral diplomacy and, 358–366
    Gorbachev and, 368, 369, 371–380,
        382–386

    guerrilla units in, 7
    heavy industry in, 91, 151, 164
    ideological challenge to USSR, 234
    imperial Russia and, 14
    importance of Mao Zedong Thought
        in, 172
    influence in USSR, 185, 285
    International Communist Movement
        and, 112, 175, 223, 232–234,
        239, 257, 263, 272, 280, 297
    JCP and, 262, 295, 310
    Jiang Jieshi, and USSR assistance to, 69
    Korean border, 72, 139
    MFA, Chinese embassy and, 343, 383
    Moscow and, 280
    national development strategy, 346, 347
    needs for military equipment, 138
    North Vietnam and, 262, 291, 295,
        296, 300, 308
    nuclear facilities, 315–317
    Paris Peace Conference and, 3, 5, 6
    People's Commune Movement, 253
    Poland and, 79, 176, 180, 181, 185,
        186, 191, 365
    "Proposals for Improving Sino-Soviet
        Relations," 340
    reform, 6
    Sino-Soviet cooperation to aid
        Vietnam, 294
    so-called "true socialism" and, 349
    socialist bloc and, 125, 130, 133, 147,
        173, 175, 176, 183, 198, 202,
        209, 223, 281, 296, 297, 309
    sovereignty of, 8, 11, 12, 14, 88, 89,
        129, 150, 242, 256, 298
    Soviet pledge of non-use of nuclear
        weapons against, 316
    Soviet Revolution in, 1, 39–53
    strategic global position of, 346
    strategic regions, 272
    students trained on USSR, 143
    trade debts of, 331
    USSR and development of Chinese
        politics, 2
    USSR diplomatic relations with,
        198, 327
    USSR loans to, 112, 130, 131,
        155, 156
    Vietnam and, 96, 272, 285, 290,
        293–296, 300, 322, 333–335,

347, 348, 352–354, 371, 372, 376, 377, 382, 383
war preparedness of, 269, 271, 310, 315
war scare, Chinese leaders and, 318
withdrawal from Cold War, 370
work for unity of International Communist Movement, 277
after world War II, 56
China White Paper, 117
Chinese Academy of Science (CAS), 151
Chinese colleges and universities, 307
Chinese Communist Party (CCP)
Albania and, 259, 262
anarchists and, 8
armed separatism and, 51
aspiration for special status in International Communist Movement, 286
Brezhnev, L., interest in improving relations with, 280
Brezhnev, L., on, 258, 279, 282, 289, 303, 304, 358
capitalist class, CCP not compromising with, 20
Central Executive Committee, 21–23, 27, 29
central leadership of, 186
Chinese Communist Army, 34, 35, 74, 110, 190
concessions at Moscow Conference, 246n28
condemned by Suslov, 274, 292
confidence in polemics, 257, 259, 261, 262, 264, 265, 274, 277, 281, 292
on declaration of equality among socialist states, 173, 178
Eighth CCP Congress, 161–173, 199, 204, 206n10, 213, 256, 272, 297
expansion of, 79
First CCP Congress, 8, 20, 21
fraying of CCP-CPSU ideological connections, 265
JCP and, 295
Jiang Jieshi and, 34, 64–67, 74
Khrushchev, 198
"The Leaders of the CPSU are the Greatest Splitters of Our Times," 274
Mao Zedong and, 40, 78, 97, 193

MFA and, 21, 359
Moscow and, 56, 76, 118, 287
after Moscow Declaration, 229, 235, 239, 261, 290
Nationalist Party and, 19, 20, 22, 23, 26, 29, 34, 35, 62, 63, 65, 67, 75, 76, 91, 95, 97, 99, 100, 103
Ninth CCP Congress, 314
Northeast Bureau of, 102, 103, 114
Northeast China and, 55, 111, 113, 114, 123, 268
Organization Bureau of, 16
Politburo Standing Committee of, 203, 241
political flexibility for, 61
prestige in International Communist Movement, 145
on secret speech, 161, 167
Seventh Congress of, 60, 61, 91
split in International Communist Movement and, 243, 244
Stalin; on leadership, 41; on Nationalist Party and, 97
Sun Yatsen and, 16
Tenth CCP Congress, 332
U.S. and, 121n24
on USSR under Khrushchev, 218, 256
Chinese Communist Party Central Committee (CCP CC)
Chinese Revolution and, 33, 47, 91
"Circular on Carrying Out Anti-Revisionist Education Work Inside and Outside the Party," 259
Comintern and, 27, 32, 33, 35, 41, 42, 46, 49, 50, 56, 60, 61, 63, 64, 67, 74–76, 84
"Congress of the Soviet Regions," 49
internal affairs of, 83
"May 16 Notification," 305
Nationalist Party, Provisional CCP CC and, 27, 33, 55–57, 60, 74, 97
Northeast Bureau of, 113, 117
Northern Bureau of, 310
Politburo of, 56, 67, 97; enlarged meeting of, 138, 167, 183, 250, 270
Presidium of, 149, 153, 219, 274
Propaganda Department of, 157, 233, 245n12

Chinese Communist Party Central
Committee (CCP CC) (*cont.*)
Provisional CC of, 39, 41, 52, 53, 56, 57
SED and, 261, 266n19
"Several Issues Raised in the Socialist
Education Movement in the
Countryside," 273
Shanghai and, 33, 39, 46, 49, 51,
56, 240
Social Department of, 84
United Front Work Department of, 255
USSR and, 82, 97, 152
work conference, 230, 249, 269
Chinese Communist Party Manifesto, 7
Chinese Communist Revolution,
8, 110, 111
Chinese Eastern Railway
China and, 8, 11, 12, 44
incident, 43–47, 53n3
Japan and, 58
price, 13
stations, 44
status quo on, 16
Chinese Foreign Ministry, 179, 206n6,
219, 308, 316
Chinese media, 4, 14, 234, 288, 349
Chinese Ministry of Higher Education, 307
Chinese National Congress, 64
Chinese National Defense Government, 64
Chinese National People's Congress
(NPC), 231, 337, 358
Chinese Navy, 45, 143, 157, 216
Chinese People's Political Consultative
Conference, 129
Chinese People's Volunteers (CPV)
38th parallel and, 134, 139–141
UN forces and, 139, 140
Chinese Revolution
CCP CC and, 20, 33, 47, 91
Chinese Soviet Revolution, 50
Stalin and, 40, 50, 210
U.S. and, 116
victory of, 83, 130
world revolution and, 306
Chinese Revolutionary Alliance, 15
Chinese Revolutionary Party, 4
Chinese Soviet Republic
Provisional Government of, 50, 57, 60
Ch'oe Yong-gŏn, 317

Chongqing, 80, 85, 95–99, 170
Christensen, Thomas, 294, 301n13
Chronicle of the Life of Deng Xiaoping
(Party Literature Research Center),
345, 373
Chronicle of the Life of Zhou Enlai (Party
Literature Research Center), 330
Chuikov, Vasily Ivanovich, 71
CIA, *see* Central Intelligence Agency
"Circular on Carrying Out Anti-Revisionist
Education Work Inside and Outside
the Party" (CCP CC), 27, 32–35, 39,
41–43, 46, 47, 49–53, 56, 57, 60–67,
74–78, 82–84, 91, 96–98, 100, 101,
103, 112, 113, 117, 120n10, 124,
151–154, 157, 158, 159n11, 163,
167, 173, 174n9, 177, 183, 185,
186n4, 187n10, 206n16, 217, 221,
222, 225n16, 230, 231, 233,
235–238, 240, 242, 245n12,
248–252, 255, 258–261, 264,
266n12, 266n19, 268–270, 272,
273, 276, 278, 279, 287, 288, 293,
294, 297, 304–306, 308, 310, 312,
315–317, 331, 334, 336, 347, 348,
358, 359, 374
Civil Aviation Company, 149
Class struggle, v, 22, 34, 56, 162, 249,
254–256, 272–274
CMC, *see* Central Military Commission
Coalition Government of Democratic
Kampuchea (CGDK), 375–377
Cold War
China withdrawal from, 370
development of, 162
escalation of, 269, 357
imperialism and, 205
international politics of, 161, 332
Sino-Soviet Cold War, 322
Collaboration, vi, 4, 6, 16, 18, 36, 81,
82, 92, 189, 209, 294
Colonial countries, 115
Cominform, *see* Communist Information
Bureau
Comintern, *see* Communist International
Communist Information Bureau
(Cominform), 162, 190, 191, 193,
204, 205n4, 248
"Cominform in the East," 190

Communist International (Comintern)
  AUCP b and, 26, 41
  CCP CC and, 41, 61, 63, 64
  Comintern Eastern Department,
      21, 28, 75
  dissolution of, 83, 84, 190
  Eastern Department, 21, 28
  Executive Committee of, 32, 33
  political flexibility toward CCP, 61
  Resolution of the Left-Wing
      Nationalist Party and the Issues of
      Soviet Slogans, 48
  Seventh Congress of, 60, 61, 63
  Seventh Expanded Meeting of
      Executive Committee of, 32, 33
  Seventh Plenum of, 59
  Social Democratic parties and, 59
  USSR and, 42, 82–84
The Communist Manifesto (Marx and
  Engels), 7
The Communist Party (publication), 7
Communist Party of Burma, 298
Communist Party of Czechoslovakia
  (KSČ), 168, 202, 257–259
Communist Party of Germany, 58
Communist Party of Indonesia (PKI),
  285, 298–300
Communist Party of Soviet Union
  (CPSU)
  and CCP, 265
  Deng Xiaoping on Twentieth CPSU
      Congress, 167, 172, 203, 242
  General Line of International
      Communist Movement and,
      280, 286
  International Communist Movement,
      CPSU program as guiding principle
      of, 235, 292; unity in, 277
  LCY and, 192, 193, 204
  leadership role of, 175
  Mao Zedong contempt for, 175, 209,
      230, 257, 304, 309
  after Moscow Declaration, 196, 203,
      240, 242
  Nineteenth CPSU Congress, 162
  Presidium of, 125, 183–185,
      191–195, 197, 202, 232,
      233, 239, 289
  on problems under Stalin, 170–172

  Third World and, 300
  Twentieth CPSU Congress, 152, 157,
      158, 161–173, 182, 190, 196,
      198, 200, 203–205, 206n10,
      206n11, 235, 239, 242, 244,
      250, 263
  Twenty-first CPSU Congress, 214,
      215, 225n4, 229
  Twenty-fourth CPSU Congress, 333
  Twenty-third CPSU Congress, 285,
      293, 303–305, 309
  Zhou Enlai and, 170, 180, 192, 241,
      277–279, 288, 293
Communist Party of the Soviet Union
  Central Committee (CPSU CC)
  International Department of, 289
  "On Measures for Normalization of
      Soviet-Chinese Relations," 289
  on People's Commune Movement, 255
  Presidium of, 149, 153, 167, 219,
      274, 277
  See also Communist Party of Soviet
      Union (CPSU)
Communist Party of Spain, 166
Communist Party of Thailand, 298
"Comrade Kang Sheng Talks about the
      Current International Situation at
      the Political Consultative Committee
      Conference of the Warsaw Treaty
      Member Countries," 232
Congress of the Laborers in
      Transbaikalia, 8
Conference of World Communist and
      Workers' Parties, 175, 185, 186,
      240, 248, 262, 287, 289, 290, 309,
      311, 312
"Congress of the Soviet Regions," 49
Constitution Protection Movement, 16
Counterrevolution, 32, 179
CPSU, *see* Communist Party of Soviet
      Union
CPSU CC, *see* Communist Party of
      Soviet Union Central Committee
CPV, *see* Chinese People's Volunteers
Crimean Peninsula, 85
Cuba, 237, 264, 266n16
  missile crisis, 256, 257, 259, 261, 264,
      266n15
Cuéllar, Pérez de, 379

Czechoslovakia, 98, 135, 168, 202, 233, 257, 259, 260, 262, 288, 306, 310–312, 316, 365
  USSR and, 306, 310–312, 316

D

Daily Worker (newspaper), 167
Dalian
  Agreement, 110
  shipyard, 149
  troops in, 125, 128, 149
  USSR and, 89, 110, 115, 126, 128
Dalian Shipyard, 149
de Gaulle, Charles, 98
"Declaration on the Principles for Mutual Relations" (USSR), 340
Democratic Coalition Army, 103
Democratic People's Republic of Korea (DPRK), 233, 317
  Supreme People's Assembly of, 317
Democratic Republic of China, 64
Deng Fa, 50
Deng Wenyi, 62, 63
Deng Xiaoping, 42, 167, 172, 175, 177, 197, 203, 211, 236, 242, 243, 244n3, 250, 252, 254, 266n8, 274, 279, 336, 338–340, 345, 346, 348–355, 358–360, 363, 364, 367–374, 377, 379, 380, 384
  on bilateral relations, 336, 339, 353
  Ceauşescu and, 346, 352, 355, 368, 373, 377
  Chervonenko and, 250, 252
  Chronicle of the Life of Deng Xiaoping (Party Literature Research Center), 345, 373
  Gorbachev and, 368, 369, 371, 373, 380, 384
  Huang Hua and, 345, 353, 359, 360
  Jackson and, 363
  Kim Il-sung and, 353, 355, 364
  Liu Shaoqi and, 167, 172, 242
  normalization and, 338, 346, 360, 384
  political status of, 339
  Shevardnadze and, 384
  on Sino-U.S. relations, 349, 351
  Sonoda and, 336

three major obstacles and, 359, 364, 367, 369, 373
  on Twentieth CPSU Congress, 203
  U.S., and, 339, 340, 349–352
Department for Economic Liaisons with People's Democratic Countries, 149
Department for Liaison with Communist and Workers' Parties in the Socialist Bloc, 252, 309
Department of Soviet and East European Affairs, 292, 352
De-Stalinization, 162, 165, 167, 172, 173, 191
  Mao Zedong and, 173
The Diary of Yang Shangkun (Party Literature Research Center), 155
"The Dictatorship of the Proletarian and the Great Proletarian Cultural Revolution" (*Red Flag*), 306
Dimitrov, Georgi, 59, 64, 67, 74, 76, 77, 83, 84
Dinh Nho Liem, 383
Diplomatic History of the People's Republic of China, 1957–1969 (Wang Taiping), 155, 156
"Directives on Formulating the Fifteen-Year Long-term Development Program of the Chinese Academy of Science," 151
Division of labor, 115
DPRK, *see* Democratic People's Republic of Korea
Dratvin, M. I., 71
Du Yuming, 101
Duan Qirui, 5, 15, 25
Duljinevskii, Vsevolod, 126
Dulles, John F., 219

E

East China group, 255
Eastern Europe, 5, 113, 124, 162, 166, 168, 175, 176, 180–182, 187n21, 310
Eastern Expeditions, 30, 36n9
Eastern Turkistan Islamic People's Republic, 81
Economic aid, 144, 147, 152, 173, 248

Economic cooperation, 102, 316, 331, 361, 366
Economic crises, 241
Economic development
  of China, 115, 144, 150, 151, 153, 154, 209–212, 254, 256, 273, 369, 371
  socialism and, 254, 256
  during Stalin era, 171
Economic Problems of Socialism in the USSR (Stalin), 167, 211
Economic reconstruction (China), 114, 164, 171
Egypt, 140, 302n28
18 September incident (Japanese Kwantung Army), 46, 55–58, 66, 82
Eighth Route Army, 76, 77, 82, 96, 104
Eight-Party Conference, 152
Eisenhower, Dwight, 84, 220, 234, 245n10
Elizavetin, Aleksei, 316
Engels, Friedrich, 170
Entente powers, 4, 9
Europe
  advanced capitalist nations of, 7
  Chen Lifu in, 63
  Eastern, 5, 113, 162, 166, 168, 175, 176, 180–182, 187n21, 310
  USSR and, 57, 63, 98
  war against fascism in, 84
Exterritorial rights, 14

F
Far East Bureau, 42, 49, 219
Far East Department, 309
Far Eastern Commerce Bureau, 44
Far Eastern Kerosene Bureau, 44
Far East region, 6, 10, 57, 129
  USSR Far Eastern policy, 57
Far East Republic, 8–10, 18n1
February Revolution, 4
Fedorenko, Nikolai, 149, 200
Feng Yuxiang, 15, 24–26, 29, 31, 34, 35, 36n7, 58, 67n2
  Jiang Jieshi and, 35
  rise of, 25
Fengman Hydroelectric Power Station, 213

Feng-Russian Agreement, *see* Agreement between the Provincial Government of the Three Eastern Provinces of the Republic of China and the Government of the Soviet Socialist Federation
Fengtian (Shenyang), 11, 14, 15, 25, 26, 28, 29, 31, 43, 47, 56
Feudalism, 91
Finance and Economics Committee of the Government Administration Council, 148
Finance Bureau, 152
Finland, 79, 307
Five Principles of Peaceful Coexistence, 203, 329, 332, 333, 385
  normalization and, 333
Five-year Plan (FYP)
  economic cooperation during, 316
  First, 148, 150–152
  of Petroleum Ministry, 152
  "Proposal on the Second FYP for Developing the National Economy (1958–1962) (Revised Draft)," 154
  Second, 151–154
Foreign aid, 298
Foreign Cooperation in Contemporary China, 155
Foreign trade, 113, 245n13
Foundation for Strategic Research, 312
Four Cleanups Movement, 274
Fraternal parties
  differences among, 250, 251
  growing pessimism among, 173
  Mao Zedong blocking conference of, 280, 290
  Party of Labor of Albania and, 251, 262
French Communist Party (leftist), 262
French Communist Party (PCF), 98, 99, 191, 206n10
French Revolution, 4
Friedman, Jeremy, vi, 298, 321
Friendship Daily (newspaper), 226n32
Fugh, Philip, 116, 117
Funeral diplomacy, 358–366
Fushun Coal Mines, 102
FYP, *see* Five-year Plan

G

Galen (General), 28, 30, 31, 37n10, 41, 45, 62, 70
Gao Gang, 111, 114, 138, 139, 141
  Stalin and, 114, 141
Gapon, F. I., 7
General Agreement on Solutions to the Unresolved Issues Between China and Russia (15 articles), 13
General Line of the International Communist Movement, 239, 261, 280, 286, 290, 297, 299
General strikes, 46
Geneva Conference, 148, 163
Germany, 5–7, 11, 55, 56, 58, 62, 73, 78, 79, 82, 84, 85, 89, 243, 257, 262, 266n19
Gomułka, Władysław, 176, 180, 181, 193, 195, 197, 198, 201, 202, 206n14, 214, 268
  Khrushchev and, 176, 180, 181, 195, 197, 201, 214, 268
  Mao Zedong and, 202
  Polish-Hungarian relations and, 181
Gorbachev, Mikhail, 368, 369, 371–380, 382–386
  bilateral relations, and, 369, 374, 384, 385
  China and, 368, 369, 371–379, 383, 384
  Deng Xiaoping and, 384
  Li Peng and, 368, 373, 374, 384
  reform measures of, 375
  resignation of, 386
Great Britain, 12, 70, 83, 84, 86, 93n2, 98, 190, 202, 204, 210
  formal recognition of USSR by, 12
Great Leap Forward
  economic crises from, 241
  Khrushchev and, 209, 212, 215, 253, 264
  USSR and, 171, 209, 210, 212, 213, 244, 264
Great Proletarian Cultural Revolution
  Brezhnev, L., on, 304
  diplomatic pressure on Khrushchev and, 276
  foreign policy of, 111, 232, 257, 347
  in full swing, 307
  launch of, 274–276, 281, 305
  objectives of, 305, 321
  polemics and, 274, 292, 306
  purpose of, 253, 274, 292, 304
  research institutes abolished during, 343
  Soviet embassy and, 307
  ultra-leftist atmosphere of, 311
Great Purge, 162
Great Wall, 11, 61, 88, 95, 98–101, 104
  peace within, 100
Greece, 98
Grishin, Viktor, 236
Gromyko, Andrei, 104, 127, 142, 219–222, 334, 337, 359–362, 365
  Wang Youping and, 337
  Wu Xueqian and, 365
Gu Mu, 348
Gu Weijun (Wellington Koo), 11, 13, 42
Guangdong, 17, 24, 27, 29, 30, 32, 34, 36n9, 41, 48, 56, 64, 85
  rebellion in, 41, 48, 64
Guangzhou
  defeat of rebellion in, 17, 24, 41, 48, 49
  uprising, 41
Guangzhou Merchant Association, 24
Guerrilla warfare, 40, 50, 52, 56, 82
  Korean People's Army and, 136
Guo Songling, 26, 29

H

Hanoi, 295, 296, 324n28, 375, 376, 379–381
Hao Deqing, 176
Harriman, W. Averell, 84, 110
He Jian, 35, 49, 63
He Long, 278
Heath, Edward, 367, 368
Heavy industry, 151, 164, 171
Hebei warlords, 10, 11, 24, 25
Heilongjiang Provincial Military District, 312
Heixiazi Island, 275
Heng Samrin, 375
He-Umezu Agreement, 61
High frequency telephone links, 316
A History of Soviet-Chinese Economic and Trade Relations, 1917–1974, 155
Hitler, Adolf, 58, 78

Ho Chi Minh, 242, 250, 324n28
Hoxha, Enver, 248, 250, 252
Hu Hanmin, 26
Hu Qiaomu, 193, 206n8, 233, 360
Hu Yaobang, 368, 373, 375, 376
Hua Guofeng, 338, 341n2
Huang Hua, 116, 117, 120n20, 336,
    337, 341n3, 345, 353, 356,
    358–362, 364
  Andropov and, 360–362
  Brezhnev, L., funeral and, 360
  Deng Xiaoping and, 336, 345, 353,
    359, 360
  three major obstacles and, 359, 361, 362
Huang Kecheng, 152
Huang Ping, 48
Huang Yongsheng, 317
Huanggutun incident, 43
Huangpu (Whampoa) Military Academy
  Moscow and, 24, 30, 36n6
  National Revolutionary Army and, 30
Hubei, 31, 32, 34, 35, 41, 42, 49, 52
Hungary
  danger of capitalist restoration in, 185
  Hungarian People's Republic, 176
  Hungarian Revolution, 7, 176, 186n3
  Hungarian Socialist Workers' Party, 257
  Kádár and, 180, 181, 258
  Khrushchev and, 177, 179, 181, 185
  military intervention in, 177
  Polish-Hungarian relations, 181
Hurley, Patrick J., 84, 86, 91
Hussein (King), 363
Hydraulic power, 339

I
Ibarruri, Dolores, 166
ILD, see International Liaison
    Department
Ili Military Command, 271
Ilichev, Leonid, 344, 353–356
  normalization and, 356
Imperialism
  anti-imperialism, 236, 250, 254, 267,
    271, 293, 296, 299, 300, 305
  Anti-Imperialism Day, 46
  Cold War and, 205
  imperialist camp, 105, 118

imperialist countries, 33, 116
  international, 273, 281
  joint actions against, 312
  revisionism and, 270
  Soviet "social imperialism," 312
  threat of, 236
  of U.S., 145, 197, 236, 255, 257, 260,
    263, 281
Imperial Russia, 14, 85
Imperial system, abolition of, 5
"An Important Step toward the Unity of
    World Communism" (*Pravda*), 292
Inchon landing, 137
India, 125, 140, 190, 221, 222, 224,
    226n19, 229–232, 241, 264, 321, 344
  See also Sino-Indian border conflict
Indochina, 241, 295, 314, 335, 371,
    372, 374–377, 379
  Beijing and, 371
  Sino-Soviet normalization and, 369
  War, 201, 349
Indonesia, 190, 201, 260, 262, 290, 321
  reactionaries in, 299
Indonesia Committee of Supporters of
    Peace, 298
Industrial development, 113
Industrial raw materials, 131
Industrial workers, 49
Information Bureau for Communist and
    Workers' Parties, 105
Instructions on Our Countermoves to
    Reagan's Strengthening of Ties with
    Taiwan (MFA), 350
Intercontinental missiles, 310
Interkit, *see* International on China
Intermediate-range missiles, 310, 363
"Internal Publication for
    Safe-Keeping," 167
Internal Reference (publication),
    167, 170, 235
International Communist Movement
  CCP and split in, 243, 285, 286, 293
  CCP aspiration for special status in, 286
  China and, 175, 223, 232, 280
  common program of, 232, 263, 291
  CPSU work for unity in, 277
  de-Stalinization and, 162
  formation of leftist contingents in,
    257, 262–264, 286

International Communist Movement (*cont.*)
General Line of, 239, 261, 287, 290, 297, 299
guiding principles of, 235, 292
leadership of, 204, 238, 247, 261, 263, 286, 290, 311
left-leaning political parties in, 286, 299
Mao Zedong and, 262, 286, 311
Moscow Conference of World Communist and Workers' Parties and, 186
parallel leadership centers of, 186
prestige of CCP in, 241
revisionism and, 259
scope of, 297
Sino-Soviet split, 244
split, 243, 281, 285, 286, 293, 296, 300
strategies and tactics of, 240
traditional road of, 288
unity of, 280, 288, 291, 292
International Conference of Seventy-five Communist and Workers' Parties, 312
International Liaison Committee, 23
International Liaison Department (ILD), 192, 215, 231, 254, 257, 277, 288, 310
International on China (Interkit), 309
International relations, v–vii, 133, 164, 224, 333
Inter-socialist-state relations, 329
Iran, 320
Israeli Communist Party, 203
Ita Incident, *see* "Tacheng Incident in the Ili Region"
Italian Communist Party (leftist), 205n4, 206n10, 259, 262, 266n16, 290, 378
Izvestia (newspaper), 379

J
Jackson, Harry, 363
Japan
anti-Japanese forces, 57, 58
cease-fire proposal from, 73
Chinese Eastern Railway and, 9, 58
invasion of Northeast China, 55
Khrushchev meeting with Japanese parliamentary delegation, 271
Kwantung Army, 28, 46, 56, 72, 78, 91, 92
Nineteenth Division, 72
surrender of, 90, 92, 93, 96
westward aggression of, 82
Japanese Communist Party (JCP), 295, 310, 323n3
CCP and, 262, 295
Japanese Socialist Party, 270
JCP, *see* Japanese Communist Party
Jersild, Austin, vi, 149, 158n4, 226n28
Jiang Jieshi, 1, 17, 18, 26–31, 33–35, 37n10, 44–46, 51, 52, 55, 60–67, 67n2, 70, 73–75, 77, 79, 80, 83, 86–90, 93n1, 93n2, 95–104, 110, 210, 219, 241
aggressive actions of, 104
Bogomolov and, 61–63
CCP and, 33, 34, 63, 64, 77
Eighth Route Army, 82
Feng Yuxiang and, 35
Mao Zedong and, 77, 82, 96, 97, 99
Nanjing Nationalist government and, 45
Song Ziwen and, 67, 87–90
U.S. and, 79, 242, 269
USSR assistance to China and, 79
Xi'an incident and, 69
Jiang Jingguo, 90, 102
Jiang Tingfu, 61, 69
Jiang Zemin, 385
Jiangxi Soviet Region, 50
Jinmen
failure of battle of, 120n14
liberation of, 225n16
shelling of, 210, 219–220
Joffe, Adolf, 11, 12, 16
Joint fleet, 216–219, 225n8, 242
Journal of the Socialist Youth League, 23

K
Kachanov, K. M., 71
Kádár, János, 180, 181, 258
Kaganovich, Lazar, 153, 162, 182, 250
Kamanga, Reuben C., 307
Kang Sheng, 167, 231, 232, 238, 255
Kapitsa, Mikhail, 120n13, 219, 221, 343, 353, 363, 364, 378
Karakhan, Leo, 12–14, 25, 26
Kardelj, Edvard, 193, 198, 199, 206n17
Kasimi, Ahmatjan, 100
Kaunda, Kenneth, 380

Kenji, Miyamoto, 295, 310
Khmer Rouge, 375, 378, 379, 381, 382
Khrushchev, Nikita, v, 145, 147–158,
    161–169, 171–173, 175–186,
    189–205, 209, 210, 212, 214–224,
    225n4, 225n7, 225n8, 230–235,
    237–244, 245n10, 248–251,
    253–257, 259–264, 266n16, 268,
    271, 274–282, 287, 288, 291, 292,
    294, 300, 305, 306, 321
  accused of opportunism, 222
  Albania and, 248, 251, 261
  Bucharest Conference of Communist
    and Workers' Parties of Socialist
    Countries and, 238
  CCP on USSR under, 212, 215, 218,
    230, 232, 233, 248, 256, 264
  criticism of Stalin, 165, 167, 169,
    173, 250
  diplomatic pressure on, 276
  fall from power of, 271
  Gomułka and, 214, 268
  Great Leap Forward and, 209, 212,
    215, 253, 264
  Hungary and, 262
  influence of CCP and, 173, 218, 255
  "Khrushchevism without
    Khrushchev," 279
  Liu Shaoqi and, 167, 223, 230, 240,
    242, 248, 274
  Mao Zedong and, 163, 170, 193, 196,
    219, 225n8, 230, 255, 263
  meeting with Japanese parliamentary
    delegation, 271
  on Moscow Conference declaration,
    189–205, 209, 216, 224, 253,
    261, 287, 300
  Nehru and, 222, 232, 257
  Party of Labor of Albania and,
    248, 250, 251, 287
  Peng Dehuai and, 172, 215
  on People's Commune Movement,
    253, 255, 256
  People's Daily condemnation of, 251
  polemics and, 277, 279, 292
  Sino-Indian border conflict and, 210,
    221, 222, 224, 230, 266n16
  Sino-Soviet split and, 173, 282
  U.S. and, 199, 221, 222, 232, 234,
    255, 281, 321

  U-2 spy plane incident and, 234–235
  Yugoslavia and, 199, 235, 248, 260
  Zhou Enlai and, 217, 222, 231, 250,
    276–281, 288, 294
  Zhukov and, 184
  See also Secret speech
Kim Il-sung, 133, 141, 142, 144,
    146n15, 251, 269
  Deng Xiaoping and, 353, 355, 364
  Mao Zedong and, 133, 142
  Stalin and, 133, 141, 142, 144, 145
  USSR and, 141, 142, 269
Kirchschläger, Rudolf, 370
Kirk, Alan, 142, 146n17
Kisanka (N. V. Kuybyshev), 28, 29
Kissinger, Henry, 315, 318–322
  Mao Zedong and, 319–321
  Nixon and, 318, 319, 321
  secret trip to Beijing, 321
Kohler, Foy D., 278
Komatsubara, Michitaro, 73
Kong Xiangxi, 61
Kongha Rebellion, 81
Korea
  border with China, 72, 139
  guerrilla units in, 7
  Japanese Nineteenth Division and, 72
  Mao Zedong and, 131, 133–139, 144,
    145, 147
  U.S. intervention in, 134, 135
Korean People's Army, 134–137
Korean War
  armistice talks, 145
  Moscow and, 131, 133, 136, 144
  outbreak of, 131, 134, 190
  status of PRC and, 147, 218
Korean Workers' Party
  Politburo of, 136
  at Twenty-third CPSU Congress,
    304, 305
Kosygin, Aleksei, 277–279, 282, 289,
    290, 294, 306, 315–317, 324n28,
    330, 331
  Beijing and, 289, 294, 306, 316, 317,
    330–332
  Mao Zedong and, 279, 306, 330
  Zhou Enlai and, 277, 278, 289, 294,
    316, 324n28, 330
Koval, K. I., 149
Kovalev, Evgenii, 112

Kovalev, Ivan, 111–114, 116, 119n4, 124, 125
Kovda, V. A., 151
Kozlov, Frol, 233, 239, 250, 266n16
Kremlin, 129, 147, 162, 200, 278, 318
Kropotkin, Peter, 4
KSČ, see Communist Party of Czechoslovakia
Kuo, Mercy, 176, 186n2, 187n21
Kurile Islands, 85, 86, 124, 270, 283n8
Kuusinen, Otto, 257, 258

L
Laborers, 6, 8, 32
Lapin, Sergey, 293
Latin America, 235, 237, 244, 255, 260, 262, 263, 286, 288, 296, 297
Lazarenko (adviser), 151
"The Leaders of the CPSU are the Greatest Splitters of Our Times" (CCP), 274
League of Communists of Yugoslavia (LCY)
  CPSU and, 192, 193
  Mao Zedong and, 193, 199
League of Nations, 59
League of Yugoslav Communists, 261
Lebowski, Andrei, 116
LCY, see League of Communists of Yugoslavia
Le Duan, 251, 372, 377
Lenin, V. I., 3, 15, 25, 83, 165, 170, 196, 230, 232, 233, 239, 250, 260
  commemoration of, 230, 233
  polemics, 233
  Sun Yatsen and, 4
Leninism, 1, 20, 161, 211, 233, 263, 305
  See also Marxism-Leninism
"A Letter to All Countrymen on Resisting Japan and Saving the Nation," 60
"Let Us Unite on the Basis of the Moscow Declaration and Moscow Statement" (People's Daily), 261
Li Dazhao, 5, 7, 20, 25, 34, 36n1, 36n3
Li Fenglin, 359
Li Fuchun, 42, 128, 148, 152–154, 272, 273

Li Lianqing, 314
Li Lisan, 42, 49
  on Soviets, 49
Li Peng, 368, 370, 373, 374, 381, 384, 385
  Gorbachev and, 368, 373, 374
Li Qiang, 150, 213
Li Shichun, 383
Li Xiannian, 363
Li Yueran, 187n10, 197
Li Zhangda, 16
Li Zhilong, 28, 29
Liao Zhongkai, 26, 36n4
Liaoning warlords, 10, 11
Liberation Daily (newspaper), 313
Lin Biao, 137, 269, 270, 308, 314, 324n24
  "Urgent Directive Regarding Strengthening Combat Readiness to Prevent a Surprise Attack by the Enemy," 317
Lin Boqu, 20, 43
Litvinov, M. M., 69, 70
Liu Changsheng, 237
Liu Ningyi, 236, 237, 245n18, 254
Liu Shaoqi, 109, 114–116, 118, 119, 124, 129, 131n5, 151, 156, 172, 177–179, 183, 190, 193, 194, 210, 211, 223, 230, 236, 240, 242, 243, 246n27, 248, 253, 254, 258, 260, 266n12, 276, 277, 280, 293, 295
  Abrasimov and, 183, 193
  Deng Xiaoping and, 167, 172, 175, 211, 242, 274
  Khrushchev and, 177
  Mikoyan and, 112, 113, 169
  on polemics, 264
  revisionism and, 262
  Stalin and, 116
Liu Xiao, 180, 231, 240, 249, 251, 252, 288
  Chervonenko and, 288
  Warsaw Pact and, 249
Living standards, 32, 298
Loans, 24, 35, 36n6, 70, 71, 79, 112, 114, 118, 127, 128, 130, 138, 149, 155–157, 218
Long March, 60, 61, 66, 75

"Long-term Program for the Development of Science and Technology from 1956 to 1967," 151
Long-wave radio, 210, 216–219, 225n8, 225n9, 242
Louis, Victor, 316
Lu Dingyi, 157, 158, 233
Luo Fu, 76
Lüshun, *see* Port Arthur
Lushan Conference, 255
Lüthi, Lorenz, vi, 162, 256, 266n16, 279, 282, 291

M
Ma Xusheng, 336, 353, 359, 362
Malaya, 190, 262
Malayan Communist Party, 298
Malenkov, Georgii, 153, 162, 163, 182, 195, 250
Malik, Jacob, 141, 142, 146n16
Malinovskii, Rodion, 278, 279, 282, 287
Maltsev, Viktor, 353
Manchu Qing dynasty, 5
Manchukuo, 58, 67n2, 72, 73, 79
Manchuria
    invasion of, 310, 315
    South Manchuria Railway, 9, 43, 56, 85–89, 91, 119n2
    USSR and, 17, 44, 57, 78, 104
    withdrawal from, 102
Mao Zedong, 52, 76, 95, 109, 123, 133–137, 147, 162, 175, 189, 209, 230, 249, 267–282, 286, 303, 330, 348, 370
    anti-revisionist position of, 262
    blocking conference of fraternal parties, 280
    CCP and, 1, 2, 76, 84, 96, 97, 113, 116, 133, 134, 137, 144, 147, 167, 169–173, 175, 181, 183, 191, 193, 194, 196, 198, 204, 238, 243, 262, 263, 272, 273, 288, 290, 305, 317
    compromise with USSR, 244, 276
    contempt for CPSU, 304
    death of, 333, 334, 358
    on defensive war against USSR, 270
    de-Stalinization and, 162, 167
    diplomatic strategy of, 297, 303

Eighth Route Army and, 82
    foreign policy of, 111, 116, 222, 254, 297, 310, 334
    Gomułka and, 181, 197, 198, 201
    International Communist Movement and, 145, 168, 173, 223, 238, 240, 244, 262, 263, 265, 272, 286, 287, 290, 294, 299, 311
    Jiang Jieshi and, 77, 95–97, 99, 104, 269
    Khrushchev and, 182, 185, 193, 197, 222, 230
    Kim Il-sung and, 141, 269
    Kissinger and, 319–321
    Korea and, 131, 133–139, 145, 145n4
    Kosygin and, 282, 289, 290, 294, 301n3, 314, 316
    LCY and, 199
    learning from USSR, 221
    Mikoyan and, 112, 113, 116, 120n18, 125, 169, 183
    Moscow and, 40, 50, 67n1, 76, 78, 82, 84, 109, 112, 116, 118, 119, 120n14, 123, 124, 139, 167, 189–205, 210, 223
    Moscow Conference and, 175, 189–205, 209, 224
    "On the People's Democratic Dictatorship," 116
    "On the Ten Major Relationships," 157, 164, 171, 172
    personality cult and, 166–170, 172, 274
    rise within CCP, 2
    Second FYP and, 152, 154
    on secret speech, 167
    on Sino-Soviet alliance, 116, 130, 131, 144, 145, 147
    Sino-Soviet border and, 270, 282, 317, 330
    Sino-U.S. relations and, 352
    socialist bloc and, 147, 173, 183, 198, 202, 205, 209, 223, 224, 256
    Stalin and, 124, 131, 268
    third world, Mao leader of, 306
    three worlds theory of, 334
    on unequal treaties, 275, 276
    USSR and, 82, 83, 124, 129, 130, 178, 193, 196, 198, 202, 206n20, 210–212, 218, 223, 242, 244, 253, 254, 264, 269, 270, 281, 303

Mao Zedong (*cont.*)
　U-2 spy plane incident and, 234–235
　Wang Jiaxiang and, 50, 125, 266n9
　world revolution and, 170, 263, 300, 306, 320
　Yudin and, 157, 169, 184, 193, 194, 217
　on Zhenbao Island, 313, 321
　"Mao Zedong on the Foundation of the Chinese People's Democratic Dictatorship" (*Novoe vremia*), 118
Mao Zedong Thought, 172, 173, 255, 257, 262, 263, 265, 299, 306
Maring, H. (Henk Sneevliet), 16, 20, 36n1
Marosán, Gyorgy, 181
Marshall, George, 99, 100, 102, 105
Marx, Karl, 83, 170
Marxism
　debates on Marxist theory, 281
　orthodox, 229
Marxism-Leninism
　currents, 259
　interpretations of, 247
　principles of, 230
　two-stage theory of, 18n2
　world revolution and, 262, 263
May Instructions (Stalin), 31–36
"May 16 Notification" (CCP CC), 305
McMahon Line, 221, 226n19
Mechanized troops, 310
"Memorandum from the Department of the People's Commissioners of Foreign Affairs of the Soviet Russian Federative Socialist Republic," 10
"Methods for Planning and Organizing Scientific Research in the People's Republic of China," 151
MFA, *see* Ministry of Foreign Affairs
Mićunović, Veljko, 180
Mif, Pavel, 75
Mikoyan, Anastas, 112–114, 118, 120n18, 128, 129, 131n5, 148, 149, 152, 167, 178, 179, 182–184, 190, 191, 250, 277, 279
　Liu Shaoqi and, 109, 112, 113, 131n5, 169
　Mao Zedong and, 112, 113, 116, 125, 183
　on Stalin, 112, 113, 118, 167, 170

　in Xibaipo, 109, 112–114, 118, 119n8, 120n18
Mikunis, Shmuel, 203
Military assistance, 63, 70, 78, 111, 118, 143
Military bases, 17, 339
Military Commission, 70, 101
Military equipment, 71, 120n14, 137, 138, 143, 308
Military intervention, 177, 301n6
Military revolution, 43
Military struggle, 40
Ministry of Foreign Affairs (MFA)
　CCP and, 21
　Chinese embassy and, 343, 383
　"Instructions on Our Countermoves to Reagan's Strengthening of Ties with Taiwan," 350
　internal deliberations by, 336, 345
　"Report on Negotiating Sino-Soviet State-to-State Relations," 338
　"Request for Instructions Regarding Not Renewing the Sino-Soviet Treaty of Friendship, Alliance, and Mutual Assistance," 336
　Zhou Enlai address to, 130
Ministry of Railways, 126
Modernization, 143, 348, 370, 371
Molotov, Vyacheslav, 84, 86, 125, 126, 162, 163, 182, 183, 195, 201, 202, 250
Mondale, Walter, 339
Mongolia
　independence of, 81
　Red Army and, 10–12, 17, 65
　USSR military cooperation with, 276
　See also Outer Mongolia
Mongolian People's Republic, 115, 118, 315
Mongolian People's Revolutionary Party, 269
"More on the Historical Experience of Proletarian Dictatorship" (*People's Daily*), 175, 179
Moscow
　Beijing border negotiations with, 276, 317, 377
　Beijing feeling threat from, 321

bottom line for restoring relations with China, 280
CCP and, 39, 40, 43, 52, 56, 58–60, 63, 64, 75, 76, 84, 109, 117, 183, 192, 204, 209, 242, 252, 279, 280, 317
foreign policy of, 300, 357
Hanoi and, 296, 376, 379, 380
Huangpu (Whampoa) Military Academy and, 24, 30, 36n6
Korean War and, 133, 144, 147
Mao Zedong and, 40, 76, 78, 82, 84
March Conference, 292, 293
May Instructions, 35
military principles of, 52
political situation in, 181, 357
pressure on Beijing, 316
Sun Yatsen and, 16
Vietnam and, 290, 293, 324n28, 380, 383
Vietnam War and, 294
Washington and, 317, 318
Xi'an incident and, 67
Moscow Conference of World Communist and Workers' Parties
CCP concessions at, 253
as display of unity, 194
draft declaration of, 193, 238
International Communist Movement and, 204, 244, 286–293, 300
Mao Zedong and, 175, 189–205, 209, 224
March Moscow Conference, 291–293, 300
in 1965, 300
Sino-Soviet alliance and, 189, 204
Yugoslav delegation to, 199
Moscow Declaration
accusations of betrayal, 189
ambiguities of, 200
CCP and CPSU after, 229
Peace Manifesto and, 189
peaceful coexistence and, 261
Moscow Olympics, 348
Moscow Radio, 312
Moscow Statement, 261, 286, 290, 291
Muhsin, Turk, 81
Mutual-assistance, 6, 62, 63, 69, 70, 73, 74, 93n1, 147, 185

N
Nagy, Imre, 178, 185
Nanchang Uprising, 36, 41
Nanjing, 34, 35, 40, 41, 44–46, 56–59, 61–65, 67, 70, 73, 96, 116–118
Nanjing Nationalist government, 34, 41, 44, 45, 57–59, 61–64, 118
National Daily (newspaper), 4
National democratic revolutionary movements, 115
Nationalism, 81, 89, 218
Nationalist Army, 15, 24, 25, 31, 33, 41, 52, 57, 61, 65, 66, 71, 85, 101, 103
Second Army of, 25
Nationalist Assembly, 103
Nationalist countries, 296, 297, 305
Nationalist Party
anti-Soviet demonstrations by, 45
CC of, 17, 26–28, 33–35, 46, 47, 56, 62, 64, 67, 77, 82, 84
CCP and, 1, 3, 19–23, 26, 27, 29, 33–36, 36n4, 40, 55, 57–65, 67, 69, 74–78, 82, 91, 95, 97, 99–101, 103, 104
Central Executive Committee, 21–23, 26, 27, 29, 36n4
Fifth National Congress of, 76
First National Congress of, 20–23
Fourth Plenary Session of the First Congress, 26
ideological preparation for, 17
lack of leadership of, 19
Provisional CCP CC and, 41, 57
Outer Mongolia and, 22
Revolutionary Committee of, 36, 41
Second National Congress, 23, 27
Second Plenary Session of First Congress, 23
Stalin on CCP and, 34, 40, 65, 97, 99, 104
USSR and, 19, 22, 24, 30, 55, 61–63, 69, 74, 82, 101, 103
National Liberation Movement, 15, 22, 25, 235, 263, 291, 296, 297
National liberation struggles
in Third World, 296, 298
wars of national liberation, 60
National People's Army, 25, 26, 31, 34

"National Program Committee for Scientific Research Work," 151
National Resurrection Group, 80
National Revolutionary Army, 27–31, 34, 67n1
  Huangpu (Whampoa) Military Academy and, 30
National security, 119, 242, 253, 264, 269–272, 281, 282, 315, 332, 338, 339, 349, 350, 370
Nation of Great Mongolia, 9
Nazism
  in Germany, 84
  rise of, 55
Nehru, Jawaharlal, 221, 222, 226n19, 232, 255, 257
  Khrushchev and, 222, 232
Neo-colonialism, 297
New China, 111–113, 116, 118, 120n10, 123, 266n7
New Fourth Army, 76–78, 96
New villages, 6
New Zealand Communist Party, 225n8
Nguyen Co Thach, 380, 383
Nguyễn Dy Niên, 375
Nineteenth Route Army, 56
"9 September" rebellion, 41
Nixon, Richard, 303, 318–321, 325n37, 325n39, 339
  Kissinger and, 318–321, 325n39
  Shanghai Communiqué and, 319
  withdrawal of U.S. forces from Vietnam and, 318
  Zhou Enlai and, 318
No. 1 Campaign, 85
Normalization
  of bilateral relations, vii, 15, 290, 327, 330, 332, 337, 338, 353, 355, 356, 358, 376, 380, 381, 384
  Carter and, 349
  characteristics of, 328
  Deng Xiaoping and, 338, 339, 345, 346, 349, 353, 360, 367, 369, 384
  differences in attitudes toward, 355
  discussions about, 331, 332, 346
  factors behind, vii, 339, 373
  first reference to, 330
  Five Principles of Peaceful Coexistence and, 332, 333, 385

  gradual, 289, 346, 355, 359, 361
  guiding principles for, 333
  Ilichev and, 356
  Indochina and, 349, 369
  norms of international relations and, 333
  preconditions for, 356, 369
  Sino-U.S. relations and, 349
  of Sino-Vietnamese relations, 376, 379
  strategic benefits from, 371
  talks on, 338
Northeast Area People's Democratic Authority, 111
Northeast China
  CCP and, 55, 109, 111, 114, 268
  truce talks, 103
Northeast Executive Commission, 44
Northeast People's Revolutionary Army, 57
Northern Bureau, CCP CC, 310
Northern Expedition
  Northern Expedition Army, 30, 31
  Second Northern Expedition, 43
Northern Sea warlords, 5
North Korea, 134–137, 140–142, 144, 251, 260, 262, 290, 295, 355
North Korean People's Army, 134
North Territories dispute, 283n8
North Vietnam, 262, 291, 295, 296, 300, 308
  China and, 262, 296, 300, 308
Northward Resisting-Japan Advance Force, 52
Northwestern Suppression Headquarters, 64
Novoe vremia (newspaper), 118
Novotný, Antonín, 202, 258, 259
NPC, *see* Chinese National People's Congress
Nuclear facilities, 315
Nuclear power, 312
Nuclear protection, 220
Nuclear submarines, 205, 217
Nuclear war
  preemptive nuclear strike, 316
  Soviet pledge of non-use of nuclear weapons against China, 316
Nuomenkan incident, 72, 78

O

October Revolution
anarchists and, 4
anniversary of, 104, 278, 310
Chinese Eastern Railway and, 8, 9
fiftieth anniversary of, 309
Ōhira, Masayoshi, 320
"On Measures for Normalization of
Soviet-Chinese Relations" (CPSU
CC), 289
"On the CCP Leadership's Splittism in
the International Communist
Movement and the Position of the
Mongolian People's Revolutionary
Party" (Mongolian People's
Revolutionary Party), 269
"On the Divisive Moscow Conference"
(*People's Daily*), 292
"On the Historical Experience of the
Dictatorship of the Proletariat"
(*People's Daily*), 168, 173
"On the People's Democratic
Dictatorship" (Mao Zedong),
113, 116
"On the Ten Major Relationships"
(Mao Zedong), 157, 159n13,
164, 171, 172
"Open Door" policy, 100, 102
Opium War, 3, 5
Opportunism, 197, 222, 255
Orlov, Andrei, 113
Outer Mongolia
eruption of problems in, 10
independence of, 9, 11, 17, 81, 87–90,
110, 115
Nationalist Party and, 17, 22, 65
Outer Mongolian Border Army, 72
problems in, 10
recovery of, 13
Red Army in, 10–12, 17, 65

P

Pacific War, 69, 80, 84
Paikes, Lenin Aleksandr, 11
Pak Hon-yong, 141
Pak Il-u, 137
Pakistan, 320, 380
Pan-labor, 6

Panmunjom, 142
Panyushkin, Alexander, 83
Paris Peace Conference, 3, 6
China and, 5
Paris Summit, 234, 245n10
Party Literature Research Center, 330
Party of Labor of Albania
fraternal parties and, 251
Khrushchev and, 248, 251
Party Reform Strategy Drafting
Committee, 20
Party-to-party relations, vii, 147, 230,
267, 281
Pavlov (General), 30
PCF, *see* French Communist Party
Peaceful coexistence, 163, 164, 167,
168, 199, 203, 221, 223, 229, 231,
236, 237, 239, 242, 248, 251, 260,
261, 293, 296, 298, 313, 385
Peaceful transition, 163, 164, 174n4,
195, 196, 229, 236, 239, 240, 242,
248, 261
Peace Manifesto, 189, 195, 199, 235, 239
Moscow Declaration and, 240
Peasants
peasant governments, 49
peasant movements, 32, 34, 35, 50
rich, 273
Peng Dehuai, 49, 136, 138–141, 172,
192, 215–217, 255, 256, 266n12
Khrushchev and, 215
Malinovsky and, 216, 217
rehabilitation of, 255
Stalin and, 141
Peng Pai, 48
Peng Zhen, 157, 167, 223, 239, 240,
248, 251, 284n25
People's Commune Movement
CPSU CC on, 214
Khrushchev on, 255, 256
USSR and, 253
People's Daily
condemnation of Khrushchev, 251
"Let Us Unite on the Basis of the
Moscow Declaration and Moscow
Statement," 261
"More on the Historical Experience
of Proletarian Dictatorship,"
175, 179

People's Daily (*cont.*)
"On the Divisive Moscow
Conference," 292
"On the Historical Experience of the
Dictatorship of the Proletariat,"
168, 173
"To Advance Forward Along the Road
Opened Up by the October
Socialist Revolution," 306
"Workers of All Countries Unite, Oppose
Our Common Enemy," 259
People's Republic of China (PRC)
Constitution of, 157
founding of, v, 1, 109, 114, 123, 145,
156, 222, 327, 348, 352
Korean War and, 147
representation at UN, 140
strategic triangle among USSR, U.S.,
and, 328, 346, 350, 357, 370
USSR and, 109, 114, 123, 125, 130,
147, 205, 216–220, 251, 319,
327, 328, 385
People's Liberation Army (PLA),
111, 139, 152, 270, 271, 312,
317, 369, 370
People's Republic of Tuva, 81
Personality cult, 162, 166, 168–170,
172, 191
Mao Zedong and, 166–170,
172, 274
Petroleum Ministry, 152
Phnom Penh, 334, 380, 382
Pietrow (Ambassador), 86
PKI, *see* Communist Party of Indonesia
PLA, *see* People's Liberation Army
Poland
China and, 180, 181, 365
crisis in, 176
Polish-Hungarian relations, 166, 179,
181, 191
Polemics
CCP confidence in, 262
commemoration of Lenin's birthday
and, 233
Great Cultural Revolution and, 274
intensification of, 264, 332
international implications of, 281
Khrushchev and, 257, 277
onset of, 257–262, 331

Polish United Workers' Party, 176, 195
Political Consultative Committee, 191,
232, 248
Politics and Law Commission, 157
Pol Pot, 375
Ponomarev, Boris, 193
Port Arthur
Agreement, 127
Stalin and, 87, 89, 130
troops in, 149
Positional warfare, 52
Pospelov, Pyotr, 200, 232
Poverty, 32
POW, *see* Prisoners of war
Powers, Francis Gary, 234
Pravda (newspaper), 31, 118, 168, 179,
183, 191, 215, 260, 261, 269, 270,
277, 281, 298, 300, 308, 312, 315,
363, 379
"An Important Step toward the Unity
of World Communism," 292
PRC, *see* People's Republic of China
Preemptive nuclear strike, 315, 316
Prisoners of war (POW), 101, 142
Problems of Peace and Socialism
(publication), 206n18, 280
"Proclamation on Developing and
Further Strengthening the
Friendship and Cooperation
between the Soviet Union and
the Other Socialist States"
(USSR), 329
Proletarian dictatorship, v, 20, 249,
272, 297
revisionist, 273
Proletarian internationalism, 203, 251,
278, 327, 329
Proletarian leadership, 48
Propaganda activities, 44, 45
Propaganda Department of CCP CC,
157, 233, 245n12
"A Proposal Concerning the General Line
of the International Communist
Movement" (CCP), 261
"Proposal on the Second FYP for
Developing the National Economy
(1958–1962) (Revised Draft)," 154
"Proposals for Improving Sino-Soviet
Relations" (China), 340

"Protocol Confirming the Validity of an Agreement on the Chinese Changchun Railway," 126
Provisional Government of the Islamic People's Republic of Eastern Turkistan, 81
Psychological warfare, 117
Pyongyang, 133, 135, 138, 139
  Beijing and, 144

Q
Qian Qichen, 345, 351, 353–356, 360–362, 371, 374, 378, 380–383
Qiao Guanhua, 316, 318, 354
Qiliqin Island, 311
Qin-Doihara (Chin-Doihara) Agreement, 61
Qing dynasty, Tsarist government and, 275
Qu Qiubai, 5, 36n3, 41–43, 50

R
Radchenko, Sergey, vi, 131n4, 261, 282, 282n3, 290, 310
Railway communications, 315
Rakhmanin, Oleg, 309
Rákosi, Mátyás, 176
Ranković, Aleksandar, 193, 199
Reactionaries
  Indonesian, 299
  reactionary tactics, 257
Reagan, Ronald, 349–351, 365, 371, 380
  Zhao Ziyang and, 357
Rectification Campaign, 83, 84, 172
Red Army
  in Central Soviet Area, 52, 53
  fighting capability of, 65, 75
  Mongolia and, 10, 11
  in Outer Mongolia, 10, 11, 17, 65, 72
  in Russian Turkistan, 16
  Second Corps of, 65
  Siberia and, 7, 10
  Soviet Republic of China and, 51
  and Zhang Xueliang, 66
Red Flag (journal)
  "The Dictatorship of the Proletarian and the Great Proletarian Cultural Revolution," 306
  "Why Did Khrushchev Fall?," 281

Red Flag Far East Special Corps, 45
Red Guards, 307, 308, 323n9
  Chen Yi and, 308
Red Square, 200, 277, 307
  Red Square incident, 308
Reform and opening policy, v, 346, 347, 365
Ren Bishi, 42, 112, 172
"Report on Negotiating Sino-Soviet State-to-State Relations" (MFA), 338
Republic of China, 14, 51, 140
Republic of Eastern Turkistan, 85
"Request for Instructions Regarding Not Renewing the Sino-Soviet Treaty of Friendship, Alliance, and Mutual Assistance" (MFA), 336
Resist Japan and Oppose Jiang Movement, 60, 64
Resist Japan Coalition Army, 60, 64, 66
Resolution on Comrades Working in the Nationalist Party and Their Attitude (Socialist Youth League), 23
Resolution on the Nationalist Movement and the Nationalist Party (Socialist Youth League), 23
Revisionism
  anti-revisionism, 267, 271, 290, 305
  emergence of, 273, 274
  failure of, 281
  guarding against, 273, 274, 305, 321
  imperialism and, 257, 263, 270, 306, 309, 321
  International Communist Movement and, 263
  political campaign to eliminate, 272
  semi-revisionism, 237
  Socialist Education Movement and, 274
  struggles against, 233, 254, 262, 309
  threat to proletarian dictatorship, 273
Revolutionary Committee of Nationalist Party, 36
Revolutionary Military Commission of the Central People's Government, 137
Revolutionary struggles, 48, 196, 286, 288
Revolution of 1911, 4, 16
Ridgway, Matthew, 142
Rogachev, Igor, 368, 378, 380–382
Rokossovsky, Konstantin, 180
Romania, 78, 98, 233, 290, 355
Romanian Communist Party, 288

Romanian Workers' Party, 238, 239
Rongzhen, Nie, 43, 139, 141, 167, 313
Roosevelt, Franklin, 86, 110
Roshchin, Nikolai, 125, 134, 135, 137, 138
Roy, M. N., 35
Russian Communist Party (Bolsheviks),
    8, 15, 16, 18n4
  CC of, 7, 17
Russian Revolution
  Chinese media attitude toward, 4
  impact of, 5
  information about, 6
  See also October Revolution
Russian Siberian Railroad, 8
Russian Turkistan, 16
Russo-Chinese Kyakhta Border
    Agreement, 9
Russo-German Non-Aggression Treaty, 78
Russo-German War, 69, 71, 74, 78–84
Russo-Japanese Neutrality Pact, 78, 79
Russo-Japanese War of 1904, 85

S
Saillant, Louis, 236
Saint Petersburg, 4, 268
Sanmenxia Key Water Control Project, 213
Sary-Ozek, 71
Shcherbakov, Iljia, 336, 337, 341
Science and technology reference
    materials, 150
Second Afro-Asian Conference, 299, 300
Second Opium War, 81
Secret "additional agreement," 129
Secret speech
  CCP on, 161, 167, 181
  distribution of, 167
  Mao Zedong on, 167–169
  surprise nature of, 166
SED, see Socialist Unity Party of Germany
Selected Writings of Deng Xiaoping, 384
Self-criticism, 64, 173, 182, 266n9
Self-determination, 5, 115
Self-reliance, 39, 154, 241
Serov, Ivan A., 177, 182
"7 July incident," 70
"Several Issues Raised in the Socialist
    Education Movement in the
    Countryside" (CCP CC), 273

Shahidia, Burhan, 100
Shanghai
  general strike in, 46
  Shanghai General Union, 34
Shanghai Communiqué, 319
Shanhaiguan, 43, 46, 98, 101
Shen Dexie, 70
Shen Honglie, 53n2
Sheng Shicai, 79, 80
Shepilov, Dmitri, 192
Shevardnadze, Eduard, 380, 384
Shi Zhe, 43, 112, 177–179
Short History of the All-Union Communist
    Party (Bolsheviks) (Stalin), 167
Shtykov, Terentii, 135, 136
Siberia, 7, 10, 80, 222
  Russian Siberian Railroad, 8
Sihanouk, Norodom, 375, 378, 379,
    381, 382
Sino-American ambassadorial talks, 313
Sino-American Commerce Treaty, 104
Sino-American rapprochement
  potential for, 316
  USSR seeking to undermine, 322
  Washington uncompromising in, 317
Sino-American strategic cooperation, 333
Sino-Indian border conflict
  Cuban missile crisis and, 256
  Khrushchev and, 222
  McMahon Line and, 221
  USSR neutrality in, 210, 221
Sino-Japanese war, 5, 73, 74
Sino-Mongolian border, 90, 268, 281,
    310, 367
Sino-Mongolian relations, 269
Sino-Russian Agreement on an Outline
    for Resolving All Existing Issues and
    the Temporary Agreement on the
    Management of the Chinese Eastern
    Railway, 13
Sino-Russian non-aggression treaty, 59
Sino-Russian Treaty of Peking, 268
Sino-Soviet Agreement on Science and
    Technology Cooperation, 150
Sino-Soviet Agreement on the
    Changchun Railroad, 90
Sino-Soviet alliance
  collapse of, 281
  consolidation of, 150

deterioration of, 276, 303
economic foundation of, 109–119,
    133, 144
growth of, 145
guidelines of, 327
interests of, 119
Mao and Stalin on, 119
Moscow Conference and, 186, 189, 204
strength of, 220
Sino-Soviet border
Beijing lowering military tensions
    along, 315
breakdown of negotiations on,
    vii, 274, 281, 282, 303
clashes, 221–223, 244n3, 310–312
Mao Zedong and, 270, 282, 310,
    312, 317
military conflicts along, 312, 331
negotiations, vii, 274, 281, 282, 317,
    322, 344, 385
settlement of disputes on, 330, 378
Soviet troops deployed along, 317
Zhou Enlai and, 322, 330
Sino-Soviet Cold War, 322
Sino-Soviet Committee on Economic,
    Trade, and Scientific and
    Technology Cooperation, 365
Sino-Soviet detente, 243, 244, 249, 250,
    252, 280
Sino-Soviet hotline, 314
Sino-Soviet Joint Stock Xinjiang
    Petroleum Company, 149
Sino-Soviet Military Committee, 90
Sino-Soviet non-aggression and
    non-use-of-force treaty, 337
Sino-Soviet political negotiations,
    354, 360, 365
Sino-Soviet Protocol on Conditions for
    Exchanging Engineering and
    Technical Personnel, 365
Sino-Soviet split
evolution of, v, vi, 161, 229, 230,
    278, 371
International Communist Movement
    and, 161, 165, 179, 204, 205,
    235, 241, 244, 247, 281
Khrushchev and, 161, 233, 282
seeds of, 63, 130, 173, 196
Sino-Soviet State Relations Negotiation
    Office, 338

Sino-Soviet strategic cooperation, 115
Sino-Soviet Treaty of Friendship,
    Alliance, and Mutual Assistance,
    99, 109, 110, 317, 340
expiration of, 335, 337
talks on terminating, 329
Sino-Soviet Treaty of 1945, 115
Sino-U.S. relations
Deng Xiaoping on, 339, 349–352
Mao Zedong and, 352
normalization and, 349, 351, 352, 354
progress in, 339, 351
stabilizing, 350, 354
Sino-Vietnamese relations, 294, 372,
    376, 379
Sino-Vietnamese War, 336
Social Democratic Party of Germany, 59
Socialism
China, so-called "true socialism"
    and, 349
construction of, 142, 164, 256
declaration of equality among socialist
    states, 173, 178
diverse socialist models, 349
economic development and, 256
ideology, 15, 168
moving from capitalism to, 195
Russian-style, 5
socialist countries, 47, 150, 158n1,
    168, 171, 173, 177, 178, 183,
    185, 186, 191, 196–198, 210,
    213, 223, 234–236, 238, 252,
    257, 267, 293, 294, 299, 309,
    310, 329, 344
socialist development, 163–165, 173,
    180, 214, 349
struggle for, 229, 237
transition to, 194, 195, 212, 229,
    237, 240
Socialist bloc
China and, 130, 133, 202
intra-bloc issues, 204
Korean War and, 133
Mao Zedong and, 198, 223, 224
political crises in, 173
secret speech and, 161
Socialist camp, 144, 165, 168, 173, 176,
    179, 180, 184, 186, 189–191, 194,
    196, 198, 206n13, 209, 212, 218, 268
Socialist Education Movement, 274

Socialist Party International, 59
Socialist revolutions, 4–7, 164, 186, 195, 213, 297
Socialist Unity Party of Germany (SED)
CCP CC and, 261, 266n19
Sixth Congress of, 257, 260
Socialist Youth League, 7, 20, 21
Society for China's Resurrection, 15
Song Qingling, 80, 200, 207n21
Song Ziwen, 79, 86–88, 90
Jiang Jieshi and, 67, 87, 88, 90
Stalin and, 86–89
Wang Shijie and, 90
Sonoda, Sunao, 336
South Anhui incident, 78
South Korean Army, 138
South Manchuria Railway, 9, 43, 56, 85–89, 91, 119n2
Sovereignty, viii, 12, 45, 100, 101, 150, 298
of China, 8, 11, 12, 14, 129, 242, 256
Soviet air force, 120n14, 133, 134, 137–139, 143, 144
Soviet-American collusion, 315
Soviet Army, 16, 45, 46, 53n3, 72, 84, 85, 90–93, 96, 100–103, 110, 124, 143, 147, 150, 312, 338, 340, 374
Soviet Aviation Bureau, 44
Soviet-China Friendship Association, 213
Soviet-Chinese assets, 127
Soviet-Chinese Friendship, 214, 224
Soviet Far East Army, 70
Soviet Frontier Defense Army, 312
Soviet-German Non-Aggression Treaty, 73, 79
Soviet-Japanese Neutrality Pact, 78
Soviet-Polish relations, 181, 194
Soviet Republic of China
Provisional Central Government of, 50, 60
Red Army and, 49, 50
Soviet Revolution, 1, 39–53, 60, 65
Soviet Russia
foreign affairs of, 44, 295
government of, 10, 13
Soviet Russian Communist Party (Bolsheviks), 4, 7, 8, 16, 17, 18n4, 40, 43, 48

Soviet Russian People's Diplomatic Commission, 11
Soviets (assemblies), 48
Soviet State Planning Commission, 153
Soviet Union (USSR)
Albania, relations with, 248, 250, 252
Beijing and, 10–12, 14, 22, 41, 144, 154, 176, 213, 264, 285, 289, 294, 365, 371, 373, 377
Beijing, Soviet leadership in, 299, 308, 345
Boxer Indemnity and, 13, 14
Brezhnev, L., on China relations with, 289, 344
CCP CC and, 43, 97, 173, 221, 270, 294
CCP on USSR under Khrushchev, 147–158, 170–172, 175–186, 197, 248
Chen Yi on, 222, 243
China, anti-Soviet international united front and, 334, 335, 348, 370
China assistance from, 62, 64, 66, 70, 73, 74, 111, 129, 213
China combat-ready for war with, 314
China diplomatic relations with, 3–18, 23, 308, 321
China four-point policy toward, 319
China ideological challenge to, 234
China influence in, 185
China on danger of Soviet hegemony, 333
Chinese students trained in, 42
Comintern and, 56, 59, 83
Czechoslovakia and, 98, 310, 311
Dalian and, 85–88, 110
"Declaration on the Principles for Mutual Relations," 340
development of Chinese politics and, 2
diplomatic concessions of, 102
diplomatic ties with China, 41, 45
disintegration of, 312, 386
domestic policy of, 209, 223, 232, 292, 345
Europe and, 57, 63, 83, 85, 98, 124, 152, 162, 168, 175, 180, 182, 223, 320, 363
expansionism, 319, 320, 335, 349

experts from, 71, 114, 127, 130,
  143, 150, 156–158, 158n6,
  241, 244, 331
Far Eastern policy, 123
Feng and, 15, 25, 26, 31, 35, 58
foreign policy of, 59, 61, 111, 116,
  223, 254, 264, 296, 346, 358,
  370, 382
formal recognition of, 12
Great Leap Forward and, 209, 212,
  244, 253
intra-party activities, 163
invasion of Afghanistan, 343, 347
Jiang Jieshi, USSR assistance to China
  and, 79
Kim Il-sung and, 269
League of the Nations and, 59
loans to China, 127, 155, 156
Manchuria and, 44, 57, 58, 78, 104
Mao Zedong and, 82, 83, 124, 129,
  130, 178, 193, 196, 198, 202,
  206n20, 210–212, 218, 221, 223,
  242, 244, 253, 254, 264, 269,
  270, 281, 303; Albania, relations
  with, 248, 250, 252
media and, 239, 258, 379
military advisers from, 18, 25, 29, 31,
  51–53, 71, 82, 135, 139, 140, 216
military aid from, 118, 143, 252, 291,
  293, 296, 308
military aid to North Vietnam, 291, 308
military cooperation with Mongolia, 276
naming of, 12, 230, 295
Nationalist Party and, 17–19, 23, 30,
  47, 63, 82
Nationalist Party, anti-Soviet
  demonstrations by, 45
National People's Army and, 31
neutrality in Sino-Indian border
  conflict, 210, 222
People's Commune Movement and, 213
perceived threat from, 320
pledge of non-use of nuclear weapons
  against China, 316
political crisis in, 182
PRC and, v, 114, 130, 147, 190, 205,
  216, 217, 219, 220, 251, 319,
  327, 328
pressure on PRC, 319

"Proclamation on Developing and
  Further Strengthening the
  Friendship and Cooperation
  between the Soviet Union and the
  Other Socialist States," 329
secret speech and Soviet society, 165
and Sino-American rapprochement, 322
Sino-Soviet cooperation to aid
  Vietnam, 294
"Soviet imperialism," 312, 334
strategic triangle among PRC, U.S.,
  and, 328, 332, 336, 346, 350,
  357, 370
Sun Yatsen and, 19–25
troops deployed along border, 317
U.S. and, 98, 100, 101, 103–105,
  110, 133, 136, 142–144, 162,
  201, 221, 222, 224, 232, 234,
  236, 267, 271, 294, 298, 309,
  313, 319–321, 328, 334,
  349–351, 357, 379, 380
Vietnam and, 285, 294–296, 299,
  300, 334, 335, 353, 354, 361,
  372, 374, 383
war against warlords by, 47
Xinjiang and, 79, 80, 87, 99, 129
Yugoslavia, relations with, 193, 198, 199
Zhang Xueliang agreement with, 46, 64
Soviet-Vietnamese Treaty of Friendship
  and Cooperation, 334
Stalin, Joseph, 32, 40, 58, 74, 95, 109,
  123, 133, 147, 161, 181, 190, 210,
  239, 250, 278, 307
Chinese Revolution and, 40, 50, 111,
  170, 210
Comintern dissolved by, 83
concessions made by, 110, 118, 125
CPSU on problems under, 170
criticism of, 161, 165, 167–171, 173, 250
economic development under, 171
Gao Gang and, 141
Kim Il-sung and, 141, 142
on leadership of CCP, 41, 114, 118
Liu Shaoqi and, 116
Mao Zedong and, 98, 131, 168
May Instructions, 34
Mikoyan and, 114, 170
on Nationalist Party and the CCP,
  34, 97, 99

Stalin, Joseph (*cont.*)
  Nineteenth CPSU Congress, 162
  North Korea and, 134
  Peng Dehuai and, 49, 139, 141,
    167, 172
  Politburo of Korean Workers' Party
    and, 136
  Port Arthur and, 87, 89, 118
  on Sino-Soviet alliance, 116
  Song Ziwen and, 86–90
  Yalta Agreement and, 87, 99, 110
  See also De-Stalinization
State Council of China, 294
"Statement from the Soviet Russian
    Federative Socialist Republic
    Government to the Chinese People
    and the Governments in North and
    South China," 6
State Planning Commission, 148,
    151–153, 158n3, 213, 272
  Basic Construction Planning Bureau
    of, 152
State-to-state relations, vii, viii, 147,
    241, 244, 253, 256, 281, 289,
    290, 329, 337
Stern, Manfred, 51–53
Strategic triangle between USSR, PRC
    and U.S., 328
Stuart, John L., 116, 117, 121n25
Stykalin, Aleksandr, 185, 187n19
Suburban peasants, 56
Sudarikov, Nikolai, 249, 251
Sun Ke, 93n2
Sun Yatsen, 3, 4, 15–27, 29, 30, 36n1,
    43, 202
  Borodin and, 18, 24, 26
  CCP and, 3, 19–22, 42, 43
  death of, 25, 26
  Lenin and, 4
  military bases and, 17
  Moscow and, 16
Sun Yatsen University, 42, 43
Supreme People's Assembly of DPRK, 317
Supreme Soviet, 81, 231, 234, 277, 337,
    338, 379
Suslov, Mikhail, 178, 182, 192, 194,
    195, 197, 230, 238, 242, 257,
    274, 292, 293
  CCP condemned by, 274, 292

T
"Tacheng Incident in the Ili Region"
    (Ita Incident), 253
Taiwan
  arms sales to, 351, 352
  Brezhnev, L., and, 344
Taiwan Relations Act (U.S.), 344, 349, 350
Taiwan Strait, 134, 222–224
Tanggu Truce, 61
Tang Shengzhi, 35
Tannu Uriankhai, 80, 81, 90
Tashkent, 343–345
TASS, 125, 131n4, 221, 222, 231, 232,
    244n3, 363
Technical aid, 75, 109, 148, 150–154
Technology cooperation, 150, 331
Temporary Agreement on the
    Management of the Chinese
    Eastern Railway (11 articles
    and 7 addenda), 13
TFD. *See* Third Front of Defense (TFD)
Third Front of Defense (TFD), 269, 271
Third World
  CCP and, 98, 297, 298
  CPSU and, 300, 306
  Mao Zedong as leader of, 137, 297, 305
  national liberation struggles in,
    60, 296, 298
38th parallel
  stalemate along, 141
  UN troops and, 144
Thorez, Maurice, 98, 99, 191
Three major obstacles
  Andropov and, 363, 364
  Ceauşescu and, 346, 352, 371
  Deng Xiaoping and, 346, 359, 364,
    367, 369, 373
  Huang Hua and, 361, 362
  Qian Qichen and, 355, 361, 374
  removal of, 346, 353, 355, 357–359,
    361–364, 367, 377
  resolution of, 346, 375
  strategic concerns over, 369
Three Principles of Hirota, 62
Three Principles of the People, 16, 29
Three worlds theory, 334
Time (magazine), 335, 373
Tito, Josip Broz, 190, 193, 198, 204,
    260, 261

Titoism, 176
"To Advance Forward Along the Road
    Opened Up by the October Socialist
    Revolution" (*People's Daily*), 306
Togliatti, Palmiro, 205n4, 266n16
Togo, Shigenori, 78
Töre, Elihan, 81
*To Strive for Permanent Peace, To Strive for
    People's Democracy!* (journal), 191
Trade relations, 70, 316, 330, 331,
    340, 365
Trade Union Movement, 237
Transbaikal Front, 314
Treaty of Aigun (Aihui), 268
Treaty of Brest-Litovsk, 11
Treaty of Friendship, Alliance, and Mutual
    Assistance Between the People's
    Republic of China and the Union of
    Soviet Socialist Republics, 128
Treaty of Friendship, Commerce, and
    Navigation, 104
Treaty of Friendship, Cooperation, and
    Mutual Assistance with Mongolia,
    126, 310
Treaty of Ili, 268
Trotsky, Leon, 33, 34, 170
Trotskyism, 236
Truman, Harry S, 86, 96, 104, 105n1,
    120n23
Tsarist government
    overthrow of, 4, 5
    Qing dynasty and, 5, 81
    sphere of influence, 30, 110
Tsedenbal, Yumjaagiin, 268, 269, 282n3
Tumen River, 72
Turkey, 28, 320
Twentieth CPSU Congress, 152, 157,
    158, 161–173, 182, 190, 196, 198,
    200, 203–205, 206n10, 206n11,
    235, 239, 242, 244, 250, 263
"20 March" incident, 25–29, 33

U
Ulanfu, 358
Ulbricht, Walter, 166, 260, 266n17
Ultra-leftism, 311
    in China, 321

UN, *see* United Nations
Unequal treaties, 13, 268, 275, 276
Union members, 22
United Arab Republic, 298, 302n28
United Front Work Department of CCP
    CC, 255
United Nations (UN)
    CPV and, 139–141
    General Assembly, 140, 365
    PRC representation in, 140
    UN forces, 133, 139–142, 144
United States (U.S.)
    CCP and, 95, 97–99, 103, 104, 116,
        117, 121n24, 130, 145, 210,
        264, 299, 304, 352
    China alignment with, 318
    Chinese distrust of, 357
    Chinese Revolution and, 50, 116
    danger of aggressive war by, 314
    Deng Xiaoping and, 197, 350, 352
    imperialism of, 91, 145, 197, 222,
        236, 255, 257, 260, 263, 281,
        309, 321
    intervention in Korea, 135
    Jiang Jieshi and, 79, 85, 86, 97, 110,
        242, 269
    Khrushchev and, 199, 202, 209, 217,
        219, 221, 222, 224, 226n20, 232,
        234, 254, 255, 257, 264, 281
    military forces, 142, 220
    Soviet summits, 320
    State Department, 117, 225n4
    strategic triangle among USSR and
        PRC, 328
    Taiwan Relations Act, 344, 349
    USSR and, 103, 110, 116, 130, 140,
        210, 255, 271, 281, 298, 328
    Vietnam War and, 269, 271, 299, 318
Ural Mountains, 6, 363
"Urgent Directive Regarding
    Strengthening Combat Readiness to
    Prevent a Surprise Attack by the
    Enemy" (Lin Biao), 317
U.S., *see* United States
USSR, *see* Soviet Union
Ussuri River, 303, 311
U-2 spy plane incident, 234–235
Uygur "Liberation Organization," 81

V

Vietnam
  aid to, 285, 291, 293–295, 300, 308
  bilateral aid cooperation for, 331
  Cambodia and, 335, 339, 340,
      352–354, 356, 361, 362,
      367–369, 371–383
  China and, 271, 294, 296, 300, 334,
      371, 376, 377, 382, 383
  expansionism of, 361
  Moscow and, 293
  North Vietnam, 262, 295
  USSR and, 373
  withdrawal of U.S. forces from, 318
  Zhou Enlai and, 250, 294
Vietnamese Communist Party, 296, 372
Vietnamese Workers' Party, 242, 290,
    293, 301n6, 305
  at Twenty-third CPSU Congress, 305
Vietnam War
  escalation of, 269, 299, 300
  last phase of, 296
  Moscow and, 294, 299
  U.S., and, 269, 271, 272
Vilensky, V. D., 7
Vishinski, Andrei, 114
Voitinsky, Grigori (Wu Tingkang), 7, 16,
    22, 27
Volkogonov, Dmitri, 225n7, 226n22
Voroshilov, Kliment, 182

W

Walt, Stephen, 158
Wan Li, 364
Wang Jiaxiang, 42, 50, 74, 76, 120n10,
    124, 125, 192, 215, 254, 255, 264,
    266n7, 266n9
  Mao Zedong and, 50, 76
Wang Jingwei, 26–29, 35
Wang Jinqing, 325n50, 359
Wang Ming, 42, 43, 60, 75, 76, 82, 83
Wang Shijie, 90
Wang Taiping, 155, 156
Wang Youping, 337, 338, 354
Wang Zhengting, 12, 13
Ward, Angus, 117
Warlords
  USSR war against, 26, 28, 30, 31, 63
  Zhili (Hebei province), 15, 26

War of Resistance Against Japan, 2
Warsaw Pact
  Albania and, 248
  Liu Xiao, 178, 249
Warsaw Treaty Organization, 191
Washington
  Moscow and, 142, 222, 317, 318, 322
  regarding in Sino-American
      rapprochement, 316
Wedemeyer, Albert, 96
Wei Daoming, 86
Westad, Odd A., 131, 132n15, 158n7,
    301n12
Western powers, 113, 125
WFTU, *see* World Federation of Trade
    Unions
Whiting, Allen S., 245n8
"Why Did Khrushchev Fall?"
    (*Red Flag*), 281
Wilcox, Victor, 225n8
Wilson, Woodrow, 5, 283n12, 324n23
"Workers of All Countries Unite, Oppose
    Our Common Enemy" (*People's
    Daily*), 259
Workers-Peasants Red Army, 48
Work-study, 6
World Communist and Workers' Parties,
    Conference of, 175, 185, 186, 193,
    238, 240, 248, 262, 287, 289, 290,
    309, 311, 312
World Communist Party, 7
World Federation of Trade Unions
    (WFTU), 235–240, 243, 245n12,
    245n16, 249
  Beijing Conference of, 235, 239,
      240, 243
World revolution
  Chinese Revolution and, 33, 306
  Mao Zedong and, 163, 255,
      263, 265
  Marxism-Leninism and, 265
  promotion of, 300
World War I
  end of, 4
  entente powers and, 4, 9
World War II
  China after, 56
  Transbaikal Front, 314
Wu Peifu, 25, 26
Wu Tingkang, *see* Voitinsky, Grigori

Wu Xiuquan, 43, 231, 254, 258, 259, 266n18, 276, 277, 283n23
  Chervonenko and, 231, 276, 283n23
  Yugoslavia and, 260
Wu Xueqian, 365, 374, 377, 378
Wubalao Island, 311
Wuhan, 8, 30, 32, 34–36, 37n10, 40, 71, 72, 74

X
Xia Douyin, 34
Xiang Zhongfa, 42, 43, 47, 49
Xi'an incident
  Jiang Jieshi and, 66, 67, 69
  Moscow and, 67
Xiao Xiangrong, 183
Xibaipo, 109, 112–114, 118, 119, 119n8, 120n18
Xie Fuzhi, 268
Xingang Statement, 220
Xinhua News Agency, 166, 359, 360
Xinjiang
  Joint Government, 99
  rebellion in, 80, 88
  separatist forces in, 85, 99
  Sheng Shicai and, 80
  territorial claims to, 118
  USSR and, 80, 89
Xinjiang Military Command, 271
Xinjiang Nonferrous Metal and Rare Metal Joint Stock Company, 127, 149
Xiong Shihui, 101
Xu Congzhi, 26
Xu Kexiang, 34, 35
Xu Teli, 43

Y
Yalta Agreement
  framework of, 123
  Stalin and, 86, 87, 98, 99, 110, 123
Yan Mingfu, 220
Yan'an Rectification Campaign, 83
Yang Chengwu, 270
Yang Hucheng, 66, 67
Yang Jie, 70
Yang Kuisong, vi, 130

Yang Shangkun, 42, 155, 197, 200, 248
Yang Shouzheng, 360
Ye Jianying, 43, 313, 318, 324n23
Ye Ting, 48
Yegorov, Alexander, 31
Yellow River, 65, 66, 76, 77
Yining incident, 99
Yining Liberation Organization, 81
Youth League, CCP, 7, 20, 21, 23, 39, 42–44, 174n9, 213
Yu Hongliang, 352, 353, 361, 362
Yu Zhan, 278, 292, 337, 354
  Chervonenko and, 292
Yuan Shikai, 5
Yudin, Pavel, 157, 169, 184, 193, 194, 210, 217, 218, 225n6
Yugoslavia
  delegation to Moscow Conference, 199, 248
  Khrushchev and, 199, 204, 235, 248
  socialist camp and, 180, 194, 198
  Wu Xiuquan and, 260
  See also League of Communists of Yugoslavia
Yurin Mission, 9
Yu-Xiang-Gui (Hunan-Henan-Guizhou) Campaign, 85

Z
Zakharov, Matvei V., 137, 139–141, 278, 314
Zeng Yongquan, 275, 276
Zhang Chong, 62
Zhang Haifeng, 340–341
Zhang Hao, 61
Zhang Ji, 20
Zhang Tailei, 20, 48, 49
Zhang Wentian, 42, 111, 152, 158n2, 163, 172
Zhang Xueliang, 40, 43–46, 64, 66, 67, 67n3
  agreement with USSR, 46
Zhang Zhizhong, 99, 100
Zhang Zuolin, 11, 14, 25, 26, 28, 29, 43, 66, 67n3
  death of, 43

Zhanggufeng incident, 72
Zhao Ziyang, 357, 378, 384
Zhenbao Island
  incident on, 311–313, 315, 321
  Mao Zedong on, 313, 321
Zhili (Hebei province), 15, 26
Zhivkov, Todor, 378, 379
Zhou Enlai, 67, 74, 82, 84, 97, 112,
    123, 124, 128–130, 131n5, 134,
    135, 137–141, 144, 148, 151, 152,
    154, 158n2, 158n3, 163, 164, 166,
    167, 172, 175, 179–182, 186,
    187n9, 187n13, 187n14, 187n21,
    192, 193, 217, 220, 222, 223, 230,
    231, 236, 241, 242, 250–252, 254,
    262, 269, 270, 275, 276, 278,
    284n25, 293, 295, 298, 307, 308,
    310, 313, 315–322, 324n28,
    325n39, 330–333
  address to MFA, 130
  Africa and, 298
  Brezhnev, L., and, 288
  in Chongqing, 97

Chronicle of the Life of Zhou Enlai
    (Party Literature Research
    Center), 330
  CPSU and, 170, 181, 192
  delegation led by, 250, 278, 324n28
  formal protest against CPSU, 279
  Khrushchev and, 148, 179, 250,
    276–281
  Kosygin and, 289, 294, 314–317,
    324n28, 330–333
  on March Conference, 293
  Nixon and, 318, 319, 325n39
  Northern Bureau, CCP CC and, 310
  revisionism and, 294
  Sino-Soviet border and, 310, 322
  Vietnamese leaders and, 250, 294
Zhou Wenyong, 48
Zhu De, 42, 50, 67n1, 96, 104, 112,
    124, 170, 172, 277
Zhu Shaoliang, 80
Zhukov, Georgii, 73, 82, 177, 182, 184
Zinoviev, Grigori, 33
Zyrianov, Pavel, 275

CPSIA information can be obtained
at www.ICGtesting.com
Printed in the USA
LVHW020436050821
694513LV00004B/192